Dialogues WITH THE Living Earth

Praise for

Dialogues with the Living Earth

"A variety of compelling approaches that sharpen our awareness that the Earth's and our destiny are inextricably connected. I highly recommend this book."

—Laura Huxley, President and Founder, Our Ultimate Investment, a nonprofit organization for nurturing the possible human

"Once again, James and Roberta Swan show us how important it is to respect and live within the boundaries of our planet. This selection of essays goes a long way toward giving readers the necessary proofs for understanding, appreciating, and conducting their lives to sustain the bountiful yet fragile system in which we live."

—Allen Bassing, Ph.D., Director of Public Programs, The Renwick Gallery, The Smithsonian Institution, Washington, D.C.

"The personal quest for inspiration from nature and the harmony, tranquility, and power of the great places in the world are documented on these pages."

—Richard L. Wade, Ph.D., Ecotourism Consultant, Associate Professor, University of California

Dialogues with the Living Earth

New Ideas on the Spirit of Place

from Designers, Architects, & Innovators

Compiled by

James Swan & Roberta Swan

A publication supported by
The Kern Foundation

Quest Books
Theosophical Publishing House

Wheaton, Illinois ♦ Madras, India

First Quest Edition 1996

The Theosophical Publishing House
P.O. Box 270
Wheaton, IL 60189-0270

A publication of the Theosophical Publishing House,
a department of the Theosophical Society in America

Library of Congress Cataloging-in-Publication Data

Dialogues with the living earth : new ideas on the spirit of place from designers, architects, and innovators / James Swan and Roberta Swan, [compilers].—1st Quest ed.

p. cm.

"A publication supported by the Kern Foundation."

"Quest books."

Based on the five-year Spirit of Place Symposium series which took place in the United States and Japan between 1988 and 1993.

Includes bibliographical references and index.

ISBN 0-8356-0728-3

1. Sacred space—Congresses. 2. Architecture—Psychological aspects—Congresses. I. Swan, James A. II. Swan, Roberta. III. Spirit of Place Symposium.

BL580.D53 1996

291.3'5—dc20 96-2935

CIP

6 5 4 3 2 1 * 96 97 98 99 00 01 02

Printed in the United States of America

Contents

Acknowledgments ix

Contributing Authors xi

Introduction: Working with the Spirit of Place 1

Part One: The Power of Place Around the World 11

1. Shamans, Sacred Places, and the Healing Earth
   Stanley Krippner 13
2. The Spirit of Space and Place Among the Inuit
   Nancy C. Zak 22
3. The Spirit of Sustainability and the Female Principle Among the Southwest Pueblos
   Nancy C. Zak 38
4. Iṣẹ Kekere Kan Ati Aṣẹ Ayie: The Ifá Concept of Work and the Power of the Earth
   Awo Fa'lokun Fatunmbi 62
5. A World View of Bliss for God and Humankind: The Teachings of Tenrikyo and Its Sacred Place
   Akira Kaneko 75
6. The Ganga River and the Spirit of Sustainability in Hinduism: A Study of Banaras (Varanasi)
   Rana P. B. Singh 86

Part Two: Honoring the Spirit of Place 109

7. Study Where You Live
   Robert Sommer 111
8. But You, O Bethlehem of Ephrathah: Bethlehem as a Sacred Place
   Roger Wharton 123

9. From Huacas to Mesas: Altars as Mirrors of Ecstatic Experience
Debra D. Carroll 136

10. Creating a Living Temenos
Roberta Shoemaker-Beal 159

Part Three: Designing with the Spirit of Place 165

11. Building with a Soul
Tom Bender 167

12. Organic Development of Place
Christopher Day 184

13. House: Symbol of the Soul
Anthony Lawlor 192

14. The Uses of Plants for Transcendental Functions from the Black Sect Feng Shui Perspective
Linda Juratovac 199

15. House Reading: A Spiritual Approach to Residential Design in Traditional Japan
Fumio Suda and Colin Carpenter 217

16. Embodiment of a Sacred Vision: The John E. Fetzer Institute
James B. Beal 229

17. Interviews by Roberta Swan
Brent Smith 243
Sim Van der Ryn 252
James Hubbell 258
Nader Khalili 270
Architecture and Design Conclusions 280

Part Four: Translating New Ideas into Public Policy 281

18. Facing Up to the Challenge of Translating the "Living Earth" Idea into Policies and Programs
Donald N. Michael 283

19. Spirit of the Forest: Integrating Spiritual Values into Natural Resource Management and Research
Herbert W. Schroeder 294

20. Finding Peace in Our Craft: Architecture for Tourism as an Expression of Harmony with Place
David Andersen 307

21. The World Needs This Mountain
Michelle Berditschevsky and Charles M. Miller 326

Conclusion: Lessons from the Spirit of Place
James and Roberta Swan 350

Index 355

Acknowledgments

This book is the consequence of producing the five-year Spirit of Place Symposium series, which took place in the United States and Japan between 1988 and 1993. These programs could not have been possible without the support of many individuals and organizations including: The Beldon Fund; the JRH Foundation; the L. G. and Mary C. Skaggs Foundation; Lawrence Rockefeller; The University of California at Davis Extension Service; Grace Cathedral in San Francisco; Robert Heyder, Superintendent of Mesa Verde National Park; Fumio Suda; the many people of the City of Sendai, Japan, who worked long hours to make the 1991 program the largest environmental meeting of the year in Japan; Quest Books, especially Brenda Rosen, Shirley Nicholson, John White, and Mary Holden for their support and guidance to publish the presentations; the nearly three hundred speakers who presented in these programs, especially Master Thomas Lin Yun, Tom Bender, Kenneth Cooper, and Elizabeth Rauscher; and the artists who enchanted audiences with music and dance honoring the power of place—Paul Horn, Anna Halprin, Steven Halpern, R. Carlos Nakai, Earth Spirit, and the children's production in Sendai, Japan, of an original musical/dance play "Torah." We also appreciate the assistance and support of Celeste McMahon, Sara Segal, and Linda Allen.

Contributing Authors

Compilers

James A. Swan, Ph.D., is an environmental psychologist who has taught at the Universities of Michigan, Western Washington State, Oregon, and Washington and at the California Institute of Integral Studies. He is the author of several books including *Nature As Teacher and Healer*, *The Power of Place*, and *Sacred Places*, and co-author of *Bound to The Earth* with his wife Roberta, with whom he co-produced the Spirit of Place Symposiums.

Roberta Swan, M.Arch., has taught design and women's studies at the Universities of Oregon and Washington State. She has produced symposiums, conferences, and expositions on health and fitness, natural childbirth, and energy conservation. She has also taught energy conservation and designed interiors for health centers. She is the co-author of *Bound To The Earth* and co-producer of the Spirit of Place Symposiums. Roberta also has been a featured guest on the *Donahue* show.

Contributors

David Andersen is an architect internationally known for his research and design work on ecotourism facilities. He has presented numerous papers and conducted workshops on ecotourism for many organizations all around the globe. Mr. Andersen is a contributing author to *Ecotourism: A Guide For Planners and Managers*, and an advisor to the board of the Ecotourism Society. He is past-president of the Minneapolis chapter of the American Institute of Architects (AIA) and a principal in The Andersen Group Architects Ltd. in Minneapolis, Minnesota.

James B. Beal is a former aerospace engineer for the Martin Marietta Corporation and an Associate of the Monroe Institute, and is considered by many to be one of the foremost authorities on the effects of subtle environmental fields on health. He consulted with the Fetzer Institute on the design of the environmental fields within the research facility to maximize health and creativity. Previously he spent ten years with NASA (the National Aeronautics and Space Administration) at the Marshall Space Flight Center in Huntsville, Alabama, where he worked on the Saturn V Apollo Space Program.

Thomas Bender is an architect in private practice who lives on Neahkahnie Mountain in Nehalem, Oregon. In 1993 he won the Sustainable Community Solutions, International Competition, which was sponsored by the American Institute of Architects and Union Internationale des Architects (International Union of Architects). He is one of the founders of the appropriate technology magazine *Rain* and the author of *The Environmental Design Primer.*

Michelle Berditschevsky is a poet, former college professor, and founder of Save Mount Shasta, where she lives.

Colin Carpenter, M. Arch., is an architect associated with the Zero Design Group in New York City. He has considerable experience in a wide variety of projects in the United States and abroad and has studied Japanese traditional design methods for a number of years.

Debra D. Carroll, M.A., is an expressive arts therapist and dancer. She is the former editor of *Shaman's Drum* and *Sun World* magazines and has led many groups to study with the Peruvian shaman Don Eduardo Calderone.

Christopher Day is trained in architecture and sculpture and works in both Britain and the United States. In addition to designing buildings, he has built seven of them, including two Steiner schools. He is in international demand as a lecturer. He is the author of two books, *Place of the Soul* and *Building With Heart.*

Awo Fa'lokun Fatunmbi is the author of *Ifa Quest: The Search for the Source Santeria and Lucumi* and an initiate in the Order of Ogun of the Yoruba Tribe of West Africa.

James Hubbell is an internationally known artist, sculptor, designer-builder, and poet. With an intuitive, nature-sensitive approach, he has designed restaurants, private homes, churches, and an award-winning chapel. The complex of buildings that comprise his family residence on the top of a hill in Southern California, and the fantastical doors in Abu Dhabi have been the subject of two books. KPBS in San Diego documented his work in a half-hour film which was shown nationally in January, 1990.

Linda Juratovac has been a practicing certified horticulturist, licensed landscape contractor, and designer since 1973. Linda began studying the traditional compass-astrology school of Feng Shui with J. S. Shiah in 1986. In 1987 she began studying Black Sect Feng Shui with the Grand Master Thomas Lin Yun. She is a Feng Shui consultant, working with interior and exterior environments for commercial and residential clients.

Nader Khalili, California architect/author, is the world-renowned Earth Architecture teacher and creator of the Geltaflan Earth and Fire System, known as Ceramic Houses, and of the "superblock" construction system. For this work he received the 1984 California Council of the American Institute of Architects Award for "Excellence in Technology." He is a United Nations consultant for Earth Architecture, Ceramic Houses, and Superblock Technologies. He has written three books: *Racing Alone*, *Ceramic Houses and Earth Architecture: How to Build Your Own*, and *Sidewalks on the Moon.*

Akira Kaneko, Ph.D., is lecturer of Liberal Arts at Tenri University in Nara, Japan. His major interests are ethics, religious philosophy, and Japanese intellectual history. He and his wife Juri translated Dr. James A. Swan's *Nature As Teacher and Healer* into Japanese.

Stanley Krippner, Ph.D., is Professor of Psychology at the Saybrook Institute and Distinguished Professor of Psychology at the California Institute of Integral Studies in San Francisco, California. He is the past-president of the Association for Humanistic Psychology and author of numerous books including *Personal Mythology*, *Dreamworking*, *Human Possibilities*, *The Kirlian Aura*, and *Realms of Healing.*

Anthony Lawlor is a practicing architect and principal of Lawlor/Weller Design Group in Fairfield, Iowa. He has received awards from the American Institute of Architects and the Institute of Business Designers, and is the author of *The Temple In The House.*

Donald N. Michael, Ph.D., is Professor Emeritus of Planning and Public Policy from the University of Michigan, and a member of the Club of Rome. He is the author of *Learning To Plan: Planning to Learn*, *The Next Generation*, and *Cybernation: The Silent Conquest.*

Charles M. Miller, J.D., is an attorney in practice with Petit and Martin in San Francisco. He is also legal counsel to Save Mount Shasta, and a leading force in seeking to create a new land use category that acknowledges that some places may be sacred to all people.

Herbert W. Schroeder, Ph.D., is an environmental psychologist with the North Central Forest Experiment Station of the United States Department of Agriculture Forest Service in Chicago, Illinois. Since completing his doctorate at the University of Arizona in 1980, he has been conducting research on people's experiences and perceptions of trees and forests. His current research focuses on the symbolic, experiential, and spiritual values of natural environments.

Roberta J. H. Shoemaker-Beal, M.F.A., is a clinical art therapist and consultant who lives in Louisiana. Her professional career has paralleled the developing field of art therapy. She has done clinical work with a variety of psychiatric populations, taught graduate art therapy programs, done research, and presented workshops from coast to coast. Between 1990 and 1994, she served as coordinator of the Greater New Orleans Creative Arts Therapies Institute.

Rana P. B. Singh, Ph.D., is the Executive Editor of the National Geographical Journal of India, and an instructor at Banaras Hindu University, where he is also the Director of the Institute for Pilgrimage Studies. He is the author of numerous articles and books and in January 1995 he organized an international symposium entitled "The Spirit and Power of Place."

Brent Smith, B.Arch., is an award-winning building designer who has specialized in making very small, energy-efficient living spaces which are full of spirit. He has taught at University of California at Davis and at Sierra College in Rockland, California. His current project for cottages for the homeless in Sacramento, California has won awards for design excellence and the American Society for Interior Designers (ASID) Service Award.

Robert Sommer, Ph.D., is Professor of Psychology and Chairman of Environmental Design at the University of California at Davis. One of the originators of the concept of environmental psychology, he is the author of several books including *Personal Space, Social Design, The Mind's Eye,* and *Design Awareness* as well as numerous research articles that shed light on how people and the environment are interrelated.

Fumio Suda, M.S.Arch., is an architect who consults with Tan-Pri International in San Rafael, California, and Sho Architects Lab in Sendai, Japan. He is also an accomplished artist whose drawings have been shown in galleries in the United States and Japan. He has designed album cover art for Japanese recording artist Jun Hirose. In 1991 he was the co-producer of the Spirit of Place Symposium held in Sendai, Japan.

Sim Van der Ryn is a noted environmental architect, teacher, and author. He is Professor Emeritus of Architecture at University of California Berkeley, where he has taught for thirty-three years. Currently he is President of the Ecological Design Institute which is actively extending the concept of ecologically based design through education and research. He is the author of five books including *Ecological Design.*

Roger Wharton, D.Min., is an Episcopal priest who leads people on wilderness treks to discover and deepen spirituality through his company, Wilderness Manna. He has had parishes in Wisconsin and Alaska.

Nancy C. Zak, Ph.D., is a writer and storyteller who has a Ph.D. in Comparative Literature from the University of California at Berkeley. She has taught at the Institute of American Indian Arts in Santa Fe, New Mexico, for a number of years. She has Inuit ancestry and has been a frequent speaker at Spirit of Place Symposiums, as well as many other colleges and universities.

Introduction: Working with the Spirit of Place

James A. Swan, Ph.D.

We are by nature ground-loving animals, and insofar as we court the ground, know the ground and sympathize with what it has to give us and produce in what we do to it, we are utilizing our birth rite.

—FRANK LLOYD WRIGHT,
THE FUTURE OF ARCHITECTURE

SEVERAL YEARS AGO I had the pleasure of producing two public lecture programs for the noted mythologist Joseph Campbell. A special reward for this work was having dinner with Campbell. One evening I told him that I had been studying the meaning and value of place in human life as it seemed there was a loss of place consciousness in modern society. Campbell heartily agreed, and referred to the work of East Indian scholar Ananda Coomaraswamy, who had pointed out that myths were frequently linked to certain places, and coined the phrase "land-nam," a term derived from the Icelandic tradition of claiming ownership of a place through weaving together a mythic metaphor of plants, animals, and geography of a place into a unique mythic story. I then asked Campbell if he had any special places. He thought for a moment, musing over a glass of French wine, and said that his three favorite places in the world were Delphi in Greece, Palenque in Mexico, and Lasceaux in France. When pressed as to why these places were important to him, after another draft of wine and some quiet reflection Campbell replied, "Because I, Joe Campbell, felt more powerful there, and I don't know quite why."

Psychiatrist Carl Jung said that he felt people often tended to have dreams and visions of a similar character associated with the same place, and coined the term "psychic localization" to describe the connection between place and the psyche. The ancient Greeks spoke of the "genus loci," or spirit of a place. The artist's mind is not so encumbered by the constraints of intellectual reasoning and so it is a clearer channel for the voice of the spirit of place. For anyone who has lived through the wet winters and walked among the giant trees of the Pacific Northwest rain forests, the dramatic masks and huge carvings of the Indian peoples of that region are very understandable. The spirit is different among the Pueblo Indians of the Southwest, and similarly unique for the circumpolar Eskimos, and their art shows this. The sensuous choral singing and dancing of Samoa is bred by the warm tropical trade winds, the steady rhythmic pulse of the waves lapping on the sand beaches, the swaying of the stately palm trees, and the thrust of the volcanic mountains which rise up sharply above all this. This must help explain why a characteristic style of art seems to arise from a geographic region, for each region has a voice that speaks to us through indigenous art.

We moderns use the word "spirit" to describe energy and vitality when we speak of community spirit, or the enthusiasm that builds for a football game. The root of the word "spirit" is the Latin word "spirarae," which means to "breathe together." "Spirits," disincarnate entities, are foreign to us. For us, spirits are sold in taverns, where good spirit is cultivated, and spirit is generated at sports pep rallies.

Regardless of whether you believe in spirits or not, to speak of spirit is to speak of an inspiring force. It would be difficult to find someone who would argue that places do not affect the emotions. There are dismal, gloomy places, that seem to breed depression and loneliness. Some towns have a phlegmatic character that chills the heart. The noted biologist Konrad Lorenz once remarked, "You find the highest incidence of crime in the ugliest parts of town."[1] The question of whether the place *causes* ugliness or ugliness causes the place is a question that is not taken seriously enough in modern planning and design. On a recent visit to England, world Master of Black Sect Tantric Buddhism Thomas Lin Yun, a renowned expert on Chinese geomancy, Feng Shui, was asked if the special feelings one often has when visiting an old castle are due to the architecture, the people who have lived and prayed there, or a special quality of nature at that place. Master Lin's response was that the people had made a difference and the architecture seemed inspired, but none of it could have happened if a place had not first drawn people to it.

There are places that make the soul soar: snow-capped mountains, lush verdant valleys, crystal caves, bubbling brooks, tumbling waterfalls, and sensuous sandy beaches dotted with palm trees that stir us to the core. "I Left My Heart in San Francisco," "Chicago," and "The Wichita Lineman," are a fraction of the countless songs written about places. Some places, like Lourdes in France, the Oyasato shrine at Tenri in Japan, and Chimayo in New Mexico even seem to have a quality that facilitates healing. "The spirit of place is a great reality," proclaimed D. H. Lawrence.[2]

Whole religious traditions are built upon paying homage to a special place. For some people, making a pilgrimage to a special place like Mecca, the Ganges at Banaras, Mount Kalias, Mount Fuji, Macchu Picchu, or Jerusalem is the quest of a lifetime. Recognizing our connection to place, it seems strange that Western psychology has built up precious little theory about the relationship between people and places, and has even less to say about the psychology of the love of nature. The unconscious awareness of place is part of human nature. The sights, sounds, odors, plants, animals, stones, and land forms of a place seep into our consciousness, sometimes vividly reminding us of their importance in dreams. In a modern world, where science and technology have become so powerful and pollution so problematic, we must recover our conscious awareness of the subtle power of place to be able to design our lives and built environment to live in harmony with nature.

For most of us who live in urban environments, having special places in nature where you can retreat to rest and recreate is essential to mental and physical health. As actor James Earl Jones puts it: "I have always thought it quite wonderful and necessary to keep connected to nature, to a place in a country landscape where one can rest and muse and listen."[3]

As wild places are threatened with destruction by modern society's ravenous appetite for resources, we search for reasons to justify saving natural areas. The simple truth is that aside from being biological reserves for animals and gene pools, these places are perceptual baselines for human consciousness. Their beauty and inspiring spirit enables us to know, firsthand, the power and value of nature in human life. Each has its own special potential to make the human spirit soar, and that in itself is justification to save wild places of unusual quality.

In 1988, my wife Roberta and I began producing a five-year annual symposium series—The Spirit of Place: The Modern Relevance of An Ancient Concept—seeking to help restore the wisdom of the past about the significance of place and explore its meaning in modern times. Each symposium was begun with an open call for papers, inviting people from all disciplines and cultural backgrounds to share in a quest to restore a key element in our guidance system for living in harmony with nature. Nearly three hundred speakers participated in the programs, four of which were held in the United States—at the University of California at Davis, Grace Cathedral, Mesa Verde National Park, and at the San Rafael, California, Marin Civic Center designed by Frank Lloyd Wright. The other program was held in Sendai, Japan. Speakers represented disciplines as diverse as aerospace engineering, biophysics, psychology, architecture, biology, law, history, anthropology, music, dance, and art. Members of twenty different

American Indian tribes participated with speeches, music, singing, and dancing, along with others from Eskimo, African, Polynesian, and Oriental ethnic backgrounds. The rule that was used to organize such a diverse group of presenters was that they had to respect each other as peers—equal experts in whatever their profession. Thus, panels blending a salmon fisherman with a physicist, and an aerospace engineer with a priest and a farmer became a common search for truth where many new alliances were forged. A total of about nine thousand people attended these symposiums.

An earlier anthology, *The Power of Place*, published by Quest Books in 1991, is a selection from papers presented during the first two years as we sought to establish the validity of the unique qualities of a place and their relationship with our lives.[4] Some additional papers also were published in the Quest anthology *Gaia's Hidden Life*, edited by Shirley Nicholson and Brenda Rosen.[5] The overwhelming conclusion of all these presentations was that modern society and science should take the spirit of place concept very seriously, as it represented a theme for ecologically conscious behavior that had enormous cross-cultural and historical precedent. The material gathered from the symposiums also represents a significant amount of information which has not previously been integrated into modern environmental philosophy or design and represents a new way of looking at right relationship with place. When people reach agreement from so many different perspectives, there is something important that deserves attention.

After you realize that an important truth exists, action must follow. The selections in this anthology take the next step. Beyond increasing our awareness of the importance of the spirit of place theme, these articles provide strategies and recipes for reintegrating the spirit of place concept into modern society, addressing the question of how we should act to maximize our relationship with the spirit of a place. You will find a wide variety of responses, ranging from trekking long distances to sacred places to planting trees, from mindful home construction to using the political and legal processes to save a country's resources. The unifying theme running through all these essays is that by finding ways to identify the spirit of a place and creatively engage its kinship, we will then be using that natural energy and intelligence and be bringing it into our lives in a way that is sorely missing for many people and places.

Vancouver, British Columbia, is for me one of those places with which I feel a strong, powerful, positive resonance. Set at the mouth of a river that supports a salmon run and ringed by snow-capped mountains on three sides and the Pacific Ocean on the other, Vancouver is a place where the voice of nature speaks loudly. Also, one never gets lost for long in Vancouver because of the ever-present orienting presence of the mountains to the north, east, and south. Yet on a recent trip, a heavy blanket of fog settled on Vancouver, and I found myself downtown not quite knowing where I was, as all familiar landmarks had disappeared. By chance (some people assert that nothing is ever an accident), I walked into an older stone building at the corner of Burrard and West Hastings, hoping to get directions back to the hotel. Suddenly, without talking with anyone, I knew exactly where I was, for I was standing in the middle of a giant golden compass laid into the marble floor of the lobby, surrounded by art deco images of the rising sun and signs of the zodiac like one might find on an old mariner's compass. I soon learned that I was standing in the Maritime Building, a building that for decades has been a nexus of communications and commerce for the shipping trade. What a fitting way to design a building that seeks to guide ships at sea! It was later pointed out to me that the bricks on the top of the building are a lighter color than those near the ground. This color change was designed to harmonize with the surrounding snow-capped mountains. When we plan and design to blend the spirit of a place with human needs and succeed, magic happens and our lives are enriched as a result.

These essays seek to help us understand the special magic of the spirit of place and what we can do to align our lives with its subtle influence. In the first section we learn about other cultures who are more familiar with the spirit of place, and how their cultural perspectives express their desires for collaboration with places. Taking this global journey, look for the common themes as well as the culturally unique. This will help you gain more value from the second section that looks at how on a personal level people seek to honor places. Here we explore several ways to begin to more fully acknowledge the voice of places: drawing to express our sense of place, undertaking pilgrimages to special places, and making altars to focus the energies of place by creating what Joseph Campbell called a microcosm of the macrocosm. Good architecture and design, we should point out, is ultimately ritual shaped into form. And so in a third section we move to more ambitious design. Here we see that good design is a vessel for spirit, an affirmation of both natural energies and human values. How sad it is that we have all too often allowed what Frank Lloyd Wright called "cash and carry architecture" to rule our landscape, ignoring the personality of each place. One cannot help but wonder if such neglect in recognizing uniqueness in place is a contributing factor to the tension that chokes some communities. This need not be so, we discover, as we look at alternatives in construction that should offer hope that design and spirit can work together. As you read this section, looking through the eyes and minds of designers who are on the cutting edge of design, you will learn how homes and workplaces can be transformed into nourishing spaces of meaning and inspiration, and learn about how art can be used to focus and celebrate the spirit of each place.

In the final section we turn to the nuts and bolts of making things happen. We live in a social context and its rules and constraints can make or break ideas. Making good ideas become reality in terms of law, public policy, and personal stewardship for the earth is where all the work comes to fruition. When the spirit of place can be a working reality in daily life, expressed in our art, law, design, public policy, and community identity, we will find peace and an important root of how we can establish a sustainable society. While modern science has taken us forward in some directions, it may have overlooked some very pragmatic aspects of living in harmony with nature that must be acknowledged before we can establish a firm foundation for an ecologically sustainable society. People all throughout history and around the world believe that the spirit of place is real and alive and important. We can't go back to the past, but we can bring the wisdom of the past into the present and integrate nature and human nature into an exquisite harmony. It can be done. It must be done.

Increasing Your Sensitivity to Place

One of the favorite speakers at Spirit of Place programs was Kenneth Cooper, or Cha-Das-Ka-Dum, in his native Lummi Indian tribal language. Cha-Das-Ka-Dum is a cultural historian for the Lummi, and Seyowyn Spirit Dancer. According to the wisdom of the land of giant trees, water, and snow-capped mountains where the Lummi live, to become healthy and fully alive, you must learn to listen with your "third ear," which is the heart. The unique art that comes from the Pacific Northwest people who have learned to sense and feel the spirit of that region has the common form of trees, celestial bodies, mythic beings, and animals drawn with many eyes scattered throughout their bodies. This style suggests that to sense the special, subtle energies of place one must learn to use the entire body as an organ of awareness. Mastering this kind of seeing, one eventually develops a state of mind which the Pacific Northwest tribes called *skalatitude.* Roughly translated, this means that when one is in harmony and right relationship with the places where one lives, there is magic and beauty everywhere. In the English language there is no similar term, which suggests our loss of awareness of the sense of place in our lives.

Caught up in the labor of adapting to modern society and answering the call to join the Information Superhighway and its printed and broadcast images, it is all too easy for us to forget to listen to the softer voices of nature and allow them to play us like musical notes and help us find joy in our lives. Yet we can remember to listen to these voices. We must remember if we are ever to find harmony with nature.

In Japan, a "shimenewa," or ceremonial straw rope, is frequently hung to mark special places of spiritual power, such as this waterfall. Photo by Bradley Cox.

Learning to listen with the third ear is not so hard as one might think. During the Spirit of Place symposiums, we learned that both award-winning landscaper Lawrence Halprin and psychologist Robert Sommer recommend sketching places that are important to us. It is not necessary to replicate it in exact detail to get a sense of a place. Instead, focus on the feelings that the place awakens and put them on paper. This is a good first step to heightening place consciousness.

Our speakers also agreed that if you can learn to observe nature you can gain important insights into your self and the spirit of a place. Listen to the birds calling. Watch the squirrels or the chipmunks feeding. Smell the flowers. Feel the sun and wind on your face. Research has found that spending as little as half an hour a week in a pleasing natural place can have a beneficial influence on your emotional health. Just looking out the window at pleasing scenery can lessen tension at work. Learn to relax and enjoy the sensory pleasures of nature.

Become more aware of what the birds and animals are doing. Animals have highly developed sensory awareness. They must, as for them it is often a matter of life and death. One area of agreement among all the representatives of traditional cultures in the Spirit of Place programs is that an abundance of animals in a place is a sign of its special power—the sheer numbers as well as the diversity of species. For example, in the Golden Gate National Seashore just north of San Francisco, as one turns off Highway 101 at the Pelican Inn and takes the road to Muir Beach, one soon crosses a stream. Immediately on the right there is a stand of pine and oak trees on the southeast side of the bluff where a number of seaside homes are sited. Every winter, in December and January, one frequently finds these trees glowing with a vibrant orange color. On closer inspection, one discovers that they are covered by thousands of orange and black monarch butterflies, which for some reason stop right here in their annual migration. These trees are much smaller and offer much less shelter than the nearby grove of towering redwoods in Muir Woods National Monument, yet the butterflies gather on these same trees year after year. As the butterfly is a symbol of emerging creativity, one wonders if these butterflies are not embodiments of the spirit of Muir Beach, which is an artists' colony.

Anyone who is buying land or thinking of buying land should go out and sleep on it a night or two before signing a contract. When you are there, lying on the ground, do you feel peaceful or not? Trust your feelings, they may be telling you something that only later will become apparent. One couple who had bought some land in northern California reported that despite the apparent beauty of the place, every time they went there they got into a fight. Dowsers suggest such conditions may be due to underground streams of water. In Europe, many people consult dowsers for fear they will build on top of a "pathogenic zone," which is believed to cause illness if you spend too much time in that place.

Dreams, too, may yield valuable information about places. The symbols and metaphors of dreams sometimes speak loudest about the spirit of a place. One couple who were thinking of buying some land went out and spent the night sleeping on the ground. One of them had a dream about seeing a stump crying. In the dream, the prospective buyer talked to the stump, and it said that it was sad that all the native redwood trees had been cut down. The stump suggested a tension existed because the shade of the native trees had vanished. The couple bought the land and immediately planted redwood saplings. Almost immediately they reported feeling more peaceful on their new property. Nature can be a teacher and healer if we can learn to listen to the many voices that speak to us as we walk through a natural area.

Visiting a Place of Power

Every place has a special identity, perhaps a spirit. Some places, however, are extraordinary. Stonehenge in England, Macchu Picchu in Peru, Lasceaux and Lourdes in France, Ayres Rock in Australia, the pyramids in Egypt, and Mount Fuji in Japan, draw people by the millions each year. In the United States, the Grand Canyon, the Black Hills of South Dakota, Yosemite Valley, the Serpent Mound in Southern Ohio, Denali or Mount McKinley in Alaska, and Mesa Verde in Colorado are just a few of what the Hopi Indians call "spots of the fawn"—sacred places.

Approaching a place of power, often you will find that an indigenous culture or a religious faith has established a long-standing association with that place. When you walk into a massive cathedral, mosque, or shrine, leave an offering in the collection box as a way of expressing respect. The amount does not have to be much. The feeling behind it is more important. If no such collection box is present, there may be a nearby store that sells arts and crafts. In some cases, the same sentiments can be expressed by mailing a donation to an appropriate charity. Sacrifice of some kind is an ancient tradition in religious practice.

While visiting a sacred place, be sure to respect the traditions. Arriving at Bear Butte State Park in the Black Hills of South Dakota, or Mount Fuji in Japan, you will almost certainly find people deeply engaged in prayer and ritual. Treat them as you yourself would like to be treated. Often, photos of special places are not permitted. Objections may be raised to placing crystals or other objects in the ground and making loud noises. Park rangers in Hawaii tell stories of getting heavy packages sent from all around the world. Opening the packages, they find stones with letters asking the rangers to please return the stones to where they came from. In native Hawaiian culture, it is said that tourists who take away rocks for souvenirs will have bad fortune. The lesson seems to be that if you want to take something away from a special place, pick up some trash.

People visit special places in hopes of special experiences—inspiration, synchronicities, visions, dreams, encounters with animals, and even healings. I have interviewed well over a hundred people who have had unusual experiences while visiting special places. Anything is possible, but if you visit a place of power with respect and nothing out of the ordinary seems to happen, you did not do anything wrong. As Mick Jagger of the Rolling Stones sings, "You can't always get what you want, but if you try sometimes, you just might find, you get what you need."

A miracle may happen when you are in a special place, but what seems to be often more important is what happens afterwards. Undertaking a pilgrimage to a special place is an invocation. It makes a statement that you wish to blend your personal presence with another presence, forming a unity that results in something larger than normal. Following a visit to a special place, sometimes there is an "answer" to your pilgrimage. It may be a phone call from someone, a creative insight, or a synchronous meeting with someone. If one believes that the earth is alive and that we all are part of a great golden chain of natural systems, then making a special effort to visit a sacred place is like a prayer. The Sufis, a mystical order of the Middle East, say that making a pilgrimage may make a good man better, but it may make a bad one better or worse, depending on the sincerity of his heart. In this age, when we have such great technological power, one learns from the special places of the earth that humility is always a good attitude to have when dealing with power.

Notes

1. Kurt Mundl (in conversation with Konrad Lorenz), *On Life and Living* (New York: Saint Martin's Press, 1988), 38.
2. D. H. Lawrence, *Studies In Classical American Literature* (New York: Thomas Seltzer and Sons, 1923), 8, 9.
3. James Earl Jones, *Voices and Silences* (New York: Chas. Scribner's Sons, 1993), 358.
4. James A. Swan, *The Power of Place: Sacred Ground In Natural and Human Environments* (Wheaton, Ill.: Quest Books, 1991).
5. Shirley Nicholson and Brenda Rosen, eds., *Gaia's Hidden Life* (Wheaton, Ill.: Quest Books, 1992).

PART ONE:

The Power of Place Around the World

NORTH AMERICAN CULTURE populated by immigrant Europeans is a relatively new culture. In contrast to the earlier indigenous inhabitants and other cultures all around the world, we are very new to the place where we live, and the late psychiatrist Carl Jung felt that until we came into harmony with the place we live, there will be an unconscious tension between people and the land that will prevent us from finding peace.

One discovers the spirit of a place slowly; in your dreams and daydreams, by watching wildlife, through art, and in how you think and feel at each place you visit. Another way of discovering how important the influence of place is in our lives is to learn about how other people who have resided in one place for a very long time have come to relate to the place where they live. In this section authors describe how people in different cultures develop special feelings for a place and then express their feelings in unique ways. We carry the place ties of our ancestry within us. Their symbols appear in our dreams, even when we think that we are only from the place where we now live. By blending ancestral heritage perceptions of place with the experience of the here and now, we achieve the root of how to know what is the right thing to be done for each place, time, and person.

1. Shamans, Sacred Places, and the Healing Earth

Stanley Krippner, Ph.D.

Editor's Note

Carl Jung believed that there was a "spiritual instinct" in man, and that honoring such a deep-seated motivation was essential to health and happiness. In this first article psychologist Stanley Krippner traces the origins of reverence for the earth and its sacred places to early shamans, who believed that certain places aided their abilities to perform magico-religious acts. Shaman or not, each of us can recognize that places have their own special powers. But because of shamans' special abilities to access and utilize altered states of awareness, we all can learn a great deal from studying their wisdom.

FOR TRIBAL SHAMANS, nature was sacred; Earth was alive and special spots were engulfed with "power," filled with "energy," or inhabited by "spirits." Although soil, water, and air all partook of the divine, some spots were especially numinous and these sacred places were visited by shamans for renewal, communication with the "other world," or entry into altered states of consciousness.[1] Shamans, both past and present, were socially designated practitioners who voluntarily altered their consciousness to enter the "other world," bringing back knowledge that they used to serve the needs of their community. Shamans were exceptionally sensitive to what biologist Rene DuBos.referred to as "the spirit of place."[2]

Many shamans regarded the Earth as their mother. There were hills that looked like breasts, crags that looked like faces, rivers that could have been life-giving milk. But the concept of Mother Earth was not universal; each indigenous culture worked out its pantheon of deities in its own way, albeit with frequent interactions with other cultures.[3] Mother Earth was given visibility in North America by the Wanapum prophet Smohalla and the Shawnee cultural leader Tecumseh, although it had much earlier roots in the Pocahontas myth. However, many Native American tribes do not have a maternal Earth deity even though they have long traditions of respect for nature and care for the land.

In Ancient Egypt, Geb was the Earth Father. All the world's vegetation sprouted from Geb's back as he was lying on his stomach, prone. The Algonquin Indians worshipped Nokomis, the Earth Mother, and believed that all living things fed from her bosom. Balkan peasants considered Earth each person's parent and spouse, dressing the corpse for a wedding before burying it. Indeed, the first people who developed skills in the healing arts held a special reverence for Earth deities, whether they were male, female, or both.

Animism was a perspective that saw nature as alive and sacred; it was associated with hunting and gathering tribes, especially those in the Old and Middle Stone Ages (i.e., Paleolithic and Mesolithic Ages). Totemism, an evolved strand of animism, conceptualized various animal species as related to particular clans. For the mythologist Joseph Campbell, the bear skull sanctuaries of Paleolithic times provide the earliest evidence of the veneration of a divine being.[4] Shamanism was associated with both animism and totemism and has been called "applied animism."[5] Many contemporary writers refer to the living planet Earth as "Gaia," pointing out that active feedback processes operate to keep Earth temperature, oxidation state, and acidity constant while solar energy sustains comfortable conditions for life.[6] The Gaia concept is the most recent in a long tradition of perspectives that views Earth as a living organism whose capabilities include the ability to bear, sustain, and heal human beings.

This is a far different world view than that held by the Europeans who conquered the Americas. Despite the evidence of long-established, city-based civilizations like those of the Inca, the Aztec, and the Maya, European settlers regarded Native Americans as people with no real homes. This provided justification for "civilizing" the Indians "for their own good" into "ordered communities."[7] No other approach could save as many souls; and no other approach could further the territorial and economic interests of the conquerors. The invaders overlooked the architectural accomplishments of Native Americans, such as building their homes in concert with nature rather than in opposition to nature, placing doorways towards the east where the sun rose, and devising floor plans so that when people awoke they would feel as though they had been reborn.

The Healing Earth and Treatment Practices

Pablo Amaringo is a contemporary shaman who has made a considerable effort to preserve the Amazonian ecosystem. Over the years, Amaringo has utilized a powerful mind-altering brew, *ayahuasca*, in his work, and painted several of his ayahuasca visions. A book containing forty-nine of these paintings presents hundreds of animals, plants, spirits, and mythological beings.[8] Journeys to various underwater, subterranean, and outer-space worlds are graphically detailed in these paintings. After retiring as a healer, Amaringo organized an art school in Pucallpa, Peru, dedicated to documenting the ways of Amazonian life. The school's philosophy is the education of local youths in the care and preservation of the Amazonian ecosystem.

The concept of the healing Earth has entered into treatment procedures used by indigenous shamans and other magico-religious practitioners since prehistoric times. For example, the central element in the Navajo healing ceremony is sand painting. This painting represents, simultaneously, the spiritual and physical landscape in which the patients and their transgressions exist as well as the etiology of the disease and the mythic meaning of the procedure that has been chosen for its cure. Stones, plants, and sacred objects often are placed inside the painting. Mythological relationships among the elements are represented in colored sand. The sand figures may be clouds or snakes or whatever is needed to portray the path of the disease as it proceeds through time and space.

Dangers and diseases have their place in the matrix as well; if they have been the cause of illness or misfortune, they alone can correct it. Chanting, drumming, and a vigil bring the elements together. Patients become aware of the pattern of their sickness and their life, and how both are joined in the cosmos. Usually patients are surrounded by their friends, neighbors, and relatives who sing and pray to that purpose.[9,10]

A variation of the sand painting is the ground painting constructed by the Southern California Diegueno Indians during the puberty ritual of young tribesmen. They convey the design of their world by representing the horizon as a circle. Also included are the world's edge, various heavenly bodies, power animals (especially the crow, coyote, snake, and wolf), and the mortar and pestle used to grind up the mind-altering plants used in these ceremonies.[11]

Some psychohistorians believe that the placenta is represented in these Indian medicine wheels—both in the temporary sand and ground paintings and in the longer-lasting constructions, of which about fifty still exist in the western parts of the United States and Canada. These structures are composed of stones placed on the ground to form a small central circle, with lines of stones radiating outward; sometimes there is an outer circle around the circumference.[12] Used for ceremonies involving renewal and rebirth, some of the medicine wheels are said to "look more like placenta than any other religious symbols derived from intra-uterine life, including the tree of life, the pagan cross, and the sacred pole."[13] Medicine lodges are built each summer by the Plains Indians for sacred ceremonies; these lodges feature a central tree or pole—often with as many rafters as the medicine wheels have lines of stones. Although these designs could also emulate the sun, anthropologist R. B. McFarland says that he favors

> . . . the placenta as the origin of the sacred circle, everyone starts life dependent on their placenta for nourishment and life's blood, long before we see the sun, and the sun doesn't have a central pole. The circle and the tree of life are both symbols of the placenta, the umbilical cord, and the network of blood vessels resembling the roots and branches of a tree.[14]

I found a similar concern in the songs of Maria Sabina, the Mazatec Indian shaman I interviewed in 1980 and whose sacred mushroom *veladas* were recorded and transcribed before her death. Many of her verses reveal her close association with nature:

> Living Mother . . . ,
> Mother of sap, Mother of the dew . . . ,
> Mother who gave birth to us . . . ,
> Green Mother, budding Mother . . . ,
> These are my children . . . ,
> These are my babies . . . ,
> These are my offshoots . . . ,
> My buds . . . ,
> I am only asking, examining . . . ,
> About his business as well . . . ,
> I begin in the depth of the water . . . ,
> I begin where the primordial sounds forth . . . ,
> When the sacred sounds forth . . . ,
> I am a little woman who goes through the water . . . ,
> I am a little woman who goes through the stream . . . ,
> I bring my light . . . ,
> Ah, Jesus Christ . . . ,
> Medicinal herbs and sacred herbs of Christ . . . ,
> I'm going to thunder . . . ,
> I'm going to play music . . . ,
> I'm going to shout . . . ,
> I'm going to whistle . . . ,
> It is a matter of tenderness, a matter of clarity . . . ,
> There is no resentment . . . ,
> There is no rancor . . . ,
> There is no argument . . . ,
> There is no anger . . . ,

It is life and well-being . . . ,
It is a matter of sap . . . ,
It is a matter of dew . . .[15]

These excerpts from several of Maria Sabina's songs reveal a woman who reveres the Mother who gives birth to us, a woman who has entered the primordial waters of oceanic consciousness but who does not stay there. The true nature of her consciousness is oriented toward service, toward healing, toward her community, and toward the children and babies to whom she strives to bring life and well-being. For her, the human being is a part of the natural world and must join its quest for life and well-being.

In general, North American Indians felt that nature-in-movement had magical power, hence the importance given the Deer Dance by the Huichols, the Buffalo Dance by the Hopis, and the Sun Dance by the Plains Indians. The Naniamo shamanic apprentices of Vancouver Island believed that their tutelaries were mythical monsters rather than the animal spirits who assisted other members of their tribe. When I visited the Cuna Indians of Panama in 1985, I observed a dance in which each tribal member moved to the spirit of his or her power animals, bringing the energy and knowledge from the "other world" into communal activity.

The Nature of Sacred Places

Some locations in what shamans call Middle Earth are held to be more sacred than others. Shamans frequently locate "power spots" and use them in their healing ceremonies. These are the areas that are said to contain more "energy" and "vital force" than surrounding geographic locations. Taking the position that "ancient peoples are still offering us their wisdom through their sacred sites and landscapes," mythologist Paul Devereux has found that they differentiated between the physical landscape as constituted by consensual agreements, i.e., the ordinary reality of the world, and the visionary landscape of the human mind.

For example, the Balinese language contains a well-developed sensibility of dual worlds (*niskala* and *sekala*). But English can only call the alternative visionary world "symbolic," at best. By whatever name it is called, Devereux suggests that a rediscovery of the human capacity to "see" as the ancients could "see," would assist residents of industrialized societies to understand that the existence of these other landscapes rests essentially on one's willingness to believe in them. Devereux does not simply dismiss the phenomenon of the symbolic reality as existing only in the imagination; he also documents the presence of naturally magnetic stones at a variety of recognized sacred spots, and presents reasonable explanations for the verified presence of strange bright lights at some "power spots." The nearby magnetic stones could have been employed both for healing work and for altering people's consciousness.

The well-preserved Neolithic landscape of Avebury in southern England is undeniably recognized as having been a ceremonial landscape for its ancient inhabitants. It follows from Devereux's argument that it was also a landscape of the mind. This is only one example of the legacy that Devereux believes native people left the world in their sacred sites and landscapes.

A contemporary example of such a site is given by Alfonso Ortiz, who as a child in his Pueblo village had a vision that was directed to the mountaintop, the place where the paths of the living and the dead were said to converge. Ortiz recalled:

> A wise elder among my people, the Tewa, frequently . . . smiled and said, "Whatever life's challenges you may face, remember always to look to the mountaintop; in doing so you look to greatness. Remember this, and let no problem, however great it may seem, discourage you . . ." Although he knew I was too young to understand, he also knew there was not much time left to impart this message to me and, perhaps, to others like me. In accordance with our beliefs, the ancestors were waiting for him at the edge of the village the day he died, waiting to take him on a final four-day journey to the four sacred mountains of the Tewa world. A Tewa must either be a medicine man in a state of purity or he must be dead before he can safely ascend the sacred mountain.[16]

Ortiz's statement implies that the shaman can utilize sacred geographical spots such as the mountaintop. These spots are also the places where tribal "ancestors" can be found by the shaman and consulted in time of need. James Swan has reviewed more than one hundred case histories of people having unusual experiences at power spots, and he observes that the most common experiences reported were feelings of ecstasy, unification with nature, interspecies communication, waking visions, profound dreams, the ability to seemingly influence the weather, feeling unusual "energies," and hearing words, voices, music, and songs.[17]

One explanation of the nature of sacred places can be found in the creation myth of the Hopi Indian tribe. In the beginning, it is told, Tiowa, the Creator, saw a need to assign a guardian for Earth and he gave the position to a wise old woman named Spider Grandmother. Descending to Earth, Spider Grandmother saw that she would need help with her task as a steward. She reached down, picked up two handfuls of soil and spit into each of them. From each hand sprang a handsome young man. The three sat quietly in meditation for a time, attuning their minds to that of Tiowa. Then Spider Grandmother sent one young man clothed in shimmering silver, Poqanghoya, to the North Pole to work his magic of giving structure and form to Earth, holding the planet together. The other, Palongwhoya, wearing an equally spectacular costume of fiery red, carried a drum with him as he was sent to the South Pole. When Palongwhoya reached the South Pole, he sat in meditation for a time, reaching his heart-mind out into the universe. When he heard the heart beat of Tiowa, he began to imitate that rhythm on his drum, creating a harmony. Whenever two or more things come into harmony, energy is exchanged, and so Palongwhoya's drum directed energy from the heart of the Creator into the Earth through the drum beat. This stream of life-force energy coursed downward to the very center of the Earth. Striking the center, they radiated outward again, like the seeds of an dandelion. As they emerged from the Earth's crust, they were more concentrated at some places than at others. These places are the strongest sacred places, known to the Hopis as the "spots on the fawn," places of light as on the back of a young deer.[18]

The Exploitation of the Living Earth

Some contemporary humans claim that their needs permit them to ravish nature. As former U.S. Secretary of the Interior, Manuel Lujan, Jr., stated, "I think that God gave us dominion over these creatures." Lujan also remained unconvinced that every species needs to be preserved, saying "Nobody's told me the difference between a red squirrel, a black one, or a brown one."[19]

In a San Francisco interview with several social scientists on May 8, 1992, former Soviet leader Mikhail Gorbachev took a different position, when he said:

> We must continue to move ahead on this issue in the spirit of innovative thinking. The destruction of the environment is a dramatic problem. We need to work toward a single global vision. For example, the Siberian taiga and the Amazonian rainforest are the twin lungs of the planet. In our new Foundation, we have a Center for Global Problems devoted to these issues. This is a global problem and it must be solved with global approaches.[20]

This vision of the living Earth is also implicit in the work of Nobel laureate Barbara McClintock. In studying genetic transportation, she focused on corn (a sacred food to many Native American tribes), working with nature to determine how genetic structures respond to the needs of the organism. In commenting on her work, biographer E. F. Keller states that nature is on the side of scientists like McClintock—although her underlying philosophy alarmed her peers (especially the male geneticists) and regulated her to the periphery of genetic research for many decades.[21]

Mythologist Elizabeth Sahtouris observed how Earth's relatively constant temperature and chemical balance is favorable to life. For her, Earth meets the biological definition of a loving organism, as a self-producing and self-renewing system.[22] Earth is the only planet in its solar system that had the right size, density, composition, fluidity of elements, and "the right distancing and balancing of energy with its sun star and satellite moon to come alive and stay so."[23] Mythologist Charlene Spretnak adds that on the smaller celestial bodies, the electromagnetic interaction overpowered gravity's pull; on the larger ones, the opposite relationship developed. Only on Earth were the two in balance.[24]

Western scientists and philosophers who agree with the shamanic conception of Earth as a living being are in a minority. But they, in consort with indigenous people, call for awareness and sensitivity on the part of human beings in regard to the balance that must be maintained. The ancient Greeks believed that in the beginning there was darkness, personified by the god Chaos. Then appeared Gaia, the Earth goddess. Western cultures have used their technology to insulate themselves from any limitations imposed by nature. Spretnak contends that the Western stance has been that if societies let down their guard, they would again be engulfed by chaos. But this is a misreading of nature and a dysfunctional mythology; humankind's destruction is more likely if the living, healing Earth is ignored.

Notes

1. Paul Devereux, *Shamanism and the Mystery Lines: Ley Lines, Spirit Paths, Shape-Shifting and Out-of-Body Travel* (St. Paul, Minn.: Llewellyn, 1993).
2. Rene Dubos, "The Spirit of Place." *Parabola* (winter 1993, originally published 1972), 66–68.
3. S. D. Gill, *Mother Earth: An American Story* (Chicago: University of Illinois Press, 1987).
4. Joseph Campbell, *The Way of the Animal Powers* (New York: Harper and Row, 1988).
5. Neville Drury, *The Shaman and the Magician: Journeys Between Worlds* (London: Routledge and Kegan Paul, 1982).
6. Elizabeth Sahtouris, *Gaia: The Human Journey from Chaos to Cosmos* (New York: Pocket Books, 1989).
7. J. Bruhac, "The Families Gathered Together," *Parabola* (winter 1992), 36.
8. Luis E. Luna and Pablo Amaringo, *Ayahuasca Visions: The Religious Iconography of a Peruvian Shaman* (Berkeley, Calif.: North Atlantic Books, 1991).

9. Richard Grossinger, *Planet Medicine: From Stone Age Shamanism to Post-Industrial Healing*, rev. ed. (Boulder, Colo.: Shambhala, 1982), 105–106.
10. Donald Sander, *Navaho Symbols of Healing* (New York: Harvest/Harcourt Brace Jovanovich, 1979).
11. Joan Halifax, *Shaman: The Wounded Healer* (New York: Crossroads, 1982).
12. R. B. McFarland, "Indian Medicine Wheels and Placentas: How the Tree of Life and the Circle of Life Are Related," *Journal of Psychohistory* 20, 1993, 543–564.
13. Ibid., 456.
14. Ibid., 462.
15. Alanso Estrada, *Maria Sabina: Her Life and Chants* (Santa Barbara, Calif.: Ross-Erickson, 1981), 107, 136, 150–151, 165, 175–176.
16. Halifax, 30.
17. James A. Swan, *Sacred Places* (Santa Fe, N.M.: Bear and Co., 1990).
18. Ibid.
19. T. Gup, "The Stealth Secretary," *Time*, May 25, 1992, 57–59.
20. Personal communication, May 8, 1992.
21. E. F. Keller, *Feeling The Organism: The Life and Work of Barbara McClintock* (New York: W.H. Freeman, 1983).
22. Elizabeth Sahtouris, "The Dance of Life," in *Gaia's Hidden Life: The Unseen Intelligence of Nature*, eds. Shirley Nicholson and Brenda Rosen (Wheaton, Ill.: Quest Books, 1992), 18.
23. Ibid., 23.
24. Charlene Spretnak, *States of Grace* (San Francisco: HarperSanFrancisco, 1991).

2. The Spirit of Space and Place Among the Inuit

Nancy C. Zak, Ph.D.

Editor's Note

In the Arctic, the place where the cold cleansing wind—the great bear's breath—arises, life and death are often not far apart. Storms, ice packs, and sub-zero temperatures all can take life very quickly. Food is often either a feast, as when the caribou herds are near, the ducks and geese swarm on the ephemeral tundra to nest and molt, and schools of salmon and Arctic char surge up icy cold streams to spawn; or a famine, when a thick blanket of ice and snow covers everything and the ghostly northern lights provide the only illumination in the dark Arctic sky. Under these conditions, people must learn to get along with each other and live in harmony with nature, or death will quickly take them.

The Eskimo or Inuit are a quiet, shy people whose success in surviving in a land where most of us would could not imagine living is evidence of a wisdom that has much to teach us. In contrast to other Native Americans, there is relatively little written about the Inuit. In this paper, writer and storyteller Nancy Zak draws upon her own family background as well as scholarly research to guide us through life under the northern lights in circumpolar realms and explain Inuit beliefs about right relationship with the spirit of place.

BEFORE I BEGIN I would like to tell you a little about myself. I have Inuit blood. My grandmother was a full-blooded Inupiaq woman from northern Alaska. My father John Carpenter was born above the Arctic Circle. His native name is Nanoona, which means "Little Polar Bear." I would like to dedicate this presentation to my Aunt Mary, whose native name was Turagana. I sincerely hope that this presentation will do honor to my relatives and ancestors and to the spirit of the Inuit people.

The term *Inuit* means "the people," or "the real people," and is the original people's name for themselves. It has long been held that the term

Eskimo comes from the Algonkian dialect of the Cree people, neighbors of the Inuit. In Cree, *Eskimo* means "people who eat raw fish"; in fact, the word *Eskimo* comes from a Montagnais form of the Algonkian language meaning "snowshoe-netter."[1] Research by ethnolinguists suggests another meaning for the term *Eskimo*—"one who speaks the language of a foreign land."[2] I prefer to use the term *Inuit* rather than *Eskimo*, since my father experienced the latter designation as a mark of shame and reproach.

In this paper I will discuss some of the ways in which the Inuit people from Siberia to Greenland have experienced and envisaged what we might call the spirit of space and place. Although I will focus my attention on traditional views of the concepts of spaces and place, I will also include modern ideas and experiences. It has been said that traditional Inuit people accord the importance to space that modern man lavishes on time.[3] I believe there is a great deal of truth to this statement. I hope that as a result of reading my article you will come to understand why this is so.

The Inuit people are a hunting people, most of whom by necessity and inclination have traveled from place to place throughout the year according to the dictates of the seasons and the food resources available. This people, who inhabit what some have called a vast desert of ice and snow, have lived in more varied ways and more varied ecological zones than the average person might imagine. For example, the Yup'ik Eskimos of Siberia have traditionally been semi-sedentary rather than purely nomadic. There are mountain Eskimos in Alaska, former slave-owning and Raven-honoring tribes in the Pacific, landlocked bands in Alaska and Canada, those who hunt the caribou, the mountain goat and sheep, moose and elk, and those who hunt the seal, whale, or walrus.

Elaine Jahner, a scholar of the Lakota, has observed that "what lies at the heart of the religion of hunting peoples is the notion that a spiritual landscape exists within the physical landscape."[4] An understanding of this spiritual landscape is vitally necessary to any understanding of the Inuit people and their concepts of space and place.

In order to gain an idea of the nature of this landscape, we will begin by considering aspects of the spiritual life of the Bering Sea Eskimo.[5] Their general beliefs and attitudes are shared by large groups of Inuit people.

The Bering Sea or Yup'ik Eskimo live along a shallow coastline which excludes the presence of the bowhead whale and most walrus. Their waters abound in a variety of seals, beluga whales, some walrus, and sea lions. The daily lives of the Yup'ik have been focused on taking these sea mammals as well as a large variety of fish, land mammals, and waterfowl. The Bering Sea Eskimo see themselves in a collaborative relationship with the animals. The various animals give themselves to the hunter in response to the hunter's respectful treatment of them.

In the Yup'ik world view human and nonhuman persons share many traits. Their flesh is perishable, their souls immortal. All living beings participate "in an endless cycle of birth and rebirth of which the souls of animals and men are a part, continent on right thought and action by others as well as self." Both men and animals possess a soul with a specific anatomical locus, the bladder. In human and nonhuman persons, the soul remains "in the vicinity of the body for a specified time after death before going to an extraterrestrial realm to await rebirth." Among human beings, an essential aspect of the person is reborn in the next generation. The newborn child has "regularly received both the name and with it the soul of a recently deceased relative in the ascending generation." Inanimate objects are also believed to possess souls. As a result, hunting implements have been decorated "not only to please or attract animals but also to impart life into and please the objects themselves."[6]

The Bering Sea Inuit believe that men, animals, and what westerners call inanimate objects possess awareness. As Joe Friday of Chevak put it in a 1985 interview: "We felt that all things were like us people, to the small animals like the mouse and the things like wood we liken to people as having a sense of awareness." He believes "The wood is glad to the person who is using it and the person using it is grateful to the wood for being there to be used."[7]

Both humans and animals have been subject to many prescriptions and prohibitions for living life in a way that is appropriate as they grow to and live in maturity and awareness. Three concepts predominate: (1) the power of a person's thought; (2) the importance of thoughtful action in order not to injure another's mind; and (3) the danger inherent in following one's own mind. A person's attitude has had as much significance as his actions. As young men perform their daily tasks, they have been admonished to "keep the thought of the seals" first in their minds. By doing so they are "making a way for the seals" whom they will one day hunt. In like manner, a pregnant woman must keep the thought of her unborn child first in her mind to assure its well-being.[8]

As we have noted above, in the Inuit world view, everything is alive and, despite appearances to the contrary, it is generally believed that there is no empty space. Spirits live everywhere. Everything needs to be treated with respect, as everything is sacred, holy, and powerful, and possesses a soul. Potent sacred beings such as the Man in the Moon, the Woman of the Sea, and the powers residing in the air need to be treated with great respect.[9]

At this point we will explore the cosmic interconnections of the spiritual and physical landscapes, taking the Copper people of the Central Arctic of Canada as an example. For these people, in the words of Arctic explorer Knud Rasmussen:

> The great world in which mankind lives consists of *nuna*, *tarajoq* and *hila*.
>
> *Nuna* is the world itself. It stretches without end far out to the north and to the south, to the west and to the east. Of this enormous world we only know the lands that border upon the districts where we hunt the caribou. . . . It is not only men and women who live on *nuna*; there are different kinds of spirits too, and mankind has to take notice of them all. And *nuna* herself has her own spirit, who does not like people to busy themselves too much with earth and stones, especially when the caribou are wandering; if people work too much with the earth in that period, the spirit of the world makes the caribou disappear and man has to starve.
>
> *Tarajoq* is the salt sea that washes against *nuna*; there live the seals that are hunted from the breathing holes when the ice comes. Like *nuna*, the sea has its spirits which demand great respect from both hunters and women. The mightiest of all these spirits is *Arnakaepshaluk*, who is the mother and guardian of the sea beasts.
>
> *Hila* is all that space above *nuna* and *tarajoq*. *Hila* is held up by immense pillars that stand out at the ends of the world in the four corners of the wind; its uppermost arch is called *qilaek*: the sky. *Hila* is not empty space as one might think; it is the dwelling place of *hilaep inue*, supernatural beings who all seem to be united through a great power: *hilaep inua* itself: the spirit of *hila*. It governs the weather that makes it possible for people to live. It is not only the cause of the good weather that allows a man to go hunting, but bad weather too, especially blizzards, which cause the dwellers of the earth to suffer want.
>
> Up in *qilaek* live the sun, the moon and the stars; these are all people who once died a "supernatural," an inexplicable or a violent death and who in death have become shining spirits. The sun is a woman, the moon a man. The stars are almost all men, dogs, bears or caribou.
>
> The Moon Spirit is the one that is easiest to see; for at the time of full moon the shadow of a man and his dog stands out clearly in the lunar circle.[10]

Incidentally, for the Netsilik people of the Central Arctic, "the moon was assumed to bring luck to the hunter. For this reason, women were not allowed to sleep exposed to the moon, as it was believed they would become pregnant."[11]

To return to the Copper Inuit, according to Rasmussen:

> The aurora borealis is called *Arsharneq* or *Arshaet*. It is personified in a powerful spirit who is in great demand as a helping spirit for the best shamans. We believe that the aurora borealis is alive just as men and women are. . . . *Arnakaepshaluk*: the big, bad woman, is the origin of all taboo.

> Of all the spirits, people are most afraid of her. She lives on a rock at the bottom of the sea in a . . . little bubble. There she lives with her husband . . . and a small child. She is sovereign over all the sea beasts and therefore is particularly feared in winter, when the ice comes and sealing begins.
>
> Should it happen that people break their taboo—she is especially touchy about unclean women—she gathers up all the women's sewing things and the men's work and covers the seals over them so that they cannot get out. All the sea beasts can be hidden under her side-platform, and they are shut up there when a taboo has been broken, the space under the side-platform then being blocked up with the [taboo] word that was . . . [spoken] under the taboo.[12] This does not mean literally the sewing materials or the implements or tools that the men have worked with, but simply the souls of these things. The materials remain with the people and they do not notice that their souls are being piled up in the house of the Sea Woman. But suddenly hunting fails, and then the people can only be saved if a shaman forces *Arnakaepshaluk* up to the top of the sea.[13]

The Netsilik have a female deity called Nuliajuk living in the depth of the sea; she is considered to be the mother of all animals and the mistress of both the sea and the land. A similar goddess, Sedna, lives in eastern Canada and Greenland; she is considered to be the mother of all marine mammals. In other parts of Inuit country, for example, in the Bering Strait, it is the male Moon Spirit who controls the animals and has to be visited by the shaman.

Traditional life has been structured around the avoidance of numerous taboos. Many spirits have been considered hostile: "If all the taboos were obeyed, animals allowed themselves to be killed, and good health and prosperity descended upon the hunter and his family. If some were broken, no matter how innocently, famine or accident or sickness were certain to follow."[14]

Life in the Arctic even in the late twentieth century is hazardous: "A sudden drop in temperature can turn a family outing into tragedy within hours, a loose dog can tear a child to pieces in moments [This almost happened to one of my cousins as a very small child; as a result my cousin still feels very uncomfortable around dogs, even gentle ones.], life is fragile and unfair."[15]

Traditionally Inuit people have believed in an afterlife and in the existence of afterworlds, and, in some cases, several afterworlds, located in specific physical places. For instance, the Netsilik people believe in the existence of three afterworlds well known to shamans since the latter have visited them. Asen Balikci, a student of these people, learned the following:

> *Agneriartarfik*, or the village one can always return to, is located high in the sky. There is plenty of game at all times, the caribou in particular

> roaming in great herds. Hunting is invariably very good, and whenever the dead become tired of caribou meat and wish a different food, the moon spirit helps them down to the sea where they can kill seals. The country is beautiful up there, the weather good, and the dead continuously happy. They play at all sorts of games, everything is happiness and fun, and in all respects it is a land of pleasure. The people who go there are the clever and energetic hunters, especially those who have died violent deaths. As for women, only those with large and beautiful tattooings have access, this because they had the courage to endure the suffering involved in the tattooing technique. [Tattooing was a widespread practice throughout the Arctic: it had powerful ritual significance.] The dead remain there forever at the age that they were when they died. . . . *Aglermiut* is an underworld located very deep under the tundra. Living conditions for the dead are as good as for those living in the sky. There is plenty of caribou, and salmon fishing is very rewarding. The dead live there in joy and abundance. The seasons are reversed from those on earth whenever there is winter among the Netsilik, there is summer in the underworld. The same good hunters and tattooed women who go up into the sky live here. *Noqumiut* are called the dead who live in a different underworld, located just below the crust of the earth. They always sit huddled up with hanging heads. Their eyes are closed. Their only food is the butterfly, which is caught when it comes too close to the head of a dead man. The *noqumiut* are perpetually hungry, idle, and apathetic. Lazy hunters go here, along with the women who would not endure the suffering of getting tattooed.[16]

Now that we have an idea of the conceptual and spiritual world of the Inuit people, we will go on a brief tour of this world from Siberia to Greenland, focusing on notions of space and place. First we will "visit" the Asiatic Eskimos of Siberia and St. Lawrence Island, an American Island in the Bering Sea. These people are called the Siberian Yup'ik. Although St. Lawrence Island is officially part of the United States, the Inuit people of this island belong to the Asiatic Eskimo culture. By tradition the people of this culture are divided into kin groups or *nalku.* This feature is absent in all other Inuit groups. Patrilineal clans have determined rights and access to resources, residence areas in the villages, and even cemetery plots. The oldest, most powerful clans have controlled "the most convenient locations in a given community and used separate burial grounds from other clans. They [have] controlled access to hunting and fishing areas and [have] determined the composition of whaling crews, war parties, and trade partnerships." Clan politics have dominated "community decisions, and the ancestral traditions and legends of each clan were maintained separately from those of other clans and were expressed in distinctive rituals and beliefs."[17]

Traditional Asiatic Inuit housing differs from Alaskan housing: "Ancient forms were large, round semi-subterranean structures occupied by communal families of given clans. . . . Another departure from Alaskan Eskimo tradition was the absence of the *kashim*, the men's communal workplace, residence, and community center. . . . "[18]

As to the spiritual landscape, it is similar to what was described above: "Most features of observable nature were thought to have indwelling spiritual essences, in some cases capable of taking diverse forms. Rocks, mountains, and other features of landscape were included under such a spiritual umbrella."[19]

At this point we turn to Alaska where, as is true of the Arctic, the year is characterized by the cycles of dark and light. The wind is an ever-present element.[20] People are always listening to it and for it. One definition of an Inuit person is that he or she is a listener: "We have survived because we know how to listen."[21] Yet visual acuity is also important.[22] Literature on the Inuit abounds in numerous examples of Inuit hunters' extraordinary powers of visual perception, their ability to "navigate" on sleds in seemingly undifferentiated landscapes of snow, their ability to draw detailed maps of coastlines where they hunt or fish. Inuit children and adults learn to pay close attention to subtle differences in cloud and weather formations, and thus know when storms are approaching, and the type of storm they will face.

The land is peopled with fantastic creatures. For example, for the Inupiat of the interior of North Alaska, the land abounds in ghosts, dragons, birds, and giant fish.[23] In general there has been a prohibition against hunting, eating, or working on the animals of the land and the sea in one and the same day.[24]

Ancient traditions associate tattooing or joint markings with social transformation: the first kill for a boy, the first menstrual cycle for a girl. Women are powerful in ways both positive and negative throughout the Inuit world. Their menstrual cycle can affect the hunt or otherwise disturb the balance. Powerful taboos surround women and birth as well as death. "On Kodiak Island and the north Bering Sea . . . the whalers kept their whaling implements, amulets and mummies or human images that gave them their power in secret places away from the settlements."[25]

Due to weather and resources, traditional dwellings are smaller in the north, and larger in the south. Among the Inuit there has been a general pattern of winter aggregation and summer dispersal. Throughout Inuit country "special structures housed social and religious gatherings. These assembly chambers were known as *kashim* [or *qasgiq*] in south Alaska, *qaggi* in coastal Canada, and *qashe* in Greenland, and were generally more circular in plan in eastern areas and more rectangular in Alaska. . . . " It was in Alaska that "the kashim developed into a vital social institution for men . . . . There the young underwent initiation rites, and it was also a men's club, sweathouse, gambling house, workshop, and temple for major religious and curing ceremonies." In some areas in the south men and boys above a certain age lived in the kashim.[26]

Traditional Inuit houses served and still serve "many functions and cultural dimensions—they were [and are] homes, workshops, social environments, sanctuaries from evil spirits, theaters for religious ceremonies . . . " writes anthropologist Aron Crowell. During ceremonies the "*qasgiq* . . . became a nexus between the secular and sacred worlds. In hunting festivals such as the Eskimo Bladder Festival . . . animal spirits were entertained in the house as honored guests." The celebrants' passage through house orifices symbolized "passage between worlds and different states of being." On special occasions "the Yup'ik Eskimo shaman rose through the skylight of the qasgiq or descended into the entrance passage to enter the undersea world of the seal spirits." At times "The house could also become . . . a representation of the cosmos, as when a hooped and feathered model of the sky world was suspended from the ceiling in the Yup'ik Eskimo Doll Festival . . . "[27]

Among the Bering Sea Eskimo, women's small houses were analogous to wombs in which "biological, social, and spiritual production were accomplished." At times the hunter's wife was "equated with the hunter's prey, her inactivity directly related to the inactivity (and subsequent huntability) of the animals her husband sought . . . " In the Bering Sea area the ringed center motif in art connoted "spiritual vision and movement between worlds"; in addition, "the act of encircling was also performed in various contexts to produce enhanced spiritual vision or as protection from spiritual invasion."[28]

One Inuit custom offers an angry person release by allowing him to walk "the motion out of his . . . system in a straight line across the landscape; the point at which the anger is conquered is marked with a stick, bearing witness to the strength or length of the rage."[29]

Before we leave Alaska, we will explore the symbolic meaning of clothing in the Inuit world: "The link between clothing and identity can be understood in reference to the ideology of spiritual transformation." People, animals, and spirits are subject to metamorphosis. No being has a single, invariable shape. Garments, like masks, can affect or make reference to spiritual transformation. Cosmological links between humans and the animal world are also evident in the requirement that the clothing be carefully and beautifully made to please the spirits of the animals upon whom the group has depended for survival. Animal skin, transformed into a second skin for humans by the work of the seamstress, maintains its animal identity. The use of tailored animal parts to cover the corresponding parts of the human body has been extremely common. For example, leggings and boots have traditionally been made of animal leg skin; mittens from reindeer leg skin or bear paws; hoods "from the skin of the head of a caribou, fox, dog, or wolf, on which the ears . . . [are] often preserved."[30]

In Alaska an impressive effect is obtained by the gores—wedgelike inserts of both male and female Eskimo parkas, which imitate walrus tusks. Labrets, ornaments worn in holes pierced on or near the lip, which both men and women once wore under their lower lips, reinforced the walrus image. Clothing has served as an interface between power and identity and protected him or her from evil spirits. Iconographic motifs, colors, and ornaments are added to clothing to serve these functions. The material and the cut of the clothing also convey cosmological meanings. In northern Alaska, among the Inupiat Eskimo, the parka is a representational three-dimensional piece of art adapted to the human body and is charged with the meaning contained in the various pieces of fur in its symbolic cut. A man-walrus, man-reindeer, or woman-bear illustrates, as does a visual pun on an Eskimo carving, the transformational quality of the inhabitants of this world.[31]

We now move on to Canada where there is a strong prohibition against mixing the products of the land and those of the sea. We even see this reflected in the traditional distribution of space in the snow block house known as the *igloo.*[32] The dropped floor area is known as *natiq* and is associated with men and hunting, marine mammals, men's tools, the sea, the winter, the dark, and the moon. The moon tends to be male in much of Inuit culture, while the sun tends to be female. The raised sleeping platform is called *ikliq* and is associated with women, their soapstone lamps and gear, sewing, the land, the light, the sun, the short season of summer, and fur-bearing mammals. The room inside the igloo has been almost equally divided between sleeping porch and floor, that is, between feminine and masculine domains.[33]

As among the Bering Sea Yup'ik, for the Inuit of the Central Arctic, the house has symbolic links with the womb: "If a man . . . [desires] many children he . . . [uses] a serrated knife to cut the first block [of ice of the snow house igloo] for the broad side, slicing outward so the household will not suffer bad fortune. . . ." The final building step merits special attention: "The opening for the keystone block . . . [has] to be as large as possible to ensure easy childbirth for the women."[34]

Among the Copper Inuit, houses generally have been placed in a cluster so that no evil spirits can harm villagers as they wander in the darkness from one house to another.[35] Furthermore, every home has been regarded as sacred: no one is ever attacked there. If a man attacks his enemy in his own home, he will himself be caught by vengeance some day when at home, suspecting nothing.[36]

When strangers used to visit the Netsilik, women who were mothers would run around the newcomers' loaded sleds in a wide circle. The Netsilik believed that the tracks left by these women would encompass any evil spirits that had pursued the strangers across the ice, thus keeping these spirits out of the settlement.[37]

Graves have been and still are at times considered to be potentially and highly dangerous because of the possibility that the evil spirits of the dead might lurk there.[38] A common ritual when visiting a grave has been to walk around it one or more times in a prescribed direction.[39] On Queen Maud Gulf, Knud Rasmussen discovered a "row of stone cairns which had been erected as monuments to the memory of dead persons lost at sea."[40]

Inukshuk—stones piled up and arranged in the shape of human beings—dot the Central and Eastern Arctic. Sometimes people build them as directional markers, sometimes to lessen loneliness, to create company for themselves.[41] Yet again, "They once funneled herds of caribou into depressions or rock corrals and marked shores at points where fishing was good."[42]

Other *inukshuit* (the plural of *inukshuk*) are as tall as a man: "These are places which must be seen from a great distance and in winter, because they mean that an important thing like food, has been left there. . . . you can see them along the coast and inland where caribou are taken."[43]

Canadian photographer and writer Courtney Milne states that the term *inukshuk* means "acting in the capacity of a human." Milne calls these stone formations "the visual language of the people." He reports that they can function as "personal message centers to hunters," as well as "indicators to kayakers in sight of land." The Canadian writer observes that "Some are revered as locations of power, never to be touched or approached. Others are believed to bring good fortune and are venerated and given gifts." Milne believes that "the best way to describe the significance of these landmarks is in the words of an Inuit hunter." The man pointed to an inukshuk and said, " 'This attaches me to my ancestors and to the land.' " Milne observes that "In English we have no word for the Inuit [expression] *unganaqtuq nyna*," which means "a deep and total attachment to the earth."[44]

At times a hunter must set out on a trip over land without his wife or children. He will tell his family when to follow, and describe how they will find their way, making a "pointer," or *tikotit*, in the direction of his camp, or as a warning of danger ahead, or as a sign that the hunter has set up camp in another direction. A tikotit is "a tall rock leaning in the right direction, or a small rock on top of another which points in the direction of the hunter's camp."[45]

Once an Inuit from the Central Arctic told Canadian official Norman Hallendy, "You asked if there were any strange inukshuit, and my partner told you about the man who made inukshuit in the likeness of the spirits which possessed his father." The man confided in Hallendy that:

> "Yes, there are some strange *inukshuit* in the nearby hills of old camps. They are very small and in the shapes of birds and animals. No, they have not been made by an *inugaruvligak* (dwarf); they were made by children." They are the children of a child's imagination. ("Umm," a lovely sound of agreement followed by a smile came from all who were listening.)

I believe that this last remark reveals that the Inuit know from experience of the existence of the inner child.

South of Wales, a village in northern Alaska, you can see Siberia if the weather is clear. The men of Wales placed inukshuit "at intervals up the seaward face of the cape." They placed figures resembling Eskimo warriors in parkas "half crouched with arms outstretched in the classic alert-and-prepared position." Enemies approaching this area from the Bering Sea, "such as the dreaded Siberian Chukchi Eskimo would believe the men of the cape to be ever alert and ready. Not wishing to risk heavy losses in open battle, the enemy raiders would turn back."[46]

Why is a certain location sacred? For the Inuit people of Igloolik in eastern Canada, a sacred space is one that is usually apart from the community, since it is a snowy area with no trace of any kind on it—only clear, fresh snow.[47] Why or how does a certain object or location become sacred? Generally, some inexplicable peculiarity it has leads to the belief that it is possessed of a spirit or a soul. For example, "Where . . . there are inordinately bountiful food resources, supernatural forces must reside; furthermore, where many living creatures are killed many souls are apt to accumulate."[48] For this reason King William Island is felt to be a "sacred spot because the fishing there often provides those reserves of food that may be indispensable in winter should the caribou hunting fail . . . "[49] There is a small island off the west coast of Hudson Bay, Sentry Island, where some of the Caribou Inuit live every summer when hunting aquatic mammals. The island has a large boulder, a holy stone, where men used to leave such items as tobacco, baking powder, knives, files, in order to ensure good luck in hunting.[50] In a like manner, certain spots are considered sacred because they are particularly rich in caribou.

We end our tour with a stop in Greenland, where "According to Eskimo notions, in every part of the human body (particularly in every joint, as for instance, in every finger joint) there resides a little soul."[51] Among the Inuit of Greenland there has not been as strong a separation of land and sea animals and the activities pertaining to them as there has been in Canada; however, there have been local examples of similar taboo rules.[52] The shaman has served as intermediary between people and the higher powers: Sea Woman and Moon Man. Kaj Birket-Smith observed in the 1930s that "When passing places where there are dangerous current holes or ice fjords, the *inue* [souls/*genii loci*] of these localities should be given an offering, though it be a mere trifle, a piece of blubber or the like."[53]

According to Peter Freuchen: "Basically the Eskimos regard the land and the game as belonging to everybody, inasmuch as they are all at the mercy of the 'great woman who lives at the bottom of the sea and who sends out the game.' "[54]

Jean Malaurie, who lived with the Polar Inuit in 1950 and 1951, has declared that "The sacred group had priority of claim on everything: the subsoil, the water, the hunting areas, the game belonged to it." When a hunter went after seal, "he did not say 'I am going to try to catch a seal' but [I am going] 'to have my share of seal.' " To prevent a man from becoming too possessively attached to a particular area, "there was a rotation of dwellings every five or six years; a given igloo was never the permanent property of any one family. Authority as well could be accepted only on a delegated and temporary basis." Malaurie further states that "The Thule Eskimos preserved their individuality over thousands of years by clinging to an anarcho-communalism that was at once supportive and constraining. The group was all-powerful, the individual never more than its mouthpiece. Each person's thought, each personality, coalesced with that of others in order to contribute to the good of all." The words by Malaurie which I am about to cite are very important, since by our words, by our language, we create the world we live in and the possibilities inherent in living there: "One did not say 'I think' but 'the group thinks,' thus suppressing one's personal ideas. I myself was gradually brought around to doing this; to behave otherwise would have seemed incongruous, inviting ridicule."[55]

Malaurie observes that "For the Eskimo everything [pertaining to the natural world] is a sign." When the hunters "meet in the evening and are all together, the collective consciousness of the group, like a giant computer, reinterprets these signs. . . . these men . . . have been able, on various occasions, to predict far-ranging changes in climate several years in advance."[56]

There were special customs surrounding birth and death. As elsewhere in Inuit country, strong taboos surrounded women. When a woman was about to give birth, she had to move out of the house she shared with her husband. If it was summer, a little tent was erected over her; if winter, a snow house was built. As soon as the birth was over, she was at liberty to return home.[57]

When a man died, his relatives and companions set him in a stone grave in the scree. They didn't leave him for five days because for five days the spirit of the dead was said to hover around the corpse, and if any taboo was broken during that time, it became an evil spirit that would wreak terrible revenge upon mankind. In order to give the spirit peace, all tools and kayaks were turned inland as a sign of no activity, and nobody stirred unnecessarily.[58]

Knud Rasmussen discovered that the Inuit believe the earth—nuna—is very sensitive. She is composed of living matter and is grieved by death. Since the village is attached to the earth, traditionally it has not been permitted that the skins of dead animals be laid directly on the ground "except on islands or in areas separated from the village by a glacier; if this rule . . . [is] not followed the spirits of the dead animals . . . afflict the earth."[59]

Peter Freuchen remarked that he often saw men and women sit in quiet meditation on the rock of Agpat behind Thule, where dead people were stone-set. The men and women "would dress in their newest and most beautiful clothes, and then sit quite still, staring out over land and sea for hours on end. They believed that during this stillness they received the wisdom of the ancestors."[60]

Our tour is at an end. As you can see from our trek through the Arctic landscape and soulscape, concepts of space and place have played and do play significant roles in the lives of my relatives and ancestors. There is an inherent unity of Inuit thought and belief—the spiritual landscape at the heart of the physical landscape, which consists of a basic respect for all that is.

Notes

1. Ann Fienup-Riordan, "Eskimo Essays, Yup'ik Lives and How We See Them" (New Brunswick and London: Rutgers University Press, 1990), 5.
2. In this respect, see J. Mailhot, "L'etymologie de 'Esquimau' revue et corrigee," *Etudes/Inuit Studies* 2, no. 2 (1978): 59–68.
3. Edmund Carpenter in *Eskimo*, by Edmund Carpenter, Frederick Varley, and Robert Flaherty (Toronto: University of Toronto Press, 1959), 14.
4. Cited in Barry Lopez, *Arctic Dreams, Imagination and Desire in a Northern Landscape* (Toronto, New York: Bantam Books, 1987), 245.
5. The material in this section on the Bering Sea Yup'ik stems from Ann Fienup-Riordan, "Eye of the Dance: Spiritual Life of the Bering Sea Eskimo," in *Crossroads of Continents, Cultures of Siberia and Alaska*, eds. William W. Fitzhugh and Aron Crowell (Washington, D.C.: Smithsonian Institution, 1988), 256–270.
6. Ibid.
7. Ibid.
8. Ibid.
9. For the Central Yup'ik of the interior of Southwest Alaska, the moon is female, the sun male: Lecture, Chuna McIntyre, January 18, 1994, Institute

of American Indian and Alaska Native Culture and Arts Development, Santa Fe, New Mexico.

10. Knud Rasmussen, *Intellectual Culture of the Copper Eskimos, Report of the Fifth Thule Expedition 1921–24* (Copenhagen: Gyldendalske Boghandel, Nordisk Forlag, 1932), 22–23.
11. Asen Balikci, *The Netsilik Eskimo* (Garden City, N.Y.: The Natural History Press, 1970), 207.
12. For example, hunters did not use the word "bear" during a polar bear hunt because they believed the polar bear would hear the word and flee.
13. Rasmussen, 23–24.
14. Ernest S. Burch, Jr., *The Eskimos* (Norman, Okla.: University of Oklahoma Press, 1988), 96.
15. Robin Gedalof McGrath, "Introduction," *More Tales from the Igloo*, as told and illustrated by Agnes Nanogak (Edmonton, Canada: Hurtig Publishers, 1986), x. Also see *Northern Quebec Inuit Elders Conference, Kangirsujuaq, Quebec, August 30-September 6, 1983*, tr. Sarah Naluktuk (Inukjuak, Quebec, Canada: Avataq Cultural Institute, 1985), 162ff.
16. Balikci, 214–215.
17. William W. Fitzhugh, "Eskimos: Hunters of the Frozen Coasts," in *Crossroads of Continents*, 46.
18. Fitzhugh.
19. Charles C. Hughes, "Saint Lawrence Island Eskimo" *Arctic*, ed. David Damas, vol. 5, *Handbook of the American Indians*, ed. William C. Sturtevant (Washington, D.C.: Smithsonian Institution, 1984), 273.
20. Robert Coles, *The Last and First Eskimos* (Boston: New York Graphic Society, 1978), 106. In *Arctic Dreams*, 230, Barry Lopez comments on this as well and eloquently, citing an Inuit from Anaktuvuk Pass, Alaska. Edmund Carpenter also cites Inuit people, the Aivilik of Canada, on the important role of listening, in the segment on "Acoustic Space," in *Eskimo*, 14.
21. Coles, 106. See Coles, 106, and Carpenter, 10, for the important role the wind plays in Inuit culture and vocabulary.
22. Dorothy Jean Ray, written communication, October 31, 1994.
23. Edwin S. Hall, "Interior North Alaska Eskimo," in *Arctic*, 343.
24. Dorothy Jean Ray, telephone interview, March 9, 1989.
25. Margaret Lantis, *Alaskan Eskimo Ceremonialism* (Seattle and London: University of Washington Press, 1947), Monographs of the American Ethnological Society, vol. 11:32.
26. The material in this paragraph stems from Peter Nabokov and Robert Easton, *Native American Architecture* (New York, Oxford: Oxford University Press, 1988), 203.

27. The material in this paragraph stems from Aron Crowell, "Dwellings, Settlements, and Domestic Life," in *Crossroads of Continents*, 194.
28. The material in this paragraph stems from Fienup-Riordan, 260ff.
29. Lucy R. Lippard, *Overlay, Contemporary Art and the Art of Prehistory* (New York: Pantheon Books, 1983), 129–130.
30. The material in this paragraph stems from Valerie Chaussonnet, "Needles and Animals: Women's Magic," in *Crossroads of Continents*, 210ff.
31. The material in this paragraph stems from Chaussonnet, 216 and 226.
32. According to Nabokov and Easton, *Native American Architecture*, p. 194, "The Eskimo word *igloo* originally meant any permanent roofed dwelling made of solid materials—in brief, any winter home." In the summertime, people might dwell in tents made out of caribou skin or other natural materials. Today in the Arctic, winter hunters may build snow house igloos as an overnight shelter. However, most Inuit people today live in western-style dwellings.
33. Nabokov and Easton, 196 and 199.
34. The material in this paragraph stems from Nabokov and Easton, 195.
35. Diamond Jenness, *The People of the Twilight* (Chicago: Phoenix Books, 1928, reprint 1961), 75.
36. Rasmussen, 18.
37. Edward Moffat Weyer, Jr., *The Eskimos, Their Environment and Folkways* (Hamden, Conn.: Archon Books, 1932, reprint 1962), 161.
38. Telephone interview, Mary Carpenter, spring 1988.
39. Weyer, 259.
40. Weyer, 277.
41. Jean L. Briggs, *Never in Anger, Portrait of an Eskimo Family* (Cambridge, Mass.: Harvard University Press, 1970), 35.
42. Lopez, 260. Also see *In the Middle, The Eskimo Today* (Boston: David R. Godine, 1983) for remarks by Stephen Guion Williams and Edmund Carpenter on the inukshuk, and Jimmy Muckpah, cited in Steltzer, 122.
43. Norman Hallendy, "Silent Messengers," *Reflections, Shades and Shadows* [a collection of conversations with some of the elders of Cape Dorset, Pangnirtung, Holman Island, and Pelly Bay], (No place listed: self-published, 1982), 32.
44. Courtney Milne, *Sacred Places in North America, A Journey into the Medicine Wheel* (New York: Stewart, Tabori & Chang: 1994, 1995), 119.
45. The material in this and the following paragraph on inukshuit and tiktotit is taken from Hallendy, "Silent Messengers," 32. For further information on inukshuit, see Luke Suluk, "Inukhuit," in *Inuktuit*, no. 76 (1993):10–19. *Inuksuit* is a dialectical variation in the spelling of *inukshuit.*

46. Material in this paragraph comes from Shannon Lowry, *Natives of the Far North, Alaska's Vanishing Culture Through the Eye of Edward Sheriff Curtis*, photos by Edward S. Curtis (Mechanicsburg, Pa.: Stackpole Books, 1994), 101–102.
47. Bernard Saladin d'Anglure, "Penser le 'feminin' chamanique," *Recherches amerindiennes au Quebec*, vol. XVIII, nos. 2–3 (1988):23.
48. Weyer, 302.
49. Ibid.
50. Kaj Birket-Smith, *The Eskimos*, rev. and enl., trans. W. E. Calvert (London: Methuen & Co. Ltd., 1961), 171 and 173.
51. William Thalbitzer, cited in Fienup-Riordan 261.
52. Inge Kleivan, "West Greenland Before 1950," in *Arctic*, 617.
53. Birket-Smith, 170.
54. *Peter Freuchen's Book of the Eskimos*, ed. and with a preface by Dagmar Freuchen (Greenwich, Conn.: Fawcett Premier, 1961), 108.
55. The material in this paragraph stems from Jean Malaurie, *The Last Kings of Thule, With the Polar Eskimos As They Face Their Destiny*, trans. Adrienne Foulke (New York: E. P. Dutton, Inc., 1982), 134. The author has made a good faith effort to obtain permission to reprint this excerpt. If permission is eventually received, proper acknowledgment will gratefully be made in future editions.
56. The material in this paragraph stems from Malaurie, 197–198.
57. Knud Rasmussen, *The People of the Polar North, A Record*, compiled from the Danish originals and ed. by G. Herring (Detroit, Mich.: Gale Research Company, 1908, reprint 1975), 119.
58. Freuchen, 162.
59. Rasmussen, cited in Malaurie, 218.
60. Freuchen, 156.

The author gratefully acknowledges permission granted by the publishers to reprint quotations cited above.

3. The Spirit of Sustainability and the Female Principle Among the Southwest Pueblos

Nancy C. Zak, Ph.D.

Editor's Note

Dr. Nancy Zak has studied and written about the people of her own ancestry, the Inuit, and the peoples of the Pueblos where she has lived for a number of years. This article gives a number of insights into the long-term success of the Pueblo culture of the Southwest in maintaining a sustainable society in which the traditional farming culture is honored in an annual round of ceremonies.

THE TERM "PUEBLO" IS the Spanish word for people or village. The Pueblo peoples have survived and sustained themselves in a harsh environment over long centuries by living out their ideal of conduct. In this paper, I will talk about the Pueblo people of today, as well as certain traditional beliefs and attitudes. I will also discuss ideals of conduct and female roles in Pueblo life. I dedicate this article to the spirit of the Pueblo peoples.

The Pueblo peoples have lived for untold centuries in northeastern Arizona, and west central, central, and northern New Mexico. Their tribal names and languages are Hopi, Zuni, Keresan, and the Tanoan dialects of Tiwa, Tewa, and Towa.

The Hopi people live in villages on First, Second, and Third Mesa in northeastern Arizona. The Zuni live in west central New Mexico near the Arizona border; the largest city close to them is Gallup, New Mexico. Keresan pueblos west of Albuquerque include Acoma and Laguna. Keresan villages along or near the Rio Grande between Albuquerque and Santa Fe include Santa Ana, Zia, San Felipe, Santo Domingo, and Cochiti.

The Tiwa have two southern-speaking pueblos—Sandia, which borders northwest Albuquerque, and Isleta, which lies to the southwest of the city. The two northern Tiwa-speaking pueblos include Taos, which adjoins the famous artists' colony and skiing mecca, and Picuris, which lies in mountainous country southeast of its sister pueblo.

The Tewa pueblos which lie north and west of Santa Fe include Tesuque, Nambe, Pojoaque, Santa Clara, San Ildefonso, and San Juan. In addition, the Hopi have one Tewa-speaking village on First Mesa called Hano.

The sole Towa-speaking pueblo of Jemez lies in Keresan country, northwest of Santa Fe and southwest of Los Alamos.

Members of these tribes live close together in adobe villages where people value the long-term life of the community over and above that of the individual. Rina Swentzell, who is an environmental architect from Santa Clara Pueblo, states that:

> . . . the old ones did not see human beings as the primary expression of the life force. Life, for them, was not defined in hierarchical terms. . . . This attitude of the equal status of all life expressions extends also to human-built spaces and structures. . . . Individual house units are balanced by the communal kiva and plaza spaces. The age-old human dilemma of the individual versus the group is resolved by advocating a balanced interaction of the two. The individual person or house unit cannot be justified without its context of the community or village form, and the community form has no meaning without the individual units.[1]

Swentzell specifically discusses the cultural significance of the village in architectural terms. Its adobe structures flow out of the earth; it is often difficult to see where the ground stops and where the structures begin: "As we are synonymous with and born of the earth, so are we made of the same stuff as our houses." Swentzell goes on to say that these structures are interactive: "We built them, tasted them, talked with them, climbed on them, lived with them, and watched them die. . . . The entire community was the house."[2]

The ceremonial year of each pueblo entails many obligations.[3] People do not only dance, sing, and pray for themselves—they dance, sing, and pray for the entire world. They do so with the help of kachinas who are messengers to the gods.

Anthropologists divide this world into the western pueblos, which comprise Hopi, Zuni, Acoma, and Laguna, and the eastern pueblos—all the rest. The former tend to be more matrifocal and matrilineal than their eastern relatives. The western pueblos also emphasize the kachina cult and the need for rain more than their relatives: this may be due to the extraordinarily arid climate which prevails in the west.

The Hopi, Tewa, and, apparantly, the Tiwa, believe we are in the fourth world, having successfully emerged from the three previous worlds which lie directly below us. The Zuni and the Keresans believe we are in the fifth world, having successfully emerged from the four previous worlds. The Towa appear to believe that there are two worlds: this world and the world below.[4]

The heart or center of this world is the plaza of one's particular village. The center relates to the Pueblo experience of the soul, an idea/reality/image which is difficult to put into words. Western pueblos have rectangular chambers or *kivas* for the men's rites, while the eastern pueblos have circular kivas; in the center, according to witnesses, lies the *sipapu*, the navel-like opening symbolizing the place of emergence from the lower world(s). Author Stephen Trimble writes that:

> In the plaza, often, stands the kiva, its ladder reaching upward toward a lapis sky filled with life-giving clouds, its inner chamber sunk in the secure and sacred earth. Inconspicuous in the dust of the plaza, a half-buried rock with a scatter of prayer feathers and cornmeal indicates the center of the center, the "navel of navels," the symbol of the emergence place. Here "is where cosmic regions intersect; where the heartbeat of the earth is felt."[5]

Every Pueblo person is born into a clan and usually belongs to his or her mother's clan. In some pueblos property is inherited by women through the mother; in some it is inherited by men; and in some it is inherited by both women and men. Most pueblos have curing societies, hunting societies, war societies, and women's societies, as well as initiation rites of various kinds.

Tanoan people are born into summer or winter *moieties* or divisions: the villages are divided into Summer People and Winter People. Clans are less important in the eastern than the western pueblos. The eastern Keresan pueblos still tend to emphasize the mother. So do the Tanoan pueblos in their own ways.

Each Pueblo has a civil and a religious government. Male religious leaders are called "fathers and mothers."[6] There can be divisions between the so-called traditional branch of the tribe and the progressive one. For example, most of these tribes run their own school systems. Some, such as the Tewa of San Juan Pueblo, write down their language and teach and speak it in the schools. Traditional pueblos such as Santo Domingo forbid putting their language into print and teaching it this way to their children. Due to persecutions by the Spanish and the Americans, Pueblo people have learned to keep many of their spiritual beliefs, attitudes, and practices to themselves. In this respect I cite a poem by Taos poet Howard Rainer. It is entitled "Beyond the Adobe Wall":

Far from an outsider's reach
Is guarded Tiwa tradition;
Embedded in mud, straw, and stone.

Old secrets and ceremonies
Still fastened to closed lips,
Hidden within the heart of the Tiwa people.

A sea of strangers
Have come and gone,
Their curiosity wanting to capture
A culture centuries old.

But Tiwa tradition
Still lives beyond the old adobe wall,
the inhabitants holding firm,
The key to unlocked treasures.[7]

Pueblo people of today can be highly educated by mainstream standards. Some still live at the pueblo of their birth; others marry out of the pueblo and live in other pueblos or in mainstream culture, returning home to participate in important religious events.

Corn is the staple crop of these tribes and the basis of their spiritual life. Traditional western Pueblo ways of life include dry farming of corn, beans, and squash: to dry farm means to farm with little water, only the rain that falls from the sky. Eastern pueblos have the great advantage of being near a river and thus being able to divert water to their farming plots.

Pueblo life centers around the growth of corn, that miraculous plant given the people by the gods, or, according to other myths, chosen by the people themselves. This sacred food requires a great deal of patience, care, and attention in order to plant and harvest. Traditionally it is the men who plant and care for the corn; once they harvest it, it belongs to the woman of the household. Hopi men treat corn like a beloved child, a living being. They sing songs to it as it grows. It comes in many colors: blue, purple, yellow, white, red. Just as the corn emerges from the earth, so did the people emerge from the lower world(s). This agricultural metaphor is central to Pueblo life and thought.

According to tribal traditions, everything is alive and worthy of respect, every rock, tree, animal, insect, person—even what mainstream Americans call "inanimate objects." Respect entails awe and obligation. The poem, "What My Uncle Tony Told My Sister and Me," by Acoma poet Simon Ortiz, defines what life is for a Pueblo Indian:

Respect your mother and father.
Respect your brothers and sisters.
Respect your uncles and aunts.
Respect your land, the beginning.
Respect what is taught you.

> Respect what you are named.
> Respect the gods.
> Respect yourself.
> Everything that is around you
> is part of you.[8]

Vickie Downey, an elder of Tesuque Pueblo says, "The Instructions . . . at the beginning, were to love and respect one another even with all the differences, different cultures, different languages."[9] Once Jemez artist Laura Fragua asked that one of her works be returned from customers who broke an agreement with her. She sent them back their money, informing them that she didn't consider them to be "proper caretakers for her sculpture."[10]

Self-knowledge is highly valued among the Pueblos. Pablita Velarde, the celebrated artist from Santa Clara Pueblo, communicates this in her rendering of the traditional tale, "Enchanted Hunter," from her collection *Old Father Story Teller*:

> Old Father sat smoking a corn husk tobacco cigarette while the children around the fireplace waited patiently for him to begin a story. [The practice of telling sacred stories is accompanied by ceremonial smoking.[11]] He was thinking of how each one must learn to awaken to his senses, to know himself as he is, good or bad, weak or strong; of how one must be alert, guarding against bodily harm and against the evil that can disturb the *e-ve-hanuh*, the inner self.[12]

Life is meant to be lived in a joyous manner while experiencing humor, beauty, and happiness. Pleasure and delight are highly valued. Pueblo men and women are reserved but sensuous people who are handsome and beautiful to look at. Pueblo women tend to wear joyous and beautiful colors. The gods do not wish to visit sad faces or downcast dispositions. For example, Ben Marcus, an elder of Taos, loved to dance—dancing was in his blood. He often went up to his roof early in the morning to dance the sun up.[13]

Traditionally brought-up people tend to concentrate on the good rather than dwelling on the bad: they visualize and anticipate the good. Humor has a place in Pueblo culture even in sacred moments, witness the at times outrageous, scandalous, and scatological conduct of summer and winter clowns. Hopi artist Michael Kabotie calls the clowns "priests of life." He discloses the prayer of the clown: "With one smile may there be enlightenment."[14]

Pueblo people love to laugh; they joke, and make puns. People especially laugh at their own misfortunes; this is a potent survival mechanism.[15] Many a time I have roared with laughter as I joked with Joe Sando of Jemez, Otellie Loloma of Shipaulovi, a Hopi village, and Manuelita Lovato of Santo Domingo.

The day before Hopi wedding festivities is traditionally set aside for the aunts of the groom to descend on those of the bride, and then to figuratively and literally sling mud at each other—to hurl verbal abuse at the respective bride or groom while literally slinging mud at people inside or outside the house. This is quite an enjoyable and humorous occasion. It certainly serves a useful purpose: Hopi people fling mud at each other's families before, and not after, a wedding. Of course, Hopi weddings are a long time coming, so that by the time there is a wedding, people know each other rather well: they know what mud to fling and where to aim the blows.[16]

To return to the corn, how do you successfully care for it and everything that grows? You nurture it. Thus, the Pueblo ideal of conduct is to be a nurturer: this, of course, is a female ideal, that of the good mother. Swentzell declares that "Human life, in the traditional Pueblo world, is based on philosophical premises that promote consideration, compassion, and gentleness toward both human and nonhuman beings."[17]

Pueblo traits which are highly valued include generosity, reciprocity, harmony, sharing, all-inclusiveness, willingness to work together with others when the need arises, the importance of the family, and thinking, deciding, and speaking from the heart. The Tewa definition of health is balance, harmony, and connectedness.[18] In the words of Rina Swentzell, the Tewa believe that "the breath of life, the *powaha*, flows through all life expressions—even village forms." The term *powaha* means "water-wind-breath." "Water-wind-breath" energizes all life, touching and emanating from rocks, trees, and houses: "It is not discriminatory and does not remain exclusively in the human context."[19]

The world view we are exploring is concerned with dualities: summer and winter; Mother Earth and Father Sky; this world and the next world; this world and that of the ancestors; this world and the previous world(s) up to the emergence; the traditionalists and the progressives, or the hostiles and the friendlies; what is male and what is female. For example, the Tewa and the Zuni view the cosmos as a spherical unit: "The male sky is referred to as a basket, while the female earth is a bowl."[20]

Rina Swentzell believes that opposites or dualities create tension and are the source of movement and continual transformation. She reveals that:

> Winter and Summer, as the social/political organizing principle of the Tewa Pueblos, assure psychical and political movement within the human context. Each equinox the Winter group which consists of approximately half of the members of the community, takes or gives the decision-making power to the Summer people. Stasis is avoided.[21]

I now consider female ways of being and doing among the Pueblos, with an emphasis on the Keresan and Zuni peoples. At times I will of course refer to what is considered male in this world.

In the Pueblo world everything is male or female—rain, mountains, rivers, colors, plants, rites, and customs. Let's hear what Paula Gunn Allen of Laguna Pueblo has to say on this topic:

> For the Laguna Pueblos, everything has male and female manifestations. Rocks and hard things, salt, crystals, cohesiveness, and thought are female. The soft gardener's rain that goes slowly into the earth and waters everything: that's female rain. Male is the rain that goes *Wham*! and runs down the arroyos [ditches]. It's wonderful and terribly exciting, but then it's gone. Female lightning is sheet lightning that fills everything. Male lightning is the jagged arrow, the bolt. The female seems to be more inclusive, and it's always big. The female never dies; the male is born and dies. And both things are true. Things are always coming into being and passing away. That's male. But things are always staying right where they are in a sense, and that's female. Men are warriors because it's important to them to go out and keep testing their transitoriness. I don't think it's that men get to do all the exciting things and women have to do all the dull things. That's not how my grandma thought. In America, the ones who get on radio and TV and get to be president are the men, and they've convinced us [women that] that's really important. But at Laguna it was important, maybe more important, to grind the corn and feed everybody.[22]

As mentioned above, the Pueblo ideal of conduct is that of motherhood. In this respect, Allen declares that "where I come from the ideal of manhood is motherness."[23] We have seen that male Pueblo religious leaders are called "fathers and mothers." Indeed Simon Ortiz has written a poem entitled "The Expectant Father." According to the poet, the way the prospective father behaves, thinks, and feels, is just as important as the way the expectant mother behaves, thinks, and feels; it affects the soul, mind, body, heart, and spirit of the developing fetus just as much. Here is the poem:

> I am an expectant father.
>
> Pray then:
> Smile for all good things,
> note the wind,
> note the rain,
> touch the gentleness with care;
> be good. . . .

When the child comes, expectant father,
tell the child.
When I have awoken in the early mornings,
I have felt the child's flutter at the small of my back,
the mother's belly pressed against me.
The child is a butterfly, cupped in the Mother's hands.
Be kind, Naya; be kind, this morning
and for all mornings of our—your—children's lives.

When it rains in a soft wind,
it feels so good.[24]

Laguna Pueblo writer Leslie Marmon Silko, in her masterwork *Ceremony*, portrays the traditional male storyteller is pregnant with sacred stories which are the life of the people:

I will tell you something about stories,
[he said]
They aren't just entertainment.
Don't be fooled.
They are all we have, you see,
all we have to fight off
illness and death.

You don't have anything
if you don't have the stories.
Their evil is mighty
but it can't stand up to our stories.
So they try to destroy the stories
let the stories be confused or forgotten.
They would like that
They would be happy
Because we would be defenseless then.

He rubbed his belly.
I keep them here
[he said]
Here, put your hand on it
See, it is moving
There is life here
for the people.

And in the belly of this story
the rituals and the ceremony
are still growing.[25]

To return to the overall Pueblo ideal of conduct, in a paper by Rina Swentzell and her brother Tito Naranjo, also from Santa Clara Pueblo, the two authors declare that being a mother or *gia* (a Tewa pueblo term) "is the essence of Pueblo thought and being. It is manifested in the family, community and religious aspects of . . . [life in the Pueblo]. It describes the ideal person and outlines the goal for that society."[26]

The fascinating etymological parallel between *gia* and *Gaia* is supported by the meaning ascribed to the Tewa term by the two authors:

> The Santa Clara Tewa word "gia" in its most frequent and simple usage is synonymous with "mother". . . . It refers to a person who gives, loves, provides, protects, and assures balance and harmony—a person who gives food, life and health. According to Pueblo thinking, the word is not exclusively used to designate female nurturers but rather is also applied to particular groups of males, or spiritual entities, and is even used in reference to the ultimate nurturer—the Earth. . . . The Earth is the ultimate nurturer. She is our mother, or *nung be gia.* We humans move in and out of her womb as told in the emergence myths of the Pueblos. She is constant, reliable, and always giving and forgiving. She protects and heals.[27]

Another Tewa word for the earth is *nan*: this term means the living, pulsating earth.[28]

Unsurprisingly, in *The Sacred Hoop* Allen acknowledges that

> At Laguna Pueblo in New Mexico, "Who is your mother?" is an important question. At Laguna, one of several of the ancient Keres gynocratic societies of the region, your mother's identity is the key to your own identity. Among the Keres, every individual has a place within the universe—human and nonhuman—and that place is defined by clan membership. In turn, clan membership is dependent on matrilineal descent. Of course, your mother is not only that woman whose womb formed and released you—the term refers in every individual case to an entire generation of women whose psyches, and consequently, physical "shape" made the psychic existence of the following generation possible. But naming your own mother (or her equivalent) enables people to place you precisely within the universal web of your life, in each of its dimensions: cultural, personal, and historical.[29]

At the Catholic mission of San Diego at Jemez Pueblo, people show their concern for the mother. In the traditional Nativity scene at Christmas the statue of the Virgin Mary is placed face-up while she rests lying down, her torso wrapped in a blanket, as she is recovering from childbirth. It is touching to see such loving concern for the mother. Such caring attention does give one pause: in comparison, there is something distinctly odd about traditional European-oriented Nativity statues of the Virgin Mary, who is depicted as standing up, or kneeling, just after she has given birth. Traditionally it has been the Pueblo mother's role to rest rather extensively after labor.[30]

The earth in New Mexico is not the same as the earth near the California coast with its soft rolling hills. As Allen declares:

> Where I come from the earth is female; you look at the landscape and its stone mesas, it's vast and huge and terrifyingly powerful. . . . You're looking at these enormous mountains and these vast plains, where in the old days before smog you could see 150 miles. Where I come from, God is a woman. To understand the native people you have to understand female force, female intelligence in native systems. It is tribal and female-focused or female-centered. It's not about all these tough women who beat up on men. It's about balance and mutual respect and reciprocal obligation. Our relationship to the Animal People and to the Spirit People is reciprocal. Where I come from, God who is the woman is not Mother Earth, but Spider Grandmother. We don't call her Mother Earth. We call her *I-yati-kooh* or Corn Woman. Before her, in the beginning there was Thought Woman; she had two medicine bundles, and in each of these bundles was a woman, a spirit, a god. And each of these God women had sacred bundles. And the Spider sang them into life. She's not their mother. She's their sister [in other words, their co-creator]! It's about sisters. Into their bundles, they sing the heavens, the firmament, the languages, the mountains, the rivers, and all that into being.[31]

Women play invaluable roles in Pueblo and Keresan cultures. Let us begin by considering some of the divine roles they play in Laguna culture. Thought Woman, the creator deity, is primarily female, yet she contains both male and female qualities. She creates the universe, the world, and their stories. She is the "Great Spirit." The pan-Pueblo Spider Woman is also female: in Keresan religious thought, she is the secular version of Thought Woman.[32] At the beginning of *Ceremony*, Leslie Silko declares:

> *Ts'its'tsi'nako,* Thought-Woman,
> is sitting in her room
> and whatever she thinks about appears.
>
> She thought of her sisters,
> *Nau'ts'ity'i* and *I'tcts'ity'i,*

and together they created the Universe
this world
and the four worlds below.

Thought-Woman, the spider,
named things and
as she named them
they appeared.
She is sitting in her room
thinking of a story now

I'm telling you the story
she is thinking.[33]

To return to other God women, Mother Corn, or Iyatiku, is female; so is the pan-Pueblo Salt Woman, the pan-Pueblo Clay Lady, and, of course the Keresan figure of Yellow Woman.

A Laguna version of the legend of Ship'apu, as told by Paul Johnson to his clanswoman Miriam Marmon, reveals the role played by God women in the initiation and ongoing maintenance of creation:

> According to tradition, my people came from a land of the North many, many years ago, from a place called *Ship'apu. Ship'apu* was in an underground pit or chamber, and in this underground chamber dwelt the Indians. The mother of these people was a beautiful woman, *Nau tzi tee* by name . . . . Reason, [that is, Thought Creation Woman] a great power—the Great Spirit, we might call it—had created the earth, the sun, the stars, and all living creatures. *Nau tzi tee* saw that everything was beautiful. She saw the sun in the sky, but she wondered where it would look the best. She tried having the sun rise in the north, but that was not becoming to the earth. Then she tried the west and the south, which also failed to be effective. She then tried the east, and that was very becoming and beautiful. A beautiful light glowed clear across the eastern horizon. Thus the first day came and went.[34]

In the Keresan creation story, the co-creator or God woman named Nau tzi tee takes aesthetic pleasure in her creation. She is depicted as an artist and a playful experimentalist. Incidentally, this Laguna myth about Nau tzi tee and the sun could be a coded way of saying that there have been four worlds or ages, and that in each world or age the sun has risen and set in a different direction than in the previous worlds or ages. The legend continues:

> *Ship'apu* being in an underground chamber, how were the people to come out of this dwelling place? *Nau tzi tee*, the mother of these people—the

> *Katsina* people—said, "Who shall open a way out of here so that we may ascend from this cavern?" She asked *E sto a mut* (Arrow Boy) to pierce a hole through the Earth. *E sto a mut* did as he was told, and at once pierced a hole through the earth, but the hole was too small. *Nau tzi tee* then called on the badger to make the opening larger. He at once began scratching and digging upward through the earth with his sharp claws. The opening was large enough now, and *Nau tzi tee* and her children came forth. As they came forth, she said to her children, "Go now your way in all directions, each taking with you your customs and ways, but always remember that you forget not your home here. Cast your thoughts and prayers back here often, for I am ready always to hear you."[35]

Nau tzi tee births her people into a new world and, like all good mothers, she assures her children of her continued concern for, and responsiveness to, their plight.

Spider Grandmother's role in the Keresan world is described by Acoma poet and potter Angelina Medina's moving and insightful work "Spread Peace":

> Mother's Spirit
>
> Spirals through the universe
>
> Silver Thread
>
> Connects us to all
>
> Feel the freedom
> See the expanse of eternity
> Experience our bond
>
> Humble beings are we all
> Yet immense is the power we hold
> If we but use it well
> To give abundant harmony
> She can then spread peace[36]

The Keresan goddess Iyatiku told the people at the beginning as she gave the religious leader an ear of corn: "Take this. . . . This corn is my heart. This is what you will live on; its milk shall be to you as milk from my breasts."[37]

Salt Woman is another important pan-Pueblo female entity. Physically unattractive, rough and scaly, yet magically powerful, she gives up of herself so that the people may live. She makes us question ideals of physical beauty: does the outer truly reflect the inner? Salt Woman makes food flavorful and tasty. Hers is a hard yet vital substance. When the people make a heartfelt and appropriate pilgrimage to her lake, she offers them parts of herself. When the people dishonor her, they are visited by destructive storms and a dearth of crops, as they were during the Great Depression.[38] Without her, food has no taste.

The Clay Lady lives on in each piece of clay pottery reverently made in the traditional manner; she inspires and advises her potters what to do with each piece of clay. Renowned Cochiti potter Helen Cordero, who created the original Pueblo storyteller doll, says that her clay figures talk to her and tell her to make just what the Clay Lady wants.[39] Barbara Babcock has observed that "every recorded Pueblo origin myth . . . describes the creation of life itself as occurring in part through the process of pottery making."[40]

Santa Clara Pueblo poet and potter Nora Naranjo-Morse has revealed that

> Even today, when . . . [an appropriate] vein [of clay to use for pottery] is located and uncovered, a prayer is offered to *Nan chu Kweejo* (Clay Mother), acknowledging her generous gifts to us. . . . This prayer continually renews our relationship to the earth, her gifts, and . . . [the people].[41]

Here is the English translation of this Tewa prayer:

> Clay Mother,
> I have come to the center of your abode,
> feed and clothe me
> and in the end you will absorb me
> into your center.
> However far you travel,
> do not go crying.[42]

The last lines of this prayer underline the inherent value of pleasure and happiness in the Pueblo world view.

Before we leave the divine women of the Keresans, I would like to introduce you to Yellow Woman. In this culture yellow is the color of the Northwest and yellow is the color for woman; thus, as Allen has remarked, the name Yellow Woman or *Kochinninako* in Keresan means "Woman-Woman."[43] She plays many roles in Keresan culture:

> [Kochinninako] lives in New Mexico . . . She is a Spirit, a Mother, a blessed ear of corn, an archetype, a person, a daughter of a main clan, an agent of change and of obscure events, a wanton, an outcast, a girl who runs off with Navajos, or Zunis, or . . . Mexicans. She is also . . . consort of the sun [and thus mother of the twin war gods], granddaughter of the one who plays with stars, [and she is] somehow . . . related to Grandmother Spider, the

> Woman Who Thinks Us As We Are Being . . .[44] Yellow Woman [figures] in many narratives concerned with rituals related to wilderness and natural surroundings of the pueblo.[45]

Kochinninako is the "goddess of the game, giver of women's dress, baskets, and place-names"; she is "a mountain spirit with yellow face," often associated with Arrow Boy, who seems to be her brother or husband.[46] Yellow Woman is an independent divine being.[47] It is she who brought the buffalo to the people.[48] Today we would call her a "wild woman," a "woman who runs with the wolves."[49]

Now that we have considered the roles of divine Pueblo women, we will look at both traditional and contemporary roles Pueblo women play. We will begin with the former, primarily focusing on Zuni Pueblo. Anthropologist Ruth Bunzel has called Zuni "a woman's society" where "The women have a great deal of power and influence."[50] Archeologist Florence Hawley Ellis has declared, "I think the Pueblo men think of women as good advisors."[51]

Traditionally girls have been the preferred offspring at Zuni.[52] Edmund Ladd, anthropologist and member of Zuni Pueblo, has discussed women's traditional roles there. As mentioned above, a child belongs to his mother's clan. According to Ladd,

> Women play a very special religious role. They must know the proper words of prayers to keep the corn maidens from running away. (In legend, the corn maidens ran away from Zuni because they were not respected and properly cared for. A great famine occurred until they were coaxed back to Zuni by the . . . galaxy society.) The women must also bless the newborn with water and present them to the Sun Father with proper prayers. They must prepare the bodies of their deceased clan relatives for burial. They must prepare food offerings for the gods, feed the ancestors at every meal at the table or the fireplace, and also greet the morning sunrise. Men are responsible for the universe. Women are responsible for the family and the tribe. All life is traced through the mother. Thus, one's mother's household is the center of all major religious and ceremonial events.[53]

Ladd goes on to say that "Women, regardless of age, offer prayer meal and prayer sticks to the ancestors and to the moon. . . . The prayer sticks offered by women are prepared for them by male relatives."[54]

Pueblo woman up to a ripe old age plaster walls and repair roofs.

> The house and housekeeping are associated with women. Clay is the flesh of a female supernatural and clay processes, brick making or laying or plastering, and pottery making are women's work. There are indications in sacerdotal circles that painting is or was thought of as a feminine

> activity. Corn, like clay, is the flesh of female supernaturals, and the corn is associated with women. Even men corn growers are duty bound to bring their product to their wife or mother. Women or women impersonators figure in corn rituals. . . . Today . . . the preparation of corn as of other food is women's work.[55]

Women have sex-specific tasks, expressions, and skills. Female relatives usually name the baby. Caring for the children, cooking, and being in charge of the house, as well as work on embroidery, pottery making, and sewing clothes, have traditionally been female occcupations.

When a woman is pregnant, movement on the right side indicates the child will be a girl; movement on the left reveals the child will be a boy.[56] Among the Keresans and the Tewa, right is the side of life, or the flesh, while left is the side of death, or the spirit: when a woman dies her traditional dress or manta is fastened on the left.[57] In 1919, Elsie Clews Parsons related that

> [Immediately] after . . . birth [at Zuni], a boy is sprinkled on the penis with cold water that the parts may be small, and a girl has placed over the vulva a gourd cup, that the parts may be large. These requirements in physical proportion are distinctively feminine, as men will say to women, "Why do you want us small and yourselves large?"[58]

Female heads of clans daily feed the important paraphernalia belonging to the clan. Women also feed the household fetishes or power objects.

Needless to say, the prototype of the Pueblo woman is not the slim, seemingly ageless creature of mainstream Western culture. In this respect I cite Allen's poem, "The Beautiful Woman Who Sings":

> a beautiful woman at Laguna
> isn't much like a beautiful woman
> in L.A. except for some parts
> of it, of her, who carried
> beauty in her eyes. the strength
> of her hands. not gentle, though,
> of course gentle, but power.
> those women were large. big.
> round. smiling. serious.
> selfcontained. private.
> kept right on. with what they
> were. doing. beautiful.
> not for its own sake. not
> devoid of meaning. ovoid. not

void. full. not empty. but
not noisy either. maybe that
was the beauty of them.
not full of noise. laughing,
to be sure . . . and sure the
beautiful women. beautiful corn
woman. woman like corn:
ripe and full. sweet. self
generating. tasseled.
blowing in the wind. meeting.
juicy. feeding. coming back
every time. coming home.
filling the fields with green.
making the people dance.
gathering.
making the children laugh.
making butterflies sing.[59]

Angelina Medina's poem "Big Eyes Bust/Curly Hair" reveals more of the Keresan concept of womanly beauty:

. . . Regardless of the ads
I try to live my life
According to the Pueblo teachings
Knowing I am accepted as a worthy human being
Because of what I say and do
And not because of how I look

My wise old grandmother
Has always reminded me that a woman who is
Truthful and honest
Thoughtful and considerate
Respectful and unselfish
Is truly beautiful[60]

Pueblo women's societies traditionally deal with fertility, reproduction, favorable weather, war, and curing. Santa Ana Pueblo is the sole pueblo with masked dances involving women.[61] Women at Zuni are buried on the north side of the cemetery, men on the south.[62]

At many western pueblos the choice of marriage and sexual partners is with the woman.[63] At contemporary western Pueblo bars in Gallup and elsewhere

where people dance with partners[64] to contemporary music, dancing pueblo style is always ladies' choice.

In the mid-1800s the Hopi village of Moenkopi chose a woman—Nashile-owi—as its political spokesperson. More recently Verna Williamson of Isleta Pueblo was elected and served as the first modern Pueblo tribal chairwoman.[65]

According to anthropologist Alfonso Ortiz of San Juan, among the Tewa winter, strength, hunting, meat as a food, as well as mountains, shrines, and lakes of the north and east are associated with maleness; summer, weakness, agriculture, wild and cultivated plants, and mountains, shrines, and lakes of the south and west are associated with femaleness. Winter People are called Ice Strong People, East Side People, Ice People, and Turquoise People; White Corn Maiden of Winter has male characteristics: she is something of an Amazon. Summer People are called Summer Strong People, West Side People, Sun People, and Squash People; Blue Corn Woman of Summer has female characteristics.[66]

Joseph (Beautiful Painted Arrow) Rael, a teacher, healer, and storyteller of Ute/Picuris blood, who grew up with his relatives at Picuris Pueblo, says that at Picuris men embody and represent the "essence of expanding light," while women embody and represent the "essence of descending light."[67] For the Tiwa people of Picuris, the houses traditionally have been "square, the shape symbolic of the masculine." The kivas, on the other hand, where boys and men go for their spiritual training, have been "round, the shape symbolic of the feminine."[68]

Nowadays, even at pueblos as traditional as Taos, men are beginning to help out with the housework or work as "househusbands."[69] Women work in the world, some as artists, some in professional capacities. We have noted that the Pueblo ideal is to be a nurturer, a mother. Mothers serve as role models for their sons.

Pueblo mothers can have close relationships with their sons. I once observed a particularly gracious Pueblo secretary at the Institute of American Indian Arts working at the Xerox machine while talking with her son. She quietly told him how she had received her professional training—on the job. Her son ultimately joined the Armed Forces to get his education and training on the job, just as his mother had. This woman is not a single mother; she is happily married to a Pueblo man.

In the fall of 1982 when I first began teaching at the Institute, I shared an office space with an Indian man from the Midwest; he was a counselor who had married a Pueblo woman. She had just given birth to their son. When I was at my desk during those first days after their son's birth, I often heard my officemate telephone his wife to gently and patiently ask and remind her to name their baby.

A particular secretary with whom I have worked at the Institute embodies the glory and beauty of Pueblo womanhood. She radiates a quiet, gentle strength, a feeling of peace, balance, universal love, and harmony. These are very unusual qualities which are not always recognized, appreciated, or understood by the mainstream-focused individual.

A few years ago my superior was a Pueblo man who holds a Ph.D. in social science. Every one of us who worked with him—for we worked with him, rather than under him—experienced a high point in his or her professional life. This man really cares for the people with whom he works. He encouraged us to learn, grow, contribute, flourish, and prosper. I know a gentle elder from the same pueblo with much the same characteristics. The former chairman of the All-Indian Pueblo Council of New Mexico, a distinguished gentleman, has the same sweet wisdom and quietly powerful demeanor as those of the two men I have just mentioned.

I will always remember the time in the early 1980s when Joseph Rael visited my Institute class in Native American visionary literature and experience. He did not demand a fee for his lecture. When he came, he gently spoke to us about the cosmovision of the Pueblo peoples, related some incidents about his life, answered a few questions, and, as he was leaving the room, removed his beautiful, large, light-blue, turquoise-nugget-adorned bolo tie, and gave it to a student in the class who had said little during Joseph's lecture, but who, nonetheless, was going through a hard time. Such humble generosity and quiet thoughtfulness are typical of Pueblo people.

The men I have described are not what Robert Bly calls "soft men"—on the contrary, they are very attractive because of the balance of masculine and feminine qualities in their personalities. Another important reason for their attractiveness and charm may be that their role models include the buffalo, the deer, the eagle, Kokopelli[70], and the Sun God, as well, of course, as the Earth Mother. As Regis Pecos, a gentle and powerful young man from Cochiti Pueblo, has stated: "We believe duality to be a means of balance; others see it as something where conflict evolves."[71]

To emphasize this point, I would like to quote Joseph Rael of Picuris, who states that

> Even as a boy of six or seven, already the round structure of my femininity was expanding the potential in my masculinity because alchemically I was growing into my opposite, that I might learn balance of male and female. What was being taught was that one first accepts the energy that he/she is born into and then learns its opposite, so that one can become integrated and balanced.[72]

Now that I have described the Pueblos, their ideals of conduct, and the traditional and contemporary roles women play in Pueblo life, I can ask the question: How have the Pueblo Indians survived for centuries in such an arduous climate? For Allen, the way of the Pueblo people is "The way of respect, the way of nonviolation."[73] Simon Ortiz was continually told as he grew up at Acoma that his people exist because "our ancestors loved, cared, and prepared for us. They loved themselves, their land, and their way of life; they lived responsibly so that life would regenerate and flourish. And we . . . [are] expected to do the same."[74] His ancestors survived because they were nurturers.

Silko states that "Pueblo cultures seek to include rather than exclude. [The ideal mother loves all her children: she is inclusive.] The Pueblo impulse is to accept and incorporate what works, because human survival in the Southwestern climate is so arduous and risky." She goes on to affirm that "Hopi [and, by implication, all Pueblo peoples] . . . are the people who would not die, the people who do not change, because they are always changing."[75]

To link this concept to my own line of argument, which beings are always changing? Of course, humanity in general as well as man in particular changes: man is born, grows up, matures, ripens, dies, and falls back into the earth. The Earth Mother changes; the seasons change. Woman in particular is always changing. By virtue of her primordial physical, spiritual, and emotional role as mother, with its concomitant stages of infancy, childhood, adolescence, and the onset of menstruation with its cycles of menstruation, pregnancy, and birth, which ultimately result in menopause, the law of woman is both the law of transformation and the law of adaptation to changing circumstances.[76] These two laws are the laws of Pueblo life.

Silko has declared that "What is essential to all Pueblo people is that generation after generation they will continue to remember and to tell one another who they are, who they have been, and who they may become."[77] In the Pueblo world view it is primarily the mother as well as the spirit of motherhood as embodied in everyday life, which ensures that life continues and unfolds from generation to generation. This then is the meaning of the spirit of sustainability and the female principle among the Southwest Pueblos.

Notes

1. *Ancient Land, Ancestral Places, Paul Logsdon in the Pueblo Southwest*, essays by Stephen H. Lekson and Rina Swentzell, photographic text by Catherine M. Cameron (Santa Fe: Museum of New Mexico Press, 1993), 142.
2. All references in this paragraph are from Rina Swentzell, cited in *The People, Indians of the American Southwest* by Stephen Trimble (Santa Fe: School of American Research Press, 1993), 44.

3. See, for example, Barton Wright, *Kachinas of the Zuni* (Flagstaff, Ariz.: Northland Press, 1985) to get an idea of such obligations.
4. For the Hopi, see Harold Courlander, *The Fourth World of the Hopis, The Epic Story of the Hopi Indians as Preserved in Their Legends and Traditions* (Albuquerque: University of New Mexico Press, 1971). For the Zuni, see: Dennis Tedlock, "Zuni Religion and World View," *Southwest*, vol. 9:499. For the Keresans, see Leslie A. White, "The World of the Keresan Pueblo Indians," *Primitive Views of the World*, ed. Stanley Diamond (New York and London: Columbia University Press, 1969). For the Tewa, see Rina Swentzell, "Prehistoric Architecture with Unknown Function," in *Mesa Verde Symposium on Anasazi Architecture and American Design*, Baker H. Morrow and V. B. Price, eds. (Albuquerque, N. Mex.: Morrow and Co., Ltd., 1992), 150. For the Tiwa, see Nancy Wood, "Fire Fire of the First World," *Hollering Sun* (New York: Simon and Schuster, 1972). For the Towa, see Joe S. Sando, *Nee Hemish, A History of Jemez Pueblo* (Albuquerque: University of New Mexico Press, 1982), 4.
5. Trimble and Swentzell, cited in Trimble, *The People*, 53.
6. Unpublished paper, Rina Swentzell and Tito Naranjo.
7. Howard Rainer and Sharon Reyna, *Beyond the Adobe Wall, A Tribute to Taos Pueblo in Art and Prose* (Taos: H and R Productions, no date), 4.
8. Simon J. Ortiz, *Woven Stone* (Tucson & London: The University of Arizona Press), 47.
9. Vickie Downey, cited in *Wisdom's Daughters, Conversations with Women Elders of Native America*, written and photographed by Steve Wall (New York: HarperCollins Publishers, Inc., 1993), 2.
10. Laura Fragua, cited in *Crosswinds*, August 1993, vol. 5, no. 9:27.
11. Barbara A. Babcock, and Guy and Doris Monthan, *The Pueblo Storyteller, Development of a Figurative Tradition* (Tucson: The University of Arizona Press, 1986), 31.
12. Pablita Velarde, *Old Father Story Teller* (Santa Fe: Clear Light Publishers), 24–26.
13. Nancy Wood, *Taos Pueblo*, with an introduction by Vine Deloria, Jr. (New York: Alfred A. Knopf, 1987), xix-xx.
14. Trimble, *The People*, 53.
15. Personal communication, Joe Sando.
16. Susanne and Jake Page, *Hopi* (New York: Harry N. Abrams, Inc., Publishers, 1982), 168ff.
17. Lekson and Swentzell, *Ancient Land, Ancestral Places*, 141.
18. Trimble, *The People*, 115.
19. Lekson and Swentzell, *Ancient Land, Ancestral Places*, 141. For an intro-

duction to the rich metaphorical nature of the Tiwa language and way of life at Picuris Pueblo, see *Beautiful Painted Arrow, Stories & Teachings From the Native American Tradition*, by Joseph E. Rael (Shaftesbury, Dorset, and Rockport, Mass.: Element, Inc., 1992). In *Indian Tales from Picuris Pueblo*, collected by John P. Harrington, with musical transcriptions by Helen H. Roberts, ed. Marta Weigle (Santa Fe, N. Mex.: Ancient City Press, 1989). Harrington, p. 9, discusses the "versatility of the [Tiwa] language, which is capable of expressing the most intricate and poetic thought."

20. Swentzell, cited in *Ancient Land, Ancestral Places*, 145; Ruth L. Bunzel, "Introduction to Zuni Ceremonialism," in *Zuni Ceremonialism, Three Studies*, introduction by Nancy J. Parezo (Albuquerque: University of New Mexico Press, 1992), 487.
21. Lekson and Swentzell, *Ancient Lands, Ancestral Places.* John Collier, former Commissioner of Indian Affairs, saw Pueblo society as a utopia. He felt it could provide a model for American society. Collier "believed that the Pueblos had found the perfect balance between individual and community identity, a balance that was lacking in urbanized, industrialized America": cited by Alfonso Ortiz, *The Pueblo*, in vol. 9 of *Indians of North America*, general ed. Frank W. Porter III (New York and Philadelphia: Chelsea House Publishers, 1994), 105.
22. Paula Gunn Allen, "Where I Come From, God Is a Woman," *Whole Earth Review*, no. 74, spring 1992:44.
23. An interview with Paula Gunn Allen, by Patrice Wynne, "Recovering Spirituality in Native American Traditions," *Woman of Power, a Magazine of Feminism, Spirituality, and Politics*, Issue Eight, *ReVisioning the Dark*, winter 1988:69.
24. Simon Ortiz, 47–48.
25. Leslie Marmon Silko, *Ceremony* (New York: New American Library, 1977), 2.
26. Swentzell and Naranjo.
27. Swentzell and Naranjo, "Nurturing: The *Gia* at Santa Clara Pueblo," *El Palacio*, vol. 92(1):36
28. Cited in Alejandro Lopez, "Tewa Women United, The Breath of Life," *The Sun* (Santa Fe), March 1993:19.
29. Allen, *The Sacred Hoop, Recovering the Feminine in American Indian Traditions* (Boston: Beacon Press, 1986), 209.
30. See, for example, Elsie Clews Parsons, "Hopi Mothers and Children (1921)," in *Pueblo Mothers and Children, Essays by Elsie Clews Parsons 1915–1924*, ed. Barbara A. Babcock (Santa Fe, N. Mex.: Ancient City Press, 1991), 111.
31. Allen, *Whole Earth Review*, 45.

32. See Anthony F. Purley, "Keres Pueblo Concepts of Deity," *American Indian Culture and Research Journal* I (1974):1. Also see Laguna creation myth which follows in the text.
33. Silko, *Ceremony*, 1.
34. Bertha P. Dutton and Miriam A. Marmon, *The Laguna Calendar*, The University of New Mexico Bulletin, Anthropological Series, 1936, vol. 1(2):20.
35. Ibid.
36. Angelina Medina, *Angelina Sings, Poetry of a Pueblo Sculptress* (Zuni, N. Mex.: 1991), Book Two: 20.
37. White, *Primitive Views of the World*, 85.
38. See Dutton and Marmon, *The Laguna Calendar.*
39. Personal communication, Helen Cordero.
40. Barbara Babcock, and Guy and Doris Monthan, *The Pueblo Storyteller*, 9.
41. Nora Naranjo-Morse, *Mud Woman, Poems from the Clay* (Tucson & London: The University of Arizona Press, 1992), 9.
42. Ibid., 9.
43. Allen, cited in Marta Weigle, "Southwest Native American Mythology," in *The Feminist Companion to Mythology*, ed. Carolyne Larrington (London: Pandora, 1992), 347.
44. Allen, ed., *Spider Woman's Granddaughters, Traditional Tales and Contemporary Writing by Native American Women*, with an introduction by the editor (Boston: Beacon Press, 1989), 182.
45. Allen, *Grandmothers of the Light, A Medicine Woman's Sourcebook* (Boston: Beacon Press, 1991), 241.
46. Kenneth Lincoln, *Native American Renaissance* (Berkeley, Los Angeles, and London: University of California Press, 1983), 244.
47. Allen, *Grandmothers of the Light*, 244.
48. Leslie Marmon Silko, "Cottonwood Part Two: Buffalo Story," *Storyteller* (New York: Seaver Books, 1981), 67ff.
49. Clarissa Pinkola Estes, Ph.D., *Women Who Run With the Wolves: Myths and Stories of the Wild Woman Archetype* (New York: Ballantine Books, 1992).
50. Ruth Bunzel, cited in *Daughters of the Desert, Women Anthropologists and the Native American Southwest, 1880–1980, An Illustrated Catalogue*, by Barbara A. Babcock and Nancy J. Parezo (Albuquerque: University of N. Mex. Press, 1988), 41.
51. Florence Hawley Ellis, cited in *Daughters of the Desert*, 125.
52. Elsie Clews Parsons, "Zuni Conception and Pregnancy Beliefs (1915)," in *Pueblo Mothers and Children*, 35.
53. Edmund Ladd, "Zuni Religion and Philosophy," in *Zuni and El Morro, Past*

& Present, eds. David Grant Noble and Richard B. Woodbury (Santa Fe, N. Mex.: Ancient City Press, 1983), 28.

54. Ibid., 30.
55. Parsons, "Waiyautitsa of Zuni, N. Mex. (1919)," in *Pueblo Mothers and Children*, 103.
56. Parsons, "Mothers and Children at Zuni, New Mexico (1919)," in *Pueblo Mothers and Children*, 79.
57. Ruth Underhill, *Life in the Pueblos* (1946; Santa Fe, N. Mex.: Ancient City Press, 1991), 145. For the Keresan view, see Allen, *Grandmothers of the Light*, 57–58.
58. Parsons, "Mothers and Children at Zuni, New Mexico (1919)," in *Pueblo Mothers and Children*, 79.
59. Allen, cited in *That's What She Said, Contemporary Poetry and Fiction by Native American Women*, ed. Rayna Green (Bloomington: Indiana University Press, 1984), 23.
60. Medina, *Angelina Sings Poetry*, 66.
61. Pauline Turner Strong, "Santa Ana Pueblo," in *Southwest*, ed. Alfonso Ortiz, *Handbook of North American Indians*, vol. 9:452.
62. Parsons, "Waiyautitsa," in *Pueblo Mothers and Children*, 100.
63. Ibid.
64. Barbara Tedlock, *The Beautiful and the Dangerous, Dialogues with the Zuni Indians* (New York and London: Penguin Books, 1993), 222.
65. References in this paragraph are to Trimble, 113.
66. Alfonso Ortiz, cited in Edward P. Dozier, *The Pueblo Indians of North America* (Prospect Heights, Ill.: Waveland Press, 1983), 107.
67. All references in this paragraph are to Joseph Rael, with Mary Elizabeth Marlow, *Being and Vibration* (Tulsa, Okla.: Council Oak Books, 1993), 149.
68. Ibid., 20.
69. Wood, *Taos Pueblo*, 122.
70. Kokopelli is the Humped-Backed Flute Player seen widely in rock art and ancient pottery throughout the Southwest. He carries a flute and at times is represented as ithyphallic. He represents fertility in all ways—he brings seeds and also can seduce women.
71. Trimble, *The People*, 105.
72. Rael, *Being and Vibration*, 20.
73. Allen, cited in *A Circle of Nations, Voices and Visions of American Indians, North American Native Writers & Photographers*, ed. John Gattuso (Hillsboro, Ore.: Beyond Words Publishing, Inc., 1993), 75.
74. Simon Ortiz, cited in *A Circle of Nations*, 27.
75. Leslie Marmon Silko, cited in *A Circle of Nations*, 6–7.

76. Allen, cited in *A Circle of Nations*, 72.
77. Silko, cited in *A Circle of Nations*, 7.

The author gratefully acknowledges permission granted by the publishers to reprint quotations cited above.

4. Iṣẹ Kekere Kan Ati Aṣẹ Ayie: The Ifá Concept of Work and the Power of the Earth

Awo Fa'lokun Fatunmbi

Editor's Note

In all traditions there are strong religious ties to the earth that hold wisdom which could be of value to modern society. There are values common to all traditions, but each culture also has unique contributions. This article brings an unwritten reservoir of knowledge into the light, helping African-Americans, as well as anyone else, by introducing the roots of earth wisdom among the Yoruba of West Africa.

In 1989 I made the first of several journeys to the African rain forest in Nigeria. I traveled to this region to study *Ifá,* the indigenous spiritual tradition of Yoruba culture. My initial interest was to explore the wisdom of Ifá as a methodology for personal transformation. The experience of being in Africa made it clear to me that Ifá considers personal development to be dependant upon one's ability to live in harmony with family, community, and the natural environment. I believe it is a system of thought and action that may offer important clues to finding ways to structure support systems in an urban environment that is less directly interactive with its use of natural resources.

As a tradition, Ifá is based on the concept of developing *iwa-pele,* which means "good character." According to Ifá, iwa-pele is the foundation for interaction with family, community, and the Forces in Nature that generate and sustain life. Personal growth is viewed by Ifá as a consequence of the interactive polarity between self and world. The foundation of this polarity is the idea that if someone else's life improves, my life improves and if someone else suffers, then I suffer. This belief is not limited to human interactions. It includes the interaction between animals, plants, and the earth itself because Ifá teaches that everything that exists has some form of consciousness.

Ifá is a system of both religious wisdom and technical knowledge. It is an integration of the information needed to support life in the West African rain forest. In the region where I have studied Ifá, the rain forest stretches to the horizon in every direction. As you leave the town and enter the bush, the layers of vegetation block the sky. There are iroko trees with trunks the size of a house, surrounded by ferns and thick, fan-shaped leaves. Literally thousands of plants, animals, and insects share an ecological web at any given spot. Ifá teaches that this web is a matrix of spiritual power called *ase.* These invisible lines of integration that exist in the rain forest create what Ifá calls an opening into the "invisible realm," or *Ikole Orun.* These openings are called *Igbodu,* which means "sacred grove." It is within these groves that humans, animals, and plants join together in the ritual process of creating harmony, balance, and community.

There is no literal translation for the word *Ifá.* It refers to a religious tradition, an understanding of ethics, a process of spiritual transformation, and a set of sacred stories that are the basis for a complex process of divination, technical information necessary for farming, as well as an understanding of indigenous herbal medicine, the structure of government, self-defense, and the preservation of trade skills. It is a world view that embraces spirituality, science, and art in a way that honors the past, while remaining open to the evolution of consciousness as well as an understanding of environmental change.

Ifá is found in Nigeria, Benin, Ghana, and Togo. Prior to colonization, the Yoruba Nation was a federation of city-states that was originally centered in the capitol city of Ile Ife. According to Ifá history, the Yoruba migrated to Ile Ife under the leadership of a warrior chief named Oduduwa. It is difficult to date the time of this migration because of limited archaeological research on the subject. Estimates range from between sixteen hundred to twenty-five hundred years ago. It is likely that migration took place over a number of generations. As the population grew, each new city-state that became part of the Yoruba Federation was governed by a king who was initiated into the mysteries of Oba.

Ifá myths also suggest that the Yorubas were not the original people who settled in the region of Ile Ife. These two historical accounts are not necessarily contradictory. Together they suggest that there was a blending of cultures that occurred in the region. Many historians have given the impression that African societies were isolated from each other and developed independently. There is clear evidence from an evaluation of oral traditions in the region that suggests cross-cultural interaction was extensive and that it occurred over most of the continent. For example, there are stories about Ifá sages traveling to Mecca, as well as references to desert floods. Because Ifá is both science and religion, it accumulated external and internal influences based on both need and accessibility. It is a synthesis of indigenous wisdom that has arisen from the land itself, coupled with a cosmopolitan sense of other cultures and diverse systems of learning.

Within the discipline of Ifá, there is a body of wisdom called *awo*, which means "mystery." In traditional Yoruba culture, awo refers to the hidden principles that explain the Mystery of Creation and Evolution. Awo also refers to the rituals used to create direct communication with Forces in Nature such as earth, air, fire, and water. It is the study of the invisible forces that sustain dynamics and form within Nature. The essence of these intangible forces is believed to remain elusive, awesome in their power to transform, and in possession of their own form of consciousness that can communicate directly with humans.

Ifá teaches that all Forces in Nature come into Being through the manifestation of energy patterns called *Odu*. Ifá has identified and labeled 256 different Odu which can be thought of as different expressions of primal consciousness. This is based on the Ifá belief that everything that has existence, has consciousness. Divination and trance serve as the basis for establishing the communication with Forces in Nature that is needed to sustain balance and harmony between the self and the world.

According to Ifá, it is not possible to abuse the environment without receiving some form of warning from the Nature Itself. These warnings may appear in a number of ways: dreams, unusual occurrences in the forest, prophetic voices, and through divination. Abuse of the environment is considered an expression of poor character. Ifá teaches that those who ignore the responsibility of developing good character run the risk of creating illness, accidents, poverty, and shortened life expectancy. Those who work at developing good character will receive blessings of long life, abundance, and children.

These blessings are believed to originate from the land of the Immortals, who are called *Orisha*. Yoruba Creation Myth states that the first Orisha to make the journey from the land of the Immortals to the land of earth was the Spirit of Obatala which means "King of the White Cloth." White Cloth is a mythic reference to sunlight. When Obatala made the journey, he traveled on a long chain for guidance and when he arrived near earth, he discovered that it was covered with water. He reached inside of a snail shell that was filled with dirt and sprinkled the soil on the water. Obatala then dropped a bird on the land, who scratched the dirt, creating a larger land mass. When the land was stable, he scattered seed for a palm tree. The seeds sprouted and produced a tree, allowing Obatala to release himself from the chain and climb into the tree and from there descend to earth.

In this traditional Creation story, we have an ancient expression of the idea that the earth's ecology was regulated by the effect of the sun on primal elements that existed on the planet. The place where Obatala first set foot on earth is the sacred city of Ile Ife. The words *Ile Ife* mean "spreading earth." Geologists who have studied African land formations theorize that three land masses pushed up from the bottom of the ocean many millions of years ago. Eventually the land masses expanded and united to form a giant continent which eventually broke apart, forming what is now known as Africa and South America. One of the three primal land masses is located in the area that Yoruba sacred history identifies as the original spreading earth, the city of Ile Ife.

It was at Ile Ife that an historical Prophet named Orunmila established the traditions of Ifá. The oral history surrounding Orunmila has clear elements of sacred myth, legend, and the historical record of actual events. One of the stories concerning Orunmila's journey to Ile Ife indicates that he survived a flood, then settled in the West African rain forest following the deluge. This suggest that the early sources of Ifá are ancient, because the only clear evidence of massive flooding on the African continent dates back nine thousand years.

The various disciplines that are incorporated within the wisdom of Ifá are preserved orally through the use of a system of divination called *dafa*. This system is based on the polarity between the forces of expansion that are symbolized by a single line (I), and the forces of contraction that are symbolized by a double line (II). These lines are grouped together in two sets of quadragrams, making an octogram. The octogram is called *Odu*, meaning "womb of creation." An example of Odu would appear as follows:

I I
II II
I I
I II

The use of this format generates 256 different patterns of Odu made up of various combinations of single and double lines. Each Odu is believed to represent a Primal Force in Nature. Ifá teaches that these Primal Forces come into being at every level of evolution. For example, the Spirit of Fire came into being during the Big Bang at the moment of Creation. Fire is reborn at the core of a star, born again in the fire at the center of the earth, manifest as fire on earth and reflected in the passions that form part of the inspiration for human development.

Within Ifá, Primal Forces in Nature or Odu are personified as Spiritual Beings. Spirits are then grouped together according to their function within the unfolding process of Creation and Evolution. Ifá clearly expresses the idea that Spirits are the physical and knowable manifestation of a single Creator called *Olorun*. This suggests that what is seen and known in the physical world is an approximation of a deeper mystery that remains illusive.

When used as the basis for divination, each Odu is associated with a set of religious verses called *Ese Odu.* These poetic verses preserve the spiritual and metaphysical understanding of each Odu. The pattern of the Odu itself forms a mandala or graphic representation of the energy patterns that actually occur in Nature. Most traditional Yoruba communities have a society of Ifá initiates who preserve the inner secrets of this system and insure that it is passed on to future generations. Those who are chosen to memorize the text associated with Odu begin the process when they are between seven and ten years old. The training period lasts for ten to fifteen years. Once the study process has started, it continues on a daily basis through oral instruction from an elder.

After the primary religious material has been memorized, there is a period of specialization, where the information related to science, medicine, government, farming, martial arts, and astrology are studied. Generally each student takes on one or two disciplines for study. These disciplines are delegated to a dozen or more initiates to insure that the entire body of collective wisdom and knowledge is preserved from one generation to the next. The system itself is fluid, allowing for the addition of new verses to each Odu as new insights are developed. For example, Odu related to hunting includes information on the use of bow and arrows as well as muskets.

It is this collective body of information that establishes the guidelines for maintaining a balanced relationship between self and world. The economy of Yoruba communities in the rain forest is based on farming. The style of farming is to clear a plot of land outside of the village and to work the land through the joint effort of the extended family. Staple crops include yams and corn. This diet is supplemented by gathering palm nuts, plantains, cola nuts, and assorted fruits and vegetables that grow in abundance in the forest. Some food is produced through the domestication of goats, sheep, pigs, and chickens and a limited amount of wildlife is gathered through hunting. The most common forms of wild animals eaten on a regular basis are snails and rodents.

The holistic approach to farming, hunting, and spiritual belief has been disrupted to some extent by Christian and Islamic proselytization in the region. However, the traditional relationships between indigenous religion, land management, and politics still exert a strong influence on daily life outside of the large cities. This relationship is extremely intricate and subtle. Yoruba culture places a high value on maintaining civility and decorum in public. For this reason, the inner workings of communal interaction usually take place behind closed doors. As a result, much of what has been written about Yoruba culture describes outward appearances and misses a deeper layer of wisdom, understanding, and cooperation.

Much of Western spiritual discipline is centered upon the idea of the individual, self-directed spiritual quest. In Yoruba culture such a quest would be considered vain and unproductive. Ifá teaches that life is a journey and that individuals can expect the guidance of those elders who have traveled along a significant leg of that journey, exhibiting the qualities of good character and humility.

In traditional Yoruba culture, good character is related to the idea that the earth is sacred. An expression of this world view is the Ifá doctrine that Nature provides abundance for those who live in harmony with Natural Law. This belief affects the way that land is managed, which in turn affects the way communities are organized, which in turn supports the ongoing ritual and ceremonial life within traditional culture.

Twenty million Yoruba-speaking people live along the northwestern rim of the African rain forest. The influence of Western technology is clearly evident in the region, because it is the source of some of the highest grade oil on earth. Villages that were once predominantly constructed of mud brick are now constructed with cement blocks and metal roofs. In spite of this influence, the earth-centered traditional spiritual values remain very much in evidence.

All three of my visits to the regions were spent in the city of Ode Remo. It is one hour's drive east of the port of Lagos in Nigeria. Ode Remo is located in the midst of a dense rain forest that surrounds that town in all four directions. The political structure of Ode Remo centers around the concept of a divine king. Most anthropological descriptions of this political station assume that it is similar to the European model of hierarchical monarchies. This assumption is inaccurate. In Yoruba culture the position of the king is usually called *Oba.* The prefix *O* in the Yoruba language is usually translated to mean "owner." However, this translation is misleading because the prefix more accurately expresses the idea of one who possesses a secret, or one who knows the mystery concealed within a particular aspect of physical reality. In Yoruba language, the concept of ownership refers to the idea of possessing an awareness of the essential nature of some object or realm of life experience. It does not necessarily refer to possession of the thing itself. The suffix *ba* means "to hide." Therefore, the term Oba suggests one who has wisdom related to hidden matters.

The installation of an Oba takes the form of a religious initiation transforming the initiate into a child of Oduduwa. In Ifá sacred history, Oduduwa is the original ancestor of the Yoruba people. The word *Oduduwa* means "owner of black character." Again "owner" suggests knowing the essential mystery, "black" is a reference to that which is "invisible," and "character" is considered the foundation of human potential. The initiation of the Oba provides the spiritual transformation that gives the monarch the wisdom to support the growth of the community. It is an initiation into the meaning of good character.

This is a noble idea and to insure that it is not corrupted by the human tendency towards an abuse of power, the position of Oba is regulated by an intricate system of checks and balances. The selection of Oba is not from a single family, but circulates on a rotating basis between sixteen different families within a given community. Once someone from a particular family has been chosen, that family goes to the end of the rotation. This process prevents a particular family from becoming entrenched in positions of political power.

Once selected, the Oba serves with the consent of the council of elders. The male council is usually called *Ogboni*, which means "wisdom of the earth." The female council of elders is usually called *Iyaami* meaning "my mothers." Both groups can make the collective judgement that the Oba is no longer qualified to serve in a position of leadership. This veto power tempers the actions of the Oba against making self-serving decisions. His true function is to act as the voice of unity following consensus.

As a further check against the abuse of power, the women of Iyaami have the ritual task of crowning the Oba each time that he appears in public for ceremonial purposes. Because the Oba must wear the crown to serve as king, the crowning ceremony becomes an effective lever in the balance of power.

The religious function of the Oba is to coordinate and facilitate the ceremonial life of the community. This is accomplished by announcing the dates of seasonal celebrations, and by personally giving a blessing at the commencement of communal ritual activity. The actual content of seasonal celebrations is the responsibility of a very elaborate network of religious collectives who preserve what is considered the inner secret of various aspects of communal life. Each of these collectives are associated with a specific Force in Nature or *Orisha*. They include: the elders of Ifá who preserve the tradition of divination; the elders of Osanyin who preserve the science of herbal medicine; the elders of Ogun who preserve the techniques of blacksmithing, hunting and self defense; the elders of Oshun and Yemoja who preserve female mysteries of health and who regulate trade skills; and the elders of Oya who run the community market and preserve methods of communication with the ancestors. This is only a partial list of complex and regionally diverse associations of religious societies that form the foundation of traditional Yoruba communal life.

The ceremonial life of each of these religious societies revolves around an Igbodu. The literal translation of the word *Igbodu* is "womb of the forest," which also suggests a sacred grove. Ifá teaches that all things in the material world have some form of consciousness, including animals, plants, rocks, fire, water, and air. Through the use of proper invocation, it is believed that it is possible to enter altered states of consciousness that facilitate direct communication with specific Forces of Nature (Orisha). This communication is believed to be enhanced by certain natural settings called *Igbodu.*

When a town is established in the Yoruba areas of the rain forest, the Ifá elders of the community search for those power spots that can be used as Igbodu. For example, the Ifá Spirit of sensuality, fertility, and abundance is called *Oshun.* The Igbodu for Oshun is usually located along a river. Once a location is selected, the area is consecrated through the use of invocation and ritual. After this occurs, only those who have been initiated into the mysteries of Oshun are allowed into Her sacred grove. Ifá teaches that this process both enhances the natural wisdom of the grove itself and preserves the interaction that occurs there over time between humans and nature. This creates a reciprocity in which a source of natural power becomes more accessible through human interaction.

Igbodu Oshun in the city of Oshogbo is located in a cluster of trees along a bend in the Oshun River. The exposed roots of ancient trees appear to be long fingers leading to the water. Mud statues of mythic events in the life of Oshun are woven into the natural setting of the forest. The floors of the shrine room are covered with mosaics done with dried *ikin* which are the fruit of the Ifá tree of life. Igbodu Ogun at the Oba's palace in Ile Ife contains what appear to be iron meteorites. *Ogun* is the Spirit of Iron and throughout Africa there is the belief that Iron from the Heavens landed on earth as the seed of biological life. Igbodu Ifá in Ode Remo is a small room in the center of town. It has been the site of Ifá initiations into antiquity and the city seems to have grown up around the sacred grove so that it is no longer in the forest. The space is still used because of the spiritual power that has been sustained there over generations. When this small room is used for ritual purposes, ancient altar objects are brought into the grove that give it an otherworldly dimension.

Each town that I have visited in Nigeria has its own unique collection of sacred groves and there is some variation in those Forces of Nature (Orisha) that are honored depending on the survival needs of a particular region. When the Oba comes forward to make community policy, it is assumed that he is speaking for the extended families of the community and that each family is involved in an ongoing effort to remain in harmony with those Forces of Nature that are invoked in Igbodu.

To facilitate the coordination of this complex network of religious, social, and political systems, the traditional Yoruba community is built upon the concept of family districts. The Yoruba language has no words for uncle, aunt, or cousin. Each person in an extended family is either *Baba* meaning "father," *Iya* meaning "mother," *ara okunrin,* meaning "brother," or *ara obinrin,* meaning "sister." Those grandfathers and grandmothers are called *Babagba* and *Iyagba* respectively. Most members of an extended family live in a compound called *agbole.* The agbole is usually a collection of houses formed around a square courtyard.

Usually the Babagba and Iyagba of the compound are initiated elders in a particular priesthood that sanctions the economic activity of the extended family. That extended family will have one or more Igbodu that is used as a gathering place for both ritual and learning. Within a given community there would be extended families that specialize in divination, medicine, hunting, blacksmith trades, wood carving, textile production, and martial arts. Each extended family has a compound within the town, a collective farm outside the town, and access to the communal market. The extended family also has the responsibility of caring for their Igbodu and to present annual festivals for the family Spirit on behalf of the entire community.

It is recognized within Yoruba culture that not everyone within a particular extended family has the same destiny as the family itself. This is usually determined through divination. When such a determination is made, the child is sent to apprentice with another family that specializes in the skills that match the child's aptitude. During the apprentice years, the child is treated as a member of the new family during the day and where possible returns to the birth family either at night or on weekends. This is a reflection of the Ifá proverb that says, "It takes a village to raise a child."

In rural areas, most extended families engage in farming as the foundation of support for the family. Farms are communal plots located outside the city. There is generally a strict division of labor within the agricultural process. The men do the planting, weeding, and harvesting. The women do the processing and market the surplus. Within the West African rain forest, there are two dry seasons and two wet seasons. This allows for the production of two annual crops. The planting and harvesting that occur during each segment of the year are marked by communal rituals that invoke fertility and good fortune. This is done by making offerings to the earth, giving thanks for the abundance of the past year, and asking that it return again. The divination associated with these rituals is used to anticipate potential problems during the upcoming seasons.

In traditional Yoruba communities there is a direct correlation between the challenges of personal growth, the needs of the extended family, and the natural cycles of nature. This integration is directly related to the survival needs of the individual, the extended family, and the overall community. As a result of this integration, there is direct experience of the value of communal ritual and direct feedback on the efficacy of collective effort. This level of integration has been disrupted in the larger cities of Nigeria as it has in Western urban environments. When there is no direct interaction with Nature as a necessity of survival, the importance of communal ritual related to earth-centered principals is lost. Also lost is the need to remain bonded to an extended family. The collective needs for survival are replaced by the individual needs for survival, and this shift in emphasis is, I believe, the source of much of the alienation and violence that occurs in contemporary urban communities. The people of Ode Remo have very little earned income in the form of currency. But within this network of shared responsibilities there is no homelessness, no hunger, and very little crime.

Both culturally and spiritually, the extended family is viewed by traditional Yorubas as an eternal structure that forms the foundation for growth within a particular lineage. Ifá has a strong belief in *atunwa*, which translates as "character is born again." This is a reference to a belief in reincarnation, based on the idea that humans return to earth within the same family and that coming to earth is a positive experience. Each of the priestly positions within the extended family is seen as an eternal post that must be filled by succeeding generations. It is the responsibility of each elder initiate to insure that the younger generations are fully trained and fully prepared to assume their position as future elders within the family.

The process of teaching is carried on through observation and the gradual introduction of increased responsibility. For example, herbal doctors take young children with them into the forest until they are able to recognize specific herbs. At a certain point they are told to gather the medicine on their own. They watch during the preparations of the medicine, until they are able to prepare the medicine without supervision. The more competent an elder becomes, the more students the elder is likely to have and the less work the elder will engage in directly. An elder's competence is then judged by the skill of the students.

In 1989 I was initiated into the mysteries of Ifá during a seven-day ceremony that involved thirty men and fifty women. The seven- to ten-year-olds led the first portion of the ritual, guided by the teenagers. The teenagers led the next segment of the ritual, guided by the young adults. It was only during the key moments of the transfer of power that the senior priest stepped forward to lead the initiation. By taking a minor role in the ceremony, he was insuring that the younger members of the religious society learned all the ritual procedures of initiation. This guarantees that the process will be passed on from one generation to the next and creates a situation where the community is not dependent on a single person. In a culture that is based on oral instruction, the untimely loss of an expert could result in the loss of generations of wisdom. The awareness of this possibility appears to create a strong communal emphasis on the need to properly train children of all ages.

Ifá teaches that initiations occur in two distinct arenas. There are initiations into the mysteries associated with specific Forces of Nature (Orisha) and there are initiations into rites of passage. Initiations into the mysteries of Orisha are considered a form of spiritual rebirth. That which is reborn is the latent potential inside the individual that corresponds with the manifest potential of the Orisha. For example, *Ogun* is the "spirit of iron." Initiation into the Mysteries of Ogun reveals the spiritual nature of iron and is considered a prerequisite for anyone who shows potential as a blacksmith. In addition, iron represents strength and determination. The initiation process can kindle these latent character traits and teach the discipline and methodology to use iron as a constant source of inspiration and motivation in these matters.

Rites of passage are designed to educate and illuminate the shift in personal and communal responsibilities that occur with age. They include naming ceremonies at birth, puberty rites, marriages, installation of elders, and funerals. It is believed that the life of most individuals passes through these stages and that the transition can be facilitated through the use of communal ritual. The wisdom needed to transform consciousness is presented in a symbolic form in a way that unlocks the latent understanding of these stages that is buried in consciousness itself. It also provides guidance from those who have effectively moved through the rite of passage earlier in their life.

The effectiveness of this system is clear to me, based on observations of the maturity of children and young adults in Ode Remo. I saw little indication of domestic violence, no indication of sexual abuse, and no organized criminal activity. It is possible to go anywhere in Ode Remo, day or night, without fear for personal safety. It is apparent by any standard of measure that the traditional Yoruba residents of Ode Remo have discovered a way to live in harmony with their environment and with each other and that they have done so without creating the problems that plague life in urban cities around the world.

It is my belief that much can be learned by studying the social-spiritual systems that do work and applying the lessons to life in different settings. In my experience, this cannot be done in a romanticized way. The first difficulty that I encountered when I attempted to make use of Ifá as a methodology for personal and communal transformation was language. The language of Ifá ritual, like the language of most earth-centered traditions, makes use of religious terms that have no clear English equivalent. For example, the Yoruba word *Orun* is usually translated to mean "Heaven." In the West the word "Heaven" has distinct religious and culture associations related to "salvation" and the belief in specific "doctrines." In Ifá the concept of Orun refers to the invisible realm of reality that supports the visible world. It includes the possibility of interaction with Spirit and the possibility of opening windows between the two dimensions. It is actually closer to the scientific understanding of energy fields and force fields than it is to the idea of a home for Angels.

I would encourage anyone who is seeking inspiration and guidance from earth-centered traditions to spend some time examining the original meanings of words in that traditions. For example, Eskimos in Alaska have over thirty words to describe snow. The language itself is able to give insight into the use and function of snow as an important aspect of that particular environment. It is estimated that the rain forest in West Africa has over two hundred thousand plants that are unknown to Western science. Many of these plants have African names that usually reflect the practical and spiritual use of the plant.

The examination of language may seem to be a straightforward task. However, many of the dictionaries created for traditional cultures were written by missionaries as a basis for translating the Bible into different languages. These dictionaries often have a strong religious bias that distorts traditional religious concepts. For example, the Yoruba word for Spiritual Forces in Nature is *Orisha.* The Dictionary of the Yoruba language published by University Press in the city of Ibadan, Nigeria defines Orisha as "an object of worship, an idol." The use of the word "idol" is prejudicial and does nothing to illuminate the deeper meaning of the term. Ifá teaches that the sculpture used in shrines are meant to act as a focal point for prayers, and there is no suggestion that they are the Spirit Itself.

In most urban communities survival is dependant on earning a living to pay for food and shelter and knowing how to shop for food and where to put out the garbage. In a community like Ode Remo, survival is tied into an intricate web of interpersonal relationships that are ultimately linked to spiritual powers. The market in Ode Remo is open twice a week and supplies a limited amount of food to the community. To maintain the supply of food, attention is given to the weather, the seasons, availability of water, preservations of seeds, plant disease, marauding wild animals, fertilization of the soil, and food preservation. No family can sustain this system without cooperation from the extended family and without the cooperation of the entire community. This collective effort is supported by constant attention to the spiritual forces that work through nature so that nothing is done to create drought, famine, and contagious disease.

It was not until I experienced this level of cooperation that I was able to notice the level of non-cooperation that occurs in urban city life. There is a tendency among people to assume that the social rules that guide our immediate social interactions are either the only systems of community possible or the best systems of community ever created. This seems to be especially true when comparisons are made between African culture and Western culture. Both the media and academia in the West have tended to present a view of African culture and spirituality that suggests that it is "evil," "violent," and rooted in "superstition." My direct experience of African spirituality as it continues to be practiced in Ode Remo is that it is founded on clear principles of good character, that good character has a personal as well as a communal component, and that the concept of community includes the natural environment as well as the people who live in it.

The ethnocentric world views that tend to denigrate other cultures are not only divisive to the world community; they also are having a negative impact on the health of the earth itself. Some media attention has been given to the concern of indigenous people in the rain forest of Brazil related to the global effect of deforestation in South America. What is less known is that when a single tree is cut in Brazil, the West African rain forest responds by producing more oxygen to compensate for the loss. This compensation puts a drain on the natural resources in Africa and is one of the factors that has contributed to draught and famine in the regions that border the African rain forest. The healers and medicine people who live in the African rain forest know about this imbalance; they are in communication with the spirits of the forest in an effort to restore health, and they have the tools to implement the messages that they receive. It is an effort that deserves both respect and support, if for no other reason than it is based on thousands of years of successful living in an environment that is vital to the health of the planet.

5. A World View of Bliss for God and Humankind: The Teachings of Tenrikyo and Its Sacred Place

Akira Kaneko, Ph.D.
translated from the Japanese by Tamio Kinoshita

Editor's Note

The city of Nara in the southern part of Honshu, the main island of Japan, has a long history of being a place of importance. Nara was once the capital of Japan, and in the hills surrounding the city there are many sei-chi *or sacred places, marked by Shinto shrines and Buddhist temples, and many* onsen *or hot springs bubble up from the ground. One of the best-known spiritual features of Nara are its sacred deer, preserved in a sanctuary in Nara Park. The modern deer who eagerly await your arrival and expect gifts of crackers are descendants of a white deer who, it is said, once transported a god whose wisdom was very important to Japan.*

Things do not happen by chance, and so it would seem to not be a mere coincidence that Nara Valley is also the site of the founding of one of the fastest growing new religions of the world, Tenrikyo. In this article Dr. Akira Kaneko, lecturer of Liberal Arts at Tenri University at Tenri in Nara Prefecture, describes this new faith and its connections to a very special sacred place that serves as the nexus for Tenrikyo, the Oyasato. Aside from being one of the largest wooden buildings in the world, crafted with extreme love and care, visitors to Oyasato also sometimes experience healings and many report feeling peace of mind and joy. One afternoon at sundown in November of 1992, I (JAS) sat in prayer in this wondrous temple for the evening service and experienced the presence of spirit in the air. It warmed body and soul in a fashion that is found only in those wondrous special places of the earth that draw us to them like magnets for reasons we know not why—Lourdes, Macchu Picchu, Delphi, Stonehenge, and other places of similar potency. In this article we are introduced to the energies of Tenrikyo and also given special insights into the workings of an important new religion grounded in a special physical place.

Oyasato: The Home of All Humankind

With mountains to the east, Tenri is a small city located in the middle section of the Nara Basin, a valley that reminds one of the womb when viewed from a satellite. Six miles north of Tenri is Nara, which was an ancient capital of Japan between 710 and 784 A.D. Located to the south of Tenri are Asuka and Fujiwara, which were also capitals of Japan prior to Nara. From the late third century to the middle sixth century, a powerful ancient family dwelled in Tenri, and there are still old Shinto shrines and quite a few tombs including the emperors' burial mounds, as well as Japan's oldest road. Overlooking the Nara Basin is Mount Miwa, that is itself said to be the divine body. To make the ascent to the summit, one must wear a special white scarf to insure protection and guidance from the powerful spiritual forces present there. There are also many other sacred places nearby, marked by a wide variety of shrines and temples.

Tenri is also the home of the Tenrikyo Religion, whose sacred place is located along the foot of the green, hedge-like mountains that form part of a nationally designated park. The sacred place is called Oyasato, the Home of the Parent, and its central spot is called the Jiba, or the original place of human conception.

When the morning mist disappears, the morning service begins at sunrise. The morning sunshine is brightly reflected on the roof tiles of the huge main sanctuary of Tenrikyo Church Headquarters. The main sanctuary, comprised of the sanctuary proper and four connecting worship halls, has a total floor space of about 92,700 square feet. "*Ashiki o harote tasuke tamae, Tenri-O-no-Mikoto.*" ("Sweeping away evils, please save us, Tenri-O-no-Mikoto.") This simple, yet expressive melody of the origin of life is chanted twenty-one times to the music of wooden clappers, a large drum, and other musical instruments. Every morning thousands of worshippers gather in the main sanctuary to attend the morning service and worship the Jiba-Kanrodai from all four directions. The focus of worship is the eight-foot, two-inch tall wooden Kanrodai pillar erected in an open space in the middle of the main sanctuary. In many Japanese shrines and temples, people usually worship towards an object which is placed against a wall. But the Tenrikyo sanctuary is unusual in that the Jiba-Kanrodai is in the center and worshippers can see other worshippers who face them at the other side of the sanctuary. Right above the Kanrodai is an opening in the ceiling of the sanctuary. The Kanrodai thus bridges heaven and earth.

According to the teachings of Tenrikyo, the Jiba is the place where human beings were originally conceived by God the Parent at the beginning of time. Miki Nakayama, the foundress of Tenrikyo who began the teachings in 1838 based on revelations, gave the sacred name of *Tenri-O-no-Mikoto* to the Jiba. As proof of human creation, she built the Kanrodai on the spot. Together with the Jiba, the Kanrodai is the object of worship for Tenrikyo followers. The Kanrodai is a hexagonal pedestal to receive the *kanro* or the heavenly *amrita* (the dew of immortality that also allows one to withstand illness or weakness) when the minds of all human beings are purified.

Daily prayers occur at sunrise and sunset. On the twenty-sixth day of each month, ten selected service performers (five men and five women) dance to the joyous music of nine musical instruments, expressing the workings of God the Parent through their hand gestures. The service with this dance is called "the Service around the Kanrodai" and is performed only at the Jiba. Following the service around the Kanrodai, another dance service called the *Teodori* is performed to the music of the nine musical instruments as well as to the joyous singing of the *Mikagura-uta*, which consists of a eight-verse prelude and the twelve ten-verse songs for the service. Partaking in the deep meaning of the service which is conducted in the main sanctuary of the Church Headquarters, the service is also performed on at each of 17,000 Tenrikyo churches around the world (of which about 16,700 churches are in Japan).

The Truth of Creation in Tenrikyo

According to the doctrine of Tenrikyo, this world in the beginning was an immense expanse of chaotic muddy ocean. Only aquatic animals were living. God the Parent took the form of a huge dragon and a huge serpent in the muddy ocean. Finding this chaotic situation tasteless, God decided to create human beings and an orderly world. God's purpose is explained in a verse of the *Ofudesaki*, the Book of Revelation, which is comprised of 1,711 poems written by Miki Nakayama,

> The purpose for which I, Tsuki-Hi, created human beings is to see them live joyfully in harmony with nature.
>
> —*Ofudesaki* XIV:25

God wanted to share in their joy and be respected as God.

In the muddy ocean there were numerous loaches. Their number was nine hundred million, ninety-nine thousand, nine hundred, and ninety-nine. This number symbolically signifies an extremely large number. Looking further through the muddy ocean, God saw an *uo* (fish), a *mi* (white snake), a *shachi* (orca), a *kame* (turtle), an *unagi* (eel), a *karei* (flatfish), a *kurogutsuna* (black snake), and a *fugu* (globe-fish). God summoned these aquatic animals one after another. After testing the flavors of their nature, God assigned to them the roles of the physical functions of human beings and the orderly law of nature in the world. The orca, for example, is very vigorous, stiff, and rigid, which represents the function of support. God the Parent therefore decided to use it as the instrument of the male organ and of the bones and support in the human body. The turtle has very strong skin and rarely turns over. God the Parent decided to use it as the instrument of the female organ and of the skin and joining. In the world, the turtle represents the function of joining in general. The loaches were all made to become the seeds of human beings. God especially assigned the fish and the white snake the models of husband and wife, promising that when years equal to the number of their first-born had elapsed, they would be returned to the original place of human conception and would be adored by their posterity. According to this promise, God the Parent gave them sacred names. By manifesting in heaven as the moon and the sun, God the Parent sheds God's benevolent light on all parts of the world and nurtures all creation with warmth and moisture.

In the second part of the *Mikagura-uta*, it is sung:

> This world's heaven and earth as the model
> I have created husband and wife.
> This is the beginning of the world.

Hand gestures accompany these recited verses. In the part "This world's," index fingers are moved horizontally to signify equality as the basis for all human society. In the phrase "heaven and earth as the model," the creation of husband and wife is expressed by gestures with both hands facing each other. A fundamental unit of human beings is the husband and wife whose significance is compared to heaven and earth.

In his lecture entitled "Cosmology for the Soul" delivered during an international symposium held at Tenri University in 1986, James Hillman, a psychologist of the Jungian school, played the role of a patient who, dissatisfied with philosophers, scientists, and theologians, sought treatment in the form of therapeutic cosmology, or cosmotherapy.[1] The patient is the soul or the psyche.

"I venture the idea that a cosmology for soul gives special attention to animals," Hillman said. "I propose that any acceptable new cosmology will have to receive approval from the animal kingdom." I agree that to give cosmological significance to animals is the proper step, and that such a step is appropriate for religion in general. According to Genesis 6:18–22, God asked Noah to build an ark in order to save animals as well as Noah and his family. Plato describes "the symbolic image of the soul" as a many-headed animal. In *Republic* (vol. 9, chapter 12), Plato indicates that, by taking into consideration the many-headed animals—the souls—inside human beings, they would be provided with nourishment while the mutual relationship of friendship is maintained. In polytheism, animals are gods. In totems and constellations, the close relationships between human beings and animals are depicted. There are also numerous narratives around the world that refer to the marriage between humankind and animals.

In the Truth of Creation in the teachings of Tenrikyo, animals were all initially aquatic. The forms of these animals evoke the image of the phallus whereas their figures swimming in the muddy waters, especially the countless numbers of loaches, can be likened to sperm. The fish also has a spiritual connotation, like the fish symbolism associated with Jesus Christ. Human salvation stories through the spiritual reproduction functions are told in the Truth of Creation. Human beings were created out of aquatic animals by God who existed in perpetual time. Although human beings were all born about only half an inch tall at first, they gradually grew through repeated deaths and rebirths. In the process of their growth, they were reborn eight thousand and eight times (this also symbolizes an extremely large number) as worms, birds, and other animals. After that, they all died and only a she-monkey was left behind. She conceived five males and five females—this is the number of the performers for the Service around the Kanrodai—and her offspring continued their growth to become human beings. This she-monkey is the original mother of human beings who ensured the continuation of life in the fundamental past, and Tenrikyo foundress Miki Nakayama is the motherly existence who guides the lives of human beings from the present to the world of Joyous Life in the future.

Salvation through the Body

Through the senses the human body is connected with the outside world. Not only do human beings perceive through the nose, ears, eyes, and tongue, but they also touch with their hands and walk on their feet. Senses of internal organs play similar roles. Connecting the mouth and the anus are the esophagus, stomach, duodenum, small intestines, large intestines, and rectum. This series of human organs connects the inside and the outside of the human body. Through this series the human body is opened to the outside world.

According to Tenrikyo's Truth of Creation, functions of the human body are correlated with workings of the human world. For example, the functions of eating, elimination, and digestion in the human body correspond to the rise and fall of moisture in the human world. The functions of breathing and speaking in the human body correspond to the working of wind and atmosphere in the human world. Similarly, the providence of constancy of bodily temperature is equivalent to the providence of fire, whereas the functions of the eyes and fluids in the body are equivalent to the providence of water in the world. The functions of the female sexual organ and the joining of skin are linked with the function of every joining in this world, whereas the functions of the male sexual organ and the support of bones are related to the working of every support in the world.

God the Parent gave a sacred name to each function, indicating that they are all providences and workings of God. Further, the creation of human beings and that of the world are explained in parallel with each other. The world is the body of God and was formed in conjunction with the bodily and spiritual growth of humankind. God is incorporated here with the developing body as the concept of mediation. Not only is this world a thing created by God but also it is the body of God. Although human beings are also created by God, their bodies are lent to them by God. This human body, therefore, has the same characteristics as those of this reality. This is the Tenrikyo teaching on the human body, which is called "a thing lent, a thing borrowed." This teaching is based on the following verses of the *Ofudesaki*, the Book of Revelation:

> Step by step, reflect deeply on all things:
> the universe is truly the body of God.
>
> The bodies of all human beings are things lent by God.
> For what purposes are you using them?
>
> —*Ofudesaki* III: 40–41

There is an orally transmitted story regarding the relationship between the human body and this world:

> When one of the followers asked the foundress, "How far is it from east to west and from south to north?" She replied, "It is like when you lie down, stretching both of your arms." So, when we human beings sleep by stretching both arms, it is the same as east, west, south and north. This represents roundness of truth. On another occasion the foundress also said, "The earth is like the human body. Gold and other minerals correspond to nails in the human body. Hot springs are like the prime organ; trees and plants are like human hair; and rivers are like blood vessels. They have the same truth."[2]

When this analogy is applied, I understand that the Jiba is the navel of this world as the spot of human creation.

The navel is located in the center of the body and is the place filled with power, where the spirit gathers. The navel plays the role of lifeline through which nutrition is supplied in the interior of the womb. After birth, however, the navel is no longer necessary, and therefore, it may seem silly for modern human beings to return to the navel—the Jiba—the place of human conception. Without that place, however, we could not have existed and so honoring it affirms our heritage. In his book entitled *Nature as Teacher and Healer*, James Swan says, "You can't fully appreciate the spirit of a place by intellectualizing it, you have to let it creep into your body and allow it to cast a spell on your soul."[3] As it is stated here, such a place as the Jiba should be approached with reverence as it is the spiritual origin for our present existence, and we are renewed in its presence.

As Oyasato, the Home of the Parent, is the original home for all human beings, pilgrims flock to this place from all around the world to vitalize their spiritual sensibility and refresh their minds and bodies. During the Sechi Festival, held every year from January 6 to 8, as many as 150,000 followers return to the Jiba to eat ceremonial rice cakes offered for the New Year's Day service. The spring grand service on January 26 is held to commemorate the day the foundress shed her physical being, at 90 years of age. On April 18 a special celebration is held to celebrate the birthday of the foundress. And on October 26, the autumn grand service is held to commemorate the founding of Tenrikyo. A children's pilgrimage is held during the summer school vacation time. Annually between July 26 and August 4 some 300,000 young pilgrims come to Tenri. Millions of people come to Tenri during these pilgrimages, and so guideposts in the city are written in Japanese, Korean, English, and Portuguese. The 100th anniversary of the foundress's passing was held between January 26 and February 18 in 1986. During this time three million people returned to Oyasato not only from all over Japan but from some forty other countries.

While the foundress Miki Nakayama was physically alive, she often demonstrated healings and other spiritual abilities such as clairvoyance. Even after she withdrew from physical life in 1887, followers have been taught that the soul of Miki is everlasting at Oyasato and continues to watch over everyone in the world. Even today in the Foundress' Sanctuary, attendants prepare her bath, meals, and bedding each day, as if she were physically alive. The Foundress' Sanctuary is located on the north side of the main sanctuary. This sacred chamber and the Memorial Hall to honor the memories of deceased members of the Nakayama family and other followers are connected with the main sanctuary by a 2,640-foot long corridor also crafted from elaborate woodworking, the beauty of which affirms the powers of this place to inspire the soul.

In Tenrikyo there is a three-month spiritual development course called *Shuyoka*. Many of the people who attend this course have physical problems. After graduating from the three-month spiritual training, however, many have regained healthy physical bodies. Displayed at the corner of the Shuyoka building are a number of discarded items for the physically disabled, such as crutches, wheelchairs, corsets, and canes. Each discarded item is labeled for identification, such as: "Paralyzed lower body, 56-year-old man from Tokyo"; "Articular rheumatism, 68-year-old woman from Chiba Prefecture." Touched through the faith of Tenrikyo by the spiritual air of Oyasato, the minds of these people were saved, together with their bodies. The healings often begin while physically visiting the Jiba, and then patients are given further treatment at the nearby Tenri Hospital, which offers a truly holistic approach to treatment: the Medical Department, which is concerned with medical treatment, using modern clinical facilities with one thousand beds; the Religious Guidance Department, which offers the salvation of the mind through the faith in Tenrikyo; and the Service Department, which is in charge of coping with all other problems including welfare and daily living. This hospital is called *Ikoi-no-Ie* or the "House for Rest."

John Naisbitt asserts in his highly popular book *Megatrends* that in today's "high-tech" society, there must be a balancing counter-movement to restore full humanity in opposition to the increasing technological sophistication of both industry and daily life.[4] The healing resources at Tenri are developed along these lines, creating a healthy sensibility by maintaining a balance between humankind's awe of technological achievements and the spiritual aspirations of humanity developed through religion. At Tenri, the Grant of Sazuke is given to those who have acquired the teachings and purified their minds. This divine grant allows its holders to conduct a ritual of healing for the sick. Using the same hand gestures performed for the first part of the daily and monthly service, the healer's breath and the touch of his or her warm hands are transmitted to the patient, who can indulge in peaceful relief in both mind and body. In the modern Tenri Hospital, Tenrikyo ministers in the Religious Guidance Department administer Sazuke to the patients. Here, high-tech and high-touch coexist without any conflict.

But healing can no longer be administered just to the human mind and body. Healing today and in the future must also apply to the earth, the body of God, for the earth is ailing with many illnesses and disorders caused by the misuse of modern technology. Hidetake Kakihara, former vice director of an international nuclear organization, has pointed out that the present state of the earth is like a human body without veins: a lot of energy and resources are being produced and supplied to big cities, industrial areas, and everywhere else through supply systems that are like arteries. The veins of our circulatory system are used to collect wastes produced in the metabolic actions of using resources and energy. These veins, he argues, are virtually nonexistent on this earth, and so we pollute ourselves in wastes we cannot recycle into useful ends. He warns scientists and technicians who have been engaged in production and economic development that "there will be no bright future on this earth without veins."[5]

Sacred Place in Contemporary Society

On the reverse of the gold medal of the Nobel Prize for Science are embossed two goddesses. One is Natura, who is a veiled goddess, and the other is Scientia, who is about to lift Natura's veil. Between them is a cornucopia, a horn of plenty. Natura's veil hides half of the cornucopia, while the other half is exposed. This embossment vividly symbolizes the desire of humankind to unveil nature—a feminine existence—with the help of science, another feminine force. Today our world lacks balance. We have devoted all our energies to the development of technology, often paying little heed to nature, thus creating technologies that rob nature of its power and energy. A typical example of these phenomena is nuclear power plants, and their potential for catastrophic consequences as evidenced by Chernobyl and Three Mile Island.

As we seek to find ways to solve environmental problems and create a sustainable society, we must establish cultural systems that will remind us of our responsibility to nurture and support an ecological ethic. In the history of religions. Scholars of religion indicate that new religions like Tenrikyo have a life-oriented outlook for salvation.[6] According to this outlook, the cosmos/world is the ultimate existence of life of infinite abundance and is God per se. Human beings' individual lives correspond to branches running off the mainstream of life—God. The individual branches can survive only by uniting with the mainstream. In a sense, the action of joining is in accord with the optimistic and collectivistic mentality of the Japanese, which in turn accounts at least in part for the multitudes of new religions which have cropped up during the rapid economic growth of modern industry, especially in the postwar period. It is essential, however, that these new religions recognize their potential for falling into the demonistic aspect of religion. Many new religions have appeared in Japan with the modernization following the Meiji Restoration. In other words, their growth paralleled the growth of Japan's government policy for gaining wealth and military strength before World War II, and kept pace with the high economic growth policy of large corporations after the war. In this respect, many new religions in Japan seem to simply go along with the times, rather than having a firm foundation to guide their work, and their relationship with nature is uncertain.

As a sacred place, Oyasato or the Home of the Parent has an enormous power to draw people there, constantly reminding them of the teachings of the foundress. Yet at Tenri, too, we have our environmental problems. Many huge buildings have been constructed nearby and often air pollution hangs in the air, produced in part by the many vehicles driven by pilgrims returning to the holy center. These conditions are reminders of the importance of honoring one's faith.

Tenrikyo is a religion that teaches its followers to live a modest way of life. Among the orally transmitted teachings of the foundress, the following touch on the meaning of the "Joyous Life":

> The natural term of life of human beings is one hundred and fifteen. After that you may live as long as you wish.
>
> If you need rain, it will rain regularly six times while you are sleeping at night, so that you will not get wet while working on your farmland.
>
> There will be no natural disasters, and rich harvests will be assured every year.
>
> Each married couple will be blessed with a boy and a girl. Even after they get old they may be blessed with a child.
>
> You shall work joyfully until noon every day and have a pleasant rest in the afternoon.
>
> If the teachings spread, crimes will disappear from this world. Police stations, courts, and the like will become unnecessary. There will be prosperity as needed.

According to the philosopher Heidegger, the fundamental mode of human existence is "to dwell."[7] "To dwell" means that human life is finite. Such existence, the finite and corruptible existence of life on earth, is based on the divine and exists between heaven and earth. The Kanrodai, the sacred pillar erected on the spot that is the navel of the body of God, connects earth with heaven. It also delivers to the present believers the origin of human creation and the future of ultimate Joyous Life. The current Kanrodai, however, is made of wood. The sacred pillar will be replaced with one made of stone when the minds of all humans are purified at the advent of the world of Joyous Life.

Tenrikyo teaches that the earth is the body of God and that humans are allowed to live there as in the bosom of benevolent God. Humans are entrusted with keeping the earth. Being well aware of the modern illness that is affecting not only ourselves but also the earth, we have to humbly learn from nature to allow the Joyous Life to become reality for all the earth.

For the first twenty years after the first revelation, Tenrikyo was considered heretical, and very few people came to believe the teachings. During that period, Miki Nakayama's family sank to the lowest depth of poverty and their main house was dismantled. Miki herself ordered this dismantling in order to construct a new world. When their main house was dismantled, Miki's youngest daughter Kokan walked a distance of about twenty miles, crossing over a mountain pass to Osaka, to do missionary work. She set in motion a process of going out to share the teachings of the foundress, which continues today as Tenrikyo becomes an ever-growing world religion. Yet no matter how far away one travels, in this marvelous age, one is just a few hours by airplane from the sacred pillar located at the navel of the earth, the Home of God the Parent, Oyasato.

Notes

1. James Hillman, "Cosmology for the Soul: From Universe to Cosmos," *Cosmos, Life, Religion: Beyond Humanism* (Tenri: Tenri University Press, 1988), 283–301.
2. Masaichi Moroi, *Seibun'iin sho* [Excerpts from Right Oracle Literature] (Tenri: Tenrikyo Doyusha, 1970), 158–159.
3. James A. Swan, *Nature As Teacher and Healer* (New York: Villard Books, 1992), 198.
4. John Naisbitt, *Megatrends*, Japanese version, trans. Ken'ichi Takemura, (Tokyo: Mikasa Shobo, 1983), 62–79.
5. Hidetake Kakehara, "Kagaku eno hansei to shukyo eno kitai" [Reflection on Science and Hope for Religion], in Iwanami Lecture Series: *Shukyo to kagaku* [Dialogue Between Science and Religion], (Tokyo: Iwanami Shoten, 1992), 165.
6. Michihito Tsushima, Shigeru Nishiyama, Susumu Shimazato, & Hiroko Shiramizu, *Shin-Shukyo ni okeru seimeishugiteki kyusaikan* [On the View of Life-oriented Salvation in Japanese New Religion], *Shiso* 665 (1979): 92–115.
7. Martin Heidegger, "Bauen Wohnen Denken" [Build, Dwell, Think], in *Vortrage und Aufsatze* (Pfllingen: Neske, 1954), 139–156.

6. The Ganga River and the Spirit of Sustainability in Hinduism: A Study of Banaras (Varanasi)

Rana P. B. Singh

Editor's Note

Making a pilgrimage is among the oldest acts of paying reverence to the power of place. Of all the special sacred places in the world, the City of Banaras along the banks of the Ganges River in India is surely among the most popular destinations for paying spiritual homage. In this essay, Dr. Rana P. B. Singh, founding president of the Society of Pilgrimage Studies, president of the Society of Heritage Ecology, president of the Indian Society for Environment and Culture, and a cultural geographer at Banaras Hindu University, shares his special knowledge of paying homage to the Mother Ganga.

> *The Ganges, above all rivers of India, . . . has held India's heart captive and drawn uncounted millions to her banks since the dawn of history. The story of the Ganges, from her source to the sea, from old times to new, is the story of India's civilization and culture, of the rise and fall of empires, of great and proud cities, of the adventure of man and the quest of the mind which has so occupied India's thinkers, of the richness and fulfillment of life as well as its denial and renunciation, of ups and downs of growth and decay, of life and death.*
>
> —Jawaharlal Nehru, 1946[1]

THE ETHIC OF "SUSTAINABLE DEVELOPMENT," to which almost everyone subscribes today, requires this generation to use the world's environmental resources in ways which do not jeopardize the ability of future generations to meet their own needs. To be successful, this principle requires another dimension—reverence and revelation. Development should preserve, not destroy, those assets of the natural and spiritual power of our cultural heritage which future generations would also wish to enjoy and cherish. In this essay, I will speak of the need to preserve the sacred Ganga River (in the West, the Ganges River). We need to make development sustainable, both environmentally and culturally. In this way, development also has a dimension of faith and reverence.

The spirit of sustainability can be thought of as the ethic to behave in ways that help others and to realize the deeper nature of things—the cosmic integrity that is ultimately the sanctity of life. "The acceptance of the sanctity of life," says eco-philosopher Henryk Skolimowski, "promotes us to protect other forms of life and threatened habitats, as well as human environments in which life is in peril."[2] This involves a way of life and action determined by the deeper principle of realizing the intrinsic value one's actions serve. Realizing the intrinsic value requires a new moral thought which has roots in the past.

To preserve and possess a sense of the spirit of sustainability, self-realization is as indispensable to human nature as our basic urges for food or for sex. I do not think one can survive as a humane creature on this earth without special attachments to special places because they preserve the manifestable spirit of sustainability. This ability to see the past in the present—to realize that the past is not dead and is not even the past—permits Hindus to feel a sense of belonging and of sharing the past's history and traditions passing into the cyclic process of "existence-maintenance-change-continuance."

The spirit of sustainability in Hinduism is related to the creation theory of Puranic mythology. Among the five fundamental organic elements of Nature (*mahabhutas*), water is given primal importance. According to the *Bhagavata Purana* (I.3.2–5), a fourteenth-century text, Primordial Man was lying down in the water of the universe. The *Mahabharata* (XII.182.14–19), a circa fourteenth-century B.C. text, states that the Supreme God created Primordial Man who first made sky; from sky, water is then made; and from the seed of water, fire, and air—these last two together made the earth; hence in a metaphysical sense, these elements are not separated from each other.[3] The *Rig Veda* (X.90. 11–14), a circa fifteenth-century B.C. text, describes water as a unifying fluid between sky/heaven and earth. According to the *Shatapatha Brahmana* (I.8.1.1–6), a circa fifteenth-century B.C. text, Vishnu's (the protector of the Trinity) incarnation as Fish, out of ten, symbolizes the origin of life in water; in the form of Fish he saved organic life-seeds from the great cosmic flood.[4] The water is regarded as the primary materialization of Vishnu's maya-energy and is therefore a visible manifestation of the divine essence.[5]

Different kinds of myths and symbols associated with water are described in Hindu mythology.[6] In ancient Hindu mythology (circa 800 B.C.), water is described as the foundation of the whole world, the essence of plant life and the elixir of immortality (cf. *Shatapatha Brahmana* VI.8.2.2; III.6.1.7; IV.4.3, 15). The *Atharva Veda* (II.3.6.), a circa tenth-century A.D. text prays, "May the water bring us well-being!" There are many such descriptions about the quality, use, sanctity, and symbolism of water.[7] In a later period of Hindu mythology, water becomes a symbol for life, and a liquid spirit of sustainability. Water is said to be a healer (*Atharva Veda* VI.91.3.). Metaphorically and metaphysically, the ancient mythologies refer to water as the container of life, strength, and eternity, but most commonly it is perceived as the purifier. However, to reach the source and receive the merit of "living water" involves a series of consecrations, rituals, and religious activities such as pilgrimages and sacred baths. The cult of living water is described in the Vedic literature and is continued vividly in the Puranic literature. The *Rig Veda*, in its famous "River Hymn" (X.75.5–6), mentions the divine power of the Ganga. The text also eulogizes the Ganga as Gangeya, which means the "giver of all sorts of prosperity and peace"—the liquid spirit of sustainability (*Rig Veda* VI.45.31). Similar sentiments are echoed in the *Padma Purana* (Shristi 60.64–65), a circa thirteenth-century A.D. text: "We pray to you O! the Liquid-energy of the Ganga—the universal form of supreme Lord Vishnu."

The "wash away sins" quality of water is endowed with the power of sanctity and has many cosmological connotations in various mythologies. According to religious historian Mircea Eliade, "Everything that is *form* manifests itself above the waters, by detaching itself from the waters."[8] Running water in general and the waters of the Ganga in particular are described as bestowing sanctity and miracles. From mythology to tradition, a common chain of interrelationship between the river and human society is maintained by a wide variety of performances and rituals. The psychic attachment to a place and the maintenance of cultural traditions reflects the realization of the divine manifestation at the place and preserves the intrinsic value of sustainability. The intensity and level of this manifestive power are greater in certain places. Such specific places are known as *tirtha* ("holy site" or "sacred place"). The three most common factors for the popularity and acceptance of sacred places are: unique natural landscape and beauty, unique physical features of the body of water, and association with some great sage. These characteristics are eulogized in the vast arena of Hindu mythology. The holy city of Varanasi, traditionally known as Banaras, has over the centuries achieved a distinct place among the holy sites. Its location between the two tributaries of Varana and Asi and along the left bank of the northerly flow of the Ganga River, and its association with Lord Shiva (the destroyer in the Hindu Trinity) are its unique characteristics. Says the *Kurma Purana* (I.31.64), a circa eighth-century text: "There is no other holy place on this earth more sacred and powerful than Varanasi, and there would not be any in the future, too."

The Ganga River: Mythology and Intrinsic Value

In Hindu mythology all the rivers are revered as removers of pollution, but the Ganga is the most prominent as a purifying liquid power. In the *Bhagavata Gita* (X.31), while describing the cosmic form of supreme entity, Lord Krishna declares that among all the forms of liquid energy, He is the Ganga river. The Ganga is the greatest example of perceiving divine-energy (*shakti*) in nature: through our experience of shakti, she stretches out our spirit-consciousness. That is why the Ganga is called Adi-shakti, the "Primordial Divine-Energy." The Ganga is the river of the water of life, immortality, and healing from the very presence of God.

No river in the world's history has achieved the fame of the sacred river Ganga. This is especially true since the third century A.D., when the Ganga began to play a vital role in Hindu ceremonies and worship—in rituals of birth and initiation, of purification and religious merit, of marriage and death. The Ganga is known as Mother Ganga (*Ganga Mai*), bringing life in the form of sacred water.[9] The Ganga is the sacred fluid, an essential element for all the Hindu rites and rituals. The Ganga is known as "the mother who bestows prosperity (*sukh-da*), and secures salvation (*moksha-da*)"; she represents joy in this life and hope for the life to come.[10] Personifying and directing the terrestrial water, the goddess Ganga river has functioned as the sacred fluid to preserve the seed of the world. The *Mahabharata* (III.85.88–97) describes the Ganga as the savior of life.

The Ganga is often described as the river flowing in heaven, on earth and in the netherworld (*Tripathaga*). In symbolic form she is known as the Mandakini in heaven, as the Ganga on earth, and as the Bhogavati in the netherworld (cf. *Padma Purana* VI.267.47). According to Indologist Diana Eck,

> For Hindus it (the Ganga) is the River of Heaven, flowing from the foot of Vishnu, falling off the head of Shiva, touching the earth on top of the highest mountains, Mount Meru, and then generously splitting into four channels to flow in four directions, watering the whole earth with streams of blessing.[11]

Because of her grace, compassion and motherly bliss, the Ganga descended from heaven to earth, carrying with her the blessings of renewal to the weary and life to the dead.[12]

As the primordial fluid serving as the savior of life, as a divine-energy interlinking the three realms, the Ganga manifests the spirit of sustainability. "A life without savior is hardly worth living," said American cultural geographer Yi-Fu Tuan.[13] Its spatial form is manifested in five territories lying in different parts of India where the regional sacred river is known as the Ganga of that direction, i.e. the Mandakini (the Ganga of the north), the Mahanadi (the east), Kaveri (the south), the Narmada (the west), and the Godavari (the center).

This tradition of perceiving the other regional rivers as the symbol of the Ganga may be called "Gangaization."[14] The Ganga is considered "a prototype of all the rivers of India; and her magic power of salvation is shared—only to a lesser degree—by all the bodies of water in the land."[15] Says the *Matsya Purana* (102), a circa ninth-century text, that "without purificatory rite by the holy water, the mind cannot be purified, therefore a sacred bath is the first necessity before any religious act." However, in a physical sense, the Ganga is not everywhere. Hindus believe that if a person remembers the Ganga with faith and reverence, any body of water would provide the manifestive divine-energy that the Ganga transmits. The real Ganga lies out there in the hearts and minds of many Hindus who have the faith to cherish any other river as the manifestive Ganga whenever they take their holy dip.

The idea of manifestive energy at the junction of the two heavenly powers is preserved in the tradition of the special sacred bath. On the special, astrologically auspicious occasion of Kumbha, when Jupiter enters into Aries or Taurus, and the Sun/Moon into Capricorn, India's greatest fair is held at Prayaga (Allahabad), at the confluence of the Ganga and Yamuna. This takes place about every twelve years. At three other places, the Kumbha Mela also is held at intervals of six or twelve years. At these sites, purification by bathing reaches the highest level of auspiciousness and expression when reactualization of life-giving cosmic events occur. The experience of bodily touch to the cosmic event reflects the sense of "the whole"—that is how it becomes "the holy." The Ganga in its perceived spatial form represents "the whole" (either in India or as a river of the three realms), and as mother goddess, she blesses those who take part in the baths.

The Ganga is a "liquid axis mundi, a pathway connecting all spheres of reality, a presence at which or in which one may cross over to another sphere of the cosmos, ascend to heavenly worlds, or transcend human limitations.[16] The Ganga is the power center of liquid energy where one can realize true spiritual value—a source of power. This essentially means a natural place which has physical, mental, emotional, and spiritual power (energy) beyond economic value. That is how the Ganga is vital to the life force of earth. Pilgrimage to and religious activities along the Ganga provide a positive and natural return of power and energy, by recharging and recycling energy back to its original source. These activities serve as a means to help keep creation alive. The Ganga river should not be seen as an ordinary water stream; it is to be seen with the eyes of faith. A Hindu has binary vision: recognizing the ordinary as extraordinary and the extraordinary as ordinary. Hindus see the Ganga with a hermeneutical lens, which allows a correspondence to the alternative world of sacrality and power.

Only after walking along the Ganga's bank does one realize that the great-great-grandparents of today's Hindus once walked that very bank and had certain experiences, manifestations, and revelations. Revealing the Ganga as a living organism requires specific forms of communication, interaction, environmental sensitivity, and transpersonal ecological feelings. That is how the Ganga is known as the mother and soul of India. The Ganga possesses a unique history and mythology, a deep faith and divine landscape, and its own individuality together with multiplicity.

The stories of the Ganga may change, but the motherly river lives on. The story of the Ganga is the story of Indian people catching up to the older social ideals and values of the more devout Hindu world. She is a cultural symbol where every visitor has experiences and feels their harmonic relationship with nature. The story of the Ganga tells us everything about Hindu society, history, culture, and religion—their possibilities and their future. However, a living mythology is not enough; its real understanding and preservation are the human needs and the call of the time.

There are many sacred sites and centers of pilgrimage along the Ganga river from the source to the mouth. These include Gomukha, Gangotri, Devaprayaga, Rishikesh, Haridvara, Kankhala, Soron, Bithura, Prayaga/Allahabad, Vindhyachal, Chunar, Varanasi, Patna, Sultanganji, and Gangasagara. The most sacred place among all the holy places of India, however, is Varanasi—known as the microcosm of India.

The Ganga River in Varanasi

In its whole course of 2,525 kilometers, the Ganga river flows from south to north in a crescent shape only at Varanasi. The current has not left its water-edge along the left-bank cliff at Varanasi since the ancient past, while the other side is a flood-prone area. This natural condition is a result of the landform of Varanasi, which has remained the same since time immemorial.

The Ganga, the patron deity Shiva, and the sacred territory of Kashi together form the Cosmic Trinity of this great city, Varanasi. According to a twelfth-century A.D. text, the *Kashi Khanda, Kkh* (35.10):

> The Ganga, Shiva and Kashi:
> Where this trinity is watchful,
> No wonder where is found the grace,
> that leads one on to perfect bliss.[17]

With the realization of its highest mystic power of sanctity, especially in Varanasi, people from all parts of India came and got settled along the river. This resulted in the development of a social space for all of India.[18] Rich persons, lords, and kings from all parts of the country came and erected palatial buildings to serve as their resorts for performing rituals on special occasions. Thus, a series of lofty and beautiful architecture developed along the Ganges ghats.

The people of Banaras as well as Hindus all over India have a sense of rootedness and connectedness to the Ganga. Rootedness can be measured in the centuries that have lapsed since Hindus first settled along the river and by studying the mythology surrounding it. Connectedness refers to the river's emotional bondage and the mystical power. An inhabitant of Banaras expressed these feelings of rootedness and connectedness as follows:

> I am in love with this holy river Ganga; the unique face of the town and inhabitants; the unspeakable solitude of the water, and the sweet security of its bank. I would set up my tabernacle here. I am content to stand still at the age to which I am arrived; I and my friends: to be no younger/no older, no richer/no poorer, no more handsome or ugly. I do not want to be weaned by age or appearance. Any alteration, on this earth of mine, in vision or in lodging, puzzles and discomposes me. My household gods plant a sacred fixed root, and are not rooted up without this holy water.

The Ganga river front at Varanasi spreads over an arc-line of 6.4 kilometers (four miles). Along the river front are eighty-four *ghats* (steps to the river bank) between the confluences of two small tributaries—the Asi in the south and the Varana in the north. In archetypal connotation, each ghat represents one *lakh* (100,000) of the organic species as described in Hindu mythology; that is how in total all the 8.4 million species are symbolized along the 84 Ganga Ghats in Varanasi. Further, 12 zodiacs x 7 layers of atmosphere comes to 84; thus the annual cycle of the cosmic journey is completed by taking sacred baths at the 84 ghats. At these sacred sites there exist 98 water-front sacred spots. The number 98 indicates the cosmic frame linking 14 *bhuvana koshas* (sheaths) of the human body and 7 layers between the earth and heaven, thus the product 14 x 7 comes to 98.[19]

According to the *Brahma Purana* (II. 130), a ninth-century A.D. text, the mystic power of bestowing bliss increases ten times when the Ganga enters in the Vindhya region; where it follows the westerly flow it is increased to one hundred times, and when it follows a northerly flow in Varanasi, the merit increases one thousand times.[20] Following a common Hindu tradition, in the early morning at sunrise, pilgrims or devout citizens gather on the ghats to bathe in the Ganga, drink at least a few drops of the sacred water, and take blessings or religious instructions from the *ghatias* (priests at the ghats), who, while seated at the river's edge under a canopy, preside over various offerings, including ancestral offerings.[21] Pilgrims then move into the narrow lanes to take a *darshan* (auspicious sight) of the Vishvanath temple and other divine entities.

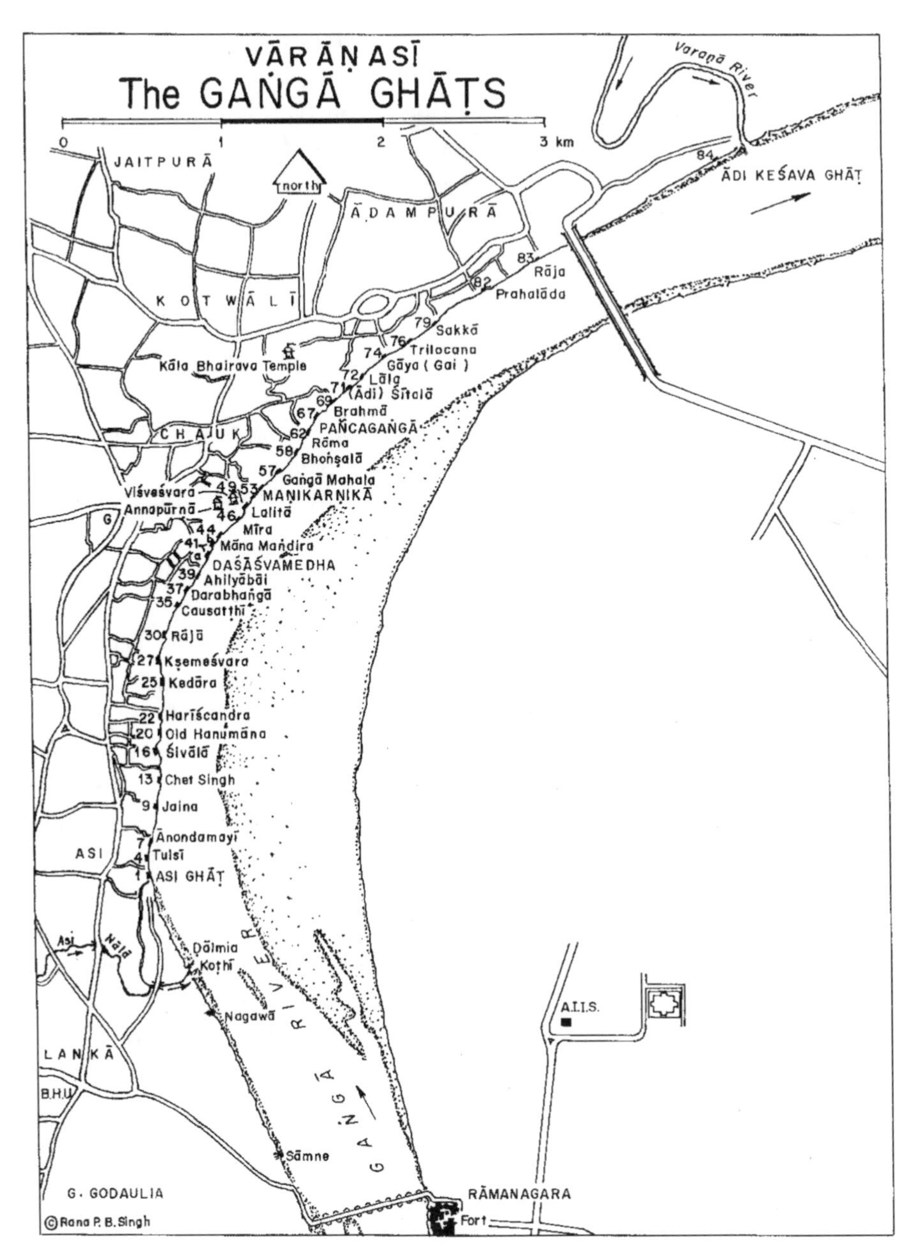

Drawing by Rana P. B. Singh.

Among the eighty-four ghats, five are considered as more auspicious; from south to north, they are: Asi, Dashasvamedha, Manikarnika, Panchaganga, and Adi Keshava. These five ghats, called the *Panchatirthis* (the five most sacred water spots), are eulogized in the Puranic mythologies (see *Kashi Kanda* 84. 108–10, and 106. 110, 114; *Matsya Purana* 185.68–65) and are still popular sites to visit.[22] The five ghats are described below in short:

1. Asi Ghat

Marking the southern edge of the sacred city in terms of the confluence of the Asi drain, this ghat was referred to in a seventeenth-century text. The palatial buildings were made by the King of Varanasi in around 1830. This is one of the famous sites for celebrating the *Surya Shashthi* (the sixth day of the Sun as mother goddess) festival, which is held on the fifth and sixth waxing fortnight of the Hindu month of Karttika (October/November), when over ten thousand mothers perform this festival for the well-being of their sons.

2. Dashashvamedha Ghat

This ghat is presumed to be the first historically recorded site associated with the myth of the ten horse-sacrifice ritual performed by Bhar Shiva Naga kings in around the second century A.D. This is also the busiest ghat. On the tenth waxing fortnight of the Jyeshtha (May/June) worship of the Ganga is celebrated on a grand scale in the Ganga temple at the top of the ghat. The sacred bath on the occasions of the solar and lunar eclipses and in the month of Magha (December/January) is also important. (See photo.)

3. Manikarnika Ghat

Known in myth as the "great cremation ground," this ghat is mentioned in the Gupta inscriptions of the fourth century A.D. This ghat has two parts: one for cremation and the other for bathing and rituals. After cremating corpses, the mourners and attendants take baths at this site. Pilgrims and devotees perform ancestral rites at this ghat, more commonly in the special period of the waning fortnight of Ashvina (September/October). There are many holy spots near this ghat.

4. Panchaganga Ghat

This ghat is frequently described in circa eleventh-century mythologies. This site was famous for the grand temple of Veni Madhava (Vishnu) which was demolished and converted into a mosque in 1670 by the Mughal king Aurangzeb. That mosque still serves as the landmark along the arc of the river. The Ganga-arati (offering oil lamps to goddess Ganga) at the time of sunrise and sunset is the most attractive scene at this ghat. In the month of Karttika (October/November)

A newly married family observing the sacred ritual of worshipping the Ganga at the Dashashvamedha Ghat.

the ritual offering of oil lamps to ancestors, arranged in the sky with bamboo stands, is performed by the ghatiyas on behalf of the devotees who patronize the cost or materials and rewards for service. Sacred baths at this ghat purify the human being in all its five fundamental organic elements of subtle substance, i.e., sky/ether, water, air, fire, and earth.

5. Adi Keshava Ghat

Since the Gahadavala period (circa eleventh century), this ghat has been famous for the temple of Vishnu Keshava, and it is assumed to be the oldest in the whole region. For Vaishnavites (followers of Vishnu), this is the most attractive site. In practice, most of the pilgrims take baths at the nearby confluence site of the Varena and the Ganga rivers, followed by visit and rituals in the Adi Keshava temple.

These five ghats symbolize the microcosmic body of Vishnu: Asi is the head, Dashashvamedha is the chest, Manikarnika is the navel, Panchaganga is the thighs, and Adi Keshava is the feet. This reminds us that Vishnu first placed his holy feet in Varanasi; this is why the area along the Ganga river is Vishnu's body.

Along the Ganga Ghats: The Festivities

Since ancient times, "time" or *kala* in Hindu theology has been thought of as both the cosmic power and the fruit of ritual action. Priest and philosopher

Raimundo Pannikar rightly observed that "The existence of the universe—and hence the history of man and the cosmos—comes under the sway of superior forces: *kala* (time) and *karma* (the act).[23] Since time is born with sacrifice and ultimately is destroyed with the sacrifice, the basic notion of worship and time helps in understanding sacrifice and man's participation in the unfolding of time.[24] The timing of rituals is critical so that their character suits the needs of the moment and the people, and their value to promote auspiciousness is at a maximum. The Hindu calendar *panchanga* is therefore essential to planning rituals for it blends together astronomical, astrological, and religious elements. In deciding the precise moment for ritual actions, the relative positions of the moon and the sun are considered. All the festivals are the result of religio-cultural needs, economic values, and sacrality in terms of space and time—altogether realized by people from time to time and eventually given a traditional identity.[25] Since water absorbs pollution, flowing water may carry it away, and the Ganga water has the highest capacity for purification. Bathing in the Ganga itself is thought of as the ritual which provides purity and religious merit, ultimately giving special power. That is why on various special occasions (*parvakala*), bathing in the Ganga is a prerequisite religious act. Following astrological theory, the precise movement of the conjunction of the sun and moon refers to possession of divine-energy, *shakti*. All the festivities are associated with the notion of auspiciousness. In writing about the Indian Almanac, Judy Pugh noted that "Auspiciousness is not an abstract quality of well-being whose meanings and expressions can be specified outside a given context of activity."[26]

Among the fifty-six most commonly celebrated Hindu festivals in Banaras, which are approximately the same in almost of all of northern Indian Hindu society, twenty-one are closely related to the sacred bath and associated religious activities along the ghats. Among these festivals, all but four fall within the waxing fortnight, for it is felt that the waxing fortnight of the moon is more auspicious than the darkening or waning time. Vishnu and Shiva are primarily the associated divinities on these occasions. This is because Hindu mythology says that the Ganga arose from the toe of Vishnu, and then takes refuge in Shiva's hair, and finally descends to earth.

According to the *Kashi Khanda* (27. 129–131) it is auspicious to bathe in the Ganga at Varanasi at any time. However, bathing during the new moon increases the merit one hundred times, at winter solstice a thousand times, during the solar and lunar eclipses ten million times, and if the eclipse falls on Monday then the merit is infinitely higher than on a normal day. The *Matsya Purana* (110.7) states that there are 350 million sacred places on the earth. Since Varanasi is the most sacred place of all, taking a holy bath in the Ganga at Varanasi directly provides contact with the divine energy the moment one touches the precious waters. Indologist Heinrich Zimmer noted that "Physical contact with the body of the goddess of the Ganga has the magic effect of transforming automatically the nature of the devotee."[27] According to the *Brahmavaivarta Purana* (Krishna-Janma Khanda, 34.13ff), a circa sixteenth-century text, Shiva himself sings a hymn in praise of the Ganga: "If a man on an auspicious day begins to bath in the Ganga, he dwells cheerfully in Vishnu's heavenly world, Vaikuntha, for the numbers of years equal to the number of his footsteps."

Eck described her own experience at Varanasi: "The power of dawn on the Ganges at Banaras is not simply the collective power of worship, but the seamless interpenetration of prayer, bathing, the river, and sunrise."[28]

The two most important occasions to bathe in the Ganga at Varanasi are Makara Samkranti (winter solstice, which in India usually happens on January 14), and Mesha Samkranti (the vernal equinox, which usually happens on April 14). The other important occasions are full-moon days (especially of October and November), new-moon days, and eclipses. On any of these occasions, more than a hundred thousand visitors take a holy dip in the Ganga.

A survey taken on the winter solstice on January 14, 1993 showed that a little less than half of the visitors belonged to the higher castes (Brahmins, Rajputs, etc.). This demonstrates that the people's strong faith leads them to Varanasi regardless of their economic means. Greater age (50 and above), lower education, and nearness to the city increased participation. Similar results were found on February 26, 1993—a new-moon day.

After taking a purificatory bath in the Ganga and worshipping her, pilgrims move on to have an auspicious glimpse (*darshana*) of the patron deity, as well as viewing Vishvanatha and auxillary shrines in and around the temple compound dedicated to *Kala Bhairava* ("the military chief" of the city and controller of Death), *Sankatamochana* (monkey-god), *Durga* (mother goddess), and others.

The birth of the Ganga, which refers to her coming on earth from heaven (Ganga Dashahara), is celebrated on the tenth waxing fortnight of Kyeshtha (May/June). Devotees believe that to bathe in the Ganga in the morning of this day gives very high merit and relief from the sins committed earlier. This day is followed by another auspicious day, Ekadashi (eleventh waxing fortnight), associated with the worship of Vishnu. The devotees coming from nearby areas or from distant areas stay in Varanasi in rest homes (*dharmashalas*) and take holy baths in the Ganga on both of these days to acquire more merit. Those who take religious vows for worshipping the Ganga, bathe and perform rituals on every day of the fortnight.

Sustainability: Some Bad Spots

The Ganga River as an environmental milieu is not simply a creature that flows across the land. The Ganga is what the Hindu culture knows to be true—and

Varanasi: The Ganga-related Festivals and Their Characteristics

Hindu Festival (Hindu Calendar)	Roman Calendar 1995, 2000	Associated divinity	Motive	Bathing and activities at the ghats
Chaitra (March/April)				
1. Mesha Samkranti (vernal equinox)	always April 14	The Ganga Sun	to purify and feel bliss	at all the ghats
Vaishakha (April/May)				
2. Amavasya (new moon day) Vaishakha K-15	April 29,1995 May 4, 2000	Shiva The Ganga	to purify	at all the ghats
3. Akshaya Tritiya (Imperishable Third) Vaishakha S-3	May 2, 1995 May 6, 2000	Shiva	to purify	at Manikarnika ghat
4. Narasimha Jayanti (birth of the Lion-headed God) Vaishakha S-14	May 13, 1995 May 16, 2000	Vishnu	removal of evil	at all the ghats, but preferably Panchaganga
5. Purnima (full moon day) Vaishakha S-15	May 14, 1995 May 18, 2000	Vishnu as Tortoise	to get bliss	at all the ghats, but preferably Panchaganga
Jyeshtha (May/June)				
6. Ganga Dashahara (Ganga's birthday) Jyeshtha S-10	June 8, 1995 June 11, 2000	The Ganga	to purify and relieve sins	bath at Dashas-vamedha, and Panchaganga ghats
Ashadha (June/July)				
7. Guru Purnima (Guru's full moon) Ashadha S-15	July 12, 1995 July 16, 2000 (lunar eclipse)	The Ganga Guru Vyasa	to get wisdom	bath at the 5 ghats, also at Ramanagar
Shravana (July/August)				
8. Purnima (full moon day) Shravana S-15	Aug. 10, 1995 Aug. 15, 2000	The Ganga Vishnu Shiva	to purify	bath at the 5 ghats
Bhadrapada (August/September)				
9. Vamana Dvadashi (12th of Dwarf) Bhadrapada S-12	Sept. 6, 1995 Sept. 10, 2000	Vishnu as Dwarf	to purify and be victorious	bath at the Varana-Ganga confluence

Ashvina (September/October)				
10. Pitripaksha, I-day (ancestral fortnight) Ashvina K-1	Sept. 10, 1995 Sept. 14, 2000	Manes	to please manes	bath and rituals at Manikarnika ghat
11. Pitrivisarjan (offering to ancestors) last day Ashvina K-15	Sept. 24, 1995 Sept. 27, 2000	Manes	to please manes	concluding ritual (same as no. 10)
12. Purnima (full moon) Ashvina S-15	Oct. 8, 1995 Oct. 13, 2000	Vishnu The Ganga	to purify	bath at the 5 ghats
Karttika (October/November)				
13. Surya Shashthi (Sun's 6th day) Karttika S-5/6	Oct. 28–29, 1995 Nov. 1–2, 2000	Sun as goddess The Ganga	mothers for their sons' well-being	at the 5 ghats on 1st day eve. and 2nd day morning
14. Prabodhani (Vishnu's waking) Karttika S-11	Nov. 3, 1995 Nov. 8, 2000	Vishnu The Ganga Tulsi	to get a new vision in life	bath at the Panchaganga ghat; Tulsi's marriage along the ghats
15. Vaikuntha Chaturdashi (14th day of Vishnu's heaven) Karttika S-14	Nov. 5, 1995 Nov. 10, 2000	Vishnu The Ganga	to acquire a place in Vishnu's abode	bath at Adi Keshava, and the 5 ghats; and for a vision go to Vishnu's temples
16. Purnima (full moon) Karttika S-15	Nov. 7, 1995 Nov. 11, 2000	Vishnu The Ganga	to purify and remove sins	bath at the 5 ghats, and all others; special at Panchaganga
Margashirsha (November/December)				
17. Purnima (full moon) Margashirsha S-15	Dec. 7, 1995 Dec. 11, 2000	The Ganga	to purify and get merit	bath at all the ghats, but common at 5 ghats

Pausha (December/January)				
18. Purnima (full moon) Pausha S-15	Jan. 5, 1995 Jan. 9, 2000 (lunar eclipse)	The Ganga Vishnu	to seek merit of the cosmic journey	bath at Matha and Dashash-vamedha ghats
Magha (January/February)				
19. Makara Samkranti (winter solstice)	always on Jan. 14	The Ganga Sun	to purify and to get Sun's blessing	at all the ghats, but common at 5 ghats
20. Purnima (full moon) Magha S-15	Feb. 4, 1996 Feb. 8, 2001	Vishnu Shiva The Ganga	to purify and get merit	bath at all the ghats, and rituals in Shiva temples
Phalguna (February/March)				
21. Maha Shiva-ratri (Shiva's marriage night) Phalguna K-13	Feb. 17, 1996 Feb. 21, 2000	Shiva Parvatti The Ganga	to seek bliss and merit	baths at all the ghats, and rituals in Shiva-temples (12 special)

S: Waxing fortnight of the lunar month, *Shuklapaksha* (light half)
K: Waning fortnight of the lunar month, *Krishnapaksha* (dark half)
Source: Hindu almanac and the author's calculations

knows this in a certain way. It is not simply a question of how the river matters to society at present (in a strict sense), it is more important to see the meanings and cultural values which have been sustained for centuries. "For it is absurd to suppose that the kind of attitude held by the Hindus to their river could be held by everyone towards everything."[29] However, it is our moral obligation to revere that attitude and maintain it in the context of the present needs, searching for a balanced relationship between man and nature within the microcosm of the Ganga river. This ideal brings together both Hindu culture and the vision of a sustainable society.

As I go down to the Ganga's banks, I see a different world. The people are not the same people as their ancestors. Oh! more materialistic and all that, but the important difference is that the people I had known were people with a deeply rooted faith. We are now faced with a new world. It has certain virtues, but also some potentially fatal defects. Two such situations I cite here.

1. A Threat to the Ganga River

American journalist Daniel Putterman has reported the current drastic environmental situation of the Ganga:

> A walk along the ghats presents another image too, one of poverty and crowding. Garbage piles high in the streets, breeding disease and vermin, and open drains carry human waste directly into the Ganga. Occasionally a corpse floats past, the legacy of a life too poor to afford wood for cremation. Besides human wastes, toxics from India's burgeoning industrial sector pour in. The river is filthy.[30]

The standard of purity set for the Ganga by the environmental ministry of India is a maximum biochemical oxygen demand (BOD) of three parts per million or three milligrams per liter. Tests conducted along the Ganga report a BOD of over 5.5 parts per million and fecal coliform counts of 5,000 to 10,000 per 100 liters (cubic centimeters) of water, while the limit for the latter is only 3,000 per 100 liters of water. At some of the sewage outlets the fecal coliform counts exceed 100,000 per 100 liters.

The Swatcha Ganga Campaign (SGC), a non-governmental organization, was launched in 1982. In 1986 the Central Ganga Authority (CGA) was created and unveiled a master plan for the cleanup with its highly-touted Ganga Action Plan (GAP) with a budget of 293 million rupees, roughly the equivalent of 18.5 million U.S. dollars. The GAP is a package of about thirty-two different plans, fourteen of which are mainly concerned with water pollution control. According to the newspapers, the monitoring statistics of the water quality at SGC are not reliable. Out of the planned 1.34 billion litres per day of waste water flow, the GAP now only treats 873 million liters daily. The State Water Authority (UP Jal Nigam) has pointed out that despite the policing of the river front, hospital and city wastes continue to be dumped near the bank of the river. In the upstream as well as downstream areas, dead bodies continue to be thrown into the river surreptitiously.[31]

In an official meeting organized by the Commissioner of Varanasi on May 2, 1994, to evaluate the GAP's work between 1988 and 1993, there was a "claim and blame" dialogue between the govenment authorities (such as UP Jal Nigam), and NGO bodies and scholars. The former group made *claims* for the great success of all 34 schemes operated during this period, which consumed 462.6 million rupees (about 15 million U.S. dollars). But the latter group *blamed*, charging that these statistics and claims are mostly on paper, and in fact a little less than half the claimed success was achieved. For the second phase (1994–1999), the UP Jal Nigam has sent a proposal to the CGA, which will cost about 536 million rupees (about 18 million U.S. dollars). The proposal inclues pollution prevention, checking and diversion of sewage outlets, and increasing the capacity of sewage treatment plants. The proposal also addresses the development of ghats and the opening of an electric crematorium, as well as an animal carcass incineration plan. Once again, surprisingly little effort was made to coordinate the CGA's efforts with that of the NGO and voluntary organizations.

The *India Express* newspaper reported that a little less than half of the GAP grant money has gone into the pockets of officials. The only visible evidence of the GAP is a huge white boat which sails up and down the Ganga with high-level authorities on board. Somehow the GAP, or even the SGC, has failed to involve people. The clean-up campaign of the Ganga has failed miserably in almost all respects. There is a lack of public participation and a lack of awareness of the river's problems. There also has been a failure to revive old theological ethics of harmony with nature and the spirit of sustainability.

But there is still hope, as millions of Hindus are spiritually tied to this river. The leader of the SGC, Veer Bhadra Mishra, who is also a professor of hydraulic engineering and a chief of a monastery, believes that "The Hindu conservation ethic has survived centuries of colonialism intact." There is an urgent need for reviving the spiritual devotion to sustainability through mass awareness and deeply-rooted public participation.

2. The Other Side of Tourism

Like most of the cultural heritage cities of the world, Banaras attracts a huge mass of foreign tourists—an average of more than 65,000 annually. Almost all of these visitors take part in the on-site package scenic tour programs, of which the Ganga ghats is the most popular. Tour organizers regard cultural heritage as something to be exploited. Yet the development and government agencies at most levels fail to plow back tourism profits into conservation. Over-promotion of tourism has led to unthinking commercialism which has had disasterous effects on natural beauty and on the centuries-old rhythm of community life. Rising prices for souvenir items and land, and the deterioration of priceless heritage sites, are also major threats. Mass tourism is now killing the goose that has laid the golden egg. The impact of tourism had led to a situation where tourists are cheated, harassed, and robbed. Rarely is any portion of revenue earned from tourism applied to the benefit of preservation and conservation of cultural heritage. The greatest share of the money goes to hotel chains and souvenir shops.

There is an ethical gap somewhere in the promotion of tourism. Tourism should have been carefully developed and promoted in the light of a spiritual perspective, where tourists become pilgrims, and issues like heritage preservation, religion, and sustainability are emphasized as part of the pilgrim's visit. In his keynote speech at the 1991 First International Symposium on World Heritage Cities, Bernard Feilden rightly warns us: "What we do today will be the history of tomorrow and ultimately it is by history that we are judged. Civilizing the city is now a cultural question. 'Where there is no vision the people perish.' "[32]

We need to experience the vision of the spirit of sustainability. However, issues like this are primarily concerned with moral understanding and self-realization. Alas! The increasing pace of ethical and moral pollution is slowly threatening the sense of culture and even the identity of humankind.

In the face of all the changes brought by modern society, one wonders whether the Ganga can retain those qualities of the spirit that have made it a heavenly-mother-goddess! One hopes that the preservation of those qualities would derive from those old impulses of tradition and belief which have made the Ganga the most powerful symbol of India's rich cultural heritage. One may also hope for a revival of the spirit of sustainability and for a recognition of our identity in comparison with our Motherly river, the Ganga. We must achieve *ecojustice*—justice for all ecological cosmology. Says Skolimowski, "Ecojustice as justice for all is a consequence of our ecological cosmology, of the idea of our responsibility for all, and of the perception of the interconnectedness of all."[33] We need the self-realization for responsibility—"a spiritual bridge which makes of rationality, human rationality, and of ethics, a nourishing river for the meaning of our lives."[34]

The Spirit of Sustainability: Sensitivity and Search

The disappearing presence of Hindu thinking about the man-nature-cosmos relationship is one of the basic causes for the present environmental crisis that is facing India today. Ethical and moral pollution by materialism and consumerism is replacing the old value system which supported sustainability. Gandhi warned us that "nature has enough for everybody's need, but not for everybody's greed."[35] During the past seven hundred years of foreign cultural domination—beginning with Islam and followed by British Christianity—the ancient Hindu value system has lost many of its facets. Nevertheless, the seeds of this ancient system of spiritual wisdom are still preserved in religious ethics found in writings and rituals. A mass awakening of awareness in the context of old cultural values would promote a new spirit of sustainability. Such a revival, however, need not turn into fundamentalism that should cause any damage to secular life.

The disposal of human wastes and other pollutants in the Ganga has been prohibited since time immemorial. According to the *Pravascitta Tatva*, a circa ninth-century text,

> One should not perform fourteen acts near the holy waters of the river Ganga, i.e., excreting in the water, brushing and gargling, removing all clothes from the body, throwing hair or dry garlands in the water, playing in the water, taking donations, performing sex, attachments to other holy places, praising other holy places, washing clothes, throwing dirty clothes, thumping water, and swimming" (*Pravascitta Tatva* 1.535).

Persons who engage in such unsocial activities and engage in acts of environmental pollution were cursed: "A person, who is engaged in killing creatures, polluting wells, and ponds, and tanks and destroying gardens, certainly goes to hell" (Padma Purana, Bhumikhanda 96.7–8).

Environmental problems result from people living out of harmony with nature. Realizing the deeper nature of things, the cosmic integrity to be researched is intrinsic value. Like most of the great systems of religious thought, Hinduism has a strong sense of the spirituality of place. It communicates feelings about the specialness of place. The spirit of a place certainly influences the unconscious in predictable ways, what Carl Jung called "psychic localization." According to Jim Swan: "The spirit of place is the result of the interplay between the spiritual world and nature, and the collective product of the interactions of the people of that area too. When all come into harmony, the spirit of place can really work its magic best."[36]

According to Hindu theology, the spirit of place exists everywhere, embuing the earth and the heaven with its unique and ineradicable sense of rhythm, mood and character; different experiences of this results in a variety of local forms of faith and traditions, but the fundamental ethic of reverence is everywhere. Disturbing the spirit and misusing the Ganga's holy water brings calamity to society. If the harmony is disturbed, the spirit of place begins to lose its power to sanctify life.

The spirit of sustainability defines development depending upon the emergence of holistic understanding and action in every segment of society.[37] The meaning of action is determined by the deeper principle of intrinsic value this action serves. After all, intrinsic value requires a new moral thought that must be rooted in place and tradition. Says American cultural geographer Yi-Fu Tuan:

> We need to be rooted in place, for without roots we cannot develop those habits and routines that are an essential component of sanity. We need to have a sense of place, because without it we shall have failed to use our unique capacity for appreciation.[38]

The Ganga is perceived as a mysterious life force for Hindu culture—the basis of the spirit of sustainability. It has special sacred value, power seemingly universal. It serves to energize the human mind into a state of unitive, intuitive consciousness where the boundaries between the spiritual and the material planes of life meet. The Ganga contains an "extra energy"—unusual environmental fields. Who is responsible for the damage to this river? Ultimately, we all are!

We want to possess the sacred without owning the ordinary. Trying to receive power from the Ganga, we want the direct experience of physically touching the river with our bodies, bathing in its waters. As a result, inevitably we look beyond everything without seeing things for what they are. That is why a preparatory and cleaning rite is prescribed before bathing in the Ganga. Only then can one get the full benefits of contact with the water. This must be an act of faith, a surrender of oneself. The reverence and faith of people in the Ganga river is an integral part of the Indian tradition and should be respected and added to the World Conservation Strategy.[39] The nearby inhabitants and their belief in the sacredness of water of the Ganga should be made part and parcel of this ambitious and important conservation program.

I saw the light along the Ganga bank; I suddenly realized that was my home, where the earth spirit meets the divine—the revelation of life. Alas! Now the feeling of attachment is superseded by consumerism. Attachment to a place is a prerequisite for developing a sense of the spirit of place. This sense of attachment provides emotional and spiritual sustainability to both individuals and the community. Attachment is an existential and phenomenological experience. The key to the future is in the commitment of human habitants living there who maintain this sense of attachment.

Reverence—the deeper vision of the sanctity of life; responsibility—the connecting link between ethics and rationality; frugality—grace without waste; and ecojustice all form the minimal core of intrinsic values for right conservation and preservation of the spirit of sustainability.[40] In fact, reverential development is unitary in the broadest and deepest sense, combining reverence and sanctity of life with contemporary economic, social, moral, cultural, and traditional premises to bring peace and harmony with nature.[41] The fact that they may be difficult to implement in practice in no way negates their importance and desirability.

To paraphrase Carl Jung: The people of India will never find true peace until they can come into a harmonious relationship with and cultivate deeper feelings of reverence for the Ganga River, which is the cradle and identity of India's culture and civilization since time immemorial.[42]

Notes

1. Jawaharlal Nehru, *The Discovery of India,* 13th ed. (New Delhi: Oxford University Press, 1993), 51.
2. Henryk Skolimowski, "Reverence for Life," *Ethics of Environment and Development,* J. Ronald Engel and J. G. Engel, eds. (Tuscon, Ariz.: University of Arizona Press), 98.
3. Rana P. B. Singh, "Nature and Cosmic Integrity: A Search In Hindu Geographic Thought," *GeoJournal* 26, no. 2 (1992): 142.
4. Singh, "Toward Myth, Cosmos, Space and Mandala In India," *National Geographical Journal of India* 33, no. 3 (1987): 307.

5. Heinrich Zimmer, *Myths and Symbols In Indian Art and Civilization* (Princeton: Princeton University Press, 1991), 34.
6. Singh, "Water Symbolism and Sacred Landscape: A Study of Banares," *Erdkunde* 48 (1994).
7. Mircea Eliade, *Patterns In Comparative Religion* (London: Sheed and Wart, 1958), 188.
8. Ibid., 131.
9. Steven G. Darian, *The Ganges in Myth and History* (Honolulu, Hawaii: University of Hawaii Press, 1978), 31.
10. Zimmer, *Myths and Symbols*, 110.
11. Diana L. Eck, *Encountering God. A Spiritual Journey from Bozeman to Banares* (Boston: Beacon Press, 1993), 231.
12. Ibid., 139.
13. Yi-Fu Tuan, "In Place, Out of Place," *Geoscience and Man* 24 (1984): 7.
14. Singh, "Toward Myth, Cosmos, Space and Mandala In India," 316–318.
15. Zimmer, *Myths and Symbols*, 111.
16. David Kinsley, *Hindu Goddesses* (Delhi, India: Motilal Banarasidass, 1987), 193.
17. Singh, ed., *Banares: Cosmic Order, Sacred City, Hindu Traditions* (Varanasi, India: Tara Book Agency, 1993), 68.
18. Singh "The Socio-Cultural Space of Varanasi," *Art & Archeological Research Papers* 17(1980): 41–46; and Singh, "Literary Images, Cultural Symbols and Intimate Sensing: The Ganga River in Varanasi," *National Geographical Journal of India*, 36, nos. 1–2 (1990): 125.
19. Singh, *Banaras: Cosmic Order*, 68.
20. Singh, "Toward Myth, Cosmos, Space and Mandala in India," 509.
21. Kelly D. Alley, "On the Bank of the Ganga," *Annals of Tourism Research* 19, no.1 (1992):126.
22. Singh, *Banaras, Cosmic Order*, 68–100.
23. Raimundo Panniker, "Time and History in the Tradition of India: Kala and Karma," *Culture and Time*, L. Gardet, et.al., eds. (Paris: The Unesco Press, 1976), 63.
24 Singh, *Banaras, Cosmic Order*, 215.
25. Ibid., 216.
26. Judy P. Pugh, "Into the Almanac: Time, Meaning, and Action In Northern Indian Society," *Contributions to Indian Sociology* 17, no. 1 (1983): 48.
27. Zimmer, *Myths and Symbols*, 110.
28. Eck, *Encountering God*, 139.
29. David E. Cooper, "The Idea of Environment," *The Environmental Question*, D. E. Cooper and J. A. Palmer, eds. (London: Routledge, 1992), 174.

30. Daniel M. Putterman, "Fighting for the Goddess By Cleaning the Soul of the Sacred Ganges," in *Trilogy* 4, no. 4 (1992): 15–16.
31. Usha Rai and Sharmilla Chandra, "And Unquiet Flows the Ganga," *Indian Express* (Delhi), 30 September1992, news development section.
32. Bernard M. Fielden, "Management of World Heritage Cities" in *Safeguarding Historic Urban Ensembles in a Time of Change*, proceedings of the 1st International Symposium on World Heritage Towns, June 30-July 4, 1991, Quebec, Canada, 19–33.
33. Skolimowski, "Reverence For Life," 101.
34. Ibid., 100.
35. Cited in O. P. Dwivedi, "Satyagraha For Conservation: Awakening the Spirit of Hinduism," in *Ethics of Environment and Development*, Engel and Engels, eds., 211.
36. James A. Swan, *Nature As Teacher and Healer* (New York: Villard-Random House, 1992), 225.
37. J. Ronald Engel, "Introduction," *Ethics of Environment and Development*, Engel and Engel, eds., 20.
38. Yi-Fu Tuan, "In Place, Out of Place," *Geoscience and Man* 24 (1984): 9.
39. The World Conservation Strategy by the International Union for the Conservation of Nature and Natural Resources and the United Nations Environment Programme, 1980.
40. Skolimowski, "Reverence for Life," 100–102.
41. Ibid., 103.
42. As cited by Swan, ed., *The Power of Place* (Wheaton, Ill.: Quest Books, 1991), 5, 304.

Puranic Sources

The details of all the references are given in Singh, *Banaras: Cosmic Order*, 319–320.

PART TWO:

Honoring the Spirit of Place

In Thailand it is generally acknowledged that each place possesses a spirit. Religious ceremonies are conducted to propitiate this spirit, and frequently small shrines called "spirit houses" are built to provide shelter for the spirits of a place. These miniature houses are replicas of traditional Thai homes and palaces. Similar spirits also may be found with rivers, caves, trees, unique stones, and mountains. When one is in the countryside and there are no spirit houses, one may leave offerings of food for these spirits to seek their favor. Such beliefs and customs are similar to the Japanese marking of a special place by hanging a shimenawa straw rope between two trees, or the custom of the Saami or Lapps of Northern Scandinavia of placing small stones on the ground or on a larger rock to honor the spirit of a place. When we recognize that a place is special it seems we need to find a way to honor its power.

In recent years there has been a large influx of people from Thailand settling in the United States. Speaking with Thai immigrants in the San Francisco Bay area, they say that in this country their spirit houses are especially important because so little is done by Americans to care for the spirits of places. Some Thais assert that failure to pay proper respect for the spirit of place is a source of anxiety and illness. Serious Thais, as a result, erect more or larger spirit houses to help us recapture our spirit of place to restore peace.

Whether one chooses to follow Thai customs or not, the desire to honor place is one of the most elemental of all human ecological urges. Being grounded in this world, the third rock from the sun, we need to root our consciousness in the soil where we live and discover how to translate our feelings into appropriate action. In this section we begin by calling upon our senses and acknowledging the value of translating them into sketches. Then we begin to seek out distant places of pilgrimage in hope of special experiences. Having touched larger dimensions of reality, we then return to hearth and home and learn to fashion simple altars to maintain connections with the greater cosmos while living in more mundane places. These actions set the stage for more serious considerations of our actions that will follow in later sections. Working with the spirit of place is a progressive process that needs to be translated into action on many different levels.

7. Study Where You Live

Robert Sommer

(Portions of this chapter were developed jointly with Allan Wicker)

Editor's Note

Modern psychology has not had much to say about the relationship between places and human behavior but, as this article suggests, sensing the spirit of a place does not require esoteric knowledge or psychic abilities. Psychologist Robert Sommer suggests you begin with paper and pencil, giving form to the feelings you have in the places you encounter. One of our findings in talking with the many gifted architects who participated in this five-year series is that Dr. Sommer's advice is very sound.

WITHIN THE FIELD of environmental psychology, place attachment has been discussed under various headings, including place identity, place dependence, psychotopia, and topophilia. Physical surroundings help to create a sense of meaning and organization in people's lives, which contributes to a sense of personal identity, since so much of what we are depends upon where we live and the experiences that we have there.[1] A useful method for studying place attachment is environmental autobiography, which can be a written or oral account of places that have been important in people's lives and why the places have been significant.[2] Writer Theodore Roszak advocates the creation of a new profession to be called ecopsychology whose practitioners combine the sensitivity of a psychotherapist with the expertise of the ecologist.[3] The first part of this essay describes some of the ways that the social sciences have approached place attachment. This serves as an introduction to the second section, which explains my attachment to Davis, California, where I have lived for the past thirty-two years. I link the two sections by showing how I have used social science techniques and concepts to study and understand Davis and its history.

Geographer Yi-Fu Tuan coined the word *topophilia* to refer to all of a person's emotional ties to a place. Those ties have sensory accompaniments, the residue of what one has seen, heard, felt, and smelled in the past, as well as symbolic connections, memories, and much else. Tuan gives examples of the attachment of different groups of people to the land. The Australian Aborigine of the Aranda tribe " . . . clings to his native soil with every fiber of his being . . . today, tears will come into his eyes when he mentions an ancestral home site which has been . . . desecrated by White usurpers of his group territory." Love of home, longing for home—these are the dominating motives that also constantly reappear in the myths of ancestors. The mountains, the springs, and the water holes are to the Aranda not merely interesting or beautiful scenic features, they are the handiwork of his ancestors. The whole countryside is his living, age-old, family tree.[4]

To illustrate the recognition of the symbolic significance of a place and place attachment, psychologists Maryanne Jacobi and Daniel Stokols contrast the experiences of a returning alumnus and a tourist visiting an older university. Both recognize the historical nature of the place and fundamental themes of the continuity of scholarship over the ages. The alumnus, however, has had extensive personal experience with the place, while the tourist has only stereotyped knowledge obtained from guidebooks, reputation, and other second-hand sources. The traditional meanings are closely linked to the alumnus' sense of identity and evoke a more emotional response than they will for the tourist, for whom the campus has general rather than personal significance. Tradition resides in people's perceptions of the links between the people who used to live there and the people who live there now.[5]

Some biologists have used evolutionary theory to explain place attachment. Survival advantages of place attachment include knowledge of predators and prey through earlier contact; improved defense of familiar areas; reduced need for exploring potentially dangerous new terrain; and a resident advantage in competition and conflict.[6] Zoo director Heini Hediger noted strong attachments to particular types of landscapes among both animals and humans. He describes these attachments as psychotopes and cites as an example, the experience of Russians from the spacious flat steppes interned during the second World War in a sub-alpine region in Switzerland, which we regard as a delightful holiday district. These people from the boundless West Asian plains felt unhappy among Swiss mountains, which to them seemed sinister and oppressive. According to Hediger, a similar eerie feeling of being oppressed, eventually becoming intolerable, is familiar to Europeans who penetrate the trackless primeval forests of Central Africa. After a few days, even thoroughly well-balanced people usually feel more or less depressed, and only regain their spirits when they see the light of day or reach open paths. The opposite is true of the pygmies, for whom the open landscape is full of fear and unbearable. Their psychotope is the thick, virgin forest. Even those accustomed to continuous contact with Europeans move through the forest if possible when going from place to place.[7]

Zoologist Gordon Orians describes how psychotope preference among different peoples develops over time through processes of natural selection. People learn those elements in the environment that are important for survival, how to adapt and use what the environment affords, with those individuals unable to adapt being selected out of the population. There develops a fit between those people in a setting and what the setting can offer, and the occupants become deeply attached to the environment upon which their survival depends. With his colleague Judith Heerwagen, Orians has been studying people's attachment to landscape through the analysis of landscape painting, garden design, and preference for tree forms.[8] Other researchers have documented the loss of contact with local flora and fauna. In cross-generational and cross-cultural comparisons of residents of the Sonoran Desert, children had less contact with plant and animal species and knew fewer plant and animal names than did their grandparents.[9] Native peoples in New Guinea who still practiced a traditional lifestyle possessed deep and detailed knowledge of plant and animal species to a degree that Westerners can only grasp with difficulty.[10]

Western psychology and sociology have had very little to say about the long-term attachment to places. Why this topic has been so neglected is not difficult to understand. The major theorists and researchers in Western psychology and sociology often were immigrants whose cosmopolitan outlook attached little value to place attachment. The serious study of people-environment relations developed less than four decades ago. Operating under a positivistic model of laboratory-based science, these researchers focused their attention upon the effects of the immediate environment, which was frequently a controlled setting whose characteristics could be varied according to the experimenter's plans. Long-term attachment did not lend itself to experimental manipulation or controlled research designs. John Bullard, city planner and former mayor of New Bedford, Massachusetts, the city where he was born and raised, described most environment-behavior researchers as hired guns moving from place to place to test their theories because they are more interested in the theories than the places.[11]

According to sociologist Alvin Gouldner, most psychological researchers are cosmopolitans, born in one place, going to graduate school in another, taking a job wherever one is available, and relocating to achieve advancement.[12] For American research psychologists like myself, there are pressures against remaining in a single location. Indeed, at Davis, we will not admit students into the psychology graduate program directly from our undergraduate program, believing that it is desirable that students should move to another location and be exposed to other ideas. When hiring a new faculty member, there would be considerable skepticism about someone who had done all their academic work at the same university. Some of the top universities such as Harvard and Berkeley had the reputation of not giving tenure to junior faculty—again, forcing them into a transient mode. Advancement, almost from the beginnings of the field of psychology, has been achieved by moving to a new location.

Another impediment to research in place attachment has been the mythology surrounding the transience of Euro-Americans.[13] If the stereotyped Euro-Americans are always on the move, there is little point in looking at their attachment to places. The mobility has been interpreted as an unfortunate, but necessary cost of personal liberty and opportunity.[14] Individualism was reflected in the willingness of people to move rather than improve an existing situation. Some have questioned the validity of this characterization, seeing more evidence for attachment than for transience among the vast majority of Euro-Americans who created settlements and remained in them. Studies have shown that most people who have been forcibly relocated from one place to another suffer various kinds of grief reactions. Most of those who relocate on their own do so within short distances and maintain earlier networks. People remain committed to environments with a high risk of flooding, fire, or other natural hazards; the unwillingness to move even in the face of repeated disasters offers additional support for attachment to place.[15]

I was uncomfortable with the transience and constant relocation my career. The marginality became most apparent to me when, as a consequence of taking a job at the Menninger Clinic in Topeka, Kansas, I ended up completing my Ph.D. at Kansas University in Lawrence, where by coincidence my great-grandfather had a store which is now a historic landmark. As a graduate student at the University and a research assistant at Menninger's, I was completely immersed in my professional activities, yet at some level I knew that I also had a connection to the place where I was living.

Feelings of marginality, of being in a place but not of it, affected me throughout a succession of jobs. I wrote about this lack of connection to place in *Expertland* which began "There is a place outside of time and space. . . . the name of that place is Expertland, the residents are called experts, and they speak a language known as expertise. . . . some people had assumed that experts would gradually become assimilated and come to think, speak, and act like real people. This has not happened and the expert is as much a stranger as he was when he lived far away."[16] I went on to describe how experts knew very few people in the places where they resided; most of their friends were within a field or profession rather than a geographic area. These friends are like shipboard companions or people waiting on the platform, waving to departing trains. "Someone is always arriving or leaving, and the streets of Expertland are full of ghosts. As the expert walks through his office building, he sees reminders of the previous occupants."[17] Living in Canada for six years increased my feelings of detachment and marginality. Not only was I a rootless professional, but I was also an American citizen, and this was resented by some of the more nationalistic Canadian psychologists. No matter how long I lived in Canada, I would never been accepted as a Canadian, only as an American.

My time in Saskatchewan and Alberta strengthened my attachment to prairie landscapes of the sort that I had found in Kansas where my great-grandfather had settled. As a perception researcher, I was very interested in the vast open spaces, the way that weather could be seen coming in over the horizon, the grand sunsets, and the still white prairie in winter.[18] It is probably no accident that I have lived in a miniature prairie, the Sacramento Valley, for the past three decades. Knowledge of this place has enriched my teaching, my research, and my writing. I have come to realize that the transient scholarship which I described with some ambivalence in *Expertland* is not the appropriate model for all science. The land grant traditions of the campus where I teach have introduced me to alternative models of scholarship based on local and regional studies. I have colleagues whose fields of study are place-centered geology, flora, fauna, and culture. I have been working with my colleague Allan Wicker to develop a model of local research for psychology, in which researchers study places where they live and share these findings with local residents as well as with other academics. The following list describes some benefits of resident research:

1. Long-term contact with a place can lead resident researchers to formulate research problems in a more sensitive and appropriate fashion. Resident researchers should be able to get more useful information because they possess the knowledge to ask the right questions and make distinctions that informants would regard as more appropriate.
2. Drawing on their local knowledge, resident researchers can select methods that yield more valuable information. Better formulated problems coupled with sensitivity to local interests and values should pay off in better information.
3. Long-term residency in a community allows researchers to study processes over time and to document change.
4. Key informants and participants are known and available to resident researchers.
5. Background information that outsiders would have to spend considerable effort to obtain and assimilate is readily available to local researchers.
6. Resident researchers can capitalize on opportunities for synergy and continuity by coupling investigations.

ımmitment and concern of resident researchers will be evident eople who often object to the exploitative aspects of research by visitors who come into a place, collect data, and then depart to report their findings in scholarly journals. These scholars may give little or nothing back to those who donated their time and surrendered a measure of their privacy to the study. Resident researchers gain credibility by casting their lot with others in the place where they and their families live.

8. Interpretation and implementation of research can be shared with local people. After the results are announced, the local researcher will be available to participate with the community in dissemination and implementation.[19]

Part 2: Davis, California and the Sacramento Valley

Applying the methods and concepts of the social sciences to the place where I live has been an ongoing project. It has been made easier by the work of professional and amateur historians, geographers, geologists, and archeologists. The Yolo County Historical Society describes my community as it has been during the millennia that preceded western settlement.[20] Before the arrival of Europeans, large numbers of native peoples inhabited the oak-covered banks of Putah Creek, which originates at the summit of Mount Cobb in Lake County, and flows eastward past what is now the city of Davis to disappear into the tule marshes of the Sacramento River. The stream dried to a trickle in drought years and became a raging torrent during the rainy season. The stream preserves the name of a branch of the Patwin Indians who dwelled on its tree-covered banks. The ancestors of the Patwins had moved into the southern Sacramento Valley from the north more than twelve hundred years ago, and lived in small autonomous villages, composed of dome-shaped, semi-subterranean houses and communal buildings made of poles covered with tule or packed earth. Like most other native peoples of California at the time, the Patwin were hunters and gatherers rather than agriculturists, who made use of the abundance that their surroundings provided. More numerous than the native peoples were the various animal species with whom they shared the banks, the stream, and the oak woodlands, which were two to five miles wide. Some valley oaks were seven and eight feet in diameter. Beyond the woodlands were swamps covering hundreds of thousands of acres, containing tule, cattails, and other aquatic plants. There were prong-horned antelope in the grassland, tule elk mostly in the swamps, and deer in the woodland thickets. California grizzly bear ranged throughout all of these environments in search of food.

Riding my bicycle around Davis today, I am barely conscious of these early scenes, but I do see many things that are no longer there. Many residential areas of town I had known as fields containing rows of tomatoes or sugar beets. The neighborhood where I live now was such a field when I first came to Davis. As I ride my bicycle from home over to campus, I pass the street where Stan, my colleague, bought a house in what was then a new development. He later moved away, got divorced, and died. On the next block is the house that Mike and Jola built. It was one of the first atrium houses made by a local builder. Dale and Donna had lived a few blocks away, and next to them was the two-story house occupied by a fellow who had a medical school appointment and was a very good teacher and left twenty years ago. I soon reach College Park which was the first housing tract in the city, built on agricultural land. I pass the family home of a good friend, who has since died, whose parents were the first Dean of Students and Dean of Women at the Agricultural School. The house has since been sold, and I'm not sure who lives in it now. As I approach the campus, I see signs of change everywhere. Mixed in with buildings under construction are images of grassy fields and earlier buildings torn down. At the Social Sciences building where I work, everything is changed because of an enormous construction project. I remember when this used to be the Physical Sciences building. If I look closely, there are vestiges of the old laboratories. The building had been part of the Manhattan Project during the second World War, circled by barbed wire and armed guards. Years later they were still clearing radioactive materials out of the vent hoods. Most of the current occupants do not know about this.

Leaving the campus, I continue downtown where everything is both changed and familiar. I pass Art Related Things which used to be Barney's Good Time Records, and which I originally knew as the Bank of Davis, before it was taken over by a larger bank from the outside. I remember the manager being very nice to my grandmother when she moved to Davis at age ninety. She died five years later at the Driftwood Convalescent Home on 8th Street, another set of memories. I used to live over in that area before I was divorced. There are a lot of associations there that I don't think about.

The store names on the main street are different from those I remember. I see the former location of what had been the only bakery in town. When I first saw the Vienna Bakery sign, I rejoiced, thinking I would get wonderful Viennese pastry *mit Shlag*. Unfortunately the bakery was named after its owner, Joe Vienna, and sold doughnuts and maple bars. The first fancy bakery was in the old Safeway store, near where they installed the first traffic light in town. That building is now the Davis Food Co-op to which I belong, but every time I visit this building I remember the old co-op store located on L Street. Nearby is a liquor store, a category of establishment that existed nowhere in Davis when I arrived. In those days, anyone in Davis who wanted beer, wine, or alcohol had to leave town to obtain it. I use sketching to connect myself to this place. Most of these are quick sketches completed in five minutes. The intent is to extract the critical features, what makes a place or building distinctive, what gives it a special character, its *genius loci.*

The one familiar landmark on the main street is Davis Lumber and Hardware, but there is now Home Plus on the awning. Two hundred feet away is the mission-style SP station, which is on the registry of historical landmarks. A hundred yards from the SP station, hidden by brush, is the old stream bed of Putah Creek, now weed-covered, full of old tires and discarded machinery. Once this was a shining stream whose abundant fish included salmon, steelhead trout, and sturgeon. Enormous numbers of waterfowl nested locally and used this as a flyover during migration. This seems like a good spot to stop, dismount from my bicycle, and reflect on the connection between what is here now and what used to be.

In order to survive I must attend to what it is here now. I cannot knock on doors and ask to see former occupants. Nor can I ride the street system as it used to be, but only as it is today. I must attend to stop signs and traffic lights that had not existed a few years ago, and ride on streets that had been fields where I would walk with the children when they were young. Knowing the state demographics and the insistent pressure from real estate developers, the city will continue to grow, and more fields will become housing tracts. There are predictions of a continuous urban strip between Sacramento and the Bay Area, into which the identities of the existing cities will be submerged. I fear what I see as the future of Davis.

Spending time studying a single location encourages travel across disciplinary boundaries. I have ventured into fields very different from what I was trained to do. This was necessary in attempting to understand local conditions. It was not possible to make an intensive study of farmers' markets without venturing into agricultural economics. When I became part of an interdisciplinary team that developed the bicycle paths on which I have been riding, I learned the jargon and methods of civil engineering. Now that I study people's responses to trees, I consult with experts in urban forestry, a subject area that I never knew existed. Yet if I imagine myself as a bird flying over Davis, looking down at the green canopy, I see an urban forest.

I have studied issues that I felt to be important, often for reasons that I could not explain to others, at least at the beginning of the research. I can see in specific instances the operation of general laws and principles. Most of my colleagues proceed in the reverse direction, in looking at what is general and then maybe—but probably not—attempting to apply this in specific instances. I take seriously the study of people's response to the environment, and this can be something as mundane as the pathway on which they walk, the store in which they shop, or their response to a distant mountain. I have studied many of these topics without going as far as I wanted, stopping before I arrived at the most important questions. My partner, Barbara Sommer, describes these avoided issues as Big Fuzzies, topics so amorphous and difficult to quantify and reduce to a journal article that one is advised to leave them alone. My research on consumer cooperation is an example of this avoidance of important issues. I can take credit for bringing social psychological research methods to bear on a topic that is personally important to me. The research was motivated by my interest in the philosophy and spirit of cooperation, rather than fame, fortune, or the approbation of my colleagues; it was certainly not motivated by the interest of the participants, whose attitudes toward the research were very similar to those of native people who cannot understand why Western researchers ask so many trivial questions.

My students and I studied all the easy issues. We compared prices at the food co-op with those at commercial supermarkets. We looked at the motives, attitudes, and demographic characteristics of shoppers. We compared interaction patterns in the co-op store with that in nearby supermarkets. We documented who did the volunteer work in the store. We did *no* research on the spirit of cooperation that had brought me into the co-op and stimulated the entire research program. The simplest explanation of this avoidance is that the spirit is difficult to study and write about. Another explanation more in accord with Native American epistemology is that the spirit is found everywhere, in all the issues that we study, in a pricing system not intended to maximize profits; in the bulk-food containers which reduce wasteful packaging; the educational programs designed to inform rather than mislead; and in the volunteer work which brings the membership directly into daily operations of the store.

Another area of study in which I have spent considerable research time involves city trees. My students and I examined what species people liked and disliked; we compared homeowner's attitudes with those of landscape architects, arborists, and professional gardeners; we asked people to make ratings of colored slide images of trees, and we used the computer to generate drawings of different shaped trees which people rated for their physical attractiveness. We published a half-dozen papers on these issues, without exploring what trees meant to people in any fundamental sense. Humans have developed in association with trees for millennia. Presumably, the vestiges of this affiliation influence their present-day attitudes, but the procedures we have used to study these attitudes make it very difficult for us to understand these deeper connections.

Looking over these lines of research, I feel we were ice skating. Our intuition led us to the right ponds at the correct season of the year and an occasional glissade brought approving glances from spectators and donations of money from those who support ice skating, but we never went below the surface. I guess ice skaters are not supposed to go below the surface and there is probably a larger truth to that. Yet there is another part of me aware of the spiritual aspects of human existence; the *plus ultra*, the something more to existence than what we can see and measure with our questionnaires.[21]

Sustainability is an important theme in discussions about the future of Davis. People strive to protect natural areas. Numerous organizations rally to preserve flora and fauna. Activists want to maintain the uniqueness of the city, to see that it does not lose its identity. There is a mythology about Davis that attracts some people and keeps away others, as the City of Bicycles, as Tree City USA, as Ecotopia, a socially concerned city dedicated to "all things right and relevant," which is the name of a thrift store run by volunteers from the mental health association.

Because of the strong influence of western positivism, all these connections to the community, to the environment, and to the cultural landscape are described in secular terms. When the citizens rallied to preserve the SP station, the old library building, or the habitat of the burrowing owl, the arguments were quasi-scientific, based on ecological principles and the environmental sciences. The spirit world is revealed more in the actions of the citizens of Davis than in their words. Any attempt to use spirit language would be ridiculed by local pundits.

People outside the writing trade often believe that a writer should know something before writing about it. In contrast, I write to learn about things, to release whatever is in hiding and can be enlisted in my cause, or to become an agent for some unidentified transmission. Pages later I can say what I know and can use it again. Writing this essay has helped me deal with the frustration I felt because my activities only seemed to touch the surface of issues. If the spirit suffuses all aspects of the world, then our study of any aspects reveals the workings of the spirit. It is important for me to realize that I was not studying merely food prices at the co-op and the behavior of bicyclists at intersections. I studied all these details, but permeating them is the spirit of the place. I tell my students that it is acceptable to study the tail, the earlobe, or the front foot of the elephant, and even to make a research specialty of this activity, so long as this is done in the context of the whole animal and its ecology.

Because of the power of the medieval church in western Europe, early science began by phrasing its objectives in spiritual terms, as if the goal of science was to document and spread the word about the majesty of the Lord. Scientists claimed to see the workings of the deity in natural forces.[22] Medieval artists described their work in similar terms, as celebrating the majesty of God. Whether or not scientists and artists believed what they said, they used spiritual terms to justify their activities.

Because the United States is a secular society, we have moved in the opposite direction in avoiding any hint of a spiritual dimension in art or science. Even when we feel the spirit, we refrain from writing about it because there are no numbers that fit, nothing that can be measured when, in fact, everything we do has a spiritual dimension for those willing to see it. These Spirit of Place conferences have opened up a dialogue in psychology between representatives of traditional wisdom and Western psychology that is long overdue. I think the time is right for these discussions to take place. The limitations of positivism are more evident than ever. The noted perception researcher James J. Gibson declared that psychology has become the study of what is convenient and controllable rather than the study of what is important or relevant.[23] Serious contact with the wisdom of traditional peoples can change the direction of Western psychology.

In this essay I have described my use of several methods to explore and document the place where I live. I undertook historical research to learn about the activities of the early residents and the buildings. I use sketches to increase my environmental awareness, to see things that might otherwise be missed. I forage for mushrooms, which keeps me in touch with the seasons. I employ the methods of modern psychology to study the behavior of the current residents. I share what I have learned in these endeavors through the spoken and written word (teach and write, babble and scribble). Allan Wicker and I have proposed local research (sometimes we call it resident research) as a research specialty in community psychology.[24] None of this precludes interest in other parts of the world or in general principles of human behavior. Knowledge of one's place in the world provides a vantage point for undertaking these investigations.

Notes

1. Francis T. McAndrew, *Environmental Psychology* (Pacific Grove, Calif.: Brooks/Cole, 1993).
2. Clare C. Marcus, "Remembrance of Landscapes Past," *Landscape* 22 (1978): 34–43.
3. Theodore Roszak, *The Voice of the Earth* (New York: Simon and Schuster, 1992).
4. Yi-Fu Tuan, *Topophilia* (Englewood Cliffs, N.J.: Prentice Hall, 1974).
5. Maryanne Jacobi and Daniel Stokols, "The Role of Tradition in Group-Environment Relations," *Environmental Psychology*, Nickolaus R. Feimer and E. Scott Geller, eds. (New York: Praeger, 1983), 157–179.
6. Sally A. Shumaker and Ralph B. Taylor, "Toward a Clarification of People-Place Relationships: A Model of Attachment to Place," in *Environmental Psychology*, Feimer and Geller, eds., 219–256.

7. Heini Hediger, *Studies of the Psychology and Behavior of Captive Animals in Zoos and Circuses* (London: Butterworths, 1955).
8. Gordon H. Orians, "An Ecological and Evolutionary Approach to Landscape Aesthetics," in *Landscape Meanings and Values*, Edmund C. Penning-Rowsell and David Lowenthal, eds. (London: Allen and Unwin, 1986). See also Judith H. Heerwagen and Gordon H. Orians, "Human Habitats and Aesthetics," in *The Biophilia Hypothesis*, Stephen R. Kellert and Edward. O. Wilson, eds. (Washington, D.C.: Island Press, 1993), 138–172.
9. Gary P. Nabhan and Sara St. Antoine, "The Loss of Flora and Fauna Story," in *The Biophilia Hypothesis*, Kellert and Wilson, eds., 229–250.
10. Jared Diamond, "New Guineans and Their Natural World," in *The Biophilia Hypothesis*, Kellert andWilson, eds., 251–271.
11. John K. Bullard, "The Speciality of Place," *Places* 7 (1991):73–79.
12. Alvin W. Gouldner, "Cosmopolitans and Locals," *Administrative Science Quarterly* 2 (1957): 281–306.
13. Edward Kopf, "Untarnishing the Dream: Mobility, Opportunity, and Order in Modern America," *Journal of Social History* 11 (1977):206–227.
14. Shumaker and Taylor, "Toward a Clarification of People-Place Relationships," in *Environmental Psychology*, Feimer and Geller, eds.
15. Ibid.
16. Robert Sommer, *Expertland* (Garden City, N.Y.: Doubleday, 1963), 1.
17. Ibid., 4.
18. Sommer, "Space-Time on Prairie Highways," *AIP Journal* (July 1967): 274–276.
19. Allen Wicker and Robert Sommer, "The Resident Researcher," *American Journal of Community Psychology* 21 (1963):469–482.
20. Joann L. Larkey, *Davisville, '68* (Davis, Calif.: Historical and Landmarks Commission, 1969).
21. Gardner Murphy, *There Is More Beyond: Selected Papers of Gardner Murphy*, Lois B. Murphy, ed. (Jefferson, N.C.: McFarland, 1989).
22. Peter Fuller, "The Geography of Mother Nature," in *The Iconography of Landscape* , Denis Cosgrove and Stephen Daniels, eds. (New York: Cambridge University Press, 1988), 11–31.
23. James J. Gibson, "Autobiography," in *Reasons for Realism*, E. Reed and R. Jones, eds. (Hillsdale, N.J.: Lawrence Erlbaum, 1982), 7–22.
24. Wicker and Sommer, "The Resident Researcher," *American Journal of Community Psychology.*

8. But You, O Bethlehem of Ephrathah: Bethlehem as a Sacred Place

Roger Wharton, D. Min.

Editor's Note

Within each religious tradition there is almost always a physical center from which invisible lines of devotion radiate outward. For those who follow Christianity, and anyone who is a seeker of spirit, Bethlehem is a touchstone. In this essay Father Roger Wharton, an Episcopal priest, describes his pilgrimage to Bethlehem. His story invites us all to think of places where each of us might find inspiration and affirmation of our faith as he did. The appearance of animals, such as the storks he finds at this holy place, is seen as a good omen in cultures all around the world.

> *But you, O Bethlehem of Ephrathah, who are one of the little clans of Judah, from you shall come forth for me one who is to rule in Israel, whose origin is from of old, from ancient days.*
>
> —Micah 5:2

THE HEBREW PEOPLE encountered God in many diverse places and circumstances. At Bethel, Jacob dreamed of a ladder reaching from earth to heaven with the angels of God ascending and descending on it (Gen. 28). On Mount Sinai (known in some traditions as Mount Horeb), God revealed his name to Moses and called on him to deliver the Hebrews from bondage in Egypt (Exod. 3). It was on on Mount Sinai, too, that Moses received the Ten Commandments (Exod. 34). The wilderness of Sinai was where the newly freed slaves wandered for forty years. These places were considered special and holy, and worthy to be commemorated as seen in the following scriptural citations.

On waking from his dream, Jacob built a stone pillar and called that place "the House of God."

> Then Jacob woke from his sleep and said, "Surely the LORD is in this place—and I did not know it!" And he was afraid, and said, "How awesome is this place! This is none other than the house of God, and this is the gate of heaven." So Jacob rose early in the morning, and he took the stone that he had put under his head and set it up for a pillar and poured oil on the top of it. He called that place Bethel. (Gen. 28:16–19a)

The Hebrew scripture is filled with place names that signify important and holy events.

Moses was told by God that the very ground was holy and that it should be reverenced.

> When the LORD saw that he had turned aside to see, God called to him out of the bush, "Moses, Moses!" And he said, "Here I am." Then he said, "Come no closer! Remove the sandals from your feet, for the place on which you are standing is holy ground." (Exod. 3:3–4)

God tells Moses that he and the Hebrews he shall help free from slavery should come to Mount Sinai to worship, thereby recognizing and honoring this sacred place.

> He said, "I will be with you; and this shall be the sign for you that it is I who sent you: when you have brought the people out of Egypt, you shall worship God on this mountain." (Exod. 3:12)

When Moses came down from Mount Sinai, the people were so grateful for the revelation of God that they built a splendid and exquisite tabernacle and ark of the covenant to house the stone tablets.

> All who are skillful among you shall come and make all that the LORD has commanded: the tabernacle, its tent and its covering, its clasps and its frames, its bars, its pillars, and its bases; the ark with its poles, the mercy seat, and the curtain for the screen; the table with its poles and all its utensils, and the bread of the Presence; the lampstand also for the light, with its utensils and its lamps, and the oil for the light; and the altar of incense, with its poles, and the anointing oil and the fragrant incense, and the screen for the entrance, the entrance of the tabernacle; the altar of burnt offering, with its grating of bronze, its poles, and all its utensils, the basin with its stand; the hangings of the court, its pillars and its bases, and the screen for the gate of the court; the pegs of the tabernacle and the pegs of the court, and their cords; the finely worked vestments for ministering in the holy place. (Exod. 35:10–19a)

This tabernacle and ark of the covenant traveled with the Israelites, but Mount Sinai remained as a holy mountain and guiding landmark during their wandering through the wilderness.

When the forty years of wandering in the wilderness came to an end, Joshua led the people through the Jordan River, which stopped flowing when the priests bearing the ark of the covenant stepped into the water. Thus the people were able to cross on dry ground. This miraculous crossing was commemorated in the following way:

> When the entire nation had finished crossing over the Jordan, the LORD said to Joshua: "Select twelve men from the people, one from each tribe, and command them, 'Take twelve stones from here out of the middle of the Jordan, from the place where the priests' feet stood, carry them over with you, and lay them down in the place where you camp tonight.' " (Josh. 4:1–3)

> Those twelve stones, which they had taken out of the Jordan, Joshua set up in Gilgal, saying to the Israelites, "When your children ask their parents in time to come, 'What do these stones mean?' then you shall let your children know, 'Israel crossed over the Jordan here on dry ground.' For the LORD your God dried up the waters of the Jordan for you until you crossed over, as the LORD your God did to the Red Sea, which he dried up for us until we crossed over, so that all the peoples of the earth may know that the hand of the LORD is mighty, and so that you may fear the LORD your God forever." (Josh. 4:20–24)

Not only were holy places marked with stone pillars and various types of shrines as shown above, but their location was recorded in oral history and in the holy scripture of the Israelites.

As the religion of the wandering Israelites developed into a religious state set within borders of the promised land and Judaism became institutionalized, wilderness holy places became less important, for two reasons. First, God's revelation was understood increasingly as a revelation of action in history for the benefit of the Hebrew people. With this new concept of history came a de-emphasis on the sacredness of place. Holy places where the living encounter with God had occurred were replaced by historical sites designating human events. Secondly, the priestly clan attempted to consolidate power on the Holy Mountain, and the kings desired to centralize rule in Jerusalem. This caused the destruction of many pre-Israelite hill shrines and even the deconsecration of some Hebrew holy places. Yet the idea of a holy place lived on in the hearts of the people as they struggled to maintain particular holy sites for inspiration. This concept lives on today not only among some Jews, but also among some of the Christians who share this early heritage with their Jewish brothers and sisters.

Well before the Christian era, the ritual attention of most of Judaism was focused on the sacred place on Mount Moriah where the temple built by Solomon stood. It was here that the grain and blood sacrifices required by Jewish law took place. Mount Moriah had a long history as a place of God's revelations. It is to this mountain that Abraham took Isaac for sacrifice.

> He said, "Take your son, your only son Isaac, whom you love, and go to the land of Moriah, and offer him there as a burnt offering on one of the mountains that I shall show you." (Gen. 22:2)

After testing Abraham's faith and obedience, God released Abraham from this command and provided a ram to replace Isaac on the altar. It is here that God renews the promise made to Abraham and Sarah of a nation of offspring living in a nation of their own.

From this beginning, Moriah becomes the center of Jewish cultic worship. Here is where God tells David to build the temple, which is built by his son Solomon.

> Solomon began to build the house of the LORD in Jerusalem on Mount Moriah, where the LORD had appeared to his father David, at the place that David had designated, on the threshing floor of Ornan the Jebusite. (2 Chron. 3:1)

Solomon built a magnificent temple on the summit of what is now Jerusalem. The temple was destroyed in 586 B.C. by King Nebuchadrezzar II of Babylon. Fifty years later the people began the rebuilding of the temple on the same sacred place. This second temple was destroyed in A.D. 70 and has never been rebuilt. Archeological excavations uncovered the wall of the temple complex. This wall is known as the Wailing Wall and is an important place of pilgrimage for the Jewish people. Orthodox Jews will not travel into the temple complex for fear of trespassing on the most holy space know as the Holy of Holies which was the innermost chamber of the temple.

This most holy mountain became the location of the central mystery of Christianity, as the place of the passion, death, and resurrection of Jesus Christ. It is also a holy place to Islam, for it is here that the Prophet Mohammed ascended into heaven on a winged steed and received the revelation of the central creeds of Islam.[1] The temple site, which became Muslim territory soon after the fall of Rome, is now covered by the Mosque of the Omar, also known as the Mosque of the Rock.

Another place which is geologically very closely related to Mount Moriah, connected by a south running ridge of about five miles, became a sacred place for Christians. For here is the town of Bethlehem, where the Messiah was born. The city sits on two hills of the ridge that forms the watershed between the Mediterranean and the Dead Sea. Bethlehem is three thousand feet above the Mediterranean Sea to the west and more than four thousand feet above the level of the Dead Sea to the east. From the top of the ridge looking east can be seen the Mountains of Moab, and of course Jerusalem and Mount Zion.[2]

Bethlehem had been the home of the shepherd David who became the greatest king of Israel and an ancestor of Jesus. It was to this place that God directed the prophet Samuel to go in order to find the young David and to anoint him the choosen one to succeed Saul as king.

> The LORD said to Samuel, "How long will you grieve over Saul? I have rejected him from being king over Israel. Fill your horn with oil and set out; I will send you to Jesse the Bethlehemite, for I have provided for myself a king among his sons." (I Sam. 16:1)

> Then Samuel took the horn of oil, and anointed him in the presence of his brothers; and the spirit of the LORD came mightily upon David from that day forward. (I Sam. 16:13a)

Bethlehem was expected to become a very special holy place, because it had long been prophesied to be the birthplace of the coming Messiah.

> But you, O Bethlehem of Ephrathah, who are one of the little clans of Judah, from you shall come forth for me one who is to rule in Israel, whose origin is from of old, from ancient days. (Mic. 5:2)

The evangelist Matthew tells us that it was indeed in Bethlehem that the Messiah was born: "In the time of King Herod, after Jesus was born in Bethlehem of Judea . . ." (Matt. 2:1a)

Christians even before the writing of Matthew's Gospel honored Bethlehem as the birthplace of the Messiah. Recently, Christian scholars have questioned not only the birthplace of Jesus but also many aspects of his life and ministry. For the purposes of this paper, it does not matter whether Jesus was born at Bethlehem or not. What matters is that Bethlehem and the Church of the Holy Nativity have been set aside as sacred places, and that the Creator uses these places to reveal his/her love to the people.

There are three classifications of holy places in Christian tradition. Each type brings it own special qualities to the sacred site. First, there are historic holy places that can be verified by historical accounts or archaeological evidence.

The village of Bethlehem falls within this category. The second classification is that of traditional holy sites. These sites cannot be scientifically verified as historical sites, but they have been connected to specific events by Christians for a long time and have acquired deep spiritual meaning. For example, Bethlehem as the birthplace of Jesus cannot be verified historically—this is a traditional site. Other examples of traditional sites would be the actual place of Christ's birth, the location of his manger in the cave, and the Shepherd's Field where his birth was announced to the shepherds by the angels. The third classification is that of pious sites. These are places that for various pious reasons have been associated with biblical events but are neither historical or traditional. The best known of these to Christians is Gordon's Calvary and tomb of Jesus. This site, established in recent history, is visited by thousands of pilgrims each day because it fits the biblical descriptions of the burial place of Jesus, although it cannot be verified and traditionally the church has recognized and honored another site about a half-mile away enclosed with the Church of the Holy Sepulcher.

The Christian cult of the first centuries was not popular with the Hebrew government, institutional Judaism, or the Roman Empire. Therefore all three groups did their best to wipe out all possible traces of historical sites that were associated with the political martyr Jesus. When Christianity became the official religion of the Roman Empire under Constantine in A.D. 324, not many of the original sites associated with the life and ministry of Jesus remained. Mount Calvary and the Holy Sepulchre had been leveled by Roman engineers on order of Hadrian after the Jewish revolt in A.D. 132 in hopes that people would soon forget the crucifixion of the carpenter from Nazareth that took place there.[3]

Constantine's mother Helena, traveling in Palestine in A.D. 326 ordered that a church be built over the place of the birth of Christ. She also located, protected, and reverenced many other Christian holy places. Even though centuries had passed since the death of Jesus, sacred sites were not difficult to locate because the persecuted Christians had passed on their location in oral tradition from generation to generation.[4] The Roman government under Hadrian (76–138) had also ironically helped to preserve the location of the very sites it hoped to destroy by building temples and shrines over them. The birthplace in Bethlehem was marked by a shrine of Adonis, making it very easy to locate.[5] Since the time of Helena, the site of Christ's birth has been honored with a church which has been built and modified over the centuries.

Although in Christian thought Bethlehem is the birthplace of the Prince of Peace, it has not been a peaceful place. It has been fought over for centuries including during the Crusades and in the 1967 War. In recent years, there has been contention over ownership between Israel and the Palestinian Liberation Army. Perhaps this heritage is further testimony to the depth of meaning people attach to sacred places. Yet in spite of all this conflict, the sacred place of the birth of the Christ has remained a place where God's love is made known to humankind in the rituals and celebrations that take place there. There is a daily procession which had is origins in the fifteenth century,[6] as well as the annual Christmas Eve celebration when thousands of pilgrims gather in the church and town squares. Less public are the personal revelations given to the pilgrims who follow the star throughout the centuries.

If such a thing is possible, the sacredness of Bethlehem was enhanced in the fifth century, when it was choosen as the place for study and work by the scholar Jerome (385–419) for the translation of Jewish and Christian sacred texts into the Latin Vulgate Bible. In this holy place, where Christians believe the Word became flesh—"And the Word became flesh and lived among us, and we have seen his glory, the glory as of a father's only son, full of grace and truth" (John 1:14)—the Word was translated so that people who where not educated in Greek and Hebrew could have access to the Good News of what God had accomplished in Christ Jesus.[7] The selection of Bethlehem for this work may again be an indication of its sacred nature, because sacred places are often the site of ongoing revelations and spiritual work.

Although it has been the Christian way to enclose sacred places within churches and buildings, Bethlehem remains unique in that it also preserves one of the few outdoor Christian holy sites. Located about two miles down the hill from the Church of the Holy Nativity are a field and cave, the traditional site where the angels announced the birth of Christ to the shepherds abiding in their field by night. Sheep still graze in this field.

The small, modern day city sits on the transition zone of semi-arid cultivated land and the desert that drops down to the lowest place on the earth, the Dead Sea. What follows is an account of a personal encounter with this sacred place and how it has affected me.

My Personal Encounter with Bethlehem

The out-of-doors has always been important to me. As a child I was fortunate in living next to a large vacant field and small pine plantation. Wood lots were also scattered throughout my neighborhood. I spent a great deal of time playing and growing up in these natural playgrounds. Insects fascinated me and formed my introduction to the exciting world of nature. As an elementary student, I caught and identified insects for high school biology students.

The spiritual connection to natural wonder and awe was cultivated by many summer church camping experiences and Boy Scout trips. When I was fourteen, I began to spend the whole summers working as a camp counselor. At the camps

I instinctually discovered places of power. In each camp I discovered those places that were especially spiritual for me. These places ranged from a grove of tulip trees, to hill tops, to a place tucked away on the edge of a pine plantation.

Nurtured by the out-of-doors, I felt a calling while in high school to become a biology and environmental education teacher. After teaching for a few years, I experienced a calling to the ordained ministry and went off to Nashotah House Seminary, which was tucked away in southern Wisconsin on the shore of a lake and surrounded by trees. Here my seminary education was enhanced by swimming, hiking, skiing, sleeping out, camping, collecting edible plants, tree planting, and making maple syrup on the seminary grounds. I also found my personal sacred places scattered around the lake and throughout the woods.

As a newly ordained Episcopal priest, I was sent off to remote northern Wisconsin, which was delightful for me. Here in the midst of natural forests, lakes, and wildlife, my formation continued with the help of the folks in my parishes. It was not long, however, before I realized that my spiritual connection and communion with the natural world were not understood by many other Christians, especially not those in leadership positions. This led me to study with Matthew Fox for a year at the Institute for Creation-Centered Spirituality in Chicago. It was here that theological reflection and language were added to my own nature-inspired Christianity and sense of the holy.

From that point on, whether serving parishes in New York or Alaska, a great deal of what I preached included inspiration from the natural world and the call to be ecologically sensitive Christians. My own experiences and education led me to develop a special outdoor environmental ministry called Wilderness Manna. By leading many wilderness trips, I realized what a powerful place the wilderness can be for teaching, inspiration, and changing lives. I experienced firsthand the need for many Christians to integrate their outdoor and nature mystical experiences with Christianity. My understanding of the power of place was enhanced by a pilgrimage to Israel in 1984.

The first week was spent with a tour group traveling quickly around the country, visiting the various holy sites. The second week I spent alone, retracing my steps to these locations and seeking out new sites of interest. I visited Bethlehem during both segments. On the tour, the visit was quick and even though it was low tourist season, the place did not have much of an opportunity to influence me. My return visit, however, was very significant as I was enfolded in the mystery of the birth of the Christ.

I arrived in Bethlehem by Arab bus from Jerusalem and proceeded to the Church of the Holy Nativity. There were few tour groups and even fewer individual pilgrims in the church when I arrived. I spent some time in the grotto with various tour groups from different countries enjoying the singing of "Silent

Night" in various languages. This is a tradition of visitors to the shrine. Eventually everyone left and no new people arrived. I was alone in this sacred place, able to pray in my own way without self-consciousness. I knelt at the silver Star of Bethlehem which surrounds a hole in the floor that marks the "very spot" on earth where it is believed the Christ was born of the God Bearer, Mary. The silver star is a replica of the one placed there in 1717. The original star disappeared in mysterious circumstances in 1847. This theft, along with other causes, led to the Crimean War.[8] I was able to place my own silver cross of the Order of the Holy Nativity on that place, making a connection that I would carry with me until this very day.

Surprised that no one yet entered, I moved to the site of the manger, where once again I was able to pray in my own way, recalling the masculine role of Joseph and the presence of the animals at the birth. It was a minor miracle that I was able to spend so much time alone in this very busy shrine touched by the power of place and the hope of peace on earth. The internal experience was one of opening and peace and feeling enfolded in a wonderful mystery. I was to learn that the Spirit had more in store for me on this holy hill.

On leaving the church, I next sought out the Field of the Shepherds. After several inquires I hired a taxi to take me the few miles down the hill to the traditional site of the shepherd's fields. It was in this field that the news of the birth of the Christ was first announced by angels to shepherds who were tending their flocks by night. The Good News or Gospel was therefore first proclaimed to the earth at this place not only to the shepherds but also to the sheep and all other plants and animals on the hillside. It was from the cave a short way up the hill that the New Creation was to pour forth, rolling down the mountain, filling the whole cosmos.

I arrived just as the final tourists were loading on to a bus. I entered the gate of this less-visited site, again encompassed in the mystery of solitude, giving thanks for the gift of being alone in such a sacred site. As I walked down the path I looked skyward and was greeted by a large flock of migrating storks who had stopped their migration to circle overhead. For a moment as I gazed upward, time was transcended. I was now standing in the field on the night of the birth of the Christ and angels were flying overhead proclaiming the Good News.

It came upon the midnight clear,
That glorious song of old,
From angels bending near the earth
To touch their harps of gold:
"Peace on the earth, good will to men,
From heav'n's all gracious King."

The world in solemn stillness lay
To hear the angels sing.

Still through the cloven skies they come
With peaceful wings unfurled,
And still their heav'nly music floats
O'er all the weary world;
Above its sad and lowly plains
They bend on hov'ring wing,
And ever ov'er its Babel sounds
The blessed angels sing!

Once again I was blessed by being enveloped in the great mystery.

> In that region there were shepherds living in the fields, keeping watch over their flock by night. Then an angel of the Lord stood before them, and the glory of the Lord shone around them, and they were terrified. But the angel said to them, "Do not be afraid; for see—I am bringing you good news of great joy for all the people: to you is born this day in the city of David a Savior, who is the Messiah, the Lord. This will be a sign for you: you will find a child wrapped in bands of cloth and lying in a manger." And suddenly there was with the angel a multitude of the heavenly host, praising God and saying, "Glory to God in the highest heaven, and on earth peace among those whom he favors!" (Luke 2:8–14)

The storks flew on and the angels departed, leaving me alone there on the hillside. For some reason no one else visited this sacred site for over the next two hours, except for one couple who stopped briefly before rushing back to their waiting taxi. This solitude permitted me once again to pray in my own ways and to make a good pilgrimage to the field, cave, and gardens of this sacred place. I was touched by the gift that had been given to me and found a deep inner peace by being able to meditate in this outdoor holy place, for the Field of the Shepherds is one of the very few holy sites that has not been covered by churches and buildings.

Several years later I have come to appreciate the appearance of the storks at Bethlehem. I have learned some of the ancient Christian symbolism that is associated with this bird which in a way has made my experience that much more powerful in retrospect. During the Christmas season, while listening to National Public Radio, I was surprised to hear of a Christmas poem about a stork.

A poem was found written by hand on the overleaf of the 1549 *Book of Common Prayer* of one of the kings of England which has not been found anyplace else. It is not known if it was written by the owner of the prayer book, or whether the king copied it down from a sermon or other source. The poem tells the story of a stork who hears the Good News of the birth of the Christ Child and wants to pay homage to the child. Being a good parent, it makes sure that its chicks are tucked into their nest and have enough food before flying off to Bethlehem. It arrives at the stable and finds the wonderful child lying in a manger. The manger is lined with scratchy straw, which the stork thinks must be uncomfortable for the baby. To soften his bed, the stork plucks its own feathers to line the nest with soft down before flying home. This stork story made the migrating storks of Bethlehem seem that much more special to me.

In *The Bestiary of Christ* is the chapter on wading birds which helps to fill in more of the mystery of the stork. The stork, like other wading birds, shares a symbolism of good struggling with evil.[9]

The wading birds are also often connected with the ideals of wisdom and guidance. In certain Asiatic regions, the stork is thought to have strange powers of insight which enable it to see clearly the state of each person's conscience. Very old traditions also connect waders with divine wisdom. Wisdom is nearly always identified with the divine Word for Christians. Thus the stork as a symbol of wisdom can also be understood as a token for the Word. The Word for Christians, as expressed in the prologue to John's Gospel, is Christ.

> In the beginning was the Word, and the Word was with God, and the Word was God. He was in the beginning with God. All things came into being through him, and without him not one thing came into being. What has come into being in him was life, and the life was the light of all people. The light shines in the darkness, and the darkness did not overcome it.
>
> There was a man sent from God, whose name was John. He came as a witness to testify to the light, so that all might believe through him. He himself was not the light, but he came to testify to the light.
>
> The true light, which enlightens everyone, was coming into the world. He was in the world, and the world came into being through him; yet the world did not know him. He came to what was his own, and his own people did not accept him. But to all who received him, who believed in his name, he gave power to become children of God, who were born, not of blood or of the will of the flesh or of the will of man, but of God.
>
> And the Word became flesh and lived among us, and we have seen his glory, the glory as of a father's only son, full of grace and truth. (John 1:1–14)

Thus the appearance of the storks to me in the Shepherd's Field was, in a sense, Christ himself. Not only does the Stork Christ speaks of its birth but also, following the Egyptian resurrection symbolism of the ibis and its connection to Osiris, it takes on the same symbolic role of speaking of resurrection and new birth. The storks circling overhead not only announce the birth of the Jesus but also speak to the inauguration of the New Creation that is to follow in the Resurrection of the Christ.

The stork in the Shepherd's Field played the role for me of a messenger from God. This role of messenger, in many cultures, is often given to birds—especially large, high-flying birds. I didn't receive a worded message. I experienced a deep peace, inspiration, and an opening for what was to follow.

My Spirit experience was not yet finished. It was getting late, and I needed to return to the Bethlehem town square to catch the last bus back to Jerusalem. My solitude at the site had been wonderful, but I had expected to catch a tour bus or taxi back up the hill, but there were none around. I was forced, therefore, to walk up the hill to Bethlehem. Soon I realized that I was retracing the steps of the shepherds to the Christ Child. The drudgery vanished. The walk became a pilgrimage in the deepest sense, and I give thanks to the Spirit again for presenting me with such a unique experience. I walked from the field to the Church of the Holy Nativity sharing the excitement of the shepherds on that most holy night.

I arrived in time to catch the next-to-last Arab bus back to the city but my Spirit experience was still not over. On the short three-mile ride to Jerusalem, our Arab bus was stopped at a Israeli roadblock. Armed soldiers entered the bus asking for indentification papers. I was scared because I did not have my identification papers on me. Fortunately as a tourist I was not asked for them. It was only the Arabs who were being queried. Here I was a short distance from the birthplace of the Prince of Peace, being reminded that there still was much work to do to bring into fulness the peace of the New Creation. I had been gifted in very special ways, and now I was reminded in a very concrete way that life involves more than just mystical experience. Christian life also means striving for justice and peace among all people and respecting the dignity of every human being.[10]

The power of place continues to work in my life. As I retell this story, I am struck once again with the power of the experience and the teaching of the Spirit. I am given new breath and inspiration to continue my life and ministry in hopes that I can help others experience the connection with the Mystery of God which is experienced in sacred places both indoors and out-of-doors.

Notes

1. Edwin Bernbaum, *Sacred Mountains of the World* (San Francisco: Sierra Club Books, 1990), 90.
2. Stewart Peronwe, *Holy Places of Christendom* (New York, 1976), 15.

3. Sabino de Sandoli, *Calvary and the Holy Sepulchre,* trans. Cormac H. McAteer (Jerusalem: Franciscan Printing Press, no date), 10.
4. Maria Teresa Petrozzi, *Bethlehem,* trans. Godfrey Kloetzly and M. T. Petrozzi (Jerusalem: Franciscan Printing Press, 1971), 30.
5. Peronwe, 16–17.
6. Petrozzi, 126.
7. Lewis Lupton, *Bethlehem to Lindisfarne* (London, 1988).
8. Horst J. Becker, *Jerusalem with Bethlehem, Hebron, Jericho, Samaria and Massada,* trans. Spurbooks Limited (Buckinghamshire, England: Spurbooks, 1973).
9. Louis Charbonneau-Lassay, *The Bestiary of Christ,* English translation (New York: Parabola Books, 1991), 267, 273.
10. *Book of Common Prayer, 1979* (New York: Seabury Press, 1979).

9. From Huacas to Mesas: Altars as Mirrors of Ecstatic Experience

Debra D. Carroll

Editor's Note

Each of us has our own special places. Their powers are often not fully realized until we arrive at the place that has called us to it. Debra Carroll is an expressive arts therapist, educator, and dancer who felt magnetically drawn to a place in Hawaii which seemed to reveal to her clues to ancient dances. Drawing on this inspiration, and her years of study with the noted Peruvian shaman don Eduardo Calderone, she shows us the rudiments of honoring the spirit of a place through the construction of altars—what some people might describe as "crystal radio sets" to focus spirit.

We had been picking our way through lava rock and low growth up a steep incline from the cove below. Ahead of us a purposely vague path of uncut rocks wound tortuously upward toward the ever-receding tower of green and black cliffs. Tangled jungle lay to the left and an upward slope of vegetation and rocks to the right. On the other side of that slope, I knew, were the terraces of a *heiau*, a stone enclosure marking a sacred place, not yet visible from where I was. Even though the heiau stood to our immediate right, our approach to it was by clambering along the slope to its left all the way to the topmost terrace.

This heiau, like most in the Hawaiian Islands, had been built centuries before the arrival of Western missionaries in the early 1800s. However, unlike many other such shrines that have fallen into ruins or been bulldozed for the construction of a golf course or tourist hotel, this heiau has been maintained. I was breathless at the mere thought of being given permission to visit the site.

I was clad simply in a hat and *pareau*, a Tahitian dress made by wrapping two yards of fabric around the body and tying two corners of the cloth either above the breasts or at the back of the neck. Around my neck was a pile of flower necklaces, or *leis.* On my feet I wore thick-soled rubber and cloth thongs, which slipped from time to time on the lava rock. This meant I had to pay attention to my step.

Even though the hike was a short one the exertion of climbing felt good. I pushed my left knee with my hands and lowered my head to ease the strain of lifting my weight over one especially large boulder. When I looked up I was startled to see just yards ahead the base of the cliff, which had looked distant only a moment ago. Now I also could see, to the right and tumbling down toward the cove from which we had just come, the wide, semi-rectangular terraces of the heiau. Short, jewel-green grass grew in the terraces bounded by supporting walls of black lava rock. Beyond, the ocean stretched out to the edge of the world.

With a few easy steps we arrived at the entrance on the left side of the topmost terrace. Standing at the entrance facing toward the heiau the cliff was to our left and ahead, inside the terrace, was a small, level platform, clearly defined by rock work. Like black pearls sewn on the earth, a seamless trail of rocks led from the narrow gate where we stood to the platform. My companion and I paused to gather both our centering and our breath.

I had been guided to this nature temple by a friend who for years had studied and performed the sacred dance of *kahiko* (ancient) *hula* with Pua and Nalani Kanaka'ole on the Big Island of Hawaii. As the daughters of a famous Hawaiian matriarch, Auntie Edith Kanaka'ole, Pua and Nalani are responsible for carrying and transmitting an interdisciplinary spiritual lineage. Their heritage includes not only the ancient oral and artistic tradition of lengthy chants and dances detailing the odyssey of the goddess Pele to her home inside Kilauea Crater on the Big Island, but also a body of wisdom including the use of herbs and the proper use of the ritual surrounding sacred dance to develop what the Hawaiians call "inner qualities."

My friend, who wishes to remain anonymous, knew that I have dedicated most of my adult life to the study of the role of creativity and the arts of ecstasy in the unfolding of human potential. She had been a participant in a process called Mythic Drama, which I developed to facilitate individual and group passages. The process uses shamanic techniques, altered states of consciousness, mask making, and awareness practice in conjunction with drama/dance improvisation to develop ritual dramas. She knew I had studied sacred dance and would be studying *hula* in Hawaii. She also knew of my interest in altars, on which I have offered courses over the past ten years.

We discussed the fact that, in a time when Western academicians and workshop gurus are writing about awakening the artist-healer within, the Kanaka'ole sisters and others like them possess a living tradition of the arts as integral to not only whole making but also cultivation of human consciousness. Healing and esoteric wisdom are held to reside in the same deep center as the creative. The Hawaiian word for this center of intelligence is *na'au*, located in the belly or instinctive center.

When I had departed the Big Island of Hawaii for the northern island of Kaua'i my friend had said, "You must go to the dance platform and make an offering to the goddess Laka, who brought us the sacred dance of hula." Through the Hawaiian grapevine I had been given permission to visit the shrine of Laka. Now I stood, a little breathless and more than a little awed, at the entrance to the very place where the native people of Hawaii believe their sacred dance form had first been conveyed to an ancient leader.

Over a period of nearly a thousand years this temple has been maintained by masters, or *kumu hula*, of the sacred dance and their students. The current caretaker Auntie Roselle, herself a kumu hula, lives on the opposite side of the island of Kaua'i from the heiau. Organizing a group of family and pupils once a month to travel a crowded two-lane road around the island to prune the plant life and clean up trash left by those ignorant of the significance of the place is no easy task, yet she does it willingly, so revered is this site.

Before important ceremonial events, dance competitions, or when they feel in need of inspiration, *kumu* from neighboring islands make pilgrimages here. After seeking permission from the caretaker, they come as humbly as novices to ask the blessing and guidance of Laka, the goddess of the dance.

After offering a flower at the gate along with a prayer for permission to enter the temple, I stepped gingerly toward what I recognized as the dance platform. It lay in front of a horizontal, chest-high gash in the cliff, filled with both fresh and decaying flowers and other unidentifiable things. Gaping in the gnarled blackness of the cliff, the altar looked like the open maw of some primordial monster.

I thought of the ballads of Eskimo shamans who, diving to the depths under the ocean, must comb the filthy hair of the sea-goddess and withstand her fetid breath to obtain her graces for a good seal hunt. That thought made me shudder as I turned to face this, the altar to the goddess of the dance. But the fragrance exuding from this mouth was sweet. Casting off fear I allowed my mind to become quiet like a still pond, and my attention to sink, a weight in the pond, into my belly.

I felt embarrassed not knowing how to address this deity properly. In silence I gently lifted over my head one of the several leis from around my neck and placed it on the altar with a quiet prayer for the use of the arts for the liberation of all sentient beings. Slowly and deliberately I did this with each one, pausing in between to feel the quieting of my own attention, until my neck was bare. Suddenly tears were streaming down my face, and I found myself turning around and moving as if pushed from behind toward the dance platform.

In the center of the platform I was twirled around to face first the altar, then the temple's terraces descending to the ocean. I felt myself sinking and swaying and immediately thought my knees were giving out, that I was going to faint. Then I noticed I was awake, albeit in an altered state of consciousness, and being brought into the "ready" position for the dance, with knees bent and body relaxed. I had been senselessly staring at the tops of the palm trees below with the ocean behind; now I realized I was swaying like a palm tree, effortlessly allowing the force of the wind to move through me. A faraway voice was saying to me, "Let yourself bend like the palm tree. Dance with the forces of nature rather than resist them."

Deep inside my solar plexus I felt something simply let go. I felt the ease of the palm tree, simultaneously bending with and buoyed by the wind. Air flowed through the fluttering fronds of my fingertips. It was as if a door opened and the wind moved right through my heart, my breath, and my body. As I surrendered to the sun-warmed ocean breeze, my spine felt soft and fluid. My shoulders and hips rotated loosely, effortlessly around the spiraling of the spine.

My senses were heightened. I could feel the air through which my fingers gestured, as if it were warm mud. I felt I was moving in slow-motion, and my awareness of each impulse of movement was intense. The awareness was of being warm, molten earth, then ocean, then air, caused by the warmth of the sun to move and expand.

It was only later that I was able to appreciate that on the dance platform I had executed very advanced combinations of hula steps which, until then, I had only seen expert dancers perform. I had, essentially, performed a series of movements corresponding to the dance styles of each of the six principal islands of Hawaii. Starting with the very strenuous, squatting (or *noho*) movements typical of the Big Island, I progressed through the vigorous, instinctive motions of Moloka'i to the fluid, sensuous motions of Kaua'i.

When I tried later to repeat the steps from the dance platform I could not. Nonetheless, something very important to me had occurred. I felt as though my physical connection with dance, which had been fragile after the trauma of a series of injuries, had been healed and bonded. The next time I saw a kumu hula dancing, the appreciation of the source and meaning of his art was deeply stirring to me.

Sacred Sites as Natural Altars

Walking back down the path to the water that afternoon, my knees and hands trembled. I felt elated, but shaken to the core of my being. As I wondered why, I thought of other sacred sites in the Americas and Europe to which I had gone as a pilgrim. At each of them I had found natural altars, some feature to which visitors were naturally drawn to meditate, make offerings, or pray. Over time I had arrived at an hypothesis that sacred sites are natural altars—the first altars, if you will.

I also had experienced an integration or healing at each sacred site I had visited. The healing for me seemed to be a result of opening into capacities greater than those with which I had previously identified myself. Those challenges to the smallness of my self-concepts had consistently prodded me into deepening reflection on how little I knew about my real being, or about anything else for that matter. Rather than injuring my self-esteem, though, the humbling of my ego within the context of an ecstatic experience repeatedly had had the effect of making me feel more centered, happier with my life, and physically healthier.

Of course, a small voice inside commented, *that is the function of altars: to challenge us to expand in heart, mind, and spirit.* The Latin root of the word *altar* is *altare*, meaning "a high place," suggesting a more elevated view from on high, or at least the raising of one's spirits. I had experienced both at each of the natural altars I had visited. Is there something at sacred sites that tends to induce numinous or transcendent experiences that leave us feeling more whole? Abraham Maslow claimed that mystical experiences and psychological health go together. Lakota medicine man Wallace Black Elk is quoted as saying of sacred sites, "The Mother Earth has special places to cleanse your body, mind and spirit."[1]

In the Greco-Roman tradition from which the word *altare* derives, temple altars were elevated structures or platforms on which offerings were made to the gods. In fact, the temples themselves were often built in high places. In the Jewish tradition the altar is the *bema*, a raised platform from which Torah is read, as a reenactment of Moses' meeting with God on Mount Sinai. The Jewish and Greco-Roman traditions converge in the Roman Catholic Church, where "the Word" is read from a raised place and wine and bread are offered up in the name of Christ on a raised altar.[2]

As I walked down the slope from yet another sacred site, the connection between high places and the elevation of altars struck me. Just as the Jews held Mount Sinai sacred because that is where Moses met God, and the ancient Greeks believed Mount Olympus to be the home of the gods, so other peoples from far-flung parts of the globe often have made pilgrimages to mountains to make offerings to the gods. Many sacred sites are located, if not on mountains or mesa tops, at least in places with views from a height of the plains or seas below, like the view from the dance platform of Laka of the vast Pacific.

Elevations as Altars

Among the Saami of Lapland in Northern Scandinavia, for example, sacrifices of reindeer were made to the deity Storjunkare (the "Vice-regent of God") on top of a holy mountain. When the mountain was too steep to climb, a stone dipped in the blood of the sacrificed animal was thrown up towards the top of the mountain.[3] The title *Storjunkare* is derived from the Norwegian name for the governor of a province, *junkare*. As an intermediary between humans and non-humans, Storjunkare could be likened to the Celtic Forest Lord. Storjunkare's permission was required to sacrifice or hunt any beast, bird, or fish.

The Saami erected shrines to their Lord of the Beasts behind their huts, and the shrines were also called Storjunkare. These shrines comprised one or more large stones surrounded by the antlers of sacrificed reindeer. Since it was believed that Storjunkare resided in places inaccessible to humans—in the rocks of high mountains, waterfalls, and the banks of lakes—sacrifices and prayers to him were made in those places. One observer counted thirty sacred sites in one district alone: hills, holy mountains, lakes, and waterfalls.[4]

In the mountains surrounding San Cristobal de las Casas in Chiapas in southeastern Mexico, the people of Zinacantan still pray to their ancestral gods at mountain shrines. Called *Totilme'il* in Tzotzil Maya, meaning "Sir Father, Madam Mother," the ancestral gods are envisioned as elders who live eternally in the hills or mountains monitoring and guarding the traditional Zinacantan way of life. The Zinacantecos make regular pilgrimages to the neighboring hills and mountains, where ritual offerings of copal incense, chickens, white candles, and cane liquor are made to the ancestral gods.[5]

The foot and the summit of the sacred mountains are littered with crosses. Visitors to the shrines light candles and copal incense at the foot of the mountain, then pray before climbing the trail to the top. At the top the same ritual is repeated, except that the prayer is similar to what one would utter at a household shrine. This is because the shrine at the summit is believed to be the household cross for the ancestral god who resides within the mountain.[6]

Not only do the ancestral gods monitor the affairs of Zinacantecos, they also care for the "animal companions," or the animal-spirit companion with which each person shares his or her inner soul. These animal-spirits—jaguars, ocelots, coyotes, and even squirrels—are kept corralled and cared for by the ancestral gods inside a sacred mountain east of Zinacanten Center.[7]

One young Zinacanteco named Romin Tanchak, recounting a dream, reveals the relationship of Zinacateco shamans to the sacred mountain:

> Whoever sees, dreams well . . .
>
> Those who are shamans see well. They see the meeting place inside Great Mountain.
>
> All our companion animal spirits are in the corral at Great Mountain. It is a big corral, they say.

> Our animal souls need to be fed. Every night the hunters go out with lassos to catch the animals' food. Sometimes they bring back cows. Sometimes they bring back deer. Sometimes dogs. The animals, there, eat dogs.
>
> The little animals that can't wait for their food get the dogs. The big animals that are patient get the cows.
>
> One night it happened that the hunters couldn't find any food. There were calves, but their mothers gored the hunters. "What can we do? We can't catch anything," the hunters said.
>
> Now there was a Chamulan looking for work at the house of one of our countrymen. He was spending the night in the sweatbath. He was sound asleep.
>
> "Sonofabitch, but a Chamulan will do!" said the hunters.
>
> They carried him off. The poor Chamulan was dead the next morning. He slept very well. His soul went to feed the animals.
>
> The catchers' souls are powerful. But it's in their dreams that they catch their prey.
>
> If there isn't a cow or sheep, then sometimes a human being is caught, a worthless person as we say.
>
> The Lords of Great Mountain are watching.
>
> The animals are cared for by the guardians. Those that wait properly for their food do well. Those that bite, that scrap and send their friends rolling, are tossed out. "Go on, you're no good—you quarrel too much with your friends!" they are told.
>
> Those who have been put out are no longer watched over. They simply look for their own meals, until they are shot. We die if our companion animal-spirit is thrown out.
>
> That's what they dream, those who see. They see the truth.[8]

Thus the Zinacantecos, like the Saami, see their very survival as dependent on maintaining a good relationship with the mountain spirits.

Hundreds of kilometers away from Zinacantan, in the region around Mexico City, the Nahuas (Aztecs) "conceived of the Sacred in terms of a 'flower world': a sunny garden filled with flowers, brightly colored tropical birds, and precious stones like jade and turquoise." The Nahuas sometimes described this sacred garden as located on a mountain; and the mythological mountain Tonacatepec, "Sustenance Mountain," was referred to as the source of food crops.[9]

According to Marghanita Laski, "The greatest religious leaders of the West all had mystical experiences on mountains."[10] Aside from the obvious effects of extreme altitudes on human physiology, I pondered whether there is something about high places that tends to induce an expansion or altering of consciousness, and whether only certain hills or mountains produce such a response. I thought of the exhilaration I always feel at high altitudes; while uplifting, it is nothing like the complete alteration of consciousness I had just experienced at the altar of Laka, only about two hundred feet above sea level.

Was it the height, or the expansive view, or something else that triggered my ecstatic dance? Again, to quote Marghanita Laski: "Ecstasy almost always takes place after contact with something regarded as beautiful or valuable or both. Typical triggers for transcendence include stately groves of trees, carpets of beautiful flowers, strong aromas, sunsets and sunrises, water of all kinds, and clouds."[11]

While the dance platform on Kaua'i possessed an elevated view and breathtaking beauty, it was while looking into the black gash of an altar that I had entered into an altered state of consciousness. And I have certainly been to some sacred sites I would describe as barren: the lines in the plains of Nazca, Peru, for example.

The commonality for me between what had just happened at the heiau and at other natural altars I had visited was that at each one I experienced contact with something or someone sentient and much greater than my individual self. I had experienced contact, even momentary communion, with the "essence," if you will, of what could be called a transpersonal presence. After the fact I was often told by the local shaman or caretaker that I had met with the guardian spirit of the place. Author and environmental psychologist Jim Swan calls this kind of experience "unification with an aspect of nature."

Swan describes unification experiences as similar to a type of shamanic journeying in which one integrates a power animal into one's mind and body. Unification with an aspect of nature is only one of nine varieties of experiences associated with sacred places listed by Swan in *Sacred Places: How the Living Earth Seeks Our Friendship*. The first of the other eight are ecstasies, of which there are three subcategories: the union ecstasy, the "adamic ecstasy"—or bottoming out of negative emotions into a moment of joyous clarity, and the knowledge ecstasy. Next come visions of mythical beings; vivid dreams; interspecies communication; sightings of monsters and UFOs; unusual odors, sounds, and ambiances; hearing voices; and death and rebirth.[12]

Pilgrim Martin Gray described a unification experience he had while attending a Shinto religious festival at the ancient Japanese shrine of Izumo Taisha, on the southwestern coast of Honshu Island. The festival occurs in late autumn, when the *Kami*, or nature spirits that inhabit specific mountains, rivers, rocks, and other natural features, journey from their natural homes to Izumo Taisha for the festivities. During the ceremony honoring the return of the Kami, Gray felt the explosive energy of their arrival. The next morning he returned to the shrine and experienced a more personal visit from the Kami:

> Then I emptied my mind of all thoughts . . . As I achieved a serene and clear state of mind and opened myself to receive any communications from the nature spirits, I began to see mental images of many different natural objects and places. Visions of mountains, trees, waterfalls, caves and lakes were clearly displayed in my mind, and I had the impression that these scenes were the locations from which the Kami spirits had come. For a while I experienced the lovely sense of playfulness of the Kami spirits, but then an extreme sadness began to pervade my being. As I allowed the sadness to flow unhindered through me, I received the clear impression the mother spirit of all the Kami was speaking to my heart. I became aware that the sadness I was feeling was really the sadness Mother Earth was experiencing because so many of her human children have become alienated from the living spirit of Nature.[13]

Gray goes on in the same article to describe another vision he had while at Athos, Greece, in which he saw that power points on the surface of the Earth were found at points of intersection of Earth's spherical surface with the vertices of the multifaceted crystalline structure of the energy field inside Earth. I have heard similar theories and visions recounted by geomancers and dowsers at earth mysteries gatherings. The veracity of their theory remains to be seen, yet it helps to explain the fact that, in addition to hills and mountains, sacred sites are also found at waterfalls, lakes, rivers, caves, and even trees.

It is tempting to say that mountains are more associated with male (and later, patriarchal religious) mysteries, and rivers and caves with female mysteries. This would neatly explain the association of the patriarchal Roman Catholic altar with elevation. Then, too, women were often excluded from mountain ceremonies, such as the sacrifices of the Saami to Storjunkare mentioned earlier.[14] There are, however, examples of deities associated with sacred sites encompassing both heights and depths. One is the worship at mountains, lakes, and caves throughout Peru of Pachamama, whose tradition predates both the Spanish and Inca conquerors.

I recall the first time I stood at the altar of Pachamama at Machu Picchu. This altar is a massive stone slab in the shape of the silhouette of a mountain in the distance behind the altar. The slab is about fifteen feet long and ten feet high, set upright in the ground. Contiguous with the front of the slab is a stone ledge two feet deep and running the length of the slab.

As I stood on the ledge, Pachamama's enveloping presence was so strong that I nearly lost consciousness in the branching of her fathomless roots. *Pachamama*, translated by some as "Earth Mother" and by others as "Inner Earth," could be best compared to Shakti in Eastern mysticism. She is the underpinning to and source of everything in our created world; she was neither created nor begotten. Although certain mountains and *apus* (mountain spirits) are masculine, Earth in its entirety, her crystal caves, agriculture, the circulation of underground streams, mineral baths, and mountain lakes are Pachamama.

I have heard her described as floating in a mountain lake, her entire body being caressed by magical serpents. Throughout Peru in areas of past or present volcanic activity there were oracles who, like the ancient Greek and Middle Eastern Sibyls, uttered prophecies while in ecstatic trances induced by breathing in volcanic fumes billowing from the caves, hot springs, or fissures where they held forth. These oracles, although they were considered spokespersons for the *apu* (mountain spirits), were associated with Pachamama.

Several ancient Peruvian tribes claim to have been birthed in one of her caves or lakes. The Incas, for example, claim to have emerged from the three caves at Picaritambo, just outside the mountain city of Cuzco. The Collas claim to have been birthed directly from the womb of Pachamama, in the waters of Lake Titicaca. The Incas later attempted to claim this site in their creation stories and changed the name of the island in the middle of Lake Titicaca from Pachamama to Island of the Sun.

It is not uncommon for the *curanderos* of northern Peru to tether themselves in their hallucinogenic visions by seeing themselves as sitting in the middle of sacred lagoons or lakes. Both don Eduardo Calderon, who lives near Trujillo, and Jose Paz Chaponan, who lives near Huanchaco describe "planting" themselves in the lagoons for protection from spiritual blows or shocks while they are engaged in shamanic flight during San Pedro ceremonies.[15]

Before the Incas and the Spaniards, Pachamama was the deity most universally worshipped in Peru.[16] This may explain the presence of small, stone, goddess carvings all over Peru. Some (male) observers have placed her at the bottom of a male hierarchy, but I have never heard her described in this way by any Peruvian curandero. In fact, I have heard her described as the very foundation on which all else rests, the source of a curandero's healing and spiritual power. Her profound mysteriousness is reflected in the complexities of Andean mysticism. As I returned to Pachamama over the years I learned to feel her presence without losing my own.

Huacas, Sibyls, and Virgins: From Nature to Temple

If sacred sites were the first altars, the question arises of how humans progressed from praying at naturally occurring formations to creating altars carved into the walls of a cliff or a cave, then out of carved, beaded, bejeweled, wrapped, and clothed objects displayed on a flat surface, later housed in a temple, and finally the altar of an individual shaman. More interestingly, how did they learn to imbue their manufactured altars with the kind of ability to affect human consciousness that had been experienced at natural places of power? How did we learn to voluntarily enter into ecstatic states of consciousness?

In indigenous cultures altars are required to have that kind of power, for they serve both spiritual and utilitarian needs. They are used by shamans, curanderos, and medicine people for divination, diagnosis, and to heal the sick. In healing ceremonies in northern Peru using the San Pedro cactus, once the altar or *mesa* has been "raised," or activated via invocation, the shaman watches the objects and staffs on the mesa to see which ones "jump" or vibrate. This allows the shaman to "see" into the unseen, to tell, for example, whether a person has been affected by sorcery or is suffering from a natural sickness and how to cure the condition.[17] The movements of the mesa objects thus allow for simultaneous divination and diagnosis. By the same means the spirits of the dead may be sent on a peaceful journey.

On a West African altar of Nigerian or Yoruba tradition the two buffalo horns of the goddess Oya ensure the instantaneous communication with and the fiery protection of the goddess of the River Niger. The powerful, unpredictable Oya, who wed the gods of both iron (Ogun) and lightning (Shango), traveled at night in the guise of a buffalo. The instant the two horns of the buffalo are struck together "Oya returns, at once," to assist and protect the supplicant, a powerful tool to have during dangerous times.[18]

When rituals to ensure a bountiful harvest of maize are performed by the Zinacantecos of Mexico, the entire field becomes the altar. The Zinacantecos believe gods hold up the four corners of the world, a belief mirrored in the saying of ritual prayers at the four corners and at the center of the maize field.[19]

There may be an historical connection between ecstatic experiences at natural altars and the use of power objects and relics in shamanic, religious, and personal altars. Clues to the possible connection lie in the languages of two Pacific cultures.

In Peru powerful places or geographical features, such as the naturally formed temple atop Huayna Picchu, are called *huacas.* In pre-Incan days there were individuals and clans dedicated to caring for such sites. Often the caretaker of a huaca was possessed of unusual personal power—the power, for example, to see and hear things others did not, to predict earthquakes, or to cause others to bow down. Then he or she was said to have *huaca.* The early Incan rulers, priests, and priestesses were said to have had tremendous huaca. If a relic were taken from a place or person of power, say, for use as a power object on a shaman's or priest's altar, then the thing would be called a huaca. Interestingly, the narcotic leaf of the coca plant was also called huaca by some.[20]

Across the Pacific in the Hawaiian language there is a similar association between the *mana*, or spiritual power, of places, persons, and sacred objects. The fact that certain places have mana is currently cited by Hawaiian activists in defending sacred sites from encroaching development. The ancient Hawaiian leaders and monarchs, or *ali'i*, were said to possess specific categories of mana, like the huaca of Peruvian leaders. However, when these special powers affected others, as in the case of the power to cause others to bow down, then that power was called a *kapu*.[21] Alae salt, kukui nuts, and other items gathered at places of power are placed on the altar of the *kahuna* (literally, "the expert")[22] and the *kumu hula* (literally, "source of dance") for their mana.

The linguistic continuity of the Peruvian term huaca and the Polynesian mana suggests an historical progression from an externalized experience of power or presences in nature, to an internalization of that power—whether through exposure to the huaca of the site or through spiritual practice—to the replication of the experience in a compact, portable form. Perhaps civilizing pressures necessitated bringing the sanctity of natural forces to the people living in communities.

Of significance in the progression from sacred sites to the religious or personal altar is the building of ancient temples or shrines near sites already observed as sacred. In some cases the constructed temple is overtly dedicated to the preexisting nature deity, as in the case of the shrine of Pachamama at Machu Picchu. In other cases there is only an implied connection. And in some cases it is difficult to tell which came first, as in the case of Zinacantan sacred mountains, which are called *vits*, a transliteration of the older Mayan word for constructed pyramids (*wits*).

A graphic example of fairly unambiguous progression stands above the Italian Bay of Naples. On an outcropping visible from the sea stand the ruins of a temple to Jupiter, built in the fifth century B.C. by Greeks who settled at Cumae three centuries earlier. In the sixth century A.D. this temple was converted to a Christian Church. Downhill from this ruin stands another, the temple of Apollo, whose date and history of construction are uncertain. Still closer to the water and the earth is the cave whose legend attracted Greeks and Romans alike: the cave of the famous oracle, the Sibyl of Cumae.

The fact that prophetic verses associated with oracles known as *Sibyllai* were known by people in Western Asia in earlier times may indicate that the tradition of the Sibyls predated the Greek patriarchal gods. No one knows for certain the origins of either the Sibyls or even the meaning of their name. What is known is that these female oracles—at Cumae, Libya, Delphi, Marpessus, and other sites—uttered their oracles while in altered states of consciousness, whether from chewing psychoactive herbs or from inhaling volcanic fumes. The Sibyls were found in caves or near springs or fissures in the ground in areas of volcanic activity.

By the time the Greeks settled in Cumae, however, the Sibyls were associated with Apollo, in his role as the god of prophecy.[23] In any case the building of temples of Apollo, Jupiter, and eventually the Christ near the site of the most famous of Sibyls offers a potent example of the historical progression from experiences of the power of altered states of consciousness, to the consecration of sites, to the building of temples housing altars to the gods.

A more enigmatic example is the Cathedral at Chartres, about ninety kilometers southwest of Paris, France. Although no one knows how or by whom Chartres was constructed, its building is linked with the mysterious Knights Templar, who spent close to ten years in the Holy Land and returned to France in 1128, possibly with secrets of sacred geometry and sacred engineering. Prior to the construction of the Gothic cathedral, there had been five other churches, each destroyed by fire, then replaced with a new one. The first Christians who, had arrived in Chartres in the third century A.D., had found in an underground grotto the image of a Druid Virgin, called The Virgin Under The Earth.

The Druids were Celtic priests of Gaul and Britain, who established a college at Chartres. The Virgin Under The Earth had been carved when Druid priests received a prophecy that a virgin would give birth to a child. The Druids then placed the Virgin beside a well within a *dolmen*, a large flat boulder supported by two or three rough stones set upright. Both the well and the dolmen had been constructed prior to the arrival of the Druids, by the same family of builders who had erected stone circles such as Stonehenge. In addition there is speculation that a natural spring preceded the construction of the well.

As interesting as the historic progression from sacred site to earthworks to church to cathedral is the fact that the sacred center of Chartres Cathedral stands thirty-seven meters above the level of water in the ancient well. Exactly the same height above the center is the pinnacle of the Gothic vault, where the pointed arches, or *ogives*, cross. This was where the original altar of the cathedral stood until it was moved in the sixteenth century.[24]

Altars as Mirrors: From Nature to Altar

The progression from direct, ecstatic experience of the sacred in nature to the personal or shamanic altar takes an equally lengthy and at times more circuitous route. The altar of the shaman or adept may, in fact, belong to a different lineage than that of the temple altar. The unrefined relics from Peruvian huacas do not end up on the altars of Roman Catholic cathedrals, even though the cathedral may have been built in some cases on top of what once was a huaca. Unlike some temples or cathedrals which draw their power from the site itself, the efficacy of the shamanic altar depends on the mental and spiritual abilities of its creator to invoke transpersonal presences distant in time and/or space.

Consider, for example, altars to the African goddesses Oya and Oshun. As already mentioned, Oya was the goddess of the River Niger, invoked by striking together two buffalo horns. Other derivative references to her brought across the Atlantic to the Americas by black slaves include the substitution of cow horns for buffalo horns and the use of the color red (the color of her fiery husband, the thunder god Shango). Because termite-mound magic helped her give birth, and because by entering the earth she became immortal, Oya may also be invoked by use of small mounds of earth.[25]

Oshun, the goddess of sweet water, dwelled in the river of the same name near the town of Oshogbo. The people of Oshogbo believe the deep places in the river to be inhabited by the spirits of all of Oshun's servants, friends, and followers. Both the depths and the spirits dwelling there are called *ibu.* The tributaries of Oshun are her fingers.

Like the sounds of water moving over river rocks, Oshun was not really one but many. According to Robert Ferris Thompson, an historian of African art at Yale:

> Wherever one stands above deep, indigo-colored portions of the river Oshun, there are avatars within. There is Oshun Abalu, the oldest Oshun. There is Oshun Jumu, a flirt; Oshun Aboto, very feminine; Oshun Opara, the youngest and most martial; Oshun Ajagura, another warrior manifestation. There is Yeye Petu, the old and quarrelsome Yeye Oga; the extremely feisty Yeye Kare, also bellicose, as is Yeye Onira. Yeye Oloko lives in the forest. Yeye Ponda is married to Oshoosi Ibu Alama, and carries a sword. Yeye Merin is another coquette, Yeye Oloke is another warrior, Yeye Lokun has no devotees, and Yeye Odo is goddess of the river's source.
>
> It is an army of marching underwater women. Some are sexual; all fight for their children and their husbands; all are Oshun. She is woman extraordinaire.[26]

From the songs once sung at the river's edge to imitate her multitude, derived the association of Oshun with the jingling sound of copper bracelets on the arm and later of coins. Hence one now finds Oshun invoked with brass or copper bracelets or coins.

In a very different association, with sweet water, Oshun was once remembered with calabashes and earthenware water jars, replaced in the long journey across the Atlantic by the stacking of porcelain plates inside porcelain bowls.[27]

Whereas contemporary African-Atlantic altars in the Americas draw on symbolic materials to invoke the mythic presences of rivers and deities on another continent, contemporary shamans in South America lean on not only symbolic objects from indigenous and Christian traditions, but also on objects from huacas, passed down for generations in the process of transmission of power.

Gathering objects from sacred sites or relics from the remains of sages may have been seen as a way to bring their power to the altar. Indeed, when I have witnessed curanderos, spiritual adepts, and shamans "raising" or "waking up" their altars, the process—which can take more than two hours—consists largely of invoking the spirit of every single object on the altar, one at a time. The place names and persons invoked often have long since passed from the memories of ordinary folk, yet their legendary power and presence are brought to life again in the activation of the altar.

The practice of invocation is essential to the creation of an altar that works, that produces an effect. Without it, an altar remains a mere collection of materials. This was understood when the early Christian disciples were creating the rituals which would become formalized in the Catholic mass. That most likely is why Catholic altars feature images of Jesus Christ, the Holy Mother, and other saints, and why their names and actions are repeated in chants. It is also probably why burning copal is offered to the four directions, and the tools of the mass are repeatedly raised and lowered. Shinto priests surely understand the same principles when they ritually invite the arrival of the Kami at Izumo Taisha.

The interrelatedness of altars and invocation may be the commonality of altars of the north, south, east, and west, as well as of religious and personal altars. For mysterious objects representing the creative, preserving, and destructive powers of cosmic deities and forces are found in altars all over the planet, in both "pagan" and "religious" cultures. They may be found as readily in residential *nichos*, tribal kivas, and lodges as in temples, stupas, and cathedrals. Altars are seen in ceremonies and silent meditation halls, and in private as well as public places. Where people gather to reflect on the source of their being, altars generally are found.

In his newly-released, landmark book on African-Atlantic art and altars, Robert Farris Thompson writes, "The altar appears in the art history of virtually all of the world." Thompson calls altars—and his book—"The Face of the Gods." He quotes *Gaanman* Gazon Matoja, paramount chief of the Ndjuka' in Suriname, South America as defining altars as "the place where you realize your belief."[28]

In this sense altars are the invisible made visible. They express the innermost mystical and spiritual insights, while also revealing the cosmological beliefs and personal projections of the human mind. Altars embody values, memories, and history of individuals, tribes, and followers of religious tradition. They commemorate the ascended and the dead.

Altars also are mirrors, reflecting the illumination hidden in the unseen regions of the human psyche. They reflect the nature and source of our enlightenment, while revealing the shadow side of our beliefs. As external expressions of internal experience, altars make visible our relationship with the source of our being, how we approach that relationship, our understanding of the nature of the creation, and our inner vision of the face of our creator. But this is a topic so large that I must address it in a subsequent article.

The Role of Huacas in the Altars of Peruvian Curanderos

Significantly for the practice of shamanism, altars represent pluralism: this reality and the other distant or invisible realities they reflect. They can simultaneously represent as true the principles of creation, preservation, and destruction, of balance and imbalance, or of health and disease. Altars also represent an intersection of multiple human realities: physical, energetic, emotional, psychological, intellectual, mythical, spiritual, and transcendent. They reflect all the dimensions in which humans and non-humans interact.

This is dramatically illustrated in the shamanic altars of South America that comprise multiple strata of symbolic abstraction. Included in each level are not only the forces of truth, healing, illumination, and life but also those of deception, disease, darkness, and death. European invaders, marching under the flag of the Inquisition, were quick to ascribe this balance of forces to the worship of evil. A more careful examination of such altars suggests their creators were possessed of a more mature world view than that of good versus evil.

A well-known example of such applied pluralism is the *mesa* of Peruvian shaman don Eduardo Calderon. Mesa means "table" in Spanish. It consists of a rectangular piece of cloth laid on the ground, on which objects are very neatly laid out according to a multidimensional plan. As documented and described sixteen years ago by Douglas Sharon in *The Wizard of the Four Winds*, don Eduardo's altar is laid out in a manner reflective not only of the polarities of life and death, light and dark, but also of levels of experience of reality. It leads the mind and the shaman's ceremony through progressive expansions of consciousness, from the invocation of historic huacas, through the dualism of ordinary reality, through the four-fold cycles of the sacred, to the cosmic axis where all levels are united. Yet don Eduardo's mesa also has the stamp of individuality.

According to Douglas Sharon,

> The spatial arrangement of Eduardo's mesa is the manifestation of a profound underlying philosophy. It has to be understood as representing two

Altar of Shaman don Eduardo Calderon. Photo by John D. Ross.

> levels of abstraction existing at the same time and in the same space. One level can be labeled "balanced dualism" and is manifest in three unequal divisions of the mesa. The other level can be labeled "the four winds and the four roads" and is manifest in four triangles converging on the center, the crucifix.[29]

In subsequent research Sharon found that the division of mesas into fields manifesting a balanced or mediated dualism is common throughout northern coastal Peru.[30] The level of balanced dualism is represented by the placement of altar objects in three sections. The key word here is "balanced," for despite the fact that the right side of don Eduardo's mesa (the side of light) is the larger section, or that the left side contains references to Satan, don Eduardo stresses that *neither* side is superior, nor can either exist in isolation from the other. While darkness cannot be allowed to triumph, neither can it be eradicated entirely.

Both curandero Jose Paz Chaponan, who lives near the north coastal town of Huanchaco, and don Eduardo place on the north side of their mesas a row of staffs and swords planted in the ground. The north side is the side furthest from the shaman and nearest to the ceremonial circle of participants. The mesa cloth itself has some value—both don Eduardo and Jose's have been passed down over generations.

Both don Eduardo and Jose divide their mesas in the same way, into right, middle, and left fields. The right side of the mesa is called the *Campo Justiciero* (Field of Divine Justice) by don Eduardo, and the *Banco Curandero* (Field of the Curer) by Jose. Artifacts on this side of the altar call forth lightness, holiness, sweetness, and order. Saints, perfumes, sugar, sweet lime, medicinal herbs, and rattles are arrayed neatly. Both Eduardo and Jose use the right-hand side of the altar for healing or whole making, purification, and initiation.

Both don Eduardo and Jose call the left side of the altar the *Campo Ganadero* (Field of the Sly Dealer). In fact, in Douglas Sharon's interviews with eight northern Peruvian curanderos other than Eduardo, he found that all eight called the left side of their mesas by the name of Ganadero. This section contains objects representing the darker aspects of existence: the underworld, sickness, unconscious action, bad luck, and the old, dark ways of sorcery. Significantly, it is on this side that power objects from ancient huacas passed down to the curanderos by their teachers are arranged. Shells, animal amulets, and cane alcohol are set out in perfect rows. These objects are associated with the power of the sorcerer to inflict harm, and it is to this side of the mesa that Eduardo and Jose go to diagnose and cure physical ailments and maladies resulting from sorcery.

The importance of the fact that the huacas are found on the left side, the side of life-threatening powers, cannot be overstated. When the curandero "raises" the mesa, he calls out to each mountain, lagoon, and ruin by name, one by one. In doing so he is calling forth both the ecstatic and terrible powers of scalding steam, molten lava, rending lightning, and the fury of water. He calls forth humankind's most primitive memories of terror in the face of nature's vastly superior power.

The terrifying and the terrible are an important ingredient in the efficacy of altars. We see their faces in Kali and Durga, and in the demons of Tibet, China,

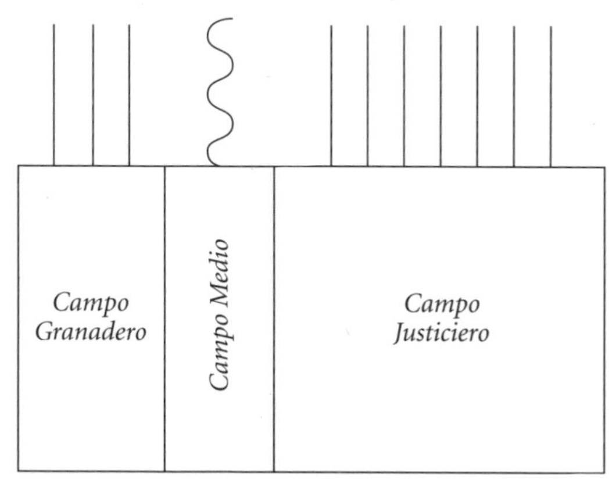

The three "fields" of Eduardo's mesa. Drawing from Douglas Sharon's *Wizard of the Four Winds*, New York: The Free Press, 1978.

and Japan. They are also seen in African altars to Shango and Ogun, and in the image of the ancient Sibyls sitting wild-eyed and disheveled over open volcanic steam vents. When seen in this light the absence of the terrible from modern Christian altars is telling.

Part of the curandero's art is anchoring terror and rage in some meaningful way to affect healing. Both don Eduardo and Jose do this by imaging[31] themselves as grounded or "planted" in the middle of a sacred lagoon, where they are protected from any blows by negative forces or any other sorcerer.

The two sides of dualistic reality are separated by the narrow center section. Called the *Campo Medio* (Middle Field) on Eduardo's mesa and the *Banco Guayanchero* (The Field of the Herbalist) on Jose's, this field is made up of objects in which the opposites of light and dark are evenly balanced or reconciled. The neutral elements of nature are represented in this field: the sun, winds, sea, and earth. This is also where each man places his *seguro*, a glass flask containing his "essence," which he periodically recharges with healing herbs, perfume, or his breath. Both men also have the figure of Saint Cyprian here. According to Christian lore, Saint Cyprian was a powerful sorcerer of the dark arts who converted to Christianity. Because of his history and skills as a sorcerer, Saint Cyprian can act as a mediator between light and dark.

Although it is the smallest of the three fields, the significance of the middle field is tremendous. As anthropologist Donald Joralemon notes, "some of the most important objects of the entire altar are placed here."[32] Don Eduardo says this is where the forces or agents affecting the situation under examination present themselves to the mediating presence of the shaman. He has described the Campo Medio as the sword's edge on which his spirit body must dance during a mesa ceremony. Thus the Middle Field is not only a neutral zone for mediation between the opposing forces of dualism but also a point of intersection of the realities of the physical and non-physical worlds. It is here that don Eduardo must concentrate his abilities as a shaman, to find a practical solution or cure.[33]

Central to both mesas is a figurine of the crucified Christ, who governs all three fields. While the preeminent position of Christ as governor of all three fields at first glance may look like an adoption from Catholicism, a deeper syncretism is at work. This Christ is a spiritual shaman who interacts equally well with the ancient huacas as with Christian figures, and who can negotiate, and if necessary do battle, with Satan.

The structure of the second level of functioning of Eduardo's mesa, that of "the four winds and the four roads," reveals a sophisticated understanding of periodicity in cycles of beginnings, growth, endings, and gestation. The association of the cardinal directions with seasons, hours of the day, and phases of the human life span is found cross-culturally, for example, in the European tradition of Wicca and in the North American Lakota Medicine Wheel. Stages in the cycle of new life, maturation, death, and rebirth are associated with the four cardinal directions of east, south, west, and north, respectively.

The four sides of the mesa correspond to the four directions, and the triangles based on each of the four sides converge in the center, the position of the Christ. The triangle on the right, or east, corresponds with the point of rebirth. The objects found within this triangle all lie within the Campo Justiciero and have to do with purification, spirituality, and rebirth. On the twenty-four hour clock rebirth occurs at midnight, the time in the San Pedro ceremony when the shaman undergoes a spiritual rebirth, leaving behind his existence as an ordinary mortal and unfolding into spiritual being.

The triangle on the bottom, or south, nearest to the shaman, corresponds with action, and the few objects within this area are predominantly practical tools used during the ceremony, such as the shells used for serving the San Pedro decoction. Some objects are used for defense or offense, like the dagger held in don Eduardo's left hand when "guarding" the ceremony.

The left-hand triangle, corresponding with the direction of west and with death, contains, not surprisingly, many objects from the Campo Ganadero having to do with mortality: stones representing organs and body parts and representations of mortals such as Saint Cyprian and don Eduardo's teacher. The west and death correspond with noon on the ceremonial clock. Between the end of the ceremony and noon the next day don Eduardo experiences the death of sacred time and a return to being an ordinary, mortal man.

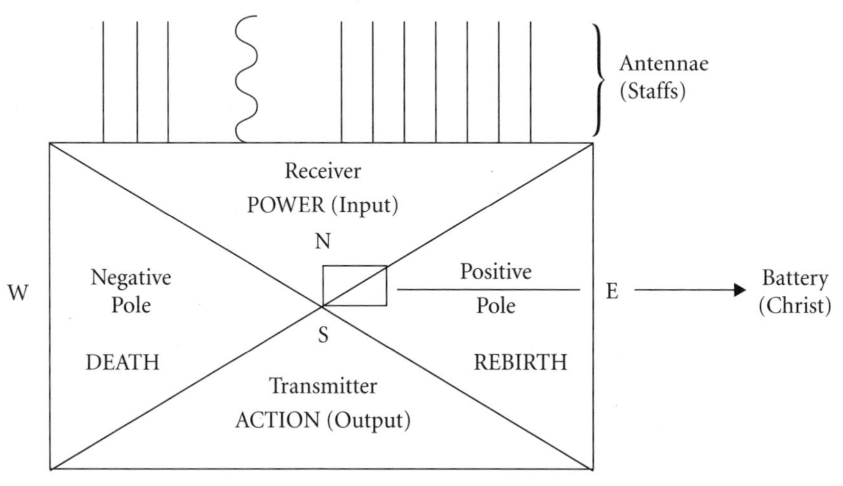

The transmitter/receiver. Drawing from Douglas Sharon's *The Wizard of the Four Winds,* New York: The Free Press, 1978.

The most noticeable feature of the triangle on the top, or north, is that the entire row of swords and staffs falls within this sector. Even cursory examination of the other objects in this triangle makes clear that for Eduardo the north is associated with power. The activating agent for the power of the entire mesa, the San Pedro cactus, is found in this quadrant. The powers of Satan's Bayonet on the one hand and the Virgin Mary on the other are balanced here by the wisdom of the serpent and the natural forces of the sun, wind, sea, and earth.

Don Eduardo's mesa represents a remarkable synthesis of abstract levels of cosmological comprehension with symbolism from native and Christian traditions. Through the collapsing of volumes of metaphysical principles and symbolic allusions into one small space, it serves as an excellent example of altars making visible the invisible, as well as of mirroring the psyche of its maker and his culture. It is a virtual repository of insight into the syncretic blending of pre-Incan, Incan, Spanish Catholic, and Western world views that is common throughout Peru and other parts of the New World.

The mesa also reveals and reflects stages in the expansion of consciousness of the shaman. Through don Eduardo's altar we can witness the pluralistic strata of his mind, including dualism, periodicity, alchemy, and the transcendent. It is also more than that. Over the years I have known him, I have watched the evolution of don Eduardo's altar. One object gives way to another, a new one is introduced, one sword is replaced by another, yet the integrity of the mesa remains intact, as does don Eduardo's capacity to affect healing through its ceremonial use.

Something ineffable that is more than the objects or the structure of the altar continues, as the man who made it and the culture from which it sprang evolve away from some of the oldest elements represented on the mesa. The huaca prized by don Eduardo's ancestors, which they reverently carried to their altars from sacred places in the form of fossils, stones, and pot shards, and which they passed down for tens of generations, remains extant.

The mesas of northern Peru are living examples of altars in the process of evolution. When we humans took bits of stone, bone, shell, and feathers from places where we experienced visions or healings and made altars with them and sang chants over them and created ritual devices for commemorating the power of our visions, perhaps we were trying to recreate a moment of experiencing essential being. In our efforts to remember being we developed altars in the form of mesas, mandalas, sand paintings, and cathedrals, along with all kinds of mental rigors to cultivate the power of invocation. And in doing all that we also developed a record of the evolution of human consciousness, both personal and transpersonal.

Notes

1. Maslow and Black Elk quoted by James A. Swan in *Sacred Places: How the Earth Seeks Our Friendship* (Santa Fe: Bear & Co., 1990), 48, 79.
2. See Robert Farris Thompson's analysis of the concept of altars in *Face of the Gods: Art and Altars of Africa and the African Americans* (New York: The Museum for African Art, 1993), 24–26.
3. Johannes Scheffer, *The History of Lapland* (Stockholm: Rediviva, 1971 facsim. reprint of 1674 ed.), 114.
4. Samuel Rheen, quoted by Scheffer, *The History of Lapland*, 100–101.
5. Evon Z. Vogt, "The Persistence of Maya Tradition in Zinacantan," *The Ancient Americas: Art From Sacred Places* (Chicago: The Art Institute of Chicago, 1992), 63–64.
6. Ibid., 64.
7. Ibid., 65.
8. Romin Tanchak, quoted by Robert Laughlin in *The People of the Bat: Mayan Tales and Dreams from Zinacantan*, Carol Karasik, ed., (Washington: Smithsonian Institution Press, 1988), 65–67.
9. Louise M. Burkhart, "The Cult of the Virgin of Guadalupe in Mexico," in *South and Meso-American Spirituality: From the Cult of the Feathered Serpent to the Theology of Liberation*, Gary H. Gossen, ed. with Miguel Leon Portilla, (1993), 210.
10. Marghanita Laski, *Ecstasy: A Study of Some Secular and Religious Experiences* (Bloomington, Indiana: Indiana University Press, 1962). Quoted by Swan in *Sacred Places*, 78.
11. Swan, *Sacred Places*, 81.
12. Ibid., 86–104.
13. Martin Gray, "Sacred Sites and Power Points: A Pilgrim's Journey for Planetary Healing," *Shaman's Drum* 25 (fall 1991):35–37.
14. Scheffer, *The History of Lapland*, 102.
15. See Eduardo Caleron, et al., *Eduardo el Curandero: The Words of a Peruvian Healer* (Richmond, Calif.: North Atlantic Books, 1982), 55, 56, and 58; and Donald Joralemon "Symbolic Space and Ritual Time in a Peruvian Healing Ceremony," *Ethnic Technology Notes No. 19* (San Diego, Calif.: San Diego Museum of Man, 1984), 9.
16. Burr Cartwright Brundage, *Empire of the Inca* (Norman, Okla.: University of Oklahoma Press, 1963), 43.
17. Caleron, et al., *Eduardo el Curandero*, 44.
18. Thompson, *Face of the Gods*, 191–192.

19. Vogt, "The Persistence of Maya Tradition in Zinacantan," 6.
20. While curanderos in northern Peru generally refer only to sacred sites or ruins as huacas, other sources extend the term in the fashion described here. Among those sources, Francisco Lopez de Gomara of Madrid, Spain associates *huaca* with *huaccay*, the wailing that would have characterized an approach to a huaca. See Brundage's 1963 analysis of the concept of *huaca* in *Empire of the Inca.*
21. The word *kapu*, which has nuances of meaning specific to the context in which it is used, unfortunately has been translated into English as "taboo," thereboy obscuring its mystical implications.
22. The term *kahu* is used to refer to an honored attendant, caregiver, or administrator. *Huna* as a noun means a minute particle, like a grain of sand, hence the etymological development of huna as hidden or secret, as hard to see as a grain of sand. *Ka* is a definite singular article, usually translated as "the." The entry for *kahuna* in the 1986 edition of the Hawaiian Dictionary by Mary Kawena Pukui and Samuel Elbert notes that in the 1845 laws, doctors, surgeons, and dentists were also called *kahuna.*
23. "Cumae: An Ancient Cave of Prophecy," *The Atlas of Mysterious Places*, Jennifer Westwood, ed. (New York: Weidenfeld & Nicholson, 1987), 48.
24. "The Symbolism of Chartres," *The Atlas of Mysterious Places*, 20–21.
25. Thompson, *Faces of the Gods*, 192–203.
26. Ibid.
27. Ibid., 206–216.
28. Ibid., 16.
29. Douglas Sharon, *The Wizard of the Four Winds* (New York: The Free Press, 1978), 62.
30. Ibid.
31. In Shamanic culture, imaging, which is the practice of conscious dreaming, is frequently used in ceremonial or healing work. Deep imaging is now used in thereapeutic settings by Western counselors.
32. Donald Joralemon, "Symbolic Space and Ritual Time," 2.
33. Ibid.; and Sharon, *Wizard of the Four Winds*, 62–72, 106–111, 159–174.

10. Creating a Living Temenos

Roberta Shoemaker-Beal

Editor's Note

We end this section with an essay by art therapist Roberta Shoemaker-Beal about how to create a personal sacred place or temenos *in your own life. In ancient Greek,* temenos *meant "a sacred precinct." C. G. Jung used this word to describe certain imagery found in the dreams of his patients as a basic organizing principle of the psyche for a space of transformation.*

PSYCHOLOGIST C. G. JUNG noted that when his patients were in great distress, circular imagery spontaneously emerged into their dreams or artwork. Characteristically, this imagery had a center and an orientation to the four directions. He named this imagery *mandala*, after the ancient Sanskrit word for "magic circle." Jung also recognized this imagery reflected the *temenos*, the word for "sacred precinct" in ancient Greek. He called a circular healing place in a dream or in his own artwork a temenos, the same root word for "temple."

A sacred place is a certain physical location which contains us by giving us a place to be safe, nurtured, and supported in our totality—body, emotions, mind, and spirit. Here we can explore anything and everything, into our deepest being and out into our farthest imaginings. Here we can reflect, without intrusion, but with the choice of the right elements, at the right time, with resonant intention, often as ritual. Being in a sacred place allows us to become resonant, again and again, with all that we feel as sacred, know to be sacred, believe to be sacred, and with all that we hold in the sacred spaces within us. Places known historically as sacred sites often have special energies and a tradition that enables us to approach and experience the Divinity there, the transcendent experience of wholeness, which evolves creative inspiration and healing that restores us to wholeness.

The holding power, the containment, offered us by circular places we intend as sacred allows for the emergence of powerful forces—forces given power often by their magnetic pull on our ever-emerging consciousness and the fear of any unknown forces seeking to guide our personal journey. According to Timothy Hatcher, minister, body-mind therapist, and philosopher at Louisiana State University,

> Sacred space is the only space that can contain the energy of the opposites, the oppositional forces of the cosmos and our psyches, and any confrontation with evil or the destuctive, without us being torn apart by these forces.

Sacred space also gives us the containment for holding the energetic forces of creative tension, so we can create and renew our lives. Tending and creating a temenos in our lives, we develop our opportunities for creativity, tapping into transcendent divine forces of healing.

To distinguish between places and spaces, let me say that outer sacred places help us sustain the inner sacred spaces within ourselves. These sacred places and sacred spaces must be held and maintained for us to sustain a life vitalized by what we revere and hold sacred in our life. In times of transition, conflict, and overwhelming circumstances, the value of the practice of sacred ceremony in sacred places to resonate with the sacred spaces within us, individually and in groups, becomes increasingly important. Participating in the dynamic processes of sacred experiences and inspired creative and healing experiences in a place we have designated as sacred enables us to keep our lives resonant with the sacred spaces within our individual and collective psyches. Our self-view, our world view, and our cosmological view can then resonate together, with clarity, with all the possibilities for the fullness of life and for wholeness with harmony, beauty, balance, and wisdom.

The Creation of a Living Temenos in Our Lives

The need for a temenos in each of our personal lives was brought home to me in my Symbol Journey class at the Jung Society of New Orleans, by a student named Angela Bose. The intent of the seminar was to teach the accessing of the symbolic life through creative expressive art work. After the initial sessions, I led the group in a guided visualization called "Journey to Your Symbolarium, treasure house of the symbols within your psyche." Angela returned from her inner visualization back into our shared place in the art room to report that she had "revisited" a circular fish pond she remembered visiting as a child with her grandmother at the Audubon Park Zoo. Because Symbol Journey class assignments ask that students incorporate their symbolic discoveries into their waking life, Angela reported to us each week the changes she was making in her dining room in front of south-facing windows. Moving her bird and newly purchased fishes there, she made a place for morning meditation, a simple and effective action.

From this experience and others, I believe that any one of us can create such a place in our lives. As long as the archetype for the temenos exists, it can be tapped by anyone when the need is felt. This matrix of universal potential can guide us at this difficult time in history to resacralize our lives and our places on this planet. But archetypes only have life if we live them, for they seem to be a product of activated conscious energy, working through our evolving species—matter and numinous energy interacting in an as yet indefinable way.

In the spirit of this intention, I have designed the following guide of experiences for creating a temenos in your life. The goal is to help you develop sensitivity to the spirit of a place, to enjoy its natural benefits and develop a relationship that expands awareness of surroundings, increasing the comfort and the joy of life, like the pleasure of watching the sun's rays dip into the darkness of a valley at dawn. Who can say when the new vision of the resacralized Earth will come from? Perhaps we need a new *imago dieu*, a consciously intended *imago naturalis mundis* for *homo naturalis sapiens*, a sustaining holistic vision in harmony with Nature.

Guide for Creating a Personal Temenos in Your Life

1. Make a commitment to get in touch with the sacred spaces inside yourself first, to explore this possibility for growth in your life. Set aside several hours for this.

2. Pick a place at home, or elsewhere, that is quiet and protected. Gather together here at least three things that you love, that inspire you and excite you. Transcribe a real or imaginary circle around this space. Shield yourself from intrusion. Bring a creative journal with you into this place to record or create out of your experiences.

3. Initially, focus on how it feels to be in this space. What is the spirit of this place? Will it support you in this work? How? Does it need modification? Make changes.

4. Get in touch with the felt need to create a temenos in your life by guiding yourself in a visualization to the memory of a place in your life that felt sacred to you, nourished you, where something significant happened that deeply affected your life. Focus on the spirit of that place where the event happened. Remember that place, in detail. What memories do you carry? Consider how being in that place supported your experience.

5. Next, tap into the great symbolic resources of your imagination. Guide yourself in a visualization to a calm place inside yourself. Go there to discover the nature and design of a sacred space inside you that could be brought out into the waking

life you choose to life. Note if the space you discovered relates to memories or dreamscapes.

6. On a 12" by 18" sheet of paper, develop a small sketch of your visualized temenos space based on your Self-discoveries from your imagination. Do not be concerned with creating art—be expressive in your sketch. Place the sketch carefully in the place you are creating. Continue to build and work on the sketch, adding to the record your visualizations and experiences. Build on this and keep it in the place emerging around you.

7. Create a modest design for a "real time and place" meditation site for yourself, like a Garden, an Altar, or an expanded creative meditation space, building on your sketches.

8. Create the temenos of your design somewhere with your own hands. Spend time and experience it on a regular basis. Let a schedule develop for yourself; weave it into your life.

9. Expand the spirit of this place out into your life, as you feel the need and ability to grow in awareness and into harmony with the places and spaces in your life.

Once you have developed this sensibility, this awareness of the temenos in your own life, it is probably time to move on and share this awareness with others. You can explore other ways to invite the guidance of the temenos archetype into your life to further develop a real-life temenos and live out the spirit of place. Here are some suggestions for this stage. Enjoy!

a. Read about and explore actual sites that others traditionally call sacred, inspiring, or healing, like Lourdes Grotto. Experience them. Incorporate elements, as you are able, into your own temenos and into your life as a regular experience of the sacredness of spaces.

b. Pick places in your life to celebrate the sacred. First celebrate alone, perhaps for an entire day without talking. Then, plan a celebration and a ceremony only with friends who respect you, love you, and nourish your spirit, in your temenos or a temenos of your choice. Include music, dance, art, and food. Plan an honoring of the place. Speak about your new-found awareness, as your honor these places and your experiences there.

c. There is music for "my little corner of the world" and simple chants to honor sacred places and spaces. Sing them where you sense the sacred.

d. Take part in a special vacation to a sacred site on the planet which has always fascinated you or which has appeared in your dreams. Research and prepare before you go. Plan a ceremony to honor that site's tradition by scheduling to be there at a festival or time that is especially energizing at that site.

e. Become active in supporting and working with people protecting the sacred places near where you live or on the planet. Being around these people creates a resonant community of awareness and supports the active awareness of the *temenos that is Gaia.* Join the Nature Conservancy or the Sierra Club and participate in their local/national events. Volunteer a vacation at an on-site project. Work in a community garden.

f. Plan a conference in your bio-region with those people who are aware and sensitive to our needed harmonious relationship with planet Earth. Invite speakers who inspire you to action.

Keep an ongoing commitment to yourself and All That Is to keep your awareness alive, resonant, and active, wherever you sense the temenos or a need for it.

Yes, I have done all these things for myself and can attest to the sense of serenity and connectedness that has developed in my life. I was puzzled for awhile when people began spontaneously, playfully calling me "Mother Earth." I do derive great pleasure and a deep enjoyment being connected to the spirit of place in my home and wherever I travel. A sense of groundedness and rootedness has helped me feel less stressed and more alive. It is a source of ongoing joy. It seems to me that across the millennia the evolution of the collective consciousness has developed the inner archetypal resonance of the temenos for a significant purpose. By bringing the spirit of place into consciousness, we can create a temenos as we live out our lives. May it be so for all that you hold dear in your places and spaces.

PART THREE:

Designing with the Spirit of Place

THERE IS REAL MAGIC to buildings that are made in tune with nature and are a reflection of the designer's deep beliefs in the spiritual essence of all life. In this section, we are fortunate to have the thoughts of architects and designers who know that buildings are for the spirit as well as the body. Nader Khalili creates shelters from clay and sand that are beautiful as well as cheap, and that resonate with the poetry of Rumi. Brent Smith uses light and an understanding of the symbols of many religions to transform the mundane into a place where the spirit can soar. And James Hubbell, guided by an intuitive sense of the spirit of man, turns sculpted concrete and broken bits of glass into places that both calm and inspire those who inhabit them.

It has been a long time since humans lived in trees and caves. We live in a world shaped by the abilities and imaginations of human beings. We are born, live, and die in buildings, each the result of decisions made during its design and construction.

The best designed structures always reflect the spirit of their place. The twentieth century has been full of buildings that were based on cost analysis and some minimal understanding of function, and we have created huge areas of wastelands in our cities and towns with such places. Only a few designers have been able to combat the sterility of design that affected most of the century. One of these was the great American architect Frank Lloyd Wright, who knew all about the spiritual side of architecture, and in his writings said that architecture was the "noble organic expression of nature," but worried that few other architects saw it for "the spiritual thing it really is . . . the idea of life itself."

The architects and designers who have written articles for this section would understand what Wright meant. They are all aware of the need to build with spirit and are actively promoting a shift in the consciousness of those who seek their services. Their entries cover both theory and practice, starting in the first part with explorations of design principles by architects Tom Bender and Christopher Day, who both have been influential in infusing the idea of spirit into the larger architectural community.

The second part of this section examines how traditions from other cultures such as Feng Shui from China and Kosa from Japan are influencing designers in the United States.

The section concludes with a series of interviews with practicing designers and architects Brent Smith, Nader Khalili, Sim Van der Ryn, and James Hubbell, who have been leaders in changing our perception of how the world can be built. They are all people who not only hold deep spiritual beliefs about their work, but are enlarging what is possible for all of us by changing building codes to accommodate their new forms, working at all levels of affordability, and even putting spiritual values into manufactured housing.

The final entry in this section is a summary of the principles learned and suggestions as to how these might be applied in everyday life.

11. Building with a Soul

Tom Bender

Editor's Note

Tom Bender is a practicing architect residing in Nehalem, Oregon. In 1992, he won the American Institute of Architects/Union Internationale des Architectes (AIA/UIA) Sustainable Community Solutions International Competition. As a founder of RAIN Magazine and author of the popular Environmental Design Primer, Mr. Bender was a leader in the early days of the movement toward ecological consciousness in building. Mr. Bender's work has now expanded to unite spirit with the need to use resources wisely. His writings have inspired architects to re-evaluate their creation of forms and use of materials. His work in Oregon gives physical examples of what it looks like to build with the spirit of the place.

In the following chapter, Mr. Bender distills his previous work into a series of principles and guidelines for building with spirit and combines these guidelines with wonderful pictures to delight and inspire the imagination.

MANY INTRACTABLE SOCIAL PROBLEMS—alcoholism, drug abuse, crime, child and spouse abuse, homelessness, obesity, poverty, failing schools—have a common root. They all arise out of lack of self-worth, lack of respect by and for others, or lack of opportunity to be of use and value to family and society. They are all diseases of the spirit.

Our built environment embodies our attitudes and manifests these same diseases. Change our surroundings to reaffirm the sacredness of our world and we can restore a sense of respect, honor, and value. This is a necessary part of solving these social problems, and necessary for sustainability.

Build schools that treat students as people and touch the excitement of discovery. Build places for health care that cherish the sick. Build work places that treat the workers as being as valuable as the machines and the boss. Give builders a chance to put something into the building they can show their children with pride. Respect the patina of age in buildings and people.

Create Magic, Touch the Heart of All You Make

Love is expressed in our surroundings, as elsewhere, in our willingness to give without condition. The most precious thing a building can convey is that sense of unstinted giving—of doing something out of love rather than calculation.

In a Head Start Center we asked ourselves what we could give that would make a kid coming in the door feel best. "The smell of good food!" was the immediate answer. We made the kitchen the physical and organizational heart of the Center. With the kitchen opening into every room, the cook represented a friend and bite of food for every kid, a cup of coffee and a sympathetic ear for every harried parent, and an extra eye for everyone's safety.

The lobby expanded into a comfortable Commons—a place to give community volunteers and staff to work, a place to give parents a moment of peace and rest in an often tumultuous day. A space just for kids—not teachers—was built. We designed it to bring them close to the earth and the sprouting spring bulbs outside a low window, with a skylight to watch clouds and rain running off the roof, and with hidden mirrors to give them new views of their world.

Give the unexpected, create magic!

Seaside Head Start Center, Seaside, Oregon

Transform Tourism

Visiting other people and places should enrich both them and ourselves through exposure to different values, conditions, and achievements. An Oregon coastal community decided that this "spirit of place" is a fundamental element of successful tourism. They concluded that people come to the Coast for its specialness, which should not be lost among look-alike tourist facilities. This visitor's center included a community hall to house events for both community and visitors, and obtained a special grant for architectural crafts to help their building more powerfully convey the unique character of the Oregon Coast.

Visitor's Center, Cannon Beach, Oregon

Make Where We *Are* Paradise

Lessen our needs for vacations, tourism, transportation, and our impact on the ever fewer remaining places of powerful natural patterns. In making our places more special, we make them of more value to us and to visitors both. Make winter gardens. Put the stars back in the night.

Ice Garden, Wilson, Wisconsin

Mirrors Distort

They focus our attention on outer, rather than inner qualities—often in our groggiest states. A window into a garden can connect us to our surroundings instead of reminding us of a hangover. Hide mirrors until needed—here inside a medicine cabinet door.

Bender/deMoll Residence, Neahkahnie Mountain, Oregon

Durability is Magic

A cathedral or palace serving twenty generations costs each one less than a hovel. Long service-life makes the generosity of quality unquestionably affordable. Remodeling rather than replacing substitutes employment for resource use. We use half the resources if our buildings last twice as long.

La Sainte Chapelle, Paris, France

Rewarding Work is Wealth

Such work requires giving an opportunity for builders and users as well as designers to contribute their skills. Durability provides the budget. Its product reflects to everyone that skill and competence is honored and valued, and it expands our belief in what is achievable.

Zenrinji Temple, Kyoto, Japan

Building with a Soul

Silence has power. It is as vital a dimension in our surroundings as space. Eliminating the sounds of TV, refrigerators, heating systems, dishwashers, and office equipment can be essential to the peace of a place. Adding bird song, the laughter of children, or the sound of the wind can give a place new life.

Give our spirits places of shelter and nurture as well as our bodies. That nourishment creates our real wealth and is the glue that holds sustainability and well-being together.

In this home, heating is by passive solar, solar hot water, and site-grown wood heat. A non-mechanical "cool box" was used for food storage, and foot valves on sinks for energy and water conservation and hygiene. Other elements included high-efficiency lighting, owner-built and state-approved compost toilet, insulating window shutters, native plant landscaping, and low-toxicity materials for indoor air quality. The quietude and freedom these technical changes gave permitted a spirit in the building to support its inhabitants and connect them to its surroundings.

Designing a building with a soul requires focused attention to each decision in design and construction, so that each element answers its need in the same spirit and relation to others.

Bender/deMoll Residence, Neahkahnie Mountain, Oregon

Connect Us with the Stars

We are their children. So are all lives and all life on our planet. Honoring these connections in making our surroundings acknowledges our place in the whole incredible dance of the universe.

Bender/deMoll Residence, Neahkahnie Mountain, Oregon

Honoring Things

Honoring things in our building empowers that attitude in our actions. Tradition honors the insights of the past. Planting trees honors hope for a future. A *tokonoma*—a space in the room reserved for art—honors our guests. Providing place for birds to nest honors the other lives that share our world. Honoring the past lives of building materials makes us aware of the beauty and struggles of all life.

Bender/deMoll Residence, Neahkahnie Mountain, Oregon

Earth, Air, Fire, and Water

These are elemental forces. Bring us closer and deeper in experience and empathy with them. The bath was made central to the design of this house, with a fireplace of wave-rounded, fire-born basalt rock beside it. Above was a sky room at the roof peak—under a ten-foot pyramidal skylight—surrounded by the ocean, fog, wind, sun, rain, and the wheeling of the stars at night.

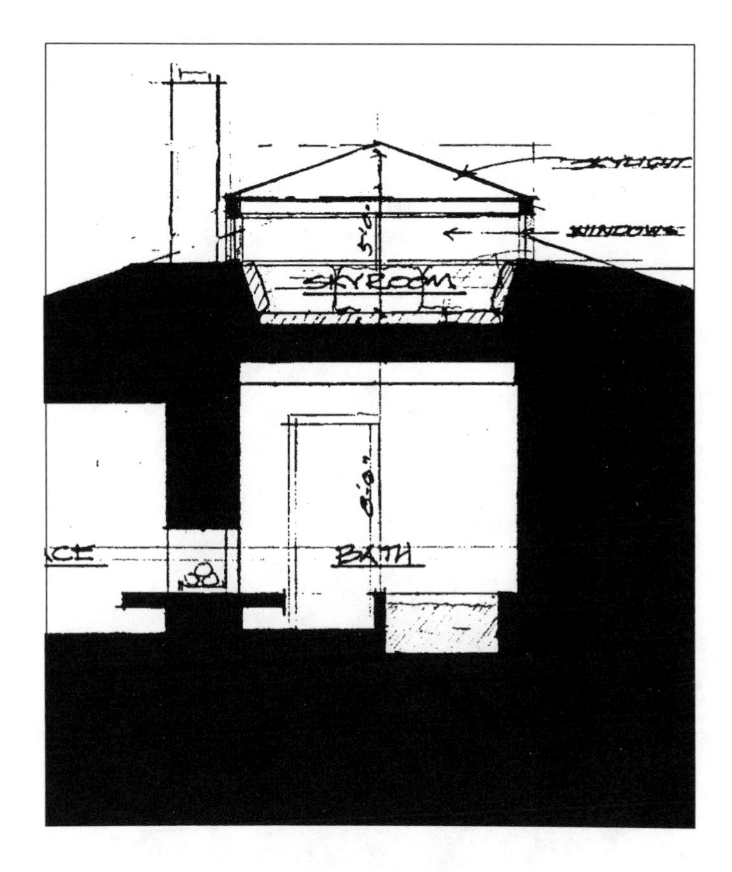

Dorscheimer Residence, Arch Cape, Oregon

Celebrate Death

It is part of life and of all cycles. Celebrate what was given and what remains with the living. Share grief. Know that the pain of loss acknowledges the wonder of the bonds that grow between us. Create a setting that touches the wonder of these events plunging deep into our hearts.

Nurse Log Garden, Neahkahnie Mountain, Oregon

Connect Us to the Life Around Us

This does not require large budgets or spaces. It needs only the desire for that connection and a willingness to evolve a life and surroundings that are unique. This native wildflower meadow needed only control of competing vegetation to reveal its beauty.

Bender/deMoll Residence, Neahkahnie Mountain, Oregon

Foundations

Making places that have a soul and that can enrich and sustain our lives *is* possible. Though such places may be outside of the experience of most of us, there are some guidelines that can help our process of learning their nature:

- Protect and enhance the *feng shui* of the site.
- Minimize waste and impact on resources and connected systems.
- Make where we *are* paradise.
- Focus on inner rather than outer qualities.
- Seek durability—build for eternity.
- Work *with* nature.
- Provide rewarding work in design, construction, and use.
- Honor all life and the power that begets it.
- Create silence and peace.
- Connect us with the stars.
- Give our spirits places of shelter and nourishment.
- Acknowledge the limits of our material world.
- Celebrate death.
- Connect us to the life around us.
- Put us in touch with the seasons.
- Touch the spirit of where we live.
- Help us touch invisible worlds.
- Create intense and fresh experiences.
- Touch the heart of all you make.
- Learn to say no—learn restraint and simplicity. Practice enoughness.
- *Give* the unexpected. Create magic.
- Affirm sacredness and meaning in our buildings.
- Create a topology which fits the use.
- Pay attention to economics rather than finance.
- Embody sustainable values; and most simply and importantly,
- Put love and energy into the place.

Touchstones—Seven Tests

Once designed, there are a few simple tests (without any right answers) that we can use to sense whether our efforts are moving in the right direction.

1. Time: The Test of Duration

This test asks if the qualities of a design are truly enduring, or a flash-in-the-pan enthusiasm which will become an embarrassment tomorrow.

Roll time back a thousand years. Does the design feel comfortable with its neighbors? Would the people find its spirit embracing the same deep-rooted values of their lives?

Roll time forward a thousand years. How does the building feel with the patina and bumps and wrinkles of time upon it? Is it mellowed and enriched, or tarnished and tattered? Did it have enough lasting value in it to be cherished and loved, or will it have been long-demolished and forgotten?

There is a hoary strength and a nourishing peacefulness in the timeless qualities of a building that truly fits our hearts and spirits. Once known, those qualities can be immediately sensed in any situation. Buildings of different periods express those qualities in unique ways specific to their time and nature, but within that uniqueness is the oneness of the same needs gaining satisfaction.

2. Arrangement: The Test of Invisibility

This test looks at serving, at our egos, the spirit of place, and the un-self-centered bringing forth of that spirit.

Like a good servant, a good place fulfills needs—giving warmth, security, happiness, and joy—without calling attention to itself. A flashy building that screams for attention may provide momentary pleasure and interest, but soon becomes tiresome. When we find ourselves again and again gravitating to a certain place, it is usually because we feel especially good being there. Even then, we may be hard pressed to figure out what invisible combination of things present and absent create that specialness.

Close your eyes. Forget what the place looks like, and feel if it does its job well and invisibly. Spend a day in it in your mind. Curl up in its sunlight. Clean house. Even if nobody else ever knew of the place, or whether you designed it, would you be happy? Think of designing a place. What qualities would permit it to escape your notice, yet attract you back to it again and again because of how good it feels and how well it fulfills its purposes?

3. Cost: The Test of Investment

This test tries to separate freedom and value from expense.

Just as between people, the relationship between people and places is richer, more rewarding, and more enduring if based on love and giving rather than economics and "payment." An older, paid-for building can be used more generously than an expensive new one. A building that does as much with one brick or one watt of electricity as another does with five conveys a sense of assurance and confidence as well as frugality and economy.

A wall that offers a place to sit as a free bonus while holding back the dirt, gives that sitting place more freely and less self-consciously than a purposefully made bench. And a place that does not demand recognition for the owner, builder, or designer is freer and more giving to those who use it. A place that gives more is loved more, and is given more in return—in our feelings towards it and in the care, maintenance, and enhancement of it in our use.

What real investment has the place required—in work, materials, energy, love, and frustrations? Has that investment been repaid? What does the place give in return? Is it old enough to be free of the demands of those who initially put resources into its making? What can it give in addition to its primary intended purposes?

The investment test asks us to see what kinds and amounts of things have been invested in a place, and how effectively that investment produces a good place. It reminds us that excess is as harmful as meagerness, and that we need to discriminate between things that harm and those that enhance our abilities, our relationships, and our lives.

4. Openness: The Test of Connection

This test looks at whether we design a place as something isolated and separate, or as something that is enriched and given meaning through its connection with other things.

Does the design of a place close people off from, or bring them into closer touch with the rest of the world and the rhythms of nature? Does the design itself adapt readily or resist changes in its use and additions to its structure? Does it gracefully accept the changes of time, or demand to be kept in the pristine condition of youth? Does it bring people together and cause good things to happen?

A good gardener plants a tree, then leaves it open to respond to the nurturing forces of its surroundings, rather than forcing it to remain in conformance to a limited preconception. A good builder does likewise.

5. Honor: The Test of Worth

This test asks how well gifts are acknowledged and repaid, and how the act of giving is itself encouraged and respected.

Does the place honor its surroundings, its materials, the things which were given up to make its existence possible? Does it honor the work that went into its making, its heritage, and the future? Does it give the people using it a sense that they and their activities are of value? Does it reflect a questioning in its design of what it can give to heal, enrich, or create greater harmony within the community of place it is joining, and to its present and future users?

6. Grace: The Test of Importance

This test asks if we are working with the right questions, and whether we have resolved the basic issues before considering refinements and less important details.

Consider the place in terms of what the *I Ching* says about grace and beauty:

> Grace—beauty of form—is necessary in any union if it is to be well ordered and pleasing rather than disordered and chaotic. Grace brings success. However, it is not the essential or fundamental thing; it is only the ornament and must therefore be used sparingly and only in little things.
>
> In human affairs, aesthetic form comes into being when traditions exist that, strong and abiding like mountains, are made pleasing by a lucid beauty.
>
> . . . beautiful form suffices to brighten and throw light upon matters of lesser moment, but important questions cannot be decided in this way. They require greater earnestness.

7. Heart: The Test of Rightness

This is the simplest and hardest test.

Set aside all the words, images, and games of our minds. Does the place have a soul? Does its personality fit and support its use, its location, and its community of life? If so, that's all we really need to know. The rest is refinement and polish.

12. Organic Development of Place

Christopher Day

Editor's Note

Christopher Day is a Welsh architect whose words and buildings have inspired people on both sides of the Atlantic. His two books, Places of the Soul *and* Building With Heart *describe his philosophy and the work he has done in the Welsh countryside where the buildings were literally constructed by hand, right down to the plaster finish that is hand-applied, giving a unique and irreproducable feeling to each room. His description of his own workspace in* Places of the Soul *gives a sense of his relationship to the theory of spirit of place.*

> *My office as a room is a silent office, even though we talk there. It is not oppressively empty when it is empty, but peacefully at rest. It is an office more like a church than a factory—and so it should be, for I want the work that comes out of it to have something of the same sacredness. If we think of work as the raising of matter, as provision of food for the human spirit, then places of work need this sort of atmosphere.*

The following essay outlines his working principles by reference to specific projects and concludes with suggestions for making a building a unique part of place. Professor Day is currently designing projects in the United States, England, and Sweden.

MODERN LIFE INCREASINGLY compartmentalizes things that should be a single unity. These range from the separation of thinking, feeling, and action by, for instance, thinking about work, listening to music, and driving a car, to the binary divisions of computer "thinking" applied to life-related issues which in reality weave between two poles and are never wholly in either.

We tend to take for granted that there are actions essential to "progress," to a large extent regardless of their environmental price. We also take for granted that some places are sacrosanct and should be preserved at all costs. The results are the wastelands of "economic" development and the museum-like ossification of places to be "preserved." Naturally the balance is not equal, but heavily weighted to the financially profitable.

Not surprisingly, we tend to view development as inevitably destructive of place. Urban development typically involves demolition and an assault on the web of memories that underpin the identity of a place. Even when the result is a genuine improvement, the disruption by the construction process, the scale of the project, and the fact that everything is completed simultaneously tend to require quite a time for the new activities housed in it to feel right in the place, and for the character of the place to become softened by human usage.

Spirit of place develops slowly. It is always changing and growing and can be built upon, but when obliterated takes a long time, possibly measured in human generations, to reestablish itself. It helps therefore to look at development sites not as opportunities to do whatever we want, but places that can be improved by conversion.

In many people's minds, development in the countryside means its destruction—a view supported by the evidence of recent years. Nonetheless, pre-industrial development has given us a heritage of beautiful farmsteads, hamlets, villages, and towns. There has been a way for development to be harmonious.

Vernacular building (and lifestyle), however, resulted from unconscious habitual intuition, wise but unfree. Nowadays we have to consciously choose to act in harmony with nature and struggle to understand how to do so.

Not all growth in demand for buildings can reasonably be confined to reclaimed derelict land, urban infill, and densification of existing settlements. As some construction inevitably must be accommodated in the countryside, it is essential that a new way be found to foster harmony between buildings, human activities, and countryside. At present, however, financial criteria, technological prowess, and de-localized consciousness cause a disregard of the time, growth, and life forces that have brought places into being, resulting in development unrelated to the reasons places have come to be the way they are, and buildings imposed without response to time or place.

There are ways of uniting buildings and surroundings so that they can belong together as inevitably as do those from the vernacular era. These involve organic growth processes, ecologically whole and visible life-support cycles underpinned by objectively sensitive techniques of studying place and developing design proposals. Some of these I can describe.

Development of Place

Dr. Margaret Colquhoun, Axel Ehwald of the Life Science Trust, and I have been working with the following process as a group activity:

Although in life, many things and themes are always mixed indissolubly together, for clarity of observation it helps to focus on issues separately. This is a discipline simple to describe but taxing to fulfill! We start the process by silent, non-judgmental listening to the place, through first impressions. Next we observe and record all the physical phenomena we can, from the range of colors to the length of the grass. We then attempt to understand how the place has been formed by the past and extrapolate this into the future—how will it change if nothing is done? If there are minimal interventions, like changing the grazing regime or restricting vehicle speed? If there are progressively more and more major interventions, from cutting single trees to major abuse?

Next we try to describe the responses invoked in us. Through this, the essential being of a place and what change it can or cannot accept can become clear.

The next stage is to work with the idea that is seeking to incarnate as a building. What is the essence of this idea? What activities does this generate? (The presence of an activity colors a whole area, even if it is invisible behind closed doors—have you ever been past a pilgrimage church or a nuclear power plant?) It is now possible to establish building edges with poles and string. These can be recorded onto scale drawings, modified to make more meaningful plans, and then developed into three dimensions in clay. The next step is to introduce eye-level views of the clay model onto drawings or paintings of the place as it is. Through this process, that which was an idea needing to be rooted on earth has become one with an evolving place in organic harmony. The idea has made its first concrete step into incarnation.

Unfortunately it is hard for many people to find the time for such a deep study and design process. Normally I have to practice a shorter version. For example, for an ecological-village project in Sweden (actually a suburb), I started by asking the eleven families to describe how they hoped to live and the qualities they hoped to find in their village. I then attempted to identify the "families" of activities that would be placed on the site. We then walked around the site and by consensus approximately located housing, parking, community facilities, etc., on site. With paper "houses" on a 1:200 (approximately 1/16-inch to 1-foot) plan, we then located buildings. We modified this on paper with respect to future influences such as adjacent high-rise housing and a new road, planned but not yet built. We then modeled our "village" in clay. In all this I could take a relative background role, although I needed to make minor suggestions and modifications to unify what initially threatened to be an unrelated group of dispirited, idiosyncratic buildings. I recorded this model with photos and sketches, and back in my office made further minor modifications, particularly with regard to building regulations, micro-climate, and trees to be retained. (Micro-climate is the climate of a small locality, such as a woodland or street. On the same day, a woodland may be cool and quiet, while a street is hot and noisy.) The village was effectively designed by the occupants, all committed to working in harmony with the forces of the place.

I have also worked with Bruce May of the Scientific and Medical Network, Richard Coleman of the Royal Fine Arts Commission, and others on trying to study the spirit of place.

As I did with Dr. Colquhoun and Axel Ehwald, we strictly divide our study into four different stages. These stages are the physical characteristics of the place, the time-life related characteristics, the feelings evoked, and the spirit of the place. Time-life related characteristics include the rhythm of spatial experience—the rhythm of expanding and contracting, and the way the space moves upward, outward, and downward. To find out the spirit of the place, we ask: if the place could speak with a human voice, how in two or three words would it describe itself?

By going through such a process, the group invariably reached a close consensus of the identity of the otherwise elusively intangible "spirit of place." This in itself is perhaps no more than interesting, but we can then reverse the process and ask: What should a hospital say? What feeling responses should it therefore invoke? What sequences of experiences should underpin these? How therefore should this be achieved in physical terms? By studying both the place and the proposed project in this way, we have an entirely new basis upon which to develop a proposal. What place says is of vital significance to the success of any project.

For example, a chapel for a retreat center should say "meditative and calm." It should support the moods of centeredness, quietness, and feeling. To accentuate the division between the outside and inside and the time it takes to pass through, the passage from outdoors to indoors can have a narrow, heavy door, a deliberate doorway, and a heavy latch. The inside can be a centered, circular space, enlivened by axial forms, quiet, and light-filled, with textured moulding—the timeless mood enhanced by durable materials.

Urban life is sustained by inputs of food, clean air, water, energy, and materials, with pollution's outputs (such as sewage, refuse, etc.). This life-supporting system is largely invisible, leading to a lack of consciousness with devastating consequences—it is at the root of the ecological crisis we are now entering. This model is increasingly duplicated even in the countryside where healthier systems are much easier to implement—indeed until a few decades ago they have been the norm. There is a strong case for requiring *all* new rural development

Photo by Christopher Day.

to be largely self-sustaining and non-polluting in its life-support systems. As such systems need to be within daily consciousness, it is important that they are attractive.

In developing a place it is easy to forget the needs of wildlife. "Wildlife" may conjure up images of lions and tigers but applies equally to birds and butterflies and indeed to every animal upon whom a balanced ecology depends. When we think of how birdsong can uplift our feelings, it is obvious that in encouraging song birds we are providing for human needs as well. For a green environment to be self-maintaining it needs not only plants but a balanced ecosystem in which birds, animals, insects, microlife, and so on all play an essential part.

While every location is different, what follows are a few general principles that are widely applicable.

For example, all life is most vigorous at the meeting of elemental qualities, just as human settlements have tended to grow from the meeting of, say, land and water, or farms from the meeting of arable and pasture land. To maximize this meeting zone, the "edge" can be extended through such means as meandering waterways, hedgerows, and belts rather than isolated blocks of trees. The more diverse the range of habitat, the better it can provide for variations of weather throughout the year. Song birds need a multilevel canopy: not only crowns of trees, but underbranches, brush, shrubs, and ground cover. Birds, in common with other creatures, also need "greenways"—animal and bird corridors which link reserves of undisturbed, wilder land or rough vegetation. They also need food supplies throughout the year. Greenways, multilayer canopies, maximized edge, and varied fruiting seasons can be interwoven with human climatic and amenity needs.

Improvement in micro-climate is often the key to improvement of a place. Every activity has certain climatic requirements—croplands need sun, but outdoor cafes may need shade; roads are noise-tolerant, but gardens are not, and so on.

One of the first things to ask is what changes to micro-climate are desirable and how we can use elements such as buildings, excavation earth, and planting. In the projects mentioned, for instance, the building layout was arranged to provide micro-climate protection. Each location had specific requirements. The eco-village in Umeå, Sweden, was laid out to ensure protection from north and east winds, maximum noon light, as well as afternon sun for amenity. The eco-village in Arnhem was likewise arranged to give protection from north winds. By mounding the site to the north, greater sun penetration was obtained. Playnooks and corners were planned to be sun-traps at the time children came out of school. In Fresno, buildings were massed to screen road noise. Footways were all leaf or building-shaded. Temperature polarity across courtyards was enhanced by warm, dark, solar chimneys on the sunny side and active water in the shade, thereby inducing cooling air movement.

Organic Development

Places have been formed by the past. Any change in the future is a development of the past—unless there is conscious human action. We now have the capacity to have ideas freed from habitual and geographical constraints. We can build anything, anywhere. We frequently do, and it is frequently harshly out of place.

Modern development can be characterized as building to enclose future life-activities such as a speculative office building, whereas vernacular development, inevitably harmonious, was building to consolidate growing life-activities such as an addition to a house for a growing family. Growth occurred from life-nodes—where activities grew, and from organic development. These principles are no less essential today.

Modern growth nodes are often existing settlements but they include such unromantic places as bus stops and car parks—places where informal activities from bottle-banks (recycling centers) to ice-cream vans spring up. Usually there is something already there, but some agricultural, research, and educational activities may develop where no obvious node previously existed. Growth nodes must be life-filled meeting points. They depend upon life—human social and economic life, and life in nature. This life is always richest at the meeting of different qualities of landscape—woodland edge, waterside, the meeting of pasture and arableland, and so on. Typically, vernacular settlements grew from such meeting points.

A vital key to successful new development is identifying meaningful growth nodes. Next comes development by strategy rather than by master plan. Here we can seek to build every stage to create a *perfect* present, yet allow scope for new paths and nodes, along with infill, densification, and intensification of use, so that the future can be even better. This is how our ancestors built, unconsciously. We can do it consciously.

Uniting Buildings and Surroundings

I have described techniques for the right placing of buildings and their related activities. The rightness of placing can be further strengthened if we use sensory "markers" such as turns in path, tree archways, etc., to strengthen the experience of approach so that buildings become the inevitable conclusion of a journey. However, to really belong, as it were, inevitably in place, they also need appropriate qualities, particularly of scale, form, color and materials, and linking elements.

In a landscape setting, building scale needs to be as small as possible. Using low buildings can help reduce perceived scale, as can siting in hollows and against backdrops, and building into slopes. Buildings need to be significantly smaller than trees, and trees vary significantly according to geographical factors. Hardness and brightness of color have a marked effect on visual impact; think of the same building, soft-edged in natural local stone and lime-washed, or smooth-rendered and sharp-edged, painted with masonry paint. In general, the brighter the color, harder the texture, or larger the scale, the quieter, softer, and smaller other qualities need to be. Curved forms, vegetated walls and roofs, earth colors, and local materials tend to blend in harmoniously as long as they don't look out of place with neighboring buildings.

Not to appear temporarily parked, buildings need to be "rooted" in the ground—traditionally by flared or stepped bases, though moulded ground form and shrubs can also be utilized. Shrubs, walls, and other landscape elements can also be used to tie buildings into place—as is easily demonstrated by drawing them onto a picture of any building disharmoniously placed in its surroundings.

Conclusion

We cannot satisfactorily imitate, but can learn from the past and translate this learning into modern forms of understanding, planning, design, and landscaping. These are based on three principles:

Photo by Christopher Day.

- marriage of past (place) and future (idea)
- ecological and aesthetic harmony and mutual responsiveness
- organic development from life-activity nodes

In the limited instances where building development is appropriate in the countryside, this approach can foster wholeness, harmony, and health of place. It can also be a model for suburban and urban development to heal the wounds already built.

More than this, it can help to overcome the schism in our thinking which assumes that the maintenance of untouched wilderness can compensate for desecrating development.

13. House: Symbol of the Soul

Anthony Lawlor, AIA

Editor's Note

Design is ultimately a magical art. It takes symbolic forms and shapes them into structures that offer spaces for us to live and work. Seldom in modern times do we give much thought to the symbolic shapes that we are creating, let alone what effect they may have upon us. In this article, Tony Lawlor guides us through designed spaces, interpreting their symbolic meanings, showing us what undeveloped potentials may be found there.

> *Sacred space is a space that is transparent to transcendence, and everything within such a space furnishes a base for meditation. . . . When you enter through the door, everything within that space is symbolic, the whole world is mythologized.*
>
> *To live in a sacred space is to live in a symbolic environment where spiritual life is possible, where everything around you speaks of the exaltation of the spirit.*
>
> *This is a place where you can simply experience and bring forth what you are and what you might be. This is the place of creative incubation. At first you might find that nothing happens there. But if you have a sacred place and use it, something eventually will happen.*
>
> *Your sacred space is where you find yourself again and again. . . .*
>
> —Joseph Campbell

SARAH'S EXUBERANT PAINTING of a house hangs on the refrigerator door—blue roof, yellow walls, bright red door; windows with delicate panes; flower boxes brim with color; a chimney touches the stars; a pathway invites entry. Ask any child in the United States to draw a house and it probably would look something like Sarah's. Perhaps, many years ago, you drew a similar image of home.

Most of us don't actually live in houses like this. We spend much of our day at work. The shoe-box apartment, the suburban house, and other dwellings we call "home" are often little more than rest stops to grab a bite to eat; sit numbly in front of the television for an hour; sleep until it's time to return to work. The house we drew as children has receded deep within the psyche, beyond the view of daily concerns.

Imaginary houses of childhood may be out of sight but they are not out of mind. The two-story colonial resting gracefully on a sparkling lawn is the advertiser's standard symbol for nurturance and fulfillment, the idyllic heaven of television commercials and magazine ads. The number of housing starts per year symbolizes the economic vitality or weakness of the nation. Absence of a house, homelessness, is an emblem of our worst fears—alienation, poverty, dereliction.

The house is a mythic archetype, "a secret opening," as Joseph Campbell writes, "through which the inexhaustible energies of the cosmos pour into human existence." Hansel and Gretel's cottage, Sleeping Beauty's castle, and other fabled dwellings are places where ordinary reality is transformed by the unseen powers that shape creation. Navajo hogans, "home places," with their circular designs, east-facing entries, and sky doors at the crown of domed roofs replicate that culture's creation story. The size, style, and neighborhood of what we consider a "good" house express the values that define our world view. The minimalist lines of a white-on-white artist's loft in Manhattan embodies one cosmos of mythic images while a rustic cabin in the Colorado Rockies exemplifies another.

Shelter and food are the essentials of material existence. From the moment we are born until the moment we pass away, we are surrounded by some sort of building or designed landscape. Except in the most benign climates, we need protection from the wind and rain, winter's cold, and summer's heat. Houses are the essential shelters. Home is the place that nourishes body and mind, fosters the companionship of family and friends, and provides the space for renewing moments of peace within a chaotic world.

Beyond shelter, houses have deep psychological and spiritual significance. Our primary impressions of life were received within the walls of a home. Footsteps in the hall, the texture of a blanket, the color of a sofa, the taste of food from the kitchen, a fragrant breeze from the garden through an open window, and the myriad of other impressions we sensed as babies helped in shaping our image of self and the world. Because of their power to influence our perceptions, our houses and apartments become sacred places on the psychological map of our existence. The demands of the workplace can be overwhelming; an exotic vacation can be exciting; but, in the back of our minds, nurturing images of home offer a haven of peace and renewal.

This haven within the psyche is the source and reference point for sacred places in the physical world. Sacred places are outer reflections of inner experiences of wholeness, unity, and vitality. The circle of stones at Stonehenge echoes the design of the primal house—the circle of the soul; the megaliths that mark the sunrise orient our psyches to a home point in time and space. Egypt's Great Pyramid is an outward diagram of the aspirations of the spirit that were kindled in our cribs as infants—the desire to rise from the diversity and groundedness of the earth to the unity and freedom of the sky.

Sacred places evoke powerful spiritual experiences because they are settings that reconnect us to the home of our being. They are places that encourage us to "find [ourselves] again and again." Entering a sacred place directs our thinking, feeling, spatial sensations, and connection to nature's cycles toward the silent depths of the soul. For example, entering a Gothic cathedral, a "house of God," our minds can contemplate the icons of Christ, Mary, and other images that speak of the soul's radiance and compassion. The rich layers of detail reflect the many levels of emotion within us. Vast interior spaces urge us to leap beyond the limited house of our bodies and enter our cosmic dwelling. The play of light through the tall windows created by the solar rhythms of day and night through the seasons reminds us of the seasons of the heart—inspiration, disappointment, insight, and joy. Touching the ancient stones, we can remember the timeless house of the soul.

In architectural terms, access to the sacred's totality is gained through perception and interaction with symbolic design forms. The soaring tower and cave-like interior of a Hindu temple define a realm "where everything around you speaks of the exaltation of the spirit." Japanese shrines, Islamic mosques, Hopi kivas, and other religious structures use a symbolic language to lead our consciousness beyond material shapes into the precinct of the spirit.

Symbolic design form works on at least three levels: cultural, personal, and universal. The cross is viewed by Christians as an emblem of redemption. It can also recall one's personal relationship to the divine. Throughout the globe the cross is perceived as a representation of the emanation of the cosmos of time and space from a dimensionless point of creation.

Emblems of sacred design are not limited to religious structures, however. Houses are constructed with architectural elements that are porous to the subtle workings of the psyche. The triangle of a gabled roof signals a place of shelter; an oak doorway offers a warm invitation to enter the interior realms; the hearth recalls the embers of vitality that glow within the depths of consciousness. But we tend to overlook spiritual connections in our living environments, to see homes as places to hang our hats instead of environments that furnish a base for meditation. We are like the fish described by Dogen Kigen, the thirteenth-century Japanese philosopher: "Now when fish see water as a palace, it is just like human beings seeing a palace. They do not think it flows. If an outsider tells them, 'What you see as a palace is running water,' the fish will be astonished."

By tracing the streams along which archetypal patterns of consciousness flow into the material forms of houses, we can discover openings to the sacred powers of life. Dwelling within rigid architectural boundaries, such as floors, walls, and furnishings can become a means of loosening restrictive inner patterns of thought and feeling. The house can serve as a means of inner transformation.

Three symbols serve as fundamental links between consciousness and house architecture—perimeter, gate, and hub of nurturance. The perimeter defines the edge of shelter, inside and outside, mine and yours, security and uncertainty. A gate allows the energies that animate human dwelling to penetrate the perimeter. Hubs of nurturance are rooms and furnishings that renew the soul through the daily actions of sleeping, bathing, cooking, eating, and gathering. On the interior, daily activities, focused around hubs of nurturance, reconnect us to the renewing forces of the soul. Perimeter, gate, and hub of nurturance are in turn constructed of sub-elements that can deepen our experience of the sacred.

The perimeter is made of four elements—floor, walls, ceiling, and ornament. Together these four create a container that cups the fluidity of the soul. They structure a vessel that protects and prompts heart and mind to engage in the alchemy of spiritual transformation. Delineating the six directions of north, south, east, west, above, and below, the perimeter defines the house's sacred space—the microcosmic seed of cosmic reality.

The floor is a symbol of stability in an ever-changing world. It offers a level and firm stage for the play of human life. Touch points between our activity and floors transform them into the horizontal surfaces of tabletops, chair seats, countertops, bookshelves, and other furnishings that uphold the processes of dwelling. Lowered floors such as those found in "sunken" living rooms and bathtubs draw our consciousness inward for gathering and revitalization. Raised floors, such as bookcases and the tops of dressers, point our attention to objects of beauty and reverence, altars to everyday experience.

The second element of the perimeter—walls—symbolizes protection and loving embrace. Walls define "mine" and "yours," what is "home" and what is "world." They form a second womb that cradles the round of daily existence. Standing away from the earth's surface, walls imitate our own stance on the landscape, representing the aspiration to overcome gravity's pull and dwell between earth and sky.

Resting atop walls, the roof and ceiling completes the perimeter of the house's enclosure. Roofs symbolize shelter and the unifying powers that span the diversity of the individual structural elements and activities that take place within a house. The shape of the ceiling can give physical form to different qualities of consciousness. Flat ceilings tend to set an upper limit, keeping our awareness within definite bounds. Peaked, or "cathedral," ceilings urge our spirits to rise heavenward to a unified point. Barrel vaults and domes invite the radiance of consciousness to expand into endless space.

Ornament grows from the meeting points of floor, walls, and ceilings. It provides the seams for the container of the soul and reveals the care and attention that has gone into the making of a house. The mindfully worked details of a Victorian cornice molding or Bauhaus style baseboard show the depth of soul that has been pouring into a living environment. The miles of "ranch"-style trim that edges the doors and windows of tract houses across America speaks of the assembly-line mentality that produces the architecture of mediocrity.

Gates pierce the perimeter of the house, enabling it to breathe the vitality of dwelling. A house without openings is a tomb. Gates are symbols of transition, transcendence, death and resurrection, and a transformation from the material to the spiritual. Three types of gates open the house to the spirit's vitality: doorways, windows, and skylights.

Doorways represent the initiation into the mysteries of dwelling. Christ said, "I am the door." The Roman god Janus held the keys to the powers of opening and closing of consciousness. The summer solstice , in the sign of Cancer, is said to be the "door of men," symbolizing death and the decrease of light. The winter solstice, in the sign of Capricorn, is called the "door of the gods," an emblem of birth, ascent, and the increase of light. "Birth and death are merely doors that we pass through," is an essential Buddhist precept. Many experiences that make home the center of our lives are connected with doors. The entry receives the love and warmth of visiting family and friends. It is the place that sends children on their first solo journey to school and where many couples share their first kiss. Notice the entries to the houses in your neighborhood and you will find a rich treasure of design and craft. Doorways between rooms—from the bedroom to the bathroom, for example—signify the transition from one expression of soul to another.

Doors are constructed of design elements that enhance their symbolic content. Twin pillars on either side of a door embody the dualities of light/dark, birth/death, yin/yang, and other polarities that must be transcended if we are to gain access to the inner realms of the sacred. At an ancient Buddhist monastery in northern India a gatekeeper would test the preparedness of those wishing to enter. So formidable was his questioning that only one in two hundred aspirants passed the test. Shrines in Japan are often flanked by two statues representing fear and desire. A crossbeam joins the twin pillars as a sign of unity. The sunburst design over the entrances to many Victorian houses recalls the solar source of light and life. The threshold marks the boundary line between the sacred and the profane, the sanctuary of home and the chaos of the world. Welcome mats enhance this symbol by offering a place to perform the common ritual of wiping the dust of the world off one's feet before entering the sanctuary of home. The door panel embodies the obstacle of matter that masks our perceptions of spirit and the veil of illusion, *maya*, that mysteriously shrouds the sacred. Hinges recall moments of spiritual insight, the instances when new knowledge or experience cracks open the boundaries of matter to reveal the inner light of existence. The lock represents the mystery to be solved, the dark center that must be pierced by a key of wisdom before passage into the house is gained. Keys recall the process of decoding scriptural knowledge; "Woe unto you, lawyer! for ye have taken away the key of knowledge" (Luke 11:52). A silver key symbolizes worldly vitality, while a gold key signifies spiritual power. In Christian iconography St. Peter holds the "keys of the gate of Heaven." According to ancient civil law a married woman was given keys by her mother-in-law, emblematic of her new status and granting her sole access to all the recesses of the house.

Windows are gates for the eyes and lungs. By providing light, views, and air to enter the house they are places of overlap between interior and exterior realms. The size and placement of windows influences how the outer world blends with inner modes of dwelling—small windows admitting limited connections and large, expansive openings tending to dissolve the boundary that divides home and world. Windows placed high in a wall connect us with the free-moving sky clouds, sunlight, birds in flight. Windows at eye level draw attention to the concerns of the earth—cycles of plant growth, people and automobiles on their way to numerous destinations. The quality of glass in a window colors our perceptions of the surroundings. Since glass is an unstable material that slowly "flows" year after year, the clear glazing of an old house can distort our picture of the surroundings. Stained glass, such as the leaded windows of the Gamble house by the Greene brothers, can create a picture within a window that masks the external. Window sills are little altars that honor the threshold of light's entry. A seashell, a bottle made of blue glass, or other translucent objects resting on the sill display the miracle of light-filled matter. Curtains, shades, and other window treatments temper a window's gateway character. The diaphanous flow of lacy curtains celebrates the subtle nuances of light and air while the precise metallic slats of a Levelor blind strictly control views and illumination.

Roof windows create doorways to the sky's expansiveness. Sunlight penetrates from on high, creating luminous axial pillars that link the cycles of earthly life to those of heaven. In Europe, an opening was often made in the roof of a dying person's house, allowing the spirit to ascend to heaven.

Within the house's perimeter and its gates are the sacred spaces that foster the soul's diverse expressions. Each room is designed to honor a different inflection of the human spirit—dreams and intimate communion in the bedroom; purification and beauty in the bathroom; the alchemy of transformation in the kitchen; savoring and devouring in the dining room; communal gathering in the living room. The size and shape of each room as well as the type and arrangement of its furnishings can be seen as the shape of the soul in material form. The spreading configuration of the bed and the softness of the pillows and covers reflect the consciousness of dreamy rest. In the kitchen, the knife expresses the incisiveness and determination of the spirit while the oven recalls the depths of its nurturing warmth.

At hubs of nurturance we engage in the archetypal activities that reconnect us to eternity. Sleeping, bathing, cooking, eating, and gathering with others of our kind are the primal human functions that inform the design of every house, from a teepee to a castle. They are also the actions of the mythic figures that enacted and fostered the creation. In India, the sleeping Vishnu dreamed the universe into being. In the Old Testament we are told that Jacob:

> . . . took the stones of that place, and put them for his pillow, and lay down in that place to sleep. And he dreamed, and behold a ladder set up on earth, and the top of it reached heaven: and behold the angels of God ascending and descending it. And, behold, the Lord stood above it, and said, "I am the Lord God of Abraham thy father, and the God of Issac; the land whereon thou liest, to thee will I give it, and to thy seed . . ." And Jacob awaked out of his sleep, and he said, "Surely the Lord is in this place . . . "(Gen. 11–16)

Bathing, the fundamental means of purification and rebirth, recalls the act of baptism. We cook with the fire that Prometheus stole from the gods. By eating the fruit of the tree in the midst of the Eden, the eyes of Adam and Eve were opened "as gods, knowing good and evil."

A house is a symbolic setting where we can re-enact sacred works and care for the full spectrum of the soul, a sacred place "where you find yourself again and again."

14. The Use of Plants for Transcendental Functions from the Black Sect Feng Shui Perspective

Linda Juratovac

Dedicated to Master Lin Yun, my teacher

Editor's Note

Linda Juratovac has been a professional horticulturist since 1973. She is co-owner of an East Bay landscape architectural firm and is also head landscape designer and horticultural consultant for the University of San Francisco's thirty-three acre campus. Linda began studying the traditional compass-astrology school of Feng Shui with J. S. Shiah in 1986. In 1987 she started her Black Sect Feng Shui studies with the Grand Master Thomas Lin Yun. She is a disciple of Master Lin and is in ongoing training with him and his senior disciple, Ho Lynn Tu. She is a Feng Shui consultant, working with interior and exterior environments for commercial and residential clients. She has documented all of her work and has hundreds of case studies on this subject. Linda's long-time study of Feng Shui makes her one of the most knowledgeable Black Sect Feng Shui practitioners in the United States today.

In this article Linda describes some of the basic principles of Black Sect Tantric Buddhism and how plants function within this system.

THROUGHOUT HISTORY, PLANTS have supported and strengthened mankind. They have provided food and clothing, as well as shelter from the weather and predators. Before chemical medicines were born, plants brought wellness to the body, mind, and spirit of souls in need.

As we progress through this century, people from Western cultures have lost awareness of the plants' true purposes and sacredness. It's unfortunate in contemporary culture that so many of us have lost contact with the wonder of nature and see plants only in terms of a few functions. Our landscapes have become a blur in our fast-paced lives. They are a meaningless background which we occasionally water when we have time.

In contrast to our limited approach, many cultures respect plants, appreciate their subtle qualities, and have developed hundreds of unorthodox uses for them. Throughout Asia, there is a wonderful form of geomancy called Feng Shui. It is the ancient Chinese art of harmonious placement, which dates back before 4000 B.C., and is still used today. The study of Feng Shui has evolved into a blend of design, ecology, mysticism, and common sense. It is both a very practical and highly spiritual art.

This sacred tradition is based on the concept of *ch'i,* or the vital life force, and acknowledges that every environment has an effect on its occupants, be it the interior of a building or an exterior plot of land. According to Feng Shui, when a town, a parcel of land, a placement of a building, or the layout within a building is positioned in harmony with nature, its occupants will prosper and enjoy a smooth and happy life. But when these elements are in disharmony with the natural forces, their lives become unbalanced, which results in constant struggle, misfortune, and ill health.

In the world of Feng Shui, there are many secret spiritual methods used to heal difficulties and enhance the environment. But before I explain these any further, I would like to provide you with:

An Introduction to the Black Sect School of Feng Shui

Professor Lin Yun is a highly spiritual being who has helped many people of all walks of life with his unlimited compassion and wisdom. He is solely responsible for bringing the Black Sect Tantric Buddhist Feng Shui teachings to the contemporary Western world.

It is important to note that within the study of Feng Shui, there are different schools which have originated in various locations throughout Asia. Many are still active in the world today. Some of these schools rely on very traditional practices such as the *Luopan,* or Chinese compass, as the main siting tool. Some lineages use the four absolute directions (north, south, east, west) as their guideline, while others adopt the use of objective shapes and tangible forms like a lot or house shape to determine a Feng Shui diagnosis.

The most unorthodox of all schools is the Black Sect Tantric Buddhist form of Feng Shui, which is the lineage from which I am writing. This oral tradition has been brought to the West by my teacher, Master Thomas Lin Yun. He is the Grand Master of Black Sect Feng Shui; he is also supreme head and spiritual leader of Tantric Buddhism, Black Sect. Master Lin Yun is a great scholar and is regarded as one of the leading contemporary Chinese philosophers in the world. He is the only source of the Black Sect Feng Shui teachings and is sought out by thousands of people all over the world. I am grateful for his teachings and invaluable guidance, which he has so generously offered me through the years.

Although other lineages are highly respected in the Black Sect school, there is one major difference between the other more traditional schools of Feng Shui and this particular form. The Black Sect lineage not only includes many thoughts, values, and practices from other traditional schools, but also explains and grounds its theories by incorporating modern fields of studies such as architecture, psychology, and scientific knowledge into its sacred teachings. It offers a graceful cultural bridge from East to West and provides remedies which are very practical. This sophisticated approach makes the ancient tradition highly effective for Westerners even though we are immersed in a rational culture and modern lifestyle.

Ch'i, the Foundation of Feng Shui

The theory of Ch'i is the foundation upon which all Black Sect Feng Shui is built. Before you can understand how these sacred cures heal many kinds of imbalances, you must first know a little of this theory.

Ch'i is the vital life force which is in us and all around us. It is in the power which creates thunder in the sky and causes volcanoes to erupt from the core of the earth. Ch'i is what keeps our hearts beating. If the ch'i in our bodies is strong, balanced, and circulating well, we will be strong and balanced. When the ch'i is blocked inside the body, illness, nervous habits, obsessions, and other imbalances may become apparent. Excessive anger or the inability to speak up for oneself are both symptoms of disharmonious ch'i in the body. If our ch'i is seriously blocked and does not flow on one side of the body, paralysis can occur on that side. And when our ch'i becomes too weak to pump our heart, the heart will stop, and death will occur.

Not only does ch'i circulate inside our bodies, it is all around us. If the ch'i does not move well in an environment, there will be a negative impact on those living or working in or near that space. In Black Sect Feng Shui, difficulties in the occupants' lives are evaluated in many ways, but a key factor will be the depth of unbalanced or negative ch'i existing in the environment. Strained relationships in the home or in the workplace, unexplained illness, unruly children, career problems, and financial difficulties are given serious attention as indicators of ch'i disturbances in the environment. The ch'i of a dwelling or workspace may be so evil that occupants become totally ineffective in their personal or professional lives; it becomes impossible for them to go forward, no matter how hard they work. If the imbalances are not corrected by a proper Feng Shui cure, the stress of this difficulty may eventually result in serious illness, financial ruin, or even death.

For a Feng Shui practitioner, the ability to read and understand ch'i is of the utmost importance. To know the appropriateness and correct placement of a sacred cure, one must develop the ability to read the ch'i of the people, environment, and situation. This skill takes years of study and rigorous internal practices bestowed by the Master and can make all the difference in a cure's successful outcome. Understanding the subtle depths of ch'i and how it affects our lives is a lifelong learning process.

Assessing the Ch'i of the Land

Feng Shui translates from the Chinese characters as "wind and water." If the Feng Shui is good, the winds are mild, the water is calm, the sun is bright, and the surrounding growth is lush. When earth ch'i, the vital force that carries the magma and water, is close to the surface of the land, life can prosper. But when earth ch'i is distant from the surface of the land, we may find water scarce, resulting in crops which will not flourish and support abundant life.

It is easy to see how people cluster naturally in areas with good ch'i. Many are intuitively attracted to a home or office built near a beautiful waterfront, surrounded by lush trees, or sited on a hill with a spectacular view. It is no secret that there is strong interest in acquiring land in which the ch'i is flourishing. Because of this universal desire, the land continues to be bought up, and built upon. It becomes more and more scarce and commands a top price almost anywhere.

In our urban areas, Feng Shui practitioners view the absence of plants as well as dead or declining growth as indicators that the ch'i of the land is weak. Blighted, depressed areas can easily permeate and bring down the good ch'i of adjacent neighborhoods. Living in or near these areas can be difficult on many levels. In Feng Shui terms, these environments may undermine well-being and severely limit the number of healthy opportunities available during the course of the occupancy.

Curing Maladies

In Black Sect Feng Shui, there are many methods to heal malevolent circumstances and bring harmony to people and places. Some of its centuries-old spiritual cures rely solely on secret meditations, while others involve the use of certain objects, usually backed by a special prayer for the highest effectiveness.

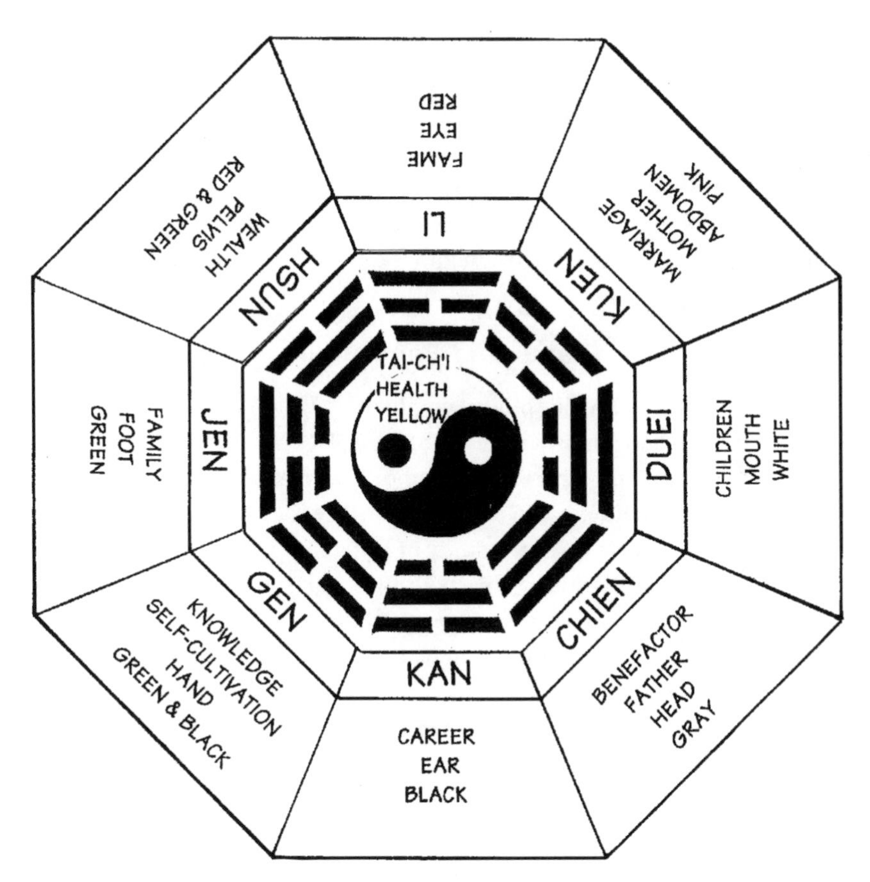

The Black Sect's Ever Changing Eight Triagrams or *Ba-gua* is a siting tool to align the practitioner with a structure, room, or parcel of land. It is used in place of the Luopan which is applied in more traditional forms of Feng Shui. This Ba-gua does not use the cardinal directions for diagnosis but emphasizes the placement of the main door for its orientation. It is one of the methods which identifies enhancing or detrimental shapes in an environment and helps resolve difficulties within a person's life.

Often these objects are placed in particular areas of a structure, on the land or on the body.

At times, the Ever Changing Eight Triagrams or Chinese Ba-gua may be used as a siting guide; while at other times a cure itself dictates the placement. The Ba-gua specifically used by the Black Sect, has eight segments plus the middle, which all relate to a person's life, and to parts of the body. Although it contains many other layers of information, I will focus on the segments which relate to the major domains of life. These segments are: wealth, fame, marriage, children, benefactors, career, knowledge, family, and health. There are certain colors that relate to each segment which can be implemented within a cure to increase its potency. Each segment on the Ba-gua is also associated with a part of the human body: hip, eye, abdomen, mouth, head, ear, hand, and foot. This layer of knowledge can be instrumental when a cure is needed to enhance or balance ch'i in the body during an illness. In a Feng Shui analysis the Black Sect Ba-gua is primarily a tool which is mentally superimposed over the lot or structure to determine conditions in the environment.

Plants and Feng Shui

Out of the myriad of tangible objects employed in Feng Shui, plants are placed high on the list as having many virtues. From the Black Sect's perspective, plants are regarded as one of the nine *Xie Zi* methods, which adjust static states of a human body, a life situation, or an environment. The *Xie Zi* method or "method of minor additions" is a part of the study of Feng Shui which teaches one how to work with sacred and ordinary objects as tools, to change negative forces into positive ch'i. With the correct cure, four ounces of a minor addition is strong enough to deflect a thousand pounds of bad influence.

While the list of minor additions is extensive, there are a few objects that are more frequently used than others. Most anyone who is familiar with Feng Shui understands that mirrors are popular because they are suitable for many types of difficult situations. Wind chimes, flutes, and faceted crystal balls are also preferred tools of the Black Sect lineage. The application of plants for transcendental functions, however, is one of the most dynamic and fascinating of all the minor additions. I must confess I am especially interested because I've been in the horticultural profession for more than twenty years, and I see that Master Lin's lineage has a solid handle on the deep and essential nature of plants.

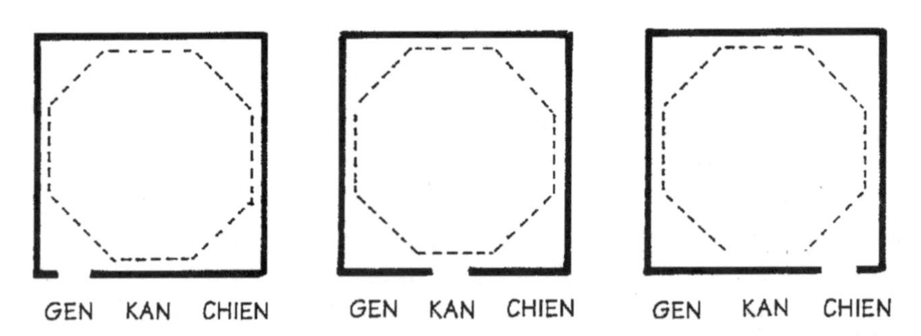

The Ba-gua is always placed with the Gen, Kan, and Chien positions on the wall of the main entry or at the base of the lot where an entrance is located.

Plant Placement in the Outdoor Environment

Plants can address a broad range of difficulties in the Black Sect tradition. They may be used in sacred cures which involve strengthening or restoring the vital life force to a situation which requires an infusion of uplifting ch'i. They can help move stagnant energy, whether it's in the body, home, workspace, or on the land. They provide a cooling effect when there is an imbalance of too much fire ch'i in a particular area, and can also balance a stubborn disposition in a person's character. It is their vital life force which gives them such an important role in this spiritual tradition.

When a plot of land or a structure is awkwardly shaped or incomplete, it may bring disharmony to its occupants. Missing *guas* are seen as devoid of ch'i, and the vital life force must be added to restore harmony to the missing positions. Very often, when people remodel their homes and offices, they create new Feng Shui problems. Once-balanced shapes become lopsided and deficient of vital ch'i. When the integrity of the shape is disrupted in the remodeling process, we see consequences in the affected areas. Additions frequently create missing wealth and marriage corners. When the *Hsun gua* (wealth corner) is absent in a structure, these construction projects may run on forever, with frequent change orders and unforeseen costs. These major overruns eventually erode the occupants' financial savings, sometimes halting the project before it is completed.

Most building architects and contractors know divorce is a common hazard in remodeling projects. Some whisper and joke about the couple's capacity to survive the remodel. Little do the architects know that they may be contributing to their clients' destiny. If a designer/contractor adds twenty-five feet to a forty-foot-wide structure, he has, in fact, taken away a necessary corner. When the designer takes out the marriage gua, he has just added another obstacle; the couple rarely makes it through the remodeling project without separation or divorce.

A Woman's Cure

In the following drawing, the residence is missing the *kuen gua*, which relates to marriage in a home, and partnership in an office building. Frequently, when this gua is absent, we find a repeated history indicating numerous divorces or dissolved partnerships. In my work I often see homes that are devoid of the kuen gua. After many years I began calling them "divorce houses," but divorce is not the only difficulty in a house of this shape. On a deeper level, the kuen position also relates to the female and mother of the household. Patterns I notice quite often include the women of the house not being supported, heard, or seen as valuable,

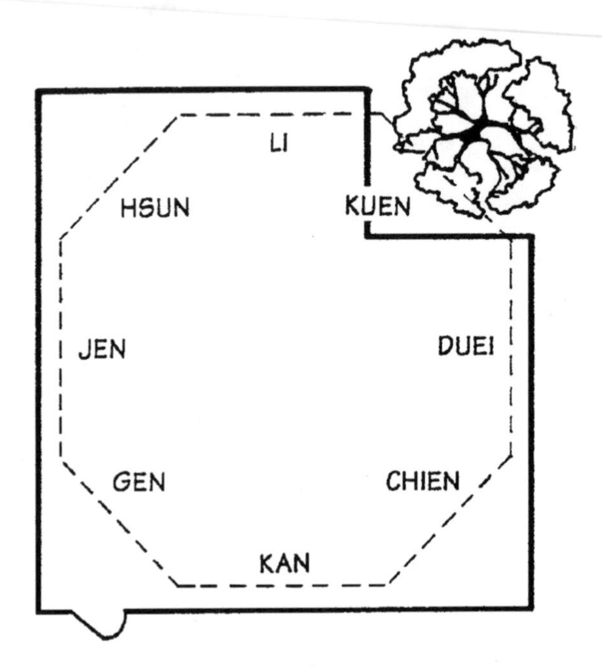

thus they are taken for granted. I see the women in these structures living with various degrees of abuse—physical or mental or both. Many times they have no careers and are stuck because they are not supported by their family, friends, community—in general, not supported by the universe. They have no place to go and no way out. They can have health problems related to the abdominal area, which may be difficult for them or their doctors to cure.

When a tree taller than the height of the owner is planted in this corner, the life force comes back to this area balancing the women and the marriage relationship. This remedy transcendentally connects the areas devoid of ch'i to the remaining areas which are whole. If one selected a tree that produced pink flowers, this would add more potency to this cure because the color pink relates in a sacred way to the kuen gua. When the vital life force is added to the kuen gua, healings can occur. The female of the house becomes empowered to go forward on her path. Even though there are other methods used to resolve this difficulty, I favor planting a tree whenever appropriate, as it also benefits our environment by helping to purify the atmosphere.

Note: I've seen all kinds of healings come in many ways after performing Feng Shui cures, including physical healings. Miracles? Yes, sometimes, but more frequently what happens is that a knowledgeable doctor or health practitioner comes on the scene. Sometimes the healing is gradual; sometimes it's just a matter of a doctor finding an error or trying a new approach. It also requires the patients' support and belief in themselves and in the Feng Shui. Balancing and enhancing a structure can also bring power and clarity to the sick person which enables her to seek out the right help—karma permitting.

Men who are single and live in a building with the kuen gua missing usually stay single. I've seen some of the nicest men have the worst luck finding the right woman when their kuen gua is missing. Their hopes for a comfortable relationship with a supportive mate are futile.

Family Support: Those Who Stand Behind You

In the Chinese culture there is a great emphasis placed on the support of the family and friends. The thought of all the burdens of daily life being placed on one family member without the help of others to lighten the load is a difficult concept for the traditional Chinese to comprehend. After all, without support, life is a slow uphill struggle and eventually one gets weary of the load. In our individualistic society, many people have moved away from their families and bear the responsibility of the daily chores (cooking, cleaning, washing, child care, etc.) alone while trying to make a living. I frequently observe people who are so overloaded with their daily tasks that they cannot explore new interests or pursue their hearts' desires. Many times these people make little headway in their careers or study because they are so occupied with the basic survival chores. They are unhappy, and their health is stressed. These people might benefit from a Feng Shui cure which brings family and friends to their aid. The placement of plants at the very back of the plot is an important remedy to help alleviate isolation and lack of support. When planting a tall hedge row or community of trees at the back of a lot, it's important to consider their size as they mature in relationship to the existing environment. Be mindful of proper scale.

Plants As Guardians Of An Entry

For centuries trees have been used to flank each side of entryways to protect the dwelling from maligned ch'i. In many traditions and folk cultures all over the world, trees protect the entire property, the threshold, and the home. They might be seen as soldiers or warriors guarding the door. Accidents and many kinds of misfortune can be dispelled by these guardians.

At the Yun Lin Temple in Berkeley, California, which is Master Lin's home base, there are two very large deodar cedars growing on either side of the stairway. These powerful trees lift the ch'i up into the heavens, supporting one's ascent up the long flight of stairs and also aiding the temple itself. They resemble a hostess welcoming the many guests who come to visit. These particular trees have a very special meaning, and they were an omen which played a part in

Professor Lin's decision to locate his temple here. Because Professor Lin's first name means "cloud" in Chinese, and his last name means "forest," these two cedars at the bottom of the main stairway suggest a forest reaching to the clouds, a very supportive path for Master Lin and his work.

Hillside Homes

In mountainous areas like the California coast, structures are built on top of hills in order to gain the widest perspective and most beautiful views. Sometimes these structures are built in a way that causes one to experience a feeling of instability, as if in danger of falling over a cliff. A grove of tall trees reaching high up to the sky planted at the base of the hill is a traditional Black Sect cure raising the ch'i and giving a feeling of support to stabilize the occupants.

Cul-De-Sac Ch'i

For the last several years it has been popular to build homes in clusters, creating numerous cul-de-sacs within large main housing developments. These small cozy neighborhoods offer residents a sense of peace, community, and security as they deflect through traffic and reduce crime by giving only those who live there or visit a reason to enter. However, Feng Shui regards the cul-de-sac as a place which moves the quickly flowing ch'i into it without having a natural way for the ch'i to flow out. When it does not have a straight path to flow in and out, it gets caught at the end of a cul-de-sac resulting in damage to those who are in its path. In order to release the energy in a healthy way, a tree placed at the end of the cul-de-sac lifts the ch'i upwards, thus allowing for a healthier flow.

Improper Plant Placement

Trees planted directly in front of doorways block ch'i. For example, in a West Coast Chinatown, street trees were being vandalized to a high extent. Puzzled tree crews kept replacing them in their inauspicious positions. The local residents

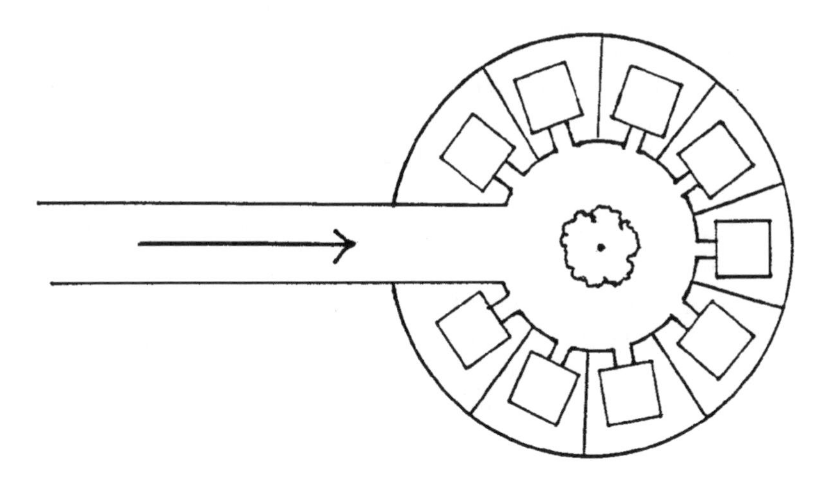

Cul-De-Sac Ch'i.

were insulted rather than grateful when new trees were planted in front of their doors. The newly installed trees continued to be vandalized. After all, they were positioned in a way to block the flow of ch'i or good opportunities from coming into their doorways. At last the city began to meet with the people in the community to discuss their cultural differences.

Trees leaning on a structure indicate pressure to occupants. A family I met had recently moved into a new home. They hadn't been there for very long when their money became very unstable. This professional family saw clients in their home and began to experience unexpected problems around their money such as bounced clients' checks and last-minute cancellations of appointments. This family was quickly losing financial ground. I was not surprised to see a large pine tree in the wealth position of their property leaning quite severely. In this case, according to the Feng Shui tradition, removal of this tree was in order, especially since there was another stronger, upright pine in competition with it, also in the wealth position. Horticulturally, the leaning pine was causing damage to the upright pine which was doubly threatening to their financial situation. They agreed to cut the tree. On top of the stump a potted plant was placed to encourage rising vital ch'i.

Note: Removal of trees requires special Feng Shui rituals to prevent the spirit of the tree from harming you. Specific blessings are performed on the tree: it's removal should be marked for an auspicious day. It is recommended that dead and dying plants be removed from the soil, as the negative dead ch'i should not be left on the property to linger. Accumulating inauspicious ch'i can affect the residents adversely.

The eerie sound of plants brushing against the house and frightening the inhabitants on a stormy night has been used in many a scary movie. In real life such sounds can create a very unsettling feeling, interrupting sleep or interfering with relaxation. In Feng Shui terms a tree or shrub looming over the house oppresses one's ch'i. If the tree is located near a window, it may block out the natural light and constrict the flow of ch'i. Conscientious pruning is a simple way to solve this problem.

Dark gloomy spaces which allow no natural light can be unhealthy and give off a constricted, cold, lifeless feeling, eventually leading to depression. On a mundane level these spaces breed mold and accumulate dust, which are taxing to the immune system. Over time, luck and opportunities, as well as health, decline.

Thresholds

What is the most heavenly, uplifting addition to a property that can give you almost immediate results? The fragrance of lovely flowers as you walk up the path, cross the courtyard into your apartment, or step into your foyer. Flowers have been used in all cultures for rituals of romance and ceremony as well as everyday occasions. Sweetly scented and brightly colored plants in the entryway can be immediately powerful, reassuring, and delightful. For me, it's nature welcoming me home after being out in the world. Plants also invite those who are not familiar with the space to feel more comfortable.

A Feng Shui cure which any one can use both to make their home more appealing or to attract potential buyers is to place pots of brightly colored flowers at the entryway. The presence of favorite flowers brings nature in, fills the space with positive ch'i, and solidifies one's relationship with the space. A client of mine is a well-known real estate broker in the Bay Area. Her reputation as a good seller is based not only on her ability to work well with her clients but also how she stages the homes she sells. *Staging* in the real estate business is defined as how one arranges the objects in a home to enhance the existing architecture or just uplift the feeling of the space. (Sounds like Feng Shui to me.) This agent can stage a home so well that she draws interested buyers very quickly. After viewing many homes, the one that may stand out or be the most distinctive in the potential buyer's memory is the one that was well-staged.

Transcendental Uses of Plants in Interior Environments

In the world of Feng Shui, no building is ever perfect unless it is built by a highly sensitive and extremely aware individual and/or a seasoned Feng

Shui practitioner. Even the most highly prized homes by famous architects and builders can be filled with imbalances that will eventually effect the ch'i of the occupants. Placement of rooms, doors, stoves, fireplaces, staircases, furnaces, etc., are critical elements when considering the delicate balance and flow of ch'i in an environment, and how well the residents will function in it day after day. When imbalances are built into the structure, Feng Shui can be used to bring wholeness and balance back to the space, thus allowing the lives of the inhabitants to smooth out and expand in a positive way.

As soon as we build walls, we cut ourselves off from our close relationships with nature. As a result we've lost touch with the plants which were our guardians, allies, healers, and companions. By severing our selves from nature, we have distanced ourselves from the vital life force. The small, inward, cavelike structures in which we spend most of our time are far more constricting than we realize. Our relationship with nature puts us in touch with the vital life force of the universe.

On the mundane level, most of our interior walls are hard and angular. For most of us this flatness and blandness dulls our senses. When we are cooped up in a small space for long periods of time, we turn ourselves off because it's difficult to feel alive and thrive. In the workplace, I see so many people confined to small cubicles and offices with no windows. Stagnant spaces breed frustrated people who eventually get sick or numb, or they become aggressive and take it out on others. Some become anxious, like caged animals who are always trying to escape. This condition is expensive emotionally and financially for both employers and employees. Confining people to small spaces constricts the flow of their vital ch'i.

When plants are brought into interiors, they can soften walls as well as the whole environment. The depth and texture they bring is essential because they transform the area into a multidimensional space, enhancing our vitality, nurturing our senses and increasing our productivity. They are very effective in bringing the great power of nature—its depth, textures, movement, and immensity—into the ordinary configuration of four walls. By introducing plants into the interior environment, you allow the sacred to be a part of daily life.

Feng Shui in the Office

I once worked with a woman named Cindy whose office was so small there was no place for plants. She was discontent and would have liked her job more if her desk was positioned somewhere in the rainforest. Although I would have loved to oblige her, the cramped space would not allow for even the simplest Feng Shui cure of a potted plant. When we put up a poster of the rainforest, we were able to give Cindy a taste of the part of nature she loved. Though this was nowhere near the real thing, it helped her remember herself throughout the day. This was an important issue, because when Cindy forgot herself at work, she became numb and didn't know what she needed to do to take care of herself when she went home at night. If Cindy didn't remember how to care properly for herself, she could not renew herself for the next day. This is one reason why corporate people get so run down. They work so hard, often in confining spaces, and stop listening to themselves until a crisis interrupts their pattern.

Balancing Interior Structures

The following Feng Shui cure is a prime example of a way plants can be used to uplift the ch'i in a space. In the Black Sect tradition, bedrooms built above a garage can pose many difficulties. The garage is often viewed as a space that harbors low or stagnant ch'i because it is usually not lived in. Unfortunately, many houses and apartments are built this way without consideration for the effect on residents' well-being. An important Feng Shui cure for this difficult situation is to paint an image of a tree inside the garage and top it off with images of foliage, flowers, or fruit on the walls of the bedroom. When they are blooming and the tree is supporting this growth from below, the vital life force in the bedroom or the studio above will be uplifted, thus helping the ch'i and health of the occupants. It is not always necessary to paint an image of a real tree; one may simply rely on colors to symbolize a strong tree. For example, one might paint the garage walls brown and the bedroom green, decorated with red flowers or red light bulbs resembling fruits.

When an interior stairway is positioned too close to a main doorway, one's savings are believed to be lost easily because money flows quickly down the stairs and right out the door. Plants should be located near the bottom step to keep earnings from slipping away.

Personal Cures for a Heart's Desire

In the interior, plants are used to give vitality to areas one desires to enhance. When one wishes to uplift a portion of their personal life such as their financial position, educational opportunities, or a child's health, a plant may be positioned in that area of the Ba-gua in the environment.

Personality Differences

Interior plant placement can help balance personality differences of family members or housemates sharing the same space. Dolores and Joseph moved into a new house. Their old residence was a tiny home which constricted their lives in many ways. When they moved into a more spacious home, they began to see their personal characteristics more clearly. I believe this was because the open living space gave them a wider, more expansive perspective on their inner qualities and life in general. Subtle aspects of their personalities became more apparent. Dolores' character was built with more exterior strength and aggression than her partner. Joseph's ch'i was smoother and softer, offering more interior strength, not so obvious to the outside world. This was not always to his advantage, as he ran a business and was at times too lenient with his employees. His personality needed more exterior stability to give him additional backbone and respect at work. Dolores was a bit too rigid, and for her health and for spiritual reasons she would be better off becoming softer and more flexible.

To help balance this couple I suggested they place nine plants in their bedroom and gave them a sacred Feng Shui prayer to recite. As time goes by, Dolores' spirit gets softer and more fluid, while Joseph's ch'i improves in a way which allows him to be more self-aware and effective with his employees and clients. Their relationship continues to grow more harmonious because Joseph has become more present and supportive and Dolores is softer and more open towards him.

Plant Allies in a Sick Room

It is customary to send plants and flowers to friends and loved ones when they are in the hospital. Instinctively, we know plants give vital life force to a sick room or hospital room. The Feng Shui perspective is that plants encourage the ill person's ch'i to rise so good health can take hold. Flowers bring joy, liveliness, and hope to the person convalescing; they also inspire the staff and visitors.

It's important for health practitioners as well as their patients that medical offices and waiting rooms be balanced with good ch'i. Many health facilities I've visited have a feeling of stagnation, which brings out dullness and other stale qualities in staff and patients alike. Dead and ailing plants are surprisingly common in these environments. In the Feng Shui tradition, what you see when you walk through the door is believed to have a great effect on a person. Imagine what patients feel when the first thing they see when they walk into the office is a dying parlor palm or ficus tree. Seeing a dying plant can bring a foreboding feeling to the patient and undermine the sense of trust in the practitioner's expertise.

One rule of thumb for health professionals is to immediately remove any plant that looks less than healthy. If they keep dying, keep replacing them. One doctor told me that after his most ill patients left his office his large Schefflera would drop its leaves and go into decline. He needed to replace it every few months. Investing in lush greenery is beneficial on many levels.

A Word about Feng Shui and Plants from a Practical Perspective

I see many clients who swear they have black thumbs and are not successful at growing plants. I also visit windowless offices and rooms where natural light is not plentiful. In these environments there may be difficulties which can be remedied or enhanced by the use of the vital life force of plants. In the Feng Shui cures, plants that won't thrive should be avoided. When the ch'i of the land is low, even house plants will struggle to stay alive. Dying plants in your environment are a very inauspicious thing.

I suggest you consider silk plants to place in those difficult areas. The floral industry is creating great reproductions these days, and it is becoming more difficult to tell the silks from the real. This is very good from the Feng Shui point of view because although they seem real, silk plants never die.

Last week I asked my husband to water the houseplants. Although he forgot a few of the real plants, all the silks were watered very well! Does this mean the silks look more real than the real ones? Horrors!

Another option is to co-mingle silks with real. This is a very effective way to enjoy lush plants with half the care, for those who wish to use some live ones but can't handle the upkeep for more than a few. If you place pots of real plants with silk plants, most people assume they are all real. I use this technique in my horticulture practice with much success when environmental conditions are less than ideal. A few years ago I saw a group of Japanese tourists in front of a planting which soared two stories high inside a well-known San Francisco hotel. For half an hour they carried on a spirited discussion which involved touching the leaves of as many plants as possible. They seemed puzzled that a planting of this scale was so immaculate and lush. The numerous silks interspersed were enough to keep the maintenance very low. Just a few live plants were strategically placed to command the eye so one would see them first and automatically assume they were all live. It's a trick of the trade that is just as effective in the home.

Conclusion

In this article I've only begun to give a taste of the ways plants are used in the Black Sect Feng Shui tradition. I have written this to help the reader to see the importance of nature-in-balance and how proper placement of plants can make a positive difference. I believe it is more important to introduce the philosophy of Feng Shui than list formulaic cures for every problem. The ability to properly read the ch'i of the land, a space, a situation, or person is far more important than finding a "quick fix." Because Black Sect Feng Shui is site-specific, formula cures can only be as successful as the practitioner's depth of intuition and training. Black Sect Feng Shui is an oral tradition, and as with most oral traditions, there are many subtle aspects which books cannot convey. Often the most significant information is transmitted to a disciple directly from the Master. This is the juice that gives one the ability to make the cures work.

In China, an herbal apprentice may sweep the floors for years before being allowed to touch the herbs or ask any questions. In our culture this practice may seem like deprivation of knowledge. Because we are in such a hurry, sweeping the floor strikes us as boring, repetitive, and "a waste of our precious time." In reality, the time spent in the Master's environment allows the student to become acquainted with the subtleties and essences of the herbs and the teaching without outward distractions. The apprentice has plenty of time to observe, feel, and witness the many complex dimensions of this healing art. Even though Feng Shui has arrived in the United States and there are many practitioners, it is still valuable to study with an authentic Master. This is because there are very few seasoned practitioners of the Master who can teach in a complete way. It's important to work hard to reach a place where one can receive the sacred information and be wise enough to appreciate it.

I believe Master Lin Yun's intent is to inspire as many people as possible to help themselves. In his teaching he emphasizes that we learn to be patient and continue to study diligently so we become deeply familiar with the material. He also gives us his full blessing to practice what we know of the Feng Shui and Black Sect teachings for ourselves and our immediate family and friends. He places importance on being clear about what we know and not to practice with information of which we are uncertain. Being centered in the heart and practicing from a place of compassion and a sincere desire to help others brings the highest results.

I have documented my Feng Shui work and have hundreds of case studies. I have found this work to be very successful for most of my clients. The information in this article comes from careful observation of how this ancient tradition fits into and can be applied to our culture. Most of my work comes from repeat clients whom I have had the opportunity to watch over time. As the Feng Shui deepens, they progress into even better balance. This long-term approach allows me to see how Feng Shui has helped transform their lives. Sometimes good situations come about immediately, and sometimes the benefits of the cures are very subtle and occur gradually.

In closing, I encourage you to become more aware of how your environment affects you and those around you. If you meditate, do it before you go out into the world, so you will be more sensitive to the ch'i around you. Allow yourself to take a walk in your neighborhood with soft eyes and notice the differences between that area and a park or forest. When you pass through blighted neighborhoods, notice the amount of hardscape that exists in relationship to greenery. What shape are the plants in? Pay attention to how work and living spaces affect you and others, noting how well you function in them and how smoothly things get accomplished there. Allow yourself the freedom to move some furniture around. Clear out clutter, open up congested spaces so you can move more freely from place to place. Every time you make a change in your environment, observe how it influences you.

15. House Reading: A Spiritual Approach to Residential Design in Traditional Japan

Fumio Suda and Colin Carpenter

Editor's Note

The spiritual parent of modern architecture and design is the ancient art of geomancy. Long dismissed as superstition, in recent years an increasing number of people all around the world are returning to consult the ancient methods for aligning human life with the cosmos and the earth. The following article contains a brief history and context for Japanese geomancy, Kaso. *What would make a fascinating study would be to compare and contrast the various geomancies of the world, seeking the common elements of wisdom shared by all.*

IN THE WEST, where the rapidity of technological advance has engendered sweeping social dislocation, the connection between architecture and society has become somewhat difficult to trace. Analysis has tended to concentrate on the material dimension in building, on relating it to highly abstract systems, and on considerations of style. In Japan, despite the influx of Western influence and the rise of technology, society remains homogenous, and the heritage of centuries of isolated development is still strong. Architecture figures prominently in the dynamic of an integrated culture. Analysis of traditional Japanese architecture, undertaken without reference to the enveloping culture, can hardly convey the essential quality of Japanese buildings.

Among the peoples of the East, particularly those of China and Japan, there exists an ancient architectural tradition of divining applied to design. Diviners typically approach their work using a methodology of involved calculation and numerical relation, or predicate their conclusions on highly refined and intensely developed powers of observation. The actual efficacy of divinatory procedures is a moot issue. Far from being an atavism of superstition or a curious aside, these procedures comprise an applied art and have been derived from the natural philosophies of that cultural system and centuries of careful observation. They hold considerable wisdom, regardless of whether they fit easily into a modern scientific paradigm.

Kaso, Japanese House Reading

By employing an obscure text, relating to the siting and construction of residential buildings, a Japanese "House Reader" makes determinations about the health and prosperity of the occupants. House Reading is the analysis of the human habitat using the criteria of elemental relation and correspondence. It seeks to engender within the envelope of the house a harmonious proportion of subtle preternatural energies. Among the tools of analysis is a decided appreciation of the inexorable influence of time, the fourth dimension of building. Relations are expressed symbolically and carry the authority of generations of unself-conscious holistic dwelling. The Japanese call it *Kaso,* a character having two components. *Ka* is "house" with a strong connotation of the surrounding site. A somewhat elusive term, *so* is translated as "phase," referring to the time of year or season, though it seems to refer to the unseen dynamics generating natural phenomena and not to the phenomena itself.

Our concern is a theoretic examination of the House Reading tradition. Throwing aside a predisposition toward the discursive methods of Western science, we ask: Do these beliefs represent a cogent and rational architectural program? What is their origin, and what is the relevance of the tradition of our age? Perhaps implicit in these prescriptions is the irreducible wisdom of the relations obtaining between people and their shelters.

In our research to identify and understand the legacy of the past, we are happy to acknowledge the invaluable assistance and inspiration afforded us by Messrs. Kenneth Isaacs, Michael Lazar, John Syvertsen, and Neil Tryba.

Principles

Looking at nature, we find that many creatures know the right time to do the right thing at the right place. Birds know when to make their nests and when to begin their long migratory journeys. Trees know when to germinate, when to cast flowers, and when to let fall their leaves. Long ago in the nearly immemorial annals of our history, human intercourse paralleled the seasonal rhythms of nature. A man built his house in accordance with the mute testimony of Heaven and thereby achieved correspondence with the universal energies. Taboos, an arcane code fully intelligible only to the initiated, deposit an essential and inescapable connection from cosmos to peoples, between which, typically, the house acts as intermediary, a kind of filter screening and reverberating the invisible animation of Earth and stars. These taboos appear superstitious and are sometimes called "mysterious instructions handed down from the past." However, history indicates that they are derived from three ancient Chinese philosophical traditions: the Five Momentum Theory, the Nine Star Theory, and the *I Ching*, which are believed to reveal deep truths about the way the universe works.

The Chinese developed the Five Momentum Theory by carefully observing the five planets visible to the eye; Mercury, Venus, Mars, Jupiter, and Saturn. As there are five planets, there are five and only five universal elements; water, metal, fire, wood, and soil. Among these elements, there are the following generative relations:

wood generates fire	wood destroys soil
fire generates soil	fire destroys metal
soil generates metal	soil destroys water
metal generates water	metal destroys wood
water generates wood	water destroys fire

Further, the theory associates these five elements with the cardinal points of the compass, where:

north corresponds to water	northeast corresponds to soil
east corresponds to wood	southeast corresponds to wood
south corresponds to fire	southwest corresponds to soil
west corresponds to metal	northwest corresponds to metal

and the center corresponds to soil.

Following this theory, the functional components of the house (bathroom, bedroom, kitchen, etc.) are arranged so that, in plan, there is harmony with the cardinal distribution of the five universal elements.

Prerequisite to an application of this theory is the interpretation of these functional components in elemental terms. The kitchen is a place of fire. It is, therefore, equated with fire and is oriented so that fire does not conflict with another universal element. The kitchen, for instance, is not related to the west. From the theory, we know that the west corresponds to metal and fire destroys metal, consequently, a kitchen to the west occasions conflict between metal and fire. Among the prohibitions of the taboos are several which warn against having a kitchen to the west. In this instance, there is an apparent empirical reason supporting the taboo: a western kitchen catches the afternoon sun, thus increasing the danger of food spoilage. What about the bathroom? The elemental equation of that function is of course, water. Water, by the theory, destroys fire and the cardinal association of fire is the south. Therefore, to avoid conflict between

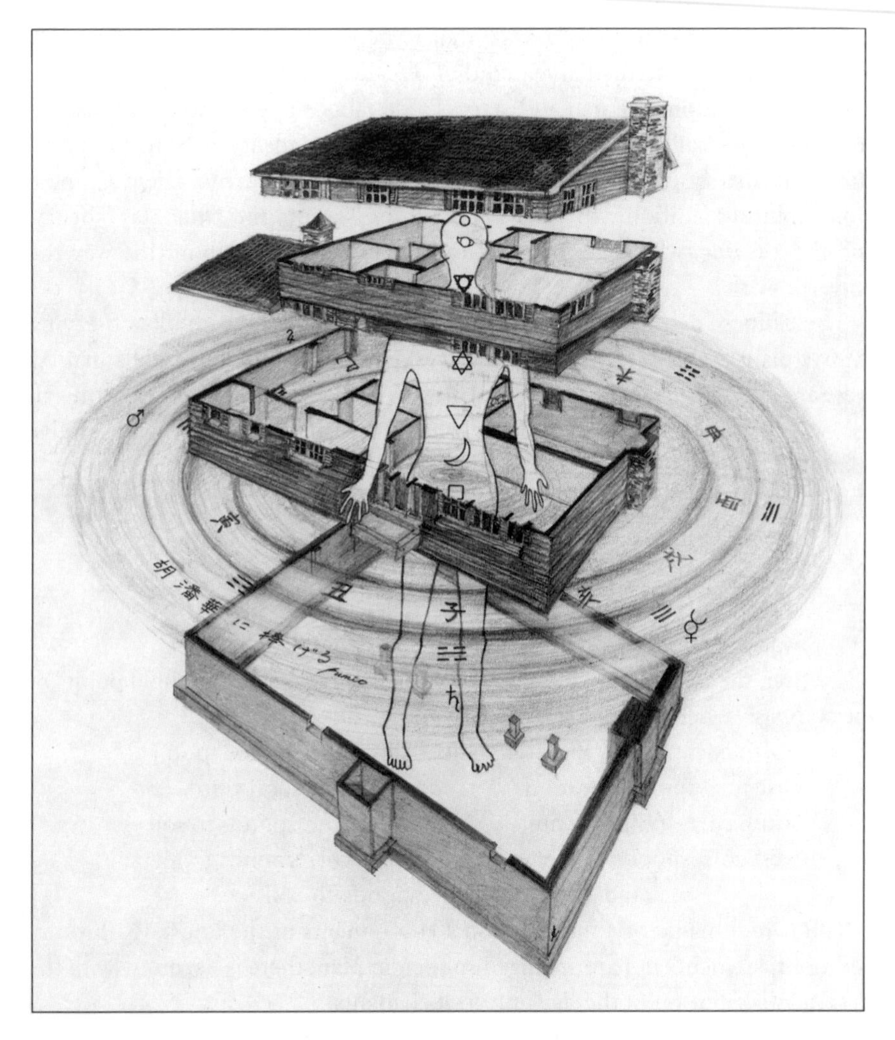

Entry: A scientific application of Feng Shui.

water and fire, do not put the WC to the south. Again, there are taboos warning against this. The idea here is to have harmony among the elements. Harmony engenders health; conflict, particularly of universal elements, brings dysfunction.

Another principle of the taboos is the Nine Star Theory. This theory is very similar to Western astrology yet uses a magic nine-square (like a tic-tac-toe game) which changes according to the changes of time. The squares are identified by number and color. Each individual is assigned to a particular number, according to his or her birthday. The cardinal directions also have numbers depending on the time of day, month, year, etc. People use this method to analyze lucky direction and unlucky direction for each individual on a certain occasion. Since House Reading is a result of analyzing cardinal direction as well as the occupant in the house, the Nine Star Theory is one of the bases of the House Reading tradition. Since there are nine numbers, there are possible nine completely distinct nine-squares, every square having a unique assignment.

By equating it with a compass, the paradigmatic nine-square becomes a spacial entity allowing its relation to the Five Momentum Theory. This theory is also from Chinese astrology. The Chinese developed a system analysis which encompasses five basic factors of phenomena, including the five basic tastes, which are sweet, salty, spicy, bitter, and sour. A combination of five tastes creates a particular taste in a food; the combination of five different forces creates a particular pheonomena in life. Here again, the harmony and modest mixture of the forces are the ideal. The associations between the nine-square and the Five Momentum Theory are as follows:

Number (Nine Star)	*Orientation* (Interface)	*Element* (Five Momentum)
One	North	Water
Eight	Northeast	Soil
Three	East	Wood
Four	Southeast	Wood
Nine	South	Fire
Two	Southwest	Soil
Seven	West	Metal
Six	Northwest	Metal
Five	Center	Soil

The *I Ching*, preeminent among the seminal influences, completes the picture. It introduces yet another array of associative relations while intimating a methodology of analysis. The *I Ching* or "Book of Changes" deals with change, not-change, chance, and simplicity. Its vehicles are the eight primary trigrams which generate sixty-four hexagrams. The trigrams, like the paradigmatic nine-square, are ranged about the compass. The orientation of trigrams and relevant associations to the Nine Star and Five Momentum theories are as follows:

The function of time in conditioning circumstance is the core of the *I Ching*. Attributed to every moment is a particular quality. The quality of the moment qualifies the events of that moment. It is the king of simultaneous causality in which the antecedent of the totality of events is a given of the moment itself. In that moment there is one future; in the next moment, there is another. Far from being exclusively quantitative, time becomes the fountainhead of the qualitative universe.

Orientation	*Trigram*	*Name Attribute*	*Family Relation*	*Corporal Assignment*
Northwest	The Creative	strong	father	head, neck, face, lungs, bones
Southwest	The Receptive	devoted	mother	stomach, spleen, flesh, ribs
East	The Arousing	movement	first son	liver, feet, hands, hair, throat
North	The Abysmal	dangerous	second son	blood, kidneys, spine, joints, genitals
Northeast	The Keeping	resting	third son	back, waist, nose, fingers, legs
Southeast	The Gentle	penetrating	first daughter	thighs, nervous system, intestines
South	The Clinging	light-giving	second daughter	eyes, heart, breasts
West	The Joyous	joyful	third daughter	tongue, teeth, chest, saliva

At birth by virtue of the singularity of the moment, every individual is given a nine-square which immediately is set in unique rotation through time. The aspect of an individual is inextricably entwined with the particular rotation of his nine-square.

In House Reading, there are fixed relations and variable circumstance. The relations of the Five Momentum Theory and the I Ching are constant. The conditions of site, structure, and occupants are constantly changing. A House Reader's virtuosity consists in superimposing one system upon another, of adjustment and emphasis, until the revelatory content of a complex web of associations is discerned. It is like piecing together a four-dimensional puzzle, its elements existing in space, but being profoundly conditioned by time. The taboos are generalizations derived from the repeatedly confirmed findings of House Readers.

History

Lao Tzu, a revered Chinese sage reputed to have lived in the sixth century B.C., said "the reality of the vessel is the void within it." The reality of traditional Japanese architecture is not only the material or technique it employs, but is found fully in its assertion of a subliminal dimension to building. One is obliged to imagine design reaching beyond the customary three dimensions. Design encompassing the plenum of processes assures health and prosperity. Taboos express the mechanics of achieving a completely integrated built environment. When we speak of the harmony of Japanese architecture, its sympathetic relation with nature, we owe it in general to the Eastern preoccupation with the immaterial and in particular to these rules.

Like much of the early culture of Japan, the taboos were carried over from China, probably by an itinerant Buddhist monk in the last decades of the sixth century. Under the regency of Shotokutaishi (593 to his death in 621), the Japanese established a government department, the purview of which included weather forecasting, disaster control, calendar revision, astronomy and astrology, and supervision of architectural projects. Having the official title "On Yo," this department had exclusive custody of the taboos and was responsible for their application in government construction. It is curious to observe the close association of architecture with the disciplines of speculative physics and even mysticism. The On Yo was disbanded circa 950.

In 794, the imperial capital was moved to Kyoto, where it remained until the Meiji Restoration of 1868. The official chronicles reveal that the On Yo consulted the taboos in siting the new city and that the taboos were then employed in designing imperial residences. According to the taboos, it is best to site a city where there is a hill to the north, a flat plane to the south, water in the east, and a heavily traveled road to the west. Kyoto is so sited, and some explain the long and happy history of the city by observing the correspondence between the city plan and the taboos. Peking, another city with a particularly stable history, was designed according to Feng Shui (the Chinese equivalent of House Reading) and was an inspiration in the planning of Kyoto.

The taboos, time and again, warn against the northeast and with somewhat less urgency against the southwest. Thus, the northeast to southwest axis is dangerous. The northeast is called "The Gate of the Devil" and the southwest is called "The Backdoor of the Devil." The northeast is associated with volition which across the spectrum of Eastern thought has strong negative connotations. Among the curious episodes of Kyoto's early history is the riot of the monks. The city fathers, to combat the pernicious attributes of the northeast, decided to locate the city's temple precinct in that quadrant. Nevertheless, there was trouble, ostensibly political, and a riot ensued. The monks ran amuck, putting entire districts to the torch, plundering, harassing men and women alike. The incident is often used by proponents of taboos to verify the wickedness of the northeast. House Readers in fact counsel against placement of significant spaces, projections, or openings either to the northeast or southwest.

The imperial house, realizing their significance, held a monopoly over the taboos until the early seventeenth century when a usurping Shogunate insisted on their dissemination. Within decades, the first books about House Readings were published. House Reading became increasingly popular particularly among the rising merchants. Carpenters having experience of imperial architecture were able to enlarge the scope of the tradition by applying it to emerging styles of residential construction. Though the emperor's advisors were deprived of authority, access to the taboos was restricted. It happened that hereditary families of carpenters became the new guardians from whose ranks are descended the House Readers of today.

The underlying impetus of House Reading's growing popularity was the cessation of strife among the Samurai. The people, rich and poor alike, were in a position to devote their energies to domestic matters. The highest quality, the imperial standard, was demanded of residential construction. Since imperial architecture utilized the taboos, so too would others. Taboos have little to do with style and were employed across the breadth of an extensively stratified society by farmers, artisans, the Samurai, the emperor, and merchants. Feudal law enforced distinctions among these groups, even obliging each to maintain a separate architectural style. The taboos enjoyed their greatest popularity between 1700 and 1850. During the 1850s, Japan discovered the West. From that time, the House Reading tradition, the cause of which was championed by Japan's highly skilled carpenters, waged a losing battle against the Western notion of building, personified, of course, by the architect.

House Reading is not a rigid tradition. Like other cultural phenomena, it is subject to change. The taboos, upon their introduction to Japan, were adapted to fit an island environment. In seeking to establish resonance with Japanese experience, House Readers were always guided by the inviolate principles. The Japanese interpretation preserves the tradition's essential meaning. By similarly referencing those principles, the taboos can presumably be modified to accord with environmental circumstance anywhere.

Since the opening of Japan to the West, there has been general neglect of Japanese custom, particularly of those traditions which Westerners found arcane or touched with superstition. The government further encouraged the flight from tradition believing that modernization would bring political parity with the European powers. House Readers receded from the building scene and were regarded with something approaching the embarrassment the parvenu feels toward his country uncle. But recently, with the failed promises of modernism becoming increasingly apparent, certain Japanese have been searching through the annals of forgotten custom for alternatives. Perhaps the taboos will provide a new direction to architects, a direction having sincerity and legitimacy and the potential of universal applicability.

In choosing to utilize taboos, the House Reading system constitutes a kind of mosaic building code. Some will make perfect sense. As one should not eat raw pork because of the danger of contracting trichinosis, one should not build where the drainage is poor (for reasons of structural stability and to avoid health problems resulting from stagnant water), and one should always orient a structure to the south, to protect occupants from cold northern winds and conserve natural energy from the sun. The sources of Japanese tradition are varied. Some of the following recommendations may not make sense, but one must understand that they originate from the Japanese intellectual culture, and without an understanding of this system of thought one cannot fully appreciate why certain taboos are established. Yet one way to explain the goals of the Japanese House Reading system is to see the house as a microcosmic entity. To maximize health and prosperity, the House Reader seeks to achieve the optimum alignments with the macocosmic universe. Taboos, then, are only the simplified expression, in somewhat juridicial form, of the dynamics of achieving this degree of increased harmony.

Twenty-five Taboos Relating to Site

1. High ground to the north and low ground to the south bring a generally fortunate result.
2. High ground to the west and low ground to the east engender wealth.
3. High ground to the west and low ground to the southeast assure victory.
4. Where there is a pond to the southeast and a hill to the northwest, happiness flows, luck predominates, and wealth is augmented.
5. A hill to the north and a distant mountain in the south; a stream to the east flowing diagonally to the southwest; and a dirt road oriented toward the mountain: a happy site. Those who live there have honor and fame.
6. Where there are hills to the northeast and northwest, a forest in the southwest, and bamboo to the southeast, there is harmony. The two kinds of universal energy have consonance.
7. A house situated on the ridge of a hill or at the mouth of a valley brings disease and misfortune.
8. If the road ends where the house begins, there will be accidents.
9. A wide street to the west brings good fortune.
10. A tall tree(s) at the gate invites calamity.
11. A house rising above the neighboring dwellings hardly ever produces wealth.
12. An old grave to the northeast surrounded by a small forest brings death to children. If there is a hill to the southwest, women have diseases of the blood, abort their children, and have fits of vomiting. If there is a pool to the west, lascivious desires afflicts the family.
13. Running water to the northeast causes diarrhea, gonorrhea, and palsy.
14. A house surrounded on its four sides by four streets has water problems and is otherwise evil. There will be drownings or hangings. The parents will vanish, leaving stammering idiots for children.

15. A grave to the north and a stream running from east to south describe an evil site. Among other things, the children have eye disease.

16. Where plum trees surround the house, there is decadence, dissipation, and erotic riots. The family will dissolve, leaving the women and the children without means.

17. A pond to the northwest and a hill at the eastern border describe an evil site. Those living there are unable to dry their tears because of continuous calamity.

18. A grave to the east is extremely dangerous to the oldest son. A grave to the west is dangerous to women and brings disease to their descendants.

19. Forests to the east and west and graves to the north and south describe an evil site. Those who live here experience reverses in business and suffer from infectious diseases and abscesses.

20. Where there is a hill, projecting onto the site from the east, and a stream in the southeast, disaster comes upon the children: the stream will swallow them up, or they will be lost in the hill.

21. A pond to the north and a street running to the southeast, bring burglaries, lawsuits, and vengeful enemies. Crowds are the source of much anxiety.

22. A triangular site, even if it is flat, causes quarrels and has the danger of fire.

23. It is exceedingly evil to redirect a stream so that it runs through the site.

24. A stone ground cover or paving conducts to the surface the inimical qualities of the earth.

25. Where the earth is sealed with stones, it becomes barren.

Twenty-eight Taboos Relating to Construction, Configuration, and Orientation

1. A stair in the center of the house brings misery.

2. A kitchen to the east is most propitious.

3. A kitchen to the southeast is ruinous since a kitchen is where food is washed and from where vapors emit.

4. Houses oriented to the south are fortunate, if the living room is to the east facing the garden.

5. If the master's bedroom and kitchen are adjacent, evil will be visited upon the children.

6. There is special providence in having the owner's study at the center of the house.

7. An entry on axis with the gateway is evil.

8. A house, either large or small and having only one entry cannot be lived in for long. The occupants will move, or the husband or wife will die young.

9. A narrow house with its entry on the long side engenders asthma.

10. There is a relation between the rooms of a house and the prospects of its occupants. A house with one room is fortunate; two rooms are fair; three or four bring sorrow; five, six, or seven are again fortunate; eight rooms are evil; and a house with nine rooms is fortunate.

11. Generally speaking, houses oriented to the south are most fortunate.

12. A house, having its entrance on the shorter side, brings abundant and lasting happiness.

13. A bathroom situated at the southwest corner of the house is ominous and will adversely affect the occupants.

14. A bathroom to the north brings unexpected troubles.

15. A bathroom on axis with the entry causes abscesses and swelling in the occupants.

16. A window facing north causes irregular menstruation in women.

17. A house oriented to the west has openings to the south or openings to both the north and south, thereby admitting sunlight and allowing through ventilation. It does not have openings only to the north.

18. A house where there is construction, particularly in the kitchen, is dangerous to a pregnant woman.

19. Floors are raised above the ground. A floor resting upon the ground transmits to the occupants the baneful qualities of the soil and causes trouble and disease.

20. A structural column is hewn from one piece of wood. It is not two connected posts, nor does it have a core of a different material.

21. Without eaves to the south, the occupants quarrel and perhaps even become estranged. But if the eaves are too long, a dissolute and sybaritic life results.

22. A very large skylight, because of a superfluity of the good, causes problems.

23. A fireplace at the center of the house is evil.

24. If a central column is visible from the outside, there will be dreadful occurrences.

25. Where there is renovation, it is imperative that no post is split or otherwise cut and then employed in the new construction. If a post is cut, the entire member must be discarded. Where an altered post is employed, tragedy and death are certainly the result.

26. Luxury is evil. Virtue consists in purity and arrangement.

27. There are two kinds of wood. One kind is positive (pine, cypress, cedar) and the other is negative (chestnut). A house is constructed from positive wood.

28. Garden walls which are very high and overshadow the house within bring poverty upon the occupants.

Speculation

Modern physics speaks of the wave phenomena of a pulsating and vibrating universe. Often the electromagnetic oscillation of waves found in the planetary field occurs at physiological frequency. The ancient Chinese speak of ch'i, an invisible current swirling and eddying about the earth. Ch'i is energy and influences everything. Where its circulation is untrammeled and flows vigorously, there is health and well-being. Studying electromagnetic waves might be the key to analyzing ch'i.

The House Reader's analysis of space involves a layering process. Diverse elements are built up and associated in an integral unit. In effect, a field is created. Within the field and conditioned by it is the distinct physiology of the occupant. Between the physical properties of the field and the physiology of the enveloped being, there is a dynamic of continuous flux. Time increasingly manifests new combinations of potentialities. The universes may be the eight hormone glands, catalysts of physiological change. They even have seasonal aspects: Some bring the florescence of youth and others the winter of age. Acting in concert, the hormones constitute a "Biological Clock," regulating an organism's physiological processes.

Using the conceptual framework of the new physics, particularly its appreciation of the covariation between space and time, it may be possible to expand the notion of the Biological Clock until it encompasses the plenum of processes and establishes the house as an organic extension of the individual. House Reading, by embracing the totality of experience, encourages transcendence of our narrowly construed causality. It teaches us to view the built environment with the wonder of a child. We may even discover something of its essence.

Resources

1. Kinkaku Matsuura, *Kaso Ichiran* (Kyoto: Kyotoshorin, 1984).
2. Matsuura, *Kaso Hidenshu* (Tokyo: Bunkashoin, 1893).
3. Toshio Mitsufuji, *Kaso Tokuhon* (Tokyo: Shokousha, 1981).
4. Kozo Okamoto, *Kaso no Sekkei* (Tokyo: Seibunsha, 1979).
5. Kiyoshi Seike, *Kaso no Kagaku* (Tokyo: Kobunsha, 1969).
6. Suburo Yamagata, *Kaso* (Tokyo: Gakugei Shuppan, 1971).

16. Embodiment of a Sacred Vision: The John E. Fetzer Institute

James B. Beal

Editor's Note

The art of architecture today is usually combined with the science of engineering and technology. Engineer James Beal has been in the forefront of exploring the best ways to make the mechanical and electrical services we depend on in our buildings free of the negative side effects of electromagnetic pollution.

His article describes the headquarters building for the Fetzer Institute where he was a Research Associate. Mr. Beal helped to set up the optimal shielding for the electrical systems in this building.

Mr. Beal also has drawn upon his lifelong quest for spiritual knowledge to describe the symbolic importance of the Fetzer building and the mission of the man who created it.

The Fetzer building is unique as a piece of architecture where the vast resources of a successful businessman, John Fetzer, were devoted to the creation of what he envisioned as the optimal working environment.

> *I wanted to bring the ideas of what the Institute stood for into a type of edifice that would bring the mission dignity and understanding.*
>
> John E. Fetzer

FROM 1983 TO 1990 I ASSISTED the Fetzer Institute as a Research Associate. I gathered information about electromagnetic field (EMF) effects, beneficial and harmful, on living systems and healing processes, and the associated monitoring/recording equipment and applications. During the initial construction phases (1985–1987) of the Institute's building near Kalamazoo, Michigan, I supplied vendor and research data to assist in decisions for the optimum bipolar, air ion generation system for improving the indoor environment.

During the "Dedication Day" open house, held at the introductory 1988 conference, my wife and I and other conference attendees were invited to tour the new building. We walked down a gentle slope through landscape plantings of native species such as flowering dogwood, willow, and hawthorn. Beyond were mature woodlands on either side of a green rolling meadow leading to a distant lake. The entrance walkway began with loosely organized large stones which became progressively smaller as we approached the building. This transition from large to small, rough to smooth, culminated in the stone of the lobby floor, fine-grained and highly polished. We were told the path also symbolized each individual's spiritual journey—from unconscious states to refined arenas of awareness.

We passed into the lobby through the red granite entry with its winged sun carving of Ra-horakhty, the Egyptian sky god, protector of the spirit and a sign of grace. The solar disk symbolizes the spiritual current of the Christ consciousness coming to full illumination. This type of entry is also similar to the Japanese torii gates signifying access to sacred places, and a welcoming statement. From the white entry passage we passed into the spacious glass-walled atrium illuminated with natural light flooding in from all sides and the roof. We beheld beautiful green and flowering plants of all sizes, which were scattered among natural artworks of wood, stone, and crystal. At the end of the central atrium, in the core of the Institute, a waterfall greeted us with its rushing sounds as it plunged down a fifty-foot wide curved wall of black granite. This gentle relaxing background music permeates the building, following us throughout our tour. We continued to the Hall of Records, which contained sculptures of famous historical individuals who inspired John Fetzer with their contributions to society. As we continued into the spacious quiet work areas and offices, our connection with nature was continually refreshed and reinforced by the outdoor panorama of woodlands, meadows, and lake views from the many windows at all levels.

Throughout the building, placed in alcoves for our contemplation, were sculptures, artworks, and lovely, yet delicate, natural metal ore specimens and crystals, symbolic of subtle, delicate, unseen radiating energies held in quiescent form. For us the peak experience with natural crystals was on the second floor at one of the apex points of the building. Here, the triangular Meditation Room was located, and at its apex end, on a black pedestal, stood a solitary, seven-foot tall, double terminated, clear selenite crystal with its delicate internal hues accentuated by indirect and natural lighting—an awe-inspiring example of Nature's creative forces, which produced in us a calming, peaceful, uplifting effect.

John E. Fetzer: The Man

John Earl Fetzer's philosophy was stated in these remarks seven days prior to his death:

> A number of years ago I had a heart attack. A young physician blithely told me that I would have a second heart attack within a year and probably it would prove fatal. I said, "I beg your pardon, young man, that is not my style. My belief system won't accommodate that." Whereupon I gave him an elementary exercise in biofield energy medicine. That probably did me more good than it did him because I don't think he heard me. But the truth is I recognized the necessity for change and immediately inaugurated a program for positive energy. I mustered up a program that had "wellness" spelled all over it. I wanted to believe that recovery was possible. I altered my lifestyle. I discovered that the quality of life must be changed and that I had to fight off fear, depression, hopelessness, panic and despair and infuse a constant stream of positive affirmation. Faith, confidence, laughter, creativity, and picturization became the order of the day.
>
> I was living a fundamental part of the Institute's mission. I believe there is a certain consciousness of synthesis that brings forth a light that some refer to as the "avatar symmetry," that is here, ready to assist all who are connected with the Institute to delineate its mission. Remember, whatever the final verdict turns out to be, its summary will be 'unconditional love'. That is our avatar of the future, because love is the unifying energy field that mobilizes the physical, emotional, mental, and spiritual resources and the caring and sharing of one another. It is an attraction of amplitude and a resonance of renewal.

An early interest in "wireless" radio led John Earl Fetzer into a deep and practical appreciation of phenomena "you can't see but know are there." His creative inventions in early radio and associated components, and his management skills in radio and interpersonal communications, provided the background, funding, and resources to further explore his special interests in electromagnetic field effects on living systems, geoelectromagnetism, and energy medicine, and to realize his visions.

He shared with others his technical accomplishments and philosophical realizations, and provided material resources during his lifetime to supply aid and supportive facilities to medical research and educational projects. He and others explored and shared the best of "the creative edge." Fetzer stated:

> Our effort is to bring into being new discoveries, starting with the field of energy medicine. As far as energy medicine is concerned, it's an effort to make discoveries about the human anatomy. The term 'body electric' describes it best. We have an opportunity to develop a whole new approach to physical health if we understand that our body is electrical as well as chemical. For too long, the emphasis in medicine has been on the chemical aspects of prevention, cure, and treatment. There is a place for that, but

> there is also a place for mind and spirit in this equation. Now we are playing catch-up. Energy medicine is an additional arm of medicine that belongs in the doctor's inventory of skills. There are new energies to be discovered and applied.

The Vision

John Fetzer was convinced that the key to humanity's future lay in the productive linkage and integration of body, mind, and spirit, and the application of this holistic approach to the problems plaguing our planet. He had the awareness and planning to combine his accomplishments to embody his vision and the continuity and inspiration to sustain the vision after his death.

In the 1930s, as a pioneer broadcaster, Fetzer established the first radio station in Kalamazoo, Michigan with equipment he mostly built himself. From this modest beginning, he set up other radio stations in Michigan and adjacent states, building a legendary career in radio and television. He was one of radio's early "test pilots," and the Institute he created is still pushing "the other side of the envelope," breaking barriers and exploring new territories. To forge ahead Fetzer had to end a chapter in his life and start a new one to realize his vision. He explained:

> I suppose to make a decision of that kind, it has to grow on you. I think it dawned on me about seven years ago [1981] that I had to do something. I was numbed for awhile at the idea of selling everything, of moving out of my industrial environment. But I mulled it over and I thought about many of my friends who operated in industrial and business circles. Many made a fatal mistake by hanging on to their businesses. When they died, their enterprises were buried with them. If you are going to be honest with yourself you must face up to it. You have to make that tough decision, probably the toughest I ever had to make, especially with an estate the size of mine. You know the kinds of complications that tie up estates in the courts. I think it is the greater part of valor and wisdom to take care of the matter while you are still alive. If there was going to be some innovative engineering done on my estate, then I was the guy who was going to do it.

Fetzer worked in the building embodying his vision for about two years before he died on February 20, 1991 at age ninety.

The Institute: The Embodiment of the Vision

> *There is a Native American saying about the need to be open to new ways of doing things only if they can grow corn. Within this approach lies the gift that*

the Institute offers the world; an open-minded skepticism, a searching for the practical applications of the mystical and the spiritual, a bridging between the east and the west, a searching for the balance point between the mainstream and the frontier where innovation and creativity flourish.

—Tom Callanan, Fetzer Director of Communications

The Fetzer Institute is a nonprofit research and educational organization dedicated to pursuing the implications of body-mind-spirit unity in a variety of arenas. The Institute's research programs focus on those approaches to health and healing that are scientifically sound and based on this essential unity. Educational activities are aimed at creating programs for health professionals, teachers, and other public leaders that address the balance of body, mind, and spirit in their lives and work. These formation programs are based upon the assumption that the effectiveness of professionals depends as much on their personal characteristics and integrity as on their experience and skills.

John Fetzer established the Fetzer Trust in 1954, modeling it after the Ford Foundation. In 1962, the Trust was incorporated into the Fetzer Foundation, which evolved into the Fetzer Institute in 1990 when the focus of its mission changed from grant making to body-mind-health education and research. The Institute, with an endowment of $250 million, spent about $12 million on sixty-five projects between 1990 and 1993. Its funding emphasis has evolved over the years, adding in 1990 a new priority of educational outreach and communications. It embodies John Fetzer's commitment to love and freedom, blending his concept of service with his vision of holistic health. The Institute was formed to pursue what John Fetzer called "spiritual freedom."

The Institute was built from the ground up to take into overall consideration:

1. The aesthetic and inspiring aspects of the outdoor environment above, below and around it,
2. The building placement regarding orientation to land, water, light, geophysical features, and geomantic attunement,
3. The highest quality of construction materials in selected symbolic stone, metal and glass patterns, and,
4. Creation of a healthy holistic indoor and proximal outdoor space for the building occupants to supply the physical body with healthy air circulation and ionization, full spectrum light, reverse osmosis water supply, and a Fitness Center for exercise and aerobics; to supply the mind with research data and related information, challenging projects, inspiring work spaces, creative art works, living-room quietness and outdoor views; and, to supply the spirit with a Meditation Room for reading, thinking, or meditating in solitude, and quiet walks outdoors by the lake or woods.

Fetzer Institute building and entry. Photo by David MacKenzie.

The 57,000-square-foot, tri-level complex, shaped like an equilateral-triangle, was designed to blend modern architectural and electronic technologies into an idyllic setting of fifty-five wooded acres around Dustin Lake, west of Kalamazoo. A rural site was selected not just for its natural beauty, but because it was remote from the noise of expressways, the glow of city lights and the electrical interference of high voltage power lines. To further the sense of seclusion, the building is nestled deeply into the site, halfway down the wooded slope and overlooking the lake. The triangular building design, symbolizing the balance between body, mind, and spirit, reinforces the Institute's holistic philosophy.

Underlying every element of the design of the Institute and the Residential Education Center was constant attention to the Institute's desire to fit all buildings and support systems into the environment with minimum deleterious impact on the beautiful wooded setting. Every effort was made to minimize tree loss and permanent forest damage, and to maximize the compatibility between building and site. Elements of the site that have been there for thousands of years were used in the construction of the buildings.

The exterior of the Institute building is clad in three colors of granite, inspired by the Aswan granite used in some of the ancient pyramids of Egypt. The black granite at the bottom represents the physical plane of existence. Further up, the gray granite symbolizes the mental and emotional aspects of the human condition. And, finally, the roof and the top of the atrium are white, symbolizing the spiritual realm. Red is a symbol of welcome and joy in many eastern cultures, so the red granite on both entrances says. "Welcome to our home."

As visitors enter the sky-lit atrium interior through the revolving doors, they hear the pleasant sound of the cascading waterfall, and it too, is steeped in symbolism. The water, containing no chemicals, runs at a slow wash over a broad expanse of vertical black granite. Used by all peoples throughout time as a purifying and cleansing agent, the waterfall represents the constant cleansing of the individual physical body and the planet as a whole. For many religions in the world, a pool of water also has been considered a mirror of the heavens and higher knowledge and of prophecy. The waterfall is a reminder of this tradition and an invitation to look beyond immediate physical reality, into the spirit, for truth.

Much of what makes the building unique, however, can't be experienced at first glance. It replicates the balance of body, mind, and spirit in the whole person, a statement in stone that integrated relationships and functions can be a many-splendored and beneficial thing. The internal environment is replete with technologies designed to make the workplace a hospitable space for creativity, contentment, and productivity.

The Hall of Records contains busts of historical figures who symbolized to Fetzer important building blocks in humanity's evolution and progress. The busts represent Socrates, Ramses II, Joseph of Arimathea, Francis I of France, Louis XIV of France, St. John of the Cross, Henry II of England, and Thomas Jefferson. In Fetzer's opinion, the eight, by their words and deeds, helped nurture and bring the human species forward to a new level of awareness and potential. The contributions of Socrates and Jefferson are well known, but the achievements of the others may not be as apparent. The room itself is patterned after the architecture of Jefferson's Monticello. The half-dome ceiling is covered in gold leaf, symbolizing the value and purity of true wisdom. The eight bronze busts are arranged in a semicircle on individual black granite pedestals. "I look at it as a continual reminder and link to the past," says Carol Hegedus, Institute Program Director.

> It is a link to older streams of knowledge, and to wisdom that serves to connect through time. And in integrating the past with the present, we come to know more fully who we are, and acknowledge those many shoulders who existed before whose work we stand on. There's the sense of timelessness and process leading to what is going on now that comes when we connect to this past.

Using classic materials (marble, granite, bronze, and imported woods), pure forms (circles, triangles, and squares), and historical references (from the pyramids to Monticello), a design was developed to reflect the concept of holism. The international nature and scope of the building serving to bring into focus John Fetzer's concern with the well-being of the whole person and the whole planet. The main dining room, for example, has been designated as the "One World Room." In it a large natural copper formation is on display, symbolizing light and life among some African peoples. The tables are made out of beautifully grained woods that have come from every continent in the world (with the exception of treeless Antarctica).

Symbolizing the mental aspect of being, The Fetzer Library and Information Center is a resource for staff and Fetzer Fellows, a rotating group of researchers and educators who assist in the development of Fetzer programs. The collection places special emphasis on the fields of psychoneuroimmunology and electromagnetic fields as related to medicine, consciousness studies, and education. Access to major national and international databases and libraries is available. Meeting rooms are available nearby, featuring front- and rear-screen projection facilities, full audio-visual services, a satellite downlink, and automated links to the Institute's computer systems and Library Information Center.

The warmth and vision of the Institute's founder John E. Fetzer is palpable in the Founder's Room. This room contains remembrances in photos and mementos of Mr. Fetzer's long-term careers in broadcasting, baseball, and public service, including the 1968 World Series trophy, won when he was sole owner of the Detroit Tigers.

In the upstairs hallways the peaked ceilings are representative of European Gothic cathedrals—another of humanity's attempts to reach for greater spiritual understanding. The ceilings have a cloth covering, much like a tent—a canopy of physical protection and warmth. All fabrics used in the Institute are of natural materials.

The windows in the second floor offices represent physical and spiritual aspects. The lower window in each office is a continuous vision strip for expansive views, at seating height, into the physical world of trees, hills, and lake. The upper "sky window" provides a view of the sky and provides natural light penetration to each space. In the spiritual sense, our gaze is directed upward so that we may become aware that we are greater than just the physical part of who we are. Allusions to monastic cells for individual contemplation are evident.

With the exception of the dining room, the wood used throughout the building is Honduran mahogany. Brass is used to represent the highly refined nature and purity of gold. The basic color of the walls—soft white—provides neutrality for decoration. The other main colors (blue, green, and burgundy) represent the mental, emotional, physical, and spiritual aspects of human well-being, as culled from the Sanskrit chakra tradition.

To create the healthiest possible working environment, there are computer-coordinated temperature and humidity controls. Special color-balanced, full-spectrum lighting is used in each work station and office along with high-density sound insulation and special acoustical treatment to provide "living-room quiet." The drinking water is purified by a reverse osmosis process and flows through stainless steel plumbing. Beyond quality mechanical and electrical systems designed to minimize acoustical interference, emphasis was also placed on minimizing and negating the effects of electromagnetic fields and the influence of electric and electronic devices on the human body. All electrical cables are underground and the Institute interior wiring is fully shielded. The air is purified in each room using balanced, bipolar ion generators. In addition, the atrium waterfall produces natural, negative ions in the core of the building. Many studies show that people enjoy an experience of well-being when they go to the seashore or mountains because of the proliferation of negative ions from crashing ocean breakers, waterfalls, and electrical storms. However, long-term occupants of the Institute with allergies report that these seem to be aggravated at certain times of the year when they go home at the end of the day. This may be because the air quality, the ion balance, and the reduced pollen level of their working environment reduces their tolerance to outside natural and variable conditions!

The Institute art collection includes a number of paintings, crystals, fossils, and pieces of sculpture. Although there is no single theme uniting the whole collection, all the pieces are meant to provide a moment of beauty, reflection, or fun for the viewer. Other natural works of art, such as a six-billion-year-old nickel-iron meteorite and 300-million-year-old fossils in shiny black marble slabs, are positioned throughout the building as both decorations and reminders of how fragile the human species is and how our existence is less than a fraction of a microscopic tick of the cosmic clock.

The entryway to the Meditation Room is a small maze, symbolizing "the straight and narrow way" mentioned in the New Testament. This is a physical reminder that entry into spiritual exploration demands conscious attention and great care. The Meditation Room is set aside as a place of retreat, contemplation, and prayer for Institute staff if they need a moment of quiet and repose in response to an emotional need. For some, the seven-foot selenite crystal, when used in connection with meditation, seems to enhance their mental clarity to better experience a sense of inner truth. This crystal and the other exquisite examples here are symbolic of what the Institute stands for—order, harmony, cosmos, enlightenment, and positive vibrations. The room's colors—white walls, blue chairs, and lavender cushions—represent the higher energy centers in some of the Eastern traditions and are colors signifying royalty in the West. The room in plainly decorated, and no single religious tradition is emphasized, so that all who choose to use the room will feel welcome. "The energetics of the room are quite unusual," Carol Hegedus adds, "it feels different than other spaces in the building. During Institute construction the workmen chose the meditation room for their breaks."

Apart from the main building is a dark stone obelisk masking the water-cooling tower for the air conditioning system. Surrounding the obelisk is a Japanese dry bed garden containing Japanese maples and ginkgo trees. The obelisk may have no special out-of-the-ordinary metaphysical message to deliver, but in many religions, it represents that part of us reaching up toward God or some higher source of energy, being, or knowledge. (The Washington Monument is a good example.) Its design is consistent with the Institute's philosophy that even functional, utilitarian objects can be aesthetically designed to complement the landscape.

While educational and research projects are conducted at major colleges and universities, much of the conceptual work for the Institute is done at the Residential Educational Center—*Seasons: A Center for Renewal.* Constructed in 1994 adjacent to the Institute's administrative office, *Seasons* provides a creative and hospitable environment for dialogue and community. Teachers and healers, scientists and scholars, leaders of public life and agents of cultural change gather at *Seasons* to participate in the Institute's planning and development work. The architects, engineers, and planners at Harley Ellington Pierce Yee Associates, Incorporated met the difficult challenge of designing both the Institute and *Seasons.* DeYoung and Bagin was the contractor for the main building, while Miller-Davis was the general contractor for *Seasons.* As an additional confirmation of how special and environmentally challenging the *Seasons* project was, in March 1995, Miller-Davis received a Build America Award, the "Oscar" of the construction industry from builders to builders.

In his dedication speech for the opening of *Seasons*, Robert Lehman, Institute President, said the following:

> I would like to suggest that no moment of our history has been without its purpose; that there is a hidden order to our history. I would propose that all of us have been students enrolled together in an invisible school of the spirit: the curriculum of this school has been a curriculum of wholeness, freedom, and love; the sacred test of this school has been the personal stories of our lives; and the students of this school have also been its teachers—our pedagogy has been to draw out the spiritual truth from one another.

John Fetzer left a strong and effective container, a temenos, a sacred place, where those who choose to enter in may be profoundly affected. (See Roberta

Shoemaker-Beal's essay on "the temenos," p. 159). The Institute may indeed serve many as their personal temenos.

Personal Experiences: Creating the Spirit of Place

Being here inspires us to be the best we can be!

—Carolyn Dailey, Administrative Assistant

In April 1995, I conducted interviews at the Institute, gathering staff personal experiences and observations about working in such a place. The comments indicated that awe and wonder are engendered in the beholder when first confronted both by the cultural mix and the dynamic symbolic architecture of the Institute. For the first time in most people's experience they encountered an unusual working environment which magnified the effect of beauty, spirit, personal responsibility, and commitment. In this sometimes boundaryless organization, everyone is expected to work and learn together as a community of self-motivating facilitators. This poses difficult challenges for many persons, because this is not the rigid hierarchy of the 'normal' business world. Teamwork and flex-time are often involved in various assignments, with everyone contributing where and when they can. According to Carol Hegedus,

> I think that the work accomplished here has actually contributed to the forming of the space; this aspect wasn't considered adequately in the early conceptualization. We have remodeled because we found that the offices the way they were conceptualized as solitary cells encouraged us to work in isolation and that we lacked spaces in our work areas for larger gatherings that weren't strictly meetings . . . the kind of conversations that happen by having coffee together. Consequently, one of the meeting rooms has been converted to a coffee-break space. Something of the place comes from who is here and what happens in the spaces. I think all of us who are here are supposed to be here as part of our destiny, both the Institute's destiny and our own destiny.

Here are some typical comments: "Working here accommodates both solitude and community." "It is so quiet, you wonder if a party is going on somewhere that you don't know about!" "After awhile you get used to it, until you go someplace else and come back with the perspective to realize what is here—the ubiquitous waterfall sound, viewing splendid sunsets and glittering ice storms from the atrium, and enjoying community in the break room." "You can cherish that you are in a process and more in touch with yourself." "This is like a school with many levels of learning and wisdom." "Every day produces a new experience from the variety of tasks in which I am involved." "The work space eventually became a sacred place for me where a growing-up process blossomed, brought about by my personal participation and recognition."

In the experience of those interviewed, there is the freedom to go from place to place inside and on the picturesque Institute grounds. Several persons, like Hegedus, indicated that they were drawn here, seemingly as part of their destiny. Initial intimidation often occurred on arrival for a hiring interview; however, once hired, personal growth occurred in all areas, due to the influences of working in a positive, supportive environment. People can find the space they needed for action or creative thought. Many of the staff have volunteered to welcome visitors and conduct tours of the Institute because in the personal dialogues and explanation of the spirit of the place their own spirit was reinforced, thus making the Institute a living place for them where the boundaries are determined by qualities of the human spirit in concert with geographic position.

Institute Program Areas

> *We are involved in studies that can enrich the practice of medicine, educational programs that teach the enriched practice, and fundamental research intended to broaden our purview of the nature of consciousness and spirit.*
>
> —Robert F. Lehman, President

The Institute works in collaboration with organizations and individuals, partnering with others as facilitators and conveners, all evolving as the field of body-mind health care evolves, pressing the field forward into the fullest possible understanding of the mind's effects on physical health.

Body-Mind-Spirit Health Research includes health research with a body-mind emphasis and health research with a spiritual emphasis. Research in alternative medical practices and their relationships to mind and spirit incorporates other medical practices and theoretical models, as well as bioelectromagnetics.

The aims of Body-Mind-Spirit Education and Formation are: education and formation for health professionals and teachers, education of the public, and attitudinal healing.

Studies in the Fundamental Nature of Consciousness and Spirit examine relationships among consciousness, spirit, and physical reality. It is expected that explorations into spiritual foundations and other fundamental issues that underlie all the other Institute activities will influence not only the Institute work but also the whole field of body-mind-spirit health and healing.

Conclusion

"We want to continue with our pioneering spirit and the questing that John Fetzer so much lived in," Hegedus says. "But our strategy has been that you can't influence the mainstream from working too far outside of it. We have become most successful from working at the edge, at the places where it takes a little push and movement to enter into the mainstream. We want to stretch the mainstream . . . reaching and working at the leading edge of it. But the other domain of our work in consciousness and in the spiritual foundations is the newest area of focus that is most central to the core of who we are."

According to Fetzer:

> There are no benchmarks for measuring what this Institute intends to do. There is no game plan, no formula to follow. Nobody is attempting the types of research and support that we are. We are plowing new ground. What we want to promote is an open mind about getting physics back into medicine where it has belonged all along. Our role will be to cluster the research, to determine what is valid and what is not, and to enlarge the network so that more players can get into the game of discovery. I think that we can truly make a difference in health care. It may take a few years, but we can do it.

All human progress results from individuals who rise above the surface of common thought to propose uncommon ideas. Every generation breeds a few men and women who challenge the rest of us to look beyond what is now. Through their conviction and determination, our knowledge is advanced and our culture enhanced. John E. Fetzer was such a person.

Acknowledgments

I wish to thank the Fetzer Institute staff and my wife, Roberta Shoemaker-Beal, M.F.A., ATR, for support and helpful suggestions.

Resources

1. The Fetzer Institute, 9292 West KL Avenue, Kalamazoo, Michigan 49009–9398, phone 616-375-2000.
2. "John Fetzer: 20–20 Visionary." *Encore*, March 1988.
3. "Fetzer Institute Administration Building Symbolism." Talk by Jim Gordon in Associate Staff Meeting, Sept. 11, 1987.

4. "A Visual Dialogue: A Tour of the Fetzer Institute." 1993 Booklet.
5. "Fetzer Institute Residential Education Center." 1994 booklet.
6. "The Institute Report." Fetzer Institute Annual Report for 1994.
7. Roberta Shoemaker-Beal, "Creating a Temenos: Sacred Places and Sacred Spaces, The Parallels Among the Sacred, the Creative, and the Therapeutic," C. G. Jung Society Lecture, New Orleans, Louisiana, January 11, 1994.

17. Interviews by Roberta Swan

Editor's Note

Brent Smith

A major problem in our built environment is that people don't realize that money is not the only variable in creating a spiritually uplifting environment. In fact many people do not really notice how the built environment is designed. If more people understood the use of design to infuse spirit into a building, they could demand it from architects and designers, and we would have a more peaceful and harmonious environment.

Brent Smith is a designer in California who has honed the art of infusing buildings with spirit over many years of practice. His current project is certainly one of his most challenging: creating low-cost, spiritually uplifting housing for the homeless.

In this interview, you will learn some of the factors that contribute to bringing spirit into building. And you will see how the work of spirit is seldom removed from real world concerns as Mr. Smith also goes over the political aspects of a controversial project, like housing for the homeless.

RS *I'd like to talk about creating a spirit in a place that would allow some transition for homeless people. Maybe we could start with how you got interested in designing something for the homeless.*

BS I had entered a competition with the idea of cottage housing for the homeless and I got nowhere with the competition, but the seeds of that idea went into my work for Loaves and Fishes, who were looking for cottage housing. But the idea had its roots in the last thirty years of my career.

First, when I did my thesis project in architecture it was on community mental health centers right when the Kennedy administration was tearing down all the old snake pit hospitals. The federal government said that the cities and counties should pick up mental health care on a local level. They said that what we are doing in the large facilities is inhumane. But cities and counties didn't pick it up, and that is one of the major reasons we have the homeless. At least forty percent of the people who are out there homeless would have been institutionalized before this change.

Second, I discovered Jung and symbolism and archetypes and got the idea that buildings are somewhat of a metaphor. My solution at that time for a building for the mentally ill was that the whole building was in a mandala configuration, generating from water at the center.

Third, I always was fascinated with mobile homes. I always thought they were terribly designed, but fascinating for some reason. I have designed and sketched prototype mobile homes for years, but couldn't connect with the industry.

And fourth was my ongoing interest in small houses. I taught courses in small houses in the late seventies, early eighties, and had at least a thousand people go through them. I was trying to get people to understand that we had to scale down, that quality had nothing or very little to do with size, and that we were just wasting our resources thinking that bigger was better. I lived for sixteen years in a very small house, only five hundred square feet, with a wife and a Great Dane. We were able to get out of debt and knew all the benefits, financial and otherwise, of living frugally in a small but delightfully designed space.

All those things came together when Leroy Chatfield of Loaves and Fishes came and asked me to expand what I had done for the public works competition. Loaves and Fishes had found from their experience working with the homeless how well small cottage spaces worked. They took over an old Hooverville of about thirty small cottages, of about three hundred square feet each that were built in the 1930s, and they rehabbed them. Many of them were converted to other uses like a clinic and a school, but twelve of them they left as individual little cottages. These cottages are now almost sixty years old.

Now they have twelve years of experience with homeless people living in a transitional state in these cottages and then moving on. They found that it just works so beautifully. And it wasn't architecture—because these buildings aren't architecture, they are just buildings. But they had their own identity, and they had their own grounding. And this brings us to the philosophy that they came to me with. They were taking people as ungrounded as anyone can be in this culture and grounding them in place as deeply as possible. Loaves and Fishes is coming from a place of the heart.

One of the things I learned in my thesis project was that what we are building here is not just housing. It is an institution taking the place of the old mental hospital, of the old skid row, of other institutions that we had, even the military. Institutions that worked in some ways, and in ways were more humane than the non-institutions that we have right now. But we lost all of those. So, if we don't understand that we are creating an institution when we house some parts of the homeless population, we can do great damage. In an institution if decisions start to be made based on what is best for the institution and not what is best for the tenant then all of a sudden we do things like lining up all the buildings in rows for the convenience of the institution, not because it is the best design solution. As we have developed this project we have had plenty of people saying, "Hey, cut the cost, line up all the buildings in rows, there will be less money going into the project if the police can see every doorway from here." But, we are saying, no, absolutely not. We start with the tenant and say that we want to create the most healing environment for someone who is totally disconnected, somebody who may be at the lowest point of their life and in many cases trying to recover from drug and alcohol abuse.

That leads us to ask the question—what can we do physically on every resource level to make the most healing environment possible? We think the answer is grounding those people as much as possible, which means giving them a place to live that truly is an extension of their individual soul. We see the cottages as their place on earth, as a very important metaphor, as an extension of their skin, and as an extension of their spirit. In designing such a dwelling there is a kind of magic that happens when all the pieces fit.

The homeless transitional living cottage is a manufactured or mobile home and in plan is a cruciform, which is both a Christian and a pre-Christian symbol. In pre-Christian iconography the cross means relationship, it's heaven and earth. And relationship is one of the things we wanted to build into this project to get these people back into communication with the bigger culture, with each other, with being responsible for themselves, committed to themselves, but also committed to those around them and to the rest of the human community and the earth. So the metaphor of the cruciform is apt, it is a very sacred form in the Christian community and an archetype of great power.

A primary concern with the buildings was to bring in light. We had people say to us—"Hey, if you build row houses, or if you build fourplexes then people could back up and have a corner to get into, and they would only have one or two sides exposed to the outside." But we said no, we want to bring people into the light, we want people to have the light around them. Where we started from was to bring in light, to infuse these buildings with light, so that people could control the light themselves. They could have the light or they could close the shades and shut themselves in.

Then we took the individual unit and formed clusters just like a normal neighborhood where the people across from you and beside you are the people that you really deal with. So, we want to cluster people into these small groups, then about three or four of these clusters become a neighborhood, and we have four neighborhoods in a village of sixty. It is a microcosm of the bigger community. At the center is the meeting hall and the washing place. Both are places where people come together. We also are incorporating a food co-op on the periphery, and a maintenance building which has a workshop to build things. We are trying to develop a place that has a sense of community, where there will be a government and the tenants will be involved in that government. They will be policing themselves—a concept that has come from the homeless. The overall plan of the village has two cross axes which again forms a cruciform with the meeting hall at its center. This is the village center, but also their healing center.

Their concerns about security and having a safe environment are stronger than those of the people in the surrounding neighborhoods who are also concerned about their own security. I saw much more concern from the homeless people who have lost everything. Most of them have been stripped of everything that they own, everything that is important to them, even photographs. When you are living in a homeless situation for a long time you have no protection.

We are trying to do the exact opposite of the old mental hospital. They used to strip the patients of their personal possessions and put them in a room at the end of a long hallway with two people to watch over sixty to eighty patients. That was the environment. We are trying to do everything we can to not let that happen again and prevent institutional deviancy.

Since there is never a big enough budget, you just have to try to get more people involved into helping it work. You start bringing in volunteers such as the master gardeners who will be working in the gardens and sharing their knowledge. You bring in people to teach cooking and other needed skills from the bigger community. You develop economic cooperative business for both jobs and the environment. This is what Loaves and Fishes is so wonderful at doing, bringing in that energy.

RS *I think people who are interested in doing projects like this one could learn a lot by hearing how you have navigated some of the political realities. What advice can you give about this aspect of the project?*

BS The concept of a village for the homeless started with Loaves and Fishes, but the city picked up on the idea and had their own design for a village of sixty units, very different from what Loaves and Fishes was doing. The project for the city was done in row houses and fourplexes. The city tentatively approved both projects and between the two projects 120 cottages had been OK'd. When Loaves and Fishes found a piece of land it could only accommodate forty-eight units.

Once Loaves and Fishes had the land we next had to get the cooperation of the people who lived near the land where we wanted to put the village. We thought the neighborhood organization that is part of the development agency was going to cooperate, but when they heard about our project they just flipped. They started writing notes to the mayor and to the council saying, "this project can't go through." So the city redevelopment agency came to us and said that they would rather not have us fight their redevelopment neighborhood organization, and they asked if we would consider doing our project on their land since our project was farther along and they liked our ideas. We then became the city's project. Which was a little more extensive than the Loaves and Fishes original plan and is part of a social service and detox center which are being designed by other groups.

We started two years ago, and it took us almost a year to get a prototype of the cottage unit built. The mayor had looked at a model of the cottage and said—this is really great, if you can produce this and it looks like this then the city will support it. But he wanted to see a prototype unit. It took us a year to find a manufacturer (Golden West Homes) and build this prototype.

The problems with the project started happening when we got into the political arena. In my opinion, a lot of people are powerful in this culture because they are very linear. They work well with the language structure and they work well with the abstract structures. But visually they are not literate. And, they tend to make their decisions based on the head and not on the heart. And I think you have to make decisions where the head and the heart come together. But for them it always comes down to bottom line of what can we do the cheapest.

If we were just doing housing for people with stable jobs and lives we wouldn't have the mandate we have here, which is to infuse as much spirit as possible into the place and make a healing environment. Most people who are healthy in this culture buy a commodity house and then they add spirit to it. But we are working with people who are really beaten down, and we need to do the very best we can to give them an environment to help them through change. Although you could likely build row houses cheaper than our cottages, there is no way you can build a single cottage with its own identity cheaper than ours. I'm not even sure that, considering the savings in the efficiencies of time and lower labor costs of manufactured housing, these cottages might be cheaper than union labor, site-built row housing.

Our [cottage] is smaller than the "Park Model" RVs [recreational vehicles] which are 400 square feet. Ours are 320 square feet and the price is the same . . . Our costs for the small unit is $72 per square foot for the house, foundation, and porch. If we go up to a 500 square foot unit, which would be a 14 feet wide instead of a 8 feet wide, we would be at $50 square foot which is cheaper than what you can build an apartment house for. But we wanted to keep the unit smaller in order to get a density of thirty units per acre. We are only using about two acres of land. Our building coverage is less than thirty percent, and we want to keep a lot

Exterior of the prototype of the cottage for the homeless while it was set up for public viewing.

of open green space. The cost of the building with porch and foundation is about $23,000—the cost of a medium-priced Buick or one year in a California prison for one inmate. The project cost, including community buildings, utilities, and landscaping is about $3 million or $50,000 per cottage.

Our units have a spirit, and they have a sense of individuality which are qualities we think are essential for this project. We want to provide a space that nurtures and really brings in light. We want the interior to have choices of places, because when you scale down into something this small you have to allow for choice of places that are psychologically different. One unarticulated room can be very demeaning. But with a choice of spaces you have an alcove where two people can sit and have an intimate conversation off the bigger space. You have another alcove where a separate activity can take place, and you have a bedroom behind double doors which is in essence a third alcove.

I think human beings have always lived in small spaces frequently with small alcoves made for various activities. Every place I've been in the world where historically people have lived in small cottages, the ones with sleeping alcoves or eating alcoves are some of the most wonderful.

RS *Something is really bothering me. You talk about the need for this little place to have as much spirit as possible because the people who are going to use it really need*

Interiors of the prototype of the cottage for the homeless while it was set up for public viewing.

that. But I wonder why should we build anything without the most spirit possible, especially when what you have just said is that the cost is not the factor.

BS The cost is not the factor—it is a minimal amount more, for these units at most $3,000 a unit out of a total cost of $23,000. We think of everything in the culture as something that is bought and sold and gotten rid of when it is useless. We can't do that anymore, our resources are too precious. Wooden buildings can last four hundred to eight hundred years. Any building standing in America right now built to code in the last fifty years should be here six hundred or seven hundred years from now. Our buildings don't last that long because we don't do the necessary routine maintenance. If it is cared about, if it is loved and people watch out for it, the building can be here for centuries and serve scores of generations. We have to develop a new economy that is not based only on the short-term bottom line or instant profit.

RS *But the ideas that a building should have as much spirit as possible and that a building should be cared for are not concepts that you frequently hear when talking about building.*

BS That is why I do what I do. I have done only single-family residence design for people who build from the heart. It is about intent. When I worked in big architectural offices after I got my degree it was all commodity, spirit was rarely the intent, and that is the way ninety-five to ninety-eight percent of our buildings are built, absolutely as commodities. This has been the view in the larger society since the end of World War II that has caused the destruction of our environment. Everything is just a commodity. And the government and the banks are the major players. Fanny Mae/Freddie Mac and the banks really design America. In the housing market alone, banks reward size over quality and hence we have these overly large, resource wasting, pretentious single-family homes being built in the last few years.

What I call "dormer disease" afflicts so many of these new houses. It's all done on a Disneyland real estate level. "Curb appeal" means the home has a winding staircase, columns, dormers, and "lick and stick" brick on the front. It is pathetic. It has nothing to do with the times we live in, with our resources, with our energy, with what our climate is all about. And it has so little to do with what our souls are all about. It is superficial.

RS *I would like to talk about symbolism in your other designs. You have worked for many years doing designs consciously or unconsciously dealing with the idea of infusion of spirit and how that gets expressed in different symbolic forms. Would you talk about some of the houses you have done and the importance of symbolism in their design?*

BS First of all I must give a disclaimer. Some of the homes I will use as examples are, to me, very large [three to four thousand square feet]. When I agree to work on a project of this scale I stipulate that the house be approached as a village of smaller houses. Zoning the home so that multi-generational living or multi-users can be easily facilitated makes the potential for better long-term use and better resource confrontation.

I think all of our homes are sacred places. What I try to do with a client is be as much a *tabula rasa* as I can. I try to bring my knowledge of architecture into the design process and leave my own style baggage behind. And I try to trust that the person coming to me really knows on a deep level what they need to tell me. It's an unfolding. There are a lot of style traps out there with confused romantic images, such as Victorian or Tudor or those of other historical periods. Style can be superficial without a deep rooting in where we live. So I try to look past style to find the deeper vocabulary we are talking about, to find the images that are coming through.

If there is to be metaphor built into a building it has to come from within the design process. It has to unfold rather than being something preconceived. I've had meetings with clients where we have sat in silence and done visualization. I've taken people through guided meditation so that I start to get their images from the deepest place I possibly can.

For example, with one client the word "gateway" came up early in the design and became the center of the design. In others the image unfolds as the building evolves if I am listening and if I am paying attention. One of the visual metaphors that developed in a design were the concentric rings of two pebbles dropped in the water. These concentric rings are interrelated to each other and yet spread out into the bigger world. The clients, the husband and wife, are tremendously dynamic people. They lead a very intense life and have three pre-teenage children, and they love the California craftsman tradition. They wrote down what their lives were like, and I was exhausted reading it. The metaphor developed from the bits and parts of the house as it came together. Parts of the house were circular forms that were broken. There were a series of posts and beams that started with a main pillar at the end of the kitchen and got wider apart as they went out towards the main view. In the center of the building was a low cupped wall with a fire from a European wood stove. So there were these three images, the interconnecting circles, the torii gate-like pillars, and the cupped wall with the fire. But there was something missing, something was not happening.

When I reach that kind of impasse I usually get up and go walk or leave it for two or three days. So I got up and walked down the street and there was a bookstore that I had never been in. I went in and found a book on symbolism. I started looking through the book and very soon came to this image which is the Sanskrit symbol for the word *Om* which is made up of the three images from the building. Om is interpreted as the symbol for creative spirit. Working with the Om symbol allowed me to integrate the three elements. Now we are going to quietly etch the Om symbol in the entry way. And the landscape architect has picked up on the concentric circles, and he has continued them out into the landscape. Metaphorically what you have is the energy of these two intense souls going out into the world, but with the home as a place of safety from which they emanate . . .

We have to find a way in our economy, in what we call economics, to factor spirit in somehow. I don't know how that is done. You either seem to be in a place where you are receptive to it and understand it deeply or you are not. I don't think we have had a lot of luck with people who don't see the necessity of spirit in the work of the world and in making decisions. We just can't afford to continue building unlovable buildings, towns, and cities.

RS *It doesn't help to expose them to places made with spirit like bringing them to see the cottage?*

BS We built the prototype for the city council to see but most of them didn't even walk across the street to go through it, however six thousand other people did come through in the four days. I watched people walk into this unit and respond with "Wow, I could live here, I want to live here, can we get one of these things and put it on our land?" They weren't talking about the homeless; they were picturing themselves there. I think on a collective unconscious level human beings have lived more at this scale than the scale that we live at now. However, others walked in and said—this is too good for the homeless. Many of those people have power in the community. We finally got a six to three vote in our favor from the council on the project. I think that if a person can visualize what it would be like for them to live in a place of spirit, they can understand how necessary it would be for a homeless person to have that kind of healing experiences. If they can't visualize or if they feel deeply personally unworthy they will not understand.

Editor's note: Brent Smith's homeless project is currently under construction, and when I checked with him before this book went to press, he asked me to add a brief statement about the evolution of the process of working with neighborhood activists.

A change in the personnel who had been working with the neighborhood activists allowed Mr. Smith to invite the activists to a meeting to create a shared vision for the community. After everyone had stated what they really wanted for their neighborhood, the most vocal of the activists were put on committees to oversee the construction of the homeless village. Now, when planning meetings happen, the needs of the neighbors are included, and common solutions are looked for between their needs and the needs of the homeless village.§

Sim Van der Ryn

Editor's note: Sim Van der Ryn has been developing solutions to architectural problems related to ecology for the past twenty years. In recent years, his concerns have widened to include the spiritual aspects of building. His newest work is a synthesis of ecology and spirituality and is best represented by the design for Real Goods, a catalog and retail store in Northern California.

Sim is a teacher, author, designer, and theoretician who has inspired architectural students and practicing designers with his constant pushing against the cultural barriers that seek to restrict innovation and creativity. In this interview he gets us to think about the need to bring magic back into our daily lives.

RS *Anybody who was in school in the 1970s had a copy of your book* The Integral Urban House. *You have been a leading figure, inspiring people to work in an ecological framework. Your new work seems to be a transition.*

SV Extension, not a transition. *The Integral Urban House* and the Farallones Institute [north of San Francisco] were first-generation ecological design and what I am doing now I would call second-generation ecological design because it pays more attention to the subtle energies, to the next level, a deeper level of integration.

How one achieves that deeper level remains somewhat of a mystery to me. It doesn't come through theory, but you find it through doing, but doing in a way that tests the truth of theory through practice. It certainly helps to keep tuning your awareness of subtle energy through constant interaction with the living world—to the point [where] it becomes second nature.

RS *The thing I'm interested in is how that extension starts to happen, and how your understanding of your own transition and extension can help other people who want to be more in touch with the mythical and mystical side of the nature of design. At one point in time you were just looking at the mechanics, and now twenty years later you are looking at something much deeper than the mechanics. What are the points along the way in which that change starts to occur?*

SV I feel that I am just coming into my own as a designer. If you read about architecture, they say it is an old man's art. You spend a lifetime doing it, and it doesn't start to mature until you are sixty. I know that is what is happening for me now. I am taking in a lot more and not through my brain, it's just happening through my body, and all my experience comes into play.

As I search for a deeper level of integration my main interest is still in designing places where nature is in the foreground, I've been writing a book that is going to come out next spring called *Ecological Design* and I've been reflecting on my experience from the time I was a kid, and I didn't want to be in cities. I feel most comfortable in those places that are interfaces, like old farms. I like places where people have been, that interface between human habitat and unspoiled nature. Those are the places where you actually learn, from a designer's point of view.

RS *But the question I wanted to ask is: How do you become sensitized to the spirit of a place?*

SV It is a somewhat mysterious process; the more time that you can spend the better, and the quieter you can get, the better. I was in Colorado a few weeks ago with John Milton, a conservationist who now studies the use of subtle energies and consciousness, who took me on a two-hour walk around where he does his vision quests, and I began to see through his eyes, at least get into his experience of it. He was showing me all these subtle ley lines and meditation seats that he says Native Americans used thousands of years ago. He told me he had lived without electricity for seventeen years, and that if you lived in a constant artificial electrical field you probably weren't going to sense subtle energy fields. He had me sit in various places and I did have some sensation, maybe that was induced by suggestion. But I am curious and hope to visit John again.

Although I cannot consciously sense the subtle energy fields, I feel that I can contact the spirit of a place. And, when I think about designing with the spirit of a place, my advice is the same as it was twenty-five years ago. Spend as much time as you can getting to know a place, different seasons, different times. To get all the information you need on a place, you need to make use of relevant technology. I use a set of technical tools. For example, the solar pathfinder allows you to do a readout in five minutes of sunpath and sun obstacles which is essential in designing ecologically. But I also use methods that are meditative, specifically sketching and walking.

Learning to design with all your senses is a closed loop. I had an insight when I wrote a poem that begins, "Skies without stars weigh me down." If you are living in an environment where you can't see the stars because of reflected light, or if you are living in environments where you never can feel natural cycles, then how can you know that something is wrong? I live in a houseboat so that I am always aware of what the tide pattern is.

We are exquisitely designed to respond to natural environments. But, now look at the stuff that turns kids on: cyborgs and things that are half machine and half human. We have designed environments that change our perceptions, change our values. At what point does that change to our environment go too far? The question I have been asking recently is, "at what point have we so modified the environment so that a human is no longer human?" [Anthropologist and philosopher Gregory] Bateson first put out the idea that one epistemological error of Darwin's was to consider organism and environment as separate entities. Bateson's point is that it is, "Organism/Environment"—it is a closely coupled system. The example of the relationship between organism and environment that I use is the controversy over saving the condor. They couldn't save the habitat so they took the eggs and hatched them in the San Diego Zoo. So we have condors sitting in the San Diego Zoo that really aren't condors without their environment. Then the next question we ask is, "is a human sitting in a concrete cage really a human? At what point have we so altered the environment so that we cease being human?" Another example of the environment changing the organism is hatchery trout. Every fly fisherman knows that the behavior of hatchery trout in a wild environment is different than the behavior of a trout that has been raised in a wild environment. I don't think these are trivial academic questions at this point in terms of the kinds of environments that we are building.

RS *What you were just saying is very much to the point as we start to construct places that take us farther and farther away from nature. We essentially begin to lose our humanness. You are posing a question—"are we going to lose our essence as humans?"*

SV Yes, I pose it as a question. And I am interested in seeing if this question can be of interest to the mainstream of people. Having spent most of my life as a teacher I am interested in affecting the mainstream, and there the issue is since people are going to be primarily urban we have to bring nature and quality into everyday urban environments where most people are going to live. The luxury that we had in the sixties that we could find a piece of cheap land out in the country somewhere isn't available to people, nor can we recreate the village experience that indigenous people had. I think the challenge is to create a new kind of experience in urban areas where people can be aware of little "n" nature versus big "N" Nature.

RS *How do you create little "n" nature?*

SV You make natural processes visible and accessible to people where they are. The typical example is you live in a suburban house where electricity, sewer, water are all underground, and storm water is carried off in a drain; the food comes from somewhere else. Those issues we were trying to bring out in *The Integral Urban House* in the seventies, but the issue is beyond self-reliance. I think it is more around awareness. It is one of the places I split with [architect] Peter Calthorpe who advocated increasing the density of urban settings for greater ecological well-being. I am interested in designing communities that are holograms of whole systems, I'm not just interested in making them dense and efficient. One part of a hologram for whole systems different from Calthorpe's proposals is growing food in the city. I think there should be community food. People should see food being grown, see it and hopefully participate in it. Ideas like that are not new ideas but I still believe in them very strongly, and they are not always being included in current day proposals.

RS *The fact that we don't have to grow food creates a very insecure system. We sit here assuming that this whole program is going to keep running.*

SV That is where I started in this whole movement. It is the big shadow that hangs over everything. The question is where you draw the line. One extreme is to become a survivalist and go hole up someplace. I am always looking for a middle ground. When I first used the word "sustainable," I envisioned it as a balance at some level of scale, the question is at what level we are achieving that balance. Which I don't think is a trivial question.

The reasons that many of our designs don't fit is that we have nature's geometry, and we have an imposed geometry. The ecological crisis arises from the fact that these two systems don't fit. Then the issue is how do you make them fit each other. When you look at nature as a marvelous whole, as a marvelous entity, you say "why is it like that, what makes it that way?" The answer lies in the scale, linking processes from the atomic level all the up to the cosmos. The design profession needs to develop a perception and a language which is talking about these processes.

RS *What are those processes?*

SV They are processes like the "waste equals food" issue. In a natural process a cell is taking nutrients in and expelling its waste. These wastes—they don't go into a sewer. They are absorbed by the next largest system. So this scale linking process has to do with material exchange, the transfer of material from one state to another. The typical scale linking process is at the edge where you have an ecotone[1] of two systems coming together. It is at this place that you have self-organization, decentralized intelligence—as in the case of the wastes from the cell that become nutrients to some other organism.

Science is just beginning to be interested in what allows natural systems to self-organize, and to the extent those questions get answered, I think they have direct implications for design. Now design operates as a series of separate, sealed compartments. Architects don't worry about where the sewage goes, the sanitary engineer doesn't worry about the roads, so we have this hierarchy, and that's the way the environment gets created. No one is thinking about wholes.

RS *Is there a spiritual level that you find yourself working from?*

SV The spiritual level is the work itself. I'm a Buddhist by osmosis. I don't follow any explicit spiritual practice. There are disciplines that I do. I have been doing watercolors for forty years. And for a few years I have been teaching watercolor outdoors. What I do is teach it as a medium to feel a place, to understand a place, and to have that kind of dialogue between you and the place. The feedback I got from architecture students was it was one of the most valuable courses they had

had. I didn't do much teaching, I just gave them the tools, critiqued them, and would do demonstrations, the act of sitting in a place and paying attention to it for a while.

RS *It seems very Zen.*

SV Watercolors is a key one for me. Another key one is taking long walks, rambles where you are not going anywhere in particular. I think walking is one of the most valuable tools you have to understand a place. The practices are things that take me out of my mental self and take me into an integral self. Watercolor is one, it is like a meditation, it is literally coming in through my fingers.

What I hope my practices allow me to express in my work is the wonder and magic of life, that is a key element that I am looking to express in my design work. In a practical sense that means shifting from designing buildings as objects to designing buildings as living entities, as something that is alive, as in magic consciousness. You can define the stages of human consciousness from archaic to magical to mythical to mental and to a new state beyond. I believe in that kind of progression. All during the eighties I was depressed thinking if we are so smart why do we behave so dumb. We are in the late stage of mental consciousness where we are persisting in the idea that somehow we are separate from the rest of life, and we are destroying life. I don't think it is possible to go back to earlier forms, to the magical consciousness that a lot of indigenous people had where to them rocks were alive, the cave painting was alive. Magic is that simultaneous reality, it is the mark on the wall but it is also the animal it represents. There is a state where we consciously reintegrate these earlier forms. Right now magical consciousness and mythical consciousness are still there but they are in a repressed form for most of us, we don't acknowledge them. The culture doesn't acknowledge them. They are repressed so they come out in other ways, like television. We are all participating in a huge myth. Sooner or later we will move to a more integrated form.

Magical thinking needs to be reintegrated into what we are doing today. That is what someone like John Milton is doing, and I realize I was resisting it. I was participating in it and saying this really can't be, this rock wasn't cleaved in two by some low-level electrical field, rationally I don't believe that. But that is what he was doing; it was magical thinking clothed in scientific language, and that is what my practices are about. The practices [watercolor and walking] are about allowing myself to lapse into magical being, because consciously I'm not going to think magic. I can't will myself to think magically. So the practices are about achieving that higher level of integration. I could be doing a watercolor of a place and I am not thinking, "By doing this watercolor this place is becoming more alive for me." My way is solitary by contrast to a lot of new age workshops that recreate mythical and magical experience with people. You can read a hundred books, you can immerse yourself in an indigenous culture but I don't think that puts you into that space. It is possible to get into that space, without drugs, but you can't get there in a conscious way. The person who does Zen Buddhism with the idea of becoming enlightened is self-defeating.

We know this is part of where we need to return to—to reintegrate the sense of magic, sense that everything is alive, to integrate everything into a shared story that we are participating in. In the sixties we hit people over the head with it; we created a new culture. The question is what are the ways we can do this today, do we have to be as crazy as we were in the sixties, do you have to be crazy or what. As a designer you can nurture the opportunity for people to experience deeper levels.

RS *Now you are working on a book. What is it called?*

SV It is called *Ecological Design* (available from Island Press), and it is both a primer and a manifesto built around these five steps: 1) knowing your place, 2) form follows flow, you need to trace the footprint of what you create, 3) design with nature, where we talk about scale linking and geometry, 4) everyone is a designer, and becoming a designer means cultivating ecological design intelligence, 5) we learn from what we create, and we find if we create denatured environments then we create denatured people. We have to work at bringing small "n" nature back in.

Notes

1. An ecotone is the boundary between two ecological communities where there is a crossover of both. The ecotone is where the richest diversity of life is located.§

James Hubbell

Editor's note: James Hubbell has been creating magical structures for the past twenty years. Trained as a sculptor, he began by building for his own family. His "boy's house" created for his own children is a building full of enchantment. The sculpted interior is covered with mosaics of mythical creatures echoed in the dragon on the floor of the swimming pool outside.

Hubbell maintains that creating beautiful environments is practical because these environments then reach the soul. His current work involves building a school that is beautiful in the slums of Tijuana and working on an outdoor amphitheater in Vladivostok to help create a spirit of openness in a city built to be a fortress.

Hubbell does not like theories and wants to teach those he works with to learn to trust their intuition. He has many practical points to make about how one comes to trust intuition. In this interview we get a good look at Hubbell's thought processes and begin to feel more confident about insisting that beauty and the spiritual benefits it brings become part of our everyday lives.

RS *You have said that the difference between Vladivostok and Tijuana is* "that unlike us they feel they are just beginning, that the world is an unsure place, but if they can find the key the future is theirs. Often I feel we have given up looking for the key. It is possible that these two places may bring a gift to us so that we may see the world like these students as a place that is just beginning." *Is that a starting point to talk about how designing for those two places is different than designing for places in San Diego, and how the spirit of those places shows itself in a way that allows you to do the kind of designing that reflects that spirit?*

JH I think that is a very good place to start. The statement that you read is about the frustration that everybody feels. And the deeper the frustration—or the feeling that you don't know—the more chance there is that you might take the next step and go to a new place where solutions for our problems might be found. We don't change unless we really have to. Now our culture is in a time of change. But it is hard for us to begin to change because we have too much in a material sense, so that we lean on what we have without taking the jump.

RS *I like that notion that we have too much—it's almost that we drown in it.*

JH And having too much saves us from actually facing the world the way it is and making the hard choices. Places like Russia don't have that, they don't have the easy out like we do. So in Russia the design must reflect the materials available, which are more likely to be from the place. But materials are only one part of design, what we really want to talk about is the art of design.

Art has to do with reinterpreting what the world is about. Mostly art has to do with artists finding themselves miserable in the world they are in and trying to make the world livable, and to do so they must reinterpret myth. Art, like nature, changes, and it either adapts or it doesn't. In man our changes are so much quicker than changes are in nature. Things like overpopulation and pollution are things that we can't adapt to physically. We adapt emotionally to them, and eventually culturally. And the artist's role really is to act like a raw nerve for the culture and to suffer through to the time when he or she has to make a new pattern that he or she can live in. It's a very personal thing, and so art in a sense is always a spiritual leap into some new place.

RS *We first met you when we saw your own house, and it was clear from what you had built that you had vision of how people might live or how structures might be created to bring art and spirit into the lives of people more directly. Was that an intent, to bring spirit into the lives of people? What was at work as you started to design these buildings?*

JH I don't want to be too broad on these answers, but I think in the beginning it is a need I have inside myself. I grew up in Connecticut and went to a Protestant Sunday School. And, I think the reason I'm so interested in Russia and Mexico is because their idea of what life is about is very different than what I experienced as a kid in Connecticut. I don't think in Russia and Mexico they see the material world the same way as we were taught. I think they see it as much more transitory, and a thing much closer to what is traditionally [the] spiritual world. I think the Protestant kind of background is really based very much on the material world and doesn't allow us to experience the spiritual world. I think most of what I have been trying to do in my life is to bring the two things together. So I think it begins there—I want to learn from the Mexicans and the Russians.

RS *What you have created in Tijuana and Russia as well as your own house are radically different than anything that is being built around them. What is important to you about how they are built and why you built them?*

JH I just do things and then later on someone asks me—why did you do it—and I try to figure out an excuse. So I'm not really sure, but I think what I usually do, for example in the boy's house, is try to figure out if I were a kid what would I want to live in, or what I would find fun. It isn't that I start with a profound idea that I'm going to communicate something. Along the way there are ideas that come, and they can be translated into theories. But I don't usually like theories, so I would like to tell you how we began work at Vladivostok.

In Vladivostok we had a bunch of students: twelve of them were Russian, eight were from the United States, and one from Mexico. In the beginning I try not to let anything go into my head. If I have ideas I put them in the back. If you have an idea about doing a certain building but if you don't know the height regulations you can get into a lot of trouble. You need to know the parameters that you are working with.

We had a site, and we spent a week just exploring the site. And, one of the things the students did was draw what they thought this park was about. The drawing at this stage was more of a feeling, nothing that needed to be built, or nothing structural. I found that the Russian students were using more organic lines than the Americans. Their drawings were more sensual and more curving. It surprised me. Partly I think that was because they live in a world that is so overly masculine, so hard. All the buildings around the site are very square, there are a lot of electric and telephone towers, it has nothing soft to it.

So when their drawings were more organic looking I began to see that they were expressing what was missing in their environment. They went to the other side from the harsh fortress nature of their environment to flowing organic lines. If we go too far we are always flipping over, and I think that is what the students were doing. Then one of the teachers took us to see a beach where there were all these wonderful stones all soft and rounded by the ocean. So to begin designing in Vladivostok, these are the things that were really critical—what the students drew, what the site looked like, what it felt like, what materials were available—and all of those coalesce into something that eventually you make physical.

RS *I guess what I hear is a process of allowing.*

JH Absolutely, if there is anything I am doing with the students, it's asking them to trust. First of all they have to trust themselves, because they have to tell me

Vladivostok amphitheater.

what they are feeling, not what they think I want them to feel, otherwise I get nothing from them. They have to trust that the other person is on their side, they have to trust the materials, they have to trust the whole process. That is all there is really.

RS *Vladivostok is a sister city of San Diego, so do you see the project as trying to build trust between the two places?*

JH Yes, but it is more than that because the trust is only the beginning of a working relationship. Without trust you are just rehashing old ideas about each other.

RS *So out of this project you are creating the basis of something bigger that can happen.*

JH Yes, it is really like a door created by a piece of music. In a sense musicians make this door that the person can walk through, and where they walk through is the important thing. If we make the right kind of door at Vladivostok then who knows what can happen.

RS *What we have talked about is the process of creating something. What is the importance of the final product that comes out of this?*

JH Well, that is hard to say. Because what comes out of it could be seen as what happens either with the individual or the community. Vladivostok since the Russo-Sino war has really been a fortress. When the head of the architecture school wanted to take us to show us relevant architecture, he showed us bunkers. That was what he thought was important. And the feeling of the town being a fortress is what you get, particularly from the hill where the amphitheater is located where you can look down on the city. The older part of the city that was done in the end of the last century isn't that way, but all of the new things are very stark and unappealing, even to the ships of war in the harbor. And we built this thing that is absolutely the opposite. It's very open; it's a very, very feminine symbol. Now what happens when you drop that kind of thing in the middle of a community that felt itself as being a fortress? What happens when you do that? Will it begin to change the fortress feeling of the city? The possibility of transformation is what is so interesting to me about the work there. It is also what is so interesting about Tijuana.

RS *It is the same kind of opening up process in Tijuana?*

JH The school in Tijuana is in a very poor place. It's a place that in a sense doesn't exist. The people live there but the city doesn't recognize it, so the city doesn't have to supply anything. There are basically no schools. They do have some water, and some electricity, but not every home. And a lot of the houses do not even have floors. It's a very poor neighborhood. And I think traditionally in that kind of place we try to solve the problem by doing the cheapest thing. But we felt that we needed to do a lot more than that. We needed to do something beautiful. I think it makes people think of themselves differently. If you were in a classroom that was just awful, but as a teacher you brought a beautiful bouquet of flowers in every morning what the students thought of themselves would change. So I think doing beautiful things is very practical and really is a powerful tool for change and one that we don't use very often.

RS *I really like that notion that doing something beautiful is practical; I think that is a really important thought.*

JH Well, if it weren't practical, nature wouldn't have gone to the trouble . . . [T]he diversity in nature is enormous. If you were a Protestant from New England, you could settle with one flower. You would only see the flower as a way of getting bees to come. I think we have taken ourselves into a dead end, where we think

Tijuana preschool.

that solving problems has to be simple and practical, and our definition is just too small.

RS *So solving problems has to do with not being simple?*

JH Well, I think it has to do with reacting to the specific problem, not to a general problem. Nature doesn't react to general problems, it reacts to specific problems.

RS *I'm assuming that the school in Tijuana, like your house and the other places you designed, had a designer behind it and then had group input to help put it together so that it represented more than just paid energy—that there was an energy of caring.*

JH Yes, and I think that comes through. I think it is true for all time and for all people. It's like the cathedrals. If you can reproduce the European cathedrals of the twelfth and the thirteenth centuries, you won't get the same thing because you don't get the energy of humans adding to it. Part of what happens when you have all of these people involved is that it happens over a period of time, and it's something that you can't do if it is done instantly. Each one brings a special gift.

RS *Does it have anything to do with everyone being in a certain state of mind or way of thinking or way of being?*

JH It is partly that, but it is also the complexity of all our uniqueness. For example, when I work with kids, if there are twenty kids I am working with, in a sense I get to work with twenty subconsciouses. And I can not only use my own, but I can use theirs. I might get them to do a clay model of what they thought the project was, and then I ask them if I can have these models. In the right circumstances I take the models and put them back into a big ball, and make something out of that. Symbolically it is saying that you are allowing me to have your thoughts about the project and that I'll do one thing that incorporates them.

RS *I like that term very much—a complexity of uniqueness—that gets at that image of everybody contributing something of their own, and it gets at that greater pattern. If you get down to the level of a group of people working on a structure or a building, again using that term, "complexity of uniqueness," it is so much different than having a machine stamp out a sidewalk. A machine comes along and stamps out the pattern, but if a whole bunch of people come along and figure out the pattern then each individual hand has a part in it. Nobody's hand is going to hold a stick the same way, so each line is going to have a uniqueness to it. It seems like that is* *what happens when you get these groups of volunteers—you get the imprint of the hand—physically and spiritually.*

JH Yes, I think the process of building is really a spiritual process especially if you can involve the people who will be part of using the structure. And you know everyone has something to give. Our culture tends to create categories and put everything in separate places to separate people from helping to build the places where they will live or work. It's like art for art's sake and science for science's sake. You can design and build whatever you want, and it's not related to what's around it. What we are trying to learn is how to bring the world back into one thing so that it is related.

RS *We have been talking about the spiritual aspect of the human energy used in creating a place, but is there a spiritual element to the materials used? And how do you decide which materials best express the spirit of a place?*

JH I really will use anything anyone will let me use, but I prefer to use something that has something to do with the area. We are doing a park in Seattle and using these absolutely marvelous granite slabs—huge, huge blocks. The forms could be built cheaper than pouring the shapes in concrete, but it also has to do with the fact that the stones are local. But the whole earth is our place so I wouldn't say I couldn't use materials not from the property.

RS *I find that very interesting because that certainly is a topic that has come up when we have had discussions about spirit of place in terms of local materials, the whole bioregional effort, and ecology where people are trying to do things closer to home. In that instance it has more to do with saving energy and using materials from a place that reflect an ecological concern. But there is also an element of wanting to use a material because it reflects the place.*

JH Well, I think that one of the things that I try to do is to give a person a sense that they are located. I think one of the things we don't do very well in our culture is locate people; by using local materials people begin to get a sense that they belong somewhere.

RS *Isn't that one of the things that made towns, cities, and states unique in the past? You would go to the southwest and you would have pueblos because adobe was what was there, and in the northeast you had houses made out of wood because that was what was there.*

JH Well, it's sort of like technology has given people the freedom to override nature. But if we use that freedom we must take responsibility for making choices. If you can keep everybody alive all the time, then you are going to have to make the decision about who is going to die; it is just that simple. If you can make an atomic warhead then you have to make the decision that you cannot have war, so it goes right down the line. If you can have materials from anywhere in the world, you have to make the choice if this is appropriate to this project. But, at the same time, I don't really like these absolutes that if it doesn't come from ten miles around that you can't use it. I just like too many materials.

I really love stuff, the material part of life. I like the feel of materials and I like what they do—how the iron bends and the way glass breaks. What they do naturally is so beautiful. But I think that I had a problem when young separating material and spiritual things. I didn't understand what they are talking about. I mean you can't pray if you don't have anywhere to kneel. It just seems like they are both expressions of the same thing. I think science is telling us that you can take matter and change it into energy and you can take energy and change it into matter. There is a difference but there is not the rigid line between them. So in a sense, if you look at a rock you are also looking at something that is energy and is a very spiritual thing. I think that also allows me to mix materials in a way so that they feel all right together because I don't give them a hierarchy. They are all part of the symphony that you have to work with.

RS *And putting them together creates a kind of music.*

JH Yes, when I talk to the kids I actually use that. Let's say you imbed a shell into the wall. Well, what you have done is maybe add a flute to the symphony. And you have to figure how you can use that shell again. Maybe you do it by repeating radiating lines in the shell. You don't just put things in. There is an inner rhythm, and when you make a decision you are not only making a decision for that one shell, but you are making a decision about how it has to be related to the larger whole. And when you get the rhythm right it can have a profound impact on people. For example, one house we did is a place a psychologist uses for patients. She said she wanted a combination of a Gothic cathedral and a Japanese shrine. After it was built she has a lot of stories about it. One of the stories is that one of her clients came in and said, "This is probably the worst day of my whole life and I came here and I can't remember why." This psychologist deals a lot with husbands and wives and when they come to this building they never yell at each other, where everywhere else she has worked with them they will yell. And, she says that changes everything. But I think that we don't use these tools that we have as human beings—beauty and respect for our souls—that is one of the reasons that we get in such trouble.

RS *Could we talk about that, why do you consider the tools that we don't use important?*

JH I think of the human being as a creature that is tied to everything and filled with all kind of surprises, and I don't want to define them in a way that answers their problems in an oversimplified way. For example in Vladivostok, part of the materials that we used were because that was all we could find. That's all there was. But if you want materials to represent the complexities of the humans present in the group—there was a girl from Mexico who was connected to Spain, and we had people from all over Russia, so that the tradition was from many places. There was somebody from Maine, there was somebody from Kansas.

RS *I hear what you are saying, the group represented so many places on the earth that to confine yourself to materials from one place would not represent the group.*

JH Part of it is that I don't really like theories too much, and I have my own way of defining what I think is organic. What we are used to in the Western world is this pyramid idea. You have the ideas on the top, you have capitalism, communism, post-modernism and you put the idea at the top of the pyramid and then everything conforms within that philosophy or system underneath it, and you try to build the world around that. But, I think organic is when you begin at the base of the pyramid, and you have to take into account everything. You take into account the people, the materials, the time, the cost, the history, the mythology, the desire of where people want to go. You build from that point. You can't really build something spiritual if all you do is think of the materials. You have to enlarge the framework so that it is no longer an intellectual framework but an intuitive framework.

RS *And intuition is very hard to discuss.*

JH It is very hard, that is why it has so much to do with trust. It is really Blake's thing of seeing the universe in a grain of sand. You no longer analyze life into little parts; you see it as this interrelated, complex, but at the same time very simple pattern. The way I work is I look for the seed and the building comes from the seed, and the seed has all the genetic material that you would have in an organism.

RS *Do most of your seeds need a long germination process?*

JH No. In nature most seeds contain generations and generations of information, but what the artist tries to do is to collect that stuff really quickly. You can only do so much of it logically—in the long run you have got to put it all together intuitively. You write down what you know technically, then you jump over to that other side. You must trust that your feelings are right.

RS *Well, obviously a lot of your feelings have been right because a lot of people like what you are doing, so that you seem to have found guiding forces in yourself that other people respond to in very positive ways.*

JH It is almost more dangerous to have people like your work than it is to dislike it. You can always fight the guy that doesn't like it, but it is very hard when everyone likes it and then you feel you must do what they like. And maybe it is not right. You always have to go inside and find out if it is right with yourself.

RS *How do you relate this to doing something public, like the school or the amphitheater; doesn't it matter in some way that people like those things?*

JH I'm not saying it doesn't matter, but it cannot be the basis of what you do. I once talked to a developer about not cutting up a piece of land into little pieces. He said that ninety percent of the people liked it this way, so this is why he did it. It's too easy to say that the last thing I did people liked so I should do it again. But, if you don't trust the voice inside yourself, which might tell you to do something different, you really short-circuit the whole thing.

RS *We are not always taught how to find that voice inside yourself, what we are taught in most schools is theories from the outside, of what somebody else did, or what is being done now, or what is approved of, and we are not really taught to listen to that voice.*

JH We are not even asked to do it and often are punished when we do.

RS *Exactly, in fact, those people who are most in touch with their inner voices frequently have a hard time being part of the larger society.*

JH What you are talking about is what we call the eccentric, which means out of center. And I think that culture and society is like a big ship, and it is going somewhere, and it is very hard to turn it. It just has such tremendous momentum.

Then you have these people you call eccentrics. They are like people out in little row boats that are paddling away in one direction or another and looking for their own thing. Now one of them comes to a waterfall and says to the big ship—look what I found, you better turn that ship. And you either listen to them, or you go into some kind of disaster.

In nature, too, that is what happens. There are offshoots that often are the thing that becomes the norm. These thoughts about spiritual things are so tied together . . . I have a friend who suggests that for the last four hundred years man has been developing his logical mind, and in that case you need a square building because you can place yourself intellectually in this building with parallel walls, but he feels that in the next century we need to develop the intuitive because things are so complex now that you can't solve them intellectually, and he says that the organic building or the amorphic building is the best kind to develop the intuitive side of the mind.

RS *Are you talking to the students you work with about developing that intuitive process?*

JH I feel I'm doing that when I try to get them to trust.

RS *And that development of trust has to do with the development of that inner voice?*

JH Yes, just believing that you can let go and it will be all right.

RS *Can we go back to Vladivostok, and see specifically how you tried to get people to trust their own inner workings—was it with building the models or with human relationship?*

JH What I found is that you can't do it too quickly. You can't just walk in and do it. What we do first are games to get to know each other and respect each other as individuals, and to have some fun. They don't have the idea that this is the end of the world. We had them go off and draw details of the city in teams, then we had them draw the site. You don't just talk about the site, you know the site. You don't just talk about the culture, you accept the culture. Doing the sketching and the models is all part of that thing of building enough complexity so that you forget what you are trying to hold on to. What I am trying to do with them is to look for the surprise, to trust that surprise. What I really like is if at the end they can't remember whose idea that it was. Then it becomes simple again. And you need some time to do that, four or five days at least.

RS *I think that is a really critical element, that notion of time. Because in our time-is-money culture, it is very hard to get the time to allow things to ripen naturally.*

JH What you are looking for is a kind of inner rhythm, and if you leave out the idea of time, you don't have the rhythm.

RS *And that is what gets lost in corporate architectural buildings, where the process doesn't allow for the type of maturing of the design idea, speed and efficiency replace time and ripeness and rhythm.*

JH It's a strange but wondrous world we live in.§

Nader Khalili

Editor's note: Nader Khalili first captured the imagination of people looking for new solutions to creating inexpensive housing by glazing and firing adobe structures like they were giant pots. His quest is to find ways to house the millions of homeless people in the world with grace, dignity, and beauty using the cheapest means possible. Coming from a Muslim background, he is strongly influenced by the writings of the Sufi poet Rumi, and his work and life are as much a personal spiritual quest as they are a quest to help solve the material problem of housing.

Nader Khalili was an architect with large corporate practices in both the United States and Iran for many years before beginning to experiment with traditional building methods. Just before the Islamic revolution in Iran, Mr. Khalili, who had been living in the United States, returned to Iran to experiment with ideas that he had for improving the mud and adobe structures common in the Iranian countryside. As he observed the structural integrity of ancient pottery kilns, he came upon the idea of firing a whole house. He returned to the United States in the early 1980s and has continued his work here.

In his desire to find ever cheaper methods of building, he has now developed what he calls "superblocks" which are long tubes of sandbag fabric filled with material from the site where a house is needed. These tubes are then coiled like upside down baskets. The "superblock" sandbag houses are currently being developed and tested in Hesperia, California by Mr. Khalili and other members of the Geltafan Foundation, which was founded to explore and expand Mr. Khalili's work. The beauty and simplicity of his designs have attracted interest from around the world. Mr. Khalili is an excellent writer and has published two books about his work: Racing Alone, *and* Sidewalks on the Moon.

In the following interview, Mr. Khalili tells the story of how he began his work and of the inner fires that keep him going. He told his story so clearly that I did not have to ask any questions.

Before I started to experiment with new forms for buildings I built many, many conventional buildings—high-rises, offices, schools, and homes, from Washington, D.C. to Hawaii, doing many different structures, designing them or working on them. Then I carried this technology to Iran, which is my native place, and opened an office there, which gave me offices in both Los Angeles and Iran. Then, just as it says in [my book] *Racing Alone*, I closed the offices, sold my shares, and went to the desert trying to learn.

At that time I had this dream of building from earth and firing the structures to become a huge ceramic bowl, turning it upside down. It would be earthquake-proof and integrate the elements of earth, water, air, and fire into structures that hold human life. And rather than making pottery as humans had always made pottery—for the hand, now this pottery—ceramic, really—is on the scale of human life. I am not a potter, but I could imagine firing and glazing a house, at the same time the ceramists and the potters would shudder thinking this is the craziest thing ever.

I had the idea of firing buildings years before; as a matter of fact, I remember it was in Los Angeles one night [in 1966] when I was crossing the street, and all of a sudden it came to my mind—the firing of a whole house. So I thought about it and talked to my friend, but at that time I did not do anything. The vision was constantly there until seven years later where I had the chance to drop everything and follow this idea.

When you are talking about sense of place, the place this idea happened was at the intersection of Hollywood and Highland. To me the place is never separated from time and never separated from humans. It isn't only the place, but it is the unity of the human soul with the time and place—that's what really makes it happen. Otherwise all the places in the world are the lands of God. And although there are special places, what is even more special is when that moment of unity when time and human soul come together. For me the unity came together first when I had the idea, then seven years later when I was able to begin work on the ideas in a right place. So I held the image in my mind for eight years and all the time I was working in many places and was very successful in the business. I was building many soulless buildings, running around collecting money, paying people to work for me. But I did not find the fulfillment of my dreams in what I was doing.

I had actually come to America, to San Francisco, in 1961, following a dream of having more than a conventional life, and by 1975, I was very successful in business. But things were happening in my mind. And I went on this journey in my native land [in 1975] a few years before the revolution. And I stopped that rat race. The story of *Racing Alone* was just that. I took my little boy to the park across the street, and the children's game became a race all of a sudden. But my son was the smallest and the slowest, and he would come in last. After the fourth time around, he came crying and said, "I want to race alone." Then I drew a line on the ground and counted one, two, three and he ran and came in even later than before. But he brought a leaf with him, and next time he found a flower. He was enjoying his race alone, at the same time I noticed that he was always coming [in] first. And that became a very important point.

At that time in Iran they were not racing alone but were totally copying the Western world, destroying everything that had existed, building high-rises. Up to thirty thousand Americans were living there and doing projects. When I pulled out and sold my business, my colleagues that had similar companies couldn't believe that I was dropping everything. So I told them if I am really serious in these dreams, quests, and visions I should follow them when I was being successful with what I was doing, not when I was a failure. And I believe that when you do that you move into anything that you want to do with a lot more power and a lot more strength.

A poet wrote, "you see a bird sit on the highest and thinnest branch because he knows if he falls he can always fly." So by getting into certain things when you have the strength, when you are powerful, when you know that you can go the other way, you can choose a direction that is within your heart or a dream that empowers you a lot more. You always have choice as far as day-to-day life is concerned, but that choice becomes very secondary to the dream.

And after each day with whatever you are doing, the dream will become the main theme. Until finally one day the change happens. But to get ready for that one day might take seven years. And for me in those seven years everything was being distilled. Just like the book *Racing Alone*—it took ten years to distill, but I wrote it in four or five weeks.

What's happening is within you, but you need a system for it. You need somewhere along the way to make the change. For me that came at the right time three years before the revolution in Iran. For two years I was in villages working, so when everyone else associated with Western ideas had to run away or was put in prison, I had no fear to stay and continue the work. During that time spiritual works, particularly of Rumi, became very important in my life.

Rumi wrote about the elements of earth, water, air, and fire and showed the importance of these elements in life—human life. Humans are made from these elements. And now I have taken these elements and brought them into a tangible form in real earth, and real air, and real water and fire. As I worked to make buildings out of these elements, it was my own transformation that was happening within me that wanted to mold these materials into a home.

And my own transformation made it possible to see more clearly how to build a home out of these elements. I am convinced if there is going to be an ideal living place or community, such a real utopia cannot take shape unless the architecture is made from these four elements. These four elements are in equilibrium with each other and they are the ones that affect the human spirit. We are always going to find them in places and times that are closest in unity with our souls. In a way the building and firing of these structures was the fire that was within me and the home that wanted to be formed. These elements are unlimited because with your imagination you can create from the smallest pot to the whole solar system out of these universal elements. As I went after this work I found a spiritual dimension that was more and more tangible in the material that I was working with. And it was at the same time that I dropped everything else.

I think my Western experience in high-rises and other technologies was as strong a backbone for my work as Persian poetry and philosophy. Their integration brought everything together for me. In 1984 I was invited by NASA [the National Aeronautics and Space Administration] to present this material at the first symposium about building on the moon. I presented how you can take fire from the sun and the dust from the moon and melt it and change it into ceramic houses. When I reached working on the moon I found out that these four elements were not there. There was only one element, and the lunar dust was that one element.

For many months I was totally disillusioned, but the answer was again in the mystic Rumi's poetry. And the answer was that there are not four elements, there is only one element, and that is the unity of all elements. Once I grasped onto that idea from him, he says "don't you see the clouds come from the fire, from water. The lightening is nothing but the fire in water, and you see the fire that burns in the earth under your feet and you can dive into water and come out through fire." These all became very important in giving me strength.

When I was working in all the villages I still thought I needed the four elements. But designing for the moon, there was the sun that was the fire, there was the lunar dust, and all these elements were in the forms of the domes and vaults that came together in the ceramic firing of the buildings. I came to see that you don't need all of these elements, one element was enough. So the structures that you are seeing me build now [in Hesperia] in Super Adobe or sandbags came from the same plan I suggested for the NASA project on the moon, in addition to ceramic building. They were Velcro bags and you just fill them and stick them together. In the very low gravity you don't need anything else. They will not blow away. They are heavy, since you need at least fifteen feet of soil on top of any structure you build on the moon to keep out the radiation, thermal extremes, and the impact of meteorites—then sandbags can be the structure as well as the shieldings.

This understanding that there is only one element crystallized on the lunar project, for building on the moon and on Mars. When I presented these ideas I only had eight minutes to explain how you can build a ceramic colony, ceramic everything, the sidewalks, the landing pads. The soil that is there is all glass and ceramics anyway, you can form it and make much, much bigger structures because of low gravity. You can make all your landing pads, your sidewalks, everything out of ceramics.

Building with sandbags, or Velcro adobe, involves arches, vaults, and domes. These forms are eternal from your eyeballs to your head to the solar system. It's all made in circles. The curvature is made by the sun. Einstein said that there is no straight line in the universe, all are curved. So that is how the heavens have been giving us the message. Do you see a rainbow in a pitched form? No, it is always curved. Everything comes in these curvatures, even the way we think is in curves, the way we dream is in curves. And once these forms are in you they brood and distill, and you become their medium. And whatever you do you are serving part of the equilibrium of the elements yourself. The work itself directs you after a while.

I have a friend who is a psychiatrist, and she was studying my work with me over eight years. One day she told me that in my mind I was trying to build houses for poor people out of earth—there are a billion people on the earth without adequate shelter, for me it was a cause to get out and build—but she said in reality you are just building yourself a safe home to hold your own fire within the ceramic crucible because your fire will not be contained by anything except ceramic. And that is why you started doing ceramic houses [she explained], this is something that came out of you.

I wanted to get out and build for people, naturally with earth, ecologically safe and balanced, using all of these things I had discovered about building with earth. But then at the same time I saw it was my own quest to know myself. So the technology that was behind me, that I learned in the Western world, connected with the spirit of poetry, and the textures and colors of the Persian rugs to help me understand both myself and what to build. Through Sufism I found that there are two ways to gain understanding: the path of knowledge and the path of love. The path of knowledge is that of Plato and Socrates; the path of love is that of Rumi and other mystics. And both paths will end in the truth. It is not one or the other. In my buildings I hope to combine the path of knowledge and the path of love.

In Iran there are probably over sixty thousand saints, every small town or village has a shrine. And I wonder where did all these saints come from. All the modern countries put together don't have as many saints as Iran. Well, the way many of these saints became recognized and have a shrine is that most of them were somebody's dream. Usually an old man of the village or a holy person would have a dream that in such and such a location somebody holy was buried and they would all walk with him till he would say—"Here." And that would become the shrine. And that would be the beginning. And this kind of dream was one of the ways that I came to Hesperia.

Before I was in Hesperia I tried to carry on the work in many places. But in none of these did what should be done take place. When I went to Hesperia, my brother was doing some work there. I used to go back and forth between there and other places until something happened between me and that area, that place. In all different ways it was right for what I wanted to do.

In my previous work in both America and Iran I found that the greatest single barrier to people who are working with earth are building departments, codes, officials, ministries of housing, that they will not give in to anything. I decided that that was the last barrier that I must conquer, and that is one of the reasons that I went to Hesperia. We found this land, and I wanted to be within the city so that I could work with the building department and get building code approval for these new ways of building with earth. As the Persian saying goes, finally you want to go to the lion's mouth, and I decided that this is the place.

I had some of my associates and students that I took out there. They saw the place and they said—"Why here? All these wonderful places exist where you were working before. Why this place, ungodly and in a desert, close to the freeway not very far from the high tension wires, why this place?" I told them this is the right place for what is the last stage of this work. And the last stage of this work is to break the barriers that stop the human from carrying on his work. And, I am staying here to build, and to test, and to show that what is here is as good, and many times better, than what is being built today. For this I have to be within the city, under the building codes, that is why I am staying here. After that day they didn't come back.

My students and associates didn't think it was a good place to be. They didn't think it was a nice living area. It was extremely hot in the summer, very, very cold in the winter, with flash storms, and very close to an earthquake fault. And that is exactly what I was looking for. This would be the best test ground for my work. At the same time I had an offer to work in New Mexico near Santa Fe. The land was given to me. I said that is a nice, comfortable, cozy place to go and to build pretty things. But it was not for me.

I need to build for the world, and the world has all these problems. If we build anything in Hesperia and it is approved, and accepted, and it works, it will work almost anywhere in the world. And this was my conviction. But they left, and I stayed. It was a difficult time. But then new associates and new students began to arrive.

During that time I had a dream that there were two very crowded freeways crossing, with one going north and one going east. In the middle of the freeway there was a piece of land, and somehow they gave me that land; they said—this land is yours, and you must build a paradise in this land, right in the middle of this land. So I think—there is this challenge—how do I build a paradise in this place? And in the dream I had solved all the problems of building on this land from pollution to structures, and when I was waking up in the morning I was just ready to solve the noise pollution. From this dream comes a new conviction that if I can build a paradise between two pieces of freeway, then I can build where we are in Hesperia. So I stayed there.

The land belongs to a fellow Iranian, and I leased his five acres for two years and started. People said—you are building everything here, who is going to own this? This place to me was like a rented piano—we rent, we play. New people came to work, and we started by digging a pit. One of the backbones of the work now is [my assistant] Iliona Outram. She was familiar with the work. She had been doing her own work on building with earth in England, so when she came and joined it was just the right time. We just started digging a pit, fifteen feet wide, three feet deep. And I kept saying, just keep digging and I'm going to start spinning, spinning in the pit.

The whole idea in the spinning is that you become like the third dimension connecting the earth and the universe. Somehow that will happen when you spin, things will happen. And it did all start to happen. We dug. Then some people gave us some bricks, and we started building with bricks. We couldn't build ceramics—it was too expensive. So I said let's just build out of what is right here. I don't want to bring anything in.

So the ideas that I had developed for the moon I was bringing down to earth. It was an important idea because places in the world where the most adobe work is happening there is not enough clay left anymore. It is mostly sand. For example in Egypt, where they started adobe building, they won't allow you to build with adobe anymore because the Nile needs the clay for agriculture. But Egypt is ninety-five percent sand. So we began to think we should be able to build with anything, anywhere. And that is when we began to consider using sand inside very long cloth sacks as building blocks. The work in Hesperia now is the closest to getting into the spirit of this place. We can build out of what is here, the best form, the most beautiful structure, the lowest cost, and the healthiest. Now healers are coming to Hesperia and studying about the health aspect of this work.

All I can tell you is that within this three years—once we chose this place and once we started working on it—we and the place became one. There was no separation from the place by trying to design things for this place. The brick dome, the Rumi dome, every brick was set and designed on spot, in this place as we went up. We were on location without any plans looking at every view, every wind that was blowing, at the sunrise, that is how it was built.

At first the building department of the city of Hesperia was totally skeptical and wouldn't let us do anything. We had to get permits by many ways. Now, less than three years later, they have turned around, and the city has given us a project to build a museum. It will be built out of sand, what we are calling superblock or megablock, the endless coil block. We will even fire and ceramic glaze the entry tower to the museum. It is unbelievable the way that things are turning around because that was the place to go to.

We tested for earthquakes there. We even got two big shocks, 7.4 and 6.9 magnitudes. Good tests for our structures. We got calculations, plans, and details, we tested them more. We had many people who came to watch and help, from space scientists to the McDonnell Douglas people to groups from Princeton. All of the tests are directed to these barriers of building codes that were not allowing us to build. Once the buildings passed the tests, the mayor and others from the city government came there and they are the ones who are promoting the work. They gave us a project, which is a miracle by itself. Instead of a place where they would not allow us to build a single building, now they are paying us and giving us projects to build.

So the power of the place is that it is never separated from the human dimension of the process. Power also comes with the integration of the five senses, where you can learn an equilibrium with the knowledge of the universe. The sense of the place that you are in, the forms that you build, and the people who come—all of this must work together. And then practical and day-to-day life solutions come from combining the spiritual dimension and the technological. A lot of our progress depends on that. So that is the story of Hesperia and the work there.

We get a lot of children now. Children come from elementary schools. We teach them how to build arches by putting their heads together, and how to make walls with their bodies. Then they understand what the structure means. Because to me a lot of us folks are fossilized in our ability to learn new things, but children can understand it very well.

The bottom line in America is always economics. You can have the best ideas, the best dreams, and someone can prove that it is uneconomical and it goes berserk. These words "It is uneconomical" are the Bible today. It is no longer the architects that build the town. It is the lawyers and banks. The Americans who first came to this country had a bunch of nails and hammers and saws, and they built everything. They had a pioneering spirit. Now the first thing they think of is the bank and the insurance company. The bank and the insurance company have nothing to do with building. They deal with polishing coins. And yet they have taken the power from the same Americans

The interior of the Rumi dome in Hesperia, built with adobe blocks then fired and glazed on the inside.

In a special program children are taught principles of architecture by building domes with sandbags.

that always built for their own family. Now they are at the mercy of all the banks and the insurance companies. Until the turn of the century everybody could build houses for themselves, but everybody is now afraid to do anything. All the power is taken.

We want to show that the barriers are the building codes. The barriers are systems that are stopping people. We have lost all these freedoms. We must gain them back. So that if you feel this is the best place for your work, you have to go and get permits. Everything needs a permit, and you should be able to get it. When you go and talk to people in that place, they don't have the first basic knowledge of what is really good for you or not. The codes are written for the large lumber, cement, and steel companies who supply the materials.

In this country you have to bring new ideas into tangible numerical values, and that is what we are trying to do with the building codes. We have to bring this whole vision and spirituality and integrate it with the language of the day. We cannot just shy away and go into a corner and be an artist. You can be an artist and a critic, but that is not going to solve the problems. They will just get worse and worse. And if an artist or a dreamer is not involved, who else has the imagination and dreams to carry on the changes that are needed?§

Architecture and Design Conclusions

In this section the authors have given guidelines that govern their particular design beliefs and practices. Each article and interview offers a wealth of insight and information to those who are interested in creating a built environment more in harmony with a sense of higher purpose and in keeping with the spirit of each place.

Although each designer's perspective is unique, there are themes that run through all of the articles, either directly stated or implied. The following six principles are ones that we feel best express those shared themes:

1) Work from the inside out, to make the built environment a reflection of our hopes, dreams, and most cherished beliefs.

2) Investigate tradition, find out what is good in the past wisdom of cultural and religious traditions and incorporate it into current design.

3) Be sensitive to the place: sit and listen, draw, sketch or watercolor it, take enough time to begin to feel in tune with the spirit of the place.

4) Make sure that what you build adds energy, grace, and beauty to the site, that when you think of what the site was like before the building, you are glad that the building is there.

5) Become one with the materials you use, use only the materials and plants that you love, and lovingly use those materials and plants.

6) Be courageous in your design and building, do not let the criticism of others deter you; if you believe you are right, change the building code, if you must, to get your idea built.

PART FOUR:

Translating New Ideas into Public Policy

WE DO NOT CREATE IDEAS; they create us, Carl Jung once said. Regardless of where ideas originate, they come to us first as individuals. Then we begin to translate those initial inspirations into forms through writing, drawing, painting, sculpture, or dance. This enables us to better grasp that spark of knowledge and share it with others. With perseverance those seeds become designs to shape the way we act, even the places where we live, work, and play.

Humans, however, are social animals. We come together in groups to form communities and cultures. To prevent chaos, we develop norms for our groups through setting goals, objectives, and policies that can become social programs that bind us together and, hopefully, nourish us. Working in creative harmony with the spirit of place is an idea that is fundamental to creating a sustainable society. In this section we show how spirit of place concepts can and must be translated into policies that can guide us to effective actions, even when that journey may require cutting through the tangled jungle of governmental bureaucracy. The creative soul may become depressed at the thought of trying to negotiate this wilderness, but only when we learn to shape policies that can respect natural laws and forces can we establish and maintain ecological harmony.

18. Facing Up to the Challenge of Translating the "Living Earth" Idea into Policies and Programs

Donald N. Michael, Ph.D.

Editor's Note

Change is the one constant in life, the I Ching *teaches. In order to find harmony with nature, then, we must be ever-inventing new and better ideas to help our lives work in cooperation with nature. In recent years, one of the most exciting ecological ideas has been a suggestion by British scientist James Lovelock that modern science should consider the entire earth to be a living being—the "Gaia Hypothesis."*[1] *In response to Lovelock's theory, numerous books and television shows have championed the living earth concept; Gaia Festivals have sprung up like mushrooms in a warm spring rain to honor the earth; and even a significant number of new children have been christened with the name "Gaia." The Gaia Hypothesis is definitely a part of life that will not disappear, but the real test of the power of an idea is how it impacts public policy. In this essay, social psychologist and futurist Donald N. Michael, walks us through the mindscape of the world of public policy and introduces us to the kinds of challenges that a new idea must face to change the shape of the way large governments and businesses work. It may seem ponderous to some, but reserve your judgment until you have finished reading David Anderson's article on ecotourism planning later in this section.*

This article is based on a keynote address to the "Is the Earth a Living Organism?" symposium held in Amherst, Massachusetts, in 1985, produced by James and Roberta Swan for the National Audubon Society Expedition Institute.

James Lovelock has challenged the scientific community by arguing that modern science and society should view the earth as acting as if it were a living organism: his Gaia Hypothesis.[2] Human societies evolve according to the times and the needs of the people. Those that survive require guiding principles to steer their course. New ideas keep society alive and vital. From a pragmatic standpoint, there are a number of steps that an idea must go through to be translated into action. And the levels of action each have their special qualities. In this essay I am going to be exploring the issues and questions that would have to be engaged if the living earth concept would be translated into the policies and programs that guide institutions, governments, and private enterprise—*not* what those policies ought to be, but what it is going to take to influence the shape of those policies.

First, let me be clear about my use of terms. By "policies," I refer not only to government policies; I include policies chosen by grass roots groups, by corporations, and by all those institutions and organizations that play a major part in determining what, of what various groups seek or reject, comes to be. And when I refer to policies, I include all those statements of principle and direction that directly or indirectly would affect the earth. Those policies might have to do with the creation of jobs, pest control, waste disposal, pollution, access to aesthetic experiences, ownership of earth rights, natural resources utilization, technology utilization, war-making, and population control, to give some examples. These are policies that, one way or another, affect the earth and so presumably would be different if the idea that the earth is living was able to influence them.

Beliefs about the living earth could have their influence in a number of ways. I am going to pose questions about three aspects. The first has to do with what qualities of *aliveness* one would want to forward to influence the shaping of policies. Just what are the attributes of aliveness when we say that the earth is alive? The second question has to do with what values apply to the formulation of policy regarding life, living, and the fact of aliveness. I refer to values held by people of all sorts of different persuasions. The third question has to do with political action in pursuit of making or changing policy.

The purpose of this exploration is to alert ourselves to general issues regarding these three areas that could play an important part whenever those who perceive the earth as alive attempt to influence and form policy. These issues and questions are very important if we hope to translate into policy beliefs that are held personally or in a group of like minds. Certainly not all groups and organizations believe and value life in a similar manner, which is not surprising considering the diversity of humankind. Not all institutions and persons are willing to pay the costs for the alleged benefits of acting as if or truly believing that the earth is alive. (I use the words "costs" and "benefits" to mean not only dollar costs and benefits, but also psychological and spiritual costs and benefits.) There are no free lunches in this world. Costs accompany any benefit, and not everybody values these the same. In an open society, the shaping of policy and the conduct of policy depend on how those costs and benefits are evaluated, allocated, adjudicated, and traded off. Given such differences, the issues and questions I shall raise are going to be very much to the point if you are interested in having your beliefs be influential beyond those who already more or less share them.

For some of you what I shall say will seem irrelevant, boring, downright annoying, or even angering. You want to get on with celebrating the earth's aliveness. Fine! Celebrating is important; we don't have enough celebration in our lives. But beyond *celebrating* what we believe we know about the earth, what *then*? If you wish to emulate those cultures that believe the earth is alive, you must deal with policy issues. Those cultures didn't call their norms of conduct policy, but the way those societies evolved and were put together resulted from shaping processes which in our complex society we call policy. If you hope to go beyond volunteeristic enthusiasm to further your beliefs and shape the ways things are chosen and done, it means you must attend to the kind of issues and questions that I am going to raise.

Lastly, lest my approach to this topic leads you to believe I am indifferent to the gut issues, so to speak, I developed this text while sitting in the botanical gardens of the city of Madrid, Spain. I chose such a setting because I am very aware of how places influence my thoughts and actions. Actually, my awareness of nature and ecology can be traced back to the first paper I ever published, which was in *Aquarium* magazine, when I was still in high school. Today, I find great pleasure in hunting wild mushrooms and other wild greens, for their taste as well as the deep satisfaction of being able to connect with nature's bounty. I am by no means indifferent to nature aesthetically or spiritually; questions about the earth's aliveness are very real for me. But my usefulness on these matters derives from the kind of evaluation I make here.

Issues Raised by the Living Earth Thesis

I now turn to the first question that is going to be important for how policy is influenced by the living earth concept: the attributes that define livingness when we say that the earth is "alive." I am going to be asking this question on behalf of those who aren't convinced that it is.

Does the adjective *living* add anything to our explanatory or predictive abilities needed for policy formulation? Does *living* add anything beyond what ecology, systems theory, biology, and the like convey? In other words, are the phrases "living earth" or "the earth is alive" something other than "catch alls" or metaphors for a complex set of concepts about interdependence, cybernetic processes, self-organizing systems, referring to a highly complex systemic mix of biological and non-biological processes? What is the meaning that is attached to "living earth," *beyond* the meanings that are already available from ecology, systems theory, biology, and the like?

If everything is alive, that is, if all the universe is alive as some argue it is, what discriminating utility has the concept "alive"? What's left to act *toward* that's not alive? In other words, has "alive" become so all embracing that it doesn't give direction and shape to policy formulation?

These are the kinds of questions doubters will ask those who say that the earth is alive. In talking this over with Roberta Swan, she made a most intriguing observation. She felt that, for those ignorant of concepts from ecology, systems theory, and the like, the idea that the earth is living appeals to the heart. That appeal engenders not only a "feelingfulness" and spiritualness, it also communicates a sense of interconnectedness, interdependency, and complexity. This is the same kind of sense that the sciences convey in their way. So, the concept of "living earth" could, perhaps, encourage some people to seek to understand these more complex scientific concepts following the initial poetic and spiritual appeal to the heart. As *an appeal to the heart*, the concept certainly adds to values aimed at respecting and protecting the earth. But besides its appeal to the heart, does the concept of the living earth add information beyond what science illuminates and documents in other terms?

Is the earth a *unique* life form? In contrast to *any* other life form, if the earth is alive, it does not reproduce itself. (Humans colonizing other planets is *not* reproducing the planet!) It is a matrix for reproduction of that which lives on it, but what about it? And if the earth doesn't reproduce itself, is it unique as a complex life form in not being sexed? The utility of sex is to provide genetic variability so that the forms *reproduced* have a greater range of variability. Some think the earth is sexed because they speak of the mother earth and the earth goddess, but is that indeed an appropriate term to help define the concept of a living earth if it is not a planet-reproducing system?

The earth is unique in another way: no earth-born life has a core of iron molten by the heat produced by its own radioactivity. Also, if the earth is alive, it is unique in being the repository of the heavy elements often toxic to life whereas other living matter is not, certainly not to the extent that the earth is. Is this another unique property of a living system radically different from all other living systems that we know?

Does its uniqueness compared to conventional life disqualify the earth from being deemed alive? It has properties like other living systems, but it also has properties that other living systems do not possess. Then the question would be asked: Is the earth simply analogous in some ways to the living systems on it, having *some* of the properties of living systems? Why *should* these unique properties be subsumed under the concept of *living*? On what scientific grounds? Of course, the earth by virtue of its uniqueness as the matrix for life could still be held precious, meriting special attention. Then the pragmatic question arises: If the term "living earth" were introduced during policy considerations, would it serve only to obfuscate the issues to be faced, thereby antagonizing others, perhaps potential allies?

Is the earth conscious? As we are? In other ways? Does it feel? Does it have thoughts? Like ours or different? Beliefs on these matters seem to run off in all directions. Nevertheless, feelings regarding these matters are intense. The implications of such beliefs are complex and serious. What part do humans have in the earth's consciousness? What part of its aliveness are we humans? Are we the earth's mind? Are we the earth's consciousness, its repository of thought and aliveness? Are we its brain? If we are not, are we part of its aliveness nevertheless? If we are part of the aliveness of the earth, what is our relationship to the other parts of the aliveness of the earth? Some have argued that, by adjusting its environment, the earth can take care of itself. As a system, it shapes itself to maintain itself as alive—or part of itself as alive. But if we are part of its aliveness in that sense, what are our entitlements and obligations as part of or separate from the living earth? (*Our* meaning "us as human beings.")

If we are the earth's mind and brain, that part of the living system, are we somehow related to the planet in ways that emancipate us from the ambiguous and conflicting (and sometimes collaborative) ways our brain and mind relate to our body? If we are not somehow emancipated from such analogous relationships, then we are indeed in trouble. There are exceptional individuals; but, by and large, I would argue that we are mediocre in attending to our physical, mental, emotional, and spiritual well-being. Most of us live with deep conflicts within ourselves. Few of us have learned to cope with the denial, projection, fear, hostility, and greed in each of us and among us. Much of this is unconscious, and we hardly know anything about it. Think of the precarious state of so many interpersonal relationships. We live poorly with our shadows. Many of us deny the shadow in ourselves. Some of us are afraid of it—do not even allow ourselves to know it is in us and in others. Few of us have learned to live with it. Can we honestly expect, if we are the mind, the consciousness, of the earth, to do better in relation to the grand system than we do in relation to ourselves as individuals and among ourselves? Today, we have profound difficulties dealing with human ethical issues, much less with the "ethical" issues that some assert exist between humans and the rest of the planet.

Clearly, there is a very large policy area, a large set of questions to be unraveled having to do with the meaning of consciousness in relation to the meaning of living earth. We must be far more clearheaded about these matters in order to defend policies appropriate for protecting a living earth.

Before I move to the next general topic, I want to emphasize a related but different point.

It is essential to keep in mind that, whatever the answers may be regarding the nature of the earth's being alive and our relation to it, these answers, and the questions we ask, are human inventions. We *create* the analogies, the metaphors, the data, from poetry, experiences, science, from whatever, for talking about the earth and its livingness. Undeniably, human beings are great storytellers. We excel at this and at coercion, the two ways we influence each other. But we are not very good truth sayers. Others have stories to tell and differing answers to give to the questions that I have raised. In an open society, the policy-making process has to adjudicate among those stories, and the questions and answers given in them. The precise meaning of the phrase "the earth is alive" must be clear when the time comes to influence and shape policies that will affect others besides ourselves, if this is to be a guiding sentiment of value to both the earth and us. Recall that besides government policies, there are those set by grassroots groups, corporations, and the like. How they respond to arguments that the earth is alive depends on how livingness *per se* is valued.

Assume for the moment there is an agreement among the earth pro-lifers on what the attributes of a living earth are. How is that aliveness valued? Consider a spectrum for valuing life. At one end are those people and institutions that say that *all* life is sacred. At the other end are those people and institutions that say that *no* life is sacred. In between are people and institutions that say *some* life is sacred. There are sacred cows, even sacred rats and mice, in some parts of the world. In other parts the same animals are hamburgers, pests, and prey for cats. There is a sacredness we ascribe to human life which is expressed in the Hippocratic Oath and practiced in the application of high technology to preserving life. We set aside wilderness areas, in part from a sense of sacredness of life. Some value systems totally oppose suicide. Others see it as among the highest forms of spiritual devotion. Euthanasia can be viewed as compassion or murder. The public conflict over abortion is perhaps the most evident example today of an emotionally charged issue where both sides assert they are spiritually correct. Another controversy involves those who say that animals have rights and we do not have the right to kill or use them for our own ends, while others assert that hunting is a spiritual act, and research with animals serves the highest ends, and so on. Just to say that such and such a thing is sacred or alive does not mean that all who hold this view will agree on how it should translate into action. Quite the contrary!

I suspect that most of us, and certainly those in the policy-shaping and policy-implementing arena, locate themselves somewhere on the spectrum where *some* life is highly valued *sometimes.* I believe this position reflects essentially the state of mind that would be the context for policy-making regarding the living earth: some life valued some of the time. I begin with this example: people regularly risk their lives and the rights of others by not wearing seatbelts in their cars or by smoking cigarettes. Second example: in the minds of many and in the law, self-defense entitles the taking of life. By extension, national interest, expressed as national defense, makes that acceptable, too. Just wars and sacred causes justify taking life or threatening to do so. Around the world in many cultures persons are prepared, even eager, to die for a cause. Most of us would be prepared to take a life to destroy another Hitler. We regularly and agreeably trade absolute protection of life for reasonable levels of profit. We routinely make life-risking decisions in terms of "cost-effectiveness," the "dollar value of life," and "acceptable risk." We do so because we feel the need to compromise between the sacredness of life and the convenience and possibility of living in some ways that entail putting life at risk and, indeed, destroying some life. But we do it, and we do it comfortably for the most part. We eat and otherwise consume living things far beyond what we need for health or for modest levels of comfort. Few of us are about to give up the additional comfort increments in order to protect all life. We kill flies, bacteria, rats, and poison ivy. In the cities of Los Angeles and San Francisco we know there are going to be earthquakes that will kill many; but we do very, very little about serious earthquake protection. Significantly, there are very few people who want very much done about earthquake protection because it would interfere with the way they live their lives.

So valuing life is not absolute, in most places in the world. There are two morals I draw from this. The first: it is not enough that something be alive *per se* to merit respect, protection, or entitlement. There is every reason to believe that policy proposals premised on the belief held by some that the earth is alive would have to face those same kinds of psychological and social tradeoffs that are implicit in the examples I have given.

The second brings us to a different issue in this policy arena. Anyone arguing that the earth is alive argues from the viewpoint that sees the world as interconnected and interactive—everything connected to everything else. Indeed, that is part of the meaning and the feeling of aliveness. In an interdependent world, entitlements, respect, and protection must be reciprocal; they are not unilateral. What, then, would the earth be expected to *give* us as well as receive from us if it were treated as alive?

We raise children to be compatible with the culture into which they are born. That has its costs, to be sure; but it gives a child an opportunity to live well in the comfort of a coherent culture and not be painfully at odds with it or destroyed by it. So we regularly shape and constrain babies, children, and indeed adults. Are humans, then, entitled to shape and constrain the earth to be compatible with human beings' needs and wants? If so, which humans and who says so?

Different cultures have very different expectations about what humans are entitled to do to shape and constrain the earth. Recall the cases of Madagascar and its rape of its timber supply; of Libya using up fossilized ground water to grow those little patches of alfalfa; of Egypt and the Aswan Dam disrupting the natural flooding of the river banks which served to fertilize the land; of Brazil, eviscerating the jungle to grow crops, mine minerals, and harvest trees—all in the name of progress and serving human needs and wants. And the old, old tribal practice of slash and burn is still rampant. For the United States there is pest control, flood control, mining, irrigation, weather modification, garbage disposal and incineration, burying radioactive wastes, and so forth. To what degree and by what means are we entitled to shape the earth so it is compatible with the culture that engages *both* the earth and human beings? And need the standards really depend on believing the earth is alive? Or, could they depend simply on prudence and on acting so as to enhance the material and aesthetic resources the earth provides?

Is the earth entitled to constrain humans, to socialize us to its culture, so to speak? How should it act to fit us to it? And who is to say so; who is to argue and interpret for the earth what it is entitled to demand of us and how we are to comply? Perhaps those who believe it is alive have the wisdom. But can they make it operative in the policy world I've been describing? And can mere mortals claiming that wisdom dispense it without falling into hubris? (Note that legitimizing such claims through group action makes those so claiming even more vulnerable to the vices of righteousness.)

So far, I have explored how the definition of aliveness and valuing life could pertain to the formulation of policy aimed at protecting the earth on the assumption that it is alive. I hope that for some of you, what I have observed makes sense, is important, and is salient for what you are doing and thinking. I'm sure there are others of you, however, for whom the issues I have raised are irrelevant. What's really relevant to you is that the earth being alive is a *spiritual fact.* That fact transcends prudence, systems analysis, and policy formulation. This way of looking at the issue comforts, gives meaning to life, and provides a basis for identity with others in a community of belief. By those very contributions, it makes the living earth true for some people. There are cultures that knew it to be true long before scientific parallels were discovered. Whether or not there are scientific parallels with other life processes is irrelevant.

Once we accept that the belief that the earth is alive is cogent and meaningful primarily as a spiritual expression, then we are in the realm of religion, myth, and ideology. Once we move into this realm, there are some special policy-influencing and implementing implications worth considering. First, note a very important difference in state of mind among those who claim on spiritual grounds that the earth is alive and those resorting to other arguments to reach the same conclusion about its aliveness. It's the difference between those who feel they *know* and those who are self-conscious about the *interpretation they make* using certain information. The former, those who feel they know, would say the earth is alive, regardless of what someone else might believe to be the case or what scientific evidence shows. The latter self-consciously *chose* an interpretation to act on, taking the question to be open. The latter see the idea of the earth's aliveness as an *invention,* a valuable story for relating us to it. The former, who *know* the earth is alive, do not think of it as a story among stories but as a discovery of truth.

An existing situation makes this distraction less abstract. Consider the differences in the state of mind between those who claim animals inherently have rights and those who acknowledge that they are humans using their values to claim rights for animals. The former see those rights as absolutely given for animals; the latter recognize that we can challenge each other about the entitlement to make claims on animals' behalf as well as the nature and validity of the claims.

Now, those who possess *the truth,* those who know, the true believers thereby possess added vitality, courage, and persistence from their convictions. Those who are self-conscious about the possibly transient or all-embracing desirability of the stories they tell bring to bear less of that unquestioning vitality and persistence. For the true believers, truth is truth, and it's not negotiable. For the storytellers, the interpretation that the earth is alive is negotiable, compromisable. Sometimes even a sense of humor accompanies their very serious mission. Therefore, a very much stronger stance regarding policy is likely to accompany those who know the earth is alive in contrast to those who say "I am making an interpretation, a story, that is valuable and I hope will prevail."

It is important to remember that many times, historically, those who knew the truth imposed it on others and sooner or later on each other as they came to differ on interpretations of what that truth *is.* In the West, wars and violence in the name of the truth have always been with us. I remind you of the Inquisition, the Crusades, the Hundred Years War, the Holocaust, social Darwinism, not to mention current assorted violences perpetrated in the name of the truth. In many cases, when places have been seen as being special reservoirs of spiritual power and significance, wars have been fought over these places, often for centuries. Perceiving the earth as having special places of uniqueness makes these places more valuable, and this may lead to conflict as well as spiritual advancement.

Open societies try to guard against ideological or spiritual domination by engaging in policy issues in a context of reason, negotiation, politics, legislation, and judicial processes. All these ways of keeping the system open turn in part on how the issues are defined and valued and what trade-offs can be contrived to deal with very different definitions of what is worthwhile and what is not. There is no doubt that power plays a big part—it always does—but it's not the only part.

I acknowledge that the whole idea of an open society and relying on reason, negotiation, politics, storytelling, etc., as means for avoiding ideological and spiritual oppression itself rests on a myth, an ideology. It is the ideology of reason, of empiricism, of systemic perspectives, and of separation of church and state. The issues we are exploring here comprise an extremely complex, self-reflexive domain. To treat them more simply does nothing less than trivialize the human condition—and the earth's.

Perhaps the image, the story, or the truth of the earth as alive will become appealing enough to enough people to contend with other images, stories, and truths about the nature of life on the earth and, thereby, to affect the policy-shaping arena. However, unavoidably, most of the actors in the policy-shaping arena will be unenlightened souls, as are most of us. It's going to be a very tough area to sort out, trade off, and work through. Of course, there are cultures that live according to their belief that the earth is alive. But what we see *now*, when we look at them, are cultures in a climax state, a climax *social* ecology, to use a term from ecology. A climax biological ecology is one that has finally balanced its contending components, such as a climax forest—one whose biological mix remains stable over time. An example of a climax social biology would be a traditional society such as certain Native American tribes before the advent of Europeans. Undoubtedly, there was a very long period of difficult and probably unpleasant learning of how to put together a set of beliefs and the mutual shaping of each. Many such efforts surely failed; we know only the successful survivors of cultural experiments. We, too, must go through such a transition period; and it is sure to be turbulent, risky, and disastrous for some. *How* we go through that period and what we learn will centrally affect whether or not we emerge with a belief system and policies that support the idea of a living earth. During that painful transition period, we *must* be learners and design our activities as learning activities.

We are going to have to learn what fits with what, who fits with whom, and how these fit in with the belief, truth, or story that the earth is alive. The ultimate challenge for those who believe the earth is alive, on whatever basis, is to learn how to fit together multiple, divergent versions of aliveness and to learn how to constructively engage those many persons and organizations that share the planet but who do not believe the earth is alive and who intend to compromise among the diverse demands made by humans and the planet. We conventionally think in terms of ecosphere and biosphere. Learning what constitutes a viable policy-sphere is the looming and compelling challenge for those who would speak for Gaia.

Notes

1. See James Lovelock, *Gaia: A New Look At Life On Earth* (New York: Oxford University Press, 1979) for the first statement of the Gaia Hypothesis.
2. Lovelock has since clarified his position, as in: James Lovelock, "What Is Gaia?" in *Gaia's Hidden Life*, edited by Shirley Nicholson and Brenda Rosen (Wheaton, Ill.: Quest Books, 1992), pp. 59–82. In contrast to his earlier formulation, his current view is this: "I have said that the biological and physical worlds are tightly coupled and that the biota operates in such a way as to insure optimum physical conditions for itself. I had in mind a biological system that works according to conventional evolutionary rules and that, like all complex systems in the universe, it has a tendency to produce stability, and to survive. I needed to show that the stability emerges from the properties of the system, not from some purposeful guiding hand." Quoted by Roger Lewin in *Complexity: Life At the Edge of Chaos* (New York: Macmillan, 1992), 115–116.

19. Spirit of the Forest: Integrating Spiritual Values into Natural Resource Management and Research

Herbert W. Schroeder, Ph.D.

Editor's Note

The development of resource management policies is usually based more on economics and politics than on a search for deeper truths. In this thoughtful article, environmental psychologist Herbert Schroeder, who works for the U.S. Forest Service, looks for spiritual principles on which to shape forest management policy.

AMERICAN INDIAN TRADITIONS describe a world filled with spirits. In these traditions the plants and animals, the rivers, the mountains, and even the rocks are living, conscious beings; and the welfare of human communities depends on how people relate to the spirits of this living world. Thus, for American Indians and other indigenous people, spiritual values are a basic part of everyday life. By contrast, the scientific world view in which most natural resource professionals are trained denies the existence of spirits or of a spirit world. Instead of spirits, modern technological cultures understand and interact with nature in terms of mechanisms of cause and effect. Nevertheless, in recent years the notion of spiritual value has begun to appear in discussions of forest management:

> *Forests are a tremendous source of wealth for a nation and its people, wealth that can be measured in economic, ecological, and spiritual terms.*
>
> —H. Salwasser, 1990[1]

> *Knowledge gained from an improved system of forestry research will enable society to choose wise use and thus to secure the environmental, economic, and spiritual benefits of forests.*
>
> —National Research Council, 1990[2]

These quotes identify spiritual values as one of the many values that forests provide for people. But what is spiritual value? Why is it important? What should we do about it? And if we take spiritual values seriously, what does this imply for a scientific view of the world?

Defining "Spiritual Value"

I want to begin by explaining what I mean when I use the term "spiritual value." I have looked at a number of discussions and descriptions of spiritual values and experiences, and there is a common theme that runs through most of them. This common theme provides a definition (of sorts) for spiritual value. *The term "spiritual value" refers to the experience of being related to an "other" that is larger or greater than oneself and that gives meaning to one's life at a deeper than intellectual level.*

Most religions identify the "other" in this definition as a supernatural deity or God. For many people, however, the "other" is a natural entity such as the earth, wilderness, or the universe. Thus spiritual value seems to come from a certain kind of experience, one which does not necessarily involve religion or a belief in the supernatural. This experience is more than just a thought or an intellectual concept. It is a nonverbal, intuitive form of experience that involves the whole person—mind, body, heart, and soul—and may evoke strong emotions.

Some psychologists now believe that human beings have a basic need for this kind of experience. Spiritual value is not something unusual or exotic, reserved for the prophet on the mountaintop, nor is it a frivolous luxury or "amenity." Spirituality, in one form or another, appears to be a natural function of the human mind and plays an important role in psychological health and well-being.

Two Modes of the Human Mind

Spiritual values are usually expressed in the language and imagery of art, music, literature, and mythology. It seems to be difficult to talk about spiritual values in the objective, analytical language of science. To understand why this is, we need to realize that the human mind can function in two very different ways. As an analogy, think of the mind as being like a computer that can operate in either a text mode or a graphics mode. Depending on which mode the computer is in, very different things will appear on the display. Similarly, the human mind can operate in either a rational-thinking mode or an intuitive-feeling mode. Depending on which of these modes a person is functioning in, you will see and hear very different things coming from the person.

The rational-thinking mode follows a deliberate, consciously planned approach. It works with intellectual concepts, submitting them to some type of rigorous analysis (e.g., logical, empirical, or mathematical). Concepts are linked together to form theories, which are expressed in precise, literal language. Science and technology are the products of this mode, and their application leads to the enhancement of material values.

The intuitive-feeling mode, on the other hand, tends to follow a spontaneous, unplanned approach. It begins with images, like those that arise in dreams and fantasies, and expresses them through some form of creative medium (e.g., painting, storytelling, or dance). At the cultural level, this leads to the formation of mythologies, which are expressed in open-ended, symbolic language. Art and ritual are the products of this mode, and their pursuit leads to the enhancement of spiritual values.

The differences between the two modes are summarized in the following table:

Rational-thinking mode	*Intuitive-feeling mode*
Conscious, deliberate	Unconscious, spontaneous
Concepts	Imagery
Rigorous analysis	Creative expression
Theory	Mythology
Literal language	Symbolic language
Science & technology	Art & ritual
Material values	Spiritual values

The formal training of scientists emphasizes the rational mode, but spiritual values are experienced mainly through the intuitive mode. Therefore, if we try to understand or talk about spiritual values in strictly objective, scientific terms, we may lose touch with the very experience that we are trying to understand. If we really want to understand and appreciate the spiritual values of natural environments, we have to be willing to explore the intuitive-feeling side of the mind on its own terms. In doing this, we cannot rely exclusively on rational, scientific methods. On the intuitive side of the mind, experiences of beauty, love, and imagination carry more weight than scientific data and statistics.

Myths of Spirit and Nature

The American Indians' belief that the natural world is filled with spirits draws on the intuitive-feeling side of the mind. This belief in nature spirits is nearly universal in cultures that have not adopted a scientific world view. Ancient traditions contain many tales about the spirits that inhabit trees and forests. A woodcutter in old Europe, for example, had to be concerned about more than just the physical task of chopping a tree down. He also had to worry about what the spirit of the tree would do, once its home had been destroyed. The woodcutter might leave an offering to make amends for the damage or might provide some food to help the spirit on its journey to a new home.

Some trees were particularly sacred. A sacred tree might be the home of a spirit that was especially beloved of a goddess or god. In that case, it was best not to cut the tree at all. Careless or disrespectful tree cutting could have dire consequences. Sometimes whole groves of trees were considered to be sacred to a particular goddess or god. Sacred groves were inviolable; tree cutting and hunting were strictly forbidden within their boundaries. Violators could be punished by both civil and religious penalties.[3]

Perhaps the most striking example of a sacred tree in mythology is the World Tree. This mythical tree appears in various forms in cultures around the world, including Europe, India, China, Siberia, the Middle East, and North America. According to myth, the World Tree stands at the center of the universe. It is the origin and the support of all life and is therefore sometimes referred to as the Tree of Life.

A common theme in mythology and folklore is that trees and forests provide a link between the ordinary world and a sacred or spirit world. The Celtic peoples of ancient Europe regarded their sacred groves as connecting points between everyday reality and a magical "Other World," which was an important feature of their stories and legends.[4] The Druids went to sacred groves in remote wilderness areas to experience "nature awe" and thereby draw closer to the Other World.

The mythic World Tree was often seen as connecting the mundane world of everyday life with spirit worlds that lay both above and below the ordinary world.[5] The roots of the World Tree extended down into the underworld, and its upper branches reached up into the realm of the gods. In some cultures, the World Tree functioned as a ladder on which the priest or shaman could climb up or down into the spirit worlds. Other elements of the natural landscape could also perform this function. Sometimes it was a mountain rather than a tree that connected the everyday world with the upper and lower spirit worlds. Bodies of water, such as pools, lakes, and streams, were common entry points to the Other World, and animals often served as guides and helpers on journeys into the spirit realm.

We can still find echoes of these mythological themes and images in the behavior and experiences of modern people. For example, when people describe their experiences in wilderness and other natural places, they often say that it is like entering a whole different world, a world that lies outside of their normal daily reality.[6] The feelings of many modern people toward wilderness areas and nature preserves are similar to the feelings that ancient people had for their sacred groves; and the special fascination that many people feel towards large, ancient trees seems to point back to the mythic image of the World Tree.

Big trees evoke powerful feelings of awe, and even a modern, scientifically trained forester may fall under the spell of a grove of large trees. The following description of a giant sequoia grove is found in an otherwise very technical forestry textbook of the 1950s:

> In their presence, all sense of proportion is lost, and smaller trees which may be 4 to 10 ft. in diameter appear dwarfed by comparison. It is small wonder, therefore, that a feeling of reverence comes over one upon entering a grove of patriarchs whose gigantic red trunks are like the supports of some vast outdoor cathedral. The emotions aroused by the silent ageless majesty of these great trees are akin to those of primitive man for whom they would have been objects of worship, and it is unlikely that many centuries of scientific training will ever completely efface this elemental feeling.[7]

In this passage we hear an echo of the nature awe that the Druids found in their sacred groves.

Symbols and Archetypes

But how are people who live in a modern culture to understand these mythological themes? In what sense is a tree or forest a connecting link between two worlds? Even if we no longer believe that a spirit world literally exists, perhaps we can find a symbolic meaning in this image. Some psychologists believe that the spirit world symbolizes an unconscious part of the human mind. That is, the spirit world is an image of a part of ourselves of which we are not ordinarily aware. If this is so, then the mythological traditions imply that contact with trees, forests, and other natural environments can draw us into a closer awareness of a hidden, unconscious world that lies within ourselves.

According to the psychologist Carl Jung, the unconscious mind contains certain basic, instinctive patterns, which give rise to the common images and themes of mythology. He called these patterns "archetypes."[8] Psychologist Robert Moore likens the archetypes to computer programs—"bioprograms" that are hard-wired into the brain at a very deep level. When an archetype is activated, it gives rise to its own characteristic pattern of emotions, imagery, and behavior. This explains why similar themes and images (for example, the World Tree) have appeared in many cultural traditions at different times and places around the world. These same themes and images also sometimes appear in people's dreams, as well as in works of art and literature. Archetypes represent the most fundamental, universal meanings and values of human existence. From this viewpoint, spiritual experience is understood as an encounter with the archetypes. The spirits, gods, and goddesses of mythology are interpreted as archetypes of the unconscious mind, personified and projected onto the natural world of trees, rivers, animals, and mountains.

Even without a literal belief in mythical gods and goddesses, natural environments still seem to provide a setting in which people can experience the archetypes of the psyche. For some people, certain settings seem to call forth the archetypal level of experience in powerful ways. The following three examples, drawn from different sources, illustrate how the archetypal images of the Tree of Life and the Sacred Grove have appeared unexpectedly at crucial moments in modern people's lives.

The first example is from the book *King, Warrior, Magician, Lover* by Robert Moore and Douglas Gilette:

> A young man . . . once told us a story about an unusual event in his childhood. When he was probably five or six years old . . . he went out into his backyard one spring afternoon yearning for something he was too young to identify but that, upon reflection later in life, he saw was a yearning for inner peace and harmony and a sense of oneness with all things. He stood with his back to a huge oak tree which grew in his yard, and he began to sing a song he made up as he went along. It was hypnotic for him. He sang his longing. He sang his sadness. And he sang a kind of minor-key deep joy. He sang a song of compassion for all living things . . . And pretty soon he began to notice that birds were coming to the tree, a few at a time. He continued singing, and as he sang, more birds came, whirling and circling around the tree and alighting in its branches. At last, the tree was filled with birds. It was alive with them. It seemed to him that they had been lured by the beauty and compassion of his song. They confirmed his beauty, and answered his yearning . . . The tree became a Tree of Life, and refreshed by this confirmation . . . he could go on.[9]

The second example is from the book *Man's Search for Meaning* by psychiatrist Viktor Frankl. While he was a prisoner in a Nazi concentration camp, Frankl had the following conversation with a fellow prisoner:

> This young woman knew that she would die in the next few days. But when I talked to her she was cheerful in spite of this knowledge. "I am grateful that fate has hit me so hard," she told me. "In my former life I was spoiled and did not take spiritual accomplishments seriously." Pointing through the window of the hut, she said, "This tree here is the only friend I have in my loneliness." Through that window she could see just one branch of a chestnut tree, and on the branch were two blossoms. "I often talk to this tree," she said to me. I was startled and didn't quite know how to

> take her words. Was she delirious? Did she have occasional hallucinations? Anxiously I asked her if the tree replied. "Yes." What did it say to her? She answered, "It said to me, 'I am here—I am here—I am life, eternal life.' "[10]

The third example is from a recent study by Paul Gobster, a social scientist with the U.S. Forest Service, and social psychologist Rick Chenoweth, in which they asked people to describe peak aesthetic experiences that they had had in outdoor settings.

> A good friend had recently lost a loved one and was feeling extremely depressed. It was about 4:00 p.m. on a warm and sunny Autumn day. Being familiar with the Morton Arboretum and with its beauty at this time of the year, I felt that a drive through the Arboretum could be both pleasant and therapeutic . . . It was almost peak fall color. While riding, we talked freely of our feelings and her present situation. As we approached the Forest area, I chose a road with no other cars or people in sight. We were able to drive slowly and soon came to the densest part of the forest where the sugar maples had turned brilliant colors of yellow and orange. Mingled in with the maples were tall green spruces; the Virginia creeper with its fall red coloring dappled the other colors. It was as if, suddenly, we were inside a large cathedral with stained-glass windows. The feeling was magnificent and awe-inspiring. Almost automatically my car came to a stop. All conversation came to a stop. The "peak" aesthetic experience occurred as the presence of a Supreme Being seemed to engulf us. The beauty of the environment and the solitude of the forest made us become "one." We were quiet and motionless for several minutes. A few tears rolled down the cheek of my friend. Quietly, she said, "Thank you, I feel better—I can face anything now." It was a profound experience for both of us.[11]

For each of these people, an imaginative experience with a tree or forest answered an intense need or longing at a difficult time in their life. These spiritual experiences clearly had tremendous value for these people.

Experiences such as these create a powerful fascination and emotional identification between a person and an environment. The physical environment becomes infused with feelings, images, and values. A forest experienced in this way is a magical place. There is a sense of enchantment, and everything is filled with meaning. When a person has experienced a forest in this way, any action (such as a timber harvest) that is perceived as threatening the forest will be experienced as an attack on the person's own self and will produce a strong emotional response.

To a scientist or a manager who is operating in the rational-thinking mode, this emotional reaction appears to be nonsensical because it is not based on a scientific understanding of the ecosystem. It is important to remember, however, that the processes of the human mind are themselves a part of nature. People have been forming these kinds of emotional and spiritual ties to the natural world for many thousands of years. This imaginative, emotional way of experiencing is a natural outcome of the evolution of the human species. It must therefore have some kind of adaptive value for people and for the ecosystems they have evolved in. To ignore, suppress, or ridicule the emotional and spiritual feelings that people have for nature may be damaging, both to people and to ecosystems.

The Myth of Erisichthon

The danger in ignoring the spiritual aspect of our relation with nature was recognized in ancient times, and is depicted symbolically in the Greek myth of Erisichthon. Erisichthon was a woodcutter who angered the goddess Demeter by cutting a grove of sacred trees. Heedless of Demeter's pleas, Erisichthon cut the ancient oak at the very center of the sacred grove, thereby killing the Dryad (wood nymph) who inhabited the tree. In retribution Demeter called upon the goddess of famine to afflict Erisichthon with insatiable hunger. Driven by the craving for food, he spent all his wealth and sold his own daughter as a slave in order to feed his hunger. But the great quantities of food that he ate gave him no satisfaction. Ultimately he died when, driven mad by hunger, he tried to devour his own body.[12]

This myth can be seen as a symbolic depiction of what happens when the intuitive, spiritual aspects of nature and psyche are devalued and repressed. Erisichthon's fault was not that he made a living by cutting trees. There would have been no problem if he had cut only trees that stood outside the sacred grove. Erisichthon suffered because he refused to respect the spiritual dimension of nature, represented by the Dryad in the oak tree. Even when Demeter herself, the goddess of vegetation, fertility, and harvest, came to plead with Erisichthon in the sacred grove, he stubbornly refused to deviate from his course. As a result, the benign goddess of harvest and plenty was replaced by an all-consuming feeling of hunger and starvation. This story represents a psychological principle, that when an archetype is repressed it does not disappear but may assume a destructive form that overwhelms the conscious ego.

This interpretation of the myth of Erisichthon suggests that modern Western culture's devaluation of the spiritual dimension has contributed to an insatiable hunger for goods and resources that is undercutting the physical basis of our survival. The story of Erisichthon foreshadows the multiplicity of compulsive and addictive behaviors that now plague modern society. Jungian psychologists tell us that many people today are experiencing spiritual famine, and that addictive behavior is a futile attempt to fill the spiritual void with an inadequate physical substitute.[13] As with Erisichthon, our consumption of the world's resources leads not to satisfaction, but to an insatiable desire for still more. Thus, in a culture that has emphasized physical commodities and resources while neglecting the spiritual side of life, one of the greatest values of natural environments may be the opportunities they provide to fill the spiritual void and to regain a deeper sense of connection with the world around us.

Integrating Science and Spirit

The spiritual connections between people and the land are as real and as important as the ecological relationships between species of plants and animals. For this reason, we need to look for ways to integrate our scientific understanding of the world with a more intuitive, spiritual way of experiencing nature. This will not be an easy task. The philosophical world views underlying the scientific and the spiritual viewpoints are very different, and often seem to be in conflict. From the perspective of scientific resource management, the natural environment is a complex system of physical and biological processes, and our goal should be to learn about these processes in order to manage, protect, and use them for the benefit of people. But from a spiritual viewpoint, nature is an "other" to be respected and loved for its own sake. From this viewpoint, our goal is not to control and manipulate nature, but to enter into a relationship with nature through which we ourselves will be changed.

Management implies control and predictability, but a spiritual attitude requires spontaneity and (at least sometimes) letting go of control. Spiritual experiences are unpredictable, and the most important ones may occur only once in a lifetime. There is an element of vulnerability in this way of experiencing. If we are truly open to it, we may find our own values and attitudes changing in unanticipated ways. Therefore, spiritual values cannot simply be subsumed into our current system of planning and management. We can't just add a term for spiritual value to our existing cost-benefit equations, because the world view that underlies spiritual values is radically different from the world view that motivates economic cost-benefit analyses. We need to grapple with the conflicts between these two world views at a deeper, philosophical level. This does not mean that we must choose one world view and reject the other. Neither of these two views is totally right or wrong. Each is valid in its own way, but neither of them gives us the whole story. Therefore, we need to draw on both scientific and spiritual views of nature and seek ways of reconciling and harmonizing them.

In doing this, perhaps we can learn something from the American Indians, who were able to integrate their practical use of natural resources with their spiritual feeling of connection to the land. Indians manipulated their environment for their own benefit, but they did this with a sense of humility, gratitude, and reciprocity. When they took something from the land they were always careful to give something back.[14]

Environmental Ethics and Education

The natural resource professions now recognize the need for an environmental ethic that will permit us to use natural resources while at the same time respecting and not damaging the environment. But the arguments put forward for a land ethic are often abstract, intellectual, and presented solely in terms of material human benefits. For an environmental ethic to be effective, I think that its motivation must come from a deeper, more intuitive level. The Indians felt, and many still feel, that the earth is a living, conscious being that speaks to them in a personal way. I do not think that a genuine land ethic is possible without some such experience of kinship with the natural world.

It is through the intuitive, imaginative side of the mind that we can find this experience of being related to the world. But the educational process for natural resource professionals virtually ignores the intuitive-feeling aspects of human experience and focuses almost exclusively on a rational-thinking approach. To promote an environmental ethic, the educational system will need to teach not only facts, concepts, and theories; but also ways of experiencing that are new for many of us.

For this purpose, we may be able to draw on the contributions of psychologists who have developed methods for exploring and working with dreams and imagination,[15] as well as nature educators who have devised ways of deepening awareness and appreciation of natural environments.[16] Techniques from experiential psychology, such as in Eugene Gendlin's book *Focusing*,[17] can also help in reaching a more intuitive experience of a natural setting.[18] Creative activities such as art, music, and storytelling have been important parts of education in virtually all human cultures prior to our own. Recently there have been calls to include the arts and humanities as part of the education of natural resource professionals.[19]

Research on Spiritual Values

Scientific research has played a central role in shaping our modern understanding of natural environments and our approaches to managing them.

Attempting to do research on the spiritual values of natural environments, however, raises some particularly interesting challenges. The usual approach to scientific research relies heavily on the rational-thinking side of the mind, stressing detachment, control, and rigor. Exclusive reliance on this approach may inhibit the intuitive-feeling side of the mind, making it harder for the researcher to appreciate the character and the importance of spiritual values. To gain a fuller understanding of spiritual values in natural resource research and management, we must learn to employ the rational and the intuitive sides of the psyche in a more balanced way, with neither function dominating the other. Towards this goal, it may be helpful to reconsider and broaden some of the underlying assumptions and attitudes of the scientific approach.

Research on the spiritual dimension of natural environments might begin by adopting a phenomenological (as opposed to physical) definition of reality. That is, the starting point for investigation would be the "life-world" as it is immediately experienced by people.[20] Psychological phenomena would be regarded as real in their own right and would be studied on their own terms, rather than being reduced to mechanistic concepts taken from the physical or biological sciences.[21]

From this starting point, the spiritual aspect of nature would be approached by listening to people describe their experiences in their own words, rather than by employing quantitative measurements and statistical models of behavior. Descriptions of experiences would be drawn from many sources, including qualitative surveys and interviews, written materials published by various groups and organizations, art, literature, and mythology. An important source of material would be the researcher's own personal experiences, intuitions, dreams, and feelings regarding nature. The researcher would not be a detached, passive observer, but would be actively involved in discovering the spiritual significance of nature in the context of his or her own life.

In the course of this exploration, the researcher would engage in an interplay between the rational and the intuitive functions of the psyche. At times it might be necessary to suspend the rational and analytical mode of thinking, to allow the intuitive process to function without interference. At other times the researcher would need to step back from the flow of intuition to clarify, organize, and evaluate the view that is emerging. The process would not proceed in a straight line. The intuitive process cannot be hurried, forced, or manipulated according to conscious plans. The researcher would need patience and a willingness to follow the process through many unexpected turns.

The findings of research on the spiritual aspect of nature may not lend themselves well to the traditional, "dry" research report. Methods for conveying the researcher's findings may require more personal, evocative, and metaphorical expressions—such as what psychologist Abraham Maslow describes as "rhapsodic isomorphic communication."[24] This approach to research on spiritual values will not produce precise predictive models or formulas, nor will it yield any final answers regarding the management of natural resources. Its underlying motive is not control or prediction. Its purpose is to explore and deepen our awareness of the intuitive relationship between humans and nature, and to discover how we ourselves might be changed by that awareness.

Conclusion

I think that it is possible for us to take the spiritual values of nature seriously without abandoning our scientific heritage. To do this, however, we need to be willing to broaden our view of the world to include ways of experiencing and knowing that lie outside the domain of science as we usually think of it. By balancing and reconciling the rational-scientific and the intuitive-spiritual viewpoints in ourselves and in our society, perhaps we can move toward a more stable and sustainable relationship between humans and the natural world.

Notes

1. Hal Salwasser, "Gaining Perspective: Forestry for the Future," *Journal of Forestry* 88, no. 11(1990):32.
2. National Research Council, *Forestry Research: A Mandate for Change* (Washington, D.C.: National Academy Press, 1990), 8.
3. J. Donald Hughes, "Artemis: Goddess of Conservation," *Forest and Conservation History* (October 1990):191–197.
4. Jay Hansford C. Vest, "Nature Awe: Historical Views of Nature," *Western Wildlands* (Spring 1983):39–43.
5. Mircea Eliade, *The Sacred and the Profane: The Nature of Religion* (New York: Harcourt Brace Jovanovich, 1959).
6. Rachel Kaplan and Stephen Kaplan, *The Experience of Nature: A Psychological Perspective* (New York: Cambridge University Press, 1989), 183–184.
7. William M. Harlow and Ellwood S. Harrar, *Textbook of Dendrology* (New York: McGraw-Hill, 1958), 202.
8. Carl G. Jung, *On the Nature of the Psyche*, vol. 8 of *The Collected Works of Carl Jung* (New York: Pantheon), 159–234.
9. Robert Moore and Douglas Gilette, *King, Warrior, Magician, Lover* (New York: Harper Collins, 1990), 21–22.

10. Viktor Frankl, *Man's Search for Meaning* (New York: Washington Square Press, 1984), 90.
11. John F. Dwyer, Herbert W. Schroeder, and Paul H. Gobster, "The Significance of Urban Trees and Forests: Toward a Deeper Understanding of Values," *Journal of Arboriculture* 17, no. 10 (1991): 277–278.
12. Thomas Bulfinch, *Mythology* (New York: Dell, 1959), 138–141; Robert Graves, *The Greek Myths*, vol. 1 (London: Penguin, 1960), 89; and Edith Hamilton, *Mythology* (London: Penguin, 1942), 284–285.
13. Lawrence W. Jaffe, *Liberating the Heart: Spirituality and Jungian Psychology* (Toronto: Inner City Books, 1990); and Robert A. Johnson, *Ecstasy: Understanding the Psychology of Joy* (San Francisco: Harper and Row, 1987).
14. Annie L. Booth and Harvey M. Jacobs, "Ties That Bind: Native American Beliefs as a Foundation for Environmental Consciousness," *Environmental Ethics* 12, no.1 (1990):23–43.
15. See, for example, Robert A. Johnson, *Inner Work: Using Dreams and Active Imagination for Personal Growth*, (San Francisco: Harper and Row, 1986).
16. See, for example, David Pepi, *Thoreau's Method: A Handbook for Nature Study* (Englewood Cliffs, N.J.: Prentice Hall, 1985).
17. Eugene T. Gendlin, *Focusing* (New York: Bantam Books, 1981).
18. Herbert W. Schroeder, "The Felt Sense of Natural Environments," in *Proceedings, Environmental Design Research Association (EDRA)* 21; 1990 April 6–9; Urbana-Champaign, Ill. (Oklahoma City: Environmental Design Research Association, 1990):192–195.
19. James E. Crowfoot, "Academia's Future in the Conservation Movement," *Renewable Resources Journal* 8, no. 4 (1990):5–9.
20. Ernest Keen, *A Primer in Phenomenological Psychology* (New York: Holt, Rinehart, and Winston, 1975).
21. Amedio Giorgi, *Psychology as a Human Science* (New York: Harper and Row, 1970); and David Seamon, "The Phenomenological Contribution to Environmental Psychology," *Journal of Environmental Psychology* 2(1982):119–140.
22. Abraham H. Maslow, *Religions, Values, and Peak Experiences* (New York: Viking Press, 1974), 84–90.

20. Finding Peace in Our Craft: Architecture for Tourism as an Expression of Harmony with Place

David Andersen, AIA

Editor's Note

In an age when transportation technologies make travel almost anywhere possible, increasing numbers of people want to visit remote wild places where cultures and landscapes are relatively uninfluenced by modern society. As a result, a multimillion dollar ecotourism industry has sprung up, transporting large numbers of people to remote areas for non-typical vacations. The potentials for personal transformation are great, and yet so is the potential for damage to the land and indigenous cultures. As this article by architect-planner David Andersen clearly shows, we can create new eco-lodges that offer a much more exciting and open-ended recreational experience, but it will take new attitudes and meticulous planning by the developers.

Prologue

The Visitor and the Host

What place is this
that links the space
between the visitor and the host?

That fills the void
created when
the soldier leaves his post . . . ?

Not left to scholars
seeking fame,

nor politicians
who play the game.

Instead *they who choose*
whom they invite . . .
whom they accept . . .
and whom they fight,

Makes this a place
a world apart . . .
That stops a race
Before it starts . . .

It is the difference
between night and day.
Are battles fought
or will children play?

It is the difference
that we value most . . .
gentle visitor,
caring host.

Faced with the collective stress of society and the abandonment of cultural values, recreation has become an increasingly important enterprise. Tourism is now the world's largest single non-military industry, with receipts expected to reach three trillion dollars by 1996, and there are no signs of this trend slackening.

We throng to well-known destinations, but an ever-growing number of people are seeking something else. The rapid growth of the transportation industry has made it possible for travelers to be exposed to environments and cultures that previously have been considered inaccessible, and growing numbers of us crave encounters with other worlds where there is more than a casino, an amusement park, or contrived nature adventures. These visitors experience the shrinking world of an environment that seeks to survive despite the cultural damage from well-intentioned missionaries and the environmental devastation from the castoff debris of a clueless society. These are places where the voiceless majority on our planet live.

This is a messy, dirty world that people seek for knowledge, with no guarantees, nothing predictable, nothing even sane by Western standards. The new breed of travelers who are coming to developing regions of the globe are not like the plundering empire builders of the past. They are visitors that defy the term "tourist" and they represent the fastest growing segment of the travel industry—a segment called "ecotourism." At best, it is a tourism experience infused with the spirit of conservation and cultural exchange that results in a net positive effect for the environment and the local economy. As might be expected, there are also potentials for disaster in this new enterprise. Critics often call ecotourism "a new form of colonialism." If this type of tourism, which is badly needed by both the recreationists and the providers, is not directed well, that criticism may be valid.

This new group of guests is not demanding room service or wake-up calls. They are thirsting for knowledge of ecosystems and exposure to different cultural values. They do not want to steal souls with their cameras, but gain friends to share their journey through time and space.

Hospitality comes easy for many cultures. The Polynesians, the Macushi, and the Inuit, for example, have cultures designed to accept the gentle visitor. While some travelers today have demonstrated that they are not always the best guests, hospitality traditions continue to be a part of the rich patchwork of cultures circling the planet. It is foolish to think that tourism alone can solve all the world's problems, but it is harder to start wars with, or turn your back on requests for aid from people when you understand and appreciate their cultural values and the places involved. In the context of ecotourism, visitors can be positive agents of change. The impact of their visits are translated into economic benefit, revalidation of local values, better relationships between peoples, and increased awareness of the diversity on this planet.

Planning for ecotourism involves great care. Often the construction of eco-lodges in remote areas is an expensive proposition. This requires outside capital investment, which then requires a return that drives up the costs of lodging. As a result, often only the affluent have access. This tends to underscore the economic distance between the visitors and hosts. It is up to the massive travel industry to decide how best to deal with this disparity, and to place the cultural exchange inherent in ecotourism in a healthy and sustainable framework. At this stage of the development of the ecotourism industry, we crucially need models to show that modest, low environmental and cultural impact lodging facilities, interpretive centers, and environmental education facilities can be built and operated in a manner that enhances the lives of both visitors and residents.

The parameters for sustainable tourism are commonly defined as a form of travel that:

- contributes to the pleasure and education of the visitor.
- has a low impact on the natural environment.
- respects and celebrates local cultural values.
- contributes to the local economy and to the welfare of local people.

- contributes to the long-term conservation of the natural environment.
- promotes understanding between visitor and host.

To quote a representative of the people most impacted by ecotourism, Lacandon Mayan Patriarch Chan K'in has said:

> What people of the city do not realize is that the roots of all living things are interconnected. When a mighty tree is felled, a star falls from the sky. Before one chops down a mahogany, one should ask permission of the guardian of the stars.

Setting the Stage for Ecotourism

> *Travel and tourism now faces major new opportunities to match its economic scope with parallel contributions to social and even political interaction among the peoples and cultures of our world.*
>
> —Queen Noor of Jordan
> International Institute of Peace through
> Tourism Second Global Conference
> Building a Sustainable World through Tourism
> Montreal, Quebec, Canada
> September 1994

In the absence of harmony with natural laws and a sensitive understanding of the spiritual qualities infused in nature's system of order, we are all too often flying blindly into an uncertain future. Numbers are important to establish credibility for environmental issues, but the heart of environmental concern must be an ability to touch the earth and feel its pulse, as well as set standards, make policies, and enforce laws.

Regulation is a human inclination. Making plans is not an inherently bad concept. But plans should be viewed for what they are: a framework for understanding a problem or issue from a specific point of view and time. Plans need to be flexible and tourism planning underscores this, as expectations of hosts and visitors are always in a state of flux. Design must be at once a common ground for human discourse, yet specific in cultural/environmental context and place.

The philosophical foundation for sustainable tourism planning should address the following points:

- Program activities should integrate cultural elements with a high level of integrity and relevance.
- The visitor experience should challenge both the spirit and the intellect of the visitor, as well as provide an active sense of adventure.

- Land stewardship activities should represent leading-edge environmental management techniques, where appropriate, and serve as living proof that the experience being presented is indeed the asset that is being managed and preserved.
- The design of structures should reflect and accommodate the natural and cultural environment and embody a sense of place.
- Accommodations should provide for essential comforts, yet preserve a sense of rustic challenge and engagement with the elements.
- Sacred places and sensitive resources should be celebrated and protected as essential assets to the long-term success of sustainable tourism development.
- Infrastructure improvements should be adequate to service the development activities without disrupting the quality of the visitor experience or the economics of a small-scale operation.
- The development of ecotourism facilities should not preclude the examination of other compatible land uses, nor should it replace other existing sustainable activities in the area around a facility. Community dependency on a tourism facility can lead to economic vulnerability.
- Care should be taken not to alter the traditional social power structure of indigenous people, or to violate sacred lands, religious restrictions, or local taboos.
- In remote areas, care should be taken to minimize the cultural and economic shock of a new tourism enterprise. In some cases remote communities may require the opportunity to adjust to cultural changes.
- Development should not infringe on the privacy of the local community.

Listening to the Earth

Architectural thought in the developed world has evolved into an abstract reflection of its unraveling cultures. The design of buildings has become increasingly viewed by the mainstream of the architectural profession as the development of objects on the landscape rather than integrated into the landscape. The design profession, with few notable exceptions, has lost touch with the energy and inspiration generated from the earth. The challenge we face is to learn to listen to the message that comes from our mother planet. There is a story being told.

The folds of the earth's terrain contain power centers—places of unusual energy and significance that have not been lost on indigenous peoples of the world. It is up to tourism facility designers to recognize these places and respect them. While there may be a temptation to capture and harness these forces, it is not a gesture taken casually, nor a concept that will automatically link guests with a special sense of place. Successful ecotourism design can only be achieved obliquely by giving the place room to breathe, and the guest the room to interpret a unique setting. Place is not a literal song, but a vague melody, that a precioūs, sensitive few can discern. Perhaps it is the ecotourist who is best prepared to appreciate the sensitivity or insensitivity of the designer's response to the spirit of place.

Just as the earth is alive with the energy that flows through it, so too should the ecotourism facility design be infused with the richness of life. The ecotourism facility should be a participatory environment that purposefully weaves together the natural and the man-made environment into a unified composition. The architecture should be an organic extension of the terrain and a product of the dynamic forces of wind, water, clouds, forest, earth, sun, and local culture. Reverence for the earth and local culture should be the underlying theme that greets the visitor.

The placement of buildings on a site is a key consideration in planning ecotourism facilities. Exterior spaces can be planned between buildings to create "outdoor rooms" to enhance the visitor's bond with nature. The design can also portray the possibilities of sustainable lifestyles: an opportunity for visitors to learn to be better stewards of the earth. In this way design goes beyond the traditional tourism formulas. The architecture is intended to be a living laboratory, with forests around the structures serving as a rich library of nature's diversity. Interpretive trails further link the visitor to the ecological spectrum of the site around the facilities.

Perhaps the most important issue that distinguishes ecotourism planning from traditional tourism development is long-term monitoring. After the completion of construction there must be a way to measure and evaluate success or failure—to continue listening to the earth. This starts by identifying the natural and cultural factors that will be monitored and determining the limits of acceptable change. This enlightened form of stewardship is a key to sustainable tourism. If humans are to be sensitive beings, they cannot set in motion a development strategy without assuring that it continues to meet economic objectives without degrading the resource that is the basis for that economic benefit.

A Framework for Enhancing a Sense of Place

The architect's mission is to graphically depict, in a logical and quantifiable manner, the spatial sequences, activity settings, contextual relationships, theme, and infrastructure for a tourism facility. The process employed should include five basic areas of examination:

- Identification of Project Scope
- Assessment and Evaluation
- Definition of Place
- Synthesis
- Long-term Monitoring

The following is an expanded outline of the issues to be considered in those five areas:

1. Identification of Project Scope
   a. Program definition
   b. Client/owner/user definition
   c. Goals and Objectives
   d. Process and products
   e. Schedule and budget parameters
2. Assessment and Evaluation
   a. Natural systems
   b. Historical/cultural systems
   c. Identification of sacred places or other site sensitivities
   d. Carrying capacity of the site and surrounding region
   e. Land use and ownership framework
   f. Visual systems and viewpoints
   g. Infrastructure/transportation issues
   h. Structure and growth opportunities
3. Definition of Place
   a. Physical aspects
   b. Unique features
   c. Linkages, connections, points of focus
   d. Symbols and icons
   e. Spiritual qualities
   f. Existing activities
   g. Imagery
4. Synthesis
   a. Composite of natural, spiritual, cultural, and visual characteristics
   b. Definition of opportunities
   c. Human partnerships/tourism interface
   d. Architectural definition
   e. Considerations and perceptions
   f. Cultural/historical/interpretive systems
   g. Open space/closure interfaces
   h. Infrastructure

   i. Conflict resolution
5. Long-term Monitoring
   a. Establish tourism project objectives
   b. Select environmental and cultural indicators
   c. Determine limits of acceptable change
   d. Monitor indicators for change
   e. Take remedial action if limits are exceeded

Learning from Indigenous Peoples

Up until recently, local cultural views of indigenous peoples were discounted by most as being uninformed or antiquated. Now there is a re-examination taking place that accounts for, and values, the wisdom of a people linked intimately to the earth. We are only now beginning to realize the vast reservoir of intellectual wealth in our planet's indigenous tribes.

The sophistication of indigenous cultures, buildings, and knowledge of the earth's hidden energies are starting to be acknowledged by architects as well. The use of space, forms, and symbols create a rich context for cultural intercourse. In some cases the specific placement of building features and spatial configuration serve to enhance a spiritual purpose. We must pause to appreciate those treasures before they are lost as part of the world's collective intellectual insight.

There are invisible structures imbedded in cultures that can only be brought to life through the spoken word, music, dance, and art. Architectural design can recognize this by providing an appropriate backdrop for the cultural exchange—a setting that accommodates the rich sequence of events that gives this exchange meaning and shape. The ceremonial cores of ancient Maya cities in Central America are a supreme example of planning for sequential human activity. The nearly one thousand miles of "spirit paths" created by the Anasazi in the American Southwest is large-scale example of indigenous people creating a framework on the landscape that replicates their origin myths. By walking this network of pathways, the Anasazi literally linked their belief system to the topography of the place.

Architecture to Facilitate Cultural Exchange

Architecture for tourism can be viewed as a portal for cultural exchange. It is potentially a common meeting ground that can provide a setting that encourages visitors to seek understanding of the cultural context. The environment must add to an authentic experience, yet not become the cultural taxidermy that one finds in amusement parks in Florida or many hotel lobbies on Waikiki Beach. This tourism instead, becomes a gathering circle where different cultures can meet in peaceful and meaningful exchange. Ecotourism is not a one-way exchange driven by a perceived need to please the visitor at any expense to the host. It is a two-way exchange driven by the motivation of the visitor to learn more about the host's way of life and the host's willingness to share. Visitor lodging, to support this notion, must therefore be designed in the distinct terms of place.

Creating a setting for cultural exchange ideally must be linked to the priorities of the host. This is not to say it does not try to accommodate the visitor. The architectural design can reinforce cultural motifs and archaeological precedents that enhance the sense of place, yet still provide certain creature comforts intended to please the visitor.

There need to be boundaries. An experience in an Amerindian village in Guyana underscored this need. When villagers were asked why a nearby tourist facility had a high fence topped with barbed wire around it; they replied, "It was to keep the tourists in." They went on to describe their experience with tourists who invaded their village without permission to capture their images on film while they bathed, did laundry, and nursed their babies. It was clear that not all visitors respect the personal territories and the perceptions of community privacy of their hosts.

Some villages in rural Belize have taken a modest but meaningful approach to receiving visitors. They have invited them to stay in their homes. It is a truly amazing conversion experience for most guests. Instead of a hit-and-run photo shoot, visitors intimately experience the day-to-day life of villagers in the most sacred of settings: the family home. Even though the small homes of the village were not specifically designed for tourism, the bonds between visitor and host are strengthened by this intimate setting for exchange.

Architecture as a Vehicle for Interpretation and Education

To create an architecture that fulfills its role as an interpretive and educational setting, an architect must focus on creating a "seamless" experience for the visitor—an experience that is authentic and avoids contradictions that might jar the visitor from the story being told. The result of this experience must be a lasting impression on the visitor that converts his/her viewpoint of the natural and cultural environment. Ideally this would have a positive net effect on the behavior of that visitor. This new awareness might further manifest itself in the buying habits or even political choices of the visitor. This approach to education and interpretation is often referred to as creating a value-based visitor experience.

Interpretation begins with the site. Trails on the site, for example, can be viewed as a conduit for direct contact between the visitor and the natural and cultural assets. Interpretive stations can be discreetly placed so as not to adversely affect the visitor's experience. At the same time they can be placed conveniently so as to enhance the visitor's appreciation of the place. Interpretive materials do not necessarily need to be totally focused on scientific data or historical fact. They also can help to frame the visitor experience in such a way as to create a sense of mystery and wonder about a place.

Interpretive centers, museums, and ecotourism lodging facilities can provide another vehicle for visitor education and understanding. Building structures should be viewed as more than site specific. They should be a manifestation of place. Siting and building configuration should respond to the spirit as well as the logistics of the site. Window placement should not just be an element to manipulate at the designer's whim, but an integral expression of the relationship between man's shelter and nature's energy.

The placement of doors and windows, for example, can reflect the sequence in which the visitor experiences a place. Experiencing this sequence of participatory learning is like pulling away layers of an onion, so that progressively the inner secrets of a special place are revealed.

Designing a Future of Relevant Technology

Technology can be intoxicating. It can be a positive agent of change, but it also can become the killer of cultures. One needs only to travel to the Amerindian villages of South America to discover radical change tearing apart the social structure and cultural belief system that has enabled these people to live in harmony with the earth for centuries. Once respected shamans are rejected by a younger population caught up in the strange sort of "cultural limbo" created when two worlds meet.

The relevant use of renewable energy resources has been an important part of ecotourism development. Frequently ecotourism facilities are located in remote areas, and, by necessity, must be off the power grid. The use of photovoltaic or wind power systems are usually the most likely candidates for employment of stand-alone alternate energy strategies. While these technologies and others are important considerations, they are but tools to be employed as appropriate for the place. Often the sensible designs of the local culture are the most effective clue to sustainability.

Architects and engineers have spent a lot of effort creating "healthy buildings." They examine the off-gassing effects of carpet and millwork. They evaluate heating, ventilation, and air conditioning systems and the kind of adhesives used. Rarely, however, do design professionals describe a healthy building in terms of the architectural soul of a structure, or the sequence and configuration of space and its relevance to the spirit of place.

H. E. Ratu Sir Kamisese Mara, the president of the Republic of Fiji, voiced his concern for relevance in our quest for sustainability at a conference on sustainable development for the Pacific island nations on August 16, 1994:

> I am in no way denigrating the efforts of so many . . . as they seek development which our planet can maintain. But I do want to remind you that, from the beach on Vanuabalavu, the pronouncements of scholars and authorities in this field seem far away indeed. And it is this need for development to be not only sustainable, but relevant that I suggest to you requires your careful consideration.

He went on to say,

> Sustainable development has become, almost overnight, it seems, the most beloved of phrases, the panacea for all ills, the Holy Grail for developing nations. Like predicting the future, it has become a growth industry in itself, providing employment for countless experts and consultants, and producing an astonishing volume of literature—and an increasing number of conferences . . .

When we can cease to look at nature only as a fuel for our society's machines, we will find a relevance in our building technology. What has been the domain of shamans, must also become the domain of architects and engineers.

Designing with the Spirit of the Earth

> *We did not receive this land from our forefathers; we have borrowed it from our children.*
>
> —traditional Native American saying

Indigenous people often point out that how we perceive time is crucial to our view of the world. If we experience time as a moment along a linear path with no connection between where we are now or have been in the past or to where we will be in the future, our actions will be short-sighted. If, however, we understand time as a circle, it becomes clear that our actions today will affect us in the future.

Architectural designs for a sustainable future should be a meditation and a reflection on life and the world around the people who will experience the structure, the land, and the sky. More than being environmentally sustainable, shelter for humans should be infused with the natural environment to become a natural extension of the building site and climate.

It is the architect's obligation to meet the needs of *all* the clients on the site. The trees, plants, animals, insects, and the air and water quality are at the mercy of the designer's sensitivity. And while they do not speak in the language of real estate, finance, or legal contracts their voices are nonetheless valuable, meaningful, and poignant. Sustainable tourism architecture must go beyond technological advances to once again harness the spirit of the earth and the state of mind and heart open to all voices. Seasonal and diurnal passages, mating and nesting habitats, aquifers and drainage soils all are the lifeblood of the animal and plant community that must be accommodated in nature's neighborhood.

A commitment to sustainable tourism architecture and planning is a commitment to the stewardship that was once an integral part of the human world view. The design process must tap into this last reserve of understanding to focus human sensitivity toward the site. To gain an understanding, one must sleep there to feel the phases of the moon, awaken there to note the springtime of glorious dawn, walk there to track the sun shadows of trees and cliffs throughout the day and, at last, to gather the melancholy of an early winter sunset turning to anticipation of a bright, starry night.

Sustainable tourism architecture should also be an opportunity to express the joy of the human experience in nature. Forms and spaces that are uplifting and that frame inspiring views, capture quiet corners and provide opportunity for fellowship should all be expressions of the human spirit as it takes delight in the site.

Sustainable built environments are about energy consciousness, balanced with the organic harmony of the site. There are unique and powerful factors at some locations that require understanding. The wind can provide energy or steal heat; the soils can support structures and pathways or destroy and erode themselves; the sun brings cheer and warmth but can bleach and age building materials; and freeze/thaw, a dynamic force for beauty in nature, if left unchecked and unanticipated will tear apart shelter, structure, and building envelope.

Mostly, sustainable tourism architecture is an architecture of modesty. Practicing sustainable architecture requires creating low-impact structures in a manner that causes no net loss of resources as a result of both construction and operation. It is a goal that continues to be debated as to its achievability. Nevertheless it is an important mindset if our species is to survive on this planet.

While architects accommodate the needs of clients with appropriate and relevant technologies, it is important to look to nature for time-tested "low-tech" solutions to providing shelter within the natural environment. In nature nothing is wasted; it is prudent to view the site as an encyclopedia of opportunities for materials, technologies, forms, structures, and techniques.

The measure of sustainable tourism architecture must go beyond technical terms of consumption of energy and materials to designs that reflect organic principles which allow the building to grow naturally from the landscape as a harmonic extension of nature itself.

Architects must listen to the ground beneath their feet to develop a relevant architecture for tourism sustainable in both form and substance which will engage the users and promote a better understanding of the natural world around them.

A Checklist for Development of Ecotourism Facilities

The following generalized criteria are suggested as a framework for more detailed standards related to specific local issues and the ecological characteristics of a given site. With some exceptions, the criteria and the principles they embody may also be applied to other environmental zones. They are intended as a general guide and should not be considered a complete list of criteria or as a substitute for professional services.

- Site buildings and other structures to avoid cutting significant trees and to minimize disruption of other natural forces.
- Use naturally felled trees whenever possible.
- Maintenance of the ecosystem should take priority over view or dramatic design statements.
- Trail systems should respect travel patterns and habitats of wildlife.
- Erosion control should be considered in all building/trail placement.
- Buildings should be spaced to allow for wildlife travel patterns and forest growth.
- Use of automobiles and other vehicles should be strictly limited.
- Provide trailhead signs to enhance appreciation of natural environment and to clearly establish rules of conduct. Provide additional rules noted in guest units.
- Provide ecologically sound restroom and trash disposal facilities at trail-heads.
- Provide facilities to accommodate "messy" activities: placement of boot scrapers, outdoor showers, etc., become a necessity for some operations.
- Pastures and corrals for horses and other grazing stock should be located so as to not pollute water sources or watersheds.
- Designate a clear area for emergency evacuation of medical emergencies. Regular on-site operation of helicopters or other air service, however, should be discouraged.
- Design should reflect seasonal variations such as rainy seasons and solar angles.

- Site lighting should be limited and controlled to avoid disruption of wildlife diurnal cycles.
- Review any potential sources of sound or smell associated with the development that may be disruptive to the environment or offensive to the visitor.
- Landscape elements should be placed to enhance natural ventilation of facilities to avoid unnecessary consumption of energy.
- Water lines should be located to minimize disruption of the earth: adjacent to trails wherever possible.
- Hydroelectric power generation techniques should be utilized with a minimal disruption to the environment.
- Provide an architecture consistent with environmental philosophies and/or scientific purposes: avoid contradictions!
- Provide adequate storage for travel gear such as backpacks, boots, and other camping equipment.
- Provide for environmentally sound methods of trash removal. Provide secure trash storage. Recycle whenever possible.
- Design of buildings should utilize local construction techniques, materials, and cultural images wherever that approach is environmentally sound.
- Provide building forms and images in harmony with the natural environment. Design buildings on long-term environmental standards.
- Limit use of air-conditioning to areas where humidity and temperature control is necessary, such as computer rooms in research facilities. Design approach should utilize natural ventilation techniques to provide for human comfort wherever possible.
- Use "low tech" design solutions wherever possible.
- Prominently post an environmental code of conduct for visitors and staff.
- Provide ecotourist with onsite reference materials for environmental studies.
- Discretely label plant/tree types around the immediate lodging facilities to acquaint visitors to species they may encounter in the surrounding preserved/protected areas.
- Hand-excavate footings wherever possible.
- Interior furnishing and equipment should represent local resources except where special purpose furnishings or equipment are not readily available from local sources.
- Facilities should take advantage of local materials, craftsmen, and artists wherever possible.
- Use of energy intensive products or hazardous materials should be avoided.

- Building practices should respect local cultural standards and morals. Involvement of local people should be encouraged to provide input for the designer as well as a sense of ownership and acceptance by local residents.
- Special design consideration should be given to insect, reptile, and rodent control. The sensitive approach to design should minimize opportunities for intrusion rather than killing the "pests."
- Facilities for handicapped individuals should be provided where practical. It is noted, however, that the rugged nature of most ecotourism or scientific sites precludes access for some disabled individuals. Educational facilities should make access equal for all whenever possible.
- Plans for future growth of the facility to minimize future demolition and waste.
- Construction specifications should reflect environmental concerns regarding the use of wood products and other building materials. Refer to "First Cut: A Primer on Tropical Wood Use and Conservation," a pamphlet prepared by the Rainforest Alliance.

Putting Principles into Practice: The Experience of Designing an Ecotourism Resort in Costa Rica

In Central America, where tourism is a $5.6-billion-a-year industry, ecotourism is about three percent of this market. Like many other parts of the world, the growth of this market niche has been limited by lack of facilities and lack of supporting infrastructure to support general tourism, and planning for ecotourism involves different values and considerations than conventional recreation planning.

In 1990 John and Karen Lewis approached Andersen Group Architects, Ltd., to design an ecotourism facility on property they had just purchased on the end of the remote Osa Peninsula in Costa Rica. The resulting design and construction of the Lapa Rios (River of the Scarlet Macaw) resort has been heralded by the press and the tourism industry as a classic case study of successful ecotourism strategy, but let us begin with the first encounter in January of 1991 to add perspective.

Situated on more than a thousand acres of virgin rainforest, Lapa Rios represents more than just an ecotourism destination—it is a vital part of the maintenance of the existing tropical rainforest and a reforestation program. After two days of driving south from the mountain valleys of San Jose on the Pan-American highway, one turns off toward the gulf and the Osa Peninsula on a paved road that soon gives way to gravel and ultimately, to rutted clay. Along this primitive artery one constantly passes logging trucks hauling away freshly cut trees. The last vestige of civilization before reaching the proposed site is Puerto Jimenez—a grass landing strip, a single public telephone, and a collection of thatched roofs and corrugated metal structures. Our arrival stirred curiosity among the local residents. Few believed that anyone would be crazy enough to build an upscale resort on the Osa.

Upon crossing the Carbonera River, which originates on the property, the team approaches a series of deep ridges that have been cleared of trees. The ridges, facing across the gulf were documented as an archaeological site along an ancient trade route that hugged the Pacific coast of Central America. A few years earlier, the tops of the ridges had been brutally bulldozed by a previous owner in search of gold artifacts. Fifteen feet of the crest of the hill had been taken off on this greedy quest. It was here the team pitched a tent that served as a field office.

From the beginning, our objective was clear: design an economically viable, low-impact facility that would become an example of sustainable tourism design techniques, provide a financial vehicle to support the local economy, and promote conservation on the Osa. It was clear from the beginning that Lapa Rios was a special place. The abundance of exotic flowers, birds (particularly scarlet macaws), monkeys, and jaguars in this last stand of virgin rainforest was amazing. It was equally clear the Osa is an island fighting a last ditch battle against the rising tide of human intrusion. As civilization approached this remote area, local people were abandoning subsistence living in favor of lumbering, mining, poaching, and other non-sustaining activities. In building Lapa Rios we intended to provide an alternative to these activities and to demonstrate that conservation of this precious ecosystem was in everyone's best long-term interest.

It was determined that the crest of the ridges would be the ideal building site. This location was already disturbed by man, required no clearing, commanded spectacular views, and allowed for natural ventilation from ocean breezes. As we were surveying the area and developing design concepts, a civil engineer determined that the Carbonera River was spring-fed and was adequate to generate electricity the year-round. Local craftsmen were then interviewed to determine the best materials and methods of building on the site.

The architect then generated a design for the Lapa Rios project. It was purposefully simple and representative of the time-tested building forms of tropical architecture in the area. Fourteen free-standing villas offer privacy as well as spectacular views of the protected beach of Golfo Dulce ("Sweet Gulf"). Some villas also have views of the rainforest canopy. Each unit has a private outdoor garden shower where visitors can bathe in the midst of tropical flora while a myriad of colorful birds keep them company with their songs.

The guest units and the main lodge have been sited along the steep ridges that mark the boundary between the rainforest and the beach area below. The main lodge punctuates the ridge line with a soaring loft observation platform. Bird

watchers and star gazers are thrilled with this commanding vantage point in an unspoiled natural setting.

Interpretive trails allow the visitors an opportunity to immerse themselves in the natural beauty of the rainforest. The private trail system extends for miles through a tapestry of virgin rainforest, cool rivers with spectacular waterfalls, and unspoiled beaches, and has been designed to accommodate all levels of physical capability. After a day of hiking or riding, a guest can enjoy a dip in the resort's swimming pool which is gravity fed by a spring on the property. This touch of luxury also serves as a water supply for gardens below and an emergency reservoir for fire protection.

Lapa Rios is a uniquely Costa Rican experience. The architecture, furnishings, food, and management reflect the input and values of Costa Rica's rich cultural heritage. The building structures all have been made with materials from the region—*suita* palm roofs are supported with the local hardwood *cara de tigre*, as well as the ironwood tree, *manu*. Truss supports were carefully harvested from mangrove swamps, and the walls were constructed with *cana blanca*, a tall grass similar to bamboo. The resort is designed as an ecologically sensitive facility using solar energy to heat water for the villas and a river turbine to generate electricity on site. The construction of the facility required removal of only one tree, which was already dead. Since its completion, the trees have been encouraged to grow back on the site so that the structures are swallowed by the forest, and a dormitory has been added to house volunteers, scientists, or university students studying the rainforest.

Lapa Rios Resort officially opened in March of 1993. Attending the celebration were Costa Rica's Minister of Tourism and David Rockefeller. The most important guests, however, were the local people of the Osa Peninsula, who believed in the project as they had helped design it, build it, and would now economically benefit from it. Today John and Karen Lewis are helping their neighbors build a school for the children on the remote Osa Peninsula.

Architecture as an Expression of Peace

In 1995 the International Institute for Peace Through Tourism in Montreal will launch its Global Peace Park program. It is a symbol of a growing movement to link this world through commonalties, rather than pull it apart by highlighting its differences. Through the smoke of continued wars and poverty, it is hard to see this peace movement taking shape. Nevertheless there is a paradigm shift that is filtering through the world's psyche. The growth of eco-cultural tourism is a small but significant reflection of this shift. This form of enlightened travel is also a contributor to the momentum of this new world view.

The Global Peace Park program seeks to establish an international linkage through the symbol of trees. Each of the two thousand parks it plans to designate or establish as Peace Parks by the year 2000 will include a *bosco sacro*, a grove of trees that symbolizes the life, creativity, and hope for the future that thrives in

peace. This is similar to the ancient Hawaiian custom of leaving a special grove of trees in the middle of prime agricultural land. In these groves native Hawaiian women traditionally went to have their babies. They are portals of new life. This is but one of many examples where the tourism formula is being changed to provide a positive net result for future generations.

Perhaps in the future there will be a different pattern on the landscape of this planet. A bird might look down from the sky to see not the crisp lines of advancing urbanism, but instead the pastoral landscape of small-scale tourism linked to sustainable agriculture and villages sensitively nestled into the contours of the terrain, and the forests will expand to cover the scars of man's rigid past planning efforts.

In this setting, visitors will see and experience authentic cultural exchange, instead of a sanitized fantasy that demeans and trivializes the very cultural values that are being promoted as a commodity. Hosts will then be able to view the land as their own domain and will invite guests to visit on their own terms (and sometimes not at all).

In this scenario, children will be left with a legacy of stewardship of land and culture that they can in turn pass on their children in a continuous circle of sustainability.

Information on the Lapa Rios Resort on the Osa Peninsula in Costa Rica can be obtained by telephone fax (011–506-78–5130) or by writing to Lapa Rios, Box 100, Puerto Jimenez, Peninsula de Osa, Costa Rica, Central America.

21. The World Needs This Mountain

Michelle Berditschevsky and Charles M. Miller, Esq.

Editor's Note

On a clear day, the majestic summit of Mount Shasta in northern California, 14,162 feet above sea level, can be seen for well over a hundred miles. This snow-capped, black volcanic cone commands respect, not only for its immense size, but for its wildlife, luxuriant forests, hot springs, and meadows of wildflowers—it is truly a striking presence.

As long as human beings have known of Mount Shasta, it has been recognized as a place of power. American Indian tribes of the area all hold Mount Shasta as a sacred place. Today, a wide variety of religions have erected retreat centers on its lower slopes to seek inspiration from the mountain. Whenever such power is available, people with a variety of agendas may come together and conflicts may arise. At Mount Arafat in the Sinai, there are plans for a massive tourist center on the summit. Fumes from a nearby aluminum plant erode the ancient statutes at Delphi in Greece. At Mount Shasta, recreational developers propose to express their appreciation for the mountain by erecting a large ski resort.

The following article by Michelle Berditschevsky and Charles Miller not only describes an all-too-typical example of a power struggle associated with use of a place of great natural power, it offers a strategy to resolve such conflicts that could change land use planning. One of the great difficulties with American land use policies is that they are based primarily on economic values and do not speak to any inherent spirit of the land as a determining force in land planning. Affirming the inherent aesthetic and spiritual qualities of the mountain not just for American Indian heritage preservation, but as a living touchstone of inspiration for all peoples, the pioneering efforts of the Save Mount Shasta association may result in the creation of a new land use category—a place in nature with recognized spiritual values to all.

THERE ARE PLACES THAT coincide with the basic human need to experience sacredness, a deeper dimension, a kinship with all living beings, a place where we can tangibly attune our senses to the earth's relationship with the divine. Symbolizing the sacred has been Mount Shasta's role from the beginnings of human inhabitation, to which long-standing Native American traditions attest. The Mountain holds a pivotal value for our times. At this end of the millennium, when a vision of sustainability is sorely needed, Mount Shasta's capacity for taking us to a level where nature still speaks wholly is a safeguard for our freedom and survival.

The quality of light, the closeness to sky, forms carved by wind, water, and ice; delicate alpine flowers; and trees that are thousands of years old, survivors of storms, eruptions, and glaciers—all contribute to a total effect that brings us into a presence of forces larger and different from the fragmented constructed world of human society. Whatever various belief systems call those experiences, they have to do with the timeless, the beautiful, and the holy—values which are in danger of extinction in our fast-paced, over industrialized society. This is what renews and inspires, heals and brings perspective, and this is present on Mount Shasta in an extraordinary way.

Rising 14,162 feet into the skies, looming high above the surrounding landscape, is magnificent Mount Shasta, the dominant landmark of Northern California. Mount Shasta is the largest volcanic peak in the continental United States—80 cubic miles spread over 200,000 acres. California's five largest glaciers are found here, and the Mountain is host to the Shasta lily, Shasta daisy, and the great trees in the Shasta red fir belt which once encircled its slopes between 6,000 and 8,000 feet. Its wildlife includes eagles, black bears, and wolves. Only legendary now are the bighorn sheep, grizzlies, and antelopes, sighted in the nineteenth century, that figure in the Native American stories. The source of waters that flow as far as San Francisco Bay, the Mountain creates weather, holds moisture, and brings fertility to the Sacramento Valley.

Since 1978, the entire geographical, cultural, and spiritual integrity of Mount Shasta stands threatened by a proposed ski resort and adjacent condominium development, complete with a shopping center and golf course. Developers have promised to set aside Panther Meadows, a major traditional ceremonial site for Native Americans. But since the natural relationships of the Mountain's elements constitute a sacred pattern, to move any of its pillars or put commercial graffiti on any of its walls or spires would be equivalent to the desecration of a temple. The spiritual nature of the Mountain cannot be preserved by protecting isolated pockets of land and creating islands in the middle of a commercial ski resort.

The struggle for Mount Shasta's preservation is a microcosm of the issues of the late twentieth century—changing views of our relationship with the Earth, the

Mount Shasta.

re-emergence of indigenous peoples and more spiritual lifeways, understanding the limits of technology and the need for its integration within a larger living whole. It is the meeting of two world views—technology and dreamtime—the view that seeks to control and subordinate nature to short-term needs, and the view which sees in nature and the universe an interconnected life web of mysterious forces with which we can cooperate.

The Mount Shasta issue has two levels. There is the level of dreamtime, or pattern thinking as some call it. This is the deeper story behind the surface. The parts we know go like this. There are the people who have lived in a sacred relationship to the Earth for tens of thousands of years and who are holding this dimension around the specific place called Mount Shasta. And there are the newcomers of the past several hundred years, many of whom have lost sight of the ways of the Earth, centuries perhaps after their own ancestors left native ways and places through the same pressures that have always threatened people and lands, pressures from authoritarian governments, empires, conquistadors, inquisitions, established religions, commercialism. . . . The present-day political situation brings us to the actual effort as we are carrying it out on legal fronts and societal forums, a struggle which reflects the indignation and resistance against violations of ethics and justice. The deeper current that runs through the effort is the process of making a place for the sacred relationship to the Earth within a secular society where the need for this is not fully understood.

The two levels of the story intertwine. We are not merely opposing domination of the Mountain by commercial development. What we are seeking to do is to make room for an ancient/new value, a relationship to the Earth that the Native American People have held to, and to which the people-who-left are beginning to return. We bring tools to the struggle: attorneys fighting for ethics and justice; anthropologists working to record Native American ways; activists in touch with the place and people, translating and interpreting values to an out-of-touch industrial society, finding out what is really going on; staying on top of the process; and together building the network that is rising, like a wave, to reclaim the Mountain for sacredness, and to find cooperation among those who value sacredness. We are making room for this sacred relationship and reconciliation to grow further and to become a prevailing force in the ecological crisis that the out-of-touch ways have brought about. This is not only an environmental issue, but also a cultural one. The Mount Shasta issue makes visible the question of our relationship to the land. In this case, culture means coming into a sustainable relationship of balance, both with a place and its native peoples. Civilizations have come and gone. Culture has remained and must remain if we are to survive.

Spirit of Place—The Cultural Meaning of a Landscape

Native Americans

Mount Shasta's solitary, mysterious dominance has been sacred to Native Americans since time immemorial as a Center, balancing the forces of the world by uniting energies of heaven and earth. The Mountain embodied the most prominent position in an interconnecting topography of Shasta, Pit River, Wintu, Karuk, and Modoc tribal territories. Mount Shasta holds great meaning in myths and legends that recall significant deeds of times past and, for some tribes, world creation.

Over generations, Native Americans have used specific sites on Mount Shasta for the training of medicine men and women, for spiritual quests, and for healing and guidance. The spiritual power of the Mountain is invoked through dancing, chanting, and prayer. Because the tribes typically left ceremonial sites in their natural state as the Creator made them, the slopes of Shasta do not appear to contain many archaeological remains. To mark a sacred place in any way would violate its spirit and power.

Floyd Buckskin, Cultural Spokesperson of the Pit River Tribe, relates how, when the world was created, Mount Shasta (*Yet Acu*) existed as a ridge on a triangular island which was the earth's only continent. The Creator lived inside the Mountain, then 22,000 feet high. Every day the Mountain greeted the people of the earth with its glory and light, emanating the power and spirit of *He wi si Takaday Ha da chi Yah weh* (The One Above Earth's Heart, I am as I am all things to all people).

But the aggression and disharmony of humankind caused the Creator to leave the world. He promised to return after a number of ages to destroy the evil work of man and to determine who would survive into the next world, the fifth world. Buckskin relates that Yet Acu remains a symbol of hope to Native Americans for the promised return of the Creator to his home on Mount Shasta, who will liberate creation and restore all things to their natural order. Until that time, they feel a responsibility to care for the Mountain.

Today Mount Shasta remains the center of the physical, cultural, and spiritual universe for the Native Americans of northern California, who continue traditional sacred activities of which the following are the best known, while others are performed in secrecy.

Every summer, Florence Jones, Spiritual Leader of the Wintu Tribe, conducts an annual renewal ceremony by the spring at Panther Meadows on *Bohem Puyuik,* or "Big Mountain." Members of the Wintu tribe camp for several days beforehand at Coonrod Flat, where they pray and dance, always facing the peak, in preparation for the rites to come. At the sacred spring, the renowned medicine woman receives guidance and healing for her people from the Creator.

The Shasta People will not venture above the tree line of the most sacred place in their world, the Mountain they called *Waka* out of reverence for the Creator, who dwells there, and they only ascend to the upper slopes for spiritual purposes.

In lower Panther Meadows, where a nearby spring runs free with holy water, Karuk medicine man Charlie Thom, Sr., annually conducts a purification ceremony. Lasting three or four days, the ceremony draws people from around the world. Thom was instructed to hold these ceremonies by his grandfather, also a medicine man.

Mount Shasta stands to the Native Americans as an interconnection between other physical and spiritual areas of the universe. It is the center of their cosmology, and actually holds the world together through its connection with other levels. An anthropological study of Mount Shasta based on interviews with Native Americans and previous field research concludes that "contemporary Indian uses of Mount Shasta are clearly rooted deeply in traditional values and beliefs."[1] "Because Mount Shasta is so intricately interconnected to the surrounding topography, [the] Wintu maintain that any disturbance to the Mountain will have disturbing consequences on other land in general, and specifically will be detrimental to connected spiritual areas which are resources of the main Mountain, Mount Shasta. Some satellite spiritual areas already no longer exist as a result of development."[2]

The literature cited by the Forest Service is replete with references to Mount Shasta as a single entity and as an "integrated whole," interconnected with other sacred sites.[3] "Mount Shasta was an important feature in the mythology of all groups whose territories bordered the Mountain," wrote Forest Service Anthropologist Wilfield Henn. His 1991 report on the Mountain concluded, "Mount Shasta was a very important feature of the mythological landscape and that today's use of the mountain for spiritual purposes is rooted in traditional practices and values."[4] Further, all tribes in Northern California, and beyond to the Hopi in Arizona and the Kikapoo in Oklahoma, attest to Mount Shasta's spiritual power and feel that any further development will disturb the energy of the Mountain and spirits who reside there. "To build a ski area in the chair of the Creator is considered by the Shasta to be the ultimate insult."[5] The proposed ski development and continued logging on the Mountain are seen as "a violation of the purity of a sacred site."[6]

Cross-Cultural Significance

Compared with other mountains of North America, Mount Shasta has been associated with the sacred by Euro-Americans as well as Natives. The Mountain stands today as a sacred monument to people the world over. Since the early nineteenth century, explorers, naturalists, artists, and seekers have added their own cultural legacy to the Mountain.

Joaquin Miller, a historian, defender of Indians, and naturalist, lived near Mount Shasta in the 1850s. He is the author of one of the most famous lines about Mount Shasta—"Lonely as God, and white as a winter moon, Mount Shasta starts up sudden and solitary from the heart of the great black forests."[7] Understanding the link between the ideal of freedom and an undeveloped mountain, he wrote: "My mountains must be free/They hurl oppression back;/They keep the boon of Liberty."[8]

"As holy as Sinai," explorer-naturalist John Muir wrote of Mount Shasta. Muir, who considered himself "married to icy Shasta," the "polestar of the landscape," founded the Sierra Club in 1897. He climbed the Mountain several times and spent weeks in its lower regions, finding there a harmony and beauty of greater dimension than the human order, as well as discovering many of the natural principles which informed his later work.[9] In 1889, appalled at the devastation from logging on Mount Shasta's lower slopes that continued unprotected, he began an attempt to have the Mountain designated as a national park. His efforts were not to succeed, yet attempts to preserve the area continue to this day.

Mount Shasta has been the source of inspiration to landscape artists and poets for over 150 years, in a tradition that for a century made it the most painted California landscape after Yosemite, with renditions by such famous names as Albert Bierstadt, William Keith, and Thomas Hill.[10]

More than any other mountain in North America, Shasta is a focal point for contemporary spirituality, encompassing individual seekers as well as a variety of religious groups with their accompanying myths and legends.[11] Mount Shasta Abbey, a Zen monastery founded in 1970, thrives there. Other organizations include the Rosecrucian Order, the I AM foundation, and the Brotherhood of the White Temple. In 1989, due to its natural spiritual attributes, Mount Shasta was selected as a site for the Tibetan Buddhist Lhasang ceremony, conducted by the twelfth Tai Situpa Rinpoche as part of his world peace pilgrimage. Mount Shasta is identified in sacred traditions that range from Tibet to Peru.

For several decades, a continuous population of individuals and groups has maintained a low-key, anonymous presence around the Mountain for the purpose of spiritual deepening, sometimes staying for one to three months, sometimes for several years. Uplifted by its unique composition of design and light, they regard Mount Shasta as a "fountainhead of cosmic energy." Thousands gathered there in 1987 to celebrate the Harmonic Convergence based on a Mayan Prophecy, which points to Mount Shasta as a power spot equivalent to Stonehenge or the Great Pyramid.

Mount Shasta's attraction for so many groups is testimony to the Mountain's enduring power and has helped to focus public attention on recognition of the Mountain's spirit of place and Native American traditions. Underlying the cultural diversity associated with Mount Shasta is a singular unifying theme: to traverse Shasta's meadows, drink its crystalline waters, or simply gaze upon its rock walls and snow-covered spires, is to be bestowed with a sense of the *sacred.*

Establishing Criteria for the Sacred

Although the National Register of Historic Places (Department of the Interior) originally designated Mount Shasta in its entirety down to the 4,000 foot elevation, some 150,000 acres, as an Historic District, severe backlash forced the boundary to 8,000 feet at tree line, reducing the area protected to 19,000 acres, covering only the peak and Panther Meadows. While Mount Shasta's peak is of great significance to Native Americans and others, to include only the area above tree line and leave out important features of the Mountain's sacred geography is insufficient. It is unacceptable to leave out its many springs, creeks, trees, animals, and their habitats, and the geographic continuity that constitutes the living being of the Mountain.

The Forest Service has supported treatment of the Mountain outside of Panther Meadows and below the 8,000 foot elevation as a "study area" in which future investigations and projects may uncover other individual sites, on a project by project basis. As we have indicated, it is well established that the entire Mountain is of vital importance to the cultural survival of the surrounding tribes.

Lack of protection leaves these sensitive sacred lands vulnerable to development and logging without proper review of effects on cultural values and the environment on which a sacred relationship to the Mountain depends. The present state of affairs places the burden of proof on Native Americans with every timber sale or other Forest Service project, and unnecessarily impacts Native American religion, which is often carried out by elders not closely associated with the political process. Many traditional cultural sites are surrounded by a veil of secrecy deemed necessary to prevent the dilution of spiritual traditions. A piecemeal approach to protection denies the living connectedness between special sites. In addition, unnecessary government interference in matters between the tribes has historically proven to be detrimental to Native American affairs. No other cultural group has to justify its culture over and over in order to obtain protection for significant places.

Too often, spiritual values sound vague or emotional to government agencies, who tend to think in terms of charts and product outputs. This is why the Native people for whom these values have a tangible meaning must gain a concrete opportunity, in the form of protection of their cultural places, to demonstrate the effectiveness of time-proven traditional practices. Decision making and management processes could evolve into a kind of partnership between tribes, local communities, and the federal government. This assumes good will on the part of the government, which most often appears to see Native American issues as a time-consuming problem for which there is a hesitancy to seek budget allocations, rather than recognizing here an opportunity to demonstrate cooperation in ecologically sound management of the land.

Recognizing that a wide gap exists between American society's and the Native American world view, Vine Deloria, Jr., has proposed four categories of descriptions for "places which have transcendent meaning," allowing that Native concepts of the sacredness of lands ultimately elude Western rational analysis. Such a link requires a willingness on the part of secular society to make room for a world view that has in the past not been fully understood by the dominant culture; a world view that includes the whole of creation which becomes an active participant in ceremonial activities, involving the "other peoples" that are birds, plants, animals, rocks, etc. Deloria's categories also establish some criteria for distinguishing critical sites, in answer to critics who fear that designation of any site would create a dangerous precedent that could imply protection for every rock and tree, since Native Americans considered the entire Earth as sacred. Often critics lose sight of the real issue: What is at stake is the definition of a "context in which the individual and group can cultivate and enhance the experience of the sacred."

In Deloria's view, one category of sacred sites are those where, within the history of a people, something of great importance took place. Such sites, made sacred by the actions of human beings, are needed to remember the past and to honor it. A second classification acknowledges sites where the sacred appeared in the lives of human beings, such as places where guidance was given to the people by higher spiritual powers, or where spiritual relationships with specific animals or plants were first established.

A third classification of sacred lands denotes "places of overwhelming Holiness where Higher Powers, on their own initiative, have revealed themselves to human beings." These places are "holy in and of themselves," locations where human beings go to communicate with higher spiritual powers. These places have the quality of regenerating people and filling them with spiritual powers. Associated with these places are ceremonies that assure survival and provide the people with the necessary information to maintain a balance in their relationship with the earth and all forms of life. A fourth category of sacred lands affirms the continuing possibility of a living relationship with higher spiritual powers and of new revelations received at new locations and new ceremonies.

On this continent, Native American religion is the context in which specific locations are hallowed with the experience of the relationship between human beings and the rest of the universe, much as the ancient Hebrew religion recognized the River Jordan, Mount Horeb, Mount Sinai, and others, as places of communion with higher powers. To deny the conditions for the practice of Native American religion, while other religions are assured of the conditions necessary to their practice, constitutes a judgment that is outside the scope of the Constitution, which does not rule on the substance of religious belief and practice and guarantees freedom for all religions.[12]

Throughout *Sacred Mountains of the World,* author Edwin Bernbaum points to a number of universal defining characteristics which sacred mountains have in common: a power to awaken an overwhelming sense of the sacred, or recognition as a place of encounter with the sacred; embodying and reflecting the highest and most central values of religions and cultures; traditionally regarded as places of revelation, centers of the universe, sources of life, pathways to heaven, abodes of the dead, temples of the gods, expressions of ultimate reality, often associated with restrictions and ritual preparations; and providing experiences of meaning, direction, and purpose in life.[13]

Religious historian Mircea Eliade defines a sacred object or place as a *hierophany*, a thing that, although an integral part of the natural world, is symbolic of *something other,* beyond itself.[14] Mount Shasta is a masterwork that stands out from the rest of the landscape, a special expression of the earth that encompasses the region's biogeographical elements—rocks, meadows, glaciers, and forests—in a natural architectural relationship to one another. The ever-changing composition of light and sky and rock seems to call down beams from the higher spheres and surround it with an atmosphere of timelessness. As a volcano, rebuilding itself every few centuries, its prevailing cultural quality continues to be *renewal.*

Mount Shasta's rise of ten thousand feet from the valley floor—as high as the great Himalayan peaks from their bases—bestows it with another attribute of a sacred place: it constitutes a break in the homogeneity of space, creating an opening to a different plane, so that three cosmic levels—earth, heaven, and underworld—are put in communication. Eliade sees a sacred mountain as an *axis mundi* connecting earth with heaven. In the Hebrew tradition, for example, Palestine, being the highest land, was not submerged by the Flood.[15] And indeed, the archival literature on Mount Shasta, both Native American and non-Native, contains several accounts of how the Mountain and its environs were spared by the great Flood.

Preservation of sacred lands necessitates a conceptual link that translates traditional spiritual world views into cultural and legal categories justifying protection in the context of modern day America. The challenge in achieving recognition for sacred lands lies in the difficulty of translating the values of Native American culture into the context of legal statutes, bureaucracies, administrative procedures, and technological approaches to land management. Our interactions with a sacred place can be said to create new cultural values, expanding the place of the sacred in our society. (Please see the section below, "Mount Shasta and the Law," for a further discussion of this link.)

Process

It is the spirit of the place that saves a place. The motivating force of a protection effort cannot be only anger at the destruction of nature and culture. Righteous indignation implies a positive vision of living values engendered by the place itself and by our human relationship to it. A deepening kinship with the Mountain has brought the presence of sacredness into the forum to protect it. The Mountain is one of the players, lending its ancient wisdom and perspective of the larger context. Through attunement to the place and focusing on the work to protect it, we receive the revelation of the spirits of the land, the grandmother springs and grandfather trees that hold the dream of the land. It has meant building the Mountain within and among ourselves, living through that sacred space, treating others, even our opponents, with respect and understanding of their position, and compassion for a perspective that denies a dimension so enriching to life.

Roots of the current conflicts started with the tragic history of the settlers' and gold miners' encounters with Native Americans, including seizing aboriginal lands during the gold rush, shooting Natives for sport, bringing diseases such as smallpox and tuberculosis, massive betrayals and disregarded treaties. Conflicts also began with logging in the late nineteenth century, first by means of oxen and horses, later supplemented by the "steam donkey," and finally replaced by railroads which opened thousands of acres of timberland and reached record volumes in the 1920s, supplying lumber all the way to the East coast and cutting large swaths out of the original forests. Perhaps, as on the Mountain, darkness is there to contrast with light, and to contrast with this dark history there is the historic resistance to invasion and the impulse to preserve the Mountain and other sites from commercial exploitation.

The U.S. Forest Service's proposal to permit development of a large-scale ski resort on public lands high on Mount Shasta's slopes has raised intense controversy ever since it was first issued in 1978 and the developer's plans revealed in 1984. An inadequate Forest Service Environmental Assessment was successfully appealed by local activists and the Audubon Society in 1986. Although Native Americans were on record as opposing the development, the Forest Service made only a nominal attempt to assess historic values and concluded that these did not exist to any significant extent on the Mountain. As a result of appeals, the Regional Forester's 1986 decision directed the Forest Service to do a full Environmental Impact Statement (EIS). When the EIS Record of Decision was issued in the fall of 1988, and at the beginning of the forty-five-day appeal period, the Forest Service awarded a permit for the first stage of the ski development to Carl Martin, a former twenty-year Forest Service Employee.

Save Mount Shasta, a grass-roots citizens' group, came on the scene in the summer of 1988 and helped organize appeals of the decision with the Sierra Club, California Wilderness Coalition, and the Wilderness Society. The California Attorney General also filed an appeal. Of major concern were plans for construction of condominium villages, shopping centers, a golf course, an RV park, and other facilities on high-elevation private land adjacent to the ski area. Initially the Save Mount Shasta group worked within the framework of the Sierra Club, raising most of the money; doing research, particularly on Native American issues; and extensive public education.

With the growing prominence of cultural issues, Save Mount Shasta played a significant part in contacting Native Americans. Together we became aware of legal rights and of opportunities to participate in the process and to create a distinct case for cultural issues. We brought the case to the attention of California Indian Legal Services, and later found legal representation for the Wintu Tribe. We have been working in a coalition comprised of Floyd Buckskin, Cultural Spokesperson for the Pit River Tribe, Karuk Medicine Man Charlie Thom, and Michelle Berditschevsky, Coordinator of Save Mount Shasta, all represented by San Francisco attorney Charles Miller.

On the organizational level, the process has meant finding ways to translate the values of the place and spiritual/cultural relationships to it into the forum. It has included creating and maintaining a working center from which the campaign can be carried out. The campaign itself has a way of organizing people according to who has time and expertise, without having to set up a structural hierarchy. The issue has its own logic, and next steps are often glaringly evident. Save Mount Shasta is a core group that works on the week-to-week needs of the issue. An adjunct committee, the Mount Shasta Heritage Council, has been formed to represent the local non-Native American community and to help educate local governments. We have been invited to participate in a broader coalition with Native Americans—the Native Coalition for Cultural Restoration of Mount Shasta. In addition, informational town meetings periodically include people who are more peripherally involved and yet want to give input and help set goals.

A quarterly newsletter mailed to an expanding constituency spreads the news and ideals that animate the work and has created some financial support. This is supplemented by educational events, such as slide shows, speakers, and conferences. The production of a video entitled "Mount Shasta—Cathedral of Wildness," gave the Mountain, Native Americans, and environmentalists a vehicle to reach a greater public. Public involvement has helped convince government agencies that this is an important issue, worthy of their attention.

Once a base of public support for the campaign is achieved, it is time to start seeking funding from foundations and larger donors. It is best to begin by asking for funds for the immediate needs or next phase of the campaign, and thus establish a track record of accomplishments and accountability. Our biggest challenge has been finding the financial support to allow us to cover all the bases in the issue. A site specific issue has difficulty competing with national issues, and we are seeking help from potential donors who feel a special commitment to Mount Shasta.

Our basic principle of working *with* the place, rather than merely *against* development, has led us to see the legal defense as a necessary space-holding action that affirms the positive values and relationships which are being protected. From this perspective, it is important not to get so caught up in the struggle that we lose sight of the essentials. The essentials are the relationships—

with the place, through participation in ceremonies and individual experience, within the communication network of groups and individuals; and with the long-term vision. Our long-term goal is a cultural management plan involving a cooperative effort to restore the ecological integrity of the Mountain. This will use a combination of restoration science and traditional Native management practices and techniques, which enhance the natural environment through cultural activities, so that it becomes more productive and more suitable for human and animal use. In cultural management, any restoration effort would work closely with knowledgeable tribal elders. The Mountain can eventually become a National Native Monument, reflecting cooperation between the newcomers and first peoples that would go a long way toward healing the wounds of a brutal history.

Coalition building is more than simply gathering support, it is a building of human bridges and cultural connections. Expanding the coalition with the Native Americans has been a vital part of the effort. Non-Natives cannot expect Native people to come to them. Working with Native Americans means finding out what their issues are—to seek to understand how they see things in the context of their history and world view. It means getting beyond the stereotypes, and understanding, as far as we can, the reality of their situation. It cannot be a superficial thing, it has to be a commitment that is capable of withstanding the inevitable tests of our sincerity. It means creating a relationship of equals, which often means finding ways to help empower people whose experience has given them repeated experiences of hardship and futility. We have sought to understand the Native concerns and values out of a deep respect for their culture and roots into the past, and to bring these into the forums, so that their input can be included in government decision-making processes. It has meant understanding administrative and legal procedures, staying on top of every step, and developing a working relationship with agencies that protect cultural values—the Advisory Council on Historic Preservation, the Native American Heritage Commission, the State Historic Preservation Officer, the National Register of Historic Places. These have led to some meaningful participation in the process, though it is never won once and for all but requires constant vigilance.

According to a Hopi myth, of which versions exist among many tribes, there was a time when human beings of all colors were together. Some of the people stayed in place. Others went around the world with a mission to record and invent things for the purpose of making life beautiful, clean, and good. These people will come back to be with those who stayed in place. However, the misuse of ceremonial symbols and the abuse of power and inventions have led to materialism with its associated corruption, greed, selfishness, and dishonesty, as well as the destruction of the land and of natural life, according to the myth.

The myth has still to be lived out. As an Australian Aborigine woman put it: "If you have come to help me you can go home again, but if you see my struggle as part of your own survival, then perhaps we can work together."

Mount Shasta and the Law

One of the most important laws used to protect Mount Shasta as a traditional cultural property[16] is the National Historic Preservation Act (NHPA), 16 U.S.C. § 470(f). Indeed, the NHPA is presently the only federal statute which expressly provides for protection of traditional cultural properties. Because of its importance, the following discussion will focus on the use of the NHPA as the principal legal tool in protecting sacred sites.

If there is a goal to this discussion it is to provide those who seek to protect sacred sites the benefit of our experience in the Mount Shasta case. Although it is far from over, those who have worked on it for so many years have tread over some now very familiar ground. For others who will walk the same ground, we offer our experience in the hope that it will guide and inform the efforts of everyone who seeks to protect the cultural heritage of Native Americans.

The Opening Salvos

In 1988, the U.S. Forest Service, Shasta-Trinity National Forests, decided to permit the construction of a ski resort on Mount Shasta. What the Forest Service had not done, however, was engage in any concerted effort to comply with NHPA.[17] This failure was brought to the attention of the California State Historic Preservation Officer (SHPO)[18] by California Indian Legal Services (CILS), a nonprofit Indian legal services agency. CILS, on November 12, 1990, wrote California SHPO, and pointed out that there was substantial evidence of Mount Shasta's historic and religious significance to Northern California Native Americans, and that the Forest Service may have failed to consider this information or not disclosed it to SHPO prior to the decision to permit construction of the resort.

Upon receipt of the CILS letter, the California SHPO informed the Forest Service that it had not completed necessary consultations on the presence of historic properties on Mount Shasta. The SHPO advised Forest Service to "take immediate actions to resolve the issue of how the [ski resort] project may affect National Register values on Mount Shasta." The SHPO specifically referred to *National Register Bulletin* 38 for guidance,[19] and stated that the Forest Service should identify properties on Mount Shasta which may be eligible for the National Register.[20]

As a direct result of the SHPO's letter, in March 1990, the Forest Service agreed to conduct a study of Mount Shasta's eligibility to the National Register because of its historic and cultural significance to California Native Americans.[21] The Forest Service subsequently contracted with two anthropologists, Drs. Dorothea Theodoratus and Nancy Evans, to conduct the study.

In March 1991, representatives of all the tribes surrounding Mount Shasta met with Forest Supervisor Robert Tyrell to directly state the sacred meaning that Mount Shasta holds for them, and their concerns about development.

In the summer of 1991, three separate lawsuits—by the Save Mount Shasta/ Native American coalition, the Wintu Tribe, and the Sierra Club—successfully challenged the denial of further appeals of the 1988 Environmental Impact Statement based on the National Environmental Policy Act in U.S. District Court in Sacramento. Save Mount Shasta's and the Wintu Tribe's lawsuits included cultural preservation issues and brought NHPA to the forefront. It was clear that cultural issues had to be resolved before a federal agency could even *consider* a project on public lands. The lawsuits were dismissed once the Forest Service agreed to open the NHPA Section 106 Process to evaluate the historic and cultural significance of Mount Shasta. Further appeals of the Mount Shasta Ski Area Environmental Impact Statement are on hold pending the result of the historic preservation process.

The outcome of these events was that thirteen years after the decision to commit a large portion of Mount Shasta's public lands to commercial ski development, the Forest Service finally began consultations with Native Americans and consideration of Mount Shasta's eligibility to the National Register of Historic Places.

An important lesson to be drawn from all this is that traditional cultural properties will not be protected unless those who want them protected stay on top of the case at all times; do not accept as fact statements made by the responsible federal agency; and seek the assistance of other agencies involved in the historic preservation process. It is an unfortunate commentary on government that it only works for those who want it to work. If local preservationists, through CILS, had not solicited the involvement of the California SHPO at an important stage in the process, the Mount Shasta ski resort may now be a reality, resulting in the destruction or damage of several Native American traditional cultural properties.

The Theodoratus/Evans Study and Comment Periods

In September 1991, Drs. Theodoratus and Evans published their "Statement of Findings—Native American Interview and Data Collection Study of Mount Shasta, California."[22]

The Theodoratus/Evans study was completed over a sixty-day period and involved interviews with thirty-nine Native Americans, representing six Northern California tribes. Theodoratus and Evans concluded that:

> Mount Shasta, in its entirety, continues to be held by Northern California Indian peoples as a sacred entity within their physical environment. The mountain figures prominently in myths and legends that recall significant deeds of time past in general, and specifically world creation for some Native American groups.

Individual sacred sites, such as Panther Meadows (located in the middle of the proposed resort) were also identified. Most importantly, the Theodoratus/Evans study documented the Native American view that the proposed Mount Shasta ski resort would be considered a desecration to the Mountain.

The Theodoratus/Evans study, the Forest Service's own literature study, and comments from Native Americans became the basis for the Forest Service's determination of what properties on Mount Shasta were eligible for the National Register.[23] Although the Theodoratus/Evans study presented strong evidence that Mount Shasta, in its entirety, was eligible to the National Register because of its historic cultural significance to Native Americans, the Forest Service declined to follow the study's lead. Rather, in early 1992, the agency issued three draft Mount Shasta National Register eligibility determinations. The first was the Panther Meadows Historic Site Eligibility Determination. The second was a finding that the area contained by the Mount Shasta Wilderness was eligible to the National Register as a Cosmological District because of the historic significance of the Mountain's higher elevations in the mythology and cosmology of many Northern California Native American beliefs.[24] Although the Forest Service did not find that all of the Mountain was eligible to the National Register, it did issue a third document in which it determined that there may be other individual historically significant Native American sites on Mount Shasta whose National Register eligibility would be evaluated in the future.

Because of widespread public concern by both Native and non-native Americans over the Mount Shasta case, the Forest Service announced a public comment period on its three Mount Shasta National Register determinations. NHPA does not require a public comment period at this stage in the historic preservation process. The Forest Service's decision to solicit comments simply underscores the importance of the public's involvement in the NHPA process; without that involvement, it is doubtful the Forest Service would have sought comments. This public comment period ended on April 21, 1992; however, the Forest Service failed to substantially change its three Mount Shasta National Register determinations, even though many public comments pointed out that all of Mount Shasta should be considered eligible to the National Register.

In the summer of 1992, the Forest Service sought the California SHPO's concurrence in its final three Mount Shasta determinations. SHPO, like the Forest Service, announced its own public comment period, which concluded in early September, 1992. Following this second comment period, SHPO agreed with the Forest Service's three Mount Shasta National Register determinations, with the exception that the boundary of the Cosmological District was changed to tree line, encompassing 19,000 acres in lieu of the previous 37,000 acres.

Even though not successful in changing the Forest Service determinations, the public comments were important for several reasons. First, they gave proponents of Mount Shasta's eligibility to the National Register an opportunity to go on record as to the deficiencies in the Forest Service's three Mount Shasta National Register determinations. This record later became important in convincing the Department of the Interior to review and substantially change the Forest Service's eligibility determinations. The comments also brought to attention of the Forest Service its complete failure to evaluate the historic significance of Mount Shasta in non-native American history. As a result, in June 1992, the Forest Service published a literature study, "Mount Shasta in Late Nineteenth and Early Twentieth-century Non-Native American History." The non-native American Report contained a resounding affirmation of Mount Shasta's historic significance to non-native Americans and concluded:

> The research for this study suggests that the Mountain has associations on various planes; a landmark seen from great distances, a focus for scientific investigation, a source of recreation and physical challenge, a boon to local and regional economies, and finally, a physical expression of energy that is ever a source of artistic, philosophical and spiritual power to humanity.

Again, proponents of Mount Shasta's eligibility to the National Register were handed additional evidence of that eligibility, as a result of Forest's own study.[25]

The well-founded criticism of the Forest Service's Mount Shasta National Register determinations, coupled with the equally widespread public interest in the Mount Shasta case, led in 1993 to a significant development. The Advisory Council on Historic Preservation[26] requested that the Keeper of the National Register (U.S. Department of Interior)[27] review the now combined Forest Service/SHPO Mount Shasta National Register determinations. Although the Keeper may review such decisions, he was not in this situation required to do so. Again, by creating widespread public involvement, coupled with the support of another federal agency, here the Advisory Council, proponents of

Mount Shasta's eligibility were able to appeal the Mount Shasta National Register determinations to Washington, D.C.

The Keeper's Decision—The Keeper's Reversal

In 1993, the Keeper's office began its lengthy review of the Mount Shasta National Register determinations. On May 10, 1993, the Advisory Council requested that the Keeper consider "whether Mount Shasta, in its entirety, warrants consideration, either as a site or a National Register district." From the beginning of this review, it was clear that its focus would be on whether Mount Shasta as a whole was eligible for the National Register.[28]

On March 11, 1994, the Keeper's office announced its historic decision. Mount Shasta, from the 4,000-foot elevation to the summit, was considered eligible as a National Register district, because of "its association with the cultural history and cultural identity of American Indian groups."[29] The Keeper's five-page decision acknowledged the strong evidence in support of Mount Shasta's eligibility.

This decision was important for proponents of protection of the Mountain. With all of the Mountain now eligible to the National Register, the Forest Service would have to consider the effects and adverse effects (and avoid or mitigate those effects) of the proposed ski resort, as well as its other activities on the Mountain (e.g., road building, logging), on the values that made Mount Shasta historically significant.[30] The Northern California Native American Community, for one of the few times in its history, received the recognition and respect its rich history and culture deserved.

But this victory did not last long. Congressman Wally Herger of Northern California, and other supporters of so-called private property interests, soon protested the Keeper's decision. These opponents wrongly believed that private property owners within the Mount Shasta Historic District would not be able to develop or use their properties.[31] This position simply ignored the fact that private property owners were free to use their property as they wished, unless they obtained federal funding or a federal permit or license for their projects. In such events, the federal agency would have to determine the effects of private property owner projects on the Mountain; surely not an insurmountable or development busting requirement.[32]

The opponents even went so far as to assert that they had not been included in the process which led to the Keeper's March 1994 decision, and that they were not told that the Keeper was considering all of Mount Shasta for eligibility to the National Register. These arguments ignored the fact that many of these same opponents had submitted written comments to the Forest Service and SHPO during the public comment periods. As for not being informed, the many public comments and local newspaper articles testify to the fact that Mount Shasta's National Register eligibility, in its entirety, was always at issue.

In response to a request from Congressman Herger, the Keeper Jerry Rogers, agreed to visit Mount Shasta on August 29 and 30, 1994. During this visit, the Keeper met with opponents of the March decision, but not with Native Americans, and then announced a new sixty-day comment period on Mount Shasta's eligibility to the National Register, which ended on October 30, 1994.

On November 18, 1994, the Keeper published his new Mount Shasta National Register eligibility determination. The March 1994 decision was substantially revised, and the Keeper adopted the three Forest Service/SHPO Mount Shasta National Register eligibility determinations: Panther Meadows; the Mountain above the tree line; and consideration of the rest of the Mountain in the future. The Keeper's rationale for the revision was simple but misplaced: the Mountain lacked integrity. In National Register parlance, integrity "is a measure of a property's authenticity and is evidenced by the survival of physical characteristics that existed during the property's period of significance." According to the Keeper, as a result of road building, logging, and other activities on the Mountain, the entire Mountain had lost integrity as a National Register property.

There is one obvious problems with the Keeper's decision. At no point did the Keeper confer with Native Americans, whose values made the Mountain historically significant, on whether Mount Shasta lacked historic integrity. This is directly contrary to *Bulletin* 38, which instructs, "The integrity of a possible traditional cultural property must be considered with reference to the views of traditional practitioners; if its integrity has not been lost in their eyes, it probably has sufficient integrity to justify further evaluation." In the eyes of Northern California Native Americans, Mount Shasta has not lost its integrity. But even if the Keeper is correct, vast portions of the Mountain remain unlogged and do not have roads. Given the Keeper's logic, should not these areas now be considered eligible to the National Register?

Even more importantly, the Keeper's November 1994 decision undermines the integrity of the National Register eligibility determination process for all Americans. If the Keeper can so quickly change his mind, then any future National Register eligibility determination is subject to change at any time. No longer can any one rely on the NHPA to protect National Register eligible properties. If integrity has been lost, it is not with Mount Shasta, but with federal law.

The Present

As this chapter is being written, we are continuing to seek review of the Keeper's November 1994 decision. Whether those efforts will be successful is yet to be seen. The Keeper's November decision can also now be seen in a broader light. It appears to be part of an effort to stop Native Americans from protecting their sacred sites. On January 18, 1995, Congressman Herger introduced House Resolution 563, which would exclude from eligibility to the National Register "any unimproved or unmodified natural landscape feature which does not contain artifacts or other evidence of human activity." Because Native Americans do not commonly leave evidence of their presence at traditional cultural properties out of respect for their sacred sites, H.R. 563, if passed, would prohibit the eligibility of many sites to the National Register. This would be an egregious outcome, since NHPA is now the only federal law which provides any degree of protection for Native American sites.

H.R. 563 also directly addresses Mount Shasta. If passed and signed into law, it would preclude from eligibility to the National Register any property on Mount Shasta, even Panther Meadows and the Mountain above tree line. Given the substantial record which supports the National Register eligibility of these properties, and the presence of numerous individual Native American traditional cultural properties on the Mountain, this bill can be seen as none other than a direct attack on Native American values and culture.

Even though the opposition to protection of Native American sacred sites such as Mount Shasta seems to be growing, the proponents of protection can and must continue their efforts to protect traditional cultural properties. The NHPA still can serve to protect sacred sites. But protection can only be realized by involvement in the process, and by building on examples such as the strategies used on the Mount Shasta case. The voices of the past and present must be heard together if Native American culture is to be protected, and if Mount Shasta is to be preserved.

For further information, please contact Save Mount Shasta, P.O. Box 1143, Mount Shasta, CA 96067. Phone: 916/926–3397.

Notes

1. Dorothea Theodoratus and Nancy Evans, *Statement of Findings, Native American Interview and Data Collection, Study of Mount Shasta, California*, (Redding, Calif.: USDA, 1991), 11.
2. Ibid., 5.
3. Ibid., 2.
4. Winfield Henn, *Native American Historic Context* (Redding, Calif.: USDA, 1991), 8.
5. Theodoratus and Evans, *Statement of Findings*, 10.

6. Ibid., 5.
7. Joaquin Miller, *Unwritten History* (Hartford: American Publishing Company, 1874).
8. Miller, *Picturesque California and the Region West of the Rocky Mountains, 1888–89*, ed. by John Muir (Philadelphia: Running Press, 1976).
9. John Muir, *Notes on My Journeying in California's Northern Mountains*, Introduction by Lawrence W. Jordan (Ashland, Ore.: Lewis Osborn, 1975).
10. William Miesse, *The Significance of Mount Shasta as a Visual Resource in 19th and Early 20th Century California*, unpublished manuscript (Mount Shasta:1989).
11. Edwin Bernbaum, *Sacred Mountains of the World* (San Francisco: Sierra Club Books, 1990), chapter 9.
12. Vine Deloria, Jr., *God is Red, A Native View of Religion,* 2nd ed. (Golden, Colo.: Fulcrum Publishing, 1994), chapter 16.
13. Bernbaum, *Sacred Mountains.*
14. Mircea Eliade, *The Sacred and the Profane: The Significance of Religious Myth, Symbolism, and Ritual within Life and Culture* (Harcourt, Brace & World, 1959), 12, 36, 37.
15. Ibid., 36–37.
16. The term "traditional cultural properties" will be used throughout this discussion to include Native American sacred or ceremonial sites.
17. The Forest Service often contests this point by pointing to an August 3, 1988, letter written by that agency to the California SHPO, in which the Forest Service sought SHPO's concurrence that it had complied with the NHPA. In the letter, the Forest Service stated that as a result of its studies, which were not identified, of Mount Shasta, "no cultural resources were recovered." The Forest Service letter failed to tell SHPO of the comments received from Native Americans since 1978 on Mount Shasta's cultural importance to Northern California Native Americans, nor did the letter mention the lack of a public participation process on Mount Shasta's eligibility to the National Register, as required in the NHPA Regulations. Because so much was left out of the August letter, the California SHPO, on September 2, 1988, agreed, based on the information provided by the Forest Service, that the proposed ski resort would have no effect on National Register eligible properties. Although misleading may be a strong word, in this case it may well apply to this Forest Service letter, given the abundant facts supporting Mount Shasta's eligibility to the National Register and known to the Forest Service as early as 1978.
18. Federal law requires each state to have a SHPO, who participates in determining eligibility of properties to the National Register. The SHPOs can also play an important role in compelling a federal agency to comply with NHPA.

19. *National Register Bulletin* 38, which provides guidance on applying the National Register criteria to traditional cultural properties, specifically states that such properties can be eligible to the National Register. Bulletin 38 is strong support for the position that Native American sacred sites, including sites associated with Native American supernatural and spiritual beings, are eligible to the National Register. The National Park Service has published several Bulletins on various aspects of the National Register eligibility determination process.
20. The NHPA contemplates two situations in which a federal agency must consider the effect of its undertakings on historic properties: first, where the undertaking may have an effect on properties already on the National Register, and second, where a property may be eligible for inclusion. Most frequently, it is the latter situation which arises in cases involving traditional cultural properties. In such cases, the responsible federal agency is required to search out and locate traditional cultural properties which may be eligible to the National Register, and determine whether the agency's proposed undertaking will have an effect upon those properties.
21. The NHPA implementing regulations, found at 36 C.F.R part 800, set forth the requirements that a federal agency must follow in locating properties which may be eligible to the National Register, and determining whether the proposed undertaking will have an effect on those properties. Pursuant to the regulations, the agency must first establish the undertaking's Area of Potential Effect (APE), which is the area within which the agency believes the federal undertaking will have an effect or impact on any culturally significant properties which may be found. 36 C.F.R. § 800.4(2)(1). The APE is not limited to the boundaries of the undertaking, but may, and often does, extend beyond those boundaries.
22. The fact that the study period was so limited, and that Theodoratus and Evans were unable to interview at least 18 other Native Americans who were identified as having information on Mount Shasta's cultural significance, became the basis for the argument that the Forest Service should contract for additional studies, to assure that all Native American traditional cultural properties on Mount Shasta were properly identified.
23. Eligibility to the National Register is determined by applying the four National Register eligibility criteria, found at 36 C.F.R. § 60.4, to the properties characteristics. Two Criteria most commonly apply to traditional cultural properties. These provide that a property is eligible to the National Register where it is "associated with events that have made a significant contribution to the broad patterns of our history," or is "associated with the lives of persons significant in our past." Bulletin 38 points out that the word

person in the National Register Criteria can be taken to refer to "persons such as gods and demigods who feature in the tradition of the [Native American] group."

24. This finding offered recognition, but virtually no additional protection to the Mountain, since the top of the Mountain was already protected under the Wilderness Act.
25. Given the costs of such studies, private individuals and non-profit public interest groups can seldom afford them. Therefore, it becomes very important for such individuals and groups to convince the responsible Federal agency to conduct the studies in order to assemble the necessary evidence in support of a traditional cultural property's National Register eligibility.
26. Another important federal agency whose input is critical to the NHPA process is the Advisory Council on Historic Preservation. Regulations provide that interested parties may request the Advisory Council's review of federal agency actions affecting eligible or potentially eligible National Register properties. The Advisory Council must review any federal agency's finding that a given undertaking will have no adverse effect on historic properties. The Council can therefore become an important ally in reviewing a federal agency's compliance with NHPA.
27. The Keeper has many responsibilities, including maintaining the National Register and reviewing Federal agency National Register eligibility determinations.
28. In addition, ACHP requested that the Keeper comment on Mount Shasta's eligibility to the National Register because of its historic significance to non-native Americans.
29. The Keeper declined to make a determination on Mount Shasta's eligibility to the National Register because of its historic significance to non-native Americans, stating that further study was needed.
30. After the historic properties have been identified, NHPA regulations require that the responsible federal agency, in consultation with the SHPO, determine if the undertaking will have an effect and adverse effect upon the historic properties. Adverse effects include destruction, damage, or alteration of all or part of the historic property; isolation of the property from its setting, or alteration of the character of the setting; and introduction of visual, audible, or atmospheric elements that are out of character with the property or alter its setting. 36 C.F.R. 800.9(b). If adverse effects are found the agency "*must* seek ways to avoid or reduce the effects on historic properties (emphasis added)." 36 C.F.R. 800.5(e). In other words, the responsible federal agency has an affirmative obligation to mitigate the undertaking's adverse effects on historic properties. Mitigation of the proposed ski resort's adverse effects

on the Mount Shasta Historic District could include relocating or even abandoning the ski resort.

31. The proposed ski resort would be on public lands, but the extensive condominium development was planned for adjacent, private land.
32. This is amply demonstrated by the fact that many commercial districts, such as Georgetown in Washington, D.C., are on the National Register of Historic Places.

Conclusion: Lessons from the Spirit of Place

James and Roberta Swan

Modern man will never find peace until he comes into harmony with the place where he lives.

—Carl Jung

WHAT GOOD ARE CONFERENCES? They take time, cost money, and require people to travel long distances. In a sense, good conferences are like pilgrimages. There are goals and objectives, but beyond these planned results, many other things occur. Before summing up what we learned, we want to tell you about the other results, in hopes that perhaps you will see the need to bring people together to discuss the spirit of the place where you live.

For Lummi Indian cultural specialist Cha-Das-Ka-Dum, whose cedar flute called all five gatherings together, these programs transformed a spirit dancer and fisherman into an international ambassador to other native peoples, a recording artist, a published author, and a featured speaker at numerous environmental meetings in many parts of the world.

For physicist Elizabeth Rauscher, who studies subtle environmental electromagnetic fields, it has led her to consult with Japanese scientists on earthquake forecasting.

Architect Tom Bender also has become a consultant on design to Japan, working on creating ecologically sensitive resorts in the mountains of that country.

At Grace Cathedral in 1989, a labyrinth maze identical to that found in Chartres Cathedral was laid out on the floor and people walked through its patterns, some experiencing unusual states of mind. Several years later, that same maze was laid out in the National Cathedral in Washington, D.C., as part of the celebration of the inauguration of President William Clinton.

At Mesa Verde National Park in 1991, the U.S. National Park Service set what seems to be a precedent by having a number of park superintendents and high-ranking administrators publicly address their views on American Indian sacred places and artifacts. We understand that this meeting has set in motion a whole series of subsequent meetings and consultations that have greatly aided recognition and preservation of sacred places and burial remains on Park Service lands.

One day we received a thank you letter from a landscape architect, along with photos of massive earth sculptures she had made out in the Great Plains. Her inspiration was attending the first conference in the series.

Even today we continue to hear from architects and landscape designers who have been influenced by the workshops of Professor Thomas Lin Yun, Grand Master of Black Sect Tantric Buddhism and Feng Shui expert extraordinaire, who taught classes on the spiritual origins of design at three of the symposiums and received a number of invitations to give lectures and do Feng Shui consultations as a result of Spirit of Place appearances.

In 1992, two years after the Grace Cathedral program that included a large concert that reenacted the creation myth of the Hopi Indians inside the cathedral's sanctuary, we received an invitation to attend the graduation ceremonies of someone completing her studies to become a minister. She wrote on the back of the invitation that on that night when Cherokee elder William Fields, former Director of Indian Affairs for the U.S. National Park Service told the story of Spider Grandmother and The Twins bringing the earth to life, accompanied by music and thirty-five costumed characters and dancers, she had a spritual experience. The writer said that at this moment she had the insight that she should go back to school and become a priest to help save the earth.

Fumio Suda, the architect who co-produced the massive symposium in Sendai, Japan, helped launch a profitable international contruction and design business by producing what turned out to be the largest environmental meeting in Japan in 1991. Fumio's rewards did not stop there, however, for he met his future wife through contacts made at that event. And, the marvelous children's musical stage play *Torah* that thrilled audiences in Sendai, was later performed at the 1992 Eco-Ed convention in Toronto, thanks to a chain of synchronous events set in motion by the Spirit of Place program.

Psychologist Robert Sommer, reflecting on the five-year series as he completed his article in this collection, concluded: "Among other personal benefits, the conferences allowed me to 'come out' and explore themes that I knew were there but didn't acknowledge." One of our hopes for this program has been to call attention to the importance of appreciation of spirit in ecological thinking. At least for some people, we feel we have been successful in achieving this goal.

Lessons of the Spirit of Place

The spirit of place concept is hardly an archaic historical concept that lost utility when ancient Greek society fell to the Romans. For many traditional cultures, honoring the power of places remains the cornerstone of their identity and spiritual practice. We moderns may now spend most of our lives indoors clustered together in urban complexes, but the spirit of places still calls out to us. World tourism authorities report that the desire to visit certain special places of spiritual and cultural value is one of, if not the most important, global tourism motivations. At each of the five symposiums researchers and designers from many disciplines asserted that the spirit of a place is a very important topic in their work, even though there are no official spirit of place associations.

In producing these programs we sought to establish the modern validity of an ancient concept that seemed to be a cornerstone of living in harmony with nature. We decided early on not to try to organize a spirit of place movement. Rather, we hope that what has taken place will inspire others to conduct programs that will carry on the remembering of the power of places. As we go to press, one such program has just taken place in India and another is being planned for Texas. Seeds have been cast. Time will tell what will grow.

In these five programs, listening to nearly three hundred speakers, formally and informally, we heard common themes emerge from many. And for those people in this group who have become voices for places, it would be nice to think that at times the earth was speaking, too, through them. The following are some of these conclusions:

1. For indigenous cultures all around the world, the belief in the existence of special places of power and spirit seems universal. This concept is less understood by modern society, and the result is that conflicts about the value of place can and do arise between traditional and modern cultures. There is a need for finding a common language and conceptual framework to promote mutual understanding about the power of place. It is easy to feed the fires of conflict in such situations. The more difficult task is to build bridges of respect and cooperation.

2. The experience of place is multi-faceted and influenced by culture, personal uniqueness, and choice of awareness. There may be many more sensory processes by which to perceive the earth and nature than modern science and psychology are willing to admit. Ancient traditions such as Feng Shui assert that we have at least one hundred senses to perceive place. In the art of Pacific Northwest Coast Indians, eyes are commonly drawn all over the bodies of men and animals to express agreement with this view. In earlier times, teachers of design

understood this and spent considerable time building the designer from the inside out. The needs of modern society for ecologically conscious design suggests we need to cultivate the inner designer as well as the practitioner with professional skills.

3. Perceiving the spirit or sense of a place is often best accomplished in non-linear, symbolic, or metaphoric terms. Modern designers must cultivate their creative faculties and sensory abilities and not sacrifice these perceptions in the name of science and math. Beauty, in the final analysis, is sensed and felt, not calculated.

4. Each place has a unique quality which in turn influences what can best be done there. Communicating the spirit of a place is one of the basic motivations of art. Art that gives voice to the spirit of a place—dance, song, sculpture, painting, landscaping, etc.—lends meaning, purpose, identity, and beauty to a place.

5. The act of making a pilgrimage to special places is among the oldest and acts of human respect for nature and spirit, and one of the least understood and appreciated by modern society, despite the fact that we undertake pilgrimages by the millions each year. Psychology needs to better understand the value of pilgrimage to human life as it may be one of the most important ways that we can discover our meaning, find health, and be inspired, as well as build reverence for nature.

6. A lack of feeling for a place, especially a place where one lives and works, can be an important source of mental and physical stress. Many ancient geomancies understand the importance of the relationship between place and personal experience and take elaborate measures to insure people are harmonized with the spirit of a place to insure health and prosperity. When principles of design from Feng Shui and other geomancies are applied to modern buildings and communities, there are positive results. We need to set aside our limiting beliefs and appreciate the power of such approaches in the same fashion that Western science has acknowledged the healing values of acupuncture, even though modern science cannot prove the existence of the life force ch'i.

7. Modern science is beginning to measure the subtle properties of place. We now know that air ions, electrical, and electromagnetic fields do influence health and well-being. More research needs to be devoted to the study of subtle environmental fields, for in documenting these existence and value of these fields, we may discover a whole new art and science of design with modern science and

ancient wisdom working hand and hand to harmonize human society with nature.

8. We need new laws and land-use categories that facilitate honoring the power of place. Creating the public policies that yield such laws will require cross-cultural communication, cooperation, and understanding unprecedented in modern society.

By rooting ourselves firmly in the earth, we allow ourselves to best explore the greater dimensions of life. May you always be at the right place at the right time.

Index

Aborigines, 112, 339
Adonis, 128
Africa, 62–74, 149–50
Allen, Paula Gunn, 44, 46, 47, 52–53
altars (as sacred places), 139–45
Ameringo, Pablo, 14–15
animism, 14
Ayres Rock, 9

Ba-gua, 203–207
Bethlehem, 123–34
Bible, 123–27, 132, 197, 198
Black Elk, Wallace, 140
Black Hills, 9
Bly, Robert, 55
Brazil, 74
Buddhism, 200–201, 332

Calderone, Don Eduardo, 145, 151–57
Campbell, Joseph, 1, 5, 14, 192, 193
Cha-Das-Ka-Dum (K. Cooper), 6, 350
Chartres Cathedral, 148
chi, 200, 201–202, 220
Chimayo, N. Mex., 2
Christ, Jesus, 79, 127, 128, 133
Christianity, 123–34, 150, 154, 194, 295
clay lady, 50
Coomaraswamy, Ananda, 1
corn, 41, 43
Costa Rica, 321–25

David, King of Israel, 127
Davis, Calif., 3, 111–20
death, 178
deer, 75
Delphi, 1, 75
Deloria, Vine Jr., 333–34
Devereux, Paul, 17–18
divining, 153–56, 217, 218–24
dowsing, 8
dreams, 9
Druids, 148
Dryad, 301

ecotourism, 309–25
edge (ecological), 188
electromagnetic fields, 237, 353–54
elemental forces, 177
Eliade, Mircea, 88, 335
environmental psychology, 111
Erisichthon, 301–302
Eskimo (Inuit), 2, 4, 22–37, 73, 138
  clothing, 29–30
  Copper, 24, 25–26, 30
  homes, 28–31
  inukshuk, 31–32
  Inupiat, 28
  Netsilik, 25–27
  sacred places, 32
  Yup'ik, 23–24, 27–28, 29, 30
"Expertland", 114–15

feng-shui, 2, 180, 199–216, 27, 352
Fetzer Institute, 229–41
Fetzer, John, 230–32, 241
five element theory (feng shui), 219

Forest Service, U.S., 300, 333–36, 339–45
Frankl, Victor, 299
Freuchen, Peter, 33, 34

Gaia, 14, 20
Gaia Hypothesis, 283–93
Gaia's Hidden Life, 4
Ganges River, 86–105
  Gangaization, 90
  festivals, 98–100
  ghats, 92–100
  pollution, 101–104
Geb, 14
genus loci, 1–2
gia, 46
Gorbachev, M., 19
Grace Cathedral, 350, 351
Grand Canyon, 9
Gray, Martin, 143–44
greenways, 189

Hawaii, 9–10, 136–39, 147
healthy buildings, 237, 316
Hebrew, 123, 124, 125, 128
Hediger, H., 112
Hegedus, Carol, 235, 239, 241
heiau, 136, 138–39
Heidegger, M., 84
Hesperia, Calif., 276–77
Hillman, James, 78
Hinduism, 87–100, 103–105
  water in Hindu mythology, 87–88
huaca, 146, 151–57
Hubbell, James, 258–70
hula, 137–39

I-Ching, 219, 221–22, 283
Ifa, 62–74
  agbole, 70
  ase, 63
  atunwa, 71
  awo, 64
  bagagbe, 69–70
  igbodu, 63, 68–69
  Iwa-pele, 62
  oba, 67
  odu, 64, 65
  Oduduwa, 67
  Ogun, 68, 69, 72
  Olorun, 65
  Orun, 72
  Orunmila, 65
  Oshun, 68, 69, 149
  Oya, 68, 149
  yemoja, 68
Institute of American Indian Arts, 54–55
Integral Urban House, 253, 255
intuition, 295–296, 303

Jacob's Ladder, 123–24, 198
Japan, 217–28
  Nara, 75–85
  Sendai, 3, 351
Jews, 126
Jiba-Kanrodi, 76–77, 79, 81–82, 84–85
Jordan River, 125
Joshua, 125
Jung, Carl, 1, 11, 13, 104, 105, 159, 244, 281, 298, 330

kahuna, 147
Kakihara, Hidetake, 82
kaso, 227–28
Khalili, Nader, 270
kiva, 40
Krishna, 89

labyrinth, 350

Ladd, Edmund, 51–52
"land-nam", 1
landscape design, 201–210
Lao Tzu, 222
Lasceaux, 1, 9
Laski, Marghanita, 142, 143
Lawrence, D. H., 3
Lin Yun, Thomas, 2, 199–216, 351
Lorenz, Konrad, 2
Lourdes (France), 2, 9, 75
Lovelock, James, 283, 284
low-cost housing, 243–52
Lujan, Manuel Jr., 19

Macchu Picchu, 9, 75, 144–45
Malaurie, Jean, 33
mana, 147
Maslow, A.H., 140, 305
McClintock Barbara, 19
McFarland, R.B., 16
Medina, Angelina, 53
medicine lodge, 15
medicine wheel, 15
mesa, 146,151–57
Mesa Verde, Colo., 3, 9, 351
Milton, John, 254, 257
mirror, 171
Moore, John, 254, 257
Moore, Robert, 298, 299
Moses, 123, 124, 140
Mosque of the Rock, 126
Mount Denali, 9
Mount Fuji, 9
Mount Moriah, 126
Mount Shasta, 326–45
Mount Sinai, 123, 124, 140, 331
Muir Beach, Calif., 8
Muir, John, 331

Naisbitt, John, 82
Nakayama, Miki, 77, 79, 81, 84–85
NASA, 273
National Historic Preservation Act, 339
National Register of Historic Places, 332, 338, 339, 341–45
Native American
  Algonquin, 14
  Cuna, 17
  Diegueno, 15
  Hopi, 17, 18–19, 43, 54
  Huichol, 17
  Karuk, 330
  Lummi, 6
  Pacific N.W. Coast, 2, 6, 17
  Patwin, 16
  Pit River, 329–30
  Pueblo, 2, 38–56
  Tewa, 46
  Wintu, 330
  Zinacanteco, 141–42, 146
Nehru, Jawaharlal, 86
nine star theory, 220–21

Oblata, 64–65
Ode Remo, Nigeria, 67–73
Orians, Gordon, 113
orisha, 64, 68, 71, 73
Ortiz, Alfonso, 18, 54
Ortiz, Simon, 41–42, 44–45, 56
Oysato, 2, 75–85

Pachamama, 144–45, 147
Palenque, 1
Panchanga (Hindu calendar), 96
peace parks, 324
The Power of Place, 4
pilgrimage, 10, 81, 86, 141, 353
place attachment, 113–14
plants (feng shui), 204–15

Plato, 78
pollution, 101–104
psychic localization, 1, 104
psychotope, 112–13
pyramids, 9

Rael, Joseph, 54, 55
Rainier, Howard, 40–41
Rasmussen, Knud, 24–25, 34
resident research, 115–16
Rig Veda, 87, 88
Rumi, 272, 278

Saami, 109, 140–41
Sabina, Maria, 16–17
sacred places, 17–19, 28, 32, 63, 76, 81, 83–84, 88, 91, 92–109, 142–43, 194, 250,288, 297, 302, 311, 329–35, 341
  Christian, 123–34
  Druids, 148
  Greece, 147–48
  Irañ, 274–75
  Mexico, 141–42
  Peru, 144–45
  Saami, 140–41
Sahtouris, Elizabeth, 20
Salt Woman, 49–50
Samoa, 2
Save Mount Shasta, 336–39
Sedna, 26
sense of place, 312–14
Serpent Mound, 9
shaman, 13–20, 32
shakti, 96
Sharon, Douglas, 151–52, 153
shimenawa, 7, 109
ship'apu, 48–49
Shiva, 88, 91, 96
shuyoka, 81
Silko, L. M., 45–46, 47–48, 56
skalalitude, 6
Smith, Brent, 243–52
Solomon, 126
Sommer, Robert, 8, 351
soul, 175
Spider Grandmother, 18–19, 49, 351
spirit of place, 2, 3, 4, 5, 13, 80–81, 109, 121, 184, 239, 317–18, 353
Spirit of Place Symposiums, 3–4, 8, 350–54
spirit paths, 314
spiritual value, 295
Spretnak, C., 20
Stonehenge, 9, 75
storks, 131–34
Sufism, 10
sustainable development, 86–87, 120
symbolism in design, 95–198, 230, 234–38, 244–45, 297, 297–301
Swan, James, 18, 80–81, 104, 143
Swan, Roberta, 286
Swentzell, Rina, 39, 43

taboo, 28
Temenos, 159–63, 238
Tenri, 2, 75, 76
Tenrikyo, 75–85
  creation myth, 77–78
  Ofudeski, 77, 80
  Shuyoka, 81
Thailand (spirit houses), 109
"third ear", 6, 8
thresholds, 210
Tijuana, Mexico, 262–63
Tokonoma, 176
totemism, 14
tourism, 102–103, 169, 307–25, 352
Tuan, Yi-Fu, 89, 104, 111–12
  topophilia, 111–12

Vancouver, B.C., 4–5
Van der Ryn, Sim, 252–58
Varanasi (Banares), 86–105
Velarde, Pablita, 42
Vishnu, 87, 95, 97
Vladivostok, Russia, 260–62, 267

Wailing Wall, 126
wildlife and design, 188
World Conservation Strategy, 105
Wright, Frank Lloyd, 1, 3, 5, 165–66

Yellow Woman, 50–51
Yoruba, 62–74
Yosemite National Park, 9
Yun Lin Temple, 207–208

QUEST BOOKS
are published by
The Theosophical Society in America,
Wheaton, Illinois 60189-0270,
a branch of a world organization
dedicated to the promotion of the unity of
humanity and the encouragement of the study of
religion, philosophy, and science, to the end that
we may better understand ourselves and our place in
the universe. The Society stands for complete
freedom of individual search and belief.
For further information about its activities,
write or call 1-800-669-1571.

*The Theosophical Publishing House
is aided by the generous support of
THE KERN FOUNDATION,
a trust established by Herbert A. Kern
and dedicated to Theosophical education.*

THE EMERALD SCEPTER

PAUL KEMPRECOS

SUSPENSE PUBLISHING

THE EMERALD SCEPTER
by
Paul Kemprecos

PAPERBACK EDITION
* * * * *
PUBLISHED BY:
Suspense Publishing

PUBLISHING HISTORY:
Suspense Publishing, Paperback and Digital Copy, May 2013

Cover Design: Shannon Raab
Cover Photographer: iStockphoto.com/Dewitt

ISBN-13: 978-0615804552
ISBN-10: 0615804551

For Christi, of course.

ACKNOWLEDGEMENTS

First of all I would like to thank my pals in the Clive Cussler Society for their continued support and for encouraging me to write a book on my own. Here it is, gang! I'm grateful to Wayne Valero, president and founder of the CCCS, for his insightful suggestions on how to improve the pile of pages I sent him. My line editor Gabe Robinson cut away thousands of words that were cluttering up the manuscript, but the surgery vastly improved the flow of my deathless prose. A special thanks to Clive Cussler who taught me during our NUMA Files collaboration to strive for a fresh point of view and avoid writing clichés like the plague. Oops! Many thanks to John and Shannon Raab at Suspense publishing for this opportunity to bring forth my first solo effort since the NUMA Files. I especially appreciate Shannon's enthusiasm, astute editorial and art sense, and her help in navigating my way around the new world of e-books and blog chats. And thanks to my wife Christi for constantly reminding me during those down spells that I am better than I think I am.

PRAISE FOR PAUL KEMPRECOS

" "The Emerald Scepter" just might be the perfect speculative thriller, offering up a seasoned blend of legend and folklore mixed brilliantly with actual historical fact. James Rollins and Clive Cussler have nothing on Paul Kemprecos who has been and continues to be a master of the form and then some. This is everything a great read should be, a riveting, tried-and true tale of quests and daring-do, of great heroes and equally contemptuous villains. There's a reason why Kemprecos is a #1 *New York Times* bestselling author and it's all on display here."

—Jon Land, bestselling author of "Pandora's Temple"

"A brilliant mystery that combines suspense with exciting adventure. Intriguing plot twists from beginning to end shrouded under genuine history."

—Clive Cussler, *New York Times* bestselling author of "Zero Hour"

"Kemprecos...writes sharp, readable prose."

—Booklist

"Absorbing...Soc is an appealing, witty protagonist...and the Cape Cod locale is rendered with panache in this face-paced enjoyable yarn."

—*Publisher's Weekly*

"Former newsman Kemprecos delivers the where, why, what, when, and finally who in a whodunit strengthened by gritty dialogue and assured depictions of suspenseful dives."

—*Boston Herald*

"Few adventures in pursuit of myth were more seductive than the quest for the mythical kingdom of Prester John."
—Daniel J. Borstin, "The Discoverers"

"How often in his long conversations with travelers and seafarers Prince Henry must have heard that name, Prester John. The search for this long-dead, or non-existent, monarch played as important a part in the history of navigation and discovery as the quest for the philosopher's stone in the history of chemistry."
—Earle Bradford, "A Wind from the North; the Life of Henry the Navigator"

THE EMERALD SCEPTER

PAUL KEMPRECOS

PROLOGUE

East of Babylon, 1179 A.D

The desert monster appeared in a glittering vortex of golden dust.

The caravan's lead scout saw the creature first. The scout had been riding a hundred yards ahead of the mile-long column of horses, camels, merchants and religious pilgrims. His head cover was pulled down over his forehead and wrapped around the lower part of his face. He was bent over the neck of his horse, squinting through the narrow opening as he scoured the high desert for the tracks of previous caravans.

The moaning wind had ramped up to a sudden squall, creating a dancing curtain of whirling dust devils. The movement caught the scout's eye. He lifted his head and saw an amorphous shape loom in the diffused sunlight, waving its appendages like the sails of a windmill.

The hulking form that emerged from the swirling cloud was bigger than the average-sized man. The head was silvery and flat on top. The face was a fiery orange-red. Metallic scales covered the body.

As the thing staggered toward the scout, it emitted a bellow like a wounded bull.

The scout was a seasoned warrior, but the tortured wail was like nothing his ears had ever heard. The hair bristled on the back of his neck and a bird-like squawk escaped from deep in his throat.

Unnerved by the blowing dust wraiths, the horse let out a pitiful whinny and reared up in fright, pawing the air with its hooves. The scout clamped his legs onto the horse's haunches and shouted for help.

The quartet of Persian mercenaries at the head of the caravan heard the wind-muted cry and saw the threatening figure advancing through the blowing sand. Four curved swords *snicked* from their leather scabbards.

With the guard sergeant taking the lead, the Persians swept past the scout. As the warriors closed in for the kill, the intruder stopped in its tracks, teetered as if being tugged in a dozen directions, took a step, stopped again and toppled over backwards.

The sergeant reined in his horse and slipped from his saddle. He cautiously approached the immobile hulk and lowered his sword. The creature lying on the sands was not a monster. It was a man. Or what was *left* of a man.

Jerusalem, Two Years Earlier

Master Philip was in a foul mood. The special emissary of Pope Alexander III hunched over a crude wooden table, quill pen poised above a blank sheet of parchment, a look of sheer agony on his face. He was struggling to find a diplomatic choice of words that would tell the Pope he'd sent Philip on a fool's errand.

He had done his best to warn the Pope. Before leaving Rome he had pleaded with Alexander one last time. "I am the papal physician, not a soldier or an adventurer," Philip had argued. "I have been trained to deal with black bile and phlegm. There are men far better suited than I to carry out your wishes."

The Pope had rejected the impassioned plea. "There is no one I would trust more for this crucial mission, Master Philip. You have the qualities I most demand. You are my friend as well as my physician. We need help to defeat the infidels beating at our door. The fate of Christendom may hinge on your success."

"All the more reason, Your Holiness, to find someone more qualified than I," Philip had countered.

Alexander had said, "Have you no faith in God?"

"In God, yes. In myself, no."

"Be not afraid." The Pope had hung a golden cross around Philip's neck. "I had this made to remind you that God moves in mysterious ways," he soothed.

With the Pope's blessing still echoing in his ears, Philip sailed from Venice across the Mediterranean to Palestine carrying a letter seeking an alliance with Prester John, the mysterious ruler of a far-off Eastern kingdom. Unfortunately, the location of Prester John's kingdom was a mystery. Not long after arriving in Jerusalem, Philip came to a reluctant conclusion. His mission was doomed to fail.

It went beyond his personal doubts. He had talked to dozens of people about the lands to the east. Day after day he had sat in his modest Jerusalem apartment and listened with growing apprehension to their hair-raising stories of travel over vast distances through unforgiving terrain, and about their encounters with blood-thirsty natives and roving bands of robbers. The conversations had convinced Phillip that his earlier misgivings were not without foundation.

He brought the quill to the parchment and waited for God to move his pen hand. But the quavering voice he heard came not from the Deity.

"Someone is here to see you, master," said his man servant, who stood in the doorway.

A bull-dog scowl came to Philip's lips. "I'm busy," he snapped.

"But Sire, I'm afraid—"

A huge hand encased in chain mail swept the servant aside like a piece of straw and a giant of a man squeezed through the doorway into the room. The stranger towered several inches over six feet. His face was hidden for the most part under a wild beard of fiery red. He filled the chamber with his bulk and unpleasant smell. A long sword hung in a scabbard diagonally across his wide chest.

The man removed a pot-shaped helmet from his neck and cradled it in his arms. Then he dropped onto one knee and pushed the mail hood back from his bowed head, revealing thick red hair that hung in uneven bangs over his forehead.

Philip felt as if he were in the presence of a creature that had sprung from a tale meant to frighten bad children.

His vocal cords seemed frozen, but he managed a loud whisper. "Who are you?"

"Thomas, son of Thomas," the giant rumbled.

Philip's gaze went to the red cross sewn onto the patched white tunic over the chain mail coat known as a *hauberk*. The symbol was the insignia of a Crusader.

He was regaining his composure. "You have taken up the Cross, I see."

Speaking in heavily-accented Latin, Thomas said, "I would take it up again to defend the Holy Land."

Philip was aware that Jerusalem swarmed with violent men like Thomas who had found themselves without employment after they had captured the city from the Saracens. He guessed that the knight was offering to hire out the long sword.

"I have no need of mercenaries," Philip said, speaking in English.

The massive head slowly lifted. Cunning lurked in the hard blue eyes.

"Perhaps not, sire. But have you need of someone who can lead you to the Prester?"

So *that* was this brute's game. Philip fumed at the boldness of the man. Word of his mission and his willingness to pay for information had quickly circulated in the ancient city.

"It is no secret in Jerusalem that I seek Prester John," Philip said, making no effort to hide the annoyance in his voice.

"But none of the others who have heard of your quest can show you the way."

"I suppose you have a map that you wish to sell," Philip scoffed.

"No map," Thomas said. "But I can lead you to the Prester's kingdom with a lodestone."

Thomas slipped a mail glove off his hand, reached under his tunic and came out with a rough-cut emerald around a half-inch across cradled in the creases of his massive palm.

Philip took the emerald from the knight's hand and studied the green stone in a shaft of light slanting through a small window. The uncut gem was of the highest quality.

"Where did you get this little bauble?" Philip said, acting as if he were only mildly curious.

"From a Greek merchant who acquired it in the Prester's kingdom."

Philip passed the emerald back.

"Get off your knee, Thomas son of Thomas. Sit on that stool and try not to break it." He turned the hour glass over on his desk. "You have until the bottom is half full."

Thomas eased his great bulk onto the creaking stool and told Philip how he had haggled over the emerald in the Constantinople bazaar. The gem merchant was vague about the source of the stone, saying only that it was east of Babylon. Intrigued, Thomas began to frequent other bazaars. He noticed emeralds of similarly unusual beauty and started a discrete inquiry as to their origin. He found a common thread. The handful of merchants who sold the gems had all been on caravans that traveled far to the east on a trade route known to be long and extremely hazardous. He went back to the Greek.

"And this merchant simply came out and told you he had reached the Kingdom of Prester John?" Philip said, not trying to hide his skepticism.

"No, sire. I had to *persuade* him."

Philip glanced at the knight's club-like hands. Thomas obviously had formidable powers of persuasion. The Greek said his supplier told him only that the gems came from a distant eastern kingdom ruled by a Christian. A handful of traders knew the way and they keep it secret.

Philip listened long after the sand had drained from the top of the hour glass. Thomas had a simple plan. Join a caravan. Identify the emerald merchants heading east of Babylon. When they neared their destination he would *persuade* the merchants to show the way to Prester John.

"We would travel together, you and I?"

Thomas nodded. "I have six loyal men who would follow me to Hell."

"And what is the cost of this journey to Hades?"

"All expenses and a fair cut of future emerald trade."

Philip's hand went to the gold cross that hung from his neck. He knew it would be madness to join a group of untamed mercenaries on a dangerous journey to nowhere. On the other hand, he was desperate. The Pope would not accept an excuse.

He wrinkled his nose; he supposed he would get used to the man's foul odor in time. "When can we leave?" he said.

"The caravan is assembling outside the city and will depart in a week." Thomas hesitated. "I'll need money for supplies and to buy a place in the caravan."

Philip gave him a handful of coins from a leather purse. "Keep in mind that even the Pope's purse has a bottom," he warned.

Thomas handed him the emerald. "This will ensure my return."

After Thomas left, Philip placed the emerald in a strong box. Before he closed the lid, he took out the folded letter inside and gazed at the Papal seal. Pope Alexander was right. God had answered his prayers by sending Thomas as His emissary. A faint smile crossed Philip's lips. The Pope said that God moved in mysterious ways, but he hadn't mentioned that the Almighty had a keen sense of humor.

Philip joined the caravan posing as a rich pilgrim traveling with his bodyguards. The arrangement aroused no suspicion. The caravans that plied the Asian trade routes were moving cities. Each with its own government, complete with bureaucrats and cooks. Private armies often accompanied merchants and traders.

Philip used Italian charm and gallons of wine to insinuate his way into this mix as the caravan plodded eastward. He identified a small group of gem traders and narrowed their number down to two close-mouthed merchants specializing in fine emeralds. Months passed. He gained the confidence of the gem merchants and every night sat with them around the campfire. He kept his ear cocked, never saying that he knew how to speak Greek. One night he overheard the two merchants hinting at their plans to slip away from the caravan.

Thomas and his men were waiting when the traders struck out on their own. One trader resisted and died. Philip was visibly upset at

Thomas, but relented when the Crusader said the man's death must have been God's will because it persuaded the other merchant to lead the way.

After weeks of travel through remote and rugged country, the travelers broke through a mountain pass into a verdant land. They followed a stone-paved road, mingling with a growing number of merchants, traders and farmers. The road led to the turreted gates of a city as large as any in Europe. A magnificent palace overlooked the city from high on a hill.

The gem trader had papers from a previous visit and the city guards allowed him to pass. He quickly disappeared through the gates, grinning at the former captors as he left them behind. Philip told the guards that he had a letter for the king. The guards took the letter and threw the strangers into a dungeon. After languishing a few days, the prisoners were visited by a black-robed man.

Speaking in a strange Latin dialect, the robed man said he was the king's minister and that he had read the Pope's letter. He had them moved to cleaner, more spacious quarters. They were well-fed and given robes to wear. Their every need was attended to, but they were still prisoners. The men gambled. Philip passed the time keeping a journal. It was not a terrible existence, but they were overjoyed when the minister sent a message saying the king wanted to see Philip and Thomas.

Guards escorted the two men to the hill palace through streets lined with opulent mansions and bustling shops. Philip had expected a throne room filled with courtiers. Instead, he and Thomas were ushered into a small, simply furnished chamber.

A middle-aged man with close-cropped gray hair and beard sat behind a dark-wood table. Unlike the minister and the guards, whose features had a faint Asian cast, the man's long handsome face was Caucasian. He wore no crown or opulent cloak, only a plain robe that differed from the others in its color, an imperial purple.

In a regal voice that was compelling, in spite of its softness, he told his guests to sit, and apologized for not seeing them sooner.

"I was away to another part of my great kingdom," he said. He placed his hand on the letter from Alexander, which lay on the table, the papal seal broken, and gazed at Philip with deep-set eyes the color of amber. "Tell me about your Pope and your long journey."

Philip related how Alexander had recruited his physician to carry the message to Prester John. The king listened intently, nodding occasionally. Only when Philip had finished his story did the king ask probing questions about European politics and religion. At the end of the interrogation, he snapped his fingers and the minister handed Philip a vellum scroll sealed in wax.

"I would like you to carry this letter to your Pope. Your journey was arduous, and I regret having to ask that you repeat it so soon," the king said. "You will have two days to rest and another three to prepare."

Philip's eyes went to the steel-bound ebony chest around three feet long that sat on a side table. The minister lifted the black box in two hands, set it in front of the king and removed the lid.

Thomas muttered a prayer, and Philip didn't blame the astonished knight. They were gazing at a golden scepter, made in the shape of a long cross and encrusted with emeralds.

"It's beautiful," Philip whispered.

A quick smile came to the king's lips. "Yes, it is beautiful, but it is more than that. It is the symbol of my power. I entrust you to carry this gift to your Pope along with other tokens of my esteem to reassure him that I will soon lead my armies to be by his side in the fight against the infidels. I wish you a safe journey and Godspeed."

He rose from the table and disappeared through a curtained door. The minister gently lowered the lid. The audience was over.

Five days later Philip and his men left the kingdom of Prester John and headed west. They were accompanied by fifty fierce-eyed horse archers clad in black-robes over light breast armor made of segmented steel plates. Steel skull caps protected their heads. They carried curved swords, but their main weapon was a short bow made of wood and horn, fashioned with the tips curved forward to exact the maximum power from the bronze-tipped arrows launched from the animal sinew strings.

The archers guarded a column of twenty mules harnessed together in pairs and several mule-drawn wooden supply carts. Each pair of mules carried an ebony chest in a hammock slung between their broad backs. The chest holding the scepter rode by itself in a mule cart positioned in the middle of the column. The horse archers called themselves the Guardians. Their sworn duty was to defend the contents of the boxes with their lives.

The iron-handed captain of the Guardians made sure the tightly-spaced column moved at double the average caravan travel speed of eight miles a day regardless of weather or physical barriers.

Philip and Thomas rode side-by-side at the head of the procession. The Italian's olive complexion had been darkened to near mahogany by years of exposure to harsh sunlight. He rode a fine-limbed chestnut Arabian horse. Like the archers, he wore a breast plate and skull cap. Thomas towered above him, sitting astride a giant Percheron of dappled gray.

As the horses jogged along, Philip looked off at the scorched hills and jagged, snow-peaked mountains. He swept his arm in the air.

"You know me to be a man of great piety, Thomas. But If God is all-powerful, why did He not bring beauty to *every* part of the world?"

The doctor's philosophical meanderings had become a familiar refrain against the clop of hooves over thousands of miles traveled together.

"Perhaps He is testing us," Thomas said.

"Well put, Thomas. Worthy of the most learned theologian. And what a test is in store for us! Just *look* at this awful place. It is difficult to imagine that God is behind every stone."

The Crusader *was* looking at the wrinkled landscape, but with the steely gaze of a military man who saw potential danger rather than the Almighty lurking behind the massive boulders and in the deep ravines. They were traveling along a path that led down into a narrowing valley hemmed in by hills that grew steeper and closer together. A ragged carpet of waist-high bushes and trees with twisted trunks covered the boulder-strewn slopes. Their guide had insisted that the canyon was the quickest way through the mountains.

Thomas saw that it was also a perfect place for an ambush. The caravan could turn back, but the search for another way through the mountains would delay their journey to Rome, and their pack animals needed the water that the guide promised they would have further into the valley.

Thomas had begrudgingly hired the guide at the last caravan stop because he spoke English he had learned from passing travelers. He said he had led many caravans. Thomas didn't trust him. He had kept a close eye on the man who was riding ahead of the caravan with a knight at his side. He watched as the guide dropped back a few paces from the knight, removed his turban and used it to wipe the sweat off his face.

As if released from a magician's hat, a flock of silver-feathered birds erupted near a clump of trees about half-way up the slope to the right. Philip watched the birds whirl into the sky, then glanced back and saw a quick on-off firefly glint in the trees.

A cut-off force was in hiding. Another force was likely hidden on the opposite side of the canyon; both were positioned to stop a retreat once the column was ambushed.

The release of the caged birds would signal the main force that the caravan was entering the trap. Thomas smiled. If he had been leading the ambush he would have made sure every shiny metal weapon that could catch sunlight had been sheathed away from the sun's rays. The lack of discipline was a good sign. The caravan would likely be facing wild bandits rather than a trained army.

Thomas raised his mail-covered fist above his head and the caravan came to a crawling halt at the signal. He leaned over in his saddle and said:

"Master Philip, if you would be so kind as to convey a message to the captain?"

The doctor was the official leader of the caravan, but he deferred to the battle-scarred ex-Crusader in all matters of security. He asked no questions and quickly relayed the message to the captain who rode back along the column to convey the orders to the Guardians.

Two archers slid from their saddles. One went over to a mule-drawn cart that carried a clay pot in a bed of sand and removed the pot cover. Heat blasted from the glowing red embers that allowed fire to be moved from camp to camp. From another cart, the second man removed a wooden bucket that held pieces of smoked meat preserved in melted fat. He carried the bucket along the lines and the archers each plunged arrows into the thick goo.

His comrade fashioned a torch from pieces of kindling and held it close to the embers until it caught fire. He followed the bucket and touched the torch to the fat-soaked arrows. As each arrow flared into flames, the Guardian holding it peeled away from the main column.

The guide galloped back to Thomas.

"Why have we stopped?" the man demanded.

Ignoring the question, Thomas said, "How much did they pay you to betray us?"

Fear flickered in the guide's dark eyes. He snapped the reins and jerked the animal's head aside, digging his heels into the mule's flanks. The move ignited the animal's reflexes. It lurched forward and broke into a fast trot.

Thomas' horse reared up on its powerful hind legs and sprang forward with an unexpected agility, covering the ground with long thundering strides. As Thomas caught up with the mule and its rider, he drew his broadsword from its chest scabbard in an exquisitely timed motion and brought it around in a sweeping arc.

The razor edge of the German-forged blade caught the guide's neck at the base of the skull. The head separated from the shoulders and hit the ground like a ripe melon.

As Thomas galloped back to the caravan, the two lines of Guardians positioned at the base of the hills on both sides of the canyon began to shoot flaming arrows into the air. Each arrow that disappeared into the tree-tops planted a fiery seed. Smoke blossomed where fire had taken hold. Tendrils of flame merged and spread, quickly turning the hillsides into infernos.

Movement rippled down the hillsides ahead of the advancing flames. The men who had been hiding in the brush were running for their lives. The moving wall of fire enveloped some men, but others made it safely to the valley floor where they brandished swords and spears and charged the horse archers in a shrieking mob. The bowmen easily picked off the attackers. Within minutes the valley was littered with bodies.

The fast-moving fire rapidly burned off the vegetation. As the rainfall of gray ash diminished and the haze thinned, the valley revealed itself to be honey-combed with openings. Men streamed from the caves and swarmed down the glowing hillsides. Shouts of anger and blood lust echoed throughout the smoke-filled valley.

The Guardians coolly adjusted their tactics for rapid fire. Each horse archer clutched a handful of arrows in his hand and drew the bow string back to his cheek instead of the ear. Killing clouds of feathered shafts descended on the attackers.

For every bandit who fell, the caves disgorged three more to take his place. Some bandits were armed with bows. While their aim was poor, the deadly cloud of arrows began to tell against the lightly armored horse archers. Several Guardians were killed outright. The others walked their horses backwards, trying to hold formation while they kept up a steady rate of fire.

Thomas saw the horse archers fade back and rallied his men, who had been guarding the panicked pack animals. The Crusader way to deal with an attack was to *attack*.

Three knights galloped off to one side of the canyon. Thomas led another trio in tight formation toward the bandits on the opposite side.

In its day, nothing devised for warfare could rival a Crusader charge in sheer shock power. A mounted knight was the medieval equivalent of a modern battle tank. The Percheron weighed at least two thousand pounds even without armor. The *Destriers* the other knights rode were nearly as big.

The horses mowed down the first rank of attackers, drove deep into the living sea, spun around and headed back, leaving splintered bones and bloody pulp in their wake. They broke into the clear, then spun around and charged again. The bandits were better prepared for the second attack. A deft spear thrust unseated the man to Thomas' left and the bandits butchered the body as the horse dragged it along.

Thomas and his men took advantage of the diversion and hacked their way into the open. The tide of battle was turning. The bandits had outflanked the archers and others were closing in on the pack animals. Philip was courageously using his short sword against three spear-carrying men on foot. Thomas rode to his aid. He cut two of the bandits practically in half and his horse trampled the third. It was too late.

A spear point had slipped through the edge of Philip's breast plate under his raised armpit. The sword dropped from his fingers and he leaned weakly on his horse's neck.

The Guardian captain fought his way over.

"Take the pack animals!" he shouted. "We'll hold the bandits off as long as we can."

Thomas grabbed the reins of Philip's horse and ordered his men to round up the pack animals carrying the black chests.

Horse archers formed ragged defensive lines to protect their retreat.

In a clatter of hooves and wagon wheels, the knights galloped further into the narrowing valley to a bend flanked by high cliffs that soared up on either side like the walls of a great cathedral. The natural stone gates had acted as fire-breaks, keeping the blaze away from the smaller section of the ravine.

Thomas hoped the archers might hold their lines until he and his men could exit the other end. His plans were dashed against a sheer vertical wall of shale hundreds of feet high. They were in a box canyon. Below the wall was a pond surrounded by reeds. The guide had been telling the truth when he said there was water.

While the men and animals refreshed themselves at the water hole, Thomas rode up one side of the canyon, then dismounted and climbed the last few hundred feet to the top. He saw a hill that reminded him of a camel's hump. His horsemen might be able to follow in his steps, but not the pack animals and carts.

On his descent he discovered an opening partially hidden by brush. He explored the cave entrance and saw that it was reinforced with timbers. A dozen paces past the entrance the cave widened dramatically. There would be plenty of room for men and animals.

He signaled his men to climb to him, and led them into the cave. Thomas lifted Philip from his horse and laid his friend out on the hard floor. He removed the doctor's armor and using the basic first aid he had learned on countless battlefields, he fashioned a compress with Philip's shirt to slow the bleeding. The lessons on how to treat wounds also made him a good judge of their severity.

Philip was dying.

Thomas removed his helmet to reveal thinning reddish gray hair. He was weary, but he kept his voice strong and reassuring.

"It's only a scratch, Master Philip. We'll be on our way after a short rest."

Philip managed a slight smile. "I've come as far as I can. You must travel the rest of the way without me. Where is the journal I've been keeping?"

Thomas held up the blood-soaked leather bag that contained Philip's daily writings.

An expression of relief came to the face of the dying man. "You must keep it safe, Thomas."

"And what of the letter to the Pope?"

A faint smile came to Philip's cracked lips. "I delivered one letter. It is up to you to deliver the reply."

The smile hardened into a grimace. Philip tensed his body and his eyes rolled up in his head. A guttural sound escaped from his throat. Thomas felt a leaden heaviness in his chest. For the first time in many years he was feeling an unusual emotion. Sadness.

Someone called his name. The scout had returned to the cave with a breathless report. "I saw no sign of the Guardians, but the bandits are not attacking."

"They know we have no place to go," Thomas said. "They will tend to their dead and rob the Guardians. Then they will rest and attack at dawn."

"We'll stand and fight to the end," the look-out said.

The other men echoed his determination with shouts of defiance.

"No. We will carry the fight to *them*," Thomas said. "But first we have some work to do."

Thomas fashioned a torch and walked further into the cave. He saw that it had been used as a tomb. Bones lay in an elevated wall niche at the end of the tomb. Clay wine vessels had been placed at the feet of the skeleton in the alcove.

While his men unloaded the chests and stacked them, Thomas swept aside the occupant of the niche. He placed Philip's body in the opening, covered his friend with his armor and bloody robe. He slipped the helmet onto Philip's head. He mumbled a soldier's prayer and made the sign of the cross.

After a moment of thought, he removed the plug from of the wine vessels. The contents had evaporated and the top was encrusted with dry resin. He placed Philip's journal in the vessel, then use his torch to melt the resin into an airtight seal when he pushed the plug back into the opening.

His men had finished unloading the chests. He unlatched the lids and allowed his men to examine the contents. They gasped when they saw the fabulous wealth in gold and jewels, but they went silent when Thomas lifted the scepter from its container.

He placed the scepter on Philip's body and the gold cross on his forehead. He took two gold coins from a chest and placed them on his friend's eyes to buy his way into heaven.

Next, he extracted the Prester John scroll from its leather bag. He dipped his finger in Philip's wound and used his friend's blood to draw a diagram on the back of the vellum. As soon as it had dried, he placed the letter back in the pouch and hung it around his neck.

After darkness had fallen, he ordered his men to move all the animals out of the cave. Ropes were tied from four mules to the vertical mine timbers at the entrance. From a safe distance, the mules pulled the timbers out and the entrance collapsed on itself. A massive boulder tumbled from above the cave, sealing the opening.

They made their way to the natural buttresses at the narrowest part of the canyon. Figures were moving around the fires that blocked the only way out. Thomas ordered the men to cut the animals loose and herd them ahead. A balky mule brayed in protest. There were shouts of alarm; their attack had been detected.

Thomas slapped the mule on its haunches with the broad side of his sword. Braying even louder than before, the mule galloped toward the fires. The other animals followed, crashing through the bandit encampment as their hooves kicked up showers of sparks.

Thomas and his men charged in behind the mules, forming a flying wedge with the giant Percheron at the point of the tight formation. Thomas swung his sword as if it were a scythe, feeling its blade bite into flesh and bone until he realized he was hacking away at empty air.

He brought his horse to a halt and looked behind him.

The camp fires were far behind him. His companions were nowhere to be seen.

He was all alone.

He touched the pouch around his neck to see if it was still there, and then urged his horse on into the looming darkness.

The Persian scout could have been forgiven for assuming that the figure in the dust vortex was a monster.

The metallic head was actually a pot-shaped steel helmet and the scales were a cloak of chain mail. The man's white tunic looked like lacework. His *coif*, or mailed hood was draped around his neck, further enhancing the reptilian appearance. A ferocious reddish beard caked with sand and dust hid the lower part of the face. Shredded blisters covered the unprotected part of his sun-blasted face and the threads of dead skin gave the man's skin a fur-like shagginess. His cloudy blue eyes were set in a vacant stare.

The man stirred and brought his right arm toward his heaving chest. The hand groped under the chain mail coat and came out with a leather pouch that hung from a broken cord. The sergeant had assumed that the man was completely blind. But when the Persian reached for the pouch a hand as big as a lion's paw whipped out and grabbed his wrist with unexpected strength.

The sergeant's companions raised their swords to strike.

"*Wait!*" the sergeant commanded.

The swords were slowly lowered.

With his free hand, the sergeant tilted the water bag into the man's mouth. A few drops made it past the parched lips and the water seemed to revive the man. His fingers uncurled from the sergeant's wrist.

"Who are you?" the guard said. He knew fragments of several languages and repeated the question until he got a response using Latin.

The cracked lips twitched, and laboriously formed a word.

"*Tho-mas*," the man whispered. "My name is Thomas."

The hollow voice seemed to issue from the grave.

The mouth produced a string of words that made no sense, as if spoken in a delirium. Then the spittle-covered lips froze in place and the words deteriorated into a mumble. The man's eyes widened in a wild glassy stare. His massive chest heaved spasmodically a few times and went still.

The sergeant removed the pouch from the dead fingers, opened the bag and pulled out a vellum scroll covered with writing and rolled around a wooden spindle.

The helmet and the mail coat were too worn and damaged to be of value. He might sell the vellum to one of the gullible pilgrims in the caravan. He was sure he could convince someone it was a holy relic. The sergeant tucked the scroll back into the pouch, tied the broken cord and looped it around his neck.

He ordered the men to bury the dead body while he rode back to get the caravan moving again. The grumbling guards used their sword points to scrape out a shallow grave and shoved the body into the hole with their feet. The reluctant grave-diggers returned to their place at the head of the caravan.

The hissing sands of the desert began to complete their unfinished task. Within minutes, a grainy shroud covered the huge body. And long before the jingling of harness bells and the shouts of camel drivers faded into the distance the desert had wrapped the man called Thomas in its timeless embrace.

Afghanistan, January, 1989

Georgi Vasilyev was seated on a camp stool in his tent, peering through a magnifying glass at the rock specimens spread out on the table in front of him, when he heard an excited voice calling out his name. Seconds later, his Afghan assistant Raheem threw the flap aside and stuck his head into the tent.

"Dr. Vasilyev. Come quick!"

The middle-aged geologist from the Soviet geological survey mission and his younger counterpart from the Afghan ministry of mining had become close friends, but Vasilyev had specifically requested that he be left undisturbed to catalogue his collection.

Before answering he picked up another specimen and jotted a note into a pad. "What is it?" he growled.

"Sorry, Dr. Vasilyev. I know you wanted no interruptions, but we made a strange find. Come. You won't be sorry."

The Russian suppressed a smile at his assistant's unabashed enthusiasm. He sighed heavily for show, followed Raheem outside and got into the passenger seat of the UAZ-469 parked next to the tent. The rugged all-terrain vehicle was the Russian equivalent of the American Jeep. Raheem drove at subsonic speed and they soon came to a large lake.

Raheem slammed on the brakes and the UAZ fish-tailed to a skidding stop alongside a BTR-152 armored personnel carrier parked a few hundred feet from the cliffs. The vehicle was used to transport the twelve-man squadron assigned to protect the survey party.

The guards stood in a rough circle with their AK-47s slung on their shoulders, alongside a group of Russian and Afghan surveyors, around the perimeter of a pit approximately fifteen feet across and a yard deep. Two Afghan laborers who'd been hired by the survey stood in the shallow crater leaning on the handles of their shovels. The hard sunlight glinted on a flat, diamond-shaped object a couple of feet long.

"What is this?" Vasilyev asked Raheem.

"Not sure. One of the men discovered it a while ago. The wind blew away the sand."

Vasilyev didn't have to be reminded of the wind blowing off the lake.

The sharp-edged breeze stabbed at his ribs and penetrated the mushroom-shaped woolen hat to his bald scalp. Vasilyev scrambled down into the pit. He was in his 60s, but ten years of field work in the harsh environment of Afghanistan had toughened him. He had shed many pounds tromping around the rugged countryside and hardly ever drank the vodka that many of his countrymen sucked down like water.

He borrowed a shovel from one of the laborers and dug around the object. Then he got down on his knees to examine what appeared to be a large winch. The name etched into the metal revealed that the winch had been manufactured in Colorado. Coiled around the winch drum were the frayed remnants of a cable. Next to the winch were some old gray wooden beams. Eye bolts had been screwed into the wood.

Vasilyev got to his feet and signaled the Afghans to widen the excavation.

There was a hollow *tung* sound as one Afghan sank his shovel blade into the earth. A minute later, he had uncovered a round metal object. Vasilyev squatted and ran his fingers over the shiny brass surface and around the glass vision ports. He furrowed his brow. A diving helmet was the *last* thing he expected to find in the desert.

He glanced off at the glittering waters of the lake trying to picture a diver descending into the depths from a boat. Why the heavy-duty winch? He had worked on mine projects and had seen similar pulleys suspended over the earth. On impulse, he stood and began to walk back and forth, moving closer to the lake with each pacing turn.

He had developed a sharp eye for detail as a geologist. After a few passes he saw a dark line in the ground. He brushed the sand away with his hand and called the laborers over. Within seconds they had uncovered a metal plate around four feet square. They removed the plate and Vasilyev looked down into a dark shaft.

One of his Russian colleagues said, "I wonder where this goes."

"Let's take a look," Vasilyev said. He ordered Raheem to round up some rope and electric torches.

As the Afghan went to carry out the request, Vasilyev heard the sound of an aircraft engine. A black dot appeared in the clear blue sky, growing in size until it morphed into the transport helicopter that brought supplies in every week. It was three days early.

The chopper landed near the troop carrier, sending up clouds of dust. A man in an army sergeant's uniform stepped out. He engaged the squad leader in conversation, then both men came over to Vasilyev.

"We have to return to Kabul," the squad leader said.

"When?"

"Now"

"I can't go now," Vasilyev said with a glance at the open shaft. "We have survey work to do."

The sergeant spoke, his voice tinged with weariness. "The survey is over. The Soviet army is leaving the country. All civilians are being evacuated."

As survey leader, the well-being of his fellow scientists was Vasilyev's responsibility. He ordered his men to cover over the shaft opening, then told the Russian and Afghan geologists to return to the base camp and gather up their belongings. He paid off the laborers and said they could keep any equipment the survey left behind.

With all the scientists aboard, the helicopter rose into the air and hovered over the abandoned jeep and troop carrier. The Afghan laborers waved at the departing chopper as it gained altitude and flew over a steeply rounded hill that rose from the generally flat terrain bordering the lake.

Kabul had been at the eye of the storm as fighting between the Soviets and Afghans raged around it. But now rockets were hitting the city on a daily basis. An army truck was waiting on the tarmac when the helicopter landed. A representative from the Soviet embassy stood next to the truck with a handful of diplomatic personnel.

He greeted Vasilyev and the other Russian geologists and handed them each a packet of papers, saying, "These are your tickets home. This is my last official job."

"I have to go back into the city to get my files," Vasilyev said.

"Impossible." The man pointed to a giant *Ilyushin* jetliner. "This will be your last chance to leave Kabul on a normal flight. Thirty thousand insurgents are massed around the city. Our troops are leaving the country. Kabul will soon fall. You don't want to be here when the *mujahideen* take over."

Vasilyev thought about the metal cabinets lining the walls of his office at the ministry. The files stuffed into the drawers bulged with maps, charts and detailed reports gathered over ten years of field expeditions to every part of the country. He turned to Raheem.

"You and the other ministry geologists must gather together the files in my cabinets and hide them. You can't let the insurgents get their hands on this material. Do you understand?"

"I'll tend to it as soon as you're safely off."

Vasilyev gave his colleague a rib-cracking Russian hug. He had sent his wife and children home weeks before his last field trip and had vacated his apartment as soon as the Soviet Union signed an accord agreeing to leave the country. The embassy staffers had climbed into the truck and were yelling at him to hurry up.

He said his sad good-byes to the Afghan geologists he'd worked with since his arrival in 1968 and climbed into the back of the truck which joined a line of vehicles pulling up to the plane to discharge refugees. The refugees loaded their own luggage in the baggage compartment and hustled up the gangway.

Chaos reigned inside the cabin. Panicked passengers claimed their unreserved seats against a backdrop of arguments and crying children. The passengers had been dressed for the cold weather and the overheated cabin reeked of perspiration and unwashed bodies.

Georgi found an empty row at the rear of the cabin, next to the bathroom, which smelled as if it hadn't been emptied in between flights. A heavy-set man squeezed in next to him. Georgi was on the portly side, but the man overflowed the arm rests and the geologist had to lean toward the bulkhead.

The man had been a bureaucrat in a government-run building company. He talked non-stop until he was cut off by the applause greeting the announcement that the plane was ready to take off. The jetliner taxied down the runway and rose at a steep angle that would gain it altitude out of gun range as quickly as possible.

Vasilyev stared morosely at the magnificent snow-capped mountains that ringed the city. He would miss Afghanistan. The country was a geologist's playground. Sitting astride massive tectonic plates, the country had some of the most complex geology in the world. He looked at the rugged terrain the same way some men might take in the curves of a beautiful woman.

"*Tovarich.*"

His seat companion waved a bottle of cheap vodka under Georgi's nose.

"No thank you," the geologist said.

The man jiggled the bottle. "You must drink to our comrades who have died."

Thousands of young Russians had been killed in the nine years since the Soviet Union invaded the country. Georgi took a swig of the vile concoction and handed the bottle back. When he looked out the window he saw only clouds.

He prayed that Raheem would heed his advice. Even after trekking from one end of the country to the other, there was much he didn't know about the ancient land. But there was one thing that he was absolutely certain of. If the material in his filing cabinets got into the wrong hands, there would be many more toasts to countless dead who were yet to be born.

CHAPTER ONE

Alexandria, Virginia, the Present

Cait Everson was running for her life.

As she raced down the center of a quiet street, the only sounds she could hear in the sleeping suburban neighborhood were the pad-pad of her bare feet on the tarmac, the quick intake and exhalation of her breath and the menacing scuffle of footsteps from behind.

She didn't know who her pursuers were, but her instincts told her that the men trying to catch her were no mere rapists or muggers. It went beyond their freakish appearance, the platinum hair and icy blue eyes. It was the sheer, predatory relentlessness she'd detected in their identical faces since the twin men had started stalking her weeks before.

The alarms clanged in her brain, urging her to greater speed, warning that if they caught Cait she would be as good as dead.

She gulped energizing mouthfuls of air into her lungs and put all her strength into her long-legged strides.

Only minutes before she had driven her five-year-old Honda Accord from Georgetown University across the Potomac River on the Francis Scott Key Bridge to Arlington, Virginia where she lived in a neat two-bedroom condo. Traffic had tapered off as she left the city, and as she stopped at a red light in a quiet residential neighborhood near her condo, hers was the only car around.

Headlights suddenly flared in her rear-view mirror.

Whump!

A big vehicle had slammed into the Accord's rear bumper. Her head snapped forward. The impact failed to activate the car's air bags, but it triggered a string of colorful oaths more suited to a sailor than a college history professor.

Cait got out of her car and strode back to inspect the damage. The bumper was a crumpled mess. She stepped out of the glare of headlights from the offending Cadillac SUV and shielded her eyes. In the reflected light, she saw the driver's blue eyes and white hair. And sitting in the passenger seat was a man with identical features.

She dashed back to her car and went to open the door. The SUV driver snapped the transmission into gear and hit the gas pedal. The door handle was ripped from her hand as the impact propelled the Honda forward several yards. The SUV's doors opened. The identical twins stepped out and walked toward her.

There was only one thing she could do.

Run.

She kicked off her low-heeled leather work shoes and sprinted along the street. Two pairs of rapid footsteps pounded the pavement behind her. Cait was in good shape—she ran five miles every day—and she slowly outdistanced her pursuers. The footsteps faded. A moment later she heard car doors slam shut and the squeal of tires from the accelerating vehicle as it took off after her.

The SUV would catch up within seconds. She ran down a dark street. The SUV followed. She could feel the headlights burning into her back. Cait changed course like a jack-rabbit being chased by a coyote and ran across the manicured front lawn of a ranch style house. The SUV drove onto the lawn. She ran around behind the house to the back yard and skirted a swimming pool. The Cadillac followed and almost drove into the pool before the driver hit the brakes and threw the SUV into reverse.

She crossed into another yard and then onto a parallel street. The SUV's engine growled in the distance, and she heard the screech of its protesting tires as it navigated a tight corner. Cait ran up to a house, punched the doorbell, and plastered herself against the wall.

The SUV sped past, braked, backed up, stopped, and accelerated. The commotion had attracted attention. Lights were starting to come on in the row houses along the street and figures could be seen in the windows. The vehicle kept moving until the sound of its engine faded.

Cait fumbled her cell phone out of her jacket and called the number the campus police officer had given her earlier that day. A sleepy female voice answered at the other end of the line.

"Douglas. Who's calling?"

"It's Dr. Everson. I talked to you this morning."

"I remember, Dr. Everson." The voice was more alert. "What's going on?"

Cait breathlessly relayed what had just happened.

"Two men are after me. The ones I told you about."

"Can you help me?"

"That's out of our jurisdiction," the officer said. "I'll call the Metro police and they'll get in touch with the Arlington cops. Where should they meet you?"

Cait told the officer she would wait in an all-night coffee shop nearby.

An Arlington police cruiser pulled up in front of the coffee shop ten minutes later and drove her back to her car. She was relieved to see her lap-top case still on the front seat. She told the police what had happened. They drove her to her condo and at the request of the university police, a cruiser was stationed in front.

She locked her door and mixed herself a stiff Cosmopolitan. Her hands shook, but a few sips of the drink calmed her down. Those men were the same ones who had been following her for days. *Why?* And who were they?

The matter had been preying on her mind. Earlier that day, a student had to repeat her name a second time to get her attention.

Cait had snapped out of the trance she'd slipped into as she'd been teaching her favorite class, an introductory course on overland and maritime silk routes. Cait hid her embarrassment with a smile. An associate professor with a doctorate degree in Central Asian history was not supposed to daydream on the job.

"*Sorry.* I must have zoned out. Could you repeat your question?"

The female student lowered her upraised hand. "I asked about the Tarim mummies."

"Yes. Fascinating stuff. The mummies were non-Mongoloid, apparently Caucasoid, found more than a hundred miles east of *Yingpan*, China. They've been dated back to 1600 B.C. Long before Alexander the Great really opened up the Silk Road. No one knows where they came from."

The student had a follow-up. "Do you think the presence of a Caucasoid in China in any way vindicates the theory that east-west contacts go back much earlier than historians are willing to admit?"

"It's an intriguing theory, but not conclusive without additional evidence. I will say that the mummies are indicative of the fact that globalization is hardly a new concept. Any more questions?"

More hands shot into the air. The class was made up of enthusiastic students in fields that included diplomacy, economics, journalism, politics and the arts. Cait had earned a reputation for bringing a contemporary global perspective to ancient events. The discussion continued until the class ended. She shooed the students from the room, gathered her papers and left the history department building, heading south through the sprawling campus until she came to Village C, the six-story brick building that housed the Georgetown University Department of Public Safety.

She took a deep breath and strode toward the entrance with purpose in her step, thinking that the worst that could happen would be that the police would think she was crazy.

Her instincts proved correct a few minutes later as she sat at a table in Room 116 across from a uniformed campus police officer who said her name was Douglas. The officer had asked what the problem was. Cait had flippantly replied that she felt as if she were in an Alfred Hitchcock movie.

Officer Douglas didn't laugh. She raised an eyebrow and read from a questionnaire.

"Have you seen a suspicious individual in your neighborhood entering an apartment, room or home?"

"Describe suspicious individual," Cait said.

"Individuals who like to seem to be lurking," the officer said, after some thought.

"Oh," Cait said. "Well then. No lurkers."

"Have you ever seen a suspicious individual entering an office without apparent purpose, or loitering in a parking lot or trying to force open a car door?"

"No, no, and no."

"Or possessing two bikes or bike parts?"

Cait emitted a strange sound that combined a laugh and a cry of disbelief.

"This is *not* about bicycles," she said with an edge to her voice.

The officer folded her hands in front of her. "What *is* it about, Professor Everson?"

"As I just explained, I think someone has been following me."

"Someone you can't identify."

"Correct. As I said, I'll be in a public place and I'll look up and see a man staring at me. When I stare back he averts his eyes. Or goes back to reading his newspaper. I know this sounds insane, but one minute he is there. The next he's not."

"He disappears into thin air?"

Cait frowned. "Please don't go there, Officer Douglas. Of *course* he doesn't vanish. He simply gets up and leaves when my attention is diverted."

"Would you go over that description again?"

The officer was looking for discrepancies in her story. It was a classic case of Town and Gown, the tension that often existed between local worker bees and the academics in their ivory towers. She described the man again.

"He has platinum white hair, cut short, but I think it's premature, because his face is younger. Almost boyish. High cheekbones and intense blue eyes. Mouth always seems to be in a half smile."

"Those are pretty good observations."

"I'm a scientist, trained to observe." She paused. "There's something else. Sometimes there are two of them. Twins, apparently."

"Twins?"

"Identical. I'm not seeing double. I have perfect eye-sight."

"That's a new one." Officer Douglas pursed her lips in thought. "From your description, he-I mean, *they*, sound handsome."

"I suppose so, in a sick stalker sort of way."

The officer leaned forward onto the table.

"I could not say this if I were a male officer. But men might stare at you simply because you are an attractive young woman."

At thirty-six, Cait was old enough to know that men found her physically attractive. She was aware, too, that a good-looking woman who had advanced to her level in academia would always be subject to envious whisperings. During her work hours, however, she tried her best to keep a low profile—she had her long hair up, wore functional glasses, hid her figure with practical but unflattering clothing, and used a minimal amount of make-up.

Some attributes were impossible to minimize. She was tall and willowy, with slightly more bust than she preferred. Her eyes were the color of a gentian flower and framed with long lashes. She had white, even teeth and a flashing smile. Had she been true to her California girl roots, her raven hair would have been dyed the color of honey, and her creamy white skin burnished with a surf bum tan. Still, even without those trappings, Cait could walk into a roomful of beautiful blondes and draw every eye in the house.

Cait dismissed the officer's suggestion. "Are you advising me to make myself *less* attractive?"

The officer frowned.

"Let's try another avenue. You said this attention started a month ago. Was there anything going on in your life, any change in a relationship or something that happened at work about then?"

"No," Cait said with a shake of her head. "Nothing like that."

Cait hoped the officer didn't hear the tic in her answer. She was well aware, though, that the surveillance began after she had sent the letter to the State Department. The officer droned on with more inane questions. Finally she sat back in her chair and pinched her chin.

"This is a tough one, Dr. Everson. I have a daughter, so I'm sympathetic. But there isn't a lot I can do at this point. No crime has been committed. There's no evidence that one *will* be committed. All you have is a *feeling* these guys are looking at you. I need more than that to go on."

Cait kept her anger in check and said she understood the dilemma. She agreed to keep a journal detailing time, place and nature of the stalking incidents. The officer gave Cait her cell phone number to call if she had further questions. After she left, Cait cursed her naiveté for assuming the police would help her. She walked across campus and was glad to get back to the sanctuary of her office. As she sat at her desk going over the fruitless meeting in her mind, a knock at the door almost sent her tumbling out her chair.

The door opened a second later and a face peered in.

"Are you busy?"

"Never too busy to chat with you, Professor Saleem. Have a seat."

The man who stepped into her office and took a chair was in his mid-fifties. He wore a misshapen autumn brown corduroy jacket, relaxed fit jeans, a blue button-down shirt, and mismatched yellow tie. Dark eyes peered out from behind owlish round plastic eyeglasses that enhanced his academic look.

The history department sought out non-American faculty to provide depth and global perspective, and in keeping with such policy, Professor Saleem was on loan from a Pakistani university. He and Cait exchanged some campus gossip, but at one point he removed his glasses and leaned forward in his chair.

"I'm curious, Dr. Everson. Has the State Department replied to your letter?"

"Not a word," Cait said with a shrug of her shoulders. "I guess they're too busy to pay attention to a lowly history professor."

He pondered her answer. "Do you think it would have helped if you were more specific with the location of your discovery?"

"I'm not sure it would have made a difference."

"Perhaps not, but it would give you credibility. Unless you think you're *wrong*."

"Not at all. I'm so close I can taste it. I just need a little more time."

"I've got good cartographical background. I may be of help."

"Thanks, Professor. But I want to be sure. In the meantime I'd prefer to keep my theories to myself so as not to attract enemy fire."

"I understand. Good luck then." The professor rose from his chair. "Let me know if there's anything I can do."

"You can help in one way." She tapped the folder on her desk. "I'll be working late tonight on some written exams. Would you let the security guard know I'm here?"

The professor said he would be glad to. After he left, Cait began to read. She was near the bottom of the pile when she heard a knock on the door.

A voice said, "Security. You okay in there, Professor?"

Cait glanced at the wall clock. It was past eleven-thirty. "I'm about done. Would you walk me to my car in about five minutes?"

"I'll check the rest of the floor and come back for you."

Cait was about to shut down the computer, but she had another thought. She called up a file that contained a number of satellite photos. She went over the photos, zooming in on an image that showed a lake shaped like a figure eight. Using a crayon from her tool bar, she drew a circle at the edge of the lake.

She sent the file as an email to the State Department and a copy to

Professor Saleem with a quick note:

"Taking you up on your offer to help. Let's talk about this."

Minutes later, the guard escorted her to the parking lot where she had left her Honda. And less than a half an hour later she was pounding breathlessly along an Arlington street in fear for her life.

Now, as she sat in the safety of her apartment, she still felt terribly vulnerable. Gradually, though, she grew angry at the unwanted violation of her life by a couple of freaks. Her fear changed to determination. She tossed down the rest of her Cosmo and placed a phone call.

A male voice answered. "Yes?"

"I need your help," she said. "Someone is after me and I want a place to hide."

"It is always a pleasure to see you, but it's a long way and it could be dangerous," the voice said, speaking English with a slight accent.

"It's safer there than here," she said.

"When?"

"*Now.*"

"I'll make arrangements."

Fifteen minutes later the phone rang and the voice said, "Fly to Zurich and my friends will take care of you." He gave her a name and number, which she jotted down.

She thanked him and hung up. Then she sent an email to the university saying she was taking a leave of absence to deal with a family matter. She got on her computer and found a first class seat on a Swiss Air flight leaving the next morning. She almost gagged at the cost, but it was the only space available. Next, she packed her biggest suitcase, mostly with field clothing and gear. Then she slept for a couple of hours. When her alarm clock sounded, she got up, showered, and dressed in comfortable traveling clothes.

An officer knocked on her door around eight to check on her.

She told him that she had decided to stay with friends and asked the police to stay a while longer while she called a taxi. As she walked out to the taxi with her bag she couldn't help reflecting on the craziness of her situation. Her peaceful life had been turned topsy-turvy and she was seeking safety in one of the most dangerous places in the world.

Afghanistan.

CHAPTER TWO

Off Cuttyhunk Island, Massachusetts

Fifty feet below the surface, the alien intruder skimmed over the sea bottom, emitting a sinister hum and scattering silvery explosions of codfish as it burbled through the water. The box-shaped object was the color of a Yellow Cab and about the size of an old steamer trunk that had been flattened in transit, and its edges had been slightly rounded. Four stubby supports, like the legs on an overweight dachshund, extended to sled runners from the plastic housing.

Printed in black on the plastic battery housing were the words: **Woods Hole Oceanographic Institution.**

The vehicle stopped in front of a sliding gate that barred the way into a maze made from a framework of pipes covered in chicken wire and joined together like an old Tinker Toy. The vehicle's camera fed the image of the gate to its computers, which sent an order to the mechanical arm at the front of the vehicle. The arm slowly unfolded, and an aluminum claw gripped the edge of the gate and pulled the barrier aside.

The vehicle swam through the opening and navigated the maze like a mouse in a lab test. Encountering a dead end, it backed out and tried another route. With each mistake, new information was added to the submersible's data base until the vehicle popped out of the maze and headed toward a plastic storage box.

Hovering above the ocean bottom around twenty feet from the maze, Matt Hawkins watched the submersible's antics through a video camera view-finder. He filmed the submersible as the mechanical claw removed the lid and pulled a plastic bag from the box. The vehicle pivoted slowly, stopped for a few seconds, then moved toward Hawkins and placed the bag on the sea floor. Hawkins patted the plastic housing and picked up the bag. The submersible then rose to the surface, plowed through the water a short distance, and slid into a horse-shoe shaped docking station floating on pontoons next to a white-hulled fishing boat.

Hawkins breast-stroked to the boat's stern ladder. He handed up the bag, unclipped his weight belt and passed it and the camera to a man wearing a tan duck-billed baseball cap. He shed his SCUBA gear, climbed the ladder onto the deck, and peeled his neoprene hood off to reveal a thick mane of salt-and pepper hair and a gray-streaked beard. He stripped down to his bathing trunks and let the summer sun bake away the drops of moisture beading a muscular body that looked as if it had been carved from oak wood.

Hawkins had inherited his warm complexion, rugged profile, and lava-black eye color from his mother's Micmac Indian forebears. His big-boned physique, with its broad shoulders and six-foot-two inch height, were gifts passed down from his English-Irish ancestors.

After stowing his dive gear in a locker, he turned to the man in the tan cap, Howard Snow—Snowy to friends—and raised his hand in a high-five. Snowy's crinkled face had been weathered by years of exposure to sun and wind as a commercial fisherman. He removed the cold stub of the cigar clenched in his teeth.

"Congratulations, Matt," he said, returning the high-five. "Watched the whole thing over the TV hookup. Fido behaved like a champ. Hell, he would have wagged his tail if he had one."

"I'll hook up a mechanical tail in time for the demo," Hawkins said. His dark eyes twinkled with good humor. "The navy brass will get a kick out of seeing a mine detection vehicle acting like a puppy-dog. Maybe I can make him pee on an admiral's leg."

Snowy chortled. He knew Hawkins was capable of doing exactly what he'd suggested.

Hawkins untied the bag and pulled out a foam cooler wrapped with plastic twine, which he cut with his dive knife. Inside the box was a bottle of double-malt whiskey.

Snowy shook his head. "Heard on the docks that Fido is worth close to half a million bucks."

The right tip of Hawkins' mouth tweaked up in a half smirk. "Let's just say that the navy owes me more than a bucket of clams for developing the little guy."

"Hope the navy doesn't mind spending that kind of dough for an underwater booze fetcher."

"Fido is a *retriever*. No one will complain after they see these tests, Snowy. The artificial intelligence that allowed Fido to navigate the maze is going to make the navy and the scientists very happy. Fido can do all sorts of things, from defusing a mine to retrieving a salinity detector. And he works cheap."

Hawkins' answer summed up the symbiotic ties between the navy and the world-renowned Woods Hole Oceanographic Institution. Using funds from the navy and the resources of the institution had allowed

Hawkins to design an Autonomous Underwater Vehicle that would serve both masters.

As one of Woods Hole's leading robotic engineers, Hawkins embodied the arrangement. His SeaBot Corporation was given wide latitude that allowed him to hire Howard Snow and buy the forty-two-foot trawler *Osprey* for sea tests. Snowy, a wiry third-generation fisherman, had an encyclopedic knowledge of the sea, and his handyman's skills were considerable. He had constructed the maze in his workshop. The *Osprey* had transported the sections to the test site over several days and they were lowered to the bottom. Hawkins dove and joined the sections together.

They winched Fido and the docking platform on board and anchored a radar buoy to warn net fishermen away from the site. Minutes later, they were cruising at twenty knots north toward Cape Cod. When they were close enough to Woods Hole to see the brick buildings that housed the institution's labs and offices, Hawkins ducked into the cuddy cabin and changed into faded jeans, a chambray work shirt and work boots. He had radioed ahead, and the Water Street drawbridge was being raised to let the boat into Eel Pond.

They tied up at the dock and used a boom to lift the submersible and docking station onto the back of a vintage fire engine red pick-up truck. Then they pulled away from the dock, hooked the anchor line onto a mooring buoy in the pond, and used a pram to get back to shore. Snowy asked Hawkins if he wanted to celebrate the tests with a beer at the venerable Captain Kidd bar that overlooked the pond.

"Maybe later," Hawkins said. "I want to work on my report while the stuff is still rattling around in my skull."

"Don't be too long. People will think that you're unsociable."

Hawkins was aware that his colleagues admired his unrelenting approach to work, but that he was also considered a lone wolf and eccentric even by Woods Hole standards. Hawkins was wrapped in his shell as tightly as a barnacle and the hard edge behind his easy quiet-spoken manner made some people nervous.

"Hell, I already *know* what they think," Hawkins said with a shrug. "They think I'm *weird*."

Snowy rolled his eyes. "Weirdness isn't exactly in short supply in these parts."

Snowy had a point. The tiny village at the heart of one of the world's most prestigious centers of ocean exploration and research was loaded with brilliant oddballs.

They parted company at the dock and Hawkins got into the 1978 three-quarter ton Ford he had painstakingly restored. He turned onto Water Street, the main drag that ran along the harbor, passed the old stone Candle House that was built in the village's whaling days, and took a right near the Georgian-style building that housed the Marine Biological Laboratory.

A few blocks back from the harbor, Hawkins turned onto a crushed shell driveway and drove into the former carriage house of a two-story mansard-roofed Victorian summer place. As he got out of the truck and walked toward the house with a slight limp, a dog ran down the porch steps and slammed into his thigh so hard that Hawkins almost lost his footing. He reached down and scratched the ears of the squirming golden retriever. The dog was a female he had adopted from the Animal Rescue League. He had called her *Quisset*, meaning Star of the Sea in the language of Cape Cod's Wampanoag Indians.

With Quisset glued to his leg, Hawkins went up the porch steps and opened the unlocked door. He went into the kitchen, put the whiskey in a cabinet, and gave Quisset some dog treats, which she noisily demolished.

Hawkins climbed to the study that took up the entire second floor.

Afternoon light streamed in through the picture window and reflected off the rows of polished bronze and brass diving helmets lined up in display cases according to year of manufacture. The helmets ranged from an antique Sander built in 1917 to a group of Discos dating back to the 1940s.

Hawkins had collected other examples of antique dive paraphernalia as well: a weight belt patented in 1898, dive lamps, single lens masks, air pumps, Frankenstein-type boots and double hose regulators like those used by Jacques-Yves Cousteau. The wall opposite the helmets had floor-to-ceiling shelves crammed with books and scale models of the shipwrecks that Hawkins' non-profit sea exploration company had discovered.

Hawkins was fascinated by the unwieldy gear both as functional art and for what it said about the earliest divers. Ever since man had crawled out of the sea humans had seemed compelled to return to their salty origins. There was no other reason a person would leave his warm, earth-bound haunts, don hundreds of pounds of encumbering equipment and descend into a hostile environment at the end of an air hose.

Hawkins flicked on a sound system. A tune by the legendary blues guitarist Mississippi John Hurt—just one entry in Hawkins' extensive collection of blues—issued from four reproduction dive helmets that housed quadraphonic speakers.

He was carrying a laptop computer that had been monitoring Fido's video cameras. He pushed aside a dive knife made by *Siebl* that he used as a letter-opener, placed the computer on a sturdy desk built of polished driftwood and settled into a chair made from the welded links of a tugboat hawser.

The dog had followed him to the study and now rested her chin on his knee.

Hawkins scratched the dog's head and thought about Snowy's

comment. He was right about Hawkins being unsociable. His real problem was his inability to trust in his fellow humans. He preferred dealing with robots. If they failed him, he could replace a part.

Maybe he *should* have gone to the bar. The thought made him thirsty. He said, "*Beer.*"

A loud hum came from a small atmospheric dive suit in a corner of the room. The suit was a scale model used to test a full-size ADS, basically an underwater vehicle with mechanical arms and legs. Hawkins had acquired the suit at auction and installed a refrigeration unit, an electric motor to give the scale model mobility and a basic audio program to pick up his commands. He had named it Mitch after the puffy-limbed Michelin man it resembled.

Mitch moved toward Hawkins on the powered roller skates attached to the bottom of its boots and stopped near his desk. Hawkins flipped back the transparent helmet and a light went on, revealing a six-pack of beer. He reached in for a bottle and said, "Thanks."

He lowered the helmet and the refrigerator rolled back to the wall. *The wonders one can accomplish with an MIT education*, he mused. He stared at the three-foot-high figure.

"Maybe I *am* as weird as people say."

He took a couple of slugs of beer, then booted up the computer and watched the video taken by the submersible's camera.

Hawkins had wanted to develop a robot that would be aware of its surroundings and change its environment when it had to. Fido had not only detected the barriers blocking its way through the maze but had also figured out how to remove them. By observing, analyzing and reacting, the little robot had come one step closer to putting real artificial intelligence on the bottom of the ocean.

Hawkins was deep into the intricacies of a communications link paradigm when his phone chirped a computerized rendition of B Flat blues. The caller ID said the call was from out of the area. He pushed the speaker button and said hello.

"This is Jack Kelly. Don't hang up on me, Matt."

Matt recognized the knife-sharp voice even though he hadn't heard it in years.

He smiled. "Why would I hang up on my favorite former commanding officer?"

"Nice try, Matt. I saw the letter you sent to the navy. It should have been written on asbestos."

Hawkins recalled that the letter had used the word "incompetent" more than might have been necessary to prove his point.

"Okay, the letter was a little over the top. But I've mellowed, Jack. I don't hate the navy brass 24/7. Only on damp days. If I count the twinges in my left leg I can forecast a storm right down to Beaufort scale."

"Glad I caught you on a good day, lieutenant. Got a big favor to ask. Urgent matter. Can you come to the War College today?"

The naval war college in Newport, Rhode Island was about an hour's drive from Woods Hole.

"What's going on, Jack? Does the navy want to make me an admiral?"

"Haven't a clue. I'm only the messenger."

Hawkins glanced at his computer. "I'm in the middle of a big project, Jack."

"Be forewarned that they intend to keep bugging you. If you say no to me, they'll go up the line of command to the Secretary of Defense."

"Who's *they*?"

"You know better than to ask me that. Consider this a personal favor to me."

"Like to accommodate you, commander, but my dealings with the navy are strictly arm's-length these days. The only guys I'll talk to are the tech people and the bean counters. Unless this has to do with my robotics work, it's nothing that will interest me. Sorry."

"Okay. Call this number if you want to reconsider."

Hawkins grunted a reply, hung up and stared into space. He'd always gotten along with Kelly. Not necessarily one of the good guys, but he wasn't bad either. But it had been five years since Hawkins had pulled a paycheck as a navy SEAL. It made no sense.

He wasn't joking when he told Kelly that the pain in his leg predicted the approach of nasty weather. The dampness in the air that presaged rain affected the metal bolts that held his bones together. He got up and went to the window.

The sky had gone from blue to tangerine.

Red sky at night, sailor's delight.

In mariner's lore, a reddish-orange sky in the evening was the sign of good weather. There was only one problem. Hawkins' leg was twanging like a bluesman plucking a guitar string, and in his experience, the sensation meant only one thing.

A storm was on its way.

CHAPTER THREE

Hawkins got the bad news over coffee early the next morning.

It came in the form of an email on his smart phone saying that his navy contract to develop Fido had been canceled because of lack of funding. After a flurry of back-and-forth emails that shed no further light on the decision, he made a series of dead-end phone calls. Everyone in the navy department was apparently out in the field.

He finally got through to an engineer he'd worked with on an earlier project and asked what happened. The engineer said he didn't know what he was talking about.

"What I'm talking about is cutting me loose after I've put a pile of my own money into this project in expectations that it would be repaid."

The engineer said he would ask around. He called back a half hour later and confirmed the cancellation and said no one could come up with an explanation. Hawkins was stewing over the announcement when Snowy called and said the *Osprey* had sunk at its mooring. Minutes later, he was standing on the dock with Snowy and a dozen or so spectators who were looking at the pilot house sticking out of the pond like the conning tower of a surfacing submarine. A salvage barge and divers came in and plugged a hole in the hull. It was early evening when they pumped out the water and re-floated the boat. It was caked with mud.

The salvagers said the boat must have hit a rock. Snowy said they were crazy. The salvagers showed them the eight inch ragged hull gap they had temporarily patched. The insurance underwriter showed up and said he might have to write the boat off as a total loss.

Hawkins thanked him, then called the number Kelly had given him the night before. When his old commander answered, Hawkins said, "When did you join the mafia, commander?"

Kelly said he didn't know what Hawkins was talking about.

When he learned about the loss of the navy contract and the *Osprey*, he said, "Wow. Double whammy. Don't blame you for being pissed. Might be just a coincidence. Run of bad luck."

"Bad luck didn't punch a hole in my boat. Where are you?"

"At the war college."

"Stay put, I'm on my way to Newport."

Hawkins steamed with anger during the drive to Rhode Island, but he couldn't contain a smile when he saw Kelly waiting at War College Gate 1. The granite-hard face was nestled in a cushion of heavy jowls, but the commander had maintained his fireplug physique and ramrod posture and he looked good in his tailored suit. Navy blue, of course.

Kelly climbed into the truck, shook Hawkins' hand, and directed him through another security checkpoint to the two-story white stone structure that had housed Newport's Asylum for the Poor until the navy took it over in 1884 for the war college. The building had been converted into a museum after the navy university and think tank expanded to a sprawl of multi-story buildings on Coasters Harbor Island, a couple of miles from the cliff mansions built by the Vanderbilts and Astors. Lights glowed in the first floor windows. Kelly led the way through the front entrance and along a hallway. He stopped in front of a closed door.

"I'm leaving you here. The folks inside are waiting for you."

"Anyone I know?"

Kelly shook his head. "Like I said, I'm only the messenger. Got a call from an old higher-up who asked me to drag you here. My job is done. Good to see you. Looking great."

Hawkins smiled at Kelly's familiar machine gun delivery.

"Looks like life's treating you well, too," Hawkins said as they shook hands.

"Couldn't be better. Terrific wife. Six beautiful grand kids. None interested in the navy. But I'm working on it." He handed Hawkins a business card.

"Consultant on naval security?" Hawkins read off the card.

"Work with the Pentagon on foreign arms deals. Sort of a respectable arms dealer." He jerked his thumb toward the closed door. "Good luck."

"Thanks, commander. Great to see you."

Kelly started down the hallway, only to stop as if he had forgotten his car keys.

"Remember what I said back in the old days about friendly fire?"

"Sure," Hawkins said. "There is never anything friendly about a bullet coming your way, no matter who fires it. What *aren't* you telling me, Jack?"

Kelly smiled but there was no mirth in his slate-gray eyes. "I hear things."

"What sort of things?"

"Never seen it like this, Matt. Real snake pit. Just watch your ass. Make sure your perimeter is secure."

His continued down the hallway, his hollow footsteps echoing on the wooden floor. With Kelly's warning lingering in his ears, Hawkins knocked softly, half expecting a python or a cobra to answer. He was almost disappointed when a woman opened the door and greeted him with a pleasant smile.

"Thank you for coming, Mr. Hawkins. My name is Anne Hilliard. We've been waiting for you. " Her voice was polite and as neutral as a telephone service recording.

Hilliard was a well-constructed woman in her fifties. She wore a canary-yellow two-piece suit with a high military-style collar. She had short hair the color of corn-silk and her face was wide and bland. She stepped aside to allow Hawkins into a room decorated with wall paintings of naval battles. Seated at a long, rectangular table of dark wood were three men and one woman.

Hilliard directed him to a vacant seat at one end of the table and took a chair at the other end.

"I'll start by introducing myself," Hilliard said. "I'm an assistant to the special counsel on security to the President. My boss advises the White House on the appropriate response to threats to our country. The people in this room constitute a task force that represents various entities charged with counter-strategy."

She turned to an apple-faced man sitting to her right. "Dr. Fletcher?"

The man gave a slight nod. "My name is Charles Fletcher, Lieutenant Hawkins. I am a retired naval officer and I am fortunate to teach naval history at this historic institution. Since age is equated with wisdom, I have been asked to moderate this discussion."

With his shiny cheeks, twinkling eyes, white goatee, tufts of cottony hair sticking out behind his ears and his prep school pseudo-British accent, Fletcher seemed to Hawkins like a character from a Dickens story. He wore a rumpled Oxford cloth shirt and striped necktie under a buff-colored vest that had a button missing,

Seated next to Fletcher was a man in his middle thirties dressed in a European cut charcoal pinstripe suit. His face was smooth and boyish and his perfectly shaped short blond hair looked as if it were painted on his head. His name was Ian Scanlon and he was with the Mid-East desk of the State Department.

A florid, heavy-set man wearing a naval officer's uniform with a captain's insignia introduced himself as Mike McCormick and said he was with naval intelligence. The last person to speak was a young woman named Natalie Glassman from the Homeland Security Department.

Hilliard picked up a dossier. "We all have been given copies of your personnel file and know about your distinguished combat career with the SEALs."

"Then you all know that my distinguished navy career ended five years ago."

"Yes," she said. "That's in the file."

Hawkins glanced at the faces around him. "In that event, could someone tell me why I'm here?"

"Fair question," Fletcher said. "If Ms. Hilliard doesn't mind, I will answer it with a question of my own. What do you know about Prester John?"

Hawkins stared at Fletcher and tweaked his mouth up in his trademark smirk. "Is that a serious question?"

"I assure you it is of the *utmost* seriousness."

Hawkins dug into his memory. "As I recall, Prester John was a mythical king who ruled over some sort of lost Shangri-La kingdom."

"Let me offer a few corrections. Prester John was *not* a myth. Nor was his kingdom. Both existed."

"Fascinating, Dr. Fletcher," Hawkins said, warily. "But I'm not sure where you're going with this."

"Bear with me, please."

Hawkins nodded to be polite.

Fletcher smiled and went on. "The legend of Prester John had its origin in 12th century Europe with rumors of a king, said to be descended from the Magi, who ruled a wealthy kingdom east of Babylon. Many expeditions tried to find him, but none were successful. Then in the 1100s, Pope Alexander III sent his physician Philip to deliver a message to the Prester asking for help fighting the infidels, who were pressing Christendom. Philip was known to have made it as far as Palestine, but was never seen again."

"Thanks for the history lesson, but I still don't know what this has to do with me."

Scanlon answered the question. "We've recently become aware of findings that suggest Philip made it to the lost kingdom. And that Prester John gave him a fabulous treasure to take back to the Pope in Rome, but it was never delivered."

Hawkins spread his hands apart. "*And?*"

The White House representative spoke.

"Your dossier said you have located a number of lost shipwrecks," Hilliard said.

"That's correct. I run a non-profit undersea exploration organization. Our goals are to expand knowledge and test new underwater equipment."

"The U.S. government would like to enlist that expertise to find the treasure of Prester John," Ms. Hilliard said.

"Since when has the U.S. government been in the treasure hunting business?"

Captain McCormick injected himself into the conversation. "Since the disposition of that treasure could have implications for national security, Hawkins."

Unlike Fletcher, the navy officer didn't use Hawkins' military title.

"Maybe you could tell me about those implications, *McCormick*."

McCormick's face glowed traffic light red. "That's *Captain* McCormick."

"And it's *Lieutenant* Hawkins, captain."

The two men exchanged hard stares. Fletcher's crisp voice broke the strained silence.

"Ms. Glassman, could you please explain the situation to the lieutenant?"

The Homeland Security representative said, "For some time now we have been picking up chatter about a plot against the United States."

"What sort of plot?" Hawkins said.

"We don't know yet. Only that it could involve even more victims than 9/11. We're still following up every lead possible, but we've determined with certainty that it is the work of a splinter terrorist group which has named the plot the Prophet's Necklace."

"Unusual name," Hawkins said. "Any idea what it means?"

"It's a parable based on an Islamic morality story," Glassman said. "In this story, a necklace given away by the Prophet's daughter Fatima was considered blessed because it clothed and fed a beggar, bestowed means instead of helplessness, freed a slave, and was ultimately returned to its owner."

Fletcher said, "We think that the perpetrators, a group which calls itself the Shadows, see this plot as their Prophet's Necklace, empowering them and freeing them from the bondage of America."

"Where does Prester John come in?" Hawkins said.

"The Shadows want to find the treasure before activating the plot. The treasure is said to include an emerald scepter that Prester John wielded as a symbol of his power. In sending it to the Pope he was saying that he was willing to join the fight to wipe Islam off the face of the earth. We think the Shadows believe that Prester John's mystical power will flow to them in their fight against the infidels."

"They wave the scepter around and *then* strike against their enemy. Not a bad display of showmanship," Hawkins said.

"These people think in terms of thousands of years, and they are always looking for historical precedent to justify their cause. In their mind we're nothing but re-born Crusaders. At the very least, having the treasure would recruit more fanatics to their failing cause."

"How did the Shadows find out about the treasure?" Hawkins said.

Scanlon, from the State Department, took over.

"We suspect they heard about research being done by a historian named Cait Everson, who teaches at Georgetown University. Dr. Everson has published books and articles in which she suggests that the Prester John legend is true."

"Did she mention the treasure in her writing?"

"Only peripherally. She was convinced that the treasure made it as far as Afghanistan. She thought State might be interested in her findings, given our country's deep involvement in the region. She sent us a report."

"Did the report say *where* in Afghanistan?" Hawkins said.

"Dr. Everson's original letter only suggested a general location," Hilliard said. "More recently she sent us an addendum pin-pointing the probable site."

Hilliard rose and dimmed the lights. Using a laptop computer, she projected onto a wall screen a satellite photo of Afghanistan with a map overlay and pointed to a section of the country in the southwest.

Hawkins said, "We kept our guys out of that neighborhood. No one was really in control last I knew."

"A drug warlord named Amir Khan controls the area, and so far he has managed to keep out both the government and insurgent factions."

"Could you put your pointer on the treasure site?' Hawkins said.

"Dr. Everson thinks the treasure is in this vicinity."

She ran the pointer in a circle around a lake shaped somewhat like a lop-sided infinity symbol. The red dot landed on the edge of the lake.

"Based on what evidence?"

"A few years ago Dr. Everson was in Afghanistan doing research on ancient trade roads. She followed a little-known route to the lake and learned that before it was flooded it was called the 'Valley of the Dead.' According to local lore, the valley earned its name as a place where bandits entrapped caravans."

Hawkins was intrigued. "Go on."

"Dr. Everson researched the history of the valley and learned of an expedition back in the 1920s financed by a mining billionaire named Kurtz. He had come into possession of a fragment of a letter, purportedly written by Prester John, which mentioned a gift of a great treasure to the Pope. There was a map on the back of the letter. This is it."

A roughly-drawn figure eight image appeared. Next to it was a drawing of what looked vaguely like an inverted U and below it, a small circle.

"What's the significance of these wavy lines?"

"The hump shown here is an odd-shaped rock outcropping that Dr. Everson saw on her visit." She pointed to the circle. "She thinks this represents a cave where the treasure could be."

"It's under water, in other words."

"That's right. Which is why Dr. Everson became even more excited when she learned that the Kurtz expedition had called for dive equipment and a diver."

"Dr. Everson is a good detective. I'd like to talk to her," Hawkins said.

"So would *we*. Dr. Everson vanished without a trace about a week ago."

"Looks like someone dropped the ball at State by not getting back to her right away," Hawkins observed.

"Wish I could say you're wrong," Scanlon said in a rueful tone. "The State Department doesn't ordinarily deal with treasure hunts, but an intelligence analyst called her report to our attention and we tried to reach her. The university said she left a message that she was taking a leave of absence. No explanation."

"No one has heard from her since?"

"We put out a trace. She flew to Zurich, but that's as far as we were able to track her."

"So you think her disappearance suggests that there is more to the story than legend."

Natalie Glassman nodded.

"Dr. Everson had complained to Georgetown's campus police about being stalked. The night before she disappeared there was an incident in Arlington, Virginia. She told the investigating officers that there had been an attempt to kidnap her."

"And you think there's some connection to the treasure and the Necklace plot?"

Heads nodded around the table.

Hawkins sat back in his chair and looked around the table, thinking he now knew how Alice must have felt at the March Hare's tea party.

"Let's see if I have this straight. You believe that if the crazies find the treasure they will pull the trigger on the necklace plot."

"That's essentially correct, lieutenant. We need to prevent that from happening."

"So you want me to go into a remote part of Afghanistan that is controlled by a warlord and surrounded by insurgents and dive into a lake to find a treasure that may or may not exist." Hearing no disagreement,

Hawkins said, "No offense folks, but that is bat shit crazy."

"Not at all," Fletcher said. "We've considered your background as a SEAL, particularly your cave combat experience in Afghanistan, and the work of your non-profit group locating wrecks. Your submersible research at Woods Hole is well-documented."

"It's been a long time since I rappelled down a line from a helicopter."

"Evidently, you've kept in shape," Fletcher said. "You've run a number of half-marathons, right?"

Damn. Is there anything that's not in that file? Hawkins thought.

"True, but I haven't won any."

"You came in near the top, though. A significant feat considering your injury, so physical incapacity is no excuse. We believe you're the perfect man for the job."

"The job you're talking about is a suicide mission."

"That's not a given," Hilliard said. "You would have all the resources of the government at your disposal. We would give you men and weapons."

"Let's talk about those resources," Hawkins said. "We have the greatest military and intelligence-gathering forces in the world, but the task of preventing a horrendous attack on the United States of America would fall on the unworthy shoulders of a forty-something ex-SEAL."

"I wouldn't exactly put it that way," Fletcher said.

"But I would. You all have my personnel file so you know I was kicked out of the navy with a psychiatric discharge. The navy said I was crazy. Good luck finding someone who's even crazier to carry out this mission."

He started to rise from his chair.

Captain McCormick snickered and looked around at the others.

"I *told* you this was the wrong guy for the job. Mr. Hawkins here doesn't like anyone telling him what to do."

"You've got me all wrong, captain. I don't like being told what to do by navy guys with a puffed-up view of themselves."

Fletcher made a palm-down gesture with his hands.

"Please hold on, gentlemen. Your comments are out of line, captain."

McCormick glared at Hawkins. "Just saying out loud what was in the record. If you'll excuse me. I need a smoke."

Hawkins watched the officer storm out of the room. He turned to Fletcher. "And I think I need some air."

Fletcher raised his hand to stay Hawkins and said to the others, "Would you allow us a few minutes? Lieutenant Hawkins and I need to have a serious talk."

Hawkins shrugged as the room cleared out. He figured that with the *Osprey* out of commission and his navy contract in question he had nothing else to do.

"Talk away, Dr. Fletcher."

CHAPTER FOUR

Instead of going out for a smoke, Captain McCormick strode briskly to a nearby office building. Moments later he entered a sparsely furnished room. A gaunt man sat in front of a computer.

"Nice acting job," the seated man said.

"Thanks." The captain pulled up a chair. "I can only stay a few minutes or the others will wonder what I'm doing. How's it going?"

The man pointed to the screen. "Pretty much as I figured. I'll rerun the part you just missed."

The screen showed Fletcher and Hawkins alone in the room.

"Sorry about the captain's rudeness, Lieutenant Hawkins."

"Thanks. But let's face it—I'm not the person you need for a job this complicated."

Fletcher tapped the dossier. "You're pretty complicated yourself. May I call you Matt? Or maybe you would prefer your full name. *Matinicus.* Named for where you were born?"

"That name was inflicted on me by my parents. I was *conceived* on Matinicus Island. My mother was a flower child before she became an ornithologist. My father was a Maine lobster fisherman."

"Then you can understand the importance of bait," Fletcher said with a smile.

He slid a sealed envelope stamped **Confidential** across the table. Printed on a white label were the words: "Report on Matinicus Hawkins, Afghanistan, 2007. Summary of Findings."

"Open it," Fletcher said. "It won't bite."

Hawkins slowly bent the metal clasp, folded the flap back, and slid out a sheaf of papers. The report was impossible to read. Line after line had been blacked out.

"Someone had some fun with a Sharpie," he said.

"I agree. It's totally useless. However, I can place in your hands a copy that has *not* been redacted. Of course, you would have to be under naval jurisdiction, if only temporarily."

Hawkins gazed at the envelope with half-lidded eyes then picked up the report. He knew more about fishing than Fletcher could ever know.

"I'd love to see the un-redacted version."

"I don't blame you. Your Afghanistan experience obviously has been gnawing away at you. You must want to know what happened."

"Yeah," Hawkins said, shifting in his chair. "Good thing this is as far as your offer goes. I feel myself weakening."

"Then let me see if I can weaken you a bit more. Name it and it is yours if at all possible."

"Okay. I want my psychiatric discharge reversed."

"That's—"

"Call it a down payment."

Fletcher frowned. "It might take a while. We're dealing with the navy bureaucracy."

"It would be in your interest as well as mine. You wouldn't want anyone to learn that a delicate mission was entrusted to a crazy man."

"You raise a valid point, Mr. Hawkins."

"I'm not through," Hawkins said. "Who owns the operation if it flops?"

"The government would need plausible deniability. The story would be that you're a rogue operation."

"In that case, let's add some truth to the spin. I want my own team and will make my own logistical arrangements."

"But as you said, this is a big, complicated job," Fletcher said.

"Which is why the simpler the better. I'll let you know if I need help."

"The situation is fluid and can tolerate no delay. We can give you a fully-equipped team ready to go as soon as you pack your toothbrush. How long will it take to pull together your own people?"

Hawkins cleared his throat. "Twenty-four hours. We can be ready to go in forty-eight."

Fletcher looked as if Hawkins had told him the moon was made of green cheese. "There's no margin for error. Everything would have to go off without a hitch."

"That's the way I want it."

"Very well. I will insist, though, on daily updates, except when absolutely impossible."

"I'll do my best, but I will insist that we remain an independent entity. Since this is a last-minute job, I will need access to back up. Someone I can call with no questions asked."

Fletcher nodded. "Very well, lieutenant. I'll put you in contact with a provider."

"I'll need financial support."

"You will have an open-ended bank account accessed by a secret number. Anything else?"

From the smile on Fletcher's face, the question was meant to be sardonic, but the smug expression vanished when Hawkins said, "Yes there is. My research contract with the navy was canceled. I want it reinstated. And someone sabotaged my boat. I want reimbursement."

"Those things are not connected with this mission."

"Maybe you can connect them."

Fletcher spread his palms apart. "I'll do my best, but I must remind you again that time is crucial."

Hawkins slid the envelope back across the polished surface of the table and rose from his chair. "In that case we'd better not waste another minute."

McCormick watched on the screen as Hawkins left, then he said, "Never expected him to demand the psychiatric discharge and the other stuff. Didn't you say he'd take the job for patriotic reasons with the report as sweetener?"

"His demands surprised me too."

"I thought you said Hawkins was predictable."

"Up to a point. He has a problem with self-control—he certainly responded to your demeaning taunts exactly the way I said he would."

"Yeah, he wanted to tear my throat out. How do you reconcile that with his obvious control in negotiating a deal?"

"Are you familiar with chaos theory?"

"Somewhat. It says it's impossible to predict accurately what a dynamic system will do. You know a hurricane is coming, but you're not always sure where it will hit. What's that got to do with anything?'

The gaunt man gestured at the screen. "Hawkins is chaos theory personified."

McCormick said, "That's not good. I read about his record in *Tora Bora*. He was with the SEAL unit that would have got Bin Laden the first time if command hadn't screwed up. He makes Rambo look like Little Lord Fauntleroy, only he's no muscle head. He thinks as well as he acts. Look at the way he just played Fletcher. I hope we've made the right choice."

"We *have*. Don't forget, I signed his psychiatric discharge papers. I know he's intelligent. But Hawkins is headstrong and impulsive as well as smart. Look at his insistence, against all logic, on forming his own team. He's like a guided missile. Point him in the right direction and he'll explode. The unknown quantity is the extent of the damage. Predictable unpredictability."

McCormick got up. "I have to get back to the meeting."

As he walked the short distance to the former poorhouse, the captain chewed over the gaunt man's assessment. He didn't like the way Hawkins had taken command of the situation. Didn't like it one bit.

But the chaos theory analogy bothered him even more. He shook his head and muttered under his breath.

"Predictable unpredictability, my ass."

CHAPTER FIVE

Quisset popped out of the doggy door on the front porch and greeted her master, then padded behind him as he climbed to his study carrying a computer disk Fletcher had given him and a glass of the whiskey Fido had liberated from the ocean bottom.

He settled behind his desk and slid the disk into the laptop. While the computer chirped through the booting up process he sipped his drink, wondering if he'd taken on the role of Johnny Carson in the old *Mission Impossible* parody, when the comedian gets stuck in the phone booth as the tape self-destructs. Funny, he thought, unless you're the one in the exploding phone booth. Hawkins was no wide-eyed child. The war college meeting stank worse than a week-old codfish. The participants could have come from a casting company. The script had been orchestrated perfectly, with the navy guy playing bad cop to Fletcher's good cop.

His instincts told him that the assignment was insane, but he needed to take it. Having his discharge reversed, his navy contract reinstated, and the *Osprey* reimbursed would be nice, but what he really wanted was to learn the truth about what happened five years ago to set him on the course to official derangement. And he was convinced he would find the answer back in Afghanistan.

The computer finished booting up, and Hawkins opened the folder on the disk. The first file it contained was a biography of Cait Everson. He gave her photograph more than a casual glance, memorizing the even features of the dark-haired woman.

Cait was a California girl. San Diego. She had majored in Middle-East and Central Asian history at UCLA, ultimately working her way up to her doctorate degree. She went on to teach at Georgetown as an associate professor. She had visited every country in the Mid-East region at least once and was fluent in or familiar with all of the region's major languages. She had written several books on her specialty, the Silk Routes. She was in her thirties and already divorced.

He looked again at the photo. Hawkins' love life had been sporadic since his divorce. Women liked his rugged good looks and his sense of humor, but they were put off when they learned that Hawkins viewed a long-term relationship as anything beyond three dates and a sleep-over.

Dr. Everson was smart as well as pretty. He hoped she hadn't come to harm.

Hawkins next clicked on the report Cait had sent the State Department. It was entitled:

A New Look at the Prester John Legend.

The report started with a detailed historic overview, fleshing out the Prester John summary Hawkins had heard in Newport. He quickly blew through this part and got right to Cait's summation, which said:

"Based on the evidence, I have come to the following conclusions. Prester John was a real historical figure who ruled a kingdom whose location is yet to be determined. He received Pope Alexander's letter and responded by sending the Pope a letter and a treasure, which disappeared in Afghanistan en route to Rome."

He scrolled down to a document marked Exhibit A and entitled **The Kurtz Expedition.**

The document contained copies of newspaper articles, dating back to the 1920s, that chronicled the expedition Kurtz had led to Afghanistan. An archeologist with the expedition described the project as "desert road archaeology." He explained that the ruins of ancient settlements often could be found along ancient caravan routes that seemingly led nowhere. The articles were arranged chronologically, spanning a number of months. The first headline read:

Mining Tycoon
Leads Archaeology
Team To Mid-East

Hiram Kurtz Looks
For Amazon Women
On His Expedition

Datelined *Ouray, Colorado,* the article said that Hiram Kurtz, 58, owned a copper mining empire, but the newspaper apparently held him in little esteem, evidenced by the headline's mocking tone. Still, it was essentially correct in describing the expedition's purpose. Kurtz was quoted as saying that he hoped to locate archaeological sites along the forgotten trade routes, but he was particularly interested in stories of legendary women warriors.

Other clips, based on dispatches from Kurtz himself, told of him sailing from New Orleans on his private yacht across the Atlantic. He sailed across the Mediterranean, and through the Suez Canal to India, where he met up with a ship carrying his expedition staff and gear, including a customized Cadillac modified for desert driving. Then came the train journey to Kabul.

The dispatches became less frequent as the expedition set off into the wild countryside, until they eventually ceased altogether. Sensing a lost explorer story, *The New York Times* got in touch with an enterprising Reuters correspondent who learned that the expedition was still intact. He came across a list of supplies that had come through Kabul for delivery to Kurtz in the field. On the list were two pieces of gear called *Schraders*. It appeared that Dr. Everson had circled this term on her report and written the words "diving gear" beside it.

Hawkins took a moment to gaze at the Schrader helmet in his collection, then he looked back at the documents. Several months later, Kurtz had been in the news again when his expedition quietly arrived back in Kabul. The Reuters reporter caught up with him and reported that the Cadillac had blown its engine and been left behind. He asked where Kurtz had been. The laconic reply became the headline as well as the story:

"I have been to the Valley of the Dead."

The article reported that a member of Kurtz's team had died in an excavation cave-in, suggesting the reason for the tycoon's mournful reply. But the expedition's misfortune didn't end there. It made tragic headlines again just a few weeks later. The archaeologist and other key expedition people died when the Kurtz company minerals carrier they were traveling on sank in the Mediterranean during a fierce *meltemi*. Kurtz was sailing separately on his yacht or he would have been lost as well. The reclusive Kurtz went back to Colorado. His health had been compromised by the rigors of travel and he died a short while later.

The next few documents detailed more of Dr. Everson's findings. In one, she described how she had been hunting for traces of lost trade routes in Afghanistan and had come across a lake that was still called the Valley of the Dead.

In another, she revealed how her research had led her to an out-of-print book about the Kurtz expedition, written in 1933, called "The Emerald Sceptre." The author had relied mostly on news reports, but he had learned from the widow of a project archaeologist about a sheet of ancient vellum the expedition found that may have been part of a longer document.

A message on the vellum, written in Latin, mentioned a great treasure that included an emerald scepter as a gift to the Pope. The letter was signed by Prester John and had what appeared to be a crude diagram on the back. Since no treasure had ever been found, the author speculated that it might have been carried on the freighter Kurtz lost. End of story. Or not.

Hawkins sat back in his chair.

The evidence was sketchy, but Cait believed it suggested that the legend of the treasure was true, and that it might still be in Afghanistan. Believed it enough, at least, to contact the State Department.

Hawkins glanced at his watch. It was one in the morning. If he was going to assemble a team, he needed to get started. He reached for his phone and punched in a name. After several rings, a female voice answered with a sleepy hello.

"Matt? Is that really you?" the voice said.

"Isn't caller ID a wonderful thing, Abby?"

"Only if you have the brains not to answer the damned phone. How's my "ex" these days?"

"*Fine.* I have to see you. How about tomorrow?"

Pause. "Hell, Matt it's *already* tomorrow. I'm in the middle of a bunch of big projects. Can it wait?"

"No. It's important."

"Where are you now?"

"In my house at Woods Hole."

Another pause. "The only time I have free is at eight tomorrow morning."

"Thanks. I'll be there," Hawkins said.

They said their good-byes and hung up.

Matt then made a quick phone call to make arrangements for the next day. After he hung up, his eye again fell on the photo of Cait Everson, and he wondered if she were dead or alive. And if she were alive, where she might be.

He ignored his instincts and took the positive view. "Good night, pretty lady," he said. "Can't wait to meet you."

Then he shut down his computer and went to bed.

CHAPTER SIX

Afghanistan

The 1921 butternut-colored Cadillac touring car with the over-sized tires churned up a dusty rooster tail as it raced across the desert at more than sixty-five miles per hour. Amir Khan had an expression of child-like joy on his face as he looked over the steering wheel down the length of the long louvered hood that covered the powerful 5.1 liter V-8 engine.

Sitting next to Amir in the seven-passenger vehicle was a ghost-like figure whose hair and face were shrouded under a light blue *keffiyah.* In the back seats were four men wearing traditional tribal garb: round *Pakol* caps, long shirts, vests and baggy pants. Cartridge belts encircled their waists and they clutched AK-47s with the barrels angled in the air.

The car swerved off the dirt track, bumped over the rough terrain, and came to a skidding stop near the edge of a large lake. The armed men jumped from the car and shouldered their guns. Each man grabbed a wooden pole from the trunk.

Amir got out next, followed by the shrouded figure who partially removed the *keffiyeh*, keeping the hair covered but exposing the face of Cait Everson. Cait unfolded a sheet of paper and glanced at a drawing that looked like a camel's hump. She compared it with the hill set back a mile or so from the lake. The mound was flatter than in the sketch, but it may have been higher in the past. She and Amir walked to the edge of a cliff that overhung the blue surface of the lake around thirty feet below. The guards stretched out in a line, roughly three feet apart, and walked slowly, striking the ground with the pole tips. Cait and Amir followed. After advancing several yards, one of the men stopped and pointed to his feet.

Amir stepped ahead and struck the ground near the guard with his cane. A hollow noise echoed up from the earth. The guards used knives to scrape away the top soil, uncovering a square metal plate around four feet across. They lifted the plate off to reveal a rectangle of darkness.

Cait produced a flashlight from under her smock and dropped to her knees. Ignoring Amir's warning to watch out for the crumbling edges, she leaned over the opening. The flashlight beam was absorbed by the darkness.

"The Kurtz mine shaft," Cait murmured. She stood up and dusted off her hands. "I'm going in."

"The mine is very old. You may be putting yourself in danger."

"The supporting timbers along the walls look okay," Cait said. "I'll be all right. You can pull me out if I get into trouble. Don't forget, I'm an experienced archaeological field worker."

Amir had mentioned the shaft to Cait over dinner the previous day. He had assumed it was the work of Russian geologists who surveyed the area years before, but Cait had become excited and insisted on seeing it. Amir had come to regard Cait almost like a daughter. And as with the pleading of his own daughters, he found it difficult to say no.

He gave an order and a man drove the car close to the shaft. Cait retrieved her duffle bag from the trunk and dug out a yellow hard hat equipped with a headlamp, and a pair of fingerless gloves, goggles and knee pads. She kept the head covering in place, but slipped out of the smock she had been wearing and shed her pajama-like pants. Underneath she wore a tan long-sleeve shirt and cargo slacks. She tucked a walkie-talkie into her shirt pocket and gave another one to Amir.

She dug into the duffle again and pulled out a nylon harness attached to a two-hundred-foot-long length of half inch manila rope. Cait's explorations of old ruins sometimes brought her into tunnels and shafts where she might need help getting out. While she buckled into the harness, Amir's men tied the other end of the rope onto the front bumper of the car. Cait put on the goggles, knee-pads and gloves and sat down at the edge of the shaft with her legs dangling. Four guards picked up the rope. She slipped over the edge and was lowered several feet until she ordered a halt to look around. As she dangled there, she reflected on the events that had brought her to this dark hole in the desert.

She had visited Afghanistan three years before to do research into the vast transcontinental network of paths that had extended more than four thousand miles between China and western Asia and Europe and northern Africa.

The routes were collectively called the Silk Road, but they had been used to transport other goods, including amber, slaves, incense and precious stones. The roads were also conduits of culture, technology, disease, such as the Black Death, and they had laid the foundation for the global economy,

Cait had been researching the southern silk route which still existed in part as the *Karakoram* Highway, a paved road connecting Pakistan and China. Using a technique known as desert road archeology, she had followed old traffic routes looking for commercial settlements around caravan stops that were often rich archaeological troves. One route in particular piqued her interest. On an old map she acquired, this route branched off from the main road for no apparent reason, eventually coming to a dead end near a lake. She suspected that the area around the lake may have been the site of commercial activity.

Returning to Kabul, she showed some Afghan colleagues her findings and said she wanted to see the site firsthand. They told her the territory was dangerous, controlled by warlords who made their living in the drug trade.

The lake was under the control of a warlord named Amir Khan. Cait expressed interest in learning more about Amir. A friend at the American embassy arranged a meeting with a cultural attaché, a title Cait knew was often a cover for CIA personnel. Frank Brady was a trim man in his fifties who had a thoughtful professorial manner that suggested he was probably an analyst rather than a field agent.

"Amir was on the American payroll during the war against the Soviets," he said. "Got wounded in action. He suffered some nerve damage and almost didn't walk again. He was brought to the United States and treated at Walter Reed hospital. Spent months in therapy. While he was recuperating, he studied at Georgetown University. From what I hear of the efficient way he runs things as a warlord, he must have majored in business administration."

Without hesitating, Cait said, "Can you get a message from me to the Amir?"

"What sort of message?" Brady said warily.

"Tell him that a Georgetown history professor is interested in doing research in his neighborhood and see what he says."

Brady chuckled. "You're serious, aren't you?"

"It never hurts to ask."

"I'll see if I can make a connection. Where are you staying?"

"At the Serena Hotel. I'll be waiting for your call."

That night Cait got a call from Brady. "You Georgetown alum must be pretty tight, Dr. Everson. The Amir would be pleased to have you as his guest."

Cait was stunned. The alumni ploy had been a gamble.

"I'd be pleased to accept his invitation," she said. "Any idea how I get there?"

"Be at the airport at seven tomorrow morning."

Cait thanked Brady, and as an afterthought, asked if he had any advice on how to deal with a warlord.

"Keep your blinders on and you'll be fine," Brady said.

Cait packed a bag with her field clothes and equipment. She spent a restless night and was awake when the sun came up over the mountains. It was only a twenty-minute taxi ride to *Khawaja Rawash* airport and she arrived well ahead of time.

What followed was like something out of a spy movie. She was met by a man who said he was the Amir's assistant in Kabul, led to a private two-engine plane, and ushered on without a word. After a two-hour flight, the plane angled down for its descent. On the approach, Cait glimpsed the figure-eight lake she had seen in the satellite photos. Minutes later, they bumped down onto a crude unpaved landing strip near a large metal hangar.

After the door was unlatched, Cait climbed down the gang way, blinking her eyes in the bright sunlight. An antique touring car was parked at the edge of the runway. Leaning against a front fender of the convertible was a tall man dressed in a traditional Afghan outfit. He waved and then walked over with the aid of a cane, and extended his hand.

"Welcome, Dr. Everson. I am Amir Khan."

His voice was deep and resonant, and he spoke in American English with a trace of an Afghan accent. He had a raffish handlebar mustache that looked bleach-white against his dark skin. He wore a flat mushroom-shaped cap over gray hair.

He opened the door on the passenger side for her, and then got behind the wheel. The car passed acres of agricultural fields and a number of large sheds. Cait heeded Brady's advice and kept her blinders on. Eventually, the car arrived at a walled cluster of buff-colored, flat-roofed buildings, passed through an unmanned gatehouse, and made its way along an unpaved street toward the largest building in the village.

The stone-and-mud house was surrounded by well-landscaped greenery. Amir pulled the car up in front of the high arched wooden door. A man appeared seemingly from nowhere and carried Cait's bag to the doorstep.

An attractive woman in her thirties opened the door. Her head was covered with an orchard silk scarf and she wore a traditional black smock. A little girl with huge brown eyes hung on her dress.

"This is my daughter Nagia and one of my granddaughters, little Yasmeen," Amir said.

Nagia bowed slightly and picked up the bag. "Please follow me," she said in English.

She led Cait along a wide marbled hallway to a room furnished with an art deco bed and a dresser that could have come from Paris. French doors looked out on a garden area. Nagia said that her father would be waiting in the garden. Cait bathed her face in cooling rose water and checked to make sure her hair wasn't a mess.

In the center of the garden was a small gazebo that shaded a carved wooden table and chairs. Cait sat in a chair and waited a minute or so before Amir appeared, trailing an elderly female servant who carried a tray with a pitcher and two glasses and a plate of pastry. The sheik had changed from his traditional outfit into tan slacks and a white shirt. The servant filled the glasses and went back into the house. They both took a sip of the amber liquid.

"Iced jasmine tea. Hope you like it."

Cait let the cooling liquid roll down her throat.

"It's delicious," she said. She glanced around the garden.

"You seem ill at ease, Dr. Everson. Is there anything wrong?"

"Not at all." She smiled. "It's just not what I imagined. Actually, I didn't know *what* to expect—"

"Of a warlord?" he said, completing her sentence. "The term is a misnomer. Most of us are not at war. Nor are we lords. In the U.S. you would call us agri-businessmen."

They both smiled. The inside joke broke the ice, and soon they were talking about their Georgetown link. That led to a discussion of Cait's work, which in turn brought up the purpose of her visit.

"I'm looking for evidence of settlements along an ancient road that branched off from the Silk Road only to end suddenly at the lake I saw flying in," she said.

"It was called The Valley of the Dead before it filled with water, supposedly released from heavy bombing during the second Anglo-Afghan war," Amir said. "Local lore has it that my ancestors would lure caravans into the valley to be trapped and looted of their riches. I don't mean to discourage you, but your trip here may have been for nothing. There's no trace of the old road."

Cait sensed that her host had satisfied his curiosity and was about to blow her off. She was pondering her next move when fate intervened.

Yasmeen had crept up behind her grandfather. She had a mischievous expression on her face as she reached around him, snatched a small cake and stuffed it into her mouth. The dry cake caught in her throat, and the look of sweet-tooth bliss in her eyes turned to one of tearful terror as her round face began to turn purple.

Amir saw what was happening. He grabbed the little girl, lifted her in the air, and gave her body a shake. Cait sprang to her feet.

"*No!*" she shouted.

She snatched Yasmeen from her grandfather's arms and applied the Heimlich method from behind, taking care not to break the girl's ribs. The greasy crumbs were expelled after a few tries. Yasmeen let out the cry that had been stuck in her throat. It was the sweetest sound Cait had ever heard.

The girl's mother came running from the house and scooped the bawling girl from Cait's arms. She and her father had a rapid conversation, then she turned to Cait, smiled, and said, "Thank you." She disappeared back into the house with the girl.

"Sorry to grab her away," Cait said. "I took a basic CPR course once."

Amir took her hand, bowed slightly and pressed it to his forehead.

"Please. No apology. I am in your debt. I would consider anything you wish to be my command."

Cait spent three nights as Amir's guest. He gave her a tour of the lake, showing her where the track once entered the valley, but there was no evidence of ruins. The bandits who had swarmed the area were nomads and left no clue behind. He said that an expedition had explored the area years before, supposedly led by a rich American named Kurtz, but it left suddenly, abandoning the touring car, which Amir had found being used as a chicken coop and restored.

He drove Cait to the air strip on the third day. Before she climbed into the plane, Amir told her that she would always be welcome. She never dreamed that three years later she would take him up on his offer.

Cait took a deep breath, exhaled, and jerked on the rope.

"Lower away," she shouted.

She began her plunge into the blackness. At one point in her descent she looked up. The opening was a rectangle of blue sky that seemed no bigger than a postage stamp and getting smaller. The dank air triggered coughing fits.

Amir's voice crackled over the walkie-talkie.

"Are you all right?" he said.

"Yes, fine."

She wasn't quite telling the truth. The support timbers were deteriorated and many were missing. She snapped off photos with her digital camera to divert her precarious state of mind. She was engrossed in her task when a shocking cold wetness enveloped her feet and ankles.

Water!

Then something grabbed at her legs. Her headlamp revealed what looked like the writhing coils of a thick black snake. She pointed the camera down and punched the shutter with a vague notion in her mind that the flash would scare it away.

She tried to dig out her radio, but in her haste it slipped from her hand. She jerked on the line. Instead of being pulled up, she continued her plunge until the water and coils were around her waist. She was almost frozen in panic. Her heart hammered in her chest. She wanted to scream, but the sound caught in her throat.

The water was nearly up to her chin when the descent stopped. The rope tenders had detected a change in tension and began to reel her up.

She popped out of the water, feeling one last horrifying brush of the coils along her legs. Her elbows and knees scraped the sides of the shaft, but she was no longer worried about a cave-in. She wanted *out!* She was shivering like a leaf when Amir's men pulled her into the sunlight.

Seeing Cait's muddied clothes and pale features, Amir said, "Are you all right?"

"I'm fi-fine, thanks," she said.

He escorted her back to the car and ordered his men to get a blanket from the car's trunk. She sat in the passenger seat, with the blanket wrapped around her body, and sipped strong tea.

Once her shivering was under control, she looked at the photo she had taken in the shaft then showed to image to Amir.

"It looks like a section of rubber hose," he said.

Cait nodded. "Kurtz dug that shaft to try to get down to the treasure cave, but the hose suggests that his diver died in a wall collapse," she said. "After that happened he wrapped up his expedition and headed home. Which is probably what I should do. I don't want to end up the same way. Sorry to waste your time, Amir."

He slid in behind the steering wheel, started the car and put it into gear. "You must not be discouraged. Remember that a river is made drop by drop."

The Kahn had sprung his enigmatic proverbs before, but she was in no mood for homespun Afghan philosophy. She had spent too many years and traveled too many miles. Her patience was exhausted.

As they drove off, she glanced at the lake with yearning eyes and made a reluctant admission to herself.

For all intents and purposes, her Prester John theory was as dead as the diver buried in the mine shaft.

CHAPTER SEVEN

Northern Virginia, the Next Day

The headquarters for Global Logistics Technologies occupied the top floor in one of the faceless buildings that cluster around Washington like suckling young around a mother sow. With its minimalist design, the three-story glass and aluminum structure easily blended in with the other corporate lairs along the Lee Highway in Fairfax, Virginia. The architectural anonymity was no accident. Many of GLT's world-wide operations handled military contracts that demanded the utmost in secrecy.

Abby liked the bee-hive atmosphere generated by the scores of offices and cubicles. The busy environment, with its sharply delineated, yet integrated roster of duties, reminded her of the aircraft carrier she had served on during her navy career and suited her no-nonsense personality. She kept the door of her comfortable but plainly-furnished office open so she could simultaneously absorb and broadcast the energy flow.

As with every morning, she had arisen at 5:30 and had a breakfast of

Kenyan coffee, fruit and whole grain toast without butter. She watched the morning news as she ran on her treadmill, then she showered and slipped into one of her conservative dark outfits that were as close as she could get to a Navy uniform without looking as if her designer was John Paul Jones.

She had driven her silver-colored Mercedes SL convertible from her country home in Leesburg, arriving in her office promptly at seven o'clock, and had glanced first thing at the agenda for the staff meeting scheduled for 8:30. She jotted a few notes and had started to go over a contract to provide army depot support when she felt what ghost-hunters call a *presence*. A feeling that she was not alone.

She looked around the edge of the oversized computer monitor. Hawkins was leaning against the door frame. He was wearing a visitor's ID in the lapel of his blue blazer and had a lopsided grin on his bearded face.

Abby's jaw sagged in disbelief. "What the hell are *you* doing here?"

"Don't you remember our phone conversation a few hours ago?"

"Of *course* I do!"

"Then you'll remember telling me I had to get here by eight." He pointed at the wall clock, which read 7:55.

"But I never imagined—"

"That I could be here as promised?"

"Well, yes."

Hawkins wouldn't have imagined it either. After he contacted Abby the night before, he had used the special number Fletcher had given him to call if he needed support services. In this case, back up had come in the form of a ride on a private jet and the use of a car with government plates. Having Fletcher's number was akin to having a genii in a magic lamp.

"How'd you get here so quickly?" Abby asked.

"I caught a ride to Washington on a Navy plane," he explained. "My

Woods Hole ID got me past your security."

Abby remembered the outrageous statements Matt had made after his Navy discharge and wondered if his off-the-wall claim was the sign of a mental relapse.

Forcing a smile onto her lips she crooned, as if talking to a dim-witted child, "Matt, you're not even *in* the Navy anymore."

Hawkins stepped into the office and flopped into a chair. "You have any coffee?"

Abby used the intercom and called for a pot of coffee and two cups, which arrived within minutes.

"You're looking well," she said, staring at Matt over the rim of her cup.

"Thanks. And you are as lovely as ever."

"Thank *you*. Tell me more about that navy ride," she said.

Hawkins had tuned into the patronizing tone, but he took a sip of coffee and said, "Please call the Naval War College in Newport and ask for Dr. Charles Fletcher. Tell Dr. Fletcher I'm thinking of using your company."

"Who's Dr. Fletcher?" she said.

He nodded toward the computer screen. "Look him up on the website."

Humor him, she thought. *Bring him gently back to reality.* With a smile frozen on her face, she Googled the war college site and clicked Fletcher's name from the staff listings. A photo and biography of Fletcher popped up.

Hawkins studied Abby as she read about Fletcher and called the war college number. Her dark red hair was parted in the middle, and cut short, curving down in points to her chin, framing the same beautiful face he had fallen in love with when they had first met on board ship. The high bridge nose and haughty upward tilt to her chin should have warned him of her strong personality, but he had been intent on her lush body. Once they were ashore, they had begun a heated courtship that culminated a short time later in their marriage.

Abby's call had gotten through.

"Matt Hawkins asked me to call you, Dr. Fletcher. He's here in my office. He says you can vouch that he is on Navy duty. Oh he's not." She smiled in triumph at Hawkins.

"I'm not officially working for the navy," Hawkins said in a low voice.

"He says he's not officially with the navy, Dr. Fletcher." The smile vanished. "Oh. He's been given a consulting assignment? Yes. I'll do that. Thank you."

She hung up and stared at Hawkins.

"Your Dr. Fletcher confirms that you are consulting for a special assignment. I'd like to know more."

Matt got up and closed the door. Then he returned to his chair and gave her an account of his meeting at the War College. Her brow darkened as he told her about the assignment to find a lost treasure in the wilds of Afghanistan. She placed her hands palm down on her desk and gazed at him with a soft expression in the big blue-green eyes that had always reminded Hawkins of tropic seas.

"We weren't married very long, but I still care a lot about you and your welfare."

"I still feel the same about you, Abby."

She allowed herself a quick smile. "What you have just described is a dangerous, may I say, insane mission. You could be killed."

"I know that. Which is why I've come here to ask for your help. I need your logistics expertise."

Abby shook her head. "Matt, look around you, for god sakes. Do you how many projects we're juggling? GLT is an international contractor.

We've got sixteen hundred employees here and around the world. We're not just military; we serve the commercial and humanitarian sectors as well. We're moving warplanes and tow tractors. Barracks and kitchens. We make sure that equipment gets where it is needed, when it is needed, anywhere in the world."

"That last phrase sounds like a marketing slogan," Hawkins said.

"It *is*," Abby replied. "I came up with it."

"I like it," Hawkins said.

"Thanks. Here's the bottom line. The government's outsourcing more and more jobs to companies like ours. In addition to keeping military supply lines open, I'm up to my ears setting up camps at a half dozen disaster locations. We've got goods and people moving on planes and ships around the world. There's no company in the U.S. that does the kind of stuff we're doing, the way we do it."

Hawkins had followed his ex-wife's career since she left the Navy, feeling an indirect pride as he watched her form one of the biggest logistics corporations in the country, eventually becoming its CEO. Her success didn't surprise anyone who had watched her meteoric rise through the Navy after graduating with honors from the Naval Academy at Annapolis.

"Hell, Abby, you just made my argument for me. It's like the Carley Simon song from that James Bond movie. No one in the world does it better than GLT."

"I won't disagree with that, but let me ask you a question. I hope you won't take this the wrong way. But given your hostile attitude towards the Navy, why did they choose you to go on a mission that has national security at stake?"

"I asked the same question. Fletcher said I was uniquely qualified, whatever that means."

"Even with the unique circumstances of your discharge?"

"Those circumstances will no longer stand after this mission." He told her about his bargain with Fletcher.

"You really are determined about this, Matt."

"I think that's self-evident."

Abby pursed her lips in thought. "I'm not saying I will take this job, but if I did, what would you offer in return?"

"Name it."

"Okay then. Two conditions. First I want you to purge your mind of that whole episode in Afghanistan."

"Easier said than done, Abby. I can lock up my memories, but I still walk with a limp."

"I'm sorry about that, but you've got to forget the past. You know how damaging your obsession has been."

Hawkins was well aware that his moods and outbursts after his return from Afghanistan had helped destroy their marriage. She had been riding high with her career and had a hard time dealing with his suspicions that her beloved Navy had not only failed him but turned on him.

"I apologize for all that," he said. "You're a good woman, Abby."

"Thanks," she said with a quick smile. "But it's *you* I care about. Your obsession will kill your chances for a normal life."

"I *have* a normal life."

"Oh *really*, Mr. Normal. When was the last time you had a meaningful romantic relationship?"

Without thinking about it, Hawkins said, "With you."

Silence ensued for a moment. Then Abby said, "Do you really believe that national security is involved in this crazy mission? That if we don't stop this treasure grab, thousands of people will die?"

"That's what I've been told, Abby. That's all I can say."

"Okay. I'll do it."

Hawkins blinked at the quick decision. He sighed with relief. "Thanks, Abby."

"Don't thank me yet. I said there was a second condition. I go to Afghanistan with you. I travel to Kabul several times of year for my work so I can call this a business trip."

Hawkins had no intention of having his ex-wife on the mission. He'd let her go as far as Kabul and dump her.

"Thanks, Abby. I'll teleconference you tomorrow night to go over strategy."

"I'll start the ball rolling as soon as you leave. Who else is on our team?"

"No one yet. You were the first one I asked."

Abby rolled her eyes. "In that case you'd better get busy."

She saw him to the door and came back to her desk. She was smiling as she punched out the number for her operations department. Seeing Matt again reminded her that life with Hawkins had never been a bed of roses. But it was seldom dull.

CHAPTER EIGHT

Department of History, Georgetown University

Professor Akram Saleem had just emerged from his classroom when he noticed the tall stranger wading through the crowd of students and academics milling along the hallway. The man's face looked as if it had been chiseled from oak and he had a physique like a longshoreman. He projected an easy confidence and there was an eagle's alertness in his dark probing eyes.

He drew nearer, walking with a slight limp, and the professor saw that he clutched a copy of the latest book Cait Everson had written on the ancient trade routes. The professor's smile clicked into place automatically and he stepped into the man's path.

"I see you're a fan of Dr. Everson's writing," Saleem said.

The man glanced at the book's cover which showed a string of camels silhouetted against a red desert sunset. The Title was: "*Trading Post Archaeology: The Role of the Silk Roads in Globalization.*"

"I picked this up at the college bookstore. Have you read it?"

"Oh yes! Some people might find it dry, but it's a well-written exposition. Dr. Everson is one of the foremost experts on ancient trade routes."

Hawkins turned the book over to show the photo of Dr. Everson on the jacket. "You sound as if you know her."

"I am Professor Akram Saleem, a colleague of Dr. Everson's."

Hawkins extended his hand in a vise grip. "Nice to meet you, Professor. My name is Matt Hawkins. I run a non-profit outfit called SeaSearch. We find lost ships, purely for educational and historical purposes."

"What brings you to the history department?"

"I was researching old trading routes and came across a reference to Dr. Everson. I happened to be in Washington, and decided to see if I could talk to her."

"I'm very sorry," the professor said. "Dr. Everson is on indefinite leave of absence."

"It was a last-minute impulse. Maybe another time. I'm not surprised she's away. She says in the introduction to the book that she spends a lot of time doing field work."

"Yes, she's fearless when it comes to research. She believes there is no substitute for physically being at a historic site. Is there any area of particular interest to you? Perhaps I could be of help."

"Thanks, Professor. Dr. Everson and I are both detectives of sorts. She researches land routes. I do the same on the sea. I wanted to compare methods."

"I can put a note in her mailbox, if you'd like."

Hawkins took a business card from his billfold, jotted down a note on the back asking her to call and handed it to the professor. They chatted a few more minutes, and then Hawkins glanced at his watch and said he had to go. Hawkins thanked the professor for his time and headed for the parking lot. The professor watched thoughtfully until Hawkins disappeared around a corner, and then went back to his office.

He looked for SeaSearch using Google and called up an impressive website that displayed photos of the dozen or so shipwrecks that Hawkins' organization had found. He clicked on a picture of Hawkins and read the biographical sketch, starting with his most recent career at Woods Hole developing robots for underwater exploration and salvage. Then he came to the part about Hawkins' service record and a frown crossed his usual smiling face.

Hawkins is a navy veteran with the rank of lieutenant. He served with a SEALs unit in Iraq and later in Afghanistan.

Saleem's eyes narrowed. Why would a former navy diver and specialist in underwater salvage come looking for Cait? Coincidence? He read the biography again and looked up a number of related links that added texture to Hawkins' background.

The professor's interest went beyond mere curiosity.

With his friendly absent-minded professorial manner and warm smile, Professor Saleem epitomized the old descriptive cliché: a gentleman and scholar. He had gained the respect of faculty and student alike for his firm grasp of Mid-East and central Asian history. He was a bona fide historian who had gone to school in the United States and had made numerous friends along the way, qualities that gave him the ideal cover for his real job as an agent for the Directorate for Inter-Services Intelligence or ISI, Pakistan's foremost intelligence agency.

He had been recruited by his cousin Mohamed, a high-ranking ISI official, who had realized the professor had the two greatest assets for a spy: accessibility and invisibility. Mohamed sent him through training and bundled him off as an exchange professor to Georgetown, hoping that his professorship would allow him to worm his way into corners of the U.S. establishment that embassy spies could never enter.

His on-going assignment was to ferret out hints of a U.S. raid that would wipe out Pakistan's nuclear capability, a paranoid fear of the ISI and the military. The arrangement promised more than it produced. Most of what he sent home was interesting but useless. He had little access to the real power centers of government, but kept his assignment secure by sending snippets of academic cocktail party gossip to his cousin.

At times the informational well went dry, and that's when he became desperate. It was during one of these dry spells that Dr. Everson told him her latest Prester John theory. He'd listened politely, not thinking there was any value to the information. When she mentioned sending a letter to the State Department, his ears perked up. He had transmitted the story to Pakistan, not because he believed that Prester John and his treasure were real but because he had nothing else at the moment. Mohamed had given the report short shrift, as expected, but when Saleem's cousin got the follow-up message pin-pointing the treasure site, he set in motion an elaborate and risky plot.

The professor reached for his phone and punched out a number. The call was patched through several blind circuits that would make it difficult to trace.

A male voice answered, "Good to hear from you, my cousin."

"You won't think so when I tell you the news. We have a problem."

"What sort of problem?"

"A very big one."

Hawkins drove directly to the airport from Georgetown. He was preoccupied with his thoughts, and unaware of the black Chrysler van that had been waiting for him at Reagan airport and had followed him, first to Global Logistics, then to Georgetown University.

The van tailed him back to the airport car rental return. The man behind the wheel had premature white hair and icy blue eyes. His passenger, who was acting as spotter, was his identical twin. The van pulled up at the departure entrance and the passenger got out. The driver made a loop around the airport and when he returned, his twin was waiting for him.

He got in the van and reported that he had followed Hawkins as far as the security line. As they drove away from the airport he called a number on his cell phone.

A gravelly voice that had been digitally altered came on the line.

"Report."

The passenger gave a detailed description of their surveillance.

There was a pause, and then the altered voice spoke again.

"I want you to concentrate on one thing and one thing only," the voice said.

"What's that?"

The order was short and chilling.

"Terminate Hawkins. Make him disappear. And do it as soon as possible."

CHAPTER NINE

Three Miles East of Norfolk, Virginia

Calvin Hayes stood in the tower of the 25,000-ton Handysize class bulk carrier and watched a man in a thirty-foot Superboat bobbing in the water below bring a pipe-shaped object to his shoulder. A starburst blossomed from the tip of the pipe and a brilliant white streak shot across the carrier's high bow. Hayes' eyes followed the rocket's trajectory and his mouth stretched in a wide grin.

He was dressed in a tailored olive suit and dark green shirt that went well with his dark chocolate complexion. A custom-made yellow silk power tie was knotted around his thick neck. Hayes was always impeccably dressed, but no one would mistake him for a fop. Hayes shaved his scalp and his ears were close to his bullet head. The nose between the high cheekbones had been flattened by a hard right during a boxing match, a match he had gone on to win. A broad-shouldered, six-foot-one physique rounded out the picture. But the tough guy look was tempered by the mischievous gleam in his molasses-colored eyes.

Hayes lowered the binoculars and turned to a pair of men dressed in conservative dark business suits.

"Gentlemen," Hayes said in his soft Louisiana drawl, "With your permission, I will proceed with the next phase of the demonstration."

The older of the two men was Hank Spence, the razor-eyed CEO of the shipping company that owned the cargo ship. His young assistant was Skyler Horton, a graduate of the Harvard Business School.

"Go ahead," Spence said with no change in his flinty expression.

Hayes nodded and turned to the ship's commander, a veteran skipper named Rollins. "Please proceed with the new defensive protocol, captain."

Rollins called the engine room and ordered full stop. The ship coasted several hundred yards before its weight and hull resistance overcame the momentum carrying it forward. As the ship lay dead in the water, the powerboat darted in.

Hayes turned back to Spence and Horton.

"Here's how the scene typically plays out in a pirate attack. The pirates shoot a real projectile across the bow, not a rocket I picked up in a fireworks shop. Then they board the stopped ship. They corral the crew, take the captain hostage and order him to bring the ship closer to land where it can be looted while ransom is being negotiated. Eventually the crew and ship may be released, but the cargo will go to the four winds." He paused for drama. "Unless you hire Secure Ocean Services to protect your investment. I'll let the captain take it from here."

Rollins picked up a microphone that would carry his orders to all parts of the ship.

"This is the captain speaking. All hands to the safe room." He repeated the order two more times, then said, "If you'll excuse us." He and his officers left the bridge in a disciplined fashion.

"Where are they going?" Spence said.

"They will join the rest of the crew in a high-security compartment. They have supplies for two weeks and communication with the outside world." He glanced out one of the big windows that wrapped around the pilot house. "The pirate grapples are hooked onto the port rail. We're about to have company."

Four men climbed over the rail. They were dressed in shorts and T-shirts, the standard uniform of Somali pirates, and wore rags around their heads. As the men slipped automatic weapons off their shoulders, the ship's engines restarted and the cargo vessel began to move.

"Forgot to mention that the captain can control the ship from the secure room," Hayes said.

"So what?" Spence said. "Those guys will get back in their boat and sink the ship with their rockets."

"Not if you've hired my company," Hayes said. He raised the radio to his lips and uttered one word. "*Now*."

The pirates had started across the deck toward the base of the bridge tower. They walked single file, AK-47s at waist level. Halfway to their destination, the last man in line crumpled to the deck. Then the pirate leader and the two men behind him collapsed like air dolls that had sprung a leak.

Spence stared at the four bodies splayed on the deck.

"What the hell just happened?"

"A two-man sniper team with sound-suppressed weapons took them out. In a real attack, the sniper team next would have gone after the man in the boat before he could get away or send a message to his friends. We would continue safely on our way, the ship effectively sanitized."

"*Sanitized*?" Spence said.

Hayes nodded. "The bodies would disappear. Word would get around pirate circles that it is unlucky to attack your ships. We've even thought about putting a decal of some sort on the hull to warn that a ship is 'pirate proof.' Maybe a skull and crossbones inside a circle with a crossbar."

Spence studied Cal's face. "You're not being facetious," he said.

"Not at all. We do whatever is in the best interests of our clients."

"By putting a gang of hired killers aboard their ships? Making bodies disappear?"

Hayes said, "My company is sensitive to the reputation of its clients. But the alternative is losing ships and cargo."

"That's why we pay the big insurance premiums, to cover our losses from these ragged-assed bastards. Ships and cargo are expendable."

"What about officers and crew?"

"Like I said, *expendable*."

Hayes pondered the answer. "I understand you built your company from scratch."

"Damn right! Started with one old rust-bucket bought at auction and turned it into an international fleet of top-notch vessels. What's that got to do with anything?"

Hayes smiled. He was ready to close the deal.

"I don't see you letting a bunch of ragged-assed bastards take your hard-earned ships without a fight. Tell you what. Let's put a team on one of your ships. Give it a test. I'll even foot the bill up front for the safe room. Run the ship through pirate territory. See how things work out. I can have a team anywhere in the world within 48-hours."

"You think I'm crazy enough to risk one of my ships?"

Hayes said nothing.

"Damned if *I'll* have anything to do with cold-blooded murder," Spence said. He gave his assistant a tight smile and stalked off.

Horton seemed unperturbed. "It's okay," he said to Hayes. "He's just covering his rear end. He wants to make a deal. What's it going to cost us?"

"The cost varies according to the size of the ship and the team. On a bigger ship you might want to have four snipers." He threw out a couple of figures. "I'll throw the hull decal in for free."

They dickered over price for a few minutes before reaching an agreement, and Horton left the bridge to find his boss. Hayes made a quick phone call to alert his home office in Bethesda that he'd secured another deal.

Business was good. Every time a pirate incident hit the headlines, he gained a client. The ragged-assed bastards had made it possible for Hayes to afford his eight-hundred-dollar suit, two-hundred-mile-per-hour Bentley Cabrio, and fast boat.

He was reaching for a microphone to tell the captain to come back to the bridge when his phone chirped. When he answered it, the voice at the other end said, "You still make the best gumbo in Louisiana, Cal?"

He brushed back non-existent hair from his shaved scalp. "Damn. Is that you, Hawk?"

"In the flesh. Maybe a little more of it around the middle than when you last saw me. How long has it been? Four years?"

"Give or take a day or two."

The call triggered a reverse switch in Cal's brain and he flashed back to a white light and loud explosion and broken men lying on the ground. He'd been deafened by the blast, but he could see their soundless screams. He swallowed hard.

"I still get flashbacks, Hawk."

"Me too. Memory is a wonderful thing. I've heard there's a pill that can wipe the brain clean of bad recollections."

"I wouldn't want to wipe out all my memories. We had some good times, man."

"That we did. How's business?"

"Can't complain. I've got job security as long as there are bad guys out there. Drive a hot car. Live in a trophy house. Alone, unfortunately. My wife gets the big alimony payments." He paused. "I owe everything to you, Hawk. You took the hit for me."

Hawkins chuckled softly. "My act of heroism was entirely involuntary, Cal. I didn't go out of my way to set off that IED."

"I didn't get your back, man."

"That's because you were standing beside me."

"Not talking about the ambush. Later. When the navy came down on you. SEALs never leave a guy behind. I let the navy chew you up and spit you out. I owe you big time."

"You may be sorry you said that once you hear my proposition."

He outlined the main points of the Afghan treasure hunt and waited for Hayes to comment, which he did after a moment's pause.

"You know something, Hawk, that is the *dumbest* mission I have ever heard of."

"I agree. I wouldn't take offense if you told me you had better things to do."

"That's not what I'm telling you."

"You're saying you're in?"

"I'm in," Hayes said. "I've got a great management staff to watch the shop. There's one other thing."

"What's that?" Hawkins said.

"I never answered your question. I still make a hell of a gumbo."

CHAPTER TEN

The setting sun was a molten ball of orange hanging over the shimmering waters of Cape Cod Bay as the executive jet made its approach to Otis air base, but the beauty of the scene was lost on Hawkins. Nearly twenty-four hours had elapsed since he'd told Fletcher he'd have a team in place.

Two down and one to go.

As he drove back to Woods Hole from Otis, he thought about his whirlwind trip to Washington. Abby and Calvin had been easier to snag than Hawkins had expected. The next call might be the most difficult, and risky.

Returning home, he fed Quisset, and then climbed to his study, sat at his desk, stared at the computer screen, and thought about his first meeting with the enigmatic Molly Sutherland.

Hawkins had refused to stop pushing for an investigation into the ambush that had nearly killed him and he'd been ordered to see a navy psychiatrist. He had limped into the waiting room of a navy medical building in Bethesda and flopped into a chair. Sitting opposite him was a young woman in her twenties, wearing army khakis, who was tapping away at a laptop computer. She was slightly plump, with a creamy white complexion and a round, pretty face framed by short black hair.

She looked up and blinked through black-framed round glasses at Hawkins with the most beautiful orchid blue eyes he had ever seen. He nodded and gave her a half smile. She gazed at him with a neutral expression, and then returned to her computer. He thumbed through an old dog-eared copy of *Guns and Ammo* magazine. He was pondering the idea of walking away from his appointment when the young woman spoke.

"He's a snake, you know."

Hawkins looked up from his magazine. "Pardon me?"

She jerked her head toward a closed door. "Dr. Mengele."

Hawkins wanted to ask the woman why she used the name of the Nazi concentration camp doctor, but a door opened and a stern-looking nurse said, "Dr. Trask will see you now, Lieutenant Hawkins." The nurse handed the woman a clipboard. "The doctor would like you to fill out this paperwork before he sees you, Corporal Sutherland."

Sutherland smirked at Hawkins. "Have a nice day."

A minute later, Hawkins was sitting in front of a mahogany desk occupied by the psychiatrist. Dr. Trask was gaunt, almost cadaverous, in appearance, with a weak chin that was diminished even further by his long face. He picked up a folder and let it drop onto the desk top.

"I've gone through your records," he said. "*Disturbing.*"

"You've done a psychiatric evaluation without talking to me?" Hawkins said.

Dr. Trask stiffened at the unexpected retort. He was used to patients cowering at his pronunciations from on high.

"I didn't *have* to talk to you. It's obvious from the statements of your superiors that you have paranoid delusions. You think someone is out to get you."

"That's not the way I look at it. I just want the Navy to investigate the circumstances of a military operation I was involved in."

Trask leaned his elbows on the desk and folded his hands in front of him. He gazed at Hawkins with slate-colored eyes. "The ambush that injured you, and resulted in the deaths of three men under your command, is making you feel inadequate and less of a man."

Hawkins had the urge to rip the man's face off with his bare hands, but he knew that the doctor was deliberately trying to prod him into making an unwise move that would support his diagnosis. He remembered the warning of Corporal Sutherland.

He's a snake, you know.

Hawkins sat back in his chair and folded his hands in imitation of the doctor.

"We can save a lot of time if you dispense with the psychobabble and get right to the point, Dr. Trask."

Trask's eyes narrowed, giving his face a predatory look.

"Very well, lieutenant. I'm sure you understand your situation. Your hostile attitude gives me no choice but to recommend a psychiatric discharge unless you stop your private vendetta against the Navy."

Hawkins understood the situation very well. Trask was a snake, but the real reptiles were the higher-ups blocking a probe.

"Thank you very much for being honest with me," Hawkins said. "I'll certainly give your warning serious consideration."

He pushed himself out of his chair and headed for the door. As he walked through the lobby he saw Corporal Sutherland look up at him with questioning eyes.

"You were right," he said. "Good luck."

She folded her laptop. "Don't worry about me. I've got snake repellant."

Hawkins was tempted to go the nearest bar and numb his brain with booze, but he waited outside for Corporal Sutherland. She emerged after less than ten minutes.

"That didn't take long. How'd you make out?" he asked.

"Medical discharge. At least it wasn't a psychiatric one like yours."

"How'd you know about that?"

"Dr. Mengele threatened me with the same thing, but held off after I used my repellant."

Hawkins grinned in spite of himself. "I could use some of that stuff myself. Can I buy you a cup of coffee?"

She cocked her head and looked at him, thinking, then said, "There's a Starbucks a couple of blocks from here."

They found a table at the back of the coffee shop. Sutherland sipped at a caramel latte coffee and watched Hawkins' face as he read the report on her computer. It had been prepared by a professional board investigating charges that Trask had a number of improper relationships with his female patients in private practice. The report recommended that his license to practice be revoked.

Hawkins studied the report. "It doesn't surprise me that he's a sleaze. Where did you get this stuff?"

"It's easy when you know how," she said with a smile. "Watch."

She tapped the computer keys and Hawkins saw his name on the screen. She scrolled down through several navy documents, going back to his SEAL training, and hospital records detailing his injuries.

"Hell," he said, not entirely pleased to see how easily details of his life could be accessed by a complete stranger. "You got all this from my last name?

"And navy rank. Didn't intend to pry, but I'm careful about who I go out to coffee with. You and I have a lot in common."

"I'd like to hear about it," he said.

She told him she was born in Wheeling, West Virginia. Her full name was Molly Sutherland Suggs. Her father had named her Molly after country singer Molly O'Day. Her mother liked film actor Donald Sutherland. Molly dropped her last name because she didn't like the way it sounded. Too hissy.

She joined the army at a young age to escape her family's cycle of poverty, received computer training and excelled at it. The army became her new family. She made corporal and was sent to Iraq. She was ambushed in the barracks and sexually assaulted by her fellow soldiers, but the army hushed up the incident and, like Matt, she was sent to counseling and threatened with a psychiatric discharge when she refused to stay silent.

"What happened to the guys who assaulted you?" he said.

"Nothing." She gave him an evil smile. "Officially, that is. I took care of it though."

"What do you mean? Took care of it."

"I got into their personnel files and inserted homosexual incidents and child pornography into their records. They're toast for the rest of their lives. Jobs. Marriages. Military service. Down the drain. One of them committed suicide."

That had been years ago, but as he sat in his study, Hawkins still remembered the dead emotionless tone of her voice and the calmness in the purple-blue eyes. He decided that something had died inside the young woman when she was attacked and pushed out of the army.

It was the only time she talked about her past. And it was the only time he had ever seen her in person. Sutherland still dropped him an email from time to time. She said nothing about what she was doing, or where she lived, and he didn't inquire. He assumed she was living on a navy disability, with her computer her only companion—a lone computer genius with a mental problem.

Desperate times call for desperate measures, he assured himself.

He took a deep breath, called up Sutherland's address and typed:

HI MOLLY.

He had barely hit the Send key when the reply appeared.

HI LIEUT. NICE 2 HEAR FROM U. WHAT'S UP?

I NEED YOUR HELP.

?

FORMING A MISSION TEAM. WOULD LIKE U TO JOIN IT.

?4U. NAVY?

Hawkins had to think of an answer. KINDA. SORTA.

;S.

?! NOT UP ON TEXTING SHORTHAND. PLZ TALK ENGLISH.

MEANS HMMM. WHY ME?

U R BEST COMPUTER PERSON I KNOW. AND TRUST.

104. MEANS THANKS. DETAILS, PLEASE. THIS IS A SECURE LINE.

Hawkins typed a summary of the expedition, starting with the call to go to Newport. He included the part about his demands for an honorable discharge. At the end of the summary he wrote:

NEED SOMEONE TO DO INSTANT RESEARCH RE PRESTER JOHN. AND WATCH WORLDWIDE COMMUNICATIONS FOR ANYTHING THAT COULD ENDANGER MISSION. PROTECT US WITH A CYBER UMBRELLA.

LOL. LOST TREASURE? EX-WIFE? COMPUTER HACKER W/TUDE!!! YOU ARE CRAZY!

BESIDE THE POINT. R U IN? There was an uncharacteristic pause before the answer appeared.

"S"

ENGLISH PLZ.

SMILE. I'M IN.

APPRECIATE IT, MOLLY.

U R ONLY ONE I WOULD DO THIS FOR. I—

He waited for her to complete the sentence, and when she didn't respond he typed: THX. SET UP SECURE TELECONFERENCE FOR TOMORROW AT 2000 HOURS WITH ABBY AND HAYES. DETAILS TO FOLLOW THEN.

A photo flashed on the screen of Sutherland in her army uniform. A second later she signed off and the picture disappeared. Hawkins felt a moment of exhilaration. His team was complete. He had the best people he knew in logistics, security and intelligence. Oddballs every one of them, but the best.

Then reality hit home. *Oh yeah*, he thought. *This merry crew is led by a man who is certifiably insane.*

He let out a groan that woke Quisset out of a sound sleep.

"We're doomed," Hawkins said.

CHAPTER ELEVEN

The next day, Hawkins and Snowy wrapped Fido in padding to prepare the submersible for travel. Later that day, a truck arrived in Woods Hole courtesy of the same special number he had called to request a jet to Washington. They watched as Fido was removed from Hawkins' workshop. As the truck drove off to Otis air base, Hawkins turned to his friend and said, "You're probably wondering what that was all about."

"Some."

"Don't blame you. I'm going to be gone for a while to work on a project. Leaving early tomorrow morning. Navy stuff, so I can't tell you the details. Or how long. I wondered if you'd pick Quisset up tomorrow and take care of her while I'm away."

"Glad to, Matt."

Hawkins shook Snowy's hand and then he and Quisset walked back into the house. He packed a bag full of clothes and another with dive gear. Then he climbed to his study and spread out some satellite photos he'd asked a geologist to prepare. Using a magnifying glass, he studied the lake and a lush-looking section of farmland that surrounded a village.

He was surprised to see an airstrip.

He spent the next few hours laying out an action plan that covered every eventuality he could think of. He took a quick dinner break and precisely at eight o'clock he called up the video conferencing link on his computer. A Cheshire cat flashed onto the screen, fading until only its enigmatic smile remained. The crescent of pointed teeth morphed into Molly's Mona Lisa smile and her full face materialized.

One never knew what to expect of Molly.

"What's with the cat?" he said.

"Virtual kitty. No feeding. No litter box."

Hawkins knew that was as far as he was going to get with the enigmatic computer genius.

"Are we all set up for the teleconference?"

Sutherland nodded slightly. Her head shrunk on the screen and moved to one side to allow space for Hawkins' face, then the screen split into quarters and Abby and Calvin appeared like a couple of CNN talking heads. Hayes hadn't changed much. The wide mouth was stretched in a grin.

"Hawk! You are looking good, man," Hayes said in his soft-spoken New Orleans drawl. "You too, Abby."

"Thank you, Cal," she said. "It's nice to see you. Thanks for arranging this reunion, Matt."

She flashed Hawkins the smile that used to get his pulse racing.

"My pleasure. I'd like to introduce you to my friend Molly Sutherland."

They both said hello, and Abby added, "How come we've never heard of you, Molly?"

"Because that's the way I prefer it," Molly said. "I like to be in the background."

Abby cocked her head. "If that's the case, how did you and Matt meet?"

"Fate," Sutherland said.

Abby's eyes narrowed. Matt saw a further question poised on his ex-wife's lips. He knew first hand about Abby's persistence and Sutherland's manic defense of her privacy and broke up the exchange before it started.

"I'll start by reviewing my own work over the last twenty-four hours."

He described their objective and outlined his plans. Get in undetected. Use the submersible to speed up the search for underwater caves. Dive into the lake. Find the treasure. Escape.

"Molly, could you give us an overview of what you've done?"

Sutherland looked pleased to be the first called upon. Her mouth turned up slightly at the corners.

"I'm putting together the comprehensive historic file on Prester John that you asked for and catalogued the data so it can be accessed forensically according to specific questions. I've also established a file on any mention of Prester John anywhere in the world in the last six months. I'll be combing that file to see if I can find anything relating to the mission."

"That will be a big help, Molly."

"Now to mission protection," she said. "I'll mine the internet for any hint that the mission has been compromised. I've established a surveillance program to keep an eye on internet traffic. If anyone is talking about us in conjunction with Prester John it will trigger a red flag."

"That sounds like a miniature version of the NSA," Abby said.

"The program is patterned after the NSA forensic search logarithms. And it's not miniature. It's a full blown data mining operation that samples all possible sources."

The quick shake of Abby's head signaled her skepticism. "That would take enormous capacity. You must have a room full of computers."

"I don't need a room. I sneak into other peoples' rooms and borrow *their* computer capacity."

Hawkins was enjoying Molly's smack-down of his hard-charging ex-wife, but he wisely kept his thoughts to himself. "Thanks, Molly. That's exactly what I had in mind. Abby?"

Abby would have liked to have learned more about Sutherland, but she got right down to business.

"My assignment was to get everyone and everything into Afghanistan without going through official channels. A charter air service my company uses will transport personnel and gear directly into Kabul. We board six o'clock tomorrow morning at Dulles. A civilian security contractor will do the in-country insertion and the extraction. Everything will be ready to go within the window of opportunity you specified." She said to Hayes, "Cal, what sort of load can we expect?"

Hayes looked as happy as a kid reciting his Christmas wish list. "I've ordered up a couple of sets of desert cammo dress uniforms," he said. "We'll be carrying CAR-15s," he added, referring to the compact version of the M-16 with the folding stock and the shortened barrel. "For side arms, I know you like the Sig Sauer 9 mm, Matt." He went down a list that included extra ammunition, a GPS, satellite phone, rations, first aid and survival items. "I've stuck in an M-203 for good luck, Matt."

The M-203 was an aluminum tube with a breech that could hurl an explosive round roughly the size of two golf balls several hundred yards.

"I'm all for good luck," Matt said. "But strictly speaking, this is not a military mission."

"Hell, Hawk, I know that. But what are you going to do if you run into some bad guys, throw a rabbit's foot at them?"

Calvin had a good point. "You can keep your little bean-shooter. You didn't mention what we're going to use to carry all that stuff."

"Saving the best for last. I'll have a DPV with extra fixings waiting for us at the airport."

The Desert Patrol Vehicle was a dune buggy on hormones with a 200-horsepower Volkswagen engine that could kick it up to a speed of ninety miles per hour.

"Sounds like you covered all the bases, Cal. Anyone have comments?"

Abby had followed the discussion closely. "One adjustment. I'd like you to order up a third line of gear. I wear a size six."

Hawkins shook his head. "I thought you'd only go as far as Kabul, Abby."

"I said I wanted to follow through on the logistical support."

"Damnit, Abby, why do you have to be so difficult? This isn't exactly a stroll in the park we're talking about."

Hawkins knew he'd said the wrong thing the second he said it. Abby's eyes narrowed. She reminded him that she had trained in covert operations and survival techniques at Annapolis, and that she was an expert marksman and an experienced diver.

"All true, Abby, but you forget that I'm in charge of this mission."

"And you forget who's organizing it. Besides, I still outrank you."

It was an unkind cut, and one Hawkins had experienced before, but he didn't rise to the bait.

"We'll have more time to talk about this on the flight to Afghanistan," Hawkins said, although he could tell from the stubborn tilt of Abby's chin that there would be no yielding on her part. "Cal, pack a third set of gear for the lady, just in case."

"See you in Washington in the morning," Abby said, setting her lips in a tight smile.

She disconnected from the teleconference. Hawkins told the other two he would send them a summary of his plans. Their pictures faded and

Hawkins shut down the teleconference. He tented his fingers, thinking, then turned back to the photos on his desk and sketched out the action plan that had been bouncing around in his head. As he worked, he heard a distant rumbling. A thunderstorm was moving in.

CHAPTER TWELVE

The storm clouds had been stacking up in the west all afternoon, even before the executive jet touched down at Barnstable Municipal Airport in Hyannis. Two passengers had gotten off the plane. They wore the standard tourist outfit: shorts, sneakers, high white socks and Hawaiian-shirts. The baseball caps pulled down over their platinum-hued hair and sun-glasses shading their intense blue eyes made it practically impossible to detect the fact that they were identical twins.

Instead of bathing suits and sun tan lotion, each man carried a Finnish-made Jatimatic machine gun and extra ammo magazines in his travel bag. The compact automatic weapon weighed slightly more than four pounds and was designed for close combat. They threw the bags in the back seat of their rental car. The pilot was told they would return in a few hours and instructed to keep his cell phone on.

Forty-five minutes later Mihovil Marzak drove the car along Water Street past the brick buildings of the Woods Hole Oceanographic Institution. His brother Mirko kept an eye on the GPS and map. Not a word passed between them, but they functioned like two pistons in a twin-cylinder engine.

The Marzaks were Serbian by birth and had come of age during the Bosnian war. As teenagers they had been recruited into the army by their father, an army officer under Ratko Mladic, and instructed in the art of wholesale homicide during the *Sbrenica* massacre. Until silenced by a NATO bomb, the elder Marzak bragged about the military prowess of his young sons, particularly Mirko, the eldest of the twins by three minutes. The age difference had created an unusual dynamic. Mirko was impulsive, almost rash, and he considered murder both his job and his hobby. Mihovil was equally as deadly, but more contemplative, a reader of poetry.

Despite the personality difference, they worked smoothly together as an efficient killing machine. After they left Bosnia, they capitalized on their skill at inflicting mass casualties, working as killers for hire until Mihovil suggested that they form a firm of their own, Gemini, which specialized in high body counts. For Gemini, a single assassination like this night's assignment was like stepping on an ant.

At a word from his brother, Mihovil turned onto a residential street and drove past a two-story Victorian style house. The name on the mailbox was Hawkins. A red pick-up truck was parked in the driveway. He turned around and went by the house again, picking a good spot for a stake-out. Then he and his brother drove around the village sizing up escape routes.

The first drops of rain from the fast-moving storm began to splat against the van's windshield. Thunder rolled in the distance and the rainfall became heavier. The inclement weather sent tourists scurrying for cover, but the twins agreed without saying that the storm was a happy coincidence. The atmospheric fireworks would cover the noise of their work.

They parked diagonally across the street from the Victorian house. A light glowed in the second floor picture window. When the lightning and thunder were at their fiercest, they got out of the car, walked quickly through the slanting rain to the front porch and climbed the steps, tensing when they saw a dark shape approach. Quisset had heard the visitors and came through the doggy door to say hello, his tail wagging.

Mirko pulled a telescoping steel spring baton from his jacket pocket.

"Come here, puppy," he said, his lips curved in a friendly smile.

"*No*," his brother warned. Attacking the dog was not part of his carefully-laid plan.

It was too late. There was a metallic blur, a wet thump, and the dog crumpled to the ground.

Hawkins looked up from his work, wondering where Quisset was. He guessed that his dog was hiding under a bed with her paws over her head. The kettle drum atmospherics had grown louder as the thunder storm crept spider-like across Vineyard Sound on long jagged legs of pure electricity. Flashes of lightning reflected eerily off the diving helmets and a drumbeat of raindrops thrummed the rooftop.

Hawkins had been working under an adjustable halogen desk lamp that cast a puddle of light around the desk. The rest of the study was in shadow. When the lightning flashed again, Hawkins glanced up instinctively and saw the otherworldly blue light illuminate the pale faces and hair of two men, one on either side of the door.

Each man held a short-barreled weapon in his hand.

The room went completely dark again, but the image engraved itself in the retinas of Hawkins' eyes. He dove for the floor and crouched behind his desk.

White-hot flowers blossomed from one gun muzzle, then the other. The thunder that followed the lightning merged with that of the bullets as they ripped into the thick wood of the desk and shot the lamp out. The computer monitor exploded in the hail of hot lead.

The gunfire stopped suddenly.

Hawkins figured the intruders were waiting for him to make a move. He thought of throwing his overturned chair off to the side as a diversion, but it would only buy him a second or two. He still had to get to the door between the gunmen.

The old wooden floor creaked. They were moving in on both sides.

He tensed every muscle in his body and prepared to vault over the desk. He thought he could maybe grab a weapon from one of the attackers, although he knew it was a frail hope. He gulped in a lungful of air and coiled his legs. A desperate plan popped into his head. Luckily there was a lull in the thunder.

He yelled, "Beer!"

He heard the sudden hum of his motorized beer cooler. He imagined the robotic diver plodding across the room like a miniature walking jukebox. There was an ear-shattering rattle of gunfire and the study was lit up by a stroboscopic effect from the muzzle flashes.

Hawkins reached a hand over the top of his desk and groped among the fragments of glass, plastic and metal. The shards cut his fingers, but he ignored the pain. His clawing hand closed on the scabbard of the Siebe-Gorman anti-magnetic knife he used as a letter opener. He pulled the scabbard off the desktop, slipped the knife out and held the tip of the blade in a pinching grip. He pushed himself up with his free hand and sprang ungracefully to his feet, snapping off the knife in a stiff-wrist throw aimed above the nearest muzzle flash.

There was as scream of pain and a gun went silent. Then a single gun began to fire. The aim was high, and the spray of bullets struck the display case. Hawkins was belly-down, hands over his head. Bullets ricocheted off the helmets in showers of sparks and the picture window disintegrated.

The firing stopped. Hawkins heard the click of a hammer on an empty chamber and then came the clink of the spent clip hitting the floor.

Hawkins was already sprinting, bent over at the waist, toward the shattered window.

He heard the racking sound of a full magazine.

He dove through the window frame head-first, leaping high to avoid the jagged points of glass. He landed on the porch roof, arms extended, and did a tumbler's roll that absorbed some of the shock of his body hitting the shingles.

He almost rolled right off the roof, but managed to twist around and grab onto the gutter, ignoring the pain in his lacerated palms. He hung there for a moment, then he dropped off onto the grass near the porch steps. Light streamed from the first-floor window and he saw a dark object on the porch. He climbed the porch stairs and discovered Quisset.

The dog's head was sticky with blood. He lifted Quisset in his arms and lurched toward the pick-up truck. He grabbed the spare set of keys he kept under the seat and started the engine. As he was backing out of the driveway, he saw movement on the front porch. A figure silhouetted in the window light dragged something out of the house, down the stairs and across the lawn, moving in the direction of a side street.

Hawkins put the truck into low gear and nailed the accelerator so hard that the spinning wheels dug a trench in the crushed shell driveway.

Minutes later he parked in front of a sign that said Emergency Veterinary services. He carried Quisset inside and told the veterinarian on duty that she had wandered off during the storm and been struck in a hit and run accident.

The vet X-rayed Quisset and said, "She's going to need surgery. There appear to be some bone fragments that could affect her cerebral cortex. We'll just have to see after we take a look. There's no guarantee Quisset will recover. She's hurt pretty bad."

Hawkins towered over the vet, but his voice was soft-spoken as he said, "Quisset and I have been through some tough times together. I'd appreciate anything you can do, including surgery."

"I'll do my best."

"That's good enough for me. Here's my problem, Doc. In about an hour I've got to catch a plane. I'm going to be away an indefinite time. I will sign any papers you need to go ahead with the surgery, and I will give you the name of someone who will be in touch with me if you have to put her to sleep."

Without waiting for an answer, Hawkins gave the vet a business card along with Snowy's name and number. He left a credit card. The doctor bent to go over the information and when he looked up again, Hawkins was gone.

CHAPTER THIRTEEN

Mirko Marzak, the man who had slugged the friendly retriever with the steel baton, was beyond medical care.

Hawkins' aim had been true. The sharp blade of the dive knife had penetrated Mirko's rib cage as neatly as a dart thrown at a target board. Mihovil had rolled his twin's warm corpse in a rug and stuffed it into the trunk of his car. Although he was anxious to get out of town, he drove with amazing control, keeping his speed exactly at the legal limit.

His brother's attack on the dog should have telegraphed Mirko's impatience and it was not surprising that he had detoured from the plan a second time, with fatal consequences. The plan had been to take Hawkins away from his house to a remote location where he could be killed and his body disposed of. But when the lightning flashed and Hawkins looked up, Mirko had started shooting, and Mihovil had to join in.

He had been puzzled at the sudden call for beer, more so at the deadly diversion when the mechanical thing hummed to life. Hawkins had reacted in an *instant*, altering the equation. Now he would have to follow suit, coming up with a plan to deal with his altered circumstances.

His first task was to get rid of the body in the trunk. He drove toward the Cape Cod Canal and turned onto a highway that paralleled the wide waterway. A number of turn-offs and parking lots offered access to the canal, and he chose a narrow dirt road and drove to the end. He pulled the knife from his brother's chest, then hauled the body from the car, removed everything from the pockets, dragged the corpse over the stone revetment that sloped down to the water, and threw his brother's body in to be carried away by the fast-moving current. The rug and knife splashed into the canal a second later.

Back in the car, he drove back onto the main road and headed to the airport. On the way he placed a call on his cell phone.

"The mission has failed," he said.

"What happened?" responded the computer-altered voice.

"My brother was killed. Hawkins was more than expected."

"And what does that make you?" the gravel voice said, dripping with sardonic contempt that even the computer couldn't disguise

"We should have been warned that Hawkins was dangerous."

"You should have acted like highly-paid professionals instead of like amateurs. Every adversary should be considered dangerous. Not every person you encounter will let you kill them."

The voice was right. He and his brother had been sloppy.

"What do you want me to do?"

"You must dispose of all the evidence."

"I've started that process."

"Good. As soon as you do that, proceed as planned."

"Even without my brother?"

"It seems that he was not much help when he was alive," the voice said.

"I can handle it alone," Marzak said. "I have a score to settle with Hawkins when I see him again."

"That's not likely. Forget Hawkins. You've had your chance. I already have a backup plan in place."

"What—?"

The line went dead.

Marzak muttered an oath, then punched out another number on his phone. A man answered. "Yes."

"This is Gemini jewelers," Marzak said. "I designed the necklace for your wife."

"We've been expecting your call."

"Sorry. I had a last minute job. I have some questions regarding the clasp. I would like to discuss them in person with you."

"Never mind the necklace for now. We're more interested in the estate items we talked about. We've learned that there is another buyer interested in the collection. When can we get together?"

"I can leave as soon as you make arrangements."

Pause. "I'll get back to you."

Marzak called the chartered jet pilot and said he would be at the airport in ten minutes.

As he drove along, he reminisced about Mirko. He and his brother had operated as a single organism, bringing death and misery to hundreds of people since going into the business of mass murder. The killing of his brother was not only a personal affront, it was an insult to his professionalism. And if word of their carelessness got out, it would be bad for business.

It could have been worse. He and his brother had put the final touches on the Prophet's Necklace plan only days before. They had been working for months on the scheme. Finding a source of sarin had been the most difficult part, and transporting the deadly poison into the U.S. almost as hard. It had given them time, though, to design the dirty bombs that would spread the toxin and figure out where and how to place them.

They had placed the bombs in six major cities stretching across the country from New York to San Francisco. Each city was a jewel in the necklace. They had picked subways, shopping malls, municipal buildings and other close quarters frequented by many people, where the effects of the toxin would be maximized. When the word was given, they would trigger the bombs remotely, one at a time as the sun moved across the country, building a wave of terror and confusion.

The whole thing depended on him now. As he considered the avalanche of challenges that would come down on him as the result of his brother's death, he could feel the growing rage in his chest. *Hawkins.* He was angry at his brother for not following the plan. They had underestimated the man, thinking that the 2-1 advantage and the element of surprise would doom their target.

He looked to his right. Like a phantom that is sometimes conjured up by the brain to replace a missing arm, he saw his brother sitting next to him.

The figure he saw in his fevered imagination had substance and sound.

"We'll know what to expect the next time around," the phantom said with a smile on its pale face.

Marzak nodded in agreement. He thought of a quote from his favorite poet, William Blake, who had said it was better to murder an infant in its cradle than nurse an unacted desire.

Marzak had murdered infants in their cradles as part of his job, and he had no intention of nursing his desire for revenge, no matter what the computer altered voice had told him about his new assignment.

Marzak would make sure he and Hawkins met again. And when they did, Hawkins would be a dead man.

CHAPTER FOURTEEN

Marjah, Afghanistan

Terrance Aloysius Murphy probably wouldn't have set out to kill someone that morning if he hadn't happened to do some personal banking on his Blackberry just before the call from the States came in with the offer of a big money job.

Although the holdings in his Swiss bank accounts were in the seven figures, Murphy figured that with his transfer home looming he was going to have to do something soon to fill the hole that his losing investments in Florida real estate had dug in the original amount.

Murphy was the leader of a two-man team from the Drug Enforcement Agency's Kabul Country Office Strike Force. After the call, he had hastily pulled the operation together, saying he had a tip that a drug kingpin suspected of Taliban connections was about to leave town.

The target was already on the hit list, waiting for a go-ahead from Murphy. He had compiled the intel on the compound in preparation for a raid, but he had always managed to divert the DEA's attention to more promising targets.

The DEA agents and a unit of Marines that included a drug-detection dog and his handler joined up with a six-man team of heavily-armed agents from the Counter Narcotics Police of Afghanistan.

The DEA agents were part of a F.A.S.T team, government shorthand for Foreign Deployed Assistance and Support. With sixty percent of heroin profits going to support the Taliban, and a government riddled with drug-related corruption, the DEA had tried going after poppy growers, but that only angered the farmers and didn't stop the heroin trade. So the agency had begun to interdict the heroin traffickers using para-military agents like Murphy.

The raiding party set out from the forward patrol base before dawn and took up positions near the compound the drug commander used as his headquarters. The intel file contained the exact lay-out of the compound. Informants had infiltrated the enclosure and identified the placement of IEDs, or improvised explosive devices, buried around the perimeter. Assuming that the booby traps would stop any intruder, the drug traffickers had grown complacent and no one was guarding the gate.

Murphy lay on his belly behind a low ridge. He was still brooding about his diminishing cash cache when someone tapped him on the shoulder. It was the platoon sergeant, a twenty-six-year-old Texas kid named Chavez.

"Five minute warning," Chavez whispered.

Murphy reached down to the speed holster at his waist and tapped the butt of his Smith and Wesson compact 9 mm. Then he wrapped his fingers around the pistol grip of his *Benelli* M3 shotgun, making sure the lever was in semi-automatic position.

A pencil-thin beam of red light sliced the darkness.

The Afghan commander had given the signal for the attack. Answering blinks came from the Marines spread out around the compound. The Afghans crawled like crabs over the ridge, then ran, crouched-over, toward the gate. The DEA agents and the dog and handler were behind the Afghan agents. The Marines moved in to establish a cordon around the compound.

The Afghan agents forced the front door of the main building. Shouts could be heard in *Pashto*, ordering someone to surrender. Moments later the Afghans prodded a short bearded man out of the house. The leader of the Afghan narcs came over to Murphy, frowning like a big-game hunter who had only bagged a rabbit.

"This man says he's only a caretaker. The one we are looking for isn't here. Only a few women and children."

"Keep an eye on the old guy and we'll check out the house," Murphy said.

The commander turned the job of room-to-room search over to the DEA and the Marine canine team, who went in first with Murphy and his teammate right behind them. They cleared the building without incident except for some screams as they entered the main living space where some women and children were huddled.

Murphy called the Afghan commander on his hand radio. Moments later, the commander appeared with a couple of police who spoke to the women and herded them into a room that had already been secured. The dog, a German shepherd, strained at his leash, pulling his handler toward a door off the main room. The dog sniffed loudly along the bottom of the door. His tail wagged with excitement.

Murphy kicked the door in, leveraging all the strength in his six-foot-three frame. He followed the leveled barrel of his shotgun into the room and found it unoccupied. The dog plunged ahead, dashing toward a pile of cloth bags. A quick swipe from Murphy's knife showed that the bags contained heroin. Other bags held hundreds of pounds of hashish.

Another door led from the room to an opium lab, where he found evidence that IEDs were assembled in the same space, linking the kingpin to the Taliban.

A voice crackled over the radio. The Marines had spotted someone trying to escape from the compound and were chasing after him. Murphy told his teammate and the Afghan commander to help the Marines, that he'd stay with the detained caretaker.

When he was alone with the old man, he spoke to him in *Pashto*.

"Who are they chasing, Abe?" he said.

The man, who had been hunched over, straightened to his full height and a crooked grin came to his lips. "I ordered my caretaker to escape, knowing he would run into your Marines."

"Pretty smart, Abe. What *isn't* smart is the fact that you've been lying to me about your operation."

"I wouldn't cheat you. I've been sending your cut of every shipment."

"You've been shaving the payments," Murphy said. "That's not holding up your end of the agreement."

"Maybe, but I'm not the only one who has failed to keep his word. You were supposed to warn me of the raid."

"And you were supposed to keep your operation out of politics. No support for the insurgents."

"I have to pay them a little to keep the operation going. Not much."

"Not talking about the *baksheesh*. You're making IEDs, and that makes you Taliban, instead of a plain old drug lord."

The grin vanished. "I was forced—"

"Not buying it," Murphy said in English. "I saw your boom-boom lab. You're one of the bad guys. Those Marines out chasing your man have been hit hard by your little surprise packages."

"No one in Afghanistan has clean hands. Not even you. If I'm arrested, I will have to tell them about our arrangement all these years."

"That's why I'm not going to arrest you. I'm going to let you go."

"You won't regret this," Abe said, a sly look in his eyes.

Murphy waited until Abe was heading for the shadows before he squeezed the trigger of his shotgun. The pellet blast caught the fleeing man dead center in the back. His arms flew in the air and he pitched forward onto the ground face first.

"I *know* I won't," Murphy said.

He went off to rejoin the rest of the strike force and encountered them escorting the terrified caretaker back to the compound. He explained to Chavez and the narc commander that the detainee had tried to get away, but in the dim light, he had misjudged his warning shot.

No one really cared as long as no citizens were killed. They had neutralized a drug and weapons factory and captured a potential informant, all with no casualties. The strike force was in a good mood on the trek back to the patrol base.

A CH-47 helicopter came in and gave the DEA men and the Afghan narcs and their prisoner a ride back to Kabul. A couple of hours after the operation, Murphy was in his apartment showering, washing the desert dust out of his short, straw-colored hair. He wrapped a towel around himself, poured a glass half full of Makers' Mark whiskey and contemplated the day's events.

The whole operation and his exchange with Abe had been nothing more than a charade to set up the drug lord's elimination.

Murphy didn't care how cozy Abe had been with the Taliban as long as he'd proved a source of revenue. But Abe had been skimming off the take, and Murphy couldn't let word get around that he could be cheated with impunity. Only thing now was that Abe's loss would cut off a supply of cash.

No matter. The payment for the job would help his bottom line. And he would easily cultivate another source: Afghanistan produced 90 percent of the world's opium and exported more heroin than Colombia exported cocaine.

He downed the contents of the glass and turned his attention to the second part of his assignment.

He started up his computer and gazed with hard blue eyes at the photograph of Matt Hawkins on the monitor. The photo had come from the Woods Hole Oceanographic website. The old Hawk had aged pretty well, whereas Murphy's broad face was weathered and crevassed from the effects of hard living. Even without the booze and women, and the blasting sunlight, the dangerous life of a DEA agent had etched premature age lines around his mouth and eyes. He experienced a rush of resentment. Hell, while he'd been chasing down drug traffickers and insurgents as many as two to three times a week, the Hawk had been leading the small town life. Not that he would ever underestimate Hawkins.

He actually liked Hawkins. He was a ballsy, competent and resourceful bastard. But the same admirable qualities made him dangerous. And now Hawkins was headed back to Afghanistan. It was a no-brainer what he would do when he got there. He would try to find out what happened years before. The trail would have led to Abe, then to Murphy, and eventually to those Swiss bank accounts.

Murphy didn't need anyone to tell him Hawkins could simply not be allowed to get that far. He would have to stop him again, although this time he would make sure Hawkins was put away for good.

CHAPTER FIFTEEN

Hawkins stood in the doorway of his darkened study and felt the cool night breeze from the shattered window against his cheeks. The salty air mingled with another, more disturbing smell. He flipped the wall switch and light from the recessed ceiling lamps flooded the room. At his feet was a dark pool of drying blood that had soaked through to the wooden floor. The rug itself was missing.

His hard gaze assessed the damage. The bullet-riddled desk might be patched with a ton of wood putty, but the walking beer cooler that had distracted the twin gunmen had gone to robot heaven. The little figure lay on its back, its bulbous aluminum skin perforated with more holes than a colander.

He walked over to inspect his collection. Shards of glass from the display cabinets crackled under his boots. Dings and dents marred the shiny brass helmets. The main damage was to the book collection on the opposite wall. The cardboard covers and pages littered the floor like confetti.

The soft chime of a wall clock that had miraculously escaped damage told Hawkins he had no time to waste. He picked up the remains of the beer cooler and stored them in a closet. Then he got out a broom and dust pan, scooped glass and paper into a trash barrel, splashed bleach on the blood spot and mopped it up. He hauled the trash down to the basement and wrestled sheets of plywood from his lumber supply up to the study. He nailed the plywood over the window frame, using quick taps to minimize the sound of nocturnal hammering.

It looked like crap, but it would have to do. He'd get Snowy to replace the window glass. He went into the bathroom and washed out the cuts in his hand. As he dabbed the lacerations with antiseptic, he happened to glance in the mirror. No wonder the vet had seemed nervous. He looked like one of those crazed Norse warriors known as berserkers. His hair and beard were competing to see which most resembled a bramble bush.

Hawkins grabbed a pair of scissors and chopped away at his beard until he could finish it off with a straight razor. The prominent chin that emerged was whiter than the rest of his face, but a few days under the Afghan sun would change that.

He took a shower and changed into fresh jeans and shirt. Then he made a quick house survey and dashed out to his truck with duffle in hand. He made good time to Otis air base on the deserted back roads. The jet had already landed. He tucked the truck into a parking space and climbed into the plane's cabin. The plane was taxiing down the runway for take-off as he buckled himself in.

Quickly gaining altitude, the plane cruised at four hundred miles per hour toward Washington. As the miles flicked by, Hawkins gazed through the window at the sparkling tapestry of cities and towns and tried to slow the thoughts churning around in his head. The would-be killers were not in Woods Hole by mistake. They knew who he was and where he lived. He knew only one reason he'd have a target on his chest.

Someone wanted to torpedo the Prester John mission.

More disturbing was the fact that someone *knew* about the assignment. So much for hush-hush security.

Borne out of desperation, his aim had been true and he had seen the dive knife strike one of the men in the chest. His eyes grew cold. He had no remorse over the kill. The destruction of property he could brush aside. Attempted murder and attacking a loyal pal like Quisset were not things he could forgive.

He called a number on his cell phone. "This is Hawkins," he said. "Sorry to bother you, doctor, but I wondered how Quisset was doing."

"No bother, Mr. Hawkins. I was about to call. They're wrapping up the surgery as we speak. Your dog will live, but her skull was severely fractured and there may be some motor impairment from the brain damage. She might not be able to function normally. You might want to think of putting her down."

"Not a chance, Doc."

"Guess that's a no. I'd probably do the same thing in your place. We'll see what we can do to bring your friend up to snuff."

"Thanks, Doc. Call me as soon as you know for sure."

The vet started to go into the details of the surgery, but Hawkins had to cut him off. The pilot had announced that the plane was making its approach to Dulles.

The plane bumped down onto the tarmac and taxied past a line of FedEx and UPS cargo jets, stopping finally near a Boeing 747. The words: **Global Logistics Technologies** were printed in black on the pale blue fuselage. Parked next to the open cargo section of the jumbo jet was the truck that had picked up the submersible and his other gear in Woods Hole.

Hawkins climbed down the gangway to the tarmac and walked over to Abby who was standing near the 747. She was wearing a pale blue jumpsuit that emphasized rather than disguised her feminine curves, and her hair was tucked under a dark blue baseball hat. She noticed that Hawkins had shaved his beard.

"What happened to the chin fuzz?"

"It got caught in a lawn-mower."

She reached out and stroked his jaw. "I like it. Never went for the werewolf look." She went back to her iPad. "I was just going over the cargo manifest. We're in good shape."

Hawkins swept the long fuselage with his eyes.

"Nice of the President to let us borrow Air Force One."

"Thought you'd like to travel in style. Global Logistics makes regular cargo runs to Kabul under government contract. I simply tweaked the schedule."

"Some tweak," Hawkins said. He was impressed but not surprised.

Abby had honed her talent for precision in the navy. The aircraft carrier she had served on was a moving base crowded with planes and the crews, where the slightest mistake could be fatal.

A cargo crew used a fork lift to load their gear onto a freight platform. Abby watched as the boxes were raised to the open cargo door and turned to Hawkins.

"Where's Calvin?" she said. "We're scheduled to take off in thirty minutes."

Hawkins glanced as his watch. Hayes was running late. He called his friend on his cell phone and asked where he was.

"*Hoo-Yah*!" Hayes yelled. "ETA is im-mi-nent."

Two pairs of headlights were approaching. A black Bentley was leading a flat-bed truck across the tarmac. The Bentley stopped next to the plane. Hayes hopped out of the car and waved in the truck, which expertly backed up to the loading platform.

The truck disgorged two men who had physiques like gorillas on steroids.

Hayes directed the unloading with shouts and arm waves. The men rolled the plastic-covered desert vehicle down a ramp at the back of the truck, and pushed it onto the cargo lift. A crew inside the plane took it from there.

Hayes peeled off some bills as payment. As the truck rumbled off, he strode over to Hawkins and Abby who had been watching the fast-moving process with amazement. He gave Hawkins a bear hug.

"Sorry I was late," Hayes said. "Had to pick up snacks for the trip." He stroked his chin. "You look different than the last time I saw you, Hawk. More clean-cut. Kinda like the two-toned skin."

Hawkins was starting to regret having shaved off his beard. "Think of it as natural camouflage."

Hayes let out a whooping laugh, then trotted over to the Bentley, tucked the car next to a storage shed and threw a protective cover over the top. He grabbed his duffle and joined Hawkins and Abby on the cargo lift. They entered the tunnel-like interior of the plane and walked past the desert vehicle, which had been parked next to stacks of cargo containers.

Abby led the way up a flight of stairs to the big passenger cabin under the fuselage hump. Instead of rows of seats, the cabin had been fitted with comfortable chairs and sofas that could be used as beds. They settled into the seats on either side of a small table. The massive Pratt and Whitney engines cranked into action and after a short warm-up, the plane taxied out onto the runway.

The pilot's voice came over the speakers, and announced that they had been cleared for take-off. The plane accelerated down the runway and lifted off the tarmac, then climbed to thirty-five thousand feet and headed east at a speed of 565 miles per hour on the route that would take it to Istanbul. With a range of more than seven thousand nautical miles, the jet would need only one fueling stop before heading across Asia to Kabul. The plane would spend around fourteen hours in the air for the seven thousand mile flight.

Hayes volunteered to make breakfast. He pulled some plastic bags out of his duffle and rattled around in the galley. Mouth-watering fragrances soon filled the cabin. Cal served a breakfast gumbo made with potatoes and sausage, and a Cajun omelet folded over crabmeat and rice, all washed down with strong coffee. As they were eating, Abby noticed the bandage on Hawkins' hand and asked about it.

"Cut myself on some window glass." Hawkins drained his cup and took in his two breakfast companions. "Thanks for the meal, Cal. And I want to thank the both of you for agreeing to come along on this mission. I couldn't ask for better back up."

Hayes stretched his legs out and laced his hands behind his head.

"Hell, Hawk. We should be thanking *you*. Flying first class on our own jumbo jet. Doesn't get any better than this."

"Before you pull out your flower shirt and sandals, I want to warn you that the mission has been compromised."

He told them about the attempt to kill him, explaining in detail exactly how he had cut his hand on window glass.

"Any idea who these two guys were?" Hayes said.

"Never saw them before. Not even in my nightmares."

"This is going to complicate things," Abby said.

"It will definitely make the mission more dangerous. I'm giving you both the option of pulling out. I'll tell Fletcher there's been a leak, and tell him to go to Plan B."

Hayes shook his head. "I'm in it if you are, Hawk."

"Thanks, Cal. I'm still in as well, but I wish you'd reconsider your decision to go along, Abby."

Abby arched an eyebrow.

"Do I have to pull rank on you again, Hawkins? I don't *do* half-missions."

Hawkins looked over at Hayes. "Can you talk some sense into her, Cal?"

"The lady's got rank on me, too, Hawk."

"Thank you, Calvin," Abby said with a smug expression.

"But this is a fool's mission," Hawkins pressed. "I have my reasons for taking it, reasons that don't concern you."

She turned to Hayes. "Calvin, do *you* think this is a fool's mission?"

Hayes greeted the question with a guffaw. "Every mission I've been on has been dumb-ass," he said.

"Matt thinks we don't know that he's trying to manipulate us with a guilt trip for his own goals. Please tell your friend that we're onto him. We know that the psycho discharge has eaten away at his brain all these years and that he's going on a mission with crazy written all over it because he wants to find out why the navy threw him to the wolves."

"I owe Hawk. I'd go along with anything he asked. I don't care why he's doing it."

"Neither do I. If it makes you feel better, Matt, I have no feelings of guilt whatsoever over our break-up."

"Happy to hear that, but there is a difference, Abby. You and I were married. Calvin and I were comrades in arms."

She gave him a stage sigh. "You've forgotten that we spent a lot of time in each other's arms, too."

Hayes saw where the conversation was heading and scooped up the plates. "I'll clean up. You can take the lunch shift."

He disappeared into the galley where he did a fairly good impression of Fats Domino singing *Blue Monday*, obviously aimed at drowning out the conversation in the main cabin. Hawkins and Abby exchanged glances and they both started laughing.

"Maybe we should put aside the serious stuff," Hawkins said. "We're going to have enough to deal with out in the field."

She flashed him a smile that could have melted an iceberg, leaned forward and kissed him on the lips longer than was necessary.

"You won't regret this, Matt."

He felt heat come into his cheeks. Another reason to regret the loss of his beard. He dug a leather portfolio case out of his duffle bag. He riffled through the dossiers until the warm glow faded from his face, and spread out the contents of the folders on a table.

When Hayes rejoined them, Matt said, "We've got the insertion and extraction down. I want to go over the dive plan."

Abby yawned. "Can we put it off until later?"

"Sure," Hawkins said. "We've got a long flight ahead of us."

"Good." She grabbed a pillow and blanket from the overhead. "I'm going to take a little nap."

She stretched out on a row of seats and promptly fell asleep. Hayes yawned and said it must be catching. He camped out on another row and a few minutes later he was snoring.

Hawkins gazed pensively at the sleeping forms. He didn't like using other people, even if they went along with it. He'd always had the feeling that it was his bad judgment five years ago that had put him in front of the oncoming freight train of a faceless entity. Now the past had caught up with the present, and he didn't want to make the same mistake again.

He was convinced that the key to his past remained in Afghanistan, where he and his unit had been ambushed. He had done everything right that day five years ago, but somehow he had screwed up. The bomb had smashed his leg and cost the lives of three men.

There had been the hot blinding light and the *kaboom* and he was flying through the air like a cannonball. When he regained consciousness, he was stone deaf and the whole scene was a silent movie. Some men were staggering to their feet. Others lay lifeless on the bloody ground.

His hearing was almost ninety-nine percent recovered when he appeared before the board of inquiry. He heard every word when the presiding officer went stone-faced and said, "This hearing is at an end."

"With all due respect sir, I believe there is more to this matter than has been presented."

"Not as far as this board is concerned. I'd advise you to count your lucky stars, try to forget this incident and get on with your life."

"Then this is the end of it?

"Correct, Lieutenant Hawkins."

The board members started to pick up their papers.

"Well it's not the end of it for me, sir. If the navy doesn't intend to get to the bottom of this, then I will."

Hawkins recalled how the guards had moved in closer as if he were a rabid dog. After the board made its escape, he sat alone in the room, alone with his thoughts, full of rage at what had just transpired. It had been a slippery slope from there, leading to the shrink's office and his discharge.

He could live without having his psych discharge reversed, but he was single-minded in his quest to find out who had shattered his leg and his navy career.

And when he did?

What then, Hawkins? he asked himself. *What then?*

He had no immediate answer. He knew only that he was going to do everything he could to make this new mission succeed, an outcome that was highly unlikely given the collection of oddballs he had assembled to back him up. The thought reminded him that he had one more thing to do. He reached for his cell phone and punched out Sutherland's number.

CHAPTER SIXTEEN

Tubac, Arizona

Sutherland lived in a one-story stucco house atop a scrub-covered hill on rolling land that was once part of an abandoned ranch about ten miles north of the Mexican border. The only people she ever saw on her property were illegal immigrants heading north and the border police in white SUVs trying to intercept them. They were the ideal visitors because they didn't linger.

She had settled in Arizona after wandering around the Southwestern desert vaguely in search of the kind of spirituality that had vanished along with her innocence. Sutherland had seen the listing for the stucco house in a real estate office window during a stopover in the artsy little town of Tubac. She rode out to take a look at the house and immediately fell in love with its isolation and panoramic view. She bought it and about five surrounding acres with her winnings from internet poker. Her navy disability pension kept her in tacos and burritos and paid the utility bills.

The quiet beauty of the desert had lulled the anxieties that seemed to hound her wherever she traveled. Inspired by the fiery vermilion of the sunsets she saw in the western sky from her patio, she had ventured into town and acquired acrylic paints, brushes and an easel in a local art supply shop. After she took a few painting lessons in a local gallery, she had been spending less time at the computer and more of her days in front of a canvas.

She painted landscapes at first. Her paintings were technically well-executed, but they made her uneasy because of what they revealed about her psyche. She didn't have to be a psychologist to detect the disturbing hints of paranoia in the beastly eyes lurking in the shadows and in the menacing postures of *saguaro* cacti. She had put her landscapes in storage and switched to another subject, the hummingbirds that darted in to dine at the dozen or so feeders she had hung around the house. It was impossible to instill menace in her paintings of the tiny birds and she captured the luminescent hues of their colors with amazing accuracy.

She had set up her computer in a small bedroom that had a window view of the crumbling walls of an old ranch house and stables in a shallow valley around a quarter of a mile away. She had carried her coffee into her office to check her computer when the call came in from Hawkins.

"We're on our way, Molly. Crossing the Atlantic. How's it going?"

"Fine. Prester John file is done. I'm setting up the internet surveillance program, but nothing has come up so far that relates to the mission."

"Great, Molly." He paused. "I've been thinking. I don't really have a handle on the folks who hired me."

"You told me about the Newport meeting."

"Yes, but those characters could have been bit players for all I know. Dumb not to vet the people at the meeting."

"Yeah, pretty dumb. No problem. I'll start files on all the names you gave me."

"That would put my mind at ease. I'll let you know when we get to Kabul."

After they said their good-byes, Sutherland turned to her computer. She compiled bios on the Newport group. Nothing popped up to catch her attention. There was one name on the meeting list that she didn't check out. Matt Hawkins.

Sutherland already knew everything there was to know about Hawkins. She had opened a file the day she met him in Trask's office, adding to it every step of his life since he'd left the navy, returned to college and established a new career. She had watched electronically from afar, only rarely corresponding with him. Her fault mostly. She was aware that she had a crush on Hawkins. *My god*, she thought, *what female wouldn't be attracted to him?* Sutherland knew Hawkins liked her, but probably more like a kid sister. She was comfortable with that arrangement, with its implicit bond of trust. It was why she had answered his IM. And the reason she took on this nutty assignment.

Although she had to admit that her heart had skipped a beat when she saw his face during the teleconference, and she was pleased to hear him praise her skill as an investigator. Out of idle curiosity, she called up the Hawkins file and clicked on the transcript of the navy hearing after the ambush in Afghanistan. She read down to the tense exchange between Hawkins and the lead officer:

Q. Lieutenant Hawkins, could you tell the board who, besides yourself, knew about the operation?

A. The only one who knew the specifics was Commander Kelly. My men were aware of the nature of the operation, but not the name of the target.

Q. So you and Commander Kelly were the only individuals in the chain of command who knew that the target was a drug runner known as Abrahim Noor Kahn.

A. Sorry. My brain is still fuzzy. There *was* one contact outside the chain of command. I consulted with a CIA agent.

Q. Can you give us his name?

A. I would have to get his permission before I did that.

Q. Unfortunately, that's not practical with our schedule.

A. I understand. For the time being, I'll use his code name. *Southie.*

Q. What was the nature of your discussions with Southie?

A. I asked him what he knew about the warlord. He said the target was a protected asset.

Q. An informer, in other words.

A. Yes sir. That was my understanding.

Q. Did you at any time tell Southie of your plans to arrest the warlord?

A. No. I told him only that Abrahim was a person of interest in connection with an ambush a few weeks earlier.

Q. What was Southie's response?

A. He advised me to look elsewhere. We checked out his leads, but they were dead ends. We pursued our mission plans.

Q. So you disregarded his advice?

A. Abrahim may have had some intelligence value, but I was convinced that the target was responsible for American deaths and could be a potential danger in the future.

Q. Have you considered that if you had called off your mission, it might not have cost the lives of three men and several injured, including yourself?

A. In every operation, you weigh the possible casualties with the outcome if the mission is not carried out. You do your best to insure the safety of your men.

Q. It was your testimony earlier that you did everything by the book, and that your mission must have been compromised. Yet you say no one knew the details of the operation. How could it then have been compromised?

A. I don't know, sir. I just don't know.

Sutherland found the rest of the testimony hard to read. The board took turns demolishing Matt's theory that dark, unknown forces had doomed the operation. Without explicitly saying so, their questions seemed to suggest that it was Matt's fault the mission went awry. Matt was still feeling guilt about his leadership. The outburst that ended his career and led to a less than honorable discharge was inevitable given his precarious mental state.

She had read the transcript before, but except for her friend's flashes of anger, it seemed straightforward. Hawkins was on the defensive, visibly frustrated with the board's unwillingness to look further into the ambush. She sat back in her chair and stared out the window.

Something was out of kilter. In reading the transcript before, she had concentrated on Hawkins and his anguished testimony rather than the facts presented at the hearing. She had the feeling she had missed something.

Sutherland glanced at her wall clock. She had to run into town for art supplies and her painting class. She snapped the cover down on her computer and pushed back from the desk. She'd get back to the hearing later. Maybe a few hours slapping paint on canvas would clear her mind.

CHAPTER SEVENTEEN

The panicked call came in a few hours after Professor Saleem had contacted his cousin to tell him about Hawkins.

"Events are moving faster than I expected," Mohamed said. "You must come home."

Saleem was standing in the history department hallway outside his classroom, phone close to his ear, after excusing himself from his pupils.

"Are you mad? I *can't* come home. I have classes to teach. What is so important that you must drag me away from my duties to my students?"

"Your duty to your country and the intelligence service you are sworn to obey."

"I thought I was fulfilling those duties with my service here at the university."

"Saleem, this is not negotiable!"

The professor had never heard his normally self-possessed cousin on the verge of hysteria.

Saleem asked Mohamed to hold on for a moment and went back into the room to dismiss his class early. When he was alone in his classroom he sat at his desk and said, "I can talk now. Please tell me what has happened. What is your situation like?"

The interlude gave his cousin a chance to settle down. "It is like trying to control a tiger with a leash made of thread. The lure of treasure had diverted our friends as we hoped. I have delayed them to this point with excuses of government bureaucracy. But now they want to move ahead immediately with a mercenary operation to secure the treasure. I can't help but think it has something to do with Hawkins."

"You said before that they were not ready to mount an operation," the professor said. "You said it would take them a while and keep them occupied while we worked on the Grand Plan. That it would keep them from hanging the Prophet's Necklace around the neck of the United States."

"True. That was what I thought until I talked to the Doctor and told him about Hawkins. He said he wants to move right away. He also said that the designer of the necklace is a mercenary named Marzak who had been hired to lead the expedition as soon as he finished putting the strands in place. It seems that he is at last free."

"If this operation slips out of our grasp it would be extremely dangerous," the professor said, trying to keep alarm from elevating his voice.

"Which is why it isn't going to happen. Our main goal remains the same. Control of the lithium fields. I want you to go on the operation and keep an eye on Marzak. A plane is flying in from London to pick you up."

"You forget that my skills are more professorial than operational, cousin."

"You've gone through training the same as the rest of us. Besides, you're the only one I can trust who can help me hold this thing together."

"I may need someone to hold *me* together."

"Be of good cheer. We may end up with the lithium *and* the treasure. The Doctor tells me he has summoned Marzak. I've arranged for him to be on the same plane as you. I told the Doctor that you will be in operational control of the treasure mission."

"What? Are you crazy?"

"Not at all. Marzak cannot be wandering about the U.S. We can't risk having him set something off that will bring the United States more into the region before we make the minerals grab. This development could be to our advantage."

"Please elucidate, dear cousin."

"You may be able to glean information about the necklace. Even if you don't, we can take care of Marzak and at the same time call the American birds in to drop their eggs on the Shadow leadership. Whether the Shadows get the treasure or not, their leaders will assemble to plan strategy and thus be vulnerable."

"I hope you are right. What about the Hawkins mission?"

"The mercenary force includes formidable air power. The American operation doesn't stand a chance. They'll be wiped out along with the drug lord, leaving the field clear for us. In the meantime, don't let Marzak out of your sight."

They chatted a few minutes longer, then Saleem hung up. His cousin had a talent for making lemonade when handed lemons, as the Americans said, but as the professor began to pack his suitcase, his thoughts of the future were pervaded by a deep sense of foreboding.

The plane his cousin had arranged for Saleem arrived in Washington to pick up a dozen Pakistani officers on their way back from a training mission with the U. S. Army. As the professor followed the officers onto the plane, he saw the man sitting toward the rear of the cabin.

Fresh from their training in Texas, the chattering officers hardly paid any attention to the man who had a baseball cap pulled down on his head and wore aviator type sunglasses. He had a copy of *The Washington Post* in his hands. Although his eyes were covered, the professor had the distinct feeling that he was not reading the newspaper, but instead was watching every person who boarded.

Saleem had no idea what Marzak looked like, but this had to be the man he was supposed to keep his eye on.

The officers settled in a group toward the front of the cabin and Saleem took a seat in a row behind them. Minutes after they boarded, the plane took off and began the first leg of its journey across the Atlantic Ocean.

Saleem had often regaled those attending his history classes that the past, present and future could not be treated separately, but as a single organism occupying space and time. Now here he was, proving his point. His present was caught up in a momentous past event that had its origins centuries before in the long lost kingdom of a legendary ruler. He preferred not to think about the future.

His cousin had asked him to watch Marzak. Easier said than done. If he turned around in his seat the man would notice. Nature in the form of a full bladder showed the way. He got up from his seat and made his way to the restroom at the rear of the cabin. As he walked down the aisle, he kept his eye on the flight attendant, who was puttering around in the space at the rear of the cabin.

He smiled at her, but at the last second, glanced at Marzak.

The man had removed his cap, revealing a platinum head of hair. He was reading a book that hid his face. Saleem was surprised to see from the cover that it was a book of poetry by William Blake. He was still looking at the title when the man lowered the book, pushed his sunglasses up onto his forehead and gazed at the professor with topaz eyes.

There was something so alien and inhuman in the gaze that the professor felt weak-kneed, much the way a rabbit must feel when it has attracted the attention of a wolf.

He brushed by the flight attendant and locked himself in the restroom where he stared at his reflection in the mirror. His face was as white as a sheet and his skin was shiny with beads of perspiration. He quickly relieved himself, and then threw cold water in his face after washing his hands.

He took a deep breath, opened the door with a shaking hand and strode down the aisle to his seat.

With every step he felt those cold blue eyes boring into the back of his skull.

He settled back into his seat and waited for his rapid heartbeat to slow down.

Don't let him out of your sight, Mohamed had said.

No worry about that, dear cousin, except for one small detail. The watcher was now the *watched.*

CHAPTER EIGHTEEN

Sutherland drove her RAV4 up the driveway and saw a dozen or so agents herding a bedraggled group of men toward a line-up of white Border Patrol SUVs. As she pulled up to the house, a middle-aged Border Patrolman approached her vehicle. His name was Ed McHugh and she knew him from previous patrols.

"Afternoon, Miss Sutherland. Sorry for all the ruckus. We're cleaning things up here as fast as we can."

She got out of the SUV carrying a bag of newly purchased paints. "Looks like you're having a busy day."

McHugh nodded.

"Can't complain. As long as these folks keep coming in, I'll have job security." He checked the progress of the round-up. "Looks like we're ready to head out. Call me if you ever need help."

She patted the shirt pocket that held her cell phone. "Got your number right here."

He plunked his hat on and rejoined the other agents. The patrol vehicles trundled off her property with their fresh catch of Mexican illegal immigrants. Within weeks the same Border Patrol officers would be rounding up the same illegal aliens. But for now, the valley was peaceful again. The lowering sun would soon dab the rugged landscape with colors from its brilliant palette.

She went into the house, popped a cold can of Tecate from the refrigerator, then sat at her computer and called up the navy board of inquiry file on Hawkins. She reread the inquiry proceedings and out of curiosity typed *Southie*, the name of Hawkins' CIA contact into a web browser.

Her West Virginia heritage had suggested that *Southie* had something to do with the southern part of the U.S. She was surprised that it was a nickname for the working class Irish neighborhood of South Boston. From the references she found, *Southie* was most famous as the home turf of gangster James "Whitey" Bulger.

Nothing there. She typed in the name Abrahim Noor Kahn and found a number of news stories on the drug lord. The most recent ones reported his death a day earlier during a DEA raid. Strange coincidence.

The New York Times story said Khan had been a CIA informant nicknamed "Honest Abe," and was a double agent working with the Taliban. Before he was unmasked, he had been paid millions, flown to Washington to meet with CIA and DEA officials, wined and dined and taken on trips to New York, supposedly to meet with his attorney.

An enterprising *Times* photographer had snapped a photo of Honest Abe coming out of Macy's. At the side of the bearded Afghan, clutching two shopping bags, was an unidentified broad-faced man. Both faces were slightly blurred.

The story on Honest Abe's death quoted his attorney as saying that his client never supported the Taliban or worked with the C.I.A. The attorney admitted that the confusion may have been caused by his client's work as a consultant to a well-connected military contractor known as Arrowhead.

Arrowhead's elaborate website said the corporation was a full service risk management company, headquartered in Plano, Texas, with hundreds of employees worldwide, and that it specialized in "Democracy Transition." Arrowhead operations were broken up into various specialties. Law enforcement. Strategic. Recruitment and Training. Anti-Terrorism. Except for scope and degree, the company was no different from any of the dozens of gun for hire groups that had sprung up around the world over the last couple of decades.

Like many regular soldiers, Sutherland considered military contractors as bottom feeders. Most mercenaries were former military men who earned big salaries for work that the people still working for Uncle Sam did for short money.

Sutherland noticed a link for The Arrowhead Foundation listed in small print on the website and clicked it. The U.S. registered charity had been set up to bring relief to war-torn environments. The list of projects included schools, water tanks, purification systems, generators and other small but important projects for poor communities.

She scrolled through the projects and stopped at one labeled Psychological Care for Children in Conflict. Sutherland had an interest in psychology stemming from her own mental issues so she clicked on the listing. The site carried a number of photos of Iraqi children with men and women who worked for an outfit called World-Wide Youth Counseling Services.

She stared with disbelief at a photo of a man handing a stuffed teddy bear to a child. The photo caption didn't name the man, just described him as a psychological counselor, but there was no mistaking the gaunt features and puny chin of Dr. Trask, the hated psychologist who had ruined Hawkins and threatened to do the same with her! The attempt at a warm smile could only be described as grotesque.

There were two other armed men in the photo. One was in the background, and the other, standing next to the girl, resembled the same wide-faced man in the photo of Honest Abe coming out of Macy's. She expanded the search on the foundation, combing the internet for any mention of the Children in Conflict site. She hit pay dirt in an online version of the Holy Cross college alumni magazine under the heading:

Alum Serves in Humanitarian Role

The article had the identical photo as the one on the Arrowhead site. The caption identified Trask only as a child psychologist, but it said the man with the gun was a BC alumni named Terrance A. Murphy. He had joined the Marines after college and served three tours in Iraq before mustering out to go to work for Arrowhead. The clip was a couple of years old and gave no indication of Murphy's movements since then.

The detail that really caught her eye was Murphy's home town. South Boston. And his nickname was *Southie*! She squinted at the screen. Was Murphy the CIA guy Hawkins talked to before going after Honest Abe? If so, his ties to the execrable Dr. Trask were disturbing. She had to know more.

Using the foundation's charitable registration number from the website, she looked up its IRS 990-PF form listing the names of the foundation's officers, directors, managers and contractors. She recognized none of the names, but noted them for a further look, then scrolled down to the list of grant recipients.

One of the recipients was World-Wide Youth Counseling Services.

She went back to the photo of Trask and found a strange coincidence. It was taken the year when, according to the alumni magazine article, Murphy was working for Arrowhead at the same time its foundation was awarding a grant to the children's organization.

When Trask had first come into her life as a hatchet man for the navy, she had prepared a comprehensive dossier on him. She went back and looked into the file. There was no mention of his tie-in to the foundation or the navy. He was described as being in private practice, but this would not prevent him from hiring out as a consultant.

Sutherland was like a hound on the scent of a rabbit. Or in this case, a *skunk*. She got up from the computer and went out onto the patio to steady her nerves. The desert was unearthly quiet. She had missed the sunset. She breathed in the scent of sagebrush and went into the house for a protein bar and a Diet Coke. Back at her computer, she limbered her plump fingers like a piano virtuoso about to play Chopin's Minute Waltz, and began to attack the computer keyboard.

She went into every aspect of the Arrowhead website. She dug further into IRS files. She used her far-ranging computer search program and picked up hundreds of references to the company. There were no other direct references linking Murphy or Trask. But she found that aside from a few projects, the organization actually did very little for children.

Sutherland decided to go right to the source, and wrote an email to the foundation director saying she wanted to donate money to the children's development fund. She included her cell phone number.

Since it was night in Texas, she didn't expect a reply, but her phone rang after a few minutes. It was the foundation director.

"I didn't think anyone would be working this late," Sutherland said.

"We're 24/7 here," the director answered. "Thank you for your offer," she said, "but you might want to donate to other foundation projects. That project ended a couple of years ago, as the situation changed in Iraq."

"Is there any way to get in touch with Dr. Trask? I saw his name on the website," she lied. "Maybe he's doing similar work that I can support."

"I'll have to do some research. I'll get back to you."

Sutherland thanked her, clicked off and stared into space. Hawkins knew *Southie*/Murphy. Murphy worked with Trask and went shopping with Honest Abe who ambushed Hawkins. She considered contacting Hawkins, but he was still in the air and she didn't have enough to go on. She just knew something wasn't right.

She wrote up a report, but decided to wait until she heard back from the foundation. If she didn't hear from Arrowhead, she'd get in touch with Hawkins in the morning.

She yawned. It was almost bedtime.

After the call from Sutherland the foundation's development officer went to the director and told him of the strange request to donate to the children's charity and the question about Trask.

The director thanked her, closed his door and made a telephone call.

Sweat formed on Dr. Trask's weak chin as he listened to the voice on the phone. How had Sutherland found him? There was no mention of his name anywhere in the company website. He thanked the director. He was calm and polite on the phone, but the moment the conversation ended, he frantically punched out a telephone number.

The phone chirped in a small, Spartan office in Falls Church, Virginia.

The hard-eyed man sitting behind a desk in the office listened intently, then said, "The 4th Protocol? You're sure of it?"

There was a verbal blast from the other end.

"I'll need clearance from upstairs first."

Trask said, "Stand by," and hung up.

A minute later, the phone rang again and it was his supervisor, following up on Trask's panicked call.

"You have the go-ahead to proceed. I'll be sending you a file. You're to act on this immediately."

"I'll take care of it."

He hung up and turned to his computer. A minute later he was looking at a photo of a woman in her twenties. The face was plump but pretty. Under the head shot was a note:

"Apply the Fourth Protocol to the subject as soon as possible."

Accompanying the photo was information on the subject. Following a pre-arranged procedure, the man began making a series of telephone calls that would bring together the personnel closest to the job into an action team.

The numbered protocols were a system of threat assessments and responses. The first protocol was meant to deal with someone who had made a casual inquiry about the business. The appropriate response was a background check.

If the inquirer persisted, the response would be quiet intimidation, mainly a suggestion that questions would be turned over to the legal department. If that didn't work, Protocol Three was invoked, calling for a physical diversion of some sort. A car would be run off the road. A house would be burned down.

The subject's inquiry by itself did not merit more than level one. But Dr. Trask's standing in the organization pushed the matter into the final category.

The Fourth Protocol.

For which the only remedy was speedy eradication.

CHAPTER NINETEEN

Kabul, Afghanistan

The pilot's voice came over the cabin intercom and announced that the 747 had been cleared for landing. Hawkins gazed out the window as if in a trance as the big plane dropped into the bowl formed by the jagged mountains that surrounded the three-thousand-year-old city.

Moments later, the massive landing gear clomped down on the tarmac at Kabul International Airport, or *Khawaja Rawash*, as the locals called it. The airport had had more lives than a roomful of cats. The Russians built it in the 1960s and controlled it for ten years before the Red Army left the country and the airport fell into the hands of various militias. The Taliban held the airport until 2001 when U.S. forces kicked them out.

Hawkins recognized the industrial-styled air traffic tower that the Soviets had constructed, but the newer terminal wasn't there the last time he had seen the airport. Since the U.S. invasion, planes from a dozen or so civilian airlines were allowed to fly in and out, but the airport was still heavily used by the military. As the plane taxied to a cargo area, it passed rows of big transport planes and muscular helicopters.

The movable stairway was rolled up to the plane and Hawkins and Calvin descended to the tarmac. Hawkins stared off toward the mountains that were nearly invisible in the haze and filled his lungs. The whiff of cool, dry Afghan air triggered memories of his first arrival in the country as part of a SEAL team.

He exhaled. “Home sweet home.”

“Place still stinks,” Calvin grumbled.

Hawkins knew he wasn’t talking about odors.

Abby bustled down the gangway and broke up their remembrance of things past. “You guys look like a couple of lost tourists. May I remind you that we’re here to get a job done.”

Calvin had a thoughtful look in his eye as he watched Abby stride purposefully over to the plane’s cargo door. “That’s some woman. How come she never made admiral? Sure as hell *acts* like one.”

“Navy’s not ready for a female John Paul Jones. Especially a pretty one. Abby’s right about getting a job done, though. Let’s give her a hand.”

They followed Abby to a mobile loading platform that had been elevated to the cargo door. The desert vehicle was moved out of the plane first, then the dollies holding the submersible and dive equipment, and finally the boxes of firearms and survival gear.

Calvin peeled the protective foam off the Desert Patrol Vehicle. “Well, what do you think?” he said.

Hawkins let his eyes roam over the wing-shaped purple fiberglass side panels emblazoned with yellow flames, the wire-spoke aluminum wheels, the burnt red lay-down seats and the chrome bumpers and headlights. The rails and roll bar were decorated with orange and black stripes.

He folded his arms and said, a pained expression on his face, “Where did you get this road rocket, Cal?”

"It's *mine*," Calvin said. "I bought it from a military supplier and customized it."

"I especially like the camouflage pattern and colors. Not bad."

Calvin lovingly placed his hand on a side panel. "This baby's more than 'not bad,' Hawk. I've squeezed some more oomph out of the 200 horsepower VW engine. You have to fight the steering wheel because of the torque, but she'll do zero to sixty in less than ten seconds and get up to over a hundred miles per hour. I've built in added fuel capacity, so she's good for more miles in between gas stations. What do you-all think, Abby?"

Abby gazed at the vehicle and pinched her chin. "I like it."

Calvin gave her a brisk salute. "Obviously you are a woman of discrimination."

Hawkins shook his head, then borrowed a fork lift to lift the plastic foam case containing Fido onto the vehicle's luggage carrier where it was secured with bungee cords and rope. The other gear was tied down to running board racks on both sides.

"What time do you want the chopper tomorrow?" Abby said.

"I want to get off the ground while it's still dark," Hawkins said. "The sun comes up around five. How about three-thirty?"

She made a quick phone call and after a brief conversation said, "You've got it. Our ride will be here at three." A smile replaced the no-nonsense set of her mouth. "The mission is all yours after that. You get the chance to boss *me* around." She pecked both men on the cheek and pointed to the terminal. "VIP immigration is through that door."

Abby had used her corporate clout and listed Hawkins and Calvin as employees of her company. They showed their passports, submitted to an automated bio data scan and entered the terminal. The scene was one of ordered chaos. There were long queues of departing passengers and dozens of armed Afghan security guards. Hawkins marveled at the duty-free boutiques that had opened since his last pass through.

Abby was leading the way to the exit, with Calvin and Hawkins right behind, when a big man cut between them. The red hair was streaked with gray, but Hawkins immediately recognized the jovial-tough face of Terrance Murphy. He caught him by the arm, and Murphy snapped his head around, a scowl on his wide face.

In a stage Irish brogue, Hawkins said, "Is it yourself off in such a rush, Mr. Murphy?"

The angry expression vanished and Murphy spread his lips in the toothy white smile that used to remind Hawkins of the Kennedy clan.

"Jesusmaryjoseph! Is that you, Hawk? And Calvin, too."

Hawkins extended his hand. "Been a long time, Murph."

"Indeed it has," Murphy said, crunching Hawkins' fingers, then Calvin's in his vise-like grip.

Abby noticed that her friends had stopped. Hawkins waved her over and introduced her to Murphy.

"This is Terrance Murphy. Murph is a pal of ours from the old days," Hawkins said.

Murphy gave Abby the full blast of his white smile. "A pleasure to meet you."

"Never expected to find you still here after all these years," Calvin said.

Murphy gave out a big laugh. "Neither did I. I'm with the DEA. I left the government after you were transferred out and worked as a private contractor. Good money, but I got tired of body-guarding the embassy crowd and applied to be a drug cop. Everyone else from the old gang is either dead or gone home."

"I saw Commander Kelly not too long ago," Hawkins said. "He's very much alive. He's a weapons consultant for the Pentagon."

"I could have done the same thing, but you know me. I've got to be where the action is."

Hawkins swept his eyes around the terminal. "Things have changed."

"Don't let this fool you. It's still like Dodge City out in the 'burbs. The bad guys sneak in to raise hell whenever they get the chance. Which leads me to inquire what prompted you to leave your cushy job to come back to this garden spot?"

Abby saved Hawkins the trouble of making up an answer.

"We're here on a job for Global Logistics."

"Great organization. Maybe I can help. I've got a lot of contacts, especially through the DEA."

"Maybe," Hawkins said. "Let's talk about it later."

"It's a deal. I've got a car outside. We can chat on the way to your hotel."

"Thanks, Mr. Murphy. I've already made arrangements," Abby interjected.

"Efficient, aren't you?" Murphy said. "Where are you staying?"

"The Serena," Abby said.

"Good choice. How about dinner?"

"We've got plans," Abby said, much to Hawkins' surprise.

They agreed to meet after dinner and parted company. A leased SUV was waiting outside the airport to take them along the heavily-trafficked main road to the city. On the ride in Abby asked about Murphy.

"Your friend seems quite the character. The operational decisions will be yours, but are you really considering bringing him into this mission?"

"Only in a limited way, for intel. As he said, he has lots of contacts. I haven't been here in five years and the place has changed a lot since then." He gestured out the window. "Murph knows who the players are."

"My impression is that he *is* one of the players."

Hawkins nodded.

"Murph came into Afghanistan with the first wave of CIA agents who turned the local tribesman against the Taliban," Hawkins said. "We shared intelligence for a number of missions. I left and he stayed."

"That's unusual to stay here all that time."

"Most people count the days. But Murphy is like a soldier of fortune back in the heyday of the British Empire."

"A mercenary, in other words."

Hawkins thought about it. "More complicated. He's just someone who was born out of time."

"Humph," Abby said, pinioning Hawkins in a narrow-eyed stare. "Your friend Murphy wasn't the *only* one born out of time."

CHAPTER TWENTY

The Hotel Serena was about a twenty-minute drive from the airport, close to government ministries and foreign embassies and overlooking a beautiful park. With its carefully landscaped gardens, swimming pool, classic Islamic architecture and cool interiors, the hotel had long been an oasis of calm away from the frenetic pace of the city. That tranquility was shattered in 2008 when a Taliban suicide squad attack killed several guests. Since then, security had been beefed up.

After being thoroughly checked out by the police guarding the entrance, the taxi pulled up under the hotel portico and its three passengers got out. The receptionist smiled when he saw Abby walk over to the desk.

"Welcome back to Kabul, Ms. McWilliams. A pleasure to see you again."

"Thank you. It's good to be back."

"You get around," Hawkins said as the clerk went to fetch the room keys.

"I stay here whenever I'm in town on business," Abby said. "I'm in Kabul two or three times a year. How about dinner in about an hour?"

Calvin shook his head. "Being my usual anal self. I'm gonna drop my stuff off and head back to airport to double-check that all my hardware made it intact. I'll grab a sandwich and catch up with you later."

Abby made dinner reservations for two in the hotel's Silk Route restaurant and told Matt to let Murphy know, then they all took the elevator up to the top floor where they had adjoining rooms. On his way to a shower, Hawkins passed a full-length mirror. His shirt looked as if it had been trampled by a buffalo and his jeans were ripe. He called the desk clerk on the hotel phone and asked if he knew of a men's clothing store nearby.

"Yes. There's a Joseph A. Banks not far from here."

Hawkins gave the clerk a list of clothes and sizes, and said he would be very happy if he could arrange delivery in forty-five minutes. He took a long hot shower and had just wiped the shaving cream off his chin when he heard a knock at the door. It was the smiling desk clerk holding a plastic bag.

Hawkins inspected the black cashmere blazer, blue shirt and olive tan slacks to make sure they were the right size and gave the clerk a fifty dollar tip. Where he was going, Hawkins wouldn't need money.

He slipped into his new clothes and looked in the mirror again. A fashionable gentleman had replaced the scruffy figure who had stared back at him earlier. Abby called and said she was almost ready. When he knocked, she came to her door dressed in a high collar patterned black velvet shift dress with partially sheer sleeves. Black stockings showcased her long slender legs. She was modest and sexy at the same time. Except for her onyx and silver earrings, she wore no jewelry, but she didn't need any ornaments.

Hawkins eyed Abby from head to toe. "You make me look like a home insurance salesman."

She took in his muscular form that filled out the shoulders and chest of his blazer.

"Not at all. You're quite dapper. The work boots are a nice touch."

"Woods Hole chic," Hawkins explained.

He offered his arm and guided her to the elevator.

The maitre d' recognized Abby who told him that they needed a quiet table with room for two more joining them after dinner. He led them across the lavishly appointed restaurant to a table covered with a starched white cloth and set in a small section separate from the dining room.

Hawkins glanced around. "I must admit that the last time I was in this country my accommodations weren't as nice as this."

"Maybe I shouldn't have brought you here. It will be a few days before we enjoy comfort like this again."

Hawkins flashed a tight smile. "Glad you brought the subject up, Abby. I wish you'd reconsider your decision to go on the operation."

"Uh-uh. Wild horses couldn't keep me away."

"Okay, but I want you to level with me. Why?"

"Despite the flip comment I made on the plane about this being no guilt trip, I do owe you for the way I cut you loose."

"I never blamed you for walking out, Abby."

"And I don't blame you for being bitter. I could deal with your fury against the navy. But not against the world."

"I'm past my Captain Queeg phase. I understand why you left me—I was bouncing off the walls—but why did you leave the navy?"

"The navy has come a long way and I made a rank that was unthinkable not long ago. But I could have commanded a carrier, and that just wasn't going to happen."

"You would have made a terrific commander."

"Thanks for your confidence.'

"And you think by taking this mission you can show the navy that they were fools to pass you over."

"Something like that," she said, a slight smirk on her lips. "God, what a fine pair we are."

They broke into laughter that made some of the other patrons look their way. Abby had to put her napkin to her lips to stifle her mirth.

The outburst caught the attention of the waiter, who hurried over to take their order. They both opted for lamb kabobs sprinkled with sumac, *palao* rice topped with fried raisins, carrots and pistachios and served with the long thin afghan bread called *naan*. Over dinner, Hawkins reminisced about his more pleasant Afghan memories. The waiter was removing the last plate when the maitre d' escorted Calvin to their table. Murphy joined them a few minutes later.

Murphy said, "My offer about helping still stands, but you'll have to fill me in on the skinny. Like where are you headed?"

"I can't tell you everything. Let me start by asking you a question. What do you know about Amir Kahn?"

"You going into Amir Kahn's neighborhood?"

Hawkins shrugged.

Murphy pushed at the air with his big hand. "None of my business, mate, but I'll tell you what you're dealing with. Amir is probably in his late sixties now, but tough as nails. He was a non-political teacher, but became a *mujadeen* during the Soviet war. Killed lots of Russians on his own long before the CIA stuck a Stinger missile launcher in his hands. He probably turned the tide on his own from what I hear."

"What happened after the war?"

"He was wounded in action and went to the U.S. to recuperate. The CIA brought him back to fight the Taliban, but he got disgusted with both sides. He went back to his home province and started raising opium. He's one of the biggest dope producers in the country."

"You're DEA now. Have you tried to stop him?"

"Whole program is about interdiction now. Tried wiping out the poppy fields and the farmers got mad as hell. Now they grow all they want, they get paid and we plug the holes where we can. Amir is a special case."

"In what way, Murph?"

"He's related to the ruling family. Cousin or something, but still close enough to make sure there's a protective shield over his operation. On top of that, he supports a private army of about two hundred tribesmen."

"Have you ever met him?"

"Once. We were after a miserable sonovabitch who had tried to kill one of our guys. Unfortunately for him, he tried to move in on Amir's territory, which adjoined his. When I caught up with him Amir had just turned him and his men into shish kebabs. When I thanked the old bandit he just looked at me with the coldest set of eyes I'd ever seen and asked me to spread the word."

"What word?"

"He said that anyone who entered his territory without invitation would be killed on sight."

"Guess we'd best stay away from Mr. Friendly," Calvin said with a drawl.

"Wise decision. The countryside is rugged as hell. Lots of ravines, canyons, gullies. Great spots for ambushes." Murphy leaned back in his chair and looked first at Hawkins, then at Calvin. "I'd suggest that you have a guide."

Hawkins shook his head. "This was designed to be a pretty tight little operation, Murph."

"A third person shouldn't make that much difference," Murphy said.

"That would be a *fourth* person," Abby said. "I'm part of this mission, too."

Murphy stared at Abby for several seconds and took a deep breath. "Guide who knows the country will help you move faster. Otherwise, you'll spend a lot of time running around in circles."

Hawkins turned to Hayes. "What do you say, Cal? Do you have room for a fourth?"

Hayes shrugged. "Sure, if we pack the desert vehicle the right way."

"Thanks, Cal. Who is this person who knows the area so well?"

"Guy grew up around the warlord's territory. He's been working as a civilian security contractor. He knows how to handle himself. "

"Could he be ready by tomorrow?"

"Why don't you ask him yourself? He's in the lounge."

"That's a coincidence," Abby said.

"Not really. He comes here every night to make connections with the movers and shakers."

Murphy made a quick call on his cell phone. Moments later, a man wearing a dark suit and white shirt with no tie approached the table. Murphy pulled over a chair and gestured for the man to sit down.

"This is Rashid," Murphy said.

Murphy's friend was in his mid-thirties. He was short and stocky and had a friendly grin that puffed out the plump cheeks on his wide, clean-shaven face. His head was shaved as well.

Hawkins quizzed the man about his background. He answered politely in a soft-spoken voice. His English was very good. He had been born in a nearby village and moved to Kabul in his teens. After a stint in the Afghan army he was hired by a contractor to provide security to government officials. Hawkins asked Rashid if he knew about the lake.

"The Valley of the Dead? Oh yes. I lived in a village around fifty kilometers from there."

"Is there a way to get to the lake without being seen?"

"Many ways. Some better than others."

Calvin asked specific questions as to terrain features he had seen on the satellite photo, and when he was finished, he said, "Man knows his stuff."

Hawkins said, "What do you think, Abby?"

"I said the mission is yours from now on."

"I don't want to put either one of you in unnecessary danger. Looks like you're joining the team, Rashid. Meet us at four am tomorrow at the airport."

Hawkins rose from his chair to signal that the meeting was over. He thanked Murphy for his help and said he would look him up when he got back to Kabul. On the elevator ride to their floor, Calvin said that he had double-checked all their weapons and gone over their survival gear. Everything was ready.

Hawkins said he would see Cal and Abby in the morning then he wrote a quick email to Sutherland, set the alarm clock, slipped beneath the sheets and quickly fell asleep.

Murphy was in a glum mood.

He was hardly a Victorian gentleman, but he loved women. Especially pretty ones like Abby. Hell, he could hardly keep his eyes off her! After leaving the dining room he had gone into the lounge. It was hard to get a real drink in Kabul, so he carried a hip flask with him. He ordered fruit juice and spiked it with bourbon. He downed the drink and ordered another, which he also doctored. The alcohol was giving him the illusion of acute mental clarity.

He looked up from his glass into Rashid's moist brown eyes. He had hired Rashid for a number of jobs. Despite his warm manner, the guide was a cold-blooded killer whose efficiency was marred only by his sadistic penchant for torturing his victims. Especially women. Murphy figured Rashid's mother must have done a real number on him. *Oh well. Can't have everything*, Murphy thought.

Speaking in a low voice, Murphy said, "When you take care of the woman, I want you to do it fast. No hanky-panky. Make it clean. Get me?"

Rashid's friendly grin was out of synch with his words. "I'll kill her so fast she won't even know it," he whispered.

Murphy stared at the Afghan for a few seconds, then slowly nodded. "See that you do," he said.

Rashid returned the nod, slid off his stool and headed for the exit.

Murphy watched him leave then poured another stiff shot into his glass.

CHAPTER TWENTY-ONE

Islamabad, Pakistan

The Pakistani plane refueled in Paris and took off on the second leg of its long journey. The professor slept. Ate the meals served to him. Watched a couple of bad movies on the small screen. Got up to stretch and chat with the army officers about their training experiences. He stayed away from the back of the plane, using the restroom near the flight deck.

When the plane landed in Islamabad, a waiting shuttle bus picked up the passengers and dropped the officers off at the terminal. The professor and Marzak were driven a short distance to a helicopter with no markings on the fuselage.

They climbed into the helicopter and buckled up. Marzak eyed the professor's civilian clothes. "Who are you?'

"I am Saleem. I'm with the intelligence services. I believe we have mutual friends we are about to see."

Marzak raised an eyebrow, but made no reply. The professor was relieved when the engine started and the spinning rotors drowned out the possibility of conversation.

The helicopter rose above the city and headed west, flying for ninety minutes before setting down in a field where they disembarked with their luggage. The helicopter took off and left them standing there in silence until a dust-covered old Chevrolet Impala raced across the field and slowed to a stop.

The car doors opened, and three men carrying AK-47s got out. The men frisked Marzak and relieved the professor of his satellite phone, then blind-folded both men and gestured for them to get in the back of the car, squeezed tightly with a guard on either side. The professor felt the car bump along for a short while, then the ride smoothed out as they left the field for a road. Fifteen minutes later the car stopped again, and they were told to get out.

The men grabbed them by their shoulders and guided them a short distance. When their blindfolds were removed, the professor saw that they were in a windowless room furnished with a small table and three wooden chairs.

The man sitting behind the table had black hair neatly cut and parted, and a short wiry beard. He was dressed in a conservative western-style black suit and wore a white shirt and no tie.

He had small delicate hands, warm, dark eyes and a soft-spoken manner. He wore no traditional headdress, suggesting that he was urban and educated, which he confirmed when he said he that they could call him the Doctor. "I am pediatrician," he said, unnecessarily adding, "I treat children."

He told his guests to have a seat and poured glasses of tea from a pitcher.

He acknowledged Saleem with a nod of his head.

"You must be the professor." Then he looked at Marzak. "And you are the Jeweler."

The professor sensed something unspoken pass between the men. Marzak's half smile grew into a broad grin, as if he had suddenly recognized an old friend in a crowd. A chill ran down the professor's spine.

"Thank you for coming all this way," the Doctor said. "We appreciate the work on the Prophet's Necklace that you and your brother have been doing for us. I'm sorry he is not with you. Is he well?"

"No," Marzak said, with no change in expression. "He is dead."

The man's heavy mono-brow formed a V. "I am sorry to hear that. An accident?"

"In a manner of speaking. He was killed during the course of an assignment."

"By an American?"

"Yes. I'm sorry, but I'm not allowed to provide more details."

"Let me tell you something," the Doctor said. "When you first made contact and offered to serve us I thought it might be a CIA trick, even after you killed an enemy of ours to persuade us of the sincerity of your intentions. You were mercenaries, working for money, and you were not of the Faith."

"I have no faith," Marzak said.

"That is not important now. We are kin, bound together by blood. The Americans killed my brother, too," the Doctor said. "And his wife and children. The cowards sent their drone airplane to bomb their house. That is how I came to be in the Shadows. We have all had friends or family killed by the Americans. Our goal is revenge."

"A laudable goal, Doctor."

"We have watched failure after failure. The shoe bomber. The underwear bomber. Pitiful attempts by amateurs. Then came the assassination of Bin Laden. We feel that if we do not act, we will become irrelevant. Which is why we are so interested in your plan. Please bring me up to date on the necklace."

"The clasp can be connected at any time. The strands run from coast to coast. There are a half dozen beads. Each one represents a location where large numbers of people gather. An explosive device in an innocent form has been hidden in each place. When the explosive is activated, it will spread sarin over a large area. Ingestion through the lungs or skin contact will be fatal."

Sarin.

The professor folded his arms in front of him in an attempt to hide his trembling hands. He needn't have worried, because the two men were deep into a discussion of the physiological effects of the deadly chemical nerve agent. He knew that sarin was 500 times more potent than cyanide and that it worked on humans the same way bug spray killed insects, but with more horrible effects leading to death.

As a member of an elite intelligence service, the professor had been exposed to the venality of every type of human behavior, ranging from suicide bombers who killed children to political assassins who killed women. But as he sat in the small room listening to a quiet discussion of how to murder scores of people, he knew he had never before been in the presence of such evil incarnate.

"How many casualties do you estimate?" the Doctor said.

"Impossible to say, but it will keep the undertakers busy for a long while."

The Doctor closed his eyes, a beatific smile on his face, then opened them. "The simple purity of your plan is appealing. How will you trigger simultaneous explosions?"

"I will call a certain telephone number and enter a code that will activate the explosions at the same second. Just give me the signal and it will be done."

"As soon as we acquire the treasure." The Doctor stared at the professor, as if reading his thoughts. "I understand that our plans must be daunting to consider."

Saleem knew better than to lie, outright.

"They are very ambitious. I worry about people of Pakistan origin who live in the U.S. and might be harmed."

"We have considered that," the Doctor said. "Those people have gone over to the infidels. They have become one with them in life and so shall they be in death."

The professor nodded.

"But don't think we are murderers. We merely want to cripple the United States. It's like disfiguring a man's wife in front of her husband to teach him a lesson in humility. Marzak understands, don't you?"

"With crystal clarity, Doctor," Marzak said.

The professor's mouth felt as if he had eaten sand. His legs wanted to carry him far away from these two madmen, but he willed his facial muscles to show no hint of the emotions roiling inside his chest.

"Have no fear. I understand as well," he said.

"Good. Now that Marzak is here we will pursue our immediate objective."

"I have contracted for an assault team I've used in other assignments," Marzak said. "Pulling together the dive team was a little more difficult, but I have four divers with combat and salvage experience. We will have three Bell Cobra helicopters and a transport helicopter."

"What do you think?" The Doctor asked Saleem. "Enough to do the job?"

"More than enough," the professor replied. "The Cobras are devastating weapons."

"Good. An assault force made up of tribesmen has arrived at a staging area closer to the target," the Doctor said. "While the Cobras deal with Amir Kahn, your divers will go into the lake to retrieve the treasure. The Cobras will also come in handy should the American mission arrive."

"A sound military strategy," Saleem said. "Since we are footing the bill for this mission, ISI maintains operational control, but I will try to stay in the background as an observer."

"Yes, yes," the Doctor said. "I'm sure the arrangement will work out fine, aren't you, Mr. Marzak?"

Marzak said, "As long as there is no interference with military decisions."

"Of course. We owe a great deal to the ISI," the Doctor said to Saleem. "Without the intelligence service we would not have known that the Americans were sending an expedition of their own. You and the Jeweler will be our guests tonight and fly out tomorrow to an advance base."

The meeting was over.

The Doctor called in a guard to show the guests to their quarters. Saleem was glad to see that his room had a bathroom with a working shower. He stripped and turned the shower up to full. He didn't know if he could wash evil away with cold water, but he tried.

As he toweled himself dry he realized that he had fulfilled the first part of his assignment faster than he could have imagined. He had important details of the Prophet's Necklace, but without his phone he had no way to share the intelligence with his cousin. He stared at the blank walls of his room, and although he was not a religious man, he began to pray for a miracle.

CHAPTER TWENTY-TWO

A few minutes after three o'clock in the morning Hawkins and Abby watched as Calvin drove the Desert Patrol Vehicle out of a shed and pulled up to the Boeing Vertol 234 model helicopter. The civilian version of the battle-tested CH47 Chinook leased by Abby's company had tandem rotors located at the front and back of the long snub-nosed fuselage.

The temperature had dropped at least thirty degrees overnight and their breath vaporized in the cold air. They were all dressed in heavy duty beige pants and shirts, tan baseball caps and matching windbreakers over fleece sweaters. The choice of clothing had been the subject of intense discussion. They ultimately chose the civilian work clothes, hoping that they might pass for engineers or archaeologists.

Calvin got out of the DPV and he and Hawkins passed a nylon sling beneath the vehicle. The rope from the sling was attached to a single length of chain with a loop at one end.

They went over the check list to make sure they had all their gear, and that the equipment was securely tied down and protected. Abby signaled the pilot with a wave of her hand. The powerful engines roared to life and the twin rotors started spinning. The team climbed into the helicopter and settled in a row of seats next to Rashid. Abby made a point of sitting far from the guide. There was something about the man she didn't like. She had caught him staring at her breasts a few times and hadn't been flattered by the attention.

The helicopter lifted off and when it was around fifty feet in the air, it shifted sideways until it was over the Desert Patrol Vehicle. A cable was lowered to the ground crew, which attached it to the sling and a winch lifted the vehicle into the air. The helicopter rose at a slow, steady rate to keep the load from swinging wildly.

The sky was going from black to a blue-gray light that revealed the jagged snow-capped peaks of the Hindu Kush mountain range rising above the city.

The racket from the tandem engines and chop of rotors ratcheted up to an ear-shattering decibel level. Hawkins put on his headphones and motioned to their hired guide to do the same.

He unfolded a laminated map of their target area and showed the guide the landing zone he had in mind.

"That's good," Rashid said. He raised his voice even though it wasn't necessary with the headphones. "It is flat here, with low hills to hide us."

"What about the terrain between the LZ and the lake?"

"Very rugged. But there is a dry river bed that goes almost all the way to the lake like a super highway."

"Any chance of someone seeing us on this highway?" Calvin asked.

"Not much. The village and the fields are on the other side of the lake."

"What about planes?" Hawkins said. "There's an airstrip near Khan's compound."

"The planes go away from the lake, toward Iran, to smuggle drugs."

"You seem to know a lot more about this territory than its topography,"

Hawkins said.

Rashid dabbed the map with his forefinger.

"I come from a village, here. Many of the men have gone to work for the Kahn."

The helicopter gained altitude and transected the mountains through a high pass to the south, before turning in a more westerly direction and following the line of the 600-mile-long mountain range running northeast to southwest across the country. They passed over green fields, flat-roofed villages and meandering rivers, but these gentle features were rare exceptions. From the air, much of Afghanistan looked like a battlefield of the gods where unimaginable forces had collided and torn the earth's crust apart, then stitched the tectonic plates back together like an insane surgeon.

Hawkins knew from experience that there was a subterranean world beneath the hard surface of the land. Parts of the country were honeycombed with caves. Some were natural. Others had been dug by men as places to live, as religious shrines, to extract lapis lazuli, to irrigate the fields, to hide in while fighting invaders. And just maybe, one had been used to hold a fabulous treasure.

As the helicopter sped southwest at a speed of a hundred-fifty-miles per hour, the scenery below changed from mountains and valleys to hills and deserts. Hawkins had been keeping tabs on their progress using his hand-held GPS set. After about two hours of flying, he rose from his seat and went to the cockpit to talk to the crew. He returned moments later and said, "ETA is fifteen minutes."

The helicopter began a long shallow descent and eventually came to a hover above a relatively flat stretch of terrain. The lake could be seen shimmering in the distance.

The winch lowered the desert vehicle until the wheels touched the ground. The automatic hook release was activated then the helicopter moved sideways fifty feet or so and descended slowly until the landing gear thumped to the ground.

The passengers disembarked one-by-one then the door closed behind them and the helicopter was in the air again.

Hawkins and Calvin checked their weapons—Sig-Sauer 9mm pistol for Hawkins and the short-barreled CAR-15 rifle for Calvin—then while Calvin stood guard at the dune buggy, Rashid led the others to some high ground that offered a wide view of the surrounding landscape. The scenery reminded Matt of the badlands found in the southwestern U.S. Rashid said the river bed ran along the base of a low ridge of sandstone bluffs.

They heard the engine start, and then the vehicle ascended the hill and skidded to a stop.

"Going my way?" Calvin said. He had a wide grin on his face.

"You're enjoying this a little too much, Cal."

"Hey, Hawk, you've got to admit it feels good to be back in the saddle."

Hawkins glanced around at the washboard topography before he climbed onto the rear of the vehicle next to Abby.

"Okay. I'll agree with you that this is pretty exciting."

Abby brought them both down to earth.

"We'll see just how long *that* lasts," she said.

Sutherland had spent a peaceful day in her studio working on a painting of a Rufus hummingbird. When she was satisfied that the colors were right, she took a break to enjoy the sunset and a cold *Tecate*. She cooked herself some vegetarian tacos, watched the Bachelor on television and sneered at the long-legged bimbos, then headed to her office desk and booted up her computer. The first thing she saw was a message from Hawkins dated several hours before.

Sorry message delay. Landed in Kabul. Long flight. All OK. Hired guide on rec of old acquaintance Terrance Murphy. Will contact you later. Incommunicado for now. Thanks. Matt.

Sutherland read the message again.

"Crap!" she said. Her fingers flew over the keyboard.

Murphy is a snake. Check attached report.

She sat back in her chair and waited for an answer knowing it would not come. Hawkins was out of reach. She raged at the screen. She should never have been away from her computer for so long. How could she be so stupid?

Now what?

Her only weapons were her old laptop and her proficiency at using it. Matt still had his satellite phone and he said he would call. She had to assume that he'd keep his promise. She spent the next few hours compiling a report on all the information she had gathered on the links between Murphy, Trask and Arrowhead. Maybe she could get it to Hawkins before he got in too deep with this Murphy character.

She murmured a prayer and pressed the Send command.

CHAPTER TWENTY-THREE

Cait sat in her room going over the photos transferred from the camera to her computer. The photo taken deep in the shaft showed the letters J. W. carved into the timber with a date, March 11, 1920, the year Kurtz launched his expedition.

She picked up her copy of "The Emerald Sceptre" and began to read. The author, a reporter for the *Denver Post* named Wayne Valero, opened the book by quoting a letter Prester John had written to the Byzantine emperor of Rome, Manuel, in 1177 in which the Prester bragged about his wealth and power and said he had vanquished the infidels who surrounded his kingdom. Skeptics pointed to parts of the letter that said the kingdom was home to men with horns and giants who had one eye, unicorns and gryphons, places where poison would not work, and a fountain of youth. According to the letter, no one in Prester John's land could tell a lie.

Valero then went on to describe how one of the many agents Kurtz employed in his worldwide quest, while foraging in a Kabul antiquities shop, came across a fragment of a letter, written in Latin on vellum. The ragged edge suggested that it had been roughly torn from a scroll. Drawn on the back of the vellum were some child-like squiggles. The letter appeared to be from Prester John. This discovery had been the catalyst for Kurtz's Prester John expedition.

The author had dogged the trail that led Kurtz to Afghanistan. His persistence paid off. He found a journalist's dream: a reliable source in the widow of an expedition archaeologist who had died at sea on the return trip. She let the reporter see papers her husband had compiled before the expedition.

The archaeologist had submitted the vellum scrap to experts who dated it to the 12th century. The same tests that verified its ancient origin led to another interesting discovery. The squiggles had been drawn in human blood. The archaeologist had copied down the message on a separate sheet of paper:

"I-John the priest, by the might and strength of God, our Lord Jesus Christ, King of earthly kings, and Lord of lords, sends to him that stands in the place of God, namely, the Ruler of Rome, through thy messenger, by the wonted munificence of our bounty, twenty casks of precious stones and gold, and this gift, in my name, so that we may strengthen ourselves mutually in our power turn by turn...."

The mention of a special gift sent Valero back to the origin of the Prester John legend in a letter written by Otto, bishop of Freisingen, who in 1145 met with a Syrian bishop. The Syrian told him about a Christian king and priest known as Presbyter John, whose kingdom lay beyond Persia and Armenia. John belonged to a Christian sect known as Nestorians and had defeated the infidels in a number of battles. He was supposedly descended from the Magi, was rich beyond belief, and used as the emblem of his power and wealth an emerald scepter.

Valero heard an echo of Otto's report in the Prester's vellum letter to the Pope: What better gift to show a willingness to share power but the fabled scepter? Or did the scepter symbolize a gift even more valuable than gold and gems: an alliance to fight the Muslim infidels?

The archaeologist's widow told Valero that one of Kurtz's historic researchers had found a clue in an old map of caravan routes that had an X labeled *Itmud*. The archaeologists nicknamed the site "It's mud" after the expedition visited the place and found a cluster of tall tower-like geological formations like those known as 'hoo-doos' in the southwestern United States. The researchers would have dismissed the map as a fake, except that the name *Itmud* meant pillar.

Intrigued by the coincidence, the researchers dug at the site and found artifacts that indicated *Itmud* may have been a trading post or a caravan stop. The map showed a dotted line leading across the desert to a valley vaguely shaped like a figure eight.

Cait skimmed through the next part of the book. Kurtz travels to the valley and discovers it full of water. Its shape matches the drawing on the back of the vellum signed by the Prester. He orders in dive equipment. The diver goes into the lake where the diagram indicates there should be a cave opening, but for some reason can't find it. Kurtz sinks a mine shaft below the odd rock formation. The shaft collapses and traps the diver.

The story ended with the tragic loss of Kurtz's archaeological crew in the sinking of one of his vessels on the return trip to the States. The rest of the book was pure speculation, with Valero postulating that Kurtz found the treasure, but it was likely lost with his ship.

Cait set the book down and reflected on what she had read, but a knock at the door pulled her thoughts back to the present. It was Amir.

"The family missed you at lunch," he said. "Especially the little one. They sent me to make sure you are coming to dinner."

"I'm sorry," she said. "I've been reviewing materials and forgot about the time. Look at this."

Amir stepped into the guest quarters, settled his long body into a chair and studied the photo on the computer screen. Cait pointed out the date of the expedition and described her theory about the mine being built because the treasure trove was not accessible from the lake.

He rubbed his beard. "Not an implausible theory, but as you discovered, the mine shaft is too dangerous to explore."

"Even dead ends are informative. Building a mine shaft is neither easy nor cheap. It tells me that Kurtz believed that there was a treasure."

"Do you think he found it?"

It was Cait's turn to rub her chin. "I don't know. But I'm determined to track it down."

Amir gazed at Cait with amusement in his dark eyes. "It seems that Mr. Kurtz is not the only one obsessed with Prester John."

"I prefer to think of it as a passion. Do you blame me?"

"Not at all. The Prester is a fascinating historical figure."

"Agreed, but no one has been able to prove that John even *existed*. My goal now is to find the rest of the vellum. Then I might be able to backtrack to the Prester's kingdom. Maybe I can locate his tomb! Even if I don't, I could be on the trail of the historical and archaeological discovery of the century."

"I will do all I can to help you, Dr. Cait. Where do you go from here?"

"Back to the beginning. Prester John."

"We're talking millions of square miles spread over several countries."

"This will be a journey in *time* rather than distance. We know the Pope sent his physician Philip east to deliver a letter to Prester John, so I went into the Vatican data base. I went through every link I could find on Pope Alexander and Master Philip. Let me show you something I turned up in my research."

She brought a letter with graceful handwriting onto the screen.

"What is it?"

"The Vatican archives had a fragment of a note, written from Philip in Jerusalem, dated 1177 *anno domini*. It was a bill which asked for papal reimbursement of expenses to Philip's bank in Rome:

"For the knight Thomas and entourage and the caravan master. I will keep a journal of further expenses and their source as they occur. Magister Phillipis."

"This proved that Philip had intentions to leave Jerusalem," Amir observed. "Who is this Thomas?"

"I wish I knew. My immediate challenge is to find Philip's journal. I need to do more research before I go back into the field. There are sources all over the world. Libraries and archives in Rome, Vienna, Paris, London and the U.S."

"Then you have made a decision to leave us?"

"Tomorrow, if possible."

"Yes, of course. I'm sorry your visit is so short. My family is quite attached to you."

"I like them, too. But I will return. I can never repay you for your hospitality and help"

"I'm the one who is in your debt, Dr. Cait. If Prester John hadn't brought you here, my granddaughter would not have lived."

Cait stared off into space. "I'm not a superstitious person, and as a historian I deal in facts, but when you study events and people over thousands of years, it's amazing how things seem to fall into place, as if they had been pre-ordained. There have been times when Prester John seems to be calling me to find him."

"Grandfather!"

They exchanged glances and started laughing.

"It seems that Prester John has the voice of a very impatient four-year-old girl," Amir said.

Cait sat cross-legged on the living room floor after dinner, engaged in an intense game of patty-cake with Amir's granddaughter. She happened to look up and noticed that the drug lord, seated in his chair, was gazing thoughtfully in her direction.

Then Amir said something in *Pashto* to the little girl, who responded with a pout that was vanquished with the offer of a sweet pastry. The little girl gave her grandfather a peck on the cheek, came over and planted a wet kiss on Cait's face, and ran off into the next room. The scene was so affecting that Cait forgot for a moment that the kindly grandfather was a hardened drug lord.

She rose to her feet.

"Thank you," she said in a breathless voice that was only partially exaggerated. "I was becoming patty-caked to exhaustion."

"Yasmeen has more energy than a young colt." He affixed her with his eagle-like gaze. "So, Dr. Cait, you still plan to leave tomorrow?"

"Yes, if I can prevail upon you to fly me out in the morning."

"I'll call the plane back from Kabul. But perhaps I can persuade you to stay another day. My granddaughter is going to miss you."

"I'll miss her, too. But my mind is set on my research. If you'll excuse me, I've got to start packing."

"Before you go to your room, I have something to show you that may be of interest."

He patted his shirt like an absent-minded professor, pulled some four-by-five inch photographs out of his pocket and handed them over.

Cait fanned the photos out on the table top.

"This picture shows an ancient bread mold," she said. "This looks like a baking oven. This photo shows ash from a fire. This oval piece is a stone name seal." She looked up from the pile. "Where were these pictures taken, Amir?"

"The objects were found at some ruins not far from the village."

He slid more pictures across the table. Cait studied the images. Most people would have seen only a maze of rectangular pits and open spaces, but in her mind's eye, Cait saw a *caravanserai.*

The high walls of the caravan stop enclosed an open space that in ancient times would have been a crowded bazaar ringed by apartments to lodge weary traders, storage space for their precious goods, and stables to house camels and other beasts of burden.

"Who took these?"

"*I* did. I'm no photographer, as you can see by the poor quality."

"Where are the objects now?"

"I've heard that the provenance of artifacts is important to an archaeologist so I left them in situ until the time the ruins can be examined professionally. I've warned the locals to stay away from the site."

"Where are the ruins in relation to the lake?"

"About twenty miles to the east."

The site was between Itmud and the Valley of the Dead. Trying to keep excitement from coloring her voice, she said, "I don't recall you mentioning these ruins before."

"Forgive me. You seemed to be focused on the old mine near the lake, and I didn't want to distract you. It's a shame that you are leaving so soon," he said with a sigh. "Perhaps you can see the ruins on your next visit. Although to my untrained eye, there is nothing there of any importance."

Amir did his best to wreath his weathered features in innocence, but it was impossible for him to mask the cunning that lurked behind the intelligent eyes. Cait wasn't fooled. The Kahn was using the ruins as bait to keep her there.

"Hard to tell much about the site from these photos. It might be a trading post or caravan stop. On the other hand, it might be part of a major settlement."

"You think that these ruins could be part of an abandoned city?"

"It's possible. Which is the reason the site is not on the caravan stop map Kurtz found. And if that's true, they could be an important piece of the Prester John puzzle."

"In what way, Dr. Cait?" He leaned forward, giving her his full attention.

"This would have been a logical place for the caravan carrying the treasure to have stopped. They would have tried to keep their presence low key, but someone might have made note of their passing through. It might be something as ordinary as a bill for supplies, but it would strengthen the foundation underlying my theory."

"Then it's done," Amir said. "You will visit the ruins tomorrow."

Cait admired the way the Kahn closed the deal. Her chances of finding evidence of Prester John in one day were slim, but historical research was like plucking at a strand of yarn and unraveling the whole sweater.

"I wouldn't want to put you to any trouble. I know how busy you are."

"No trouble at all. I shall be away tomorrow. Some of my men will take you there."

"Thank you." She smiled. "Any other ruins you have forgotten to tell me about?"

He spread his hands wide, palms up. "The sands are always shifting. One can never know what mystery lies beneath their surface until they reveal themselves. "

"No different than people," Cait observed.

Amir must have known that he was the target of her wry wit, because he confirmed the accuracy of her comment by widening his lips in a mysterious smile.

CHAPTER TWENTY-FOUR

The intruders came in the night.

Sutherland had slept a few hours only to wake up before dawn. She got out of bed and shuffled to her office like a sleep-walker, sat at her desk and booted up her computer. No message from Hawkins. She frowned. Then her sleepy eyes snapped open like window shades at the sound of her security alarm.

Bong-bong. Bong-bong.

Her security system was warning that an intruder had entered the motion detection zone. She had installed a camera at each roof corner and another at the old ranch to warn her of Border Patrol raids. The feeds came through on the seventy-two inch television screen mounted on the wall. The ranch camera had picked up the image of shadowy figures emerging from an SUV that was dark-colored, not white and green like Border Patrol vehicles.

And the figures moving toward the house wore black uniforms instead of Border Patrol khaki.

The intruders stirred up every paranoid fear Sutherland had ever encountered. She began to hyperventilate and tremble uncontrollably. Reminding herself that she was not completely defenseless, she began to get control of her emotions and silently scolded herself:

Don't be a victim. *Act.*

She reached for the phone, put in a call to 911 and reported that she had seen prowlers around the house.

"Illegals?" the dispatcher said.

"I don't know. It's dark."

"I'll call the Border Patrol and send a cruiser."

"How long?"

"Soon as possible. Keep your doors and windows locked."

Sutherland frowned at the lame advice and hung up. It would take at least fifteen minutes for anyone to reach her remote house, and during that time she would be on her own.

She looked at the monitor again. The intruders were close enough to be picked up by a camera on the front of the roof. They were approaching the electrified fence around the house. The power running through the wire strands would only give a small jolt if touched. She hadn't wanted the bodies of dead illegal immigrants or wildlife piling up outside the fence. But she had installed a switch that would allow her to ramp up power to deadly levels.

The figures were standing in a line in front of the fence, looking at the house. There were six of them, and they were carrying long-barreled weapons. One approached the fence. She increased the power level and an instant later saw a flash of light, like an insect hitting a bug zapper.

An outside microphone picked up a yell of pain. She dampened the power down until the figure fell away from the fence, then she increased it to near lethal levels again.

A couple of the intruders grabbed the limp form of the failed fence-climber and dragged it back down the trail leading to the ranch. She saw the figures get into the SUV. Then the headlights flashed on and the vehicle began to climb to the house. Moving fast.

The electronic barrier wasn't built to withstand a battering ram on wheels. The SUV crashed through the fence in a shower of sparks and slammed into the front door smashing it to splinters.

She snatched up her laptop, shoved it into a rucksack, raced down the hall and ducked into a walk-in closet. She shoved aside the hanging clothes and pushed a hidden wall button. A two-foot-wide section of shoe shelves slid open and a light switch went on automatically. She slipped through the opening into a small room and bolted the door.

Sutherland had installed the room after seeing Jody Foster fend off a gang of home invaders in the movie *Panic Room*. The chamber had eight-inch-thick steel-reinforced concrete walls, a first aid kit, food and water, a phone, cot and porta-potty. There was a chest with fresh sets of clothing and underwear.

She whipped off her pajamas and changed into jeans and sweat-shirt, keeping her eyes glued to the television screen that connected the room to cameras inside the house.

Masked figures in Ninja type uniforms burst into the house over the wreckage of the shattered front door. Caps were pulled down over their heads. The intruders searched every room, communicating with military hand signals. When they didn't find her, they gathered in the studio.

She grabbed a phone from its wall hanger and called 911 again.

The dispatcher's neutral voice said, "Hold on. A unit is on its way."

"Tell them to watch their ass. These guys have guns."

"What—?"

She clicked off and turned back to the screen. She guessed that the fence jumper must still be recuperating from shock because there were only five figures. One apparently noticed the camera high in a corner. He stared at it for a few seconds and pulled his scarf away from his lower face. There was something strangely familiar about the lopsided mouth and the yellow-toothed grin.

No. It couldn't be.

The man picked up her new painting of the hummingbird from the easel. He stepped nearer the camera, drew his arm back and punched a ragged hole in the canvas with his gloved fist. He looked at the camera again, as if daring her to come out of hiding to save her precious art work. She watched, frustrated and angry, as the other intruders ruined paintings with fists or knives and threw them into a heap.

The leader poured the contents of a can of paint thinner on the pile. He produced a lighter and snapped the flame on. He moved the lighter back and forth near the paintings, smiling all the while at the camera.

Then he touched the lighter to the pile which burst immediately into flames.

Sutherland shrieked in a voice that was part sob and part a scream of rage.

They're burning my art.

But there was nothing she could do except watch as greasy smoke filled the room and the flames spread to the curtains and consumed the easel and palette table. The intruders hastily exited the burning house.

Choking fumes were seeping into the safe room.

Sutherland hit the kill switch for the ventilation system and tried to decide what to do. Maybe the room would be safe from the fire. Maybe it wouldn't be. She wasn't going to stick around to find out.

She grabbed a flashlight from a wall bracket, then bent over and lifted a ring on the floor of the room, opening a rectangular hatch. A short stairway led down into a tight space.

A musty smell greeted her when she unlocked a steel door that guarded a tunnel. She took a deep breath and crawled fifty feet into the tunnel to another steel door, which she pushed open, emerging into another small space.

She groped for a handle above her head, found it, pushed open a hatch cover, and climbed out of the tunnel into the pump house located on the other side of the fence.

The flashlight beam played on the shiny black paint and gold scrollwork of a Harley-Davidson motorcycle resting on its kick stand next to the pump. As a young woman, she had ridden bikes back in West Virginia, and had become pretty good at it. She used her mustering out pay to buy the customized Forty-Eight model Harley. The low-slung motorcycle was built for speed rather than comfort, but she liked the retro design, low profile and the kick from its 1203-cc V-twin engine.

She slipped into leather boots and pulled on a light black leather jacket from a locker, then opened the pump house door a few inches. She let out a soft cry. Her dream house was fully enveloped in fire and her RAV4 had been torched as well. Dark figures moved against the flaming backdrop.

She had intended to wait out the intruders, but one figure had broken away from the group and was walking toward the pump house. She'd be trapped.

She swung a leg over the seat of the Harley and hit the starter. The distinctive guttural roar of the motor was ear-shattering in the close confines of the pump house and the exhaust fumes filled her nostrils. She flicked the headlight on and twisted the handle grip. The bike leaped forward and the front tire knocked the door wide open.

She popped out and headed straight for the figure in black twenty feet away. She aimed right for his crotch. He stepped aside in panic, avoiding the oncoming Harley, but Sutherland heard a satisfying yelp of pain when the handlebar slapped his mid-section.

She held the handlebars tight to keep from losing control and gunned the engine, steering to the top of the long dirt driveway that led to the road. She could feel the heat from the blaze and heard what sounded like corn popping. Gunshots. She snapped her lights off, but knew that she was still a clear target in the light of the flames. She ducked her head low over the handlebars.

Sutherland knew every turn in the driveway and made it down to the road in seconds. The bike gained speed, flying along the winding country road at nearly seventy miles an hour. She slowed at the highway on-ramp, unsure whether to head north or south.

A line of blinking lights could be seen headed south from the direction of Green Valley. The police must have called in reinforcements. She killed the Harley's lights and pulled off the road.

Two police cars and a border patrol SUV went racing by. She rode out onto the highway heading south. The cool desert air felt good on her heated forehead. She was pushing the bike at the top of its limits, when it dawned on her that she had no idea where she was going. Ahead of her was the Mexican border. Nogales. Back the other way was Phoenix.

After riding a few more miles she turned off the highway and headed southeast.

When she arrived in Tombstone, the tourists were still in bed and it was too early for the stage coach rides or the reenactment of the gunfight at the OK Corral site. She passed the office of the Tombstone *Epitaph*, and cruised past the old brothel and gambling house known as the Bird Cage back in Wyatt Earp's day. The rumble of the motorcycle exhaust echoed off the false-front old buildings.

A coffee shop was opening its doors. Inside were a couple of people in 1800s costumes who worked for the western shows. No one seemed bothered by the young woman biker with the dirty face and the wild look in her eyes. She cleaned the dirt off her pudgy cheeks and her hands in the bathroom and when she came out, bought a large coffee and blueberry muffin. She felt better after a few sips of coffee. But she was still in shock over the destruction of her house.

It was no coincidence that the attack came within twenty-four hours of her internet fishing expedition.

She remembered the squared mouth and gapped front teeth of the leader as he prepared to destroy the first painting. He had deliberately exposed his face.

As impossible as it seemed, she had to accept the evidence of her own eyes.

This was not the first time the gapped-toothed man had violated her.

A glazed expression came to her eyes.

Someone was going to pay for this.

And she knew exactly who it would be.

CHAPTER TWENTY-FIVE

The river bed wasn't quite the superhighway Rashid had described.

The pock-marked wash wound its way between lofty red cliffs and a steep rock-studded ridge. It was paved with loose stones for several miles before the old river bottom turned to sand and gravel. Calvin was eager to use the extra horsepower he had added to the DPV's engine. When the wheels rolled onto the smoother surface, he kicked the vehicle up to a higher speed.

His lead foot almost caused a disaster.

The vehicle skittered around a blind curve. A boulder that had broken off from the cliffs lay directly in the buggy's path. The rock was about six feet across and stuck out only a foot or so from the ground. It was shaped like an iceberg, with a sharp peak at the top that could have easily ripped through the vehicle's underside.

The DPV was going too fast to stop. Calvin jerked the steering wheel in a half turn then yanked it back the other way to keep from smashing into an even bigger rock. The vehicle was top-heavy from the weight of equipment and passengers but somehow defied the laws of physics and stayed upright throughout the tight S-turn.

Calvin mashed the brake pedal and brought the vehicle to a halt. He glanced in his rear-view mirror. Hawkins and Abby were still perched on top of the submersible. They would have been thrown from the vehicle if Hawkins had not tied a nylon rope around the cargo rack for a hand hold.

"Sorry about the slalom run," Calvin said. "Everyone okay back there?"

Hawkins rubbed his neck. "Nothing like whiplash to get the blood rushing. Yeah, I'm fine. How about you, Abby?"

Abby removed her baseball cap. Wild strands of hair dangled over her forehead. She swore with the gusto of an angry pirate and slapped the cap against her knee, sending up a cloud of dust that triggered a coughing fit.

Hawkins handed her a canteen. "I'll translate Abby's answer, Cal. She wants to say how happy she is to have ignored my advice and volunteered for this mission."

Abby gulped down water and then thrust the canteen back.

"Screw you, Hawkins!"

Her abrupt answer triggered another round of coughing. Hawkins handed back the canteen and advised everyone to take a stretch. He slipped off the back of the vehicle, used the "do-rag" around his head to wipe the dust from his eyes and checked the bungee straps holding the submersible in place. Fido seemed happily nestled in its bed of plastic foam.

Hawkins craned his neck to examine the face of the hill across from the cliffs. It was around eighty feet high, rising at a forty-five degree angle from the river bed. He asked Calvin to keep an eye on the vehicle, giving an almost imperceptible jerk of his head toward Rashid who sat on the ground with his back to a tire, lighting a cigarette.

"Let's go for a walk, Abby."

Hawkins went to the base of the slope, wrapped his hands around a rocky knob, stuck his toe into a horizontal crack in the rock face and began to climb up the steep hill. The bolts that held his shattered left leg together worked well enough, but his joints tended toward stiffness, even in the dry Afghan climate. The cuts on his hand were healing but his palm was still tender.

He could have sent Calvin up the hill, but he didn't want to admit to the slightest weakness, especially in front of Abby. He took his time, and although his progress was neither fast nor graceful, it was steady.

Abby had competition knotted into every strand of her DNA. She'd excelled in school sports, including traditional male ones like hockey, and had racked up an impressive record as an honor roll student. She continued to strive for first place as she blazed her way through Annapolis, and quickly advanced through the naval ranks after graduation. So it was natural for her to attempt to catch up with Hawkins and beat him to the top of the ridge.

She placed her right foot firmly on a rock outcropping, intending to use the hard muscles of her thigh to vault her body and outstretched arm closer to a hand-hold that was at the extreme end of her reach. She would have floated up the side of the steep hill like a milkweed seed if she had not glanced up at Hawkins.

His right leg and arms were strong, but the injuries to his left leg put him at a disadvantage. When his left foot slipped off a rock the stiffness in his leg prevented him from a quick save. He lost his footing, and dug his fingers into the gravel. Only a Herculean effort prevented him from slipping back down to Abby's level.

She stopped climbing and held her breath as she watched Hawkins pull himself higher, remembering his steely determination when he was recovering from his physical and psychological wounds. There was no self-pity, but she had been hurt by his refusal to ask for her help. She realized later that what he really needed was not a helping hand, but understanding. When he'd unleashed his anger against the navy, she went on the defensive. After all, she was facing difficulties enough as a woman in the navy and didn't need a husband attacking the institution that was going to be her life.

Only after their divorce and her decision to leave the navy could she admit to herself that she simply wasn't there for him in his time of need. That's why she wasn't quitting on him now. She'd been kidding herself, saying that she had signed on to cure Matt of his obsession, but the real reason, despite her disclaimer on the flight from the U.S.A., was to expunge her guilt. She was in this mission to the very end.

She saw that Matt had almost reached the top of the ridge. She took a deep breath and began to climb.

Hawkins helped her up the last few feet. Abby puffed out her cheeks and leaned on his shoulder.

"You're a hard act to follow."

Hawkins knew the gesture and comment were subtle attempts to cloak his obvious physical limitations. He didn't know whether to be angry or pleased, so he changed the subject.

"Impressive, isn't it?" he said.

"That's an understatement. It looks so....tortured."

The satellite photos and the contour lines on the chart hadn't done the surrounding countryside justice. The cool air was clear as fine crystal and as far as the eye could see, the landscape was creased and furrowed with ravines and gullies. In the distance, painfully sharp peaks raked the clear blue sky.

Abby said in an awestruck voice, "I think the chopper made a mistake and landed us on Mars."

"We're looking at what happens when continents collide. You get jumbled up pieces of tectonic crust separated by fault zones. The bedrock under Afghanistan is like a big jigsaw puzzle."

She raised an eyebrow. "You never cease to impress, Hawkins. Was geology part of your SEAL training?"

"*Survival* was. If you plan to stay alive in unfriendly country it helps to know the territory above *and* below the surface, especially if you're chasing the bad guys in tunnels and caves." He turned away from the panorama and looked into her face. "Sorry about the translation wisecrack, Abby."

"*Don't* be. I'm a big girl and shouldn't be whining because my hair gets all mussed up."

"Your hair looks fine. Just to set the record straight, and for what it's worth, I'm glad you came along."

"Coming from you, it's worth a *lot*." She glanced down the hill at Rashid. "Can't say the same for Ali Babba down there. Guy's creepy smile gives me the shivers."

Hawkins too had taken an instinctive dislike of Rashid. The guide's sly expression and fawning manner made Hawkins uneasy, but he had said nothing because as the leader of the mission he had to support unit cohesion.

"So he's not exactly Mr. Personality, but he was right about the old river bed," he said with a sweep of his arm. "If we had tried to go cross-country we'd have fallen into a deep hole."

"This isn't much better," Abby grumbled.

"In my experience, there's no beating first-hand knowledge."

He started to make his way down the hill with Abby following. Back on level ground, they went over to where Calvin was leaning against the desert vehicle.

"How far have we gone, Cal?"

"Around eight miles from the LZ. *Pitiful.*"

"Two and a half miles an hour isn't going to get us far," Hawkins said. "Let's light a fire under our rent-a-guide." He walked around the vehicle. "Looks like you were right about the river bed being the only way to go, Rashid."

The Afghan spread his lips in an I-told-you-so smile and went to light another cigarette, but Hawkins took the pack from his hand and tucked it back into Rashid's vest pocket. The guide's surprised expression turned to a glower when Hawkins ordered him to give up his seat to Abby and sit on the back.

"I can direct the way better from the front."

Hawkins pointed out that since the river bed was the only navigable route, there was no need to sit up front. "I'll keep you company," he offered.

Rashid made no further protest, but Hawkins noticed the fleeting expression of hatred in the man's eyes. All the more reason to keep close watch on him.

They started off again. Miraculously, the road improved after a mile or so. Fewer boulders blocked their path, and those they did encounter were smaller. Sand had washed down from the cliffs and covered most of the obstacles.

Calvin cautiously picked up speed. The DPV flew along at around forty miles per hour, but that ended when Calvin shouted a warning.

"Everybody hold on!"

He touched the brakes to avoid throwing the vehicle into a spin and brought them to a skidding stop. Hawkins slid off the back of the vehicle. He came around to the front and saw that a massive section of cliff had fallen into the riverbed forming a twenty-foot landslide of earth and rocks that blocked their way as effectively as a castle wall.

Hawkins turned to Rashid who had also dismounted to see why they were stopped.

"Our super highway could use some maintenance work," Hawkins said.

"This is new since I was here," Rashid said. He sounded genuinely nonplussed.

"How long ago was that, Rash?" Calvin said in his slow, Louisiana drawl.

"Maybe ten years," Rashid said.

"You know another way out of here?" Hawkins said.

Rashid answered with a vigorous shake of his bald head. "We have to turn around."

Abby batted Hawkins' earlier words back at him, "Like they say, there's nothing like local know-how."

Hawkins shrugged. "Actually, sometimes there *is* something better."

He removed the GPS unit from its dashboard holder and retrieved the topographical map that had been tucked in between the front seats. The GPS had been developed for the U.S. military. Unlike the commercial sets available in any electronics store, the GPS did not display a map, nor did it have a woman's voice telling the driver when to turn. It was used to plot how to get to grid locations on a separate paper map.

Hawkins unrolled the map and spread it out on the engine compartment. The combination map and satellite photo showed the meandering river bed had once been fed by a number of tributaries.

"This is a dendritic river drainage system," Hawkins said. "It's fed by all these tributaries that look like the branches of a tree. We're on one of these feeders now. If we get off this riverbed, and connect with another branch we can follow it to the trunk of the tree, which is the main river and leads into the flood plain where the lake is located."

Abby swept her arm around in an arc. "Too bad we can't *fly* out of here."

"You were in the regular navy too long, Abby. We SEALs don't see problems. We see *challenges*. Isn't that right, Cal?"

"Bigger the better, Hawk." He wrinkled his brow. "So what are we going to do, man?"

Hawkins shook his head. "Damned if *I* know."

Seeing she was being taken for a ride, Abby said, "This is great. Stuck out here in the wilds of Afghanistan with an all-boy act from Comedy Central." She spun on her heel. "I'm going to have breakfast. You two geniuses can let me know when you figure it out. Hopefully, before it gets dark."

She brushed by Rashid, got back into the dune buggy and started munching on a power bar.

"Lady's got a point," Calvin said.

"She doesn't understand that our boyish bantering has a purpose."

"Yeah. Gives us some stall time while we figure things out."

"Exactly."

Hawkins reached for the nylon line on the back of the desert vehicle. He started to wind it into a butterfly coil that could be carried hands-free. Calvin guessed what Hawkins had in mind. The two men had worked as a team so many times that they knew instinctively what the other was thinking and had an iron-bound trust in each other's judgment. They could joke about their situation because he knew, from past experience, that they would always come up with a solution. The scheme might be shaky, hastily improvised, risky and heavily dependent on good fortune, but at least it would be a *plan*.

Hawkins pointed to the hill. "I'd appreciate it if you could do the honors, Cal. We gimps don't do well on near vertical surfaces."

Cal took the coiled rope and tied the free ends around his body like the straps of a backpack. He scaled the hillside and disappeared over the top of the ridge, then popped out again. He waved down and called Hawkins on the hand radio,

"Looks like a go."

Hawkins got in the desert vehicle and drove it to face the slope. He got out and Calvin tossed the rope down. He tied the line to a loop in the Kevlar cable wound around a motorized drum on the front of the dune buggy, and then worked the winch controls. As the drum turned, Calvin pulled the cable up by the rope and vanished over the ridge a second time. He reappeared and called down on the radio.

"Ready, Hawk."

Hawkins turned to Abby, who was still in the passenger seat. "You may want to get out of the buggy."

She stared at Hawkins. "You're not really going to try this."

"We have no choice, Abby. It will be dark in a few hours. Our mission is to find the treasure. Going back is not an option."

Abby had often seen the stubborn set of Hawkins' jaw when they were still man and wife. Any attempt to dissuade him would be like waving a feather at a charging bull.

Hawkins got in the driver's seat, started the engine, threw the transmission into neutral, beeped the horn once to give Calvin a head's up, and activated the winch.

The front wheels rose a few inches off the ground. When the tires were about a foot in the air, he gave the winch more power. The wheels touched the side of slope and began to climb. Soon, the rear wheels were on the rock as well.

Hawkins kept a tight grip on the steering wheel, shifted into low and applied enough pressure to the accelerator to take the strain off the cable. The vehicle proceeded to inch its way up the slope, getting delayed only once when it got hung up on a half-buried rock, and twenty minutes later it was resting on top of the ridge. Hawkins got out and Calvin slapped him on the back.

"Well done, Hawk. Didn't know if she was going to make it."

Hawkins grunted his thanks and walked across to the other side of the ridge past the tall boulder used to anchor the cable. The rocky ground sloped down at a gradual angle for several hundred feet to a dry stream bed about half the size of the one they had been on. But clear of rock slides.

Calvin tossed the nylon line down to Abby. She handed the free end to Rashid, told him to tie it round his chest and to start climbing.

"I can't do it," he said.

"You *have* to do it or I'll leave you here alone," she said.

"But I'm your guide. You can't leave me."

"*Try* me," she said, reaching for the line.

He saw that she was serious and wrapped the rope around his chest. He began to climb, only to lose his balance. The men at the other end of the rope had no choice but to drag him up the hill on his belly.

The rope came down again. Abby held onto it and expertly walked her way up. She took a perverse pleasure seeing the front of Rashid's clothes were torn and soiled with dirt.

She grinned at the scowling guide. "I *told* you that you could do it."

She went over to where Hawkins stood, peering through a pair of binoculars.

"Pardon me for doubting you," Abby said. "You were great."

Hawkins handed over his glasses. "That may have been the *easy* part. The area we saw on the map looks a little different up close and personal."

Abby raised the binoculars and her eyes swept the parched maze of deep fissures and gullies spread out before them.

"Dear God," she whispered. "This must rank with the worst places in the world."

He put his arm around her and said, "Look on the bright side."

"*What* bright side?"

"At least there won't be any traffic jams."

Hawkins was forced to eat his words as their journey progressed. There was no traffic, but they had to navigate a bewildering labyrinth of intersecting gullies and washes that ate up precious time.

"Damn!" Abby said. "I'm starting to feel like a lab rat in a maze!"

"You just read my mind." Hawkins had taken over the driving while Abby navigated. He steered around a pothole big enough to swallow the city of Chicago.

The corners of Abby's lush mouth tweaked up in a bemused smile. "My psychic talents must be a hold-over from our married days."

"You could actually read my mind back then?"

"It's a talent wives develop. They can read their husbands like a book."

"My mind must have been like a Stephen King novel. Hope I didn't give you any nightmares."

"God, no, Matt! That was the problem. Toward the end, I never knew *what* you were thinking."

"Neither did I."

CHAPTER TWENTY-SIX

It was dusk when they popped out of the maze two hours later.

They exited the river system and were at the edge of the coastal plain. Hawkins called a halt among a cluster of car-size boulders that would shield the light from their campfire and offer a good defensive position if necessary. He inspected the vehicle's side and rear racks. Some of the containers had shifted position from the constant jostling.

"We'll stay here for the night and move out at dawn," Hawkins said. "What's the quartermaster serving for dinner?"

"We are in for a treat, monsieur," Calvin said.

He opened a box labeled Meal, Ready-To Eat, the operational food ration for the U.S. military, and passed out the packages inside. The MREs were warmed up in water-activated flameless heaters. Soon the fragrance of beef stew and spaghetti floated on the night air. There was little conversation as the famished travelers devoured their dinner.

Rashid sat apart from the others. As he ate his dinner he thought about how he would carry out his assignment. He had deliberately led the group into the river bed, thinking that it would be a good place to kill his companions and dispose of their bodies. He had their trust initially, but their mocking tone showed that they were more wary of him now.

He burned with a simmering anger that could only be extinguished by killing the two men. The hell with Murphy's order to make Abby's death a quick one. He would take his time with the woman, before putting an end to her life, too. His anger was stoked as he listened to their murmurings and laughter, adding fuel to the fire burning in his gut and loins.

Hawkins broke away from the others, who split up and disappeared between boulders on opposite sides of the campfire. He came over and said, "We're organizing the watch, and could use your help, Rashid. Calvin and Abby will take the first two-hour shift while we get some rest. Then it'll be our turn."

Rashid could have shouted with joy. They thought he was simply an incompetent guide. Soon they would learn he was a competent assassin.

"Yes, of course," Rashid said. "I would be glad to help. Perhaps I can make amends for my errors."

"No hard feelings, Rashid. An op wouldn't be an op if something didn't go wrong."

Hawkins had to move some of the supplies off the cargo racks to get at the sleeping bags. He stacked them neatly in a pile, planning to reload the buggy in daylight. He came back and tossed a sleeping bag to Rashid. Then he stretched another bag on the ground near the fire, zipped himself into it and was soon fast asleep.

When Abby's shift was over, she tapped Hawkins on the shoulder to wake him up. He crawled out into the cold night air. She slid into the sleeping bag.

"Thanks for warming it up for me, Matt." She zipped it shut and closed her eyes.

Calvin roused Rashid and took his place in the bag. "See you in two hours," he said.

Hawkins walked around a boulder and told Rashid to keep his eyes open and his ears cocked. He gave him a light stick and told him to wave it if he needed help. Then he walked back to where Abby had been standing watch. He found a rock roughly the size and shape of a sofa to lean against. It was better than standing, but not so comfortable that he would fall asleep on it.

His thick mane of hair was no match for the cold. He pulled a woolen cap down on his head. The stars were popping out of the heavens like rhinestones on velvet. He used to call the sight Broadway Sky back in his navy days. He always had a hard time reconciling the celestial beauty above his head with the death and destruction on earth.

He began to work out the plans for the next day. They would get underway at first light and should make it to the shores of the lake by mid-day. They would send the submersible down to sniff around, and follow up with a dive the next morning.

The following day they would come home, treasure or not.

A half hour passed and he saw a luminescent blue blur. Rashid had cracked the light stick and was waving it.

Hawkins blinked his flashlight and started toward the guide's position, walking in a wide circle around the sleeping bags so as not to disturb their occupants.

As he neared the guide, Hawkins whispered, "What's up, Rashid?"

"I thought I heard something moving."

Hawkins guessed that the guide had been spooked by a rabbit, but he drew his pistol, stepped past him and squinted into the darkness, his ears attuned to the slightest sound. He heard nothing. Not even the buzz of insects.

"Where?" he said.

"Off to the left," the guide's voice rasped in his ear. "There it is. Again. *Closer*."

Hawkins leaned slightly forward and moved his finger onto the trigger.

"I don't—"

Something hard slammed into the right side of his head and a nova blossomed before his eyes. The blow might have killed him if it had not been softened by the wool cap and if he had not shifted position a second before he was struck. As he sank to his knees he heard a loud explosion and his arm jerked backwards.

He blacked out, but the shards of pain stabbing his head shocked him back to consciousness. He heard Calvin, then Abby's voice sounding as if their mouths were full of cotton. He opened his eyes and saw a pale oval that transformed into Abby's face as his vision cleared. She was cradling his head in her lap.

"Matt. Are you all right? *Talk* to me, for godsakes!"

Hawkins reached up and removed the cap. His fingers slightly touched the tender skin and his skull felt as if it was cracked. He struggled to sit up.

"Feels like someone dropped a house on my head, but I'm okay. Rashid sucker-punched me with a rock. Where is the sneaky bastard?"

"*Gone*. Cal's after him."

They whirled at the sound of the DPV's engine turning over and barking into life, followed by gunshots. Then came the whine of spinning tires and the engine noise began to recede.

A flashlight bobbed in the darkness and footsteps pounded toward them.

"Sonofabitch stole the buggy!" Calvin shouted with breathless anger. "Fired in the air, but he kept on going. You okay, Hawk?"

"Nothing a new skull wouldn't cure."

Calvin and Abby helped him to his feet where he stood on shaky legs. He was angry for not following his instincts where Rashid was concerned. The guide had taken off with the submersible and dive gear, most of their survival equipment and a cache of weapons.

"How did you know I was in trouble?" he said.

Abby handed him his pistol. "We heard a shot and came running. I found this on the ground."

She handed over his pistol. The barrel was still warm.

"I must have fired it by accident. Damn. I don't look forward to telling the navy that their million dollar submersible got ripped off."

"Cheer up, Hawk, They'll never believe you."

"Did he get the satellite phone?"

"Yep. On the buggy."

"Then that's where we'll go. After Rashid. The DPV's tire tracks will lead us right to him."

"He's got a huge head start on us, and spare cans of fuel to keep him going," Abby said. "We'll *never* catch up with him."

"Never say never," Hawkins said. He led them to the supplies he'd stacked earlier and showed them the fuel containers.

Calvin laughed. "Rashid's going to be pissed when he runs out of gas."

"He's still got enough fuel to put some miles between us. He'll expect us to wait until light to get moving, but we'll leave now."

Abby said, "You need some first aid before we go anywhere, Matt."

The first aid consisted of a couple of aspirin, a compress to hold the swelling down and a bandage and tape. While Abby nursed Hawkins,

Calvin packed water, food and weapons. They walked to the edge of the campsite where the dune buggy had been parked, and began to follow the faint tread marks in the rocky soil.

CHAPTER TWENTY-SEVEN

Cait was much too excited to sleep. She woke up an hour before dawn, showered and got dressed in a long-sleeve tan cotton shirt, matching cargo slacks and hiking boots. Then she inventoried the contents of her duffle bag to make sure she had her digital camera, flashlight, batteries and notebook. She followed the scent of coffee through the quiet house to the kitchen. There was a fresh pot on the stove and a plate of pastry on the table. Leaning on the plate was an envelope with her name written on it. The note inside said:

"My apologies. I can't join you for breakfast. My men will show you the ruins. Best of luck. Looking forward to hearing about your explorations. A."

She tucked the folded note into her shirt pocket. Amir might be a drug lord, but the old rogue was a considerate host. After a quick breakfast of coffee and pastry, Cait filled a couple of canteens with cold water and went back to her room to collect the duffle. She pulled on a wind-breaker, tucked her hair under a Georgetown University baseball cap and stepped out the front door to wait for her ride.

It was still dark outside, and the temperature was in the forties, although once the sun rose, its heat would quickly vanquish the lingering cold of the night. The village was stirring with life. A pair of operatic roosters had begun a duet, setting off a chain reaction of barking dogs that triggered a wailing chorus of hungry babies.

The guttural rumble of a powerful engine echoed off the walls of the closely-built houses, drowning out the morning concert. Amir's Cadillac touring car drove up to the front of the house and stopped at Cait's feet.

The car's canvas top was folded down despite the cool air. Two bearded men sat in the front seat of the seven-passenger car. The driver was one of Amir's top lieutenants. His name was *Ghatool* which meant tulip in Pashto, but with his squat, troll-like physique, fierce beard and hard eyes, he was as unlike a flower as anyone could be.

The name would have more suited the handsome young man who sat in the passenger seat, his hand clutching a rifle. His name was Baht and despite his movie star good looks, his delicate features could not disguise the Afghan toughness that comes from growing up in an environment that punishes weakness.

Baht got out of the car, still holding his rifle and stored her bag in the car's trunk. Then he motioned for her to get in back and resumed his seat riding shotgun. Moments later, the car passed through the gates of the compound. The Cadillac's headlights stabbed the inky darkness as the car sped along the road between Amir's agricultural fields, then into open country, maintaining a steady pace for around fifteen minutes until it slowed to turn off onto a rutted track.

As she rode in the back seat with the air blowing in her face, Cait felt like an Oriental potentate off to inspect her vast holdings. She thought it interesting that Amir had assigned his most trusted men to the routine errand of taking his guest to visit the ruins. The gesture reaffirmed the tie that had developed since she had saved the warlord's granddaughter from choking.

The stars faded from the heavens as a golden eye peeked between gaps in the shark-tooth mountain range and the sky shifted to purple and blue. Once the sun rose above the peaks, it was as if a thousand flood lamps had been switched on.

Cait slipped on her sunglasses and took in the passing scenery. They had left the relatively flat lands of the flood plain behind and the track threaded its way through a series of linked valleys that separated low hills covered with scrub brush. The big balloon tires allowed the Cadillac to move with relative ease over the uneven ground.

Ghatool eased off the gas pedal as they rounded a bend and pointed through the windshield.

"*Look*, Dr. Cait."

It would have been impossible to miss the high crenellated walls of the citadel that rose from the earth about a quarter mile ahead. Ghatool stopped the car and they all got out. Ghatool knelt on one knee and scraped away a patch of dirt. Cait bent close to look at what he was uncovering and saw pavement stones close together.

"A road!" she said.

"Yes, yes. A road." He stood, bared his horse-toothed grin and extended his arms. "Wide."

Cait walked to her right until she came to the edge of the paving and did the same thing to her left. The roadway would have been at least twenty feet wide.

"*Very* wide," she said. She walked a short distance further where the ground sloped down to a dry wash that ran more or less parallel to the road and past the ruins.

Ghatool made a motion as if he were drinking.

"Water," Cait said. "A river."

It made perfect sense. The ancient settlements along the Silk Road were usually situated near springs or a river. Ghatool nodded and said something in *Pashto* to his friend, who smiled and gave Cait a thumb's up. They got back in the car and drove toward the high arched gate, unaware that they were being closely watched by unfriendly eyes.

Rashid lay on his belly behind a bush on the opposite side of the wash, peering through a pair of Steiner navy SEAL binoculars he had found in Calvin's stash. He focused the lenses on the two men, pausing to let his gaze linger on their weapons, and then moved on to Cait, taking in her easy, feminine stride.

Rashid seethed with anger for botching the attempt to murder Hawkins and his friends. He had planned to incapacitate Hawkins with a blow to the head and silently dispatch him with a knife. Then he'd kill the sleeping Calvin and deal with Abby. He had looked forward to hearing the insolent woman beg for her life before he killed her. The theft of the dune buggy and its valuable cargo had assuaged his rage, that is, until the vehicle ran out of gas.

He couldn't believe the turn his luck had taken. The touring car was a gift from God, he thought. He spread his thick lips in a yellow-tooth smile. He crawled backwards until he was sure he couldn't be seen, then rose to his feet and walked over to the dune buggy, which was hidden behind a cluster of rocks.

His original plan after killing Hawkins and his friends was to head for a village where he could sell his stolen goods. When he'd run out of gas, he had gathered up water and food and struck out on foot through the rugged countryside, pondering his dim prospects with each step, until he heard the sound of a car engine. He ducked behind a rock and saw the Cadillac pass by. He had followed the touring car on a parallel path, keeping out of view, until they came to the ruins.

Rashid had little interest in a bunch of old stones. He stowed the binoculars and pulled out Calvin's rifle with the sound suppressor.

He loaded the rifle, tucked a few extra shells in his pocket, and set off on a circuitous route that would take him to the ruins unseen.

Cait asked Ghatool to stop the car so she could use her camera. She stood on her seat and snapped off photos of the fort's gateway, picturing the image on the cover of the book she was outlining in her head. The title would go under the tall pointed arch of the opening, which had been built twelve feet high to allow for the passage of camels. She'd be sure to include her two colorful companions in the author photo on the back cover.

She finished taking pictures and Ghatool drove through the gateway. In the fort's heyday, armed guards would have stood at the long-gone wooden gate doors, vetting weary travelers and directing them to the fort keeper who would have assessed them a fee before passing them on to others who would require more payments for lodging and supplies.

The car entered a square courtyard around two hundred feet across. Archways lined three sides of the quadrangle, creating a shaded arcade for vendors to display their wares. Behind some of the galleries would be rooms for travelers and warehouses for their goods. At the center of the open space was a three-story, square building that probably housed the fort keeper and served as an administrative or possibly religious center.

Rather than get into a time-consuming search of the cloisters, Cait decided to concentrate on the building. Ghatool parked near a circular dry fountain around ten feet across. They all got out and Baht retrieved Cait's duffle bag and slung it onto his shoulder.

He followed Cait who walked around the tower taking photos of every side. The structure was perfectly square. Most of the plaster exterior had fallen off to expose the huge blocks used in construction. There were narrow vertical windows, the frames beveled to allow archers a clear shot in any direction. The windows on the third story were horizontal. She came back to the front of the building and got a flashlight from the duffle.

"I'm going inside to look around," she said.

Ghatool said something in *Pashto* to his friend, then he sat down on the short flight of steps that led to the entryway and crossed his rifle across his knees. With Baht leading the way, Cait climbed the steps to the doorway and flicked the flashlight on as she stepped across the threshold into the cool dark interior.

She swept the beam around the room and saw a miniature version of the outside fountain in the center of the chamber. Caravan leaders would be brought in to the reception area to sit around the fountain and refresh themselves while negotiating various fees.

A flight of cleverly-designed winding stone stairs was tucked into a corner. With Baht trailing like a devoted puppy, she climbed the stairway to the second level, which was similar to the first except for the absence of a fountain. She walked around the perimeter, her boots leaving tracks in a layer of dust that looked as if it had been undisturbed for centuries. The chamber would have housed the money-counters and scribes who tallied and recorded the flow of cash that the caravans brought in.

Baht silently watched her, an expression of curiosity on his face.

Cait reached into a pocket then pantomimed dropping imaginary coins into her palm. She described a circle with her index finger.

"Money," Baht said.

"Yes. *Big* money."

"Like Amir."

She laughed and said, "Yes. Like Amir."

Another corner stairway led to the third level. The reason for the horizontal windows visible from the outside was to allow space for the walls to be used for display. The openings had been placed so that the shafts of lights coming in from four directions fell on the opposite interior walls.

She stood in the center of the room and pivoted on her heel. What she saw was simply stunning.

She was standing in an ancient map room.

Cait clicked on her flashlight and slowly swept its beam around the room. Her heart ratcheted up several beats. This was not *any* map, but a detailed rendering, spread out over four panels, of the old Silk routes. The colors had faded through the centuries, but the details were clear.

Like most ancient examples of cartography, the proportions were out of whack, but the shape of the continents was reasonably accurate. The physical features, such as mountains, deserts and rivers, were well represented.

She walked along the walls, tracing the thousands of miles from China to the Holy land. East of China was a sliver of India, and to the west was a blue crescent, representing the eastern corner of the Mediterranean, whose ports were the jump-off for the maritime route to Rome.

The three major routes were marked with a heavy line and the branches in thinner red lines. Only major city names were identified, written in Latin and Chinese. Trading posts were represented by numerous blue dots. Some had palm trees that marked an oasis, or a drawing of a crenellated wall showing the presence of a fortified caravan stop.

The only flaw was a rectangular section of bare stones a couple of feet wide and high between China and Afghanistan. Rows of chisel marks showed that someone had methodically obliterated that part of the map from the record. The floor in front of the marred wall was covered with scattered pieces of plaster.

Cait spent several minutes making a photographic record before she tore herself away from the maps. With Baht following, she climbed to the top of the tower into the blinding sunlight. They were standing on an observation platform that offered views for miles in every direction. Any daylight threat could have been discerned, but more likely it was used to watch for approaching caravans.

As a historian, Cait had long been impressed at the ingenuity of the ancients. Without benefit of computers or powerful machines, they had managed to erect monuments that had stood for hundreds, even thousands of years. But there was another sphere in which the ancients overcame their limitations. She was standing on a formidable example of human cooperation and organization. The tower and the surrounding fortress enabled the existence of an international commercial enterprise. Caravans were tended to and protected, money exchanged, and goods passed across entire continents.

They went back down to the map room and Cait began to take more pictures. Baht cocked his head as if he were listening, and said something in Pashto, but Cait was so absorbed with her task that she only half-heard him before he disappeared down the stairway, leaving her alone. She continued with her work, unaware of the ugly danger that lurked nearby.

CHAPTER TWENTY-EIGHT

Rashid had entered the fort through a breach in a crumbling wall and was standing in the shadows of the arcade behind a stone pillar, where he could see the heavy-set man sitting on a stone bench next to the tower entrance. The man's rifle rested on his lap and he appeared to be dozing.

Rashid considered his options. If he attempted to cross the courtyard to get to the touring car, the man might wake up or someone inside the tower could see him through a window. He was pondering his move when the woman and the other man popped into view at the top of the tower.

They walked along the side of the observation platform closest to him and disappeared from his line of sight. He gambled that they would stay on the roof for a few moments and brought the rifle to his shoulder. He trained the cross-hairs of the telescopic sight on the sleeping man. He tried for a killing shot to the heart, but in his haste he aimed low.

The gun coughed softly and a millisecond later the man stiffened and his eyes popped open in surprise. His face contorted in pain and he brought his hands to his abdomen.

Rashid cursed. Damn. He'd gut shot his target. He aimed again, but his target stood, took a few steps and turned toward the door. Rashid put a second bullet between the man's shoulder blades. With superhuman effort, the fatally wounded man managed to call out something before he collapsed and died.

Rashid bided his time until the younger man soon appeared in the doorway, knelt by the dead man's side, and then looked up, a stricken expression on his face. He swept the courtyard with his eyes, then stood and brought his rifle to his shoulder, searching for a target, unaware that he had already become one. Rashid killed Baht with a single shot to the heart.

As Baht fell on top of his friend, Rashid emerged from hiding and quickly crossed to the tower door. He checked the car and found the keys in the ignition. He could have gotten in the car at that point and driven off, but his blood was up. He stepped over the warm bodies and entered the tower to look for his next victim.

Cait was shooting pictures madly, as if in a trance.

When she had all the photos she needed, she came back to the damaged wall and knelt by the pile of plaster fragments. She got a Coleman LED camp light from her duffle, which Baht had left behind, and began to examine the pieces one-by-one.

Most of the shards were blank or had squiggles representing roads or mountains drawn on them. But then she found one with letters printed on it:

PRES

She took her hat off and placed it upside down on the floor to use as a receptacle for other pieces that might have writing on them. She found a few more and guessed that they were place names, but she almost fainted with excitement when she found a fragment that said:

OH

Could it be? She placed the fragments side by side and with her finger drew the missing letters in the dust.

PRESTER J**OH**N

She was staring at the words when she heard a footfall behind her.

Without looking, she said: "Hi Baht. Can you give me a hand with this?"

When there was no answer, she turned her head and saw standing in the dimness not Baht, but a stranger who had a squat physique. He was around six feet away and held a rifle with an oddly-shaped barrel in the crook of his arm.

"Who are you?" Cait said.

"A traveler in need," said Rashid.

Cait reached for the camp light and slowly got to her feet. She raised the lantern high and in its pale blue light she could see the hungry eyes of a predator staring at her like a lion watching a gazelle. She wondered how this creep got past Baht and Ghatool. A frisson of fear went through her as she realized there was only one way that could have happened.

As if reading her thoughts, the man said, "Both your friends are dead. If you cooperate I may let you live."

Cait knew exactly what sort of cooperation he had in mind, and her revulsion at the prospect pumped up her courage.

"All right. Just don't kill me," she said, having no trouble injecting a nervous tremor into her voice. He took a couple of steps closer. When he got in range, she swung the lantern by its handle, aiming for the head. He was quicker than she expected and fended off the attack with his brawny forearm.

Cait dropped the lantern and tried to duck past him, but his hand shot out with the speed of a striking cobra and he grabbed the back of her shirt and pulled her to him. One arm wrapped around her neck and the other still held his rifle.

She snapped her head back into his nose, eliciting a yell and a satisfying crunch of cartilage, but her triumph was short-lived. He ignored the blood streaming from his ruined nose, spun her around and cuffed her cheek with a bear-like swipe of his open hand.

She was temporarily dazed from the blow and stopped fighting long enough for him to slam her shoulder blades against the wall. Then he reached down to the back of her knees so that she slipped down to a sitting position. The impact knocked the wind out of her. His hands grabbed her ankles and pulled again until she was stretched out on the floor.

Cait's hand groped along the floor, searching for the flashlight she had placed near the wall, but it found a metal object instead. She wrapped her fingers around the object and brought it up, aiming for her attacker's eyes. He was too quick, jerking his head back so the sharp end of the metal only raked his cheek. There was a cry of pain and she tried to roll aside and away, but he caught her arm with his left hand and punched her in the jaw, this time using his fist rather than his hand.

Rashid wiped the blood away from his face. His right hand slid along his belt and his fingers closed on the handle of the three-inch knife hidden in the buckle. Cait was dazed but still awake. Her eyes were fixed on the blade. *Good*, Rashid thought. *She will see what is coming*. He ripped open the front of her shirt, placed the knife-point above her breasts and moved it back and forth with just enough pressure to draw a bead of blood. Then he froze as he felt a metallic pressure at the base of his skull. A male voice said:

"Fun's over, Rashid."

Rashid couldn't believe his ears.

Hawkins.

"How did you find me?"

"I followed a bad smell. Now get up. *Slowly.* Hands in the air."

Hawkins pulled the gun away from Rashid's skull and stepped back out of reach. Rashid slowly stood, palming the knife as he reached for the ceiling.

"That's better. Now step aside," Hawkins ordered.

Rashid did as he was told. He saw Hawkins moving in from the left to tend to the woman. He still had his pistol leveled at Rashid's mid-section, but he took his eye off the man for a second as he extended his hand toward Cait. Rashid tensed, ready to swivel and slash the short blade across Hawkins' exposed throat.

Cait's eyes were open and staring. She yelled a warning.

"He's got a knife!"

Hawkins saw the glint of metal as the knife began its arc. He fired instinctively without aiming. The bullet shattered Rashid's sternum and the knife flew from his hand and clattered to the floor. Cait rolled out of the away to avoid the man's crashing body. She lay on her side, staring at Rashid's vacant eyes, then with Hawkins' help, she stood on shaky legs. Hawkins stepped over to examine the dead man so as to give Cait a moment of modesty to reassemble her clothes, then turned back and said:

"Are you okay, Dr. Everson?"

Cait was surprised to hear the man say her name. "Yes. You know me?"

"Only by your work. My name is Matt Hawkins. I stopped by Georgetown hoping to invite you to dinner so we could talk about maritime silk routes. It was quite a surprise to find you here."

"I'm very glad that you did."

"Me, too. Now we can talk about that dinner."

Cait stared at Hawkins. "Dinner," she said in a dead voice.

"That must sound a bit crazy."

"A little bit."

"No rush. I was talking about a future date, and different place, of course."

She studied the handsome, dark-complexioned face and wondered who this person was who had found her in one of the most remote places on earth, rescued her at risk to his own life, killed a man in the process and asked her out on a date. She realized that his lighthearted patter was aimed at trying to keep her from going into shock.

"You seem to know a lot more about me than I know about you, Mr. Hawkins. Who are you and what are you doing here?"

"That's a long story. I'd be glad to explain after we tend to your injuries."

"That might be a good idea." She touched her swollen jaw with her fingers and winced in pain, then glanced at Rashid, who lay face up. "I'm glad you killed that bastard."

Hawkins would have liked to have kept Rashid alive long enough to find out why he'd tried to kill him, but he couldn't blame Dr. Everson for her hard feelings.

"From the looks of his face, you got a head start."

Cait started to reply to his comment, but said instead, "I'm a bit dizzy. Maybe I should get some air."

Hawkins nodded, and took her by the arm as they made their way down to the first level. Cait gasped when she saw the bodies of Baht and Ghatool lying on the threshold, but Hawkins had more immediate concerns he had to deal with.

As he stepped into the open, he saw Calvin and Abby face down on the courtyard.

The muzzles of six automatic rifles were pointed at his heart.

Just when he thought things couldn't get any worse, he heard someone bark an order. Hawkins knew enough *Pashto* to understand the words.

"*Kill* him!"

CHAPTER TWENTY-NINE

Minutes before, Amir had driven though the front gates of the fort behind the wheel of a UAZ-469, the Russian equivalent of the American Jeep. Riding beside him was an armed guard; two more guards sat in the back.

Following close behind and protecting the smaller vehicle, was a BTR-152, a personnel carrier shielded with five tons of armor. Six more guards rode on the open top of the carrier where they were well-positioned to unleash a lethal wave of automatic gunfire in any direction. Both vehicles had been left behind during the Russian army's retreat from Afghanistan and had been restored to their original condition by the skilled mechanics who kept his fleet of trucks running.

He had wound up his latest negotiating session, with an Iranian middleman, earlier than expected and had decided to surprise Cait and visit her at the ruins. He'd been glad she'd taken his bait and prolonged her stay. His daughter and granddaughter adored her, but he was fond of her as well. Her quick intelligence and pluck reminded him of his late wife, who had attained a college degree despite the odds for an Afghan woman.

The half-grin on his lips as he anticipated her surprise changed to a deep frown when he saw the man and woman standing over the bodies of his men at the entrance of the tower building.

He hit the brakes and got out of the vehicle with amazing agility, despite his age and bad leg. He waved his cane to signal his guards from their vehicles. They went over to the man and relieved him of his weapon. The woman was unarmed. Amir's men forced the strangers face down onto the ground. Amir warned that they would be shot if they moved and ordered one of his men to check out the bodies. The man confirmed that the dead men were Ghatool and Baht and said they had been shot.

Amir seethed with anger at the murder of his two most trusted men. His unbridled fury was uncharacteristic of the drug lord, who took pride in his coolness. He told four guards to split off from the others and search the arcade. The other guards stood in a line in front of the tower doorway with orders to shoot the first person who emerged.

That's when Hawkins appeared.

He would have been dead a second later if Cait had not seen Amir and his men and stepped in front of Hawkins.

"Amir. *No!*"

Amir limped into the line of fire and waved his cane in the air.

"Stop!" he shouted.

There was a moment of bow-string tension as all parties froze in place. Then the guards slowly lowered their guns and Amir strode up to the tower.

"What is going on here, Dr, Cait?" he said.

"This man is a friend, Amir. He saved my life."

Hawkins gently placed his hand on Cait's shoulder and thanked her, then moved her aside and stepped out in front.

"And those are *my* friends," he said, pointing to Abby and Calvin. "I'd appreciate it if you would allow them to get to their feet."

Hawkins strode past the drug lord and helped Abby stand while Calvin got up on his own.

"Da-yam, that was close, Hawk!" Calvin said as he brushed the dust off his clothes. He looked over at Cait, who was in conversation with Amir, and said, "Wow! Leave it to you to find a beautiful woman in the middle of nowhere."

Abby cast an appraising glance in Cait's direction.

"Wow indeed. Who's the pretty lady?"

"That's Cait Everson, the historian who did the research into Prester John that sparked our crazy treasure hunt."

"What's she doing in this godforsaken place?"

Hawkins shook his head. "Looks like you'll have the chance to ask her yourself."

Cait came toward them, walking arm-in-arm with the older man.

"This is my friend Amir," she said. "He's a native of this area who has been helping me with my research."

Hawkins introduced himself and his friends. Abby winced when she saw Cait's swollen jaw up close.

"You need some cleaning up," she said. "I've got a make-up kit you can use after I give you some first aid."

Cait said she would be delighted to accept the offer and the two women walked off, chatting like old friends, leaving Hawkins and Cal with Amir.

"My apologies for the inconvenience." Amir said. "From what Dr. Cait told me about how you came to her rescue, I realize now that I was under a misapprehension."

"Happens to the best of us," Hawkins said in a tone that didn't match his nonchalance.

Amir picked up on the edge in Hawkins' voice. "I understand your anger." There was sadness in his eyes as he watched the bodies of Ghatool and Baht being carried to the armored vehicle. "My judgment was clouded by emotion. I was very fond of those men. They were loyal."

Amir's readiness to order him killed signified a flinty hardness of personality, but he was clearly shaken up over the death of his men. Hawkins was intrigued, too, in the way Amir spoke English, with an American accent.

Speaking in *Pashto*, Hawkins said, "A broken hand can work, but a broken heart can't."

Amir's jaw dropped. It was rare for a westerner to speak *Pashto* and even more shocking to hear the old Afghan expression of sympathy from the lips of this stranger.

"True, but in this case the hand still has work to do. To begin with, we have much to learn about each other. May I suggest some refreshments?'

The warlord clapped his hands and some of the guards who had been standing around went to the carrier and pulled out a plastic bag and a couple of coolers. Within minutes, the contents of the bag had morphed into an open-sided pavilion. Blankets and cushions were spread out in the shade.

Abby and Cait returned. They had washed the dirt off their faces, and applied touches of make-up that had improved their spirit as well as their appearance.

Amir served plates of cold spiced lamb and rice to his guests, which they washed down with ice tea. Cait chewed slowly, applying a cold pack to her sore jaw in between bites. While they dined, another cooler was passed to the guards, who had taken up stations at the fort's gate and around the courtyard.

Amir took a last bite, cleaned his fingers with a packaged hand wipe and looked around at the others.

"Now that we have fed our bodies, it is time to feed our souls with stories. Would you be so kind as to go first, Mr. Hawkins?"

Matt had been thinking how he might reply to the question that would inevitably be asked of him. Amir was too sharp to be deceived by fibs, so Hawkins decided to tell the full story, editing it here and there.

He began with a short resume of his stint as a SEAL in Afghanistan. Amir nodded when he learned how Hawkins knew *Pashto* and proverbs. He sat quietly while Hawkins told how he had been wounded and left the navy to pursue scientific studies. He touched on his work at Woods Hole and said that he had been hired by what he termed as a government group to search for the Prester John treasure in the lake. He explained without going into detail that a terrorist organization wanted the treasure as part of a scheme against America.

"To buy weapons?" Amir said.

"As I understand it, they think the treasure will give them some historical legitimacy in their attacks on the U.S."

"Are you saying that you can explore the lake waters?" Cait broke in with excitement in her voice.

"We have the equipment that will help us do that. Yes."

Amir raised his hand off his lap and held it in front of him as a gesture of disbelief.

"You plunged right into this mission without question, apparently," he said. "Weren't you skeptical?"

"Yes, I was very skeptical, until the attempt on my life."

He told how the two men had broken into his house and tried to kill him.

When he described the twin attackers, a gasp came from Cait's throat.

"Those are the same men who tried to kidnap or kill me," she said. "They are the reason I fled the country and came to Afghanistan."

"You're still here Mr. Hawkins, so the assassins must have failed," Amir said. "What happened?"

"I killed one of them. The other got away."

Amir mulled the answer for a moment, a slight smile on his lips.

"Go on with your fascinating story," he said.

Hawkins told how an acquaintance in Kabul had persuaded him to hire Rashid as a guide. He described their journey up to the theft of the desert buggy and the trek through the night to find the vehicle.

"When we arrived at the fort we found the bodies of your men," Abby explained. "We stayed outside to keep watch and Matt went in to check things out."

"It's fortunate for me that he did," Cait said. "I was so engrossed taking photos in the map room. I wish I had been paying attention, maybe I could have done something."

"You could do nothing against an armed and ruthless thug," Amir said. "Tell me, Dr. Cait, what did you think of the map room?"

"It's *wonderful*, but I'm puzzled by the vandalism to the map. Who would do such a thing?"

"I had the same thought the first time I saw the room years ago." He gazed at the tower, a thoughtful expression on his face, then he pushed himself up from the cushion with his cane. "I would like to see this Rashid person."

"I'll show you around," Hawkins volunteered.

"I'm coming with you," Cait said.

"Are you sure?"

"Yes," she said with determination in her voice. "I left my camera and my cap behind."

Hawkins shrugged and led the way to the tower entrance and up the stairs to the map room.

If the sight of Rashid's body bothered Cait, she didn't show it except for a slight wrinkle of her nostrils. Amir picked the knife from off the floor near the corpse. The blade was short but razor-sharp.

"A coward's weapon," he said with distain.

He tossed the knife aside, bent over Rashid's body and brushed away the flies settling on the mouth and lips. "This pig resembles a family of bandits that lives in a village around fifty miles distant. It's hard to tell, though. I assume you're responsible to the wounds to his face."

"No," Hawkins said. "The credit for those goes to Dr. Everson, who fought him tooth and nail."

Cait had squatted to retrieve her baseball cap and the plaster fragments. "Not exactly a nail," she said. She picked up a shiny piece of metal and stood.

"*This*."

She was holding a chisel in her hand.

"The mystery of the damaged map is apparently solved," Amir said. "This tool was used to chop away the missing section."

"That only solves part of the mystery," Cait said. "We don't know why the damage was done or who did it."

Hawkins asked if he could look at the chisel and held it under the flashlight.

"There are initials here on the shaft. K and an M. Any idea what they might stand for?"

"Yes, but it doesn't make any sense," Cait said.

"Give it a try."

"My guess is that the letters stand for *Kurtz Mining*. I found similar initials on a timber in a flooded mine shaft his expedition dug to get at the treasure."

"I read about the Kurtz expedition in your report," Hawkins said. "Why would he mess up the map?"

Cait held the two shards with the letters on them side by side. "I think the map had the location of Prester John's kingdom and Kurtz didn't want anyone else to know where it was. He was sometimes scoffed at for his pursuit of legends. Think of the glory that would come if he discovered the treasure and found Prester John's kingdom. Maybe even the Prester's tomb. My guess is that he made a paper map before covering his trail. "

"Seems like a reasonable conclusion," Hawkins said. "How far is the lake from here?"

"Two hours overland," Amir said. "I suggest we get moving immediately. How soon can you launch your search?"

"We can set up camp and start exploring the lake this afternoon."

Cait clapped her hands like a giddy child. "I've been waiting years for this moment. What are we waiting for?"

"First, I will have my men remove that animal to the desert where he can feed the vultures," Amir said. "That will be the end of it."

"Wait a second," Hawkins said. He searched Rashid's jacket and found his missing satellite phone. He cursed when he saw that the bullet that had killed the guide had smashed the phone to pieces.

Amir said, "Don't worry. I have a satellite phone you can use if you need it."

As they made their way from the map room, Hawkins glanced once more at Rashid's body. He didn't share Amir's confidence that killing the guide would put an end to it. He wasn't even sure what *it* was.

What he *was* sure of was that Murphy had produced Rashid and vouched for his character. And that Rashid had then tried to kill him.

He had expected that the main obstacle to finding the treasure would be the terrorists' rival salvage expedition, but it was clear that shadowy forces had tried to put an end to the mission even before he arrived in Afghanistan. And when that failed, they had sent in Rashid as a hit man.

None of it made sense.

His head was spinning.

He remembered the advice Jack Kelly had given him in Newport. His old commanding officer had said:

Never seen it like this, Matt. Real snake pit. Watch your ass and make sure your perimeter is secure.

As Hawkins stepped out into the courtyard behind Amir and Cait, he saw Calvin and Abby chatting like old friends with the guards who had almost killed them.

Hawkins couldn't wait to get back to Kabul and wrap his hands around Murphy's throat and shake the truth out of him. He'd ask Sutherland to dig around in the meantime. It was time he brought Sutherland up to date anyhow. He asked Amir if he could borrow his phone and tried Sutherland's number. There was no answer.

He handed the phone back to Amir. He'd try again later.

CHAPTER THIRTY

No matter how hard he scrubbed, Professor Saleem could not wash the blood from his hands. He tried different solvents and abrasives but the crimson stain persisted. He scrubbed harder. The skin dissolved, then the flesh deteriorated, and he realized to his horror that he was looking at the pure white bones of his fingers and palms.

He awoke with his heart hammering in his chest and his face bathed in a cold sweat. He knew the source of the nightmare. He had gone to sleep thinking of a spirited exchange he had had with his cousin at ISI headquarters in Islamabad over the use of violence by unpredictable men with extremist views as a cat's paw to accomplish the intelligent service's goals.

"I agree. This is a foul business," Cousin Mohamed had said, leaning back in his chair to tent his fingers. "Sometimes we get our hands dirty, but remember that we can always wash them clean."

"That's true, cousin, but sometimes the soap can be so strong that it removes the skin," the professor had rejoined.

The professor checked out his hands and was relieved to see that the flesh was attached to his fingers, then he dozed off again. He was awakened by one of the Doctor's guards carrying a tray with a glass of tea and hard cakes. He was hungry and the meager repast was like a feast to him. They must have gained the Doctor's trust because they were not blindfolded this time. It was still dark when he went outside and got into the Impala with Marzak and the Doctor.

The car took them back to the field that had been used for the helicopter drop-off the day before. The unmarked helicopter arrived within minutes. When the professor went aboard, he saw four hard-faced men wearing military uniforms that, like the helicopter, had no designations.

The professor squeezed past the SCUBA gear stacked on some of the other seats and found space to sit at the rear of the cabin. Marzak got in the front behind the pilot and co-pilot.

The helicopter lifted off and after a couple of hours in the air, began a vertical descent into a valley between snow-capped mountains, landing on a low hill next to the three Bell Cobra AHI-F guns ships. All markings on the narrow fuselages were painted over.

Several dozen bearded tribesmen came running over to meet the helicopter. Undeterred by the dust cloud stirred up by the spinning rotors, they surrounded the aircraft and shot bursts from their automatic weapons into the air to greet the landing party. The professor followed Marzak out of the helicopter. A man dressed in a flight uniform came over from one of the Cobras and spoke to Marzak. He couldn't hear their conversation, but he saw the man nodding his head.

When the conversation ended, Saleem went over to Marzak. "The Doctor's followers are excited to see us."

Marzak smiled. "They are impatient to see the show."

"Show? I don't understand."

"The Doctor asked me to have the helicopters make a practice run on that abandoned village," Marzak said, gesturing in the direction of a cluster of buildings at the foot of the hill. "He wants his men to know what they can expect when it comes to the real thing."

Within minutes, the Cobra's rotors thrummed the air. The gunships lifted off and gained elevation, then flew along the length of the valley in a single line until they diminished to the size of gnats. At the vanishing point they did a U-turn and sped back at a hundred-and-fifty miles an hour.

As they approached the village, the gunships angled down on a long descending trajectory, leveling off in a low wedge formation with the lead pilot's aircraft at point. The sound of buzz-saws cut through the chop of rotors as the Cobras fired the three-barreled Gatling cannons housed under their noses.

The guns were made to penetrate tank armor and the 20 mm slugs easily ripped through the mud-walls at the rate of more than seven hundred rounds per minute. Buildings crumbled to dust under the fierce fusillade.

As a follow-up, the Cobras unleashed seventy millimeter rockets from pods slung under their stubby wings. The rockets streaked into their targets and exploded in yellow and white blasts that produced billowing clouds of black smoke. The helicopters ended their run and banked around in a big curve.

The professor was wearing aviator sunglasses, but he averted his gaze from the blinding explosions for a second. When he looked back he could not believe his eyes. Figures were emerging from the columns of smoke. There had been people inside the buildings! Those that had survived the guns and rockets had been turned into human torches. They only made it a few steps before they fell to the ground where they burned like logs in a fire place.

All around him the bearded men shot their guns in the air and cheered. The Professor pushed his way through the throng to Marzak.

"You said the village was abandoned!" Saleem said.

Marzak shrugged.

"I was telling the truth, Professor. The village *was* abandoned by its original inhabitants. It has since been used as a prison to hold traitors while it was decided what to do with them. When I spoke to the Doctor this morning we decided what to do with them," Marzak said. "Why? Is there a problem?"

So that was what Marzak's conversation with the helicopter pilot was all about. The professor was enraged at having been made a party to murder, but he was aware of the tribesmen, who had gone menacingly silent, and were crowding in close around them.

He forced his lips into a smile.

"No," he said. "No problem."

He turned away and strode back to the transport helicopter. The deadly demonstration had only reaffirmed what he already knew, that his cousin had underestimated the ruthlessness of these men. They would stop at nothing.

Tomorrow the three Cobra helicopters would swoop in and unleash their power on the warlord's compound. The transport helicopter carrying Marzak and his newfound friend would land the dive team and their guards at the treasure site. They would be joined by the other helicopters after they had reduced Amir's compound to smoking rubble.

Professor Saleem was neither a coward nor a hero. Like most men, if sufficiently pressed, he had the potential to earn either title, but extremes of behavior were not part of his character. He preferred to occupy a safe middle ground that placed no demands on his ego or his well-being. Now, to his dismay, for the first time in his life he was having moral qualms that could not be rationalized away with clever intellectual argument.

He knew that Amir Kahn's village would have women and children. The thought of these innocents facing the same awful force as the inhabitants of the so-called abandoned village had knocked him from his precarious perch of neutrality, leaving him in a position where he was seriously entertaining the thought of *doing* something that would place him in danger.

There was only one problem. He hadn't quite decided what to do.

Or even if there were anything he *could* do.

CHAPTER THIRTY-ONE

Tombstone, Arizona

The man leaning against the wooden building next to the site of the OK Corral gunfight could have been one of Tombstone's desperado re-enactors, except for a major difference. Tyler Lee Clayton was a *real* killer.

Clayton was from Alabama where he'd knifed a man in a gambling brawl. The trial judge was a friend of the Clayton family, and said he would suspend the jail sentence if Tyler joined the army. Clayton signed up. At the time, the army was scraping the bottom of the barrel for people to send to Iraq and Clayton's anti-social behavior was seen as a boon rather than a barrier.

A thin cigar drooped from his lips as he surveyed the streets of Tombstone. He was around five feet nine, rangy in build, with stringy muscles packed on his slender frame. He had a lean face with high tight cheekbones and flat gray eyes that suggested the coiled violence of a rattlesnake.

He wore a black T-shirt and his bare arms were covered with death-themed tattoos. Without the pull-down cap, gloves and belt-knife, he bore little resemblance to the Ninja-leader who had destroyed the house in the Tubac hills a few hours earlier.

The expression of simmering anger contorting his hard features was stoked by the burning pain in his rib-cage. The handle-bar of the motorcycle had slammed into his mid-section like a steer's horn and inflicted a long, dark bruise on his pale skin. Back in the day, he never would have allowed himself to be ambushed so easily. He had been under the impression that he and his men were disposing of a defenseless young woman, not the crazed road warrior who had roared out of the outbuilding and tried to run him over. He had taken a lot of crap from his comrades before he'd silenced them with a dangerous stare.

A man was strolling toward him along the boardwalk. He was dressed in black pants and T-shirt, too. Although he was shorter and broader-shouldered than Clayton, and his complexion was olive rather than fish-belly white, he had a similar dead-eye expression on his face. His name was Vinnie Tartaglia, and he had gotten into trouble of his own in Staten Island before becoming another bottom-of-the barrel army recruit. He was not as smart as Clayton, but he was equally as violent. Vinnie said. "Talked to a guy in that restaurant. A woman came in on a Harley a few hours ago and had breakfast. She was pretty quiet, he said."

"She's going to be quiet for a long time after I catch up with her."

Vinnie snickered. "You hear from Tech?"

"Yeah. They say she left town headed southwest from here. They tracked her phone before it went dead a few miles from Fort Huachuca."

"She could have gone toward Bisbee, maybe, or doubled back to

Nogales and crossed the border. Maybe even slipped by us on the way to Tucson. She's probably hundreds of miles from here by now."

"Maybe not. I talked to our psych department. They've got the whole file on her. Crazier than a bedbug, but watch out when she's cornered!" He patted his sore ribs for emphasis. "Some people will run for as long as they can when they get scared, but she's a hunker-downer, they said. Looks for someplace she's been before where she can hide instead of run."

"This is big country. Lots of hiding spaces."

"Tech's running a check of her finances. Credit cards. Stuff like that. They'll know where she's been before. Maybe a motel or hotel. Or even a campground."

"What do you want me and the rest of the guys to do?"

"Hang out for now. Grab some lunch while we call in back up to establish a perimeter."

"Sounds good," Vinnie said. He noticed the sign on the wall. "Hey, they're doing a reenactment of the OK shoot-out in twenty minutes. Want to go see the good guys kill the bad guys?"

Clayton glanced at the sign.

"Naw," he said, flashing a gap-toothed grin. "Too violent."

After about an hour on the highway, Sutherland had pulled over and ditched her phone. She wasn't taking any chances that someone would triangulate her position using her cell phone signal, and she still had her back up phone registered under a different name and number. Then she had headed south, where she had a place in mind that might be a good hiding spot.

Sometime later, she arrived on the outskirts of Fort Huachuca, where the U.S. cavalry had set up shop in 1877 to intercept Geronimo's escape routes into Mexico. She turned off the highway south of Sierra Vista, away from the strip development along Route 92, and followed a winding narrow road into the quiet precincts of Ramsey Canyon.

At the end of the road, she parked near a low-slung building. The sign out front identified it as an inn. She had stayed at the B and B on one of her painting trips. It was a few hundred yards from a nature preserve where she had found many avian subjects for her canvas.

The middle-aged innkeeper was on her way into town, but she said no one was staying at the inn and there was plenty of room available. The hummingbirds that attracted the usual bird-watchers hadn't arrived in the canyon yet. She told Sutherland to make herself at home and to enjoy a slice of fresh-baked apple pie.

Sutherland took her up on the offer then went for a quick hike in the preserve. She was famished when she returned and polished off, not without some guilt, around half of the newly-baked pie. Then she settled into a Western print sofa opposite the stone fire place, opened her laptop and wrote a message to Hawkins, asking him again to contact her. She waited a few minutes, but there was no answer. After chewing over a few more what ifs, she consoled herself with the fact that he and Calvin were very good at what they did.

Besides, she had to watch out for her own butt.

It was clear what had happened. Lulled by the peaceful setting of her desert home, she had forgotten that the cyber network she used to detect threats was a two-way street to her front door. She had blundered in trying to get at the Arrowhead Foundation's tax status. She had set off alarms when she made the amateurish call to the Foundation, then compounded her error when she got too nosy about Trask.

She had placed filters on her phone number and email address, but anyone with a brain could have followed the trail back to her. Especially an outfit like Arrowhead which specialized in security.

Still, the speed and fury of the response surprised her.

The men who burned down her house had come to kill her; she was convinced of that. The intruder who had removed his mask before destroying her paintings was the same man who had led his fellow soldiers to attack her back in Iraq. A jerk named Clayton. She thought she had dealt with him when she salted his record with child pornography and couldn't believe he had come into her life again.

She started to shiver.

Get a grip, she told herself. *They know who you are, but you know who* they *are, too.*

Rather than look for new data, with its inherent risks, she called up the Trask file.

Trask had been born in a small town in Oklahoma. He had graduated from a run-of-the-mill university with average grades. His private practice floundered within months. No surprise. You'd have to be crazy to go to a faker like Trask. He had gone to work for the military training soldiers how to survive as prisoners. He might have disappeared into obscurity if not for 9/11 and *The New York Times*, which had published a report on the CIA use of water-boarding and sexual humiliation in interrogating terror suspects.

Trask's work became public because of a complaint filed against him with the Oklahoma State Board of Psychologists. The complaint came from another Oklahoma shrink, working with a lawyer and law professor. It documented in detail Trask's role in the harsh interrogation techniques, asking that his license to practice be pulled. It said he had misrepresented his qualifications and that his torture techniques, in addition to being immoral and illegal, lacked a scientific basis.

He was described as working as a private consultant, never replied in public to the charges, and a funny thing happened to the complaint. The state board tabled the accusation after the three filers failed to pursue the case. She looked into the background of the complainers. The professor had retired, the lawyer moved to another state and the psychologist who instigated the complaint was dead.

Cold fingers clutched at her heart. The psychologist had died in an accidental house fire.

She forced herself to keep reading.

According to the Arrowhead website, he was involved with the children's project after his work with the CIA. But in the years in between, when he supposedly worked as a consultant, he did the psychiatric evaluations of Sutherland and Hawkins that led to their discharges.

Arrowhead was a private foundation, but Sutherland was aware from her Iraqi experience that contractors occupied a twilight zone, neither civilian nor military, but something in between.

She went back to the website where she had discovered the link between Trask and Murphy. She called up the photo of Trask and the teddy bear, with Murphy guarding him from the little girl. There was another man standing in the field behind Murphy, also wearing a flak jacket.

She enhanced the photo using computer software. His mustachioed face came into focus. It looked vaguely familiar.

Hell, it couldn't be.

She opened the folder for the Newport Group. She had given each member of the group his or her own file and established preliminary bios with photos.

She clicked on the bio for Captain Michael McCormick. Hawkins had said the guy had acted like a jerk. The photo showed him wearing a navy officer uniform and his lip was clean-shaven. Instead of dark sunglasses he wore heavy-rimmed spectacles. His mouth was spread wide in the same wolfish grin he wore on the Arrowhead site.

Sutherland placed the two pictures side by side, and then looked at them upside down. They showed the same man; she was sure of it now.

Captain McCormick had worked for Arrowhead.

Trask had worked for Arrowhead.

Murphy had worked for Arrowhead.

McCormick worked for Arrowhead and the Newport group.

She started to sift in earnest through the lives of everyone in the group, following links to look for other connections to Arrowhead or to each other. It would take hours of tedious work, and she was aware her queries could be traced back to their source, but tip-toeing in and out was the kind of thing she was good at. She looked forward to the challenge. She would need to prepare herself for the task ahead, though.

She set the laptop aside, got off the sofa, went into the kitchen and cut herself another piece of apple pie.

CHAPTER THIRTY-TWO

The odd-looking convoy wound its way through a series of linked valleys, snaking between scraggly hills, eventually breaking out into countryside that was open and relatively flat. The antique Cadillac was in the lead, its convertible top down. Amir was behind the steering wheel. He had insisted that Hawkins ride beside him. Cait sat in the back seat. Next in line was the DPV, and then came the troop carrier and the Russian jeep.

Amir had quizzed Hawkins about his stiffness of leg.

"Got too close to an IED," Hawkins said. "Crude but effective. The crew at Walter Reed patched my leg back together, more or less."

"We may have had the same doctors at Reed. They reassembled my body parts after I failed to outrun a Russian rocket."

"You must have been in the hospital a long time to pick up that American accent," Hawkins observed.

"Several months, but I also spent a year studying at Georgetown University while I recuperated."

"Is Georgetown your connection with Dr. Everson?"

"Indirectly, yes," said Cait, who had been listening to the conversation.

Amir glanced in the rear-view mirror. "I've been looking at the vehicle your friend is driving. It looks very utilitarian."

"It is. *Fast*, too."

"This car too is fast. I've replaced the original V-8 engine with a much more powerful one. The suspension and wheels have been strengthened and the tires customized to allow for higher speeds, especially on rough terrain."

"I'll bet you it still isn't as fast as the DPV, even with the load the buggy is carrying," Hawkins said. He regretted the comment the second it left his lips. Amir didn't seem to be the type who would turn down a challenge, even one that was only a figure of speech. He was right.

"The wager is accepted," the warlord said.

Hawkins stalled. "We haven't agreed to the stakes."

"We'll talk about that later," Amir said. "Please hold tight, Dr. Cait."

Then he nailed the gas pedal.

The two-ton touring car didn't exactly accelerate with a whoosh, like a later model high-performance car would have done. The heavy body seemed to be waiting for the engine to persuade it to pick up speed, which it did gradually, as befitting its dignity, and quickly gained velocity. They were emerging from the valleys and the terrain was changing into an arid, grass-covered plain that allowed for faster driving.

Hawkins checked the car's speedometer. The needle was at seventy miles per hour. The Caddy was leaving a thick brown rooster tail a hundred yards behind it.

"Cal's not going to like breathing dust," Hawkins yelled at the sheik.

In reply, Amir grinned and pushed the car's speed up to eighty, but the smug smile left his face after a quick glance in the mirror revealed a pair of halogen headlights close on his tail. He gave the touring car another ten miles of speed. The headlights disappeared, only to reappear a second later off to the left as the desert vehicle emerged from the cloud.

Calvin was hunkered down low behind the wheel. Abby held onto her cap with one hand and the underside of her seat with the other.

Amir depressed the gas pedal to the floorboards, but Calvin paced them for a moment. Then he gave a wave, and passed as if they were in reverse, enveloping the Caddy in a cloud of dust.

Amir shouted something that Hawkins didn't understand. He pointed ahead and stabbed the air with his forefinger.

"The lake! The lake!"

Cait bent forward and yelled in Hawkins' ear. "Make them stop, Matt, for Godsakes! The lake is just ahead."

Hawkins knew that Cal would try to put as much distance as he could between him and the touring car just to rub it in. He had no walky-talky or telephone to warn of the impending disaster. He reached over and brought his palm down on the horn pad at the center of the steering wheel.

There was a loud, clarion beep.

He slammed the horn again, producing a quick beep, followed by two more, then three long, then three short. He repeated the SOS call again. Amir was slowing, but the dust was still thick and Hawkins had no idea whether he had been successful or not. Amir carefully braked to a complete stop.

Cait had a shell-shocked expression on her dust-smudged face. Hawkins rose from his seat and looked over the top of the double-glass windshield.

A slight breeze blew the curtain of dust aside to a point where it was opaque rather than solid. Hawkins could see the outline of a solid shape a few dozen feet ahead.

He got out of the touring car and strode to the driver's side of the dune buggy.

Calvin sat back with his feet up on the dashboard. He and Abby were covered with dust, but they were laughing hilariously.

"About time you showed up," Calvin said. "What's with the Mayday?"

"Did you need a rescue?" Abby chimed in.

Hawkins spit out a mouthful of dust.

"Nope. *You* did. You were about to pull a Thelma and Louise." He pointed ahead. The dust was settling and they could see the edge of the cliff around thirty feet from the front bumper of the desert vehicle, and the blue waters of the lake beyond.

Calvin leaned on the steering wheel.

"Man-oh-man. The DPV would have sunk right to the bottom."

"Along with Fido and months of research."

"Uh-oh," Calvin interrupted, glancing in the rear-view mirror. "Hope your pal isn't a sore loser."

Amir was walking toward the vehicle with an escort of armed guards. Cait had gotten out of the car and tailed behind. Amir had a deep frown on his face as he circled the desert vehicle, tapping the tires with his cane, but when he came back to the driver's side he flashed a smile.

"How much do you want for this wonderful chariot?" he said.

"Sorry, but she's not for sale." Calvin figured his answer was too abrupt, so he said, "But I can let you drive her."

"It's a deal. I will hold you to your offer when we have more time. Now let me show you the lake."

He hobbled to the ragged edge of the cliff and swept his cane in the air like a tour director for Cook's. The top of the bluff sloped down at a forty-five degree angle to meet the calm water twenty feet below. The lake was around two miles long and a mile wide, narrowing somewhat near the middle to give it the distinctive figure eight-shape Hawkins had seen in the satellite photos. A line of white cliffs was visible on the opposite shore.

Hawkins shielded his eyes against the sun glare. "The Valley of the Dead," he murmured.

"Yes, that's right," Amir said. "It is still called that even though the valley was flooded decades ago by artesian wells. How did you know its name?"

"I read Dr. Everson's research paper." Hawkins pivoted on his heel and gazed at the rocky hill shaped like a camel hump. "That's the land mark you mentioned, Dr. Everson. Which means the treasure cave should be under our feet."

Cait clapped her hands lightly.

"Bravo, Mr. Hawkins. If you were my student I would give you an A. But actually, the cave is about two dozen paces in *that* direction."

Cait led the way to the metal cover, which Amir's men moved aside. Hawkins knelt at the edge of the opening and winced at the foul exhalation. He could see timbers set around the walls near the top.

"Kurtz's mine shaft?" he asked Cait, who knelt beside him.

"I believe so. I explored it a few days ago. It's flooded at the bottom where the restraining timbers caved in. I found evidence that a diver might have died in the cave-in."

Hawkins brushed some rocks from the edge of the shaft and counted the seconds until he heard the echoing splash. "Deep," he said. "Why would Kurtz go through the trouble of digging this hole when his diver could have gone into the lake and found the cave entrance?"

"I'm hoping you and your friends will soon answer that question," Cait said.

"Unfortunately, I can't allow them to proceed with the treasure hunt, Dr. Cait," Amir said.

"What are you saying, Amir? We're on the verge of one of the most important historical finds of the century."

"The historical significance hasn't escaped me. But we're talking about the possibility of a fortune falling into the wrong hands."

"But that's why these people are here. To keep it *out* of the wrong hands. Do you want the Taliban or some other terrorists to get their hands on it?"

"No, of course not. No offense, Mr. Hawkins, but I consider the Americans as just another occupation force in a long line of foreigners who have taken over our country for their own purposes. When I fought the Russians, it was to have an Afghanistan for our people alone. Why should I allow you to take the treasure or allow it to go to the corrupt people in Kabul?"

"I can't argue with you there," Hawkins said. "But if you feel that way, why did you show us the lake?"

"We share a common goal to keep the treasure out of the wrong hands. The unanswered question has to do with the ultimate ownership of the treasure."

"Where would you like it to go?"

"To a place where it would benefit the people of my country."

Hawkins thought about it, then said, "Maybe I can offer an enticement to change your mind."

The sheik pinioned Hawkins with his eagle gaze. "Go ahead," he said.

"The treasure's last owner of record was Prester John. Its intended destination was the Vatican. It's in Afghan territory. So the ownership seems to be in some dispute, although I'd lean toward finders-keepers. My mission is to *find* the treasure so it can't be used by terrorists. The treasure's ultimate fate is immaterial to me."

"Then you'd turn it over to me? No conditions?"

"If it's found on your territory. Yes. No conditions."

"I'm glad to hear that is your position, because if not, I would have to take it away from you at gunpoint. You have my permission to go ahead."

"Thank you, Amir," Cait said. It would embarrass the sheik if she showed her thanks with any type of physical display so she instead threw her arms around Hawkins. Hawkins had no such reservations, and reciprocated her embrace. Then he caught Abby's glare.

The stony expression on Abby's face suggested that he had missed some signals, and despite her detached manner she retained more than a little affection for him. Or, if he were cynical, it was only her natural competitiveness. He was relieved a moment later when Cait went over and hugged Calvin, then Abby.

Hawkins glanced at the position of the sun in the western sky and turned to Amir. "We could move faster if we had a hand unloading our gear."

"*Done*." Amir relayed a series of commands.

Hawkins went around to the rear of the dune buggy and undid the bungee cords and ropes. He carefully peeled back the dust-covered tarp and he and three other men lifted the submersible and placed it near the edge of the cliff on a line with the mine shaft.

The claw-like caliper had been packed separately, as had the computer used to communicate with the submersible. While a portable generator charged Fido's batteries, Hawkins reattached the manipulator and he and his crew lowered the docking station at the end of its cable down the slope of the cliff into the water.

Calvin and his crew cleared the gear off the side carriers. Abby directed the placement, stacking the equipment in order. Food, water and other supplies. Dive gear. Gas generator. Calvin moved the lockers containing his arsenal on his own, placing them in one of the three pop-up tents that had he and Hawkins had erected.

Within an hour, they had established a search and salvage operation at the edge of the lake.

Amir circled the submersible, much as he had the desert vehicle, asking incisive questions about its operation. Hawkins explained how the vehicle would be programmed to conduct a search of the slope in a series of parallel lines. Its television cameras would make a visual record of all prominent features and side-scan sonar would probe under the slope. Once the data were analyzed, the dive could get under way.

Amir watched as the AUV was lowered into the lake. It was attached to its docking station to get its instructions and after a few minutes, backed away on its own and submerged.

"Marvelous! What next?" Amir said.

"We wait for Fido to do its job. It will run into the night. We should have a clear picture of the slope by the morning."

"I have to get back to my village," Amir said, "I'll return at dawn. Dr. Cait?"

"I think I'll go with you. I need to clean up and change."

Abby noticed the exhaustion in Cait's face. She said, "If it's okay with you, Matt, I'll go with Cait and lend a hand."

Amir ordered four of his men to remain with the troop carrier. Then he got into the touring car with his two passengers and drove off into the fading light. Dusk was falling and the surface of the lake had gone from glittering silver to pewter.

Hawkins heard the sound of his name. Calvin was stirring a pot on a camp stove and Hawkins' nostrils almost quivered like a hound's as his nose picked up a succulent fragrance.

Calvin's famous New Orleans gumbo.

CHAPTER THIRTY-THREE

Sutherland hit the wall in the wee hours of the morning. Her eyes felt as if they were on fire. The words marching across the computer screen were doing jumping jacks. She stretched out on the sofa and pulled a blanket over her body, intending to take a five minute break. The twittering of birds flocking to the window feeder woke her up. When she opened her eyes it was daytime.

She stretched her jaws in a mighty yawn, rose from the sofa and walked stiffly to the kitchen to brew a pot of coffee. The inn owner breezed in to prepare breakfast. While she stirred eggs for a vegetarian omelet, the inn-keeper said, "Most of the hummingbirds haven't arrived yet, but there may be a few in the upper reaches of the canyon, if you feel like a climb."

"Thanks. I might do that," Sutherland said, only half listening.

She munched on a slice of buttered multi-grain toast and pondered the results of her computer search. She'd found bits of information that bolstered her original findings linking Arrowhead, Trask, Murphy and the Newport Group, through Captain McCormick. She had found no connections between Arrowhead and the other members of the Newport group.

She finished breakfast and helped clean up in the kitchen. The innkeeper had an appointment in town and said she'd return in a few hours. Sutherland was alone in the inn again, staring at the beautiful sunny morning on the other side of the window. She tried to contact Hawkins on his satellite phone. No answer. *Damn you, Matt!* Didn't he know she was numb with worry?

Maybe a walk would help. She gathered up her Canon digital camera, a compact pair of powerful binoculars, a sketch pad, pencils, bottled water and protein bars, and stuffed everything into a day-pack with her computer. She slung the pack onto her shoulders and stepped outside, eyes blinking in the bright sun.

She checked on her Harley, then went over and climbed the low fence into the nature preserve, unaware that unfriendly eyes followed her every move.

Tyler Lee Clayton was a crude, violent man, but he was not stupid.

When Tech had sent the picture of Sutherland on his smart phone, it had triggered memories of the assault on the young army recruit. He remembered planning the attack as if it were military operation. He had watched her leave the barracks every night at the same time for a cigarette. He had enlisted his drunken buddies to help him, knowing it would be her word against theirs that it was consensual. He knew that she would be reluctant to report the attack because she would have to admit going out without her weapon.

And he remembered the hummingbird tattoo on the pale skin of her right shoulder.

He had flashed back on the tattoo as he burned the hummingbird painting, but gave it no further thought until he had come across the promotional brochure in the lobby of the Sierra Vista motel where he and Vinnie had taken rooms for the night.

He plucked the brochure from the case and stared at the photograph of a ruby-throated hummingbird, under the headline, "Hummingbird capital of the world." The text said that fourteen different species of the "flying jewels" could be found within the three-hundred acre nature preserve on the eastern flank of the Huachuca Mountains.

He handed the brochure to Vinnie. "I know where our little biker girl is hiding."

Tartaglia looked at the folder with the map showing that the preserve was around five miles from the motel. He wrinkled his brow.

"What makes you think she's hiding here?" he said.

Clayton put his arm around his friend's shoulder and brought his mouth to Vinnie's ear.

"A little bird told me."

Sutherland hiked along a shaded-trail and crossed a wooden bridge over Ramsey Creek, eventually breaking out of the woods after about a half a mile. She walked along the grassy floor of the canyon at the base of the mountain, past the ruined wooden buildings that harkened back to Ramsey's days as a mining camp. The mountain was a vertical stone wall, hundreds of feet high that looked as if it had been sheared by a gigantic meat cleaver. The sky was a crystalline, Delft blue.

With every breath of fresh air she pulled into her lungs she seemed to inhale the limitless energy from her wild natural surroundings. Each exhalation purged her mind and body of the memory of her burning house and blew away the dark mists that had been gathering in her brain.

The trail angled up, gradually at first, eventually going back and forth in a series of narrow, hair-pin switchbacks as the slope steepened. Log stairs helped her navigate the steeper parts. She was overweight, not in the best of physical condition, and made good use of the benches built along the trail.

A third of the way up the mountain she was startled by a loud crashing in the woods. She caught a glimpse of brownish gray and realized she had spooked a mule deer. The animal made several bounds down the mountain then stopped and froze in place. Sutherland took a few steps off the trail, raised the camera to her cheek and squinted through the viewfinder. She shot a picture of the doe and was narrowing the focus to its head when her eye caught movement beyond the animal's ear, through a break in the trees.

A speck was moving along the floor of the valley.

She got out her field-glasses and focused on a man dressed in black. He stopped to remove his cap and wipe his face with a sleeve, which is when she saw the bright red hair. She examined his face through the lenses. She couldn't see his teeth but she knew they were gapped. There was no doubt. Clayton.

More men were moving single file behind Clayton.

It began to come together. Arrowhead employed former military people. Clayton could not have found a respectable job, especially after she had altered his records, so he went to work for Arrowhead. And now he was after her again.

Clayton had scattered pairs of men around Cochise County: Tombstone, Bisbee to the south and Benson to the north, all within a quick drive of each other. With his call, they had converged in four cars at the mouth of the canyon at dawn and drove along the winding road, stopping at houses and checking cottage colonies. He recognized the motorcycle in the parking lot outside a B and B.

He and his men pulled over, melted into the woods near the inn and watched the inn-keeper leave. Minutes later, Sutherland set off for the preserve with a hiking pack and disappeared into the canyon. Clayton stepped out of the woods and went over to the Harley. Damned shame to mess up a nice machine, but he couldn't take any chances. He pulled his flip knife from his pocket and stabbed the tires.

He told Vinnie to stay behind to keep watch on their rear, then he took up the lead and the column of men entered the preserve. Clayton had studied the map and seen that it was a box canyon. He had caught a few glimpses of Sutherland moving on the upper trail, but then she disappeared. He told his men to double their speed.

Perfect.

When they caught up with her, she would be far into the woods where no one could hear her scream.

Sutherland didn't know how Clayton had found her, but there was no time to ponder. She had to keep moving.

She stepped back onto the trail and began to climb. In her panic, she tripped over an unseen root and went flying forward. She pushed herself off the ground and picked up the glasses that had fallen from her face. Her knees and palms were scraped raw. She ignored the pain and used it to help her concentrate.

Think.

There was no way she could escape. She was already winded. She needed help.

She slipped the back pack off, pulled out her spare phone, went down her list of numbers and pressed the call button. After a couple of rings a man's voice answered. He recognized her voice.

"Sutherland. What a relief. Are you okay?"

"I'm fine, Mac. I mean-no. I'm in trouble."

"We've been looking all over for you. Your house burned down."

"I *know* my house burned down!" she said. "The guys who burned it down are after me. I need help."

McHugh's cool professionalism asserted itself. "Tell me where you are."

"Ramsey Canyon."

"Who are these people who are after you?"

"I don't know," she lied; she had no time to explain. "I just need help. Please hurry, Mac." Her voice caught.

"I know where it is. That's near the major crossing for illegals. There are always patrols in those mountains. I'll contact one. Keep climbing and see if you can find a place to hide."

"Thanks, Mac, but it's too late for that."

Her pursuers had stopped. One of them was pointing up the mountain. She peered through her glasses and saw Clayton looking directly at her through a pair of binoculars. Then he and the others picked up the pace.

Sutherland started up the trail. She needed time, but she was tired. She climbed with methodical, deliberate steps and forced herself to sit for thirty seconds at each bench before pushing on.

She cursed herself for eating all that pie the day before. She squinted ahead and back, and then decided to strike off through the woods and find a place she could hunker down.

The vines and thorns tore at her bare legs, and her progress was noisy and slow. Even worse, the woods ended and a rock-studded wall a hundred feet high blocked the way. She couldn't go back, so she began to climb. There were plenty of natural hand and foot-holds and she was surprised at how quickly she was able to get to the top.

She scrambled over the ledge and stood on jelly legs. She was completely exhausted. Heat beamed from her sweaty cheeks. She put one foot in front of the other and walked twenty feet until she had to stop. She was at the flattened top of a pinnacle that dropped down hundreds of feet to the other side. The sheer rock face was smoother than the one she climbed on the way up. She was half-tempted to try to descend when she heard a wheedling voice calling.

"Suh-ther-land," the voice said. "We know where you are. Don't be shy lady hummingbird."

Sutherland gazed down from her dizzying perch, and knew what she would do if she had no other choice. The jack-hammer beat of her heart began to slow as an inner calm took hold of her fevered emotions. She walked back to the ledge and looked down at the black-clad men standing in a curved line at the bottom of the cliff. One of them stepped forward and gave her a friendly wave.

"Hello, Sutherland," he called. "Remember me?"

"I remember your ugly face, Clayton."

"Remember the *other* part of me? That must have made a big impression on you."

"Sorry, but I didn't have my microscope with me at the time."

There was a ripple of laughter from his friends, but Clayton kept his forced grin pasted on his face.

"I see you've still got the big mouth that spread lies about me."

"How did you find me?"

He flapped his arms like wings. "I remembered how much you liked the little birds. You know, like the tattoo on your pretty shoulder and the paintings I burned along with your house."

"You've already had your fun. What do you want from me?"

"We've still got a score to settle. I'm taking the balance out of your hide."

He signaled his men. Then he and his men moved forward to the base of the rock and began to climb. They looked like big black ants climbing up the side of the hill. There was no escape. She turned around and took a deep breath. She would simply make a running start and jump off into space. Clayton and his men would have made the climb for nothing.

She closed her eyes for a second and when she opened them to prepare for her leap she saw a dark spot against the cloudless sky.

She turned and faced forward. Clayton and his men were about half way up the hill.

"Hey, Clayton," she yelled down. "Did you ever tell your friends why you got kicked out of the army?"

The line of men stopped and turned toward their leader. "Don't listen to that crazy bitch."

"Not so crazy that I don't know you liked pictures of naked little boys."

She saw him reach for his holster and stepped back from the ledge. A pistol shot rang out, but the bullet harmlessly pinged off the rocks. As the echo faded she heard another, more reassuring, sound from behind her. She turned and saw that the black dot had doubled in size. She stepped forward again.

Clayton had holstered his pistol. He started to reach for it again, but realized that she could easily move out of the line of fire so he started climbing instead, moving past his men. He made it to the top of the ledge just as the Border Patrol helicopter swooped overhead in an ear-shattering clatter of rotors.

The chopper made a tight banking circle and came to a hovering stop over the side of the hill. As the men retreated down the rocks under the rotor downdraft, a stentorian voice issued from the helicopter's loudspeaker.

"Throw your guns to the ground or you'll be shot!"

Clayton's men bolted for the woods, but the helicopter anticipated the move and rotated sideways. Muzzle flashes blossomed brightly in the open side door and the bullets kicked up fountains of dirt. The men who were trying to escape tossed their weapons aside and flopped down on their bellies.

Only Clayton was left standing. He wheeled around and saw Sutherland standing at the edge of the pinnacle, a big smile on her face.

The loudspeaker voice shouted an order:

"Man with the gun. Throw your weapon down or you'll be shot."

Clayton ignored the warning. He wanted to wipe the mocking smile off of Sutherland's face, but he had learned as a soldier to deal with the bigger threat first. The helicopter was only yards away. A big noisy target. He was quick enough to spin around and snap off a round of shots. And he might have done just that if he hadn't seen Sutherland raise her hand.

She said, "You like birds, Clayton. Here's a big one for you."

He couldn't hear her words over the helicopter noise, but the gesture was unmistakable. He shouted with rage, brought his weapon up and aimed at Sutherland instead of the chopper. Before he could squeeze the trigger he was practically cut in half by hot lead.

His legs buckled, he pitched forward and in the lingering last moments before a black curtain of death fell over his eyes he saw Sutherland, still standing there with her middle finger in the air.

CHAPTER THIRTY-FOUR

While the hovering Border Patrol helicopter kept watch, the agents on the ground rounded up the attackers and marched them down the trail. The failed look-out, Vinnie Tartaglia, was already in handcuffs. Word of the Ramsey Canyon shoot-out had spread over the police radio network. The parking lot around the visitor center swarmed with sheriff's men and local police. More vehicles lined the road.

Sutherland hoped to slip away on her bike in the confusion. She would have made her escape if the Harley's tires hadn't been punctured. A deputy-sheriff told the police that Sutherland had been up on the mountain, and she was suddenly enveloped by big men in uniforms who wanted to talk to an eyewitness.

Sutherland played dumb and said she had been hiking in the preserve when a bunch of strangers started to chase her. She had called a border agent she knew and he alerted the patrols. But a deputy noticed the Harley's flat tires and that started a new round of questions.

"It looked to me like these guys were after you, specifically," the deputy said.

Sutherland stuck with her story, but she knew it was only a matter of time before someone ran a background check and pulled up her psychiatric history. They would run a fingerprint check on the dead man, or one of his thugs would start talking. More questions would follow. She breathed a sigh of relief when she saw McHugh arrive. She gave him a big hug and whispered in his ear:

"Don't mention my house burning down."

McHugh had a puzzled look in his eyes, but he nodded slightly to say he understood. He told the deputy that since he got the original call, he would interview Sutherland. He took her aside and said, "What's this all about?"

"I'll tell you later. Can we get out of here?"

By then, the first agent had lost interest in Sutherland in favor of the desperadoes. McHugh recruited a couple of men to load the motorcycle in the back of the truck and offered Sutherland a ride to Tubac.

Sutherland was steeling herself for the first glimpse of her house, but as the gutted building loomed at the top of the hill, she fought hard to stifle a whimper. The walls were standing, but black halos framed the windows where tongues of flame had blasted out the glass.

They got out of the Border Patrol truck, ducked underneath the cordon of yellow tape that surrounded the house, walked past the burned-out hulk of her RAV4, and eased through the gap that the attackers' SUV had punched in the electrified fence. They stopped at the front entrance. The stench of burned material issued from the house. McHugh pointed a powerful LED flashlight into the gutted interior of the house. The beam reflected off dozens of jagged surfaces.

He let out a low whistle. "Lots of sharp edges. Air's full of toxins. I wouldn't go inside if I were you."

"I already know what's inside," she said in a whisper. "It's the wreckage of my entire life."

The border agent shuffled his feet, unsure how to respond. "Let's go back to the truck."

Sutherland took a last look at the house. The sight dismayed her, but seeing the ruins up close had a calming effect as well, because it was a done deal and there was nothing she could do to change it. They walked to the truck where McHugh leaned against a fender and lit a cigarette.

"Thought you didn't like toxins in the air," Sutherland said.

"It's a scientific fact that tobacco is a *good* toxin." McHugh exhaled twin streams of smoke from his nostrils like a friendly dragon. "You must have had the place insured," he said, hopefully.

"Yes. I've got enough insurance to cover the cost of a new house."

"Great! You can replace this mess with an even better *casa*."

"All my artwork went up in smoke. That's something insurance can't replace."

"Hell, yes. That is tough," McHugh said. "But it could have been worse. The house and art are gone, but you're still in one piece."

"Thanks to you," she said, "You saved my butt."

"All I did was make a couple of quick phone calls. The helicopter was only a few minutes away, checking out the border fence, and there are always patrols in the mountains. They've learned to shoot first and ask questions later, since an agent got killed by smugglers."

"I also owe you for helping me slip away from the sheriff."

He chuckled and said, "That was the hard part, I'll admit. But the only thing you owe me is an explanation."

"I guess I do," Sutherland said. She'd told him what happened on the mountain and nothing more.

"You said on the phone that those guys in the canyon were the same ones who burned down your house."

"The man they shot was the leader of the arson gang. I saw his face up real close when they did this."

"Why were these guys after you?"

"It's a long story."

"I've got time."

Sutherland laid out the bare facts. She told McHugh how she had seen the attack party on her security cameras and the about the escape through the secret tunnel to the pump house. And how she went to Tombstone then Ramsey Canyon to hide.

"Why didn't you go to the police?"

"It's way out their league. This is much too big for the locals."

He scratched his chin. "Hell, I always thought it was funny, a young woman like you, living up here alone in the hills in a new house with that electric fence. You're in the witness protection program, and these were the people you've been running from."

"That's not a bad guess, even if it is wrong. Actually, I'm a computer consultant and I'm involved in a hush-hush project that involves national security. Someone got wind of what I was doing and tried to stop me."

"If this is a government deal, why can't you get the feds to protect you?"

"Because it would mean bringing more people into a project only a handful know about. That includes you. That's as much as I can say."

McHugh figured that he had hit a wall with his questioning. He pointed to the house.

"What are you going to do next?"

"I really don't know."

"I've told my wife about you. I'm sure she wouldn't mind if you stayed the night. Longer if you want to. We've got lots of room since the kids went off to college."

Sutherland suddenly realized that she hadn't had a decent sleep for two nights.

"I don't want to put you out, but I wouldn't mind a place to catch some Zs."

"No trouble at all. C'mon then. I'll call my wife on the way."

Sutherland glanced at the rear of the truck. "They did a number on my bike. I'll probably have to go to Tucson to get new tires."

"Maybe not," McHugh said. "Get in the truck and we'll see what we can do."

They drove to a garage in Nogales on the U.S. side of the border that was owned by a Mexican-American friend of McHugh's. Using an amazing mental inventory file, he plucked two slightly worn tires from the hundreds stacked on shelves. It took him another ten minutes to replace the damaged ones.

McHugh lived in a modest ranch house in Rio Rico, close to Nogales. His wife was friendly and talkative, and reminded Sutherland of some of her family back in West Virginia. She was a good cook, as well, and Sutherland asked for seconds on the tamales.

Mrs. McHugh must have noticed her guest's eyes drooping because she led her to her bedroom even though it was fairly early in the evening. Sutherland's clothes were grungy and she accepted the offer to wash them and pajamas to wear. She took a long, hot shower and slid beneath the cool sheets.

She closed her eyes and considered her situation. She was a target, and the people who were after her had a long reach. Anyone around her was in danger. She would take a short rest and do what she did best.

Disappear.

CHAPTER THIRTY-FIVE

Hawkins stirred in the cocoon-like warmth of his sleeping bag and glanced at the glowing hands of his wristwatch. He yawned, unzipped the bag, grabbed his computer and stepped out of his tent into the cold night. A welcome scent wafted on the crisp air. The guards were brewing a pot of coffee on a gas stove.

A guard waved Hawkins over and filled a mug for him. The first sip was like hitting the switch on his brain ignition. The potent concoction made the strongest Starbucks brew seem like water.

"Good?" the unlikely *barista* said.

"*More* than good," Hawkins said.

He went over to the lean-to he had erected close to the lake the day before, set his computer on a stack of boxes and booted up. He called up the data Fido had fed into the system after returning to the docking port. An orange-and-black image showed the lake floor moving under the AUV's camera. Information giving time and depth streamed along the bottom of the screen. A vertical portion of the picture off to the right showed the results of the side-scan sonar.

Calvin had emerged from his tent and followed the scent of coffee to its source. He brought his cup over to the lean-to.

"Man, this tastes like Louisiana crude."

"Yeah. We can use this stuff in the DPV if we run short on fuel." Hawkins pointed at the screen. "Have a look."

Hawkins called up the photographic image of the entire search area. Dotted parallel lines showed the path of the AUV as it moved from the bottom to the top of the slope and back down again.

"Fido was a busy little pup," Calvin said.

Calvin's finger traced several dark areas among the layers of rock strata. "These are all potential targets that could be cave openings."

Hawkins zoomed in on the individual targets, one after another. "There's one problem. You know what real estate people say. Location times three. None of these openings line up with the camel's hump or the mine shaft. They're all off to one side or the other of the mid-line."

"Maybe someone made a mistake eyeballing the hump."

"Maybe, but I can't see Kurtz sinking a mine shaft on the basis of an estimated position. Let's take a closer look at the slope directly in line with the shaft."

He went back to the over-view image and called up that section showing the path in line with the shaft. "There," he said, freezing the image on a huge boulder sitting in a depression. "Notice the shape of the shadow surrounding the rock."

Calvin squinted at screen. "The hole is rectangular, almost square. Mine opening maybe."

"That's my take on it too, Cal. It could be a mine or maybe a cave entrance modified by human beings. Only one way to know for sure."

"I'll get the dive gear ready," Calvin said.

The sun had risen, but the air was still cold and they shivered as they shimmied into their wetsuits. They ran a line down the sloping shore of the lake from the bumper of the personnel carrier. They would hold onto the rope as they made their way down to the water's edge. A couple of guards carried dive gear and waterproof flashlights to the edge of the lake. With a few strokes of the keyboard, Hawkins programmed the vehicle to return to the boulder it had discovered on its initial search.

Then he and Calvin pulled on their fins and air tanks with the attached Pegasus propulsion units, slipped into the lake and swam over to the floating dock. Fido's electric motors hummed while the computer went through its positioning procedure. Hawkins and Calvin waved at the guards lined up at the top of the cliff then they dove a few feet and tested their air supply and communications systems.

The AUV slipped below the surface with its headlights on. Propelled by the Pegasus thrusters, Hawkins and Calvin followed Fido, swimming parallel to the underwater slope. The color of the water shifted from silvery blue to navy. Their depth gauges were at one hundred fifty feet when Fido slowed to a stop and hovered with its headlight beams pointed at the massive boulder they had seen on the monitor. The rock was around twelve feet in diameter and wedged tightly into what had been the cave or mine opening.

"This explains why Kurtz sunk the shaft," Hawkins said. "There was no way he could get by this thing. And from the looks of it, neither can we."

Calvin poked his sheath knife into the tight seam between the bolder and the edge of the hole. "Where's that SEAL can-do spirit, Hawk?" He patted a pack harnessed to his chest. "Ol' Calvin packed some C-4 in his bag of goodies."

"You want to blast it? You'd need a nuke to pulverize this size rock."

"Not talking about blasting the rock. I'll set the charges around the perimeter and see if I can pop that bad boy out like a zit."

"You have a way with words, Cal. But won't the explosion bring down the whole slope above the opening?"

"Not if I set the charges right. I'll blast the ledge at the same time. The pressure will push the plug from behind, the ledge will crumble like an old cookie, and she'll roll over and out. Hopefully."

"Hopefully."

"That's the best I got, Hawk."

"Then it's good enough for me, old pal. Stay here, Fido," he said to the hovering AUV. "We'll be right back."

Hawkins pointed up. They rose up the face of the boulder, and then ascended the slope with strong, steady fin flutters. They were a few fathoms from the surface when they heard what sounded like a jackhammer. Then a buzz-saw went to work.

They hovered, listening as the combined noise grew to a stuttering sound wave that was only partially dampened by the layer of water overhead. A second later there was a flash of light and the water thudded with the vibration of an explosion. There were several more buzz saw episodes, followed by a thrashing, pulsating sound. The surface was stirred up like water in a washing machine and they backed down the slope to get away from the turbulence.

It didn't take a genius to figure out that there had been a fierce attack on land.

From the lack of sound, it appeared, too, that there was a lull. Hawkins signaled Calvin to head up the slope.

They surfaced cautiously through the roiling water. Black smoke drifted over their heads. They shed their tanks, weight belts and fins and crawled up to where they could peer over the edge of the cliff. The encampment was a scene of utter devastation.

Where there had been a dozen or so of Amir's guards were only broken bodies spread around. The troop carrier was a burning pile of blackened wreckage, and what was left of it was riddled with holes. Through the cloud of greasy smoke, Hawkins could see four helicopters circling the camel hump like hunting raptors. He recognized the slim fuselages of Cobra gunships. The larger helicopter was likely a flying command post.

Hawkins easily reconstructed the murderous assault.

The helicopters would have used the camel hump as cover and swooped in with Gatling guns blazing. The Afghans had fought back with their automatic weapons, but their defense would have been useless in the face of the withering stream of hot lead. After the guns had softened up the defenders, a missile was used to dispatch the troop carrier. The choppers had hovered over the lake for a few seconds before going into a holding pattern around the hump.

Hawkins pushed away a chilling thought. If Abby and Cait had stayed at the camp they would have been among the dead.

"Hey, Hawk. Heads up. Eleven o'clock."

Hawkins' eyes followed Calvin's pointing finger. The larger helicopter had broken from the holding pattern and was heading back toward the lake.

Without another word, Calvin scrambled over the top of the cliff and started running toward the shredded framework of their tents. The attack had concentrated mostly on the troop carrier, but shrapnel had torn through the tent fabric.

"Where the hell are you going?" Hawkins yelled at his friend's back.

Calvin raised his arm in a follow-me gesture and shouted something about needing help.

The helicopter was coming in fast.

Hawkins swore lustily and clambered over the edge of the cliff.

Calvin was at the ruined tents, and he ripped aside the tattered fabric and reached inside. He was struggling to lift a heavy metal locker when Hawkins arrived and grabbed one of the handles. They lugged the locker back toward the cliff, then down the banking to the water.

Hawkins started up toward the cliff again.

"Hey, Hawk, where the hell are *you* going?"

Calvin's voice was almost drowned out by the noise of the approaching rotors.

Hawkins gave Calvin the hand signal to stay down and raised his head slightly above the edge.

A charcoal-colored Blackhawk helicopter armed with missile pods on its stubby wings was setting down a few hundred feet from the blazing troop carrier. Seconds after the skids touched ground, the doors flew open and four men carrying AK-47s popped out. They were dressed in camouflage suits with no insignia. Black berets covered their heads. Their facial complexion and body type reflected a variety of nationalities, but they all had the hard-eyed, alert expression of professional soldiers.

Four more men got out. They were carrying duffle bags which they set on the ground. As the armed men stood guard, the quartet opened the bags and began to pull out air tanks and other dive equipment.

Finally, two more men emerged from the chopper. Hawkins couldn't believe his eyes when a portly man got out of the aircraft and he recognized the professor he had met at Georgetown University. Saleem had shed his tweeds and was dressed in a khaki army uniform, again with no insignia.

Hawkins' disbelief was further tested when he saw the last man, wearing a similar uniform emerge. The man took a few steps, stopped and swiveled his head robotically to inspect the carnage. In that fleeting second Hawkins saw the face of one of the twin assassins who had shot up his office. The man went over to the divers, who were suiting up, and pointed toward the lake.

Hawkins ducked below the ledge and slid down the slope to where Calvin was waiting.

"We've got big trouble," he said.

Over breakfast at the garden table in the courtyard of his house, Amir had been sharing reminiscences of his late wife with his two guests when he paused and looked first at Abby, then Cait.

"Tell me," he said. "If the Prester John treasure were in your hands, what would you do with it?"

"I would put it in an exhibition that traveled the world so that people everywhere could see the wonders of the past," Cait said.

"Spoken like a true seeker of knowledge. Would those people be primarily in the more affluent countries?"

"A fair question. I would make sure the exhibition goes everywhere and that poor people could see it for free."

"Better. But even if the treasure went on display, how would showing a priceless treasure better the lives of people in a poor country like Afghanistan?"

"By giving them pride in their culture. The glories of their past would show them that they once had a level of civilization that equaled or even surpassed that of Western Europe."

Amir nodded and turned to Abby. "Do you agree?"

"Cultural pride is a good thing," Abby said, "but you can't eat it. I'd slap a big price on the admission tickets and use the treasure as the basis for books, films, videos, reproductions. The money earned would go into a foundation that would distribute the income to countries where it would do the most good."

"Brilliant!" Amir said. "Could you be persuaded to run this foundation?"

"With your business background, you'd be a perfect choice," Cait said.

"Thanks for the flattering offer, but I'm pretty busy with my company."

"Not too busy to travel halfway across the world to go on a dangerous treasure hunt," Cait said.

"Matt wouldn't let me say no." She shrugged. "I guess I'm a sucker when it comes to my ex-husband."

Cait's jaw dropped. "You were married to Matt?"

"For a few years, after a whirlwind navy romance."

"You have good taste in men. He's extremely attractive."

"If you're hinting that I was a fool to give him up, you're probably right. But Matt would probably agree with me that it was the right thing to do at the time."

"At the time," Cait echoed, cocking her head.

Abby knew Cait was about to use her answer as a jumping off place to ask whether things had changed. She liked Cait, but her past was her own business, and she would not be shy about saying so. Amir may have seen the pugnacious look in her eye because he diverted the conversation back to the subject of the treasure.

"Maybe Abby would be interested in your thoughts on the exact nature of the treasure, Dr. Cait."

Abby gave Amir a smile of thanks for allowing her a graceful exit.

"Be glad to," Cait said. "Prester John described himself as being fabulously rich and said that he ruled his kingdom with an emerald-encrusted golden scepter. My research suggests that he sent some of his treasure as a gift to the Pope and the scepter as a gesture of solidarity."

"I could use a scepter like that to rule my own little kingdom," Amir said with a wry smile.

"You may have the artifact in your hands soon, if Matt's dive is successful."

"Then we should soon be on our way," Amir said. He rose from his chair and said, "My car will be here in fifteen minutes."

As Abby headed for her room, Cait reached out and touched her arm.

"Thanks for persuading me to spend the night here, and for the first aid on my face," she said. "I owe you an apology, too. I was pushing too close to your personal business."

Abby saw from Cait's expression that she was truly sorry.

"The stuff with Matt? Don't worry," she said before setting off down the hallway. "That's water under the bridge. We're just good friends, although we may not even be that by the time this adventure is over. Your face looks great by the way. Make-up is a wonderful thing. See you in ten."

Amir was at the wheel of the touring car. An armed guard sat beside him and two more tribesmen were tucked into the jump seats behind the seated women. More guards rode in the Russian Jeep, behind the Caddy, and others in the DPV, which brought up the rear.

As usual, Amir drove at breakneck speed. They were flying through the agricultural fields when suddenly a pick-up truck appeared coming in the opposite direction. The driver was blinking the headlights and leaning on the horn.

Truck and car simultaneously came to a screeching stop. Amir shouted in anger in *Pashto*. The driver babbled back at him.

Amir listened for a moment, a grim expression on his face, then he turned to Cait and Abby. "This man says smoke and noise are coming from the camp where your friends are."

He put the touring car in gear and they covered the distance to the lake in ten minutes. He stopped at the edge of the bluff and with Abby and Cait following, he hobbled to the cliff to peer through binoculars at a black cloud rising from the opposite shore.

"What's going on?" Abby said.

The Amir handed the binoculars to Abby and pointed across the lake.

"My eyes aren't what they used to be. Tell me if you see anything."

Abby studied the camp site for a moment, and said, "Too much smoke." She handed the glasses to Cait, who had no better luck.

Amir rattled off a series of orders to his men. The Russian Jeep continued on the road around the lake and the desert vehicle headed back to the compound.

"I've sent some of my men to scout out the camp and others to warn the village. Somehow, someone got past our outposts. It looks as if I will have to make an apology to Mr. Hawkins for doubting his warnings…."

Amir left off the last part of his comment, but his unspoken words hung in the air.

….If he is still alive.

CHAPTER THIRTY-SIX

As he stepped out of the helicopter and looked around at the scene of death and destruction, the professor felt as if he were spinning down into a black vortex of violence from which there was no escape. He'd failed to come up with a way to save lives.

Marzak exited behind Saleem and inhaled the oily miasma deep into his lungs as if testing the nose of a fine wine. The crackle of flames was music to his ears. His pulse raced with excitement, while his glowering eyes burned with a blue fire.

The mercenaries poured out of the helicopter to mop things up, no more emotional than cattle killers in a slaughterhouse. Marzak noticed the rope leading from the truck's bumper toward the lake. He strode to the cliff and saw where the line led into the water. He ordered the divers to suit up and get into the lake to find Hawkins.

The professor heard the order and raised his hand. "I was under the impression that we were here to look for a treasure. If we encounter the Americans we will take care of them, but it is not our primary goal."

"It is *my* primary goal. The Doctor gave me command of these men."

"And my cousin gave me control of their paychecks."

Marzak's nostrils flared in anger. He drew his pistol from his belt, aimed at a wounded man who was attempting to crawl away and dispatched him with a clean shot to the head.

The cold-blooded murder seemed to calm him down. "My apologies, professor. My brother's death still preys on my mind."

The professor was aware, especially after the cold-blooded murder he had just witnessed, that his control over Marzak was an illusion. The best he could do was delay. "I understand your feelings. I only ask that your revenge wait."

"Yes, of course. But please allow these men to do a quick search before they look for the treasure cave."

"A reasonable compromise," the professor agreed, knowing that there was little else he could do.

Marzak nodded and went over to the divers to give them their amended orders.

The four divers had donned black military style wetsuits and air tanks and were checking the loads in their APS underwater assault rifles. Developed by the Russians, the rifle had a folding butt stock and an odd-shaped oversized magazine that could hold up to twenty-six rounds. The weapon fired steel dart cartridges and had an underwater range of more than a hundred feet. Each rifle had a knife-bayonet for close combat.

The divers used the descent line to climb down to the water's edge, where they plunged in and quickly disappeared below the blue surface of the lake.

Minutes earlier, Hawkins had scrambled down the same slope and grabbed Calvin by the arm.

"We're going to have company," he warned. "Four guys packing APSes."

"Better give me a hand with this, then." Cal grabbed a strongbox handle.

Hawkins put his doubts aside, took hold of the box, and they pulled it down the slope into the water. Around the fifty feet level Calvin signaled a stop and opened the container. The object inside looked like a turbo-drive hairdryer.

Hawkins recognized the Heckler and Koch P11underwater pistol. The thick handle housed a battery pack that electrically ignited the cartridges tucked into the short, fat barrel unit. The cartridges fired steel darts around four inches long with an effective underwater range of about forty feet. Hawkins had trained on the weapon, but never used one in combat.

Calvin extracted several half-pound blocks of C-4 plastic explosive packed in foil, a time fuse, M-60 fuse lighter and blasting cap from his pack and handed them to Hawkins, who tucked them into his vest pockets.

Hawkins raised his eyes, saw four dark shapes silhouetted against the silvery surface glimmer and jerked his thumb down. They used every muscle in their legs to propel themselves to where Fido hovered next to the big boulder. Hawkins had designed the submersible with an external control panel. He doused the headlights and looked up to see a quartet of falling stars floating down into the dark water. The divers had flicked on their flashlights and were making a cautious descent, four abreast.

"I've got a dart for each one of those guys with an extra," Calvin said.

Hawkins knew from his own experience how hard it was to get a bead on a moving target with the Heckler and Koch. The four APS rifles gave the pursuing divers greater range and more than a hundred chances to make a hit.

"Stay close by and get ready to shoot when I tell you," he said.

He tilted Fido up at the front so the submersible was directed at the divers who had closed the distance by half. Hawkins waited until they were around twenty feet away, then clicked on the headlights.

The divers were clearly illuminated as they shielded their eyes against the powerful halogens with their free hands.

"*Now*!" Hawkins said.

Calvin fired his weapon at the closest diver. The dart missed by a foot or more. The divers shot at the AUV's light array using tracer darts followed by killing projectiles. Three of the darts missed, but one thunked into the plastic housing. Hawkins doused Fido's headlights. A flight of darts shot past them, missing by inches. While the rifles were recharging, Calvin pumped two shots at the darkness behind the nearest flashlight.

There was no sound to announce a hit, but the light jerked in a dozen different directions. Hawkins turned the lights on again and saw a diver clutching the shaft of the dart sticking from his rib cage. Dark blood flowed from the wound.

His companions saw the same horrible sight and kicked frantically toward the surface.

"Good shooting, Cal."

"Crap! There are still three of them."

"What would you do if you were them?" Hawkins asked.

"I'd pop some grenades into the water. Even if they miss, the blast will soften us up for a quick assault. Even better, I'd have a chopper pop a missile down our throats."

"Now what would you do if you were us?"

"Get the hell out of here!"

"We'll have to surface when our air runs out. The choppers will be patrolling the lake ready to turn us into hamburger. We need a distraction.

Follow me."

Hawkins swam toward the body of the now dead diver. He grabbed him by a fin and held the corpse steady. With the other hand he pulled the C-4 packets out of his vest and handed them to Calvin who knew exactly what his friend was thinking. While Hawkins used Fido to provide light, Calvin bundled four packets with a couple of turns of time fuse. Then he attached a tubular blasting cap to the free end of the fuse.

"This burns at around forty seconds per foot. We've got around fifty feet of water above our heads."

He did the mental calculations, cut off a length of fuse, then attached an M-60 fuse lighter to the end he'd just cut. When they were ready, Hawkins inflated the dead man's vest until the body had positive buoyancy. Timing would have to be just right.

He gave Calvin an okay signal and pushed the body off.

"You've been hanging out with us too long," he said to the dead diver. "Time to spread yourself around."

He waited to make sure the body was rising at the expected rate of speed, and then gave Calvin an okay signal. Calvin removed the safety pin, pulled back the spring-loaded firing pin and released it, lighting the fuse.

"Fire in the hole!"

Hawkins and Calvin turned Fido around. Hawkins increased speed with the external throttle. Using the power from the submersible and their Pegasus units, they began to move with agonizing slowness deeper into the lake.

The divers were furious at losing a man in an ambush.

They had forged a more prudent strategy and were stacking the grenades at the edge of the cliff, when one of them glanced at the water and shouted, “Look!”

A shiny black object bobbed to the surface around thirty feet from shore and rolled over to reveal the dead white face of the missing diver.

The divers forgot their improvised depth bomb attack, clambered down the hill, splashed into the water and began swimming toward the body.

Standing at the edge of the bluff, Marzak focused his binoculars on the dead diver and saw a thin plume of gray smoke rising from the dead man’s chest.

He threw the field glasses aside and sprinted inland away from the water.

The Doctor and Professor Saleem had wondered what the fuss was about and were walking his way when he waved his hands at them.

“Run!” he shouted.

They wheeled about and dug in their heels, not sure why.

The divers were only a few feet from the body when the C-4 exploded in a huge fireball that created a geyser of lake water, neoprene and body parts.

The shock wave from the blast surged up the cliff and rolled inland, where it slammed Marzak in the back and knocked him forward like a ball hitting a bowling pin. His face crashed into the rocky ground, breaking his nose. If the impact had not rendered him unconscious, he would have spit out the word that had been on his lips.

Hawkins.

CHAPTER THIRTY-SEVEN

Amir's scout team returned within an hour. The men gathered around the sheik, babbling in *Pashto* and jabbing their fingers toward the far shore of the lake. Amir turned to Abby and Cait.

"My men got to within a quarter a mile of the camp. They were afraid to go any further because a helicopter had landed at the encampment. The troop carrier was heavily damaged and they saw bodies lying on the ground." Anticipating the unspoken question, he added, "They were too far away to identify the bodies."

Abby was worried about her friends, but she pushed her personal misgivings aside and her military training took over.

"Did your men report anything else of interest?"

"Yes. They heard an explosion, and a short while after that the helicopter took off and flew over the camel's back."

Abby glanced up at the clear blue sky.

"The helicopter may have set down to refuel and rearm," she said. "We're totally exposed to an air attack out here. We'd better get out of sight before it returns."

"What about Matt and Calvin?" Cait said. "We can't just leave them!"

"There's nothing we can do," Amir said.

Abby put her arm around Cait's shoulders. "Matt and Cal are highly-trained soldiers. They're fully capable of taking care of themselves. They'll be fine."

"But what if they've been wounded and are just lying there?" Cait said with pleading eyes.

"If they are dead they are dead," Amir said bluntly. "We must get back to the village, see to the living and prepare a defense."

As Amir shouted orders to his men, Cait walked to the edge of the bluff and looked across at the wispy clouds of smoke rising from the far shore of the lake.

She was about to turn away, but her eye caught a strange V-shaped ripple and trail of bubbles around fifty feet from shore. Something was moving in her direction.

Keeping her eyes glued to the object, she called Abby over and pointed.

Abby squinted against the glare. "What the hell is *that* thing?"

Amir noticed the two women staring into the lake and hobbled over. He saw a light-colored blur moving toward land and called his men over. He pointed his cane at the object which became more yellow in tone as it rose to the surface.

The black muzzles of six automatic weapons tracked the object until it stopped around twenty feet away. It was a tribute to their discipline that they didn't unleash deadly fire when one head, then another, popped to the surface. A hand reached out of the water and pulled the hood back and goggles down to reveal the grinning face of Hawkins.

"Hello," he said as if returning from the dead were a normal occurrence.

Calvin pulled his mask down as well. "You-all going to stand there or give us a hand?"

The two men pushed the AUV in until it touched the bottom of the sloped bank. Amir's men hauled Fido out of the water and onto the top of the cliff. Then they helped Hawkins and Calvin who crawled out of the lake as if they were antediluvian water creatures making the transition to land. They stood on shaky legs at the top of the cliff and slipped out of their dive gear.

"This is a miracle," Amir said. "Did you swim underwater all the way across the lake?"

Hawkins patted his friend on the back. "It was nothing for a navy SEAL. Right, Calvin?"

"An *ex*-navy SEAL," Calvin corrected. "Speak for yourself, man. You said we could ride Fido all the way."

"What Cal is saying is that Fido gave us a tow until its batteries ran down," Hawkins said.

"And our propulsion units fizzled." Calvin puffed his cheeks out. "We had to drag the submersible the last couple of hundred feet. It was like moving a refrigerator underwater."

"Fido is a prototype," Hawkins explained. "Still got a few bugs to work out of its battery system."

"I'll carry some extra double AAs next time," Calvin said.

"Maybe you two could stop your bickering long enough to tell us what happened over there," Abby said.

"Sorry, Abby." Hawkins took in a lungful of air and let it out. "There was an air attack. Three Cobra gunships with missiles and Gatling guns."

Amir was familiar with the Cobra's capability and he knew better than to ask if anyone had survived. "Many of my men have wives and children in the village. The people responsible for this will pay with their lives." He clutched Hawkins by the arm. "Do you know who is behind the attack?"

"Partially. A Blackhawk helicopter landed after the Cobras did their work and three men who seemed to be in charge got out. I knew two of them. One is the twin of the man who tried to kill me. The other is a professor from Georgetown University." He looked at Cait. "His name is Saleem."

Cait gave a coughing laugh. "That's *impossible.* The professor isn't a killer and this is the last place he would be. I'm sure you're mistaken."

"I'm afraid not, Cait. I talked to Saleem a few days ago at Georgetown," Hawkins said.

"How is it that you escaped the attack?" Amir said.

Hawkins explained that they'd been underwater looking at a possible mine entrance and then told of the run-in with the dive team.

"My men said they heard an explosion," Amir said.

"We used the dead diver's body and made an improvised floating mine before the divers could make a second try at us."

"I'll bet *that* isn't in the SEAL bag of tricks," Abby said.

"Yeah, but it's in Calvin's bag," Hawkins said like a proud father.

"I had the C-4, but Hawk was the one who figured out how to use it," Calvin said. "Dumb luck."

"We won't be as lucky if the choppers come in while we're out here like sitting ducks," Hawkins said.

The sheik ordered his men to help lift the AUV onto the desert vehicle. Then they tied their dive gear onto the side carriers. Amir and the women and two guards got in the touring car. The other guards followed in the Russian jeep. Hawkins and Calvin brought up the rear in the desert vehicle.

They dashed through the countryside at a breakneck pace, prompting Calvin to say, "These guys are running as if the hounds of hell are after them."

Hawkins, who was behind the wheel, glanced in the rear-view mirror and let out an oath.

"What's wrong?" Calvin said.

"Those hounds of hell you just mentioned?"

"Yeah?"

Hawkins jerked his thumb at the black speck in the sky behind them.

"Hope you brought some dog biscuits."

He squeezed a few more miles of speed out of the desert vehicle's engine, knowing even as he did so, that there would be no escape from the helicopter closing in for the kill like a fierce-eyed Valkyrie.

CHAPTER THIRTY-EIGHT

When Marzak regained consciousness, Professor Saleem was bending over him. Sledge hammers pounded against the inside of his skull.

The professor spread Marzak's eyelids open wide with his fingers. "Do you know your name?"

Marzak slapped the arm away.

"Don't be a fool!"

"I have some first aid training and was checking for signs of dilation, which would indicate a serious condition. My guess is that it is only a concussion; although your nose may be broken. There's lots of blood."

Marzak pushed himself up to a standing position.

"*Wonderful.*" Marzak said, spreading his mouth in a grin that looked ghastly against the drying blood that streaked his upper lip. "Simply wonderful. You can send me the bill for your insightful diagnosis."

The mercenaries stood around awaiting orders, but he only gave them a glance and staggered to the edge of the cliff. Three bodies floated in the bloodied waters a few yards from shore. He couldn't believe it! Hawkins had wiped out his entire dive team.

He scanned the lake surface further from shore. Nothing. Hawkins could have swum further out, but it was doubtful he would have had the strength or the air supply to reach the far side. Marzak guessed that Hawkins was swimming parallel to the shore, looking for a safe spot to come out onto land.

He whirled around and shouted at the mercenaries to spread out along the bluff. Then he strode over to the pile of hand grenades and clipped them onto his belt. He walked along the lake and lobbed the grenades in, one-by-one, creating a line of foamy explosions. He quickly exhausted his supply of grenades, and paced up and down the shoreline, exhorting the mercenaries to keep a sharp eye out, promising a reward to the first man to report seeing a diver, dead or alive.

After a while it became clear that the reward would go unclaimed and he ordered the mercenaries to get back into the helicopter.

The professor confronted Marzak at the door of the aircraft. "What are you going to do about the treasure?"

"You saw for yourself, the dive team is no more. Kaput! We will now proceed to the next stage of our mission, the destruction of the village. Unless you want to walk home, I suggest you get into the helicopter."

A few moments later, the helicopter was rising into the air. The Cobras were taking on fuel and ammunition on the other side of the camel's back. Marzak had the pilot radio the gunships to get in the air for an attack.

While he waited to rendezvous with the Cobras, he directed the Blackhawk pilot to fly over the lake on the off-chance that his prey had actually attempted the crossing. There was no sign of anyone in the water, but at five hundred feet altitude, they had a clear view of the entire lake.

The pilot pointed at the dust cloud being kicked up on the far side of the lake and Marzak told him to check it out. As the helicopter sped across the lake, Marzak leaned out the window. In his excitement, he no longer felt the throbbing pain from the ugly bruise in his forehead and the smashed bridge of his nose.

Seconds later they caught up with the three vehicles. He had the helicopter circle around the convoy and saw the open car with two women in it, leading the way. Some of the men in the jeep raised their guns and were trying to get a bead on the helicopter.

As the helicopter banked out of range, the driver of the last vehicle looked up. Marzak recognized the tanned features immediately. Hawkins had somehow made it to safety. He ordered the pilot and mercenaries to prepare for a strafing run.

The helicopter circled around and followed the line of vehicles.

"It's Hawkins and another man," Marzak said to the professor. "They're wearing dive suits. Somehow they swam across the lake." He laughed. "It's too bad we have to spoil their day at the beach."

"Wait," Saleem said.

"No need. We can take care of Hawkins without the help of the gunships."

"No!" the professor said. "We need them both alive."

The smile froze on Marzak's lips. "*Alive?* What are you talking about?"

"Our dive team is dead. We need experienced divers to look for the treasure."

The helicopter had made its turn and was coming in at a low angle, running a parallel course that would allow the mercenaries to unleash a deadly fusillade from the doors and window.

Marzak glared at Saleem. "I know Hawkins. He's not going to dive for you," he said with unveiled contempt.

"He might if there was enough at stake. I want them alive for now. Or I'm calling this mission off."

The professor's insistent voice and hard-eyed expression told Marzak that there was no room for debate. He watched the vehicles recede to pinpoints in the distance and called on almost superhuman willpower to issue his next order.

"Lower your guns," he said.

CHAPTER THIRTY-NINE

Amir's village was in complete chaos.

The Cadillac braked to a stop just inside the gate, unable to proceed further in the traffic gridlock. Hawkins got out of the desert vehicle and strode over to the touring car.

"What's going on?" he said.

"I gave orders for women and children to move to safety," Amir said. "I assumed that the evacuation would be well under way. This is insanity. I will take care of it."

Amir rose from his seat and in a booming voice issued a series of angry commands. All commotion ceased and every eye fell on the sheik before the people once again sprang into action. Within minutes, the traffic had parted just enough for the caravan to continue to Amir's compound. His daughter Nagia stood on the veranda with his granddaughter Yasmeen. Nagia was trying to herd the aged cook and housekeeper into a khaki-colored Land Rover.

Nagia's expression of angry frustration changed to relief when she saw the procession drive up to the house. Amir and Nagia had an exchange in *Pashto*, and then he gave her a quick embrace, picked up the little girl and handed her to his daughter, who had gotten into the vehicle. He told one of his men to drive the Land Rover. As the vehicle left the compound he came back to the jeep.

"My daughter will lead the villagers to some caves a few miles from here where they can hide," Amir explained.

"Good move," Hawkins said. "The village will be a death trap if the choppers attack."

"Why didn't they shoot at us back at the lake?" Calvin said. "They had us dead in their sights."

Hawkins shook his head. "Haven't a clue, but it's only a matter of time before they return."

"We're not completely defenseless. I have something to show you that might help," Amir said.

Hawkins and Calvin were still in their wetsuits, and now they were sweating profusely under the tight neoprene coverings. "But before you do that, you don't know where we could get some street clothes?"

Amir told them to wait and disappeared into the house.

Abby and Cait got out of the touring car. "What's going on?" Abby said.

Hawkins repeated what Amir had said.

"What do you want us to do?" Abby said.

"The sheik's daughter may need a hand getting the villagers to safety. We'll follow as soon as we see what Amir has up his sleeve."

"See that you do, Matt," Cait said. "I'm holding you to that dinner invitation."

Abby shot an unfriendly glance at Cait and turned to Hawkins with narrowed eyes.

"What dinner invitation is that, Matt?"

Hawkins was struggling to come up with a diplomatic answer when Calvin came to his rescue.

"Dinner we're *all* going to have to celebrate getting out of this mess," he said.

Abby flashed an alligator smile, and then she and Cait climbed into the jeep and headed out of the village to catch up with the evacuation.

"Thanks for the save, pal," Hawkins said.

"You wouldn't be much help fighting the bad guys once Abby got through with you, Hawk. She doesn't like you hound-dogging other pretty ladies."

Hawkins told his friend to assume a position that would have been anatomically impossible.

Amir came out of the house and handed them two sets of clothing. "This is all I have, unfortunately."

Hawkins and Calvin stripped down to their bathing suits, then put on the baggy tribal trousers and robe, and the mushroom-shaped hats. They got in the car and the sheik drove to the airstrip. They stopped in front of an old hangar that Amir said the Russians had built. Amir asked for help sliding open the wide wooden door, then led the way into the darkened interior and switched on the overhead lights.

Hawkins let out a low whistle. The walls were covered with weapons that spanned centuries. More weapons were displayed on wooden shelves and in glass cabinets.

"Looks like a military museum," Hawkins said.

"Actually, it's a museum dedicated to the folly of empire. These weapons were left behind by armies that invaded my country. We're in the small arms section." He reached up and touched the sharp point of a long spear hanging from the wall. "Alexander the Great's infantry used these Macedonian *sarissa* pikes with devastating effect. Next to it is a bronze helmet and shield of the same era. This curved sword came in with the Arabs. That saddle was used by a cavalryman in the time of Genghis Kahn."

Calvin ran his fingers along the wooden stock of a rifle. "Nice Martini-Henry. We saw tribesmen still using these when we were in the SEALs."

"That weapon goes back to the British invasions," Amir said. "These are Russian weapons. *Kalashnikov* automatic rifles, *Spetsnaz* and *Malarov* pistols. Grenade launchers. Now the Taliban are using them."

"I don't see any U.S. weapons," Hawkins said.

"All in storage while the war is in progress. No doubt future insurgents will be using leftover firearms from the current war."

"No doubt," Hawkins said. "You said this is the small arms section."

"That's right. The bigger toys are in the next room."

Even if Abby had not stomped the Russian jeep's gas pedal with a lead foot, she and Cait would have had no problem catching up with the fleeing villagers. The more-or-less orderly procession had degenerated into a rout. By the time they caught up it was at a standstill. In their panic, some of the truck drivers had tried to sprint past the slower moving vehicles. The rear guard had gone after them and pulled them over like traffic cops, blocking the narrow road.

Abby drove off the road past vehicles loaded with young and old women, terrified children and wailing babies, eventually pulling up to the head of the line. Some of the armed guards were brandishing weapons at the cowering truck drivers. Amir's daughter was shouting at the guard leader. She was backed up by several women, all talking at the same time. Some of Amir's men stood behind the women shouting their side of the debate. Abby leaned on the horn to catch their attention. She took advantage of the pause in the altercation and jumped out of the jeep.

Striding over to Amir's daughter, she said, "What's going on?"

When Nagia replied in English the guard excitedly cut her off in *Pashto*. Abby joined in and within seconds, she too was shouting.

"Maybe I can help," Cait said. She said something in *Pashto* and after a moment had managed to silence both speakers who looked expectantly at Abby.

"Thanks," she said. "Now please tell the guy to move the guards away from the civilians. We will lead the parade. Everyone must stay in line."

The arrangement seemed to suit the warring parties. The procession slowly got moving again with the Russian jeep at the head of the line.

Abby glanced in the rear view mirror and allowed herself a smile. "Thanks for the help," she said.

"Anytime," Cait replied. "About that dinner with Matt."

"Before you say another word, take a deep breath, look behind us and think about where we are."

"I see what you mean," Cait said with a glance at the parade of panicked villagers and their scruffy guards. "We're a long way from the Ritz."

Abby smiled. "Couldn't have said it better myself."

Amir pressed an electrical switch and a section of wall slid back on its runners. They stepped into another section of the vast hangar and found themselves looking directly into the barrel of a gun on a massive turreted vehicle painted in camouflage green and tan.

"Whoa!" Calvin said. "Ruskie combat vehicle."

"Correct," Amir said, "It was used by Russian Special Forces. It was in bad shape from rocket grenades when I restored it, but the same mechanics who got my car and the troop carrier running rebuilt the engine. I don't have ammunition for the machine gun, unfortunately."

They walked around behind the combat vehicle and into another section of the shed occupied almost entirely by a huge biplane.

"This is a British Handley Page bomber dating to World War One. The British used planes like this to bomb villages in the second Anglo-Afghan war. Villagers found it on the other side of the lake many years ago and showed my grandfather who saved it from being cannibalized for parts. It was passed to my father, who left it to me. The body has been meticulously restored, as you can see, and the engines taken apart then reassembled."

Calvin ran his fingers along the fuselage.

"I've heard of these planes, but never saw one before in the flesh. She's in fantastic shape. Better than anything in my collection."

"You're collecting planes now?" Hawkins said.

"Got bored with cars. I've got a Sopworth and a SPAD. Still air worthy. Has anyone ever tried to fly this crate?"

"No, but my mechanics are the best and they swear it is fully operable." He moved toward a large metal storage locker and opened the doors. "This is what I wanted to show you."

The wall locker held six long metal boxes that were identical in size and color. Stenciled on the outside of the olive-drab containers were the words: Property of the U.S.A. At Amir's direction, the two men picked up a container and placed it on the floor. Amir removed the lid to reveal a Stinger missile and launcher carefully packed in foam peanuts.

Calvin lifted the missile out of the container.

The Stinger surface-to-air was only sixty inches long and a few inches in diameter, and weighed just over thirty pounds. But as the Soviets had learned to their dismay, the shoulder-fired projectile that the CIA supplied to the *mujahideen* could knock an aircraft out of the air at a range of nearly three miles and an altitude of more than twelve thousand feet.

"There are more than enough missiles here to shoot down our enemies," Amir said.

"Not so fast," Calvin said. "Shelf life of these babies is seven years. The batteries are probably dead and there could be mechanical degradation."

Calvin spent a few minutes examining each Stinger and its serial number.

Hawkins saw the slow shake of Calvin's head.

"What's wrong, Cal?"

"The news ain't good. These are all from the same lot."

"Are you saying they're useless?" Amir said.

"Probably, unless we can *throw* these puppies at the choppers."

"I've heard about degraded Stingers being rejuvenated," Hawkins said.

"Me, too. I'd be willing to give it a try."

They carried the Stingers back to the car and placed them in the rear seat. Calvin found batteries and electrical tools in a workshop. A pickup truck came screaming along the road to the hangar and braked to a stop. One of Amir's men jumped out and started shouting. Amir turned to Hawkins and Calvin.

"The helicopters have returned," he said.

Abby felt the air vibrating and a second later, three Cobra gunships flashed overhead. They followed the road for a quarter of a mile or so, then stopped and pivoted, three abreast, their Gatling guns facing toward the village procession.

Abby slammed on the brakes and stood up in the open car.

The three aircraft hovered a hundred feet above the ground like wolves about to close in on a wounded deer.

"What should we do?" Cait said.

"Not much we *can* do. They'll make the first move."

The seconds ticked by like years, then the gunships tilted down so that their guns faced the ground. They advanced at an angle and fired their guns in bursts, moving slowly ahead, the torrent of bullets kicking up fountains of dirt. They stopped firing when the fusillade was less than fifty feet from the jeep.

Abby stared at the narrow aircraft, thinking how ugly they were. "They're herding us."

"What?"

"Get out of the jeep," Abby said. "Start walking back. Tell everyone in line to get out of their cars and trucks."

"They'll kill us."

"Maybe. They could have wiped us out with a rear attack, though. Tell the guards not to fire at the choppers. Please help me, Cait."

They got out of the jeep and began to walk back along the line. Cait shouted in *Pashto* for people to abandon their vehicles. As the villagers slowly made their way back to the compound, only then did the Cobras stop firing their guns.

The sheik was visibly shaken by the news that his family was in danger and didn't protest when Hawkins slid behind the wheel of the touring car and told him to get in the back. Calvin was hanging on the running board when Hawkins took off, but he managed to get into the front seat.

They had traveled less than a mile when they heard the sound of guns and explosions. The villagers were under attack. They'd be caught in the open with no chance to escape. Black smoke billowed into the air. Hawkins had no desire to witness the scene he conjured up in his imagination, but he pushed the accelerator to the floor. Moments later, they rounded the base of a low hill.

The villagers were trekking in their direction, some running, some walking. Three Cobra gunships followed, flying abreast at an altitude of a couple of hundred feet, firing into the ground behind the villagers, herding them as if they were a flock of frightened sheep. The Blackhawk was hovering behind the Cobras. Leading the line were Abby and Cait. Nagia and her daughter, and the elderly servants were walking behind them. In the distance, the cars and trucks were ablaze.

Hawkins drove up to the head of the parade. He told Abby and the other women to get in, then he and Calvin got out to make room. Amir joined them and despite his limp, led his villagers back to the village on foot. The villagers flooded back into the settlement in a reverse version of the bedlam that had ensued during the evacuation. Amir ordered his men to get the women and children under cover. Cait and Abby went back to Amir's house with the family and staff.

The gunships flew over the village with an ear-shattering clatter, broke formation and landed out of sight. Hawkins and Calvin climbed to the top floor of the house and peered through a window. The Cobras were on opposite sides and to the rear of the village.

The Blackhawk made a slow circle over the village and set down a few hundred yards from the main village gate. Hawkins and Calvin quickly descended to the veranda.

"What did you see?" Amir asked.

"The Cobras have cut off escape on three sides," Hawkins said. "The Blackhawk is sitting just outside the front gate. Let's see what they're up to."

Hawkins and Calvin drove toward the gate and parked behind an abandoned house. Amir followed with three men. Hawkins put his back flat against the wall of the house and edged around the corner. He watched as the chopper's rotors spun to a stop, saw the door open and a man get out.

Calvin was waiting for all hell to break out, but the only sound was the oath of surprise that came from Hawkins' lips.

"What the hell's going on?" Calvin asked.

Professor Saleem was walking cautiously toward the village with a white flag in his hand.

"I think they want to surrender," Hawkins said.

CHAPTER FORTY

Professor Saleem approached the silent village, walking with the stiff-legged gait of a condemned prisoner being led to the gallows. He gulped the crisp Afghan air into his lungs, but he couldn't escape the feeling that he was about to suffocate. Sweat poured down his face, and he was nearly paralyzed with fear. He was acutely aware of Marzak in the helicopter behind him watching his every move. He didn't want to think about how many weapons behind the compound's walls were pointed his way.

His heart hammered away in his chest, and he had a forlorn hope that he might go into cardiac arrest. He was surprised that he hadn't died of heart failure when the attack on the vehicles was called off at the last second and again when it seemed the fleeing villagers would be massacred.

Marzak hadn't killed the villagers, seeing them as bargaining chips to persuade Hawkins to dive for the treasure. The professor volunteered to deliver the offer.

Saleem had fashioned a white flag from a strip of bandage from the helicopter's first aid kit. He whipped the streamer back and forth in his hand as he walked.

He was at the point where he would almost rather die than take another step, when a figure emerged from the village and began walking toward him with a slow ambling pace. The man wore tribal costume, but the professor immediately recognized the craggy features and the bark-like complexion under the mushroom-shaped hat. Matt Hawkins. *The man looks like a walking tree*, he thought.

They met fifty feet from the village. In contrast to the professor's pinched features and tense posture, Hawkins had a half smile on his lips and his hands hung loosely at his sides. He projected an unmistakable air of confidence. There was even an unexpected amusement in his dark eyes when they glanced at the make-shift truce flag. "Hello, Professor Saleem. Did you come to offer your surrender or demonstrate your talent as a cheerleader?"

Saleem bunched the bandage up and crammed it into his pants pocket.

"You have a rather mordant sense of humor," the professor said.

"You're not the first to tell me that. You're a long way from Georgetown."

Saleem managed a quick smile of his own.

"It's about the same distance to Woods Hole, Mr. Hawkins. Did you come all this way to play Lawrence of Arabia?"

"Touché," Hawkins said. "What brings you to this lovely garden spot?"

"The same thing that brought you here. *Treasure*."

"You've given up teaching history, Professor?"

"For the time being. How is my colleague Dr. Everson, by the way?"

"She's fine, but she didn't believe me when I told her that you were away from your classroom on a field trip."

"Teaching was only my day job. Actually, I work for the Pakistani intelligence service."

Hawkins cocked his head. "Are you telling me that this murderous romp is an ISI operation?"

"No! Far from it. I'll admit that elements of my service maintain contacts with extremists, but I have been dragged into this mess by the man watching us from that helicopter behind me. You know him I believe. His name is Marzak."

"He didn't introduce himself when he and his twin tried to kill me."

"He is intent on taking revenge against you for killing his brother. But first he must finish a job he was hired to do for a group that came together in the vacuum created when Osama Bin Laden was killed. They call themselves the Shadows and they would like revenge too, but against the *entire* U.S.A."

"How'd you get hooked up with these Boy Scouts, Professor?"

"Marzak and his brother were terrorists for hire. The Shadows retained them to carry out a terror plan in the U.S., but it was put on hold while they searched for the treasure. Once they have the treasure, they will move ahead with their plot. I am seen as sympathetic to their cause."

"You're telling me that you *aren't*?"

"I am nominally in charge of this expedition, but Marzak is in operational control. I am really on your side."

Hawkins took the professor's words with a grain of salt. The ISI had a reputation for double dealing, accepting American money and working with the CIA on one hand, enabling the Taliban and terrorists like Bin Laden on the other. Their goals were complicated, and were usually connected to the long-standing Cold War between Pakistan and India.

"Prove it. Tell me about the terror attack they're planning against the U.S."

"I'll tell you what I know. It's called the Prophet's Necklace. It's a scheme to use sarin gas at a number of different locations across the U.S."

The smile vanished from Hawkins' face. He knew sarin from the subway attack by a Japanese religious sect that had killed dozens of people back in the 1990s. The deadly toxin could kill within minutes of exposure.

"Do you know the targets of this attack?"

"Several American cities, but I don't know which ones. I just know that Marzak is the one who can connect the strands with a simple telephone call. "

"He's got to be stopped, Professor."

"I'll do my best, but we have to deal with the present. He sent me out here to offer a proposition."

Hawkins glanced at the helicopter. "Can't wait to hear it."

"It seems that you have wiped out the dive team that was going to find the treasure. Since you and your friend are the only divers in the area, it was thought that your help could be enlisted."

"Is that why they didn't kill us when we were driving away from the lake? And why the gunships didn't attack the villagers?"

"Correct," the professor said. "I persuaded Marzak to keep you alive so you could find the treasure."

"You and Marzak are crazier than I thought," Hawkins said.

"Not crazy at all, I'm afraid. You're very impressive, Mr. Hawkins, but you are out of your league. The real treasure at the center of this madness represents more wealth and power than anything Prester John could ever have imagined."

"You've got my attention, prof. Now maybe you can tell me what you're talking about."

"I will tell you as events unfold. We have more pressing issues now. The man watching us doesn't have a great deal of patience."

"Why would we help your friend?"

"Because if you don't, the Cobras will reduce the village to rubble and kill everyone in it. I saw them do just that in a practice run. A ground force is on its way to move in after the air assault. From what you have seen, you must know that Marzak is capable and more than willing to carry out his threat."

"What's the quid pro quo if we agree to dive?"

"They will leave with the treasure and let everyone go free."

"I admire your ability to say that with a straight face, Professor."

"It's an acquired skill," Saleem said. "We both know that they will kill you as soon as they have the treasure in hand and then proceed to wipe out every man, woman and child in the village."

"I was thinking along the same lines," Hawkins said. "Any ideas?"

"My strategy has been to stall as much as I can and hope for the best."

"How's that working out for you?"

"Not very well, I must admit."

"I thought so," Hawkins said.

He excused himself and spoke into his walky-talky. "How's the poker game going?"

"Great! I can open with a pair of aces," Calvin replied.

"Deal me in for the next hand," Hawkins said. He re-clipped the radio to his belt and said, "It's been nice talking to you, Professor."

He turned around and started to walk back to the village.

"You're going back to play poker?" Saleem said.

Hawkins stopped. "Hell, yes. I had a winning hand when you showed up."

A panicked look came to Saleem's face. "Wait! What should I tell them?"

"Tell them we agree. *Reluctantly.* To save the village. Say that we have to refill our air tanks and pull our dive gear together. It will take about an hour."

Hawkins entered a building at the edge of the village and climbed a ladder to the top story. A trio of sharp-shooters under the direction of Amir had been watching through holes in the walls, ready to act if needed. Calvin was sitting on the roof with a pile of electrical parts in front of him. He was stripping the end of a wire.

"Who was that pig?" Amir asked.

"His name is Saleem. He's with the ISI and I think he's on our side, but it's immaterial at this point."

Hawkins gave an edited version of his conversation with Saleem.

"Are you really going to find the treasure for those murderers?"

"I lied," Hawkins said. "I'm stalling for time." He turned to Calvin. "About those aces."

Calvin picked up a Stinger. "I've jury-rigged batteries to two missiles. The other systems are too far gone to fix."

"Will they work?"

"Worth a try. These guys say they know how to use them."

"Two 'maybe' missiles against four heavily-armed choppers. Not great odds."

"No, but I've been thinking about something, Hawk. It's going to sound crazy."

Calvin outlined his proposal.

"You're right. It's brilliant, but crazy."

"It's absolutely insane," Amir said. "There is so much that could go wrong."

"I agree," Hawkins said. "But at the least it will create a diversion to get the women and children out of the village. Is there any place close they can hide?"

“The agricultural sheds are not far away and they’re camouflaged from the air. They might reveal themselves under close inspection, but they could work for the time being.”

“Back to you, Cal.”

“I say we go for it. Nobody would ever expect us to do something so nutty.”

Hawkins looked at his wristwatch. “We’ve got fifty minutes to find out if you’re right.”

CHAPTER FORTY-ONE

Marzak paced back and forth near the grounded helicopter, stopping before each reverse turn to study the low-lying dun buildings. The suspicions ignited when Saleem said the offer had been accepted mounted as the minutes ticked by with no sign of Hawkins.

His wristwatch alarm chimed. Three quarters of an hour had passed since Saleem's return from his truce parley. Fifteen minutes to go. Then he'd unleash a storm of death on the village and every one in it, including Hawkins.

More pacing. The watch chimed again, signaling that the hour had gone by. Marzak called the Cobra crews on a hand radio and told them to prepare for an attack on the village. As he clicked off he heard a blatting sound that seemed to come from outside the village. He sprinted toward the chopper. The pilot and co-pilot were sitting in the doorway enjoying a cigarette. He snatched the cigarette from the pilot's lips.

"Get this thing in the air!"

The startled co-pilot ditched his cigarette and the flight crew hastily climbed into the helicopter and took their seats in the cockpit. The mercenaries who had been lounging nearby got into the cabin with their weapons.

The professor was sitting in the shade of the chopper.

"What's going on?" he said.

"We're going to punish Hawkins and his friends."

The professor paled. "I'll stay here," he said. He pointed to his head. "Air sickness."

"Suit yourself." Marzak vaulted into the cabin.

The engine cranked into action and the chopper rose into the air and hovered a hundred feet off the ground with its nose pointed toward the village. Marzak put on his communications headset and leaned out the side window. The spinning blades had kicked up a cloud of dust.

He reached forward and clamped a big hand on the pilot's shoulder.

"*Higher.* I can't see a damned thing."

The chopper lifted higher until it was above the dust.

He was pleased to see that the Cobras were aloft, noses pointed toward the village. He was about to give the command to attack when he saw a strange silhouette clawing its way into the air above the low buildings.

Marzak couldn't believe his eyes. An ungainly twin-engine biplane of impressive size was slowly circling over the rooftops. It had two sets of landing gear and a British air force insignia was painted on the boxy, chocolate-colored fuselage and mustard-hued wings. The plane was a couple of hundred feet off the ground, flying unevenly, pitching and yawing as if buffeted by a strong wind. Marzak spotted a gunner's pulpit in the nose, ahead of the pilot. The sun reflected off the metal helmet worn by someone sitting in the cockpit.

Before Marzak could bark a command, the biplane broke out of its circling pattern and did the unexpected. It flew directly toward the chopper, allowing for a clearer view of the man in the pulpit.

He was wearing an odd-looking helmet that covered the top and sides of his head, but Marzak immediately recognized the broad grin on the dark-complexioned face under the visor. Marzak was amazed at Hawkins' audacity, but pinning his hopes on that old flying crate was going to be his last mistake.

Marzak told the pilot to bring the helicopter around to position his men for a broadside attack.

During the hour Marzak was waiting, Amir passed out the operational Stinger missiles to the two men on the rooftop. He gave them instructions, made them repeat his words, and translated back into English for Hawkins and Calvin.

Moving at amazing speed, considering his age and damaged leg, Amir led the way down the stairs and got in his car with Hawkins and Calvin speeding behind him in the desert vehicle. A minute later they pulled up in front of Amir's house, which was swarming with armed guards and dozens of women and children who'd gathered there for shelter.

Cait was busy trying to comfort Amir's granddaughter, who had been crying with fright. The little girl calmed down when she saw her grandfather. Cait waved at Hawkins while Abby stepped off the porch and cut a path through the women and wailing children to greet Matt.

"What's going on, Matt?"

"They called a truce. They want us to dive on the treasure. I said I would do it."

"*What?*"

"Don't worry; it was only an excuse to buy time. We need you to organize these people and get them ready to move to the agricultural sheds while Calvin and I prepare a distraction."

"What *sort* of distraction?" Abby said.

Hawkins knew Abby wouldn't settle for an evasive answer. "Something that's risky as hell and may not work, Abby, but we've only got forty-five minutes to pull it together, so *please* don't press me on this."

Abby pinioned him with a level gaze. "You'd damn better watch your ass, Hawkins, because I'm going to pull rank and insist that you have dinner with me before anyone else."

"I never argue with a superior officer," Hawkins gave her a quick hug.

He went over to the dune buggy and Calvin handed him his CAR-15. Calvin had attached an M-203 grenade launcher—basically a fifteen-inch-long aluminum tube and breech—to the underside of the barrel.

Hawkins waved at Amir to signal that the operation was under way. Amir kissed his family good-bye, conferred with a couple of his lieutenants, then got into his car with the omnipresent bodyguards. The touring car led the way to the Folly of Empire museum.

The group bustled past the weapons display and the Soviet vehicles into the airplane hangar. Amir's men opened the wide doors leading out to the airstrip. Hawkins looked at his watch.

Thirty-five minutes.

Calvin climbed into the cockpit and familiarized himself with the controls. Hawkins got in the tank-like combat vehicle and started the engine. The sound was throaty but smooth. Maneuvering the massive vehicle was a challenge. Amir directed with waves of his cane and Hawkins drove it out of the hangar, backing it up to the front of the plane. Two cables were hooked up to the vehicle's rear bumper and the other ends attached to the twin landing gear carriages under the plane.

Hawkins began to accelerate the vehicle slowly, moving the plane inch by inch until it was out in the open. The cables were unhooked and he drove the vehicle to the side and trotted back into the hangar. Calvin was walking around the plane, making a visual inspection.

"Ready?" Hawkins said.

"Amir's head mechanic assures me that the engines are in excellent working order."

Hawkins glanced at the grease-stained man talking animatedly with Amir. "Then why does he look so nervous?"

"You don't really want me to spell it out for you, do you Hawk?"

"No I don't."

Amir had finished talking to his mechanic and hobbled over.

"My mechanic says he will ask Allah to protect you. In case He chooses not to, gentlemen, and your plan goes awry, what do you suggest as a back up?"

"It's a win-win situation, Amir," Hawkins said. "Whether we go down in flames or not, the distraction will allow you to get the villagers to the shed. Have your men lay down the heaviest fire possible. If they can nail a couple of the choppers, the others will turn tail. Sorry I can't give you better odds than that."

"They are better than I expected." Amir glanced at his watch. "You've got ten minutes."

Hawkins said, "I have a strange request to make, Amir."

Nothing these two Americans did would surprise Amir. He listened, simply nodded his head and ordered one of his men to carry out the request.

They shook hands with Amir and climbed onto the lower wing. Calvin got into the cockpit while Hawkins snugged into the tight forward pulpit and placed the CAR-15 between his knees.

Two men had been designated to start the propellers. The man on the right wing pulled the blade down, putting all his weight into the motion. Calvin fed fuel to the engine with the throttle. The man jumped out of the way as the wooden propeller rotated in a lazy spin that rapidly picked up speed. The man on his left went through the same exercise. The engines were attached to the fuselage only a few feet from the open cockpits and their sound was brain-scrambling.

The man Amir had dispatched to carry out Hawkins' request climbed onto the wing and handed him the Macedonian bronze helmet from the small arms exhibit.

Hawkins handed him his cap and pulled the helmet on. It was tight, especially around the nose guard, but it fit. The helmet would offer protection from the wind blast in the pulpit, but he was hoping at the same time that he'd benefit from its warrior spirit. He was going to need any edge he could get.

He raised his thumb in the classic OK. Calvin mimicked the gesture and fed more fuel to the carburetors. The plane crept forward. Calvin had difficulty balancing the three-hundred-sixty-horsepower Rolls-Royce engines, and the plane zigzagged in a crab-like fashion as it rolled toward the start of the landing strip. He didn't want to lose momentum, so he gunned the throttles as soon as the bomber was pointing, more or less, at the landing strip. The plane rumbled ahead at a fast run.

Hawkins put his sunglasses on to block the air blasting in his eyes. As the plane picked up speed, he bounced up and down on the hard seat as if he were sitting on a diving board. He squinted down the length of the landing strip. The plane had eaten up at least half the distance, but it seemed reluctant to leave the safety of the ground. They were bearing down on the end of the airstrip when the hundred-foot-span wings caught the air and the wheels lifted.

The plane was slow in gaining altitude and cleared the tops of the hills at the end of the runway by just a few yards. Calvin managed to keep the nose at the right pitch to allow for a climb without stalling and they were a couple of hundred feet in the air by the time they passed over the village. Hawkins had a good view of the four helicopters placed around the town. He saw figures running for the Blackhawk.

The mechanical obstacles of getting an ancient aircraft aloft and keeping it there were minor compared to Hawkins' skill at judging human nature. He had bet their lives on the guess that Marzak would want Hawkins all for himself. And that he would want to make the kill at close range, maybe even toy with him, before he blew him to pieces. He almost shouted for joy when the Blackhawk lifted off the ground. He signaled Calvin to break out of their circle.

The bomber made an agonizingly wide and very slow banking turn, waggling its wings like a gull testing the updrafts, and straightened out so that it was on a course for the rising helicopter. As the dust cleared, Hawkins saw a figure on the ground where the helicopter had been. Hawkins was close enough to see that it was Professor Saleem. He had his doubts about the professor, but he was glad the man was not on the Blackhawk, because he intended to blow it out of the sky.

The Blackhawk pivoted, presenting its side in an easy target. Calvin had added a separate sighting system that snapped onto Hawkins' rifle. Hawkins wrapped his right hand around the magazine and tried to steady the weapon as he squinted down the barrel at the helicopter.

Looking through his binoculars, Marzak saw Hawkins raise the CAR-15 over the cowling and his grin of triumph immediately faded as he recognized the dangerous significance of the thick tube slung under the barrel.

"He's got a grenade launcher!" he yelled at the pilot. "Evade! Evade!"

The pilot acted immediately, moving the control stick to the right.

The chopper leaned over into the start of a roll a second before a puff of white smoke blossomed at the front of the bomber. The projectile missed the tilted belly of the chopper by inches.

The pilot's reaction had saved the aircraft, but the helicopter banked at a dangerous angle and he fought to get it under control. As the chopper regained stability, Marzak called the Cobras on his hand radio and ordered them to call off the impending attack on the village. The Blackhawk turned and flew away from the village.

"Where are you going?" he shouted at the pilot.

"I wasn't hired for aerial combat," the pilot said.

Marzak drew his pistol from its holster and held it to the pilot's head. "You can sign a new contract when we're through. I want you to *attack*."

"Shoot me and we all die," the pilot said.

"I don't care," Marzak said.

The pilot offered no further argument, and brought the chopper around again so it faced the village.

The Cobras leapt into the air on three sides of the village. Marzak ordered them to go after the new target. It wouldn't be as satisfying as bringing Hawkins down himself, but he'd have a ringside seat for his enemy's last moments.

The helicopters flanking the slow-moving plane hovered in a hold for a moment, allowing the bomber to fly between them, and then they accelerated into a flaring climb. The tactic, called a stern conversion, would put them in position for a fast diving attack from the rear. But as they slowed to swivel into a turn, they were prime targets for the Stinger missiles that streaked into the sky from rooftops at the edge of the village.

Two Cobras exploded in bright yellow and red bursts of flame, disintegrating into fiery showers of charred metal that rained down on the village. The bomber was closing on the third, approaching it nose-to-nose.

The surviving Cobra suddenly veered off its trajectory, and darted away from the confrontation, rapidly becoming a black dot against the sky as it flew off toward the horizon.

The bomber lumbered on through the smoke-filled airspace that the gunship had occupied only seconds before.

Marzak watched as the plane made a big circle, passing over the professor. He saw Saleem wave at the big plane and noticed the return wave from Hawkins before the bomber arced back toward the village. A scowl crossed his face. He hadn't trusted the professor from the moment he had met him.

Marzak was tempted to attack the biplane, but there could be dozens of Stinger missiles ready to be launched from village rooftops and their fuel was running low. As much as he wanted Hawkins, his first priority was self-preservation. They would meet again and the next time Marzak would not be hindered by fools like the professor.

He would make sure of it right now.

Marzak told the pilot to turn back toward the figure below, and when the helicopter was in range, he stuck his rifle barrel out the window and fired. The professor, who had been waving at the approaching chopper, grabbed at his chest and crumpled to the ground.

The Blackhawk was out of sight by the time the bomber made a rough landing on the air strip and coasted to a stop.

Amir's men crowded around the plane shouting in *Pashto* and firing their guns in the air as Hawkins and Calvin descended to the ground.

Amir came over and embraced them both.

"Thanks for the loan of the plane," Hawkins said.

"Not a scratch on it," Calvin added.

"That is more than I can say for our enemies!" Amir exulted. "I only wish we were able to kill every last one of them."

They all piled in the car and headed toward the compound. As the car pulled up to Amir's house, Hawkins saw someone in a dark olive uniform stretched out on the ground. Abby and Cait were kneeling next to the professor, applying a make-shift bandage in a vain attempt to staunch the bleeding from his gaping chest wound.

Hawkins vaulted from the car and knelt by the professor. He was still alive, but from the wheezing sound issuing from his gasping mouth, he would not last long.

"They found him in front of the village and brought him in a minute ago. He's been calling for you," Abby said.

Hawkins lifted the man's head in his hand.

"I'm here," he said.

Saleem seemed to revive. His hand reached out and grabbed the front of Hawkins' shirt in a death grip.

Hawkins put his ear close to the professor's mouth.

"I understand," Hawkins said after a moment. "Thank you."

The professor tried to respond, but his words came out as an incoherent rattle. He relaxed his grip on the shirt, his eyes rolled up in their sockets and his head lolled as if his neck were made of rubber.

"What did he say?" Cait said.

Hawkins gently closed the professor's staring eyes. "He said that he was sorry."

CHAPTER FORTY-TWO

Amir surveyed the killing field on the far side of the lake, his gaze sweeping over the bullet-riddled bodies and the burned-out wreckage of the troop carrier. "It seems this Prester John treasure causes death wherever it goes. I would appreciate it if you removed the curse as quickly as possible."

"We'll start the search and survey as soon as we finish here," Hawkins said.

"Then we had better get busy with our grim task," Amir replied.

Amir supervised a work crew and Hawkins and Calvin helped collect the corpses so they could be transported by truck back to the village for a speedy burial according to Islamic custom. Amir stopped at one point to answer his chirping satellite phone. A smile replaced the frown on his face.

"One of my scouts reports that a ground force is a few miles from the village," he said.

"Those must be the guys who were supposed to mop up after the choppers destroyed your village," Hawkins said. "They don't know that the air assault was a flop."

"If you will excuse me, I must prepare a warm welcome for them," Amir said.

"Need any help?"

"The spirits of the men who died here will guide our hand," Amir said. Before getting into his car he said, "Thank you both for preventing this from happening to my village. Miss Abby and Dr. Cait have been a great help to the women and children."

"Glad to hear that. Could you send them back to give us a hand with the dive?"

Amir nodded, then put the car in gear and led the truck with its load of dead bodies back to the village. Hawkins and Calvin did a damage assessment. Calvin poked around the shredded remains of the tents and picked up a bullet-punctured MRE.

"It's not all bad news," he said. "My *jambalaya* ingredients may have survived."

"We'll have to put it off for now. Fido's hungry."

They plugged a compressor into the generator to refill their air tanks, changed the batteries in the Pegasus units and laid out their dive gear. As they were preparing to suit up, Abby and Cait arrived in the Russian jeep.

"We ran into Amir on our way here," Abby said. "He said you were looking for us."

Cait glanced around at the blasted campsite. "We saw the bodies coming back to the village. It's hard to believe the destruction."

"Amir thinks it's the curse of Prester John," Hawkins said. "I promised him that we'd dive on the treasure as soon as possible. We're about ready to check out the lake and could use a couple of dive tenders."

"I've got a better idea," Abby said. She turned to Calvin. "Would you mind if I made the first dive? I promised myself that I would see this mission through to the very end. I've passed the SEAL dive course with flying colors, of course."

Calvin shrugged. "Makes sense, Matt. I'd be more comfortable up here keeping an eye peeled for outlaws."

"I would too, Cal. Let's see if we can fit Abby out in your suit."

Abby started to peel her clothes off. "Avert your eyes, gentlemen."

The dry-suit sagged on her athletic body, but it would do the job of warding off the chill. With Calvin and Cait lending a hand, Hawkins and Abby slipped into the lake and tested their communications system, which allowed them to keep in touch with Calvin as well. Then they let the Pegasus thrusters propel them down the underwater slope. In the light from their flashlights, they saw that the boulder had disappeared, leaving an opening about eight-by-eight feet square.

Hawkins said, "There's a big hole where the boulder used to be, Cal. The booby trap explosion must have crumbled the lower ledge of the hole. Plug popped right out of the drain."

He flicked the beam of his flashlight at the opening and turned to Abby. "Shall we?"

Abby jerked her thumb in the air and with a series of strong flutter kicks she swam ahead of Hawkins. They passed through the opening into a tunnel which made a gradual turn to the right after a hundred feet. They were rounding the curve when Abby stopped so suddenly that Hawkins crashed into her.

"Hell, Abby!" Hawkins said as they untangled their arms and legs.

She made no reply, but instead pointed at the apparition blocking the way.

The figure with a bulbous one-eyed head was framed in the yellow twin halos cast by their flashlights. The thick arms and legs made a slight waving movement that gave the illusion of life.

They swam closer. The vacant sockets of a copper-hued skull peered at them through the glass of the circular visor.

"Guess we found Kurtz's diver," Hawkins said. "Time frame for the design of his gear is about right for the expedition. That's a Schrader helmet manufactured around 1918. I've got a similar one in my collection."

The diver's weighted boots had torn away from the rubberized canvas suit and the bottoms of the legs were fringed like an oriental rug. The bronze helmet and breastplate had lost their shine and were a dull brown. A couple of feet of thick black air hose dangled from the back of the helmet. The suit hung from the end of rubber-encased chain attached to the back of the breastplate.

The chain emerged from a hole in the ceiling that was packed with rocks large and small. There were more rocks below the diver on the mine floor. "Looks like the shaft caved in and cut off his air," Hawkins said.

Abby squeezed Hawkins by the arm. "What an awful way to die," she said.

"He never had a chance. Cait saw the other end of the hose when she explored the shaft from ground level. The fact that he made it this far means Kurtz accessed the tunnel and maybe the treasure."

"Yes, but was this the first dive or the last?" Abby said.

"That question may soon be answered. Let's keep going."

The discovery had tempered Abby's enthusiasm to be in the lead. They swam abreast past the forlorn figure only to stop again. The tunnel was blocked by a mound of earth that reached to within a few feet of the ceiling.

"It's going to be a tight squeeze," Hawkins said.

"We've come too far to turn back," Abby said.

"If I can make it through you'll have no problem," Hawkins said.

He swam up to the opening, which was about a yard wide. The ceiling seemed solid enough. He extended his arms like Superman in flight. Slight kicks of his fins propelled him forward inches at a time. The beam of his flashlight showed that the way actually widened after a few yards. He kept moving, crawling more than swimming. Seconds later he was through the opening. He turned around and waved his light.

"I'm in," he said. "Come ahead."

Abby navigated the passage with the ease of an eel. Hawkins tried to call Calvin, but there was no answer. They were too deep in the tunnel for their communications systems to work. They encountered no further obstructions and covered ground rapidly. After another fifty feet or so the tunnel ended abruptly in a wall. A rock shelf jutted out and behind the ledge was a large alcove around six feet long and two feet deep.

Hawkins flashed the light around the floor and walls of the empty tunnel.

"Looks like we've hit a dry hole, Abby," he said in a rueful voice.

"Damnit, Matt. Kurtz got it all."

Hawkins floated up so that he was level with the ledge and peered into the alcove. He drew his sheath knife and poked the biggest of several lumps lying in the recessed shelf. Within moments he had exposed a skull. The mud that had preserved it had colored the skull a dark brown.

"There are bones here," Hawkins said. "Someone laid out a body for burial."

He used his knife to peck away at the other chunks of concretion. The point quickly dislodged layers of hardened mud and revealed fragments of leg or arm bones. Hawkins brushed away some of the sediment and saw something shiny in the skeletal remains. He picked up an encrusted object that had a glint of gold, showed it to Abby, then put the object into his vest pocket.

Abby glanced at her wrist computer. "We'd better get back. Our friends are going to worry if they don't hear from us."

Hawkins signaled Abby to take the lead. She approached the earth barrier blocking the way and glided up and through the opening. Hawkins was right behind her. He watched her as she wiggled through, surprising himself with the thought that her backside looked good even in Calvin's oversized wetsuit.

When they emerged from the water a few minutes later, they saw Calvin and Cait waiting at the lake's edge. Hawkins crawled out and wasted no time with his report. "We found an old tomb that lies directly under the shaft and discovered what was left of the diver and another body, much older, that was apparently laid out for burial." Hawkins hated to break Cait's heart with the truth, but he had to be up front with her. "There was no treasure," he said.

Cait seemed to shrink within herself.

"Are you sure?"

He nodded. "The tunnel ends around a hundred-fifty-feet in. We went over every square foot."

"Then that's it." Her words had a hollow ring. She looked around at the devastation. "All this was for nothing."

"Maybe not. We found this with the older skeleton." He removed the lump from his vest and handed it to Cait. She examined the object, then borrowed a knife and carefully chipped away the chunk of concretion. Underneath was a gold cross. Cait translated the inscription on the long part of the cross:

"GOD SPEED PHILLIP"

Inscribed on the cross' short section was the word ALEXANDER.

"You were wrong about finding nothing," she said. "The skeleton you discovered belongs to Philip. It proves my theory that he made it as far as Afghanistan." She pursed her lips in thought. "What it *doesn't* prove is whether he was coming from or going to the kingdom of Prester John. Maybe we'll never know now, but even without the treasure, this is one of the most significant archaeological discoveries of the century."

Hawkins' eye fell on the piece of concretion that had broken off from the cross. He took the knife back and chipped away the covering. Inside was a coin. He examined the palm tree engraved one side and then flipped the coin over.

"I'm happy to say that you're wrong, Cait," he said. "Looks like the cross will be the *second* most important discovery. This is the first."

He gave Cait the coin. She studied both sides, then passed it to Abby, threw her arms around Hawkins and planted a warm kiss on his lips.

Abby was irritated at Cait's reaction until she examined the coin. She understood after she examined the side of the coin with the face pictured on it. Engraved in Latin under the profile were two words.

Presbyter Johannes.

Hawkins gave the order to break camp. They loaded the gear onto the desert vehicle and with the Russian Jeep leading the way, headed back to Amir's house. His daughter greeted them and said they had been invited for dinner and to stay the night.

After being shown to their rooms and given the chance to clean up and change, they assembled for dinner in the big dining room. Amir arrived a few minutes later. He sat down next to Cait and said that his men had ambushed a force advancing on the village. All the invaders were killed, he said.

"My men have been buried and avenged on the same day." He turned to Hawkins. "And did you find the treasure my friend?"

Before Hawkins could answer, Amir noticed that Cait's eyes were moist with tears. He put his hand on her arm. "What's wrong, Dr. Cait? Are you ill?"

Cait cleared her throat. "I'm fine, thank you. No, that's not right. I feel *terrible.* It was my research that led to the deaths of so many people. If I hadn't come up with my treasure theory, your men would still be alive."

There was a heavy silence in the room.

Hawkins had gone through a self-hatred phase and knew that once guilt got its claws into you it was hard to dislodge.

"Not so fast, Cait," he said. "You didn't ask that creep to attack you at the caravan stop. You didn't murder the men at the lake. You didn't attack the village. You have no right to blame yourself."

Her pale cheeks flushed pink. "That's easy for you to say, Matt."

"It's not easy, Cait. Not easy at all."

Calvin jumped into the discussion. "What Hawk is saying as that we've both been there. He thought it was his fault that we lost guys in an ambush back in the day. I tore myself up for years because I didn't have his back when they pushed him out of the navy."

Abby sighed loudly. "Guess I should get on the guilt band wagon. I could have tended to a deeply-wounded friend and I didn't." Abby turned her head to avoid Hawkins' surprised gaze and spoke directly to Cait. "What we're all saying is that you can't blame yourself for the actions of a bunch of sleaze-bags."

Cait threw her hands in the air. "Enough! I didn't know this was going to be an intervention. Okay, I absolve myself of blame, but the Prester John treasure still had a role in this."

"I agree," Hawkins said. "But Prester was only one in a cast of dozens. Let's not forget the professor or the twin assassins who tried to kill me."

"I never suspected that Professor Saleem was an agent with the

Pakistani intelligence. I feel so betrayed," Cait said. "He always seemed like the perfect gentleman scholar."

"Maybe that's exactly what he was," Hawkins said. "Marzak must have suspected he was on our side, and that's probably why he killed him."

"Saleem's connection to the Shadows is not surprising," Amir said. "The ISI maintains contacts with terrorists and insurgents which it sees as buffers against the greater enemy. India."

"Where does Marzak fit in?" Calvin asked.

Hawkins said, "Marzak was running the military operation for the Shadows. The professor suggested he was more than just a soldier for hire like the others."

"What did he mean?"

"Marzak's role is more complicated. He and his twin tried to kill me, which suggests that they wanted to torpedo our mission even before it started. Somehow, they knew about the operation."

"I don't get it. How could that happen?" Calvin said.

Hawkins laughed. "Because the security surrounding our top-secret expedition seems to have sprung more leaks than the *Titanic*. I suggest we go back to the beginning, the Prester John legend, and carry it to the present," Hawkins said. "As our resident historian, you have the podium, Dr. Everson."

A smile came to Cait's face. She was happy to be back on familiar territory. She went to her room for her computer, placed it on the table and pushed back the cover.

"I'll run through what we know. Let's go back to the 1100s. Rumors of Prester John circulate in Europe. The Pope writes a letter to John suggesting an alliance and entrusts it with his personal physician, a man named Philip. That fact is well recorded. So is the fact that he made it as far as Jerusalem. He disappears from sight after that. Now we know what happened to him. Defying the odds, Philip apparently found the lost kingdom of Prester John."

She opened an image on the computer.

"This is a fragment of the vellum scroll that Kurtz found in Kabul. On the front is part of a letter Philip carried from Prester John to the Pope, in which he mentions a gift that will allow for an alliance that will rally the troops against the infidels."

"The emerald scepter," Hawkins said.

"Ironic, isn't it?" Abby said. "The Shadows want to use it for the same purpose, to rally people to their flag."

Cait nodded. "History is merely the same things happening over and over. On his return trip, Philip passes through the caravan stop and sees the wall map showing a short cut to the Mediterranean coast. Somehow, he strays off the intended route into a box canyon named the Valley of the Dead, a region thick with bandits. For whatever reason, Philip takes refuge in a tomb where he dies. He or someone else draws a map on the back of the vellum and hundreds of years later, it ends up in Kabul where Kurtz finds it. Finally, we find the coin, which may have been placed on his eyes as was the custom."

"The coin proves that the treasure made it to the mine with Philip," Abby said.

"And raises the question of what became of the rest of the treasure," Calvin said.

Hawkins said, "You've got a couple of narratives here. Philip's story and Kurtz's expedition. The tomb is the nexus where those two story lines meet."

"So old Hiram ran off with the treasure?" Calvin said.

"Let's look at what we know about his expedition," Cait said. "Kurtz was looking for the Prester John treasure. We know too, from the chisel we found, that he was at the caravan stop. He sees the map of the Silk Road trade routes and uses it to track down the Prester John caravan route."

"But first he obliterates the location of Prester's kingdom with a chisel so no one will follow in his footsteps," Hawkins said.

"Exactly," Cait agreed. "He heads for the valley and finds that it is now a lake. That's when he calls in a diver who goes into the lake, but the tomb is blocked. Using the camel's back hill as a reference, Kurtz drills a shaft to the tomb, which is flooded."

"We saw what's left of the diver," Hawkins said. "It's clear that the mine shaft collapsed and plugged up access. But when Abby and I entered the shaft, there was no treasure, which suggests that Kurtz found it *before* the cave-in. Based on the historical house of cards we've built, if we follow Kurtz, we'll find the treasure."

"I'm not sure if I even care about the treasure anymore," Cait said. "I have my proof in the cross and the coin. The scepter has caused so much misery."

"It's likely to cause a lot more misery if the competition gets its hands on it," Hawkins said. "The professor told me that Marzak is going to carry out the Shadows' plot in the U.S. as soon as he finds the treasure."

"Exactly what sort of plot is this?" Abby said.

"Marzak has planted sarin bombs near U.S. population centers. The professor didn't know where, only that Marzak will trigger the explosives once he has the scepter in hand. As you said, Abby, the Shadows want to use the historic symbolism of the emerald scepter to rally extremists to their cause."

"Sarin is one of the deadliest substances on earth," Calvin said in a hushed tone. "Tens of thousands of people could die if this thing goes down."

"Damn," Abby said. "We can't let that happen."

"No argument there," Hawkins said. "We have to leave tomorrow as early as possible."

"How can we stop it, Matt?"

"Simple. We find the scepter before Marzak does."

CHAPTER FORTY-THREE

Rio Rico, Arizona

Sutherland's internal alarm clock went off at four o'clock in the morning. She switched on the light next to the bed and noticed her newly-laundered jeans, shirt, and underwear stacked on a chair. She dressed and went out to the patio. The temperature had dropped drastically during the night, and she could see her breath. The stars were like sapphires in black velvet. She focused on the North Star. Polaris seemed to beckon.

She went back inside, grabbed her computer bag and went to the kitchen where she wrote a long note thanking the McHughs and promising to keep in touch. She put on her leather jacket, wheeled the motorcycle out of the car port, but didn't start the engine until she was a hundred feet from the house. She headed north on the empty highway. The sun was coming up as she passed through the outskirts of Tucson.

As she rode along, she formed a plan of sorts to lose herself in Utah's vast back country, but she had an epiphany in the Navajo town of Chinle where she stopped to buy the makings for a picnic. She rode a few miles to *Canyon de Chelly*, pulled into the parking lot and walked out onto a bluff that overlooked the red sandstone walls of the ancient canyon.

She sat with her feet dangling over a ledge and munched contentedly on a mountainous cold-cut sandwich, gazing off at the 800-foot tall column known as Spider Rock. Not far from where she sat, the Indian fighter Kit Carson had cornered the Navajos at the blind end of the canyon, and then he drove the ones he didn't kill from their land. There was a lesson to be learned. No matter how fast and how far you run, you have to keep moving or you'll eventually be cornered.

If she didn't fight, she could end up with her back to the wall like the unfortunate Navajo.

She finished lunch, got on her motorcycle and headed north to Route 66, riding past the historic road's commercial hodge-podge until she stopped at a motel with units built in the shape of concrete wigwams. A fifties vintage car sat in front of each unit. Her kind of place. After she registered, she went out for a supply of chips and Coke, then set up her computer in the circular bedroom. No danger of being cornered here.

She wrote an account of the last few days, in case the next attempt on her life was successful and sent the file to Hawkins. At the end she wrote the words: PLS CALL.

Sutherland backed up the file using an online data storage service, and pondered where she should point her investigation. It was too dangerous to snoop around Arrowhead. After a moment of thought, she opened the Prester John folder, clicked on the TREASURE file, and went down the index until she came to a name. Hiram Kurtz.

The Kurtz history was fairly linear. Originally from Minnesota, he had studied to be an accountant, but drifted into mining when he learned he had a knack for wringing wealth out of the earth. Photos of Kurtz in the heyday of his mining career showed him with a broad, determined face, high chiseled cheek bones and intelligent eyes outlined by circular-framed wire rim glasses.

An article from the society pages described his lavish wedding to a young and beautiful debutant named Priscilla Knudson. She came from an old New York family that had made scads of money at the Wall Street end of the mining industry. He began to spend less time near his mines in Colorado and more at the house he built for his new bride. Later photos showed his Hudson River mansion, and Kurtz and his wife with a young boy whose chubby face blended the features of his parents. They traveled abroad on trips that Kurtz explained later as triggering his interest in archaeology.

In a later article there was a reference to Kurtz's late wife, which Sutherland followed to an obituary, saying Mrs. Kurtz had died giving birth to a second child, a daughter, who did not survive much longer than her mother.

The loss may have been the reason he threw himself into exploration, because after his wife died, he built a yacht to carry him to remote places and called it the *Sweet Priscilla*. It was this ship that carried him on his quest for Prester John's treasure.

The story of the treasure hunt seemed straightforward. Eccentric mining tycoon bankrolls an archaeological expedition. Nobody hears from the expedition for months. Kurtz eventually emerges from the wilderness, only for his expedition team to perish in a shipwreck during the return journey. After that, Kurtz goes home, apparently having accomplished nothing.

Sutherland compared the earlier photos of Kurtz with one taken after his Afghan expedition. The difference in his appearance was striking. The healthy-looking middle-aged man with the confident expression had turned into a thin, hollow-cheeked caricature of himself. His eyes were vacant and staring, and maybe just a little mad.

She wasn't surprised when she came across his obituary, dated a year after the expedition returned, saying he had died in Denver. With the loss of his archaeological staff at sea, Kurtz would have been the only one left with firsthand knowledge of what, if anything, the expedition had found. The secret died with him.

Sutherland sat back and gazed out the window at the rusting old Ford outside her wigwam. Something was odd about Kurtz's demise. He looked to be at death's door when he got back from Afghanistan. But he didn't stay in his comfortable riverside mansion, close to the health care available in New York City. Instead, he had hopped onto his private railroad car and headed west.

The last story she found on Kurtz was written by a reporter who had ambushed him in Denver. The headline writer got in one final jab at the ailing tycoon before Kurtz disappeared into obscurity.

AMAZON HUNTER

SAYS EXPEDITION

DEATHS JUSTIFIED

The article reported that when asked if he regretted squandering the lives of his expedition on a fruitless quest to find Amazons, Kurtz had answered that his quest had not been to look for Amazons—that had never been anything more than a line to amuse the media vultures—nor had his expedition been fruitless.

Mr. Kurtz replied further: "I regret the loss of my good friends and colleagues, but their work was not in vain."

Asked what they had found to justify his statement, he said, "Knowledge."

"What sort of knowledge? From what I have read, you found nothing."

"Don't believe everything you read in the papers."

"What are your plans, Mr. Kurtz?"

"I plan to give myself a good accounting."

Sutherland pondered the wording of his last statement. Why not say he was going to give a good accounting of himself. Why give himself a good accounting? A good accounting of *what?* And what did he mean when he said the expedition had found knowledge? Kurtz was hiding something. She entertained the possibility that he had found the treasure, which meant that Hawkins and his friends were on a wild-goose chase. But if so, what happened to it?

She returned to his obituary and found the name of his son in the list of survivors. After a quick Google search she learned that Henry Knudson Kurtz had been a drunken playboy who had inherited his father's mining company and subsequently run it into the ground. In one of his sober moments, he fathered a son who was named after his father, and he died at the age of thirty-eight of undetermined causes.

Sutherland did another search, typing in the name Henry Knudson Kurtz Junior. She was unprepared for the avalanche of results. Kurtz Junior was mentioned in hundreds of references, mostly unfavorable, as the leader of a paramilitary group named the Southwest Constitutional Militia.

Kurtz had been born in New York, studied law at an obscure southern college she had never heard of, was drafted into the army and served in a legal post in Vietnam. After his discharge, Kurtz tried to get into the FBI but his credentials were too thin. He started a one-man law practice in Denver that handled mostly cases of conspiracy and gun charges. The experience apparently convinced him the government was willing to override the Constitution to pursue its illegal aims.

He became adjutant general and legal counselor for an umbrella group that represented militias nationally and formed his own militia. On the website for his organization there was a photo of General Kurtz in a camouflage uniform, an automatic rifle cradled in his arms.

He had inherited the high cheekbones of his grandfather, but his face was narrower, and it was as creased as a piece of beef jerky. His mouth was a straight, thin line drawn across his prominent jaw. The caption described him as militia commander, and he had combined his first and last names, Hank and Kurtz, into a short hard version. *Hak. Sounds like something a cat does with a fur ball*, Sutherland thought.

Hak Kurtz's declaration of the militia's purpose was a long, rambling anti-government diatribe against the elites who were conspiring to enslave the U.S. by taking away the guns and the rights of the people. The website photos showed armed men and women in combat outfits going through training at an undisclosed site in Colorado.

Sutherland would love to see the expression on Matt's face when he learned that this dangerous nut case might hold the key to the Prester John treasure. Even better would be his surprise if *she* tracked down the treasure. It was a measure of her mental state that she found it perfectly reasonable to even consider this.

The question was how to approach Kurtz. She went over old news clips and studied maps of the original Kurtz mine holdings. The more productive mines had been sold off to a big company, but Kurtz's son had held onto the original, non-producing ones around Ouray, Colorado. She figured that'd be a good place for a militia. If she started early the next day, she could easily make Durango. Ouray was a relatively short drive through the mountains from there. What then? Go right up to the door and say she was looking for a lost treasure? Maybe she could figure something out on the ride.

She shut down her computer, slipped it into its case and left her wigwam to search for a GPS, more tortilla chips and Coke. She would head for Ouray in the morning.

CHAPTER FORTY-FOUR

The helicopter from Kabul had been delayed several hours by a security alert that grounded all civilian aircraft after a suicide bombing in the city. Amir used the time to show off the new school and water system he had built for his village. Eventually, he and his family gathered at the airstrip with their guests.

When the helicopter appeared, Amir said, "My family and I will be very sad to see all of you go."

Hawkins conferred with Calvin in a low whisper and said to Amir, "We have an idea that may soften the blow."

Hawkins handed the keys to Calvin's desert vehicle to Amir, who said, "I don't know how I can repay you."

"How about letting me borrow your satphone again and we'll call it even."

Amir handed him the phone and told him to keep it. There were tearful good-byes, then everyone climbed aboard the helicopter. As the chopper lifted off and gained altitude, Hawkins saw the desert vehicle making tight figure eights and wondered it had been a mistake to give the fast little buggy to a lead foot like Amir.

There was little conversation on the flight to Kabul. The passengers were weary from their ordeal and the engine noise made conversation difficult even using headsets. Hawkins clicked on the satellite phone and tried to reach Sutherland so he could tell her everyone was in good shape. There was no answer. He connected to his own phone number, and retrieved a texted message she had sent the day the expedition left Kabul.

MURPHY IS A SNAKE. CHECK ATTACHED REPORT

Hawkins clenched his jaw as he read on the small screen Sutherland's description of the intricate web connecting Murphy to the ambush five years ago and the attempts on her life. He cursed himself for dragging the young woman into this mess, then leaving her to fend for herself. The helicopter landed in Kabul early in the evening. Abby said she planned to go to the Global Logistics Kabul office to line up a flight home and invited Cait to go along.

"We've got a few things to take care of. We'll stay here," Hawkins said.

As soon as the two women were out of earshot, Hawkins said, "Got a big favor to ask you, Cal."

Calvin nodded as he listened to Hawkins' request, then rummaged in his luggage and handed over a thin tube-shaped object.

"Pretty serious stuff," Calvin said. "You going to need help?"

Hawkins slid the shiny cylinder into his pocket.

"Going solo on this one, Cal. Tell Abby I'll be back in an hour or so."

"What if Abby asks where you went?"

"Tell her I'm taking care of unfinished business."

He bumped fists with Calvin, then strode off to find a taxi that would take him into the city.

Murphy was at the Serena Hotel bar. He had just emptied the contents of his hip flask into his third fruit juice and was enjoying the fiery-sweet flow of liquid down his throat, when a bellhop tapped his shoulder and handed him an envelope. Folded inside was a sheet of hotel letterhead and a printed message.

"*Mission accomplished. Need to see you. No phone. Your place. Rashid.*"

"Who gave you this?" Murphy said.

The bellhop touched the top of his head. "Bald man?"

Murphy tucked the note in his pocket, tipped the bell hop and slid off his stool. He made his way erratically through the lobby and out the door to the parking lot. He fumbled with the keys to his armored Chevy Tahoe SUV. As he heaved his bulky body behind the wheel, he heard the back door open and shut. A voice spoke in his ear:

"Hi, Southie. Remember me?"

Murphy glanced in the rear-view mirror and saw Hawkins' manic grin. Struggling to keep the surprise out of his voice, the DEA agent said: "Hell, Hawk, scared the crap out of me. Didn't know you were back in town. I guess the mission went okay."

"The mission was fine."

"That's good, man. So what're you doing here? I got a note to meet Rashid."

"The note was from me. I told the bellhop to say it was from a bald man."

"Uh, what happened to Rashid?"

"Why do you think *any*thing happened to him?"

"Figure of speech. I got him the guide gig. Thought the ungrateful bastard wanted to thank me."

"He can't do that because he's vulture bait."

"Dead?"

"*Very.*"

"Jeez, what happened?"

"He got frisky with a lady friend of mine."

"Oh hell. I should have warned you that he had a problem with women."

"He had a problem with men, too. He tried to kill me and ran off with our dune buggy. I caught up with him."

Murphy dropped his hands onto his knees. "Can't say I really liked the guy."

"Too bad, because you're going to join him if you go for that gun between the seats. Pick it up by the butt with your thumb and forefinger and hold it over your shoulder. Please don't make me shoot you."

Murphy hesitated. "You're bluffing. Security guys would never let you onto the hotel grounds with a firearm."

"They'd let me get in with a special ops ball-point fitted out with a .22 caliber blank that will drive a dart into your brain. Real James Bond stuff, Murph."

Murphy winced as a sharp object dug into the base of his skull. He followed Hawkins' instructions, slowly handed the gun over his shoulder and put his hands back on the wheel.

"Glad you got the point. Now pass me the gun you carry in your belt holster."

Murphy dug out the compact .22 backup pistol and handed it to Hawkins.

"Good memory. You don't trust anyone, do you?"

Hawkins removed the magazines and emptied the rounds from each gun. "I don't want any distractions. Tell me why you sicced Rashid on us."

"Rashid was a last-minute desperation choice. I had to use the little pervert because I didn't have time to put a better plan into place."

"A plan for what?"

"To sabotage your mission."

"Who gave you the orders?"

"Dunno. I get my assignments on the phone. Someone calls. A voice gives me an ID code so I'll know it's legit, and tells me what to do. I didn't know what your mission was. Still don't."

"Did the voice tell you to kill me?"

"They used the word *neutralize*. Nothing personal."

"That makes me feel better, Murph. Someone tried to neutralize me back in the States, even before the mission got underway. You know anything about that?"

"Whaddya know, something I didn't do! I'm clueless on that score, Hawk. Maybe someone was afraid you'd dig into the past and stir things up. From what little I know, the guys I work for don't like loose ends."

"Were Abby and Cal considered loose ends, too?"

"Aw crap. Yeah," he said.

"Were you working for the same voice when we met five years ago?"

"Hard to tell. Voice is computer-altered. Could have been anyone. I was a private contractor with the Company. You know that."

"You were moonlighting for Arrowhead."

The answer caught Murphy by surprise. "How did you know that?"

"Never mind."

"Yeah, what's the big deal? Arrowhead had contracts with the CIA."

"What was your main job?"

"I was to develop local intelligence assets." He chuckled. "Basically I got paid for hanging around the hotel lounge."

"You did more than warm a bar stool. You cultivated Honest Abe as an informant. He was so important that he got wined and dined in New York. You were on his shopping trip to the Big Apple."

"You do what you have to do in this business. You know that, Hawk."

"All too well. Problem was, Honest Abe wasn't so honest. While you were showing him the bright lights of Broadway, he had been giving CIA money to the Taliban for protection. That should have neutralized him, but he became even more valuable after you turned him into a double agent. How am I doing so far?"

"Spot on, Hawk. Like I said, it's a crazy business."

"It gets even crazier when I want to bring Honest Abe in to talk about a Taliban attack on a SEAL team. My superior says, 'talk to Murphy first; he's The Man.' So that's what I did."

"I warned you Honest Abe was a protected asset, told you to stay away from him. Woulda saved a lot of trouble if you'd taken my advice. Like I said, he was valuable to us."

"Understandable. After they picked the shrapnel out of my leg, I began to wonder how he knew we were coming."

"Hard to keep a secret in these parts."

"You're the only one outside my superior officer who knew that I was contemplating a mission. You set us up, Murphy."

"I warned the bastard to get out of town. He's the one who decided to leave an IED."

"Maybe you didn't know Abe's plans, but you told him we were coming and that's just as bad."

"Chrissakes, Hawk, that's ancient history. Go home and stay there."

"You're starting to annoy me. I'm so annoyed that my finger might accidentally press the trigger. When I tried to find out how Abe knew I was coming, I ran into a brick wall. Tell me about the cover up."

Murphy's well-honed survival instincts told him that Hawkins was serious. The air seemed to go out of his body.

"You gotta go back to 9/11. Bin Laden's bragging on TV after he knocked the towers down, mocking us, saying America was filled with fear. And he was right! Everybody *was* scared. We had to hit back in a hurry. You know how it is. The wolves respect a winner. If you're seen as weak, it's all over."

"I was with a SEAL team that dispelled that notion," Hawkins said.

"Damn straight! We really kicked ass. Invaded Afghan land and pushed out the Taliban. Took a while to catch up with Bin Laden, and there was a slight detour through Iraq, but that's the stuff people knew about. There was a whole other war going on behind the scenes. Our guys decided that we had to fight dirty. Assassinations. Special rendition. Kidnapping."

"Enhanced interrogation," Hawkins added.

"I'm not afraid to call it what it was. *Torture*. But all the people wringing their hands don't get the point. Water-boarding someone wasn't *expected* to extract information. Anyone with half a brain knows you get more out of a source by giving him Twinkies and ice cream. It never *was* about intel."

"So what *was* it about?"

"*Revenge*, Hawk. We wanted to send those bastards a message. You sucker punched us, but we've tossed out the Marquis de Queensbury rules. Mess around with the U.S.A. and we won't just kill you, we'll catch you and make you wish that you had never been born. You think they went after Bin Laden so they could bring him back and put him on trial? Hell no. He had a big fat bull's-eye on his head."

"So far, you haven't told me anything new."

"Try this on for size. The stuff that went public was only the tip of the iceberg. That was a CIA-contractor op that used legalese to back it up, but they couldn't outright ignore the law. That was the job of a small sub-group within the larger operation."

"What could this group do that the others couldn't?"

"Pretty much anything they wanted to do."

"Oversight?"

"Open-end approval at the highest level with minimal oversight. Deniability was important. If they got caught, they'd say it was a rogue operation."

"Risky. With no control, it could very well go rogue."

"It was a risk the top level was willing to take. They wanted the bad guys to know that there were things worse than death."

"How big was the group?"

"Maybe six core people with on-call access to support. They called themselves Archer. Codeword for the guy who calls me is Arrowsmith."

"Archer. Arrowhead. Arrowsmith. Cute."

"Arrowhead was both the cover and the contractor. They set up an entity to take care of logistics, payroll and all that.

"The Arrowhead kids' program."

"That's right. Very impressive, Hawk. No one would suspect an outfit that helped kids."

"Where was Trask in all of this?"

"The unit needed a resident shrink with no scruples."

"He fits the bill. Tell me about Captain McCormick. Where does he fit in?"

"He was with the original black ops team and moved over to the unit."

"Did he have a role in getting me kicked out of the SEALs?"

"Probably. He was navy intel, but still attached to Archer. When the torture story went public, everyone went to the mattresses. CIA burned the videos of the torture sessions. Records were destroyed. The spin-masters came out and started spreading disinformation. Meanwhile, the Archer unit scattered to the four winds."

"Trask was on the government payroll when he saw me."

"He was in a holding pattern. A shrink in Oklahoma had dug up some stuff on Trask about his involvement with torture and tried to get him hauled up on professional misconduct. The charges were dropped when his accuser died in a house fire."

"Of suspicious origin, no doubt."

"Yeah, shit happens, Hawk. One more shrink won't be missed."

"What was your role, Murphy?"

"Arrowhead sub-contracted out my services. You don't want to know the details. Water-boarding and sexual humiliation was for amateurs. Some stuff was real medieval. All that was missing was a black hood. I've got a strong stomach, but I had to get out. They got me a job with the DEA as a reward for my work. And here I am."

Murphy took Hawkins' silence as a signal that the conversation was over.

"That sums it up, Hawk. Can I go back to the bar now?"

"Shut up." He prodded Murphy with the pen gun. "Why was Trask picked to process my psychiatric discharge?"

"Ambushing you and your guys was never in the works. Honest Abe pulled that stunt on his own to protect a stash of opium. But once you started asking questions that could have exposed the connection to Archer, you had to be stopped."

"So they decided that the best way to stop me was to say I was crazy."

"Hell, we're *all* crazy in this business. I was just a hired goon. I haven't heard from them in years until last week when they called. I was surprised as hell that you were coming back."

"It sounds as if Archer is still in business and calling the shots."

"It's been reconstituted to deal with an evolving threat."

"Talk English, Murphy."

"We've hurt the bad guys. Drone attacks have kicked the crap out of the hierarchy. Killing Bin Laden was the icing on the cake, but we've had to contend with a new reality. The leadership is more diffused, with splinter groups showing their muscle."

"Groups like the Shadows?"

"Don't know why I'm talking, Hawk. You already know everything."

"What makes the Shadows so dangerous?"

"No one knows who they are, for one thing. They've been hurt real bad and they want to hurt us. They think if they can do that it'll give the radicals a leg up in some of the Arab countries that are torn between democracy and extremism. Security made it harder to get men into the States, so they started looking for other ways to cause problems at home and in Europe. Real whack-a-mole. We had to come up with new ways to deal with their evolving tactics."

"Start bringing me home, Murphy. My hand is getting real tired."

"Patience, man. We heard chatter about the Shadows growing, getting stronger. Archer was brought together again and expanded. It's got some of the same people, but it's more like a think tank with muscle."

"Arrowhead still provides the brawn?"

"That's my understanding."

"Who provides the brains?"

"Classified. All I know is that the unit's job is to squash the plot in the U.S. and deliver a KO punch against the Shadows. "

Hawkins remembered Sutherland's report mentioning the death of Honest Abe. "I heard Abe has left this world."

"He was killed in a DEA operation a couple of days ago."

"Quite the coincidence."

"*Karma.* He's dead, Hawk. You can go home and forget about all this."

Hawkins felt a twinge in his damaged leg.

"I might be able to forget that you set me up for an ambush, Murphy, and that trusting Honest Abe was just plain stupidity on your part."

"You don't have to get insulting, Hawk."

"Here's the thing. You tried to set me up a second time, and that's unforgivable."

"It was you or me, Hawk. I didn't have any choice."

"Yes, but I do. I'm going to choose not to kill you."

Murphy puffed out his cheeks. "Damn, Hawk, I knew you couldn't pull the trigger."

Hawkins opened the door and stepped out. He skidded the guns under the car and tossed the ammunition as far as he could into the parking lot. "I'm sure you can get more ammo. You may be needing it. As you said. What goes around comes around."

"What are you talking about?"

"Think about it. You screwed up. My mission was a success. I'm still alive. You said these folks don't like loose ends. You know too much. *Bang*."

"Maybe it's time for old Murph to head for warmer climes."

"They'll find you and kill you, Murphy. But I may be able to help. They want something I've got. The deal is, you've got to do something for me."

"I'm listening."

"Tell your handlers we've talked, that I have what they want and will trade it for the guys who got me kicked out of the navy. Trask and McCormick for starters. I want their heads on a platter."

"What's in it for me?"

"I want you to be the middle-man. At the least, it will buy you time to make yourself scarce. Call my number at Woods Hole and leave a message when you hear back."

"It's a deal, man. No hard feelings?"

"This is a crazy business. Your words. One more question. Where does Marzak figure in all this?"

"Who?"

Murphy's surprise seemed genuine. Hawkins told him to forget it and got out of the car.

Murphy shook his head. "You spooked me with an old Bic, didn't you?"

Hawkins pointed the pen and pressed the trigger. There was a pop and the dart thunked into the metal just below the open window.

"Wrong again, Murph."

Abby had been watching for Hawkins from the doorway of the Global Logistics Technologies plane. She saw him striding across the tarmac toward the jumbo jet and almost tripped in her haste to meet him at the bottom of the stairway.

Her eyes were narrowed, her jaw set and her lips compressed. She seemed to be searching for something in his face.

"Sorry I'm late," he said. "Is everything okay?"

"You tell me, Matt. Calvin said you went into Kabul on an errand."

"I wanted to talk to Murphy. I had questions I needed answers to."

"I have to know, Matt. Did you kill him?"

"No, Abby. It wasn't worth it. We just talked."

Her features transformed from granite hardness back to flesh and bone.

"Damnit, Hawk!" she said, eyes brimming with tears. "I thought you'd gone off the deep end. You are the biggest pain in the ass."

Unexpectedly, she threw her arms around him and gave him a kiss on the neck that sent a tingle down to his toenails.

"I'll have to *not* kill someone more often," he said. "Let's go home."

He took her by the hand and started walking to the plane.

Calvin and Cait were already in the upper deck cabin. As Hawkins settled into the seat next to Cait, his friend hiked his eyebrows and drew his forefinger across his neck. Hawkins silently mouthed a no, which brought a wide grin from Calvin.

Abby sat next to Calvin and they all clicked their seat belts. Minutes later, the 747 was rumbling down the runway, engines at full blast as they lifted the massive plane into the skies. The sprawling city receded into the distance.

"So long, Afghan land," Calvin murmured. "We'll never forget you."

Hawkins felt his leg twinge again. "That's for *damned* sure."

CHAPTER FORTY-FIVE

The Blackhawk helicopter carrying Marzak made it back to the desert fuel dump on fumes. After refueling, the helicopter continued east over the border and put down at the field near the Doctor's house. The pilot had radioed ahead and the Doctor was waiting.

He listened to Marzak's account of the failed mission and the death of Saleem. "A pity," the Doctor said without feeling. "We must consider our next step."

"I will continue to pursue the treasure."

"My preference would be to find the treasure, but if that's impossible, it may be best to proceed with hanging the Prophet's Necklace around the throat of America."

Marzak didn't trust the Doctor. Once he had outlived his usefulness, the Shadows might decide that his continued existence might expose them to danger. There was something else. He wanted the treasure and he wanted Hawkins more than the payment for carrying out the plot.

"I will connect the strands as soon as I return to the U.S. I want to be there to follow up in case anything goes wrong."

The Doctor frowned, verifying Marzak's suspicion that he was expendable. "Do it as soon as possible, then."

The Doctor gave him a manly hug, then Marzak boarded the helicopter and was flown to the military base that had been a springboard for his mission. An ISI executive jet was waiting to fly Marzak and the remnants of his mercenary team to Islamabad. The news of Saleem's death had traveled ahead, and the professor's cousin Mohamed was at the military airport when the jet touched down. He took Marzak aside as soon as he disembarked.

"What happened to my cousin Saleem?"

"The sheik was waiting for us with ground-to-air missiles," Marzak said. "After his people destroyed the helicopters, Hawkins shot Saleem down like a dog."

"Poor Saleem. I should never have sent him on the mission."

"He fought back with everything he had, but in the end it made no difference. Unfortunately, we were unable to retrieve his body because of the intense fire."

"Of course. I don't blame you. Well, it's a good thing he has no close relatives except me. What a catastrophe! How am I going to explain the loss of three helicopters worth millions?"

Marzak clamped his hand on Mohamed's shoulder. "Don't worry," he said. "You'll simply have to ask the U.S. for an increase in its military aid package."

The comment brought a thoughtful expression to Mohamed's face. "A good idea. In the meantime, there are other more pressing matters to resolve."

He told Marzak that he had arranged a ride and hotel room for him. They would meet after a short rest to decide what to do next.

From the airport, Mohamed drove to a walled house in the affluent neighborhood where his commander lived. The commander was a big man with a square jaw and shoulders that filled out the tuxedo he was wearing for a party at his house. He took Mohamed into his study and interrogated him about the mission.

"I'm sorry for your cousin, but we have to keep in mind the big picture. The control of the mineral rights under Amir's land must be placed in the right hands. Everything else is a mere bump in the road toward that goal."

"These bumps are the size of mountains, commander."

"Then we will climb them one by one. The expedition was not a complete failure. Amir knows that he can be attacked at any time and in the future might not be so lucky. Pressure will be put on him using contacts in Kabul. He will be offered a piece of the action."

"He's a stubborn man, but it is worth a try."

"Next, this treasure business. We must keep the Shadows as potential allies, but make sure they can't cause trouble."

"A delicate balance," Mohamed grumbled.

"The Shadows won't carry out the necklace plot until they have the treasure. But if they think the treasure is out of their reach, they may proceed anyways."

"Then let's persuade them that the treasure is still *within* reach."

"How can we do that? The Americans most likely have it."

"We don't know that for a fact and I doubt the Americans will soon announce that the treasure is in their hands. As long as there is an unknown, we can use the treasure as bait. We need time to derail the Necklace plot and lure the Shadows out into the open."

"They might believe us. For a little while."

"In the meantime, we must get rid of Marzak. He's the only one who can connect the strands of the Prophet's Necklace. He must disappear without a trace. Leave that up to me."

The commander took Mohamed by the elbow and moved him toward an exit. "I have to get back to my guests. Call me in the morning."

Later, at his own house, Mohamed crawled into bed, but only slept a few hours before he was awakened by a phone call. It was the commander.

"There's been an important development concerning Marzak," he said.

"He's been arrested?"

"Not exactly. A squad went to the hotel. Apparently, he never checked into the room."

"*What*? He's gone."

"Correct. Our friend Mr. Marzak seems to have pulled his own disappearing act."

CHAPTER FORTY-SIX

Sutherland was on the move most of the day after leaving Route 66, scudding along under a cloudless sky to Durango, following Route 550 north through the San Juan national forest to Silverton where she stopped for a burger and Diet Coke before setting off again.

She caught her first glimpse of Ouray, Colorado after an exhilarating ride along a snaking stretch of mountain road known as the Million Dollar Highway. The city of Ouray calls itself the Switzerland of America, and the description works on some levels. Ouray is more than seven thousand feet above sea level, nestled in a narrow valley hemmed in on three sides by the thirteen-thousand-foot-high peaks of the San Juan mountain range, and laced with canyons, waterfalls and rushing rivers. The Victorian buildings that line the main street have a charm rivaling the quaint villages that occupy alpine valleys.

But the place lacks the green pasture gentility of its Swiss counterparts. The countryside around Ouray was shaped by volcanoes and glaciers, and later by rugged people who tore the riches from its rocky soil, leaving the evidence of their work in abandoned mines and the ruins of once-rich ghost towns.

Sutherland passed through Uncompahgre Gorge and followed a series of switchbacks to the city's main thoroughfare. She found a comfortable B and B on a side street and washed the road dust off her face. Taking her computer bag, she got on her Harley and rode to the tourist information booth next to Ouray's big hot springs pool.

She got a map showing all the abandoned mines in the area from the woman behind the desk, then she rode back to the B and B and sat on her bed with her computer. She called up the U.S. Geological Survey map of Ouray and surrounding countryside.

The Kurtz property was located off the Alpine Loop scenic byway, a sixty-five-mile-long road that winds through the northern San Juan range in the heart of mining country. Using the USGS chart for guidance, she called up satellite photos of the territory around the Kurtz mines and was able to zoom in on a section of woods at the base of a mountain. Some buildings were visible through the thick foliage.

She reread the file she had compiled on the Kurtzes. The first Kurtz mine was started in 1880 on former Ute Indian land at an elevation of 9800 feet. It closed in 1922, the same year Hiram Kurtz set off for Afghanistan, but during its decades of operation, produced nearly twenty million dollars in gold and silver, mainly, along with copper, lead and zinc as well. The peak population was nearly a thousand, and the mining town included stores, saloons, brothels and even a brick mansion for Kurtz. It was abandoned after the mines played out.

She found the old mining town using Google Earth and saw a few dirt roads and several buildings in the satellite picture. Most of the site was hidden by tree foliage. On the way out of town she stopped at a sporting goods store and bought a paper version of the survey map which she tucked into her computer bag, and a few minutes later she was back on

Route 550 heading south.

She left the main road at Animas Forks and headed east, riding around twenty minutes before she turned off onto a gravel road and traveled around fifteen miles without seeing another person or vehicle. She was riding at a fast clip and almost missed a side road that after a hundred feet or so led to a double metal gate around ten feet high.

On either side of the gate was a chain-link fence topped with razor wire. The insulators spaced along the fence indicated that it was electrified. A second fence several feet inside the first had no insulators, but sprouted antennae that could broadcast the presence of an intruder. She saw no cameras, but that didn't mean they weren't cleverly disguised to blend into the thick pine woods.

As she got off her bike and approached the gate, she heard a soft rustling patter and two Doberman Pincers as big as ponies galloped along the road on the other side of the gate. They stood up with their front paws against the second fence, and their black eyes stared at Sutherland as if she were a doggie chew.

"Nice puppies," she said in a high voice.

She backed away and walked the bike another hundred yards along the road. The dogs must have been trained to stay silent because as they paced her they didn't even growl. She had seen enough. There was no way she could penetrate security without getting electrocuted, sliced by razor wire or torn to pieces by guard dogs.

She turned around and headed out of the forest. She analyzed the problem on the ride back to Ouray. When she pulled up in front of her B and B, she knew what she had to do. She went to her room and stared at her pudgy cheeks and round glasses in the mirror. *Wussy.* Not much she could do to change her appearance, but as a student of human nature, she knew that personality is projected from the inside out.

She opened a can of diet soda, popped her laptop and began to read the Kurtz website. She allowed herself to soak up the venomous outpouring that emanated from the screen. The paranoia was the easiest for her to absorb. There were some advantages to being delusional, she reflected. She clicked the link labeled Contact Us. She took a deep breath, stifled her disgust and started typing.

She said she was a former soldier and inserted snippets of the truth as bait. Her birth in the poor coal mining state of West Virginia. Her decision to join the army. Her service in Iraq. Her distrust of the government. She said she was traveling through Colorado, had looked up organizations that shared her philosophy, learned about the Ouray camp, and asked permission to visit.

She reread what she had written and hit the SEND command.

Nothing to do but wait for Kurtz to check out her background. She was sure he had his sources. She went out for pizza and while she was finishing her last piece she checked her computer.

PERMISSION GRANTED. LOOK FORWARD TO MEETING YOU, CORPORAL SUTHERLAND. SEND ETA.

The email had been sent by Colonel Hak Kurtz.

She had set the hook, very much aware that a five-hundred-pound great white shark might be hanging on the line. She'd have to make up the rest of her plan after she got on the other side the fence.

She replied to the invitation.

THANK YOU SIR. ETA 1100 HOURS.

She checked her email and saw the message from Hawkins. She breathed a sigh of relief knowing that he was on his way home and that no one had been hurt, but she simmered over a feeling that she had been abandoned. He let her wait; she would let him wait. She imagined herself presenting himself with the emerald scepter and a shower of gold and gems.

She sent a summary of her plan to Hawkins, but clicked off before he had the chance to reply. Then she went to bed. Tomorrow was going to be a long day.

CHAPTER FORTY-SEVEN

Over the Atlantic Ocean

The 747 was flying at thirty-six-thousand feet and racing west across the skies at nearly six-hundred-miles an hour, but to Hawkins, who was worried about Marzak, the jet seemed to plod toward North America at a snail's pace. He decided to call a war council.

"First of all, I want to thank everyone for going above and beyond during this mission," he said. "But our job isn't finished. As we discussed, we've got to find the treasure before Marzak does. It's the only way to stop the Prophet's Necklace. And it might give us the chance to take out Marzak once and for all, something I know we all could go for."

Calvin made a face. "True. Only one problem, Hawk. *We* don't know where the treasure is."

"Marzak doesn't know that. We'll make him think we found the treasure. Or at least give the impression that we know where it is. The chance to get the treasure *and* me will be irresistible. He'll come to us. And he'll make mistakes."

"You know what happens when a catfish gets a hold of bait," Calvin said.

Hawkins was well aware of the danger his plan presented. "I don't know of any other way."

"How do you plan to get word to Marzak?" Abby said.

"Through the Newport Group."

"You're not serious," Abby said. "Those are the people who *hired* you."

"I'm well past the naïve stage," Hawkins said. "It was obviously a set-up. Sutherland's research confirms that Captain McCormick was tied in with Trask and Murphy. I asked Murphy to pass along a proposition to trade the treasure for Trask and McCormick. Not sure how far it will go."

"That's a long way from connecting them to a thug like Marzak."

"You would think so, wouldn't you?" Hawkins said with a wry smile on his face. "It was no accident that the Marzaks arrived at my house with guns blazing."

"McCormick?" Abby said.

"Seems like a good guess for now. I'll withhold judgment on the rest of the group."

Calvin was already thinking operationally. "What's your plan, once we get Marzak on the hook?"

"I'll leave that up to you and Abby. First, I'll see if I can even get the ball rolling."

Hawkins strolled to the back of the cabin with the satellite phone in hand.

Years seemed to have passed since he had been called to the navy War College. He remembered his go-around with McCormick and was glad that his instincts had been on the mark. Not knowing how deeply the Newport Group had been compromised, he would have to tread carefully.

He punched out Fletcher's number. The dry, patrician voice answered almost immediately.

"Hello, Lieutenant Hawkins. Nice of you to call from wherever you are."

"I'm on my way home, Dr. Fletcher."

There was a pause and Hawkins could almost hear the sound of Fletcher hiking up his bushy eyebrows.

"Then the mission was a success, I take it."

"Yes and no. We dove into the lake, but the treasure was no longer there. All we found was a coin."

"What sort of coin?"

"Gold. Inscribed with the name Prester John."

Another pause.

"Do you have any idea where the treasure is now?"

"We've got a strong lead. We'll know more when Dr. Everson has the coin verified."

"Dr. Everson? I don't understand."

"She's with us. She was in Afghanistan doing further research on Prester John and was able to help us with our explorations. She even intervened with the local drug lord."

There was a dry chuckle on the other end of the line. "You certainly never lack for surprises, Lieutenant."

"Speaking of surprises, we had problems with a dive team that tried to horn in on our operation."

"Do you know who they were?"

"My guess is that they were mercenaries. They were led by a guy named Marzak. Luckily, we drove them off without any injuries to our team. Marzak escaped."

"Too bad, but the good news is that you are all safe! Your country owes you a great debt."

"That's nice to hear, because I believe there is a payment coming my way."

"Your honorable discharge is all taken care of. I'll have the un-redacted report on what happened to you five years ago in Afghanistan. Send me a tally of other expenses. When will you arrive home?"

"We'll be in Washington in a few hours. I'm disbanding my team and heading back to Woods Hole."

"A wise decision. And Dr. Everson?"

"She will try to verify the coin and continue her research into Prester John. If you'll excuse me, Dr. Fletcher, I'm on the run. I'll send you a detailed report."

"Yes, please do. Sooner than later. I'm anxious to hear about it. And I'd like to have you up to my home in Newport within the next few days so we can toast your success. Please call when you get back."

"I will," Hawkins said, clicking off. He went to his computer and scrolled through his message board. Only one new message awaited him. It was a follow-up on Sutherland's warning about Murphy and Trask, and had been sent several hours earlier. He read her plan and the theory she developed on the treasure and her intention to visit the militia camp.

He tried to call her, and when there was no answer, sent her a quick text message. No answer. He cursed softly and walked to the other end of the cabin.

Minutes later, Hawkins had gathered everyone around a table at the forward end of the cabin. He said:

"There's been a change in plans. While we trekked through the mountains and deserts of Afghanistan, Molly Sutherland, the fourth member of our team, has been working on a theory that the treasure may have been moved to the Kurtz mines in Colorado." He opened his computer and read Molly's report.

When he was finished, Abby said, "Given what we know about Kurtz, and the fact that the treasure is no longer in the tomb, I'd say Sutherland has a pretty sound theory."

"Yes, but she's going to need help," Hawkins said.

"And I suppose you're going to need fast transportation to Colorado," Abby said.

"I think Sutherland is getting in over her head with this militia thing."

"I'll take that as a yes. I can arrange for a Gulfstream to be waiting at the airport when we arrive," Abby said.

"Thanks, Abby. Let's look at the satellite pictures Sutherland sent of the camp." He set the computer in the middle of the table. "There's a main road—the one Sutherland described in her report—and a number of off-road trails that snake around behind it and up the mountain. There's a road going to the top of mountain as well."

Calvin said, "That looks like a cleared boundary line surrounding the camp. Probably where they cut the woods back for the fence."

Another aerial photo showed several buildings in a row near a large structure.

"Those must be old mining buildings and the Kurtz mansion," Hawkins said. "Pretty far off the beaten path. From what Sutherland said about these guys, they're expecting black helicopters to drop in any day. Anyone got any ideas on how to gain entrance without getting shot?"

Abby said, "Could you go back to the aerial with the topographical overlay?"

Hawkins clicked the mouse and the screen showed the camp and surrounding terrain with contour squiggles and elevation numbers.

She studied the screen. "I think I know a way." Abby described what she had in mind. “I know it’s not the perfect plan, but it could work.” She paused. “Then again it might not.”

Calvin laughed at the disclaimer. “The possibility of a monumental failure is SOP for us special ops guys,” Calvin said. “You should have joined the SEALs, Abby.”

“I didn’t like that yucky green stuff you had to smear on your face,” she said. “Well?”

Hawkins stared at the screen, mentally working out each step of the plan.

“A thousand things could go wrong, and back in the day I would have tossed a plan like this into the shredder. Only one detail makes it worth the risk.”

“What’s that?” Abby said.

“Sutherland.”

CHAPTER FORTY-EIGHT

Ouray, Colorado

Exactly one minute before the appointed time Sutherland rode up to the gate of the Kurtz camp. She was glad to see that the Dobermans were not there to greet her.

At the stroke of eleven, her ears picked up the sound of an engine. A khaki-colored World War II Jeep with two men in it drove up to the other side of the gate. Both men were dressed in camouflage. Aviator sunglasses shaded their eyes. The driver wore a wide-brimmed fatigue hat and the other man had a do-rag tied around his head Rambo style.

The Rambo impersonator got out of the car. He had a thick muscular body and his black hair was cut close to the shiny white scalp. A droopy mustache emphasized the downward tips of his unsmiling mouth. Sutherland's eye went to the pistol holster and hunting knife at his waist.

Rambo pressed the button on a remote control. The gates swung open and he gestured for her to come inside. When she had ridden in, he closed the gates behind her and said: "Follow the vehicle."

As she trailed the Jeep, she couldn't help thinking how her poker-playing father used to say, "In for a dime, in for a dollar," an adage meaning that if a hand was worth a little bet it was worth a *big* bet.

The road sloped gradually through thick piney woods. About a mile from the gate the forest ended and the road ran between a dozen or so one-story wooden buildings that looked like worker housing. They sported a fresh coat of white paint and seemed in generally good condition.

The Jeep kept on going past the buildings and stopped at a guard house manned by two armed men in camouflage. The driver jerked his thumb at Sutherland and the guards waved them through. The driveway went through a patch of dark pine woods and led to a two-story brick Victorian mansion with a black mansard turret and roof. The lawn that surrounded the mansion was overgrown with weeds.

The Jeep stopped and Rambo got out. "Go around back. General's waiting for you."

Sutherland slid off the Harley and went to use the kick-stand, but Rambo grabbed the handlebars.

"Hey, what are you doing?" she said.

"Just putting your pretty bike away for safe keeping. General's in his shooting range. Follow the gunshots and you'll find him."

Her eyes smoldered with anger as she watched Rambo wheel the bike toward a five-port brick garage next to the mansion. Then she shouldered her pack and walked toward the *pop-pop-pop* sound coming from behind the mansion. She rounded one end of the house and saw a line of targets set up in a field.

A man wearing a fatigue hat and a matching desert camouflage uniform was firing a rifle at the targets which depicted a mean-faced man holding a pistol. The letters ATF printed in big letters across the chest identified the target as an Alcohol, Tobacco and Firearms agent.

The shooter had the M-16 rifle on automatic, firing methodically in bursts of three. As soon as he shredded one target, he moved on to the next and repeated the process.

Sutherland waited patiently. The man stopped before shooting at the last target, and turned around as if he knew she had been standing there all the time. He lowered the rifle and gestured for her to come over. He took off his safety goggles and ear protectors, handed them to Sutherland along with the rifle then pointed to the last target.

Sutherland hadn't fired a gun in years, but her army training asserted itself. She slipped on the ear protection and goggles, put her arm through the sling and felt the rifle stock snug naturally against her shoulder. She clicked the safety off, squinted through the telescopic sight, curled her finger around the trigger, ripped off three shots and clicked the safety on.

The man pushed a button and the target moved toward the firing station along a track. He thrust his forefinger through one of the tightly clustered holes in the target's forehead.

"You didn't go for the easier heart shot." He had a low, gritty voice.

"I like a challenge, sir."

"You learn that in Iraq, Corporal Sutherland?"

"I learned a *lot* of things in Iraq, sir." She smiled. "The first thing I learned was never to give up control of my weapon."

Kurtz gave Sutherland a sly smile. He took the rifle back and with the other hand he patted the holster at his belt.

"Had my eye on you every second, corporal." He made sure the weapon was unloaded and broke the action. "C'mon up to the house and have something cold to drink."

Kurtz walked with a John Wayne swagger as if he'd just gotten off a horse. He led the way toward a raised veranda that took up around a third of the back side of the mansion. He directed Sutherland to a white painted cast-iron table and chairs and went through the French doors into the house, returning a minute later with two cans of pre-sweetened iced tea. He gave a can to Sutherland, popped the other and plunked in the chair across the table from her.

He removed his hat to reveal steely gray hair in a flat top military cut. "Hope you weren't expecting anything stronger. I don't allow alcohol here at the encampment." He smiled, raised the can in the air. "*Skaol.*"

Kurtz took a sip that was almost dainty for a man who seemed to emanate a boot-camp macho masculinity. Then he knocked down the contents of the can, set it on the table and stared at Sutherland with deep-set amber colored wolf eyes under a straight brow.

Rather than challenge his piercing gaze, Sutherland glanced around as if she had been intimidated.

"I didn't expect to find a place like this way out here in the woods."

"Quite the little shack isn't it?"

"I grew up in a coal mining town. This is like a palace to me, sir."

He twitched his lips in a quick tight smile.

"Call me General Hak. I'm named after my grandfather Hiram who built this place and lived here while he developed the mines. It's fine for my purposes, but it could use a little work."

The place could use a *lot* more work, Sutherland thought. Bricks were missing, concrete trim was cracked and the panes in one of the tall windows had been replaced with plywood. The chairs they sat in were rusted where the paint had flaked off.

She simply nodded in agreement.

"I was surprised to get your email," he said. "We get a lot of queries, but not too many drop-ins."

"Like I said, sir—I mean General Hak—I was riding through the mountains. Not even sure where I'd land next."

"We did a background search to make sure you were really in the army like you said. You checked out okay." He sat back and laced his fingers behind his head. "What're you running from, corporal?"

"What makes you think I'm running from something?"

"Hell, *everyone*'s running from something."

"Guess you're right, General Hak. I joined the army to get away from West Virginia. When the army let me down, I ran away from everything."

"How'd the army let you down?"

She told him about going to Iraq, her enthusiasm for army life, and how her career hopes were dashed when she was attacked and the army not only didn't protect her, but punished her with a discharge. She didn't have to fake the emotion in her voice when she related how she had retreated to the desert isolation of southern Arizona, and how she went aimlessly on the road after her house caught fire and burned down.

The general's features hardened. "Every one of those bums who dishonored you would have been shot under my command." He sat forward in his chair. "Sorry to hear about your house. Probably some damned illegal Mexican torched it."

That set him off, and for the next half hour Sutherland sat at the table and tried to feign a tacit approval as Kurtz displayed his warped version of reality. He weighed in against the objects of his ire one after the other. He talked about restoring the honor of the Kurtz name and fortune, which must have been a veiled reference to the failures of his playboy father. She heard echoes of her own paranoia in his ramblings, when she had raged against imagined forces that were out to get her. She almost felt sorry for the pathetic old man, but she reminded herself that he was unpredictable and dangerous. He reaffirmed this when he slammed his fist down on the table so hard it made Sutherland jump.

"The only thing that's going to stop this great country from going down the drain is the militias. Are you ready to join us and make sure that doesn't happen?"

Sutherland could only nod.

Kurtz's manner changed completely. His thin lips widened in a broad smile.

He brought his hand to his chest. "I've got a bum ticker. Doctor says I could go any second. One foot in the grave the other on a banana peel. We need soldiers like you to carry on the cause when I'm gone. The militia movement's had some hard times, and it's up to folks like us to rejuvenate it. The government's been cracking down, trumping up fake charges to get us in trouble with the law. We've been trying to bring the militias together, but all this takes money. You got any money, corporal?"

"A little, General Hak."

He gave her an avuncular wink. "Just jerking your chain, corporal. What you've got is even more valuable. You've got military training and enthusiasm for the cause. You got the stomach for an intervention to help victims of the government?"

"I think so, sir."

"Good enough. In the meantime we're keeping a low visibility." He furrowed his brow. "One other thing I've got to ask. You're not a reporter, are you?"

"*No*, sir! I'll take a polygraph test if necessary."

"We caught you on camera yesterday. Why were you snooping around our gate?"

"I'm a trained soldier, General Hak. I was doing recon."

He burst into laughter, stood up and extended his hand.

"That's the kind of fighting spirit we need. You can stay here as long as you want. We'll try you out. You'll take our pledge. Most of the people are in the militia part-time, but we've got a small full-time cadre here at the base. You met a couple coming in. They'll give you a tour of the camp, get you outfitted, go through some physical tests to see where you fit in. Mess is at sunset and it's early to bed. "

She shook his hand.

"Thank you, sir. I was wondering about my motorcycle."

"You're free to leave any time, but we can't have people constantly going in and out of the compound. Besides, it's dangerous with the high voltage fence and the sentry dogs."

He snapped off a salute. She did the same, but by then he had already turned and was striding back to the French doors.

As she stared at his back, she again remembered her father's advice.

In for a dime, in for a dollar.

She tried to ignore the fact that Pop had lost his shirt at cards.

CHAPTER FORTY-NINE

Rambo led the way to the quartermaster where she picked up a couple of uniforms then to the barracks to drop off her bag and change. The man's camouflage uniform was too big, but she cinched the belt tight round her waist and rolled up the sleeves and pants. They rejoined Kurtz who proudly showed off the refurbished barracks, mess hall and the auditorium where he gave his pep-talks. Sutherland nodded like a bobble head doll, but she was more interested in the surrounding territory.

The camp was on several acres of rolling land at the base of a mountain. It was surrounded by forest that covered the lower slope of the mountain, rising to the bottom of a sheer rock face that soared up to the summit. Kurtz saw her looking at the road into the woods and said it led to the old copper mines scattered around the slopes of the mountain.

He ended the tour and dropped her off at the obstacle course which is where she met her trainer. The athletic woman was in uniform and her short blond hair was tucked under a drill sergeant cap.

"I'm Sergeant Paine, corporal, and my name is what I am," she said in introduction. She gave Sutherland a once-over, shook her head, and said: "Let's see what you are made of."

She started off with push-ups, prisoner squats, jumping jacks and planks, then Sutherland ran through the obstacle course. After she crossed the finish line, doubled over from exhaustion, Paine escorted her back to the women's barracks, told her to shower and report to the mess hall. After dinner there was a training film in the auditorium. Then it was bed time. Sutherland drifted off the moment her head hit the pillow.

A sharp-edged blast of a bugle playing reveille roused Sutherland from a sound sleep. She sat up in her cot and stared bleary-eyed out the barracks window, wondering what fool would be tooting a horn in the middle of the night. Then a woman's voice barked over the loudspeaker:

"Rise and shine, grunts!" Sergeant Paine said. "Time to stretch!"

The strains of the *Washington Post March* blared over the PA system. Sutherland put her head under the pillow which failed to muffle the rousing beat of the John Philip Sousa composition.

She sat up again and glared at the wall speaker as if she could melt it with her eyes.

There was a pounding on the door and Paine shouted, "Five minutes, Corporal Sutherland."

She pushed away the blanket and got to her feet. She was only wearing her underwear and the crisp air in the unheated barracks raised goose-bumps on her pale white skin. She got into uniform and pulled on her boots, jacket and floppy hat. Her basic training in the real army kicked into gear and she made up the cot to military standards without even thinking. Someone knocked once and the door swung open. Two people strode in. The man she called Rambo and Sergeant Paine who shouted, "Atten-shun!"

Sutherland stiffened her back, tucked her plump chin in and stared straight ahead, arms tight to her side.

The sergeant circled Sutherland, hands behind her back.

"Not bad for a newbie," she said. "At ease."

Sutherland relaxed, but kept her eyes fixed straight ahead.

"You've already met Captain Krause." She put her face close to Sutherland's. "We will be your teachers and your tormentors. When you leave here, you will have been transformed from your current sorry state into a hard-assed sonvofabitch who eats nails for breakfast."

"Yes, *sir*!" Sutherland said. "Ma'am."

"Good." The woman's voice lost its edge. "The men in this camp think women are soft. Do you think women are soft?"

"No, *ma'am*."

Paine glanced at her comrade and grinned. "We will prove them wrong. Now get your ass outside for calisthenics. *Hup*."

Sutherland marched out the door of the women's barracks, swinging her arms like a wind-up soldier, and stepped out into the cold mountain air to join the half-dozen other recruits. Krause stood in the background watching the sergeant put them through their exercises with no change in his pit bull expression. Sutherland started gasping for air after a few sets of jumping jacks. Paine cut the session short, told the recruits they were pathetic, and said they had fifteen minutes to wash up and head toward the mess hall.

Sutherland went back into the barracks and splashed cold water onto her face. She booted up her computer. Kurtz had emailed her so there must be a wireless signal. She found the link, easily figured out the entry code, which was HAK, then she logged off and put the pack holding her computer under the cot. She would feel naked without her computer, but couldn't risk damaging it. She slipped her phone under the mattress and smoothed down the blanket.

Halfway through breakfast—Froot Loops and skimmed milk–the

sergeant burst into the mess hall and ordered everyone outside. The sky was graying with a pre-dawn light. She told them to line up according to height. As the only female, Sutherland was the shortest. Paine marched the motley column past the other barracks to a road leading into the woods.

"Normally we start the day with a five-mile run, but this crew is clearly incapable of anything more strenuous than feeding your face, so we will make it a brisk three-mile walk."

Boot camp had begun.

On the road, Sutherland saw other groups, more tightly disciplined, as they trotted past with full pack and weapons. She broke the people in the camp into two groups. Some were citizens trying to look tough. Others had the easy swagger that comes with real experience as a soldier.

After the hike, they were given fake wooden rifles and put through bayonet practice. There was a short break for a lunch of protein bars and water. Next were martial arts and finally, the shooting range.

Many of the other recruits were hunters, and reasonably good shots, but they were tired from their exertion and barely able to lift their rifles. The sergeant's scorn faded when she saw the tightly grouped holes Sutherland put in the target.

"Well, we got a real Annie Oakley here." She clapped her hands. "Back to your barracks to clean up. Then supper and political orientation conducted by General Hak."

She patted Sutherland on the back and told her she had made the men look like girl scouts.

On the way to the barracks, Sutherland glanced up at the mountain, recalling from her research that it was honey-combed with mines. She wondered whether it would be possible to sneak off on an exploration. She could pretend she got lost. But as she trudged back to the barracks, she saw that she had more pressing matters to worry about.

General Hak barred the door to the barracks. Standing slightly behind him, rifle resting in the crook of his arm, was Krause. The general was holding her phone.

He growled, "What the hell are you doing with this thing?"

"You never said anything about phones."

"That's because most of them don't work out here. This one does."

"A lot of places don't have phone service, General Hak. I was a woman, traveling alone. It would have been dumb not to have communication."

He gazed thoughtfully at the phone. "Yeah, I guess, so. But we're confiscating this. For as long as you're here, there is to be no communication with the outside world."

She snapped off a salute that provoked a slight smile.

The other man who had met Sutherland in the Jeep came out of the barracks. "General. Could you come inside, sir? There's something you should see."

As she was marched through the door, Sutherland saw her laptop on the cot. The man picked the computer up and handed it to the general, who gazed at the screen then turned it to face her.

Before leaving the B and B, she had backed up all her files on a remote data storage center then eliminated them. She expected to see a blank screen except for a few icons, but someone had written her an email.

The general read the message, handed the laptop off to Krause and bore into Sutherland with narrowed eyes.

"Girl," he said in a menacing tone. "You are in deep, deep trouble."

CHAPTER FIFTY

Chantilly, Virginia

When the Global Logistics plane landed at Dulles, waiting for it was an executive jet Abby had arranged with full crew and handlers who quickly transferred gear from the big plane to the Gulfstream G150. Abby had also arranged for a taxi to take Cait to her condominium, as it had been decided that she would stay and see what she could find out about the coin while the others continued on to Colorado. Within minutes, the sleek Gulfstream leapt into the air like a fighter plane on alert and headed west.

Cait watched the plane disappear from sight, then got into the taxi and gave the driver directions to her condo. She stepped into the living room and dropped her duffle bag on the floor. As she stood there breathing in the stale air, surrounded by familiar furniture and out of date magazines and newspapers, her adventures in Afghanistan seemed like a dream.

The dashing Hawkins was like a hero from one of the bodice-ripper romances she had read as a girl, ready to swoop in and save the fair maiden from the clutches of the nasty villain. Calvin looked as if he could walk through a brick wall unscathed. She had grown to like Abby, and sensed that she still had a lot of affection for her ex-husband, although there seemed to be a barrier between them. If Abby didn't want Hawkins when they returned from their trip out west, Cait would be willing to step in.

Holding the Prester John coin in her hand to reassure herself that her adventures had not been in her mind, she called Nelson Black, a coin expert acquaintance. Cait had drawn upon Black's expertise when she was writing her Silk Road books, and his name came to mind the second she saw the Prester John coin. She had contacted him earlier from the 747 saying she had a highly unusual coin he might like to see. He tried to tease out the details, but she said he would have to wait until she arrived to examine it in person.

"Hello Nelson," she said. "Cait. I'm home."

"Please hurry. You've got me all excited with your mysterious phone call from high in the sky."

Cait smiled. "On my way."

Twenty minutes later, she arrived in National Harbor, Maryland, where Black lived. He had been impatiently awaiting her arrival and eagerly led the way to his coin vault. The spacious basement room contained the shallow drawer filing cabinets that held his collection and a wooden table he used to examine and sort coins.

"Well, what do we have, Dr. Everson?"

She handed him the Prester John coin in a plastic bag.

He slipped on a pair of rubber gloves, extracted the coin, and held it by its edges, examining both sides. Then he placed it under the magnifier, squinted through the ten-power lens for a moment, flipped it over, took it off and weighed it, rolled it between his fingers, and turned to Cait.

"If I may ask, Dr. Everson, where did you find this coin?"

"In Afghanistan."

He narrowed his gray eyes. "Specifically?"

"It was discovered in what was apparently a tomb in the central part of the country."

"Was the tomb shown to you by a local? Sometimes natives will salt a ruin with fakes."

"Its location was based on my research. The tomb seems to have been plundered, but the robbers dropped this coin."

"As you said on the phone this is a very unusual specimen. *Highly* unusual I might say. Prester John was a controversial figure. Many scholars believe that he and his kingdom never existed."

"I am in the minority that believes Prester John and his kingdom were real. I was hoping that your examination of the coin would prove it."

"I'm afraid I can't do that, but there are a number of possibilities."

"I'd like to hear them."

"This *could* be a coin from Prester John's kingdom. Or this coin could have been minted by someone who peddled it to gullible buyers. Another possibility is that it is a fantasy item, which memorializes something that may not be real. Like a winged horse or a unicorn. Bottom line, I can't confirm that this was currency minted in some long-lost kingdom."

"I knew it was a long shot."

"Don't be disheartened. What I *can* do is tell you it is, in fact, an ancient coin, not a more recent fake."

"Well, that's *something*, at least."

Black gave a crisp laugh.

"Further tests, like a spectroscopic analysis, may prove me wrong, but if I'm correct, and regardless of its origin, we are looking at one of the most important numismatic finds in the past hundred years."

Black's statement echoed in Cait's ears as she drove back to Arlington. The coin tucked in her purse seemed to be emanating rays from the past. Even if the treasure were never found, the existence of the coin would bolster her Prester John theory and spur even further research.

Back at her apartment, she slipped out of her Indiana Jones outfit, showered, and crawled into bed. She fell asleep, thinking that she couldn't wait to see the faces of her colleagues who had described her work as "pop research."

She would have slept less soundly if she had known that Marzak was only a few miles away.

Marzak had a network of contacts around the world. After slipping out of the hotel in Islamabad, he had called a number and told the person at the other end that he had to get out of Pakistan as soon as possible. He was told to hang on and after an excruciating wait, he was instructed to go directly to the airport. A first-class seat was waiting on a commercial flight to London where he caught a British Airways plane to Washington.

Upon arriving, he had taken a taxi to an apartment building on the outskirts of the city. The unit ownership was under one of his many false names, and the big beehive of an apartment complex offered a degree of anonymity. The two-bedroom unit had served as a crash pad for him and his brother and a storage place for an array of weapons that would have supplied a small army.

He checked the security camera that kept watch on the apartment, but no intruders had been recorded. He laid some weapons on his brother's bed and stretched out on the couch. He stared at the ceiling and fell into a watchful half sleep that ended when his eyes blinked open at the chirp of his cell phone.

The voice on the line belonged to one of the free-lance operators he and his brother had employed for special jobs. “We picked up a signal from the transmitter we put in Dr. Everson’s car.”

“Let me know when she reaches a destination.”

The phone chirped again an hour later.

“She went to National Harbor, stayed around forty-five minutes and drove back to her apartment.”

“Where did she stop?”

“At a private residence. We checked. It’s owned by Nelson Black, a coin expert.”

Interesting.

“Put her under surveillance,” Marzak said. “Let me know if she has visitors or if she leaves again.”

He stretched out on the couch again to martial his physical and mental resources. His prime target was Hawkins, but he had learned long ago that low-hanging fruit was better than no fruit at all.

CHAPTER FIFTY-ONE

The military jail at Camp Kurtz was a dilapidated barn-sized shed that had been used as a mausoleum for dead mining equipment. The rough-hewn building was crowded with rust-covered, derelict machines, huge wheels, cylinders, riveted boilers and spring-like coils that looked more like industrial art than the mechanical guts of a busy mining operation.

Sutherland sat on the dirt floor of the shed, her right wrist handcuffed to a giant cable spool. She had been there for hours. Slivers of light sifting through gaps in the boards had provided the only illumination, but even those had disappeared and she was in near total darkness.

She was uncomfortable, thirsty and hungry. She would have killed for a bag of potato chips. Mostly, she was angry at herself for breaking her own rule against letting her computer out of her hands. She should never have left it in the barracks. She didn't blame Hawkins for his ill-timed message. She had been hoping he would contact her, but he could never have dreamed that his words would be seen by hostile eyes. But there on the screen, for Kurtz to see, was Hawkins' mangled attempt at texting shorthand:

AAS. THX411. CONGRATS. ACKKurtz=PJ$ Home2moro. T2UL. Hawkins.

A grating sound cut into her ruminations. The shed door swung open and a flashlight beam hit her face. She shut her eyes to block the light. Boots crunched on the dirt. A hand grabbed her by the wrist, unlocked the cuff and pulled her to her feet. Her arm was yanked behind her back and she was cuffed again.

"*March*," Krause ordered.

He shoved her through the doorway. The Jeep was waiting to drive her to the mansion. They escorted Sutherland through the front entrance and down a long hallway. Wallpaper was peeling away and the corridor had a musty odor. Krause stopped in front of a door and knocked.

The general barked: "Enter!"

Krause opened the door, pushed Sutherland into the room and stepped into the hallway, closing the door behind her.

Kurtz sat behind an antique desk of gargantuan proportions that was carved with Gothic motifs. The top of the desk was bare except for a riding crop and an old-fashioned goose-neck lamp that provided the only light, but it was enough illumination for her to see that the suits of armor flanking the desk were rusty and missing parts.

"Sit," the general said, pointing to a plain wooden chair.

Sutherland did as she was told. Kurtz opened a drawer and pulled out her computer, which was on. He placed it on the desk, screen facing him.

"Who're you working for? ATF? DEA? FBI?"

"You forgot the BVD."

"What's that stand for?"

"My father wore BVD underwear. He said it stood for Buster V. Davenport." She paused. "It was a joke. Coalminer humor."

He tapped the computer with the riding crop.

"*This*," he said, "Is no joke. It's *code*. Tell me what it says."

The message from Hawkins said: *Alive and Smiling. Thanks for the information. Congratulations. Acknowledge Kurtz has Prester John treasure. Home tomorrow. Talk to you later.*

"It's not code, it's texting shorthand. Any teenage kid could tell you what it says."

"*You* tell me what it says."

"It's a message from a friend of mine. It says that he's on his way home and will call tomorrow."

"Who's your friend?"

"An ex-navy guy. I know him from Iraq."

Kurtz leaned forward and glowered.

"I might have believed you corporal, except for one thing." He slowly spun the computer around so that the screen was facing her and tapped it with his riding crop. "That's *my* family name in your friend's message. How come?"

She had been thinking how to answer the inevitable question.

"I wrote my friend that I was coming here to the old mine."

"What about the PJ dollar sign stuff?"

She had expected the question.

"Shorthand again. P means Poor. J means that I need a job so I can contribute to your cause."

He sat back, folded his arms and stared at her for a second before the grin vanished.

"Know what I think it means, corporal? It means you are lying."

Sutherland shrugged. "That's too bad, because it also means that you feel you can no longer trust me. So I'd like my motorcycle back and an escort to the gate."

"You're not going *any*where until we check you out. And if we find you are a spy, you will be brought up before a court martial."

"You have no jurisdiction over me. I'm a volunteer."

"The second you passed through the gates of this camp, you came under my authority. My word is the law here."

Sutherland's eyes narrowed behind the round glasses. She had had enough of this jerk.

"If you don't let me go, this camp will be history."

"Hah! What're talking about?"

"I've frozen all your financial assets."

"Bull crap!"

"Bull crap yourself. Check your accounts if you don't believe me." She gave him the bank name and account number and the quantity of money. "It's a pretty pitiful amount, but I took it out and I'm the only one who can put it back."

He stood up, placed his palms on the desk and loomed over her like an avenging angel. "I. Have. Had. Enough. Of. This." He smacked the riding crop down on the desk and yelled for Krause, who was outside the door and ordered him to take her back to the jail. Krause grabbed her roughly by the arm.

"Wait!" she protested. "If I'm under military arrest, I come under the army rules for treatment of prisoners. Treatment at all times should be humane. I'm hungry and thirsty and I don't like that dark hole. If I don't get better treatment, you and your men will be on food stamps when I get through with you."

They stared at each other. Kurtz knew better than to underestimate an enemy, and he didn't like the idea that Sutherland knew his bank and account information. And she was right about the military rules.

"Take the prisoner to the barracks. Give her food and water."

Krause prodded her back to the Jeep. They rode to the women's barracks and he handcuffed her to her bunk. He called someone on his hand radio. Paine showed up a few minutes later with some power bars and Gatorade, which she handed to Sutherland without saying a word or making eye contact.

Sutherland thought that maybe she shouldn't have threatened Hak. The general was even more delusional than she was. He was obviously mentally ill and she should have handled him with kid gloves, but she didn't do well with threats. She could only wish that he still had a shred of sanity and would release her once he checked on the status of his funds. She closed her eyes and dozed off.

Kurtz paced back and forth in his study, occasionally slapping his thigh with his riding crop.

The message on Sutherland's computer had sparked a long-forgotten memory. He'd been a boy when his father told him about Grandpa Hiram going to Afghanistan to look for a fabulous treasure. When he had scoffed at the story, his father gave him a book to read.

He scanned the shelves and his hand reached out for a book entitled, "The Emerald Sceptre." He sat behind his desk and leafed through the pages he had first read with youthful excitement.

He had dreamed of the Prester John treasure for weeks after reading the book. He wondered if his grandfather had actually found the treasure and what he did with it. His father had said that Hiram moved back to the mansion after he returned from Afghanistan and stayed there until he died. The family had wondered why he didn't retire to the comforts of New York instead of his played-out mines, but figured Hiram's mind had become addled from travel fever.

All of a sudden, the shorthand equation on the computer made sense.

KURTZ=PJ$

Kurtz equals the Prester John treasure.

Maybe Sutherland *wasn't* a spy. Maybe she was a treasure hunter and thought the Prester John treasure was on Kurtz's property and had lied her way into the camp to get closer to it.

He sprang from his chair and went over to an oversized lift-top cabinet. Lifting the lid, he gathered up the yellowed sheets of paper stacked inside. Printed on the three-by-two foot sheets of paper were diagrams of the mines on the Kurtz property.

He spread them out on his desk and examined each diagram under a magnifying glass. Half-way through the pile he stopped and brought the goose-neck lamp down until it was inches from the paper.

His boyhood excitement came back as he saw, scrawled in pencil at the end of a mine shaft, a penciled circle drawn around two printed letters.

P and **J**.

The sight of the simple letters was like popping a cork in his brain. This was a gift from the gods! A treasure would give him the means to defeat the forces of darkness conspiring to humble his beloved nation. With advanced weapons he could foment revolution, destroy governments and shoot down squadrons of black helicopters. And he could return honor to the Kurtz name that had been stained by the antics of his drunken father.

A maniacal light glimmered in his eyes. At any given time, he thought he was the reincarnation of many long-dead military leaders. Patton. Napoleon. George Washington. Caesar. Alexander. But as his fevered brain imagined the future, it seemed that the blood of all the great leaders who came before him now ran through his veins.

He clicked on the hand radio that connected him with Krause.

"Make preparations to march as soon as it's light," he ordered.

"We're we going?" Krause asked.

“On to glory, sergeant! On to bloody glory!”

CHAPTER FIFTY-TWO

Southwest Colorado

After a smooth three-and-a-half hour flight at a speed of Mach .80 the Gulfstream G150 landed at Montrose regional airport. A gray Jeep Wrangler sat in the parking lot, keys in the ignition. Tied down on the roof rack were two long objects wrapped in fabric bags. Attached to the rack between the bags was a cargo box.

Hawkins got behind the steering wheel. Abby slid in next to him and started going over a checklist on her IPad. Calvin sat in back doing a weapons inventory. They headed south on Route 550, passing through the sleeping town of Ouray, and continuing on the Million Dollar Highway to the connection with the Alpine Loop. The Jeep followed the same route Sutherland had taken, but near the Kurtz property, they split off on a different route.

The road was narrow, winding, rutted and at times, non-existent, devolving into a root-bound track that ascended the mountain in a series of tight switchbacks that the Jeep had to edge around in fits and starts.

As the Jeep moved higher, the tall pines thinned out, to be replaced by shorter trees, then shrubs, and finally, lichen-covered rocky slabs that were black with moisture. They entered an elevation where groping fingers of fog diffused the headlight beams and rendered them almost useless. Hawkins strained his eyes through the windshield, trying to follow an imaginary line up the middle of the road.

Abby's voice broke his concentration.

"We're here," she said.

Hawkins braked to a stop, leaned on the wheel and stared at the swirling gray mists.

"We're *where?*"

"On top of the mountain. Sun should be coming up in a few minutes. The operation is now officially yours. I got you here. The rest is up to you."

They got out of the Jeep. The temperature was at least twenty degrees colder than at the base of the mountain. They shivered as they unloaded the heavy duty plastic storage box from the luggage rack. Calvin opened the box and handed out a CAR-15 with extra ammo clips, pistol, knife and other first line gear.

Hawkins checked his altimeter and compass. "We're at ten thousand feet," he said. "The point should be about a hundred feet in that direction."

Calvin swept his flashlight at the soupy mists.

"What if it isn't?"

"Simple. We fall off the mountain."

"Good thing I know when you're joking." Pause. "You *are* joking?"

"Sure, Cal. I'm joking."

They lugged the first bag fifty feet or so, set it down and went back for the other. Abby dropped light sticks to create a path through the fog. After a couple of trips back and forth the gear was stacked and ready to go.

A silvery glow came to the mists as the new sun reflected off thousands of droplets of moisture. They moved through the pre-dawn gloom like ghosts. As the fog thinned, the mountain top materialized and they could see that they were near the edge of the domed summit.

Hawkins and Calvin walked onto a ledge, which stuck out like a huge diving platform. The vertical wall of gray rock under the ledge dropped a few hundred feet to where the mountain flared out at a forty-five degree angle.

Valley fog was pooling in a wooly layer of dark gray clouds that obscured the base of the mountain. Hawkins extended his hand and felt the air current rising up the sheer face.

"Good air flow. Should give us a nice ridge lift."

Abby's plan to jump off the top of the mountain and fly down to the Kurtz camp on hang-gliders had seemed crazy when she proposed it. But it seemed slightly less insane after she showed off a 3-D image she had created on her IPad with a GPS link to Google Earth. Abby pointed to the ledge.

"Here's your diving board. Mountain elevation is around two thousand feet. Follow the flight line I've charted to this clearing near the camp, and with the sun behind you, you should make it to the ground without being seen."

"Not bad. What about extraction?" Calvin said.

"I'm still working that out."

After Hawkins studied the maps and photos he said, "I've done enough hang-gliding to be comfortable with the flight. What about you, Cal?"

"I've tried it a few times. Can't be any worse than fast-roping from a chopper onto the deck of a ship. Let's do it."

The answer didn't surprise Hawkins. Calvin would jump into a volcano if Hawkins asked him to, and he'd do the same for his friend.

Returning to their stockpile, they unpacked the bags and assembled the gliders. The cargo box yielded camouflage one-piece jumpsuits, helmets with built-in radios that could be operated with a finger switch, and protective goggles. In addition to their weapons and ammunition, they each had a wristwatch that contained an altimeter and compass, and a helmet-mounted variometer that would track the climb and descent rate and warn the pilot with a beeping sound if the glider was in danger of stalling. Hawkins had a wrist GPS as well.

"Time, gentlemen," Abby said with a glance at her watch.

"Ready?" Hawkins asked Calvin.

"Ready."

Hawkins strapped himself into the harness, grabbed the sides of the control bar, and lifted the sixty-five pound glider over his head.

Calvin hoisted his glider, teetering as he tried to balance the assembly.

"Looking good, Cal," Hawk lied.

"Let's see if I got this right, Hawk. Push the bar down to go fast, pull it to slow down. Shift my weight to make a turn."

"You've got it. The launch is easy. Just run down the slope, jump off, and when you feel surge from the wind in the sail, drop your hands from the sides of the bar down to the horizontal bar."

"Like this?"

Calvin trotted down the ledge, keeping the wing level, and jumped off into space. The glider dipped, as the force of gravity pulled it down and forward, but the wing caught the air being deflected up the face of the mountain, and rose higher, delicately balancing on an updraft.

Calvin soared away from the mountain and over the fog-shrouded valley in a straight line. He tucked his legs into the cocoon-like bag that extended from the harness, straightened his body, rolled the wing to one side and then the other, and straightened out into a dive to gain speed, climbing in an aerobatic loop that had him flying upside down, then back again.

He lowered his left wingtip, a maneuver that brought him into a rolling turn back toward the ledge. Calvin's voice crackled over Hawkins' earphones.

"What's wrong, hawk man? Forgotten how to fly?"

Hawkins pressed the radio switch. "You said you had only flown couple of times."

"That's right, man. Liked it so much I bought my own glider."

"I didn't know bald eagles grew so big," Hawkins said, referring to his friend's shaved scalp.

"Best you can do man? Flap your wings instead of your mouth and get up here in the sky with the big birds."

Abby's voice cut into their conversation.

"It's getting light. If you two eagles don't get to the ground in a couple of minutes you'll be sitting ducks."

"Lady's got a point," Calvin said.

"So she does."

Hawk started off at a brisk walk that accelerated into a run. He leapt off the ledge and felt the surge as the sail caught the wind, arresting his downward motion. The glider lifted him higher and he headed out in a straight line, keeping his wing more or less level. It had been a while since the last time he had flown in a hang glider, and he reminded himself that his moves had to be gentle.

Within moments, he was soaring over the valley, kept aloft by the wave of air upwelling from the ground far below. Calvin had come around and was pacing him on the right side. Hawkins glanced at his wrist GPS, shifted his body weight to adjust his course, and as he neared the target, pulled back on the bar. The front of the wing tipped down, and he began to gain speed. Several times he got going too fast, or had to correct for current variability, so that the descent was more like that of a falling leaf than a bird.

Near the top of the cloud layer he looked as his altimeter. The ceiling was low, which would keep them invisible until the last few moments of flight, but the ground would come up fast.

He jerked his thumb downward, and Calvin gave him the OK sign.

Abby watched Hawkins' torturous descent from the top of the mountain. She was wondering if she'd been overconfident in coming up with this crazy plan and breathed a sigh of relief as the pair of large birds slipped out of sight in the gray clouds. She lowered the binoculars and looked around at the shreds of fog that lingered on the bleak, rocky summit.

And all at once, she felt very much alone.

She took a last glance into the chasm, muttered a quick prayer to the gods that look over mortals who have more courage than good sense, and hurried back to the Jeep.

CHAPTER FIFTY-THREE

Alexandria, Virginia

Marzak watched Cait get into her Honda and he started the engine of his rental car. He was parked across the street from her Alexandria apartment. His Washington Redskins baseball hat was pulled down low over his platinum hair and aviator sunglasses shielded his eyes.

He pulled out behind Cait, keeping back a couple of car-lengths. He followed her out to the Beltway, then toward Washington, expecting her to head for Georgetown, but she bypassed the city, and drove over the Bay Bridge, then south on the eastern shore of Maryland.

The change in expectations heightened his hunting *instincts*, especially as the countryside grew more rural and houses farther apart. She pulled over a couple of times, once into a gas station where she talked to someone in the office, then kept going.

He would pounce as soon as he sensed that the moment was right.

When Cait turned off the country road onto a narrow blacktop road that led into the woods, he knew that moment would come very soon.

Cait's decision had been impulsive.

She had every intention of driving into Georgetown to begin her research, but she changed her mind at the last second. She had been thinking about the treasure, and its long voyage from Afghanistan and across the ocean, when she remembered the fate of the Kurtz yacht.

The boat had ended up as a restaurant on the Eastern Shore of Maryland according to Sutherland's Prester John file. Cait thought the rediscovery of the yacht and its connection to the treasure would be another whole chapter in her book, and she felt herself irresistibly pulled to visit it.

She wandered the back roads, and was about to give up her search when the gas station attendant told her the restaurant had closed years before, but the boat was still there on the shore. She could hardly contain her excitement when she saw the faded old sign on the leaning post.

The Yachtsman Seafood Restaurant.

She ignored a No Trespassing sign and turned onto the road. Trees and bushes whipped both sides of her car and the wheels bumped over broken blacktop that looked like the pieces of a jigsaw puzzle.

The rank smell of the bay became stronger as she drove deeper into the woods. She traveled another quarter mile, rounded a curve and saw the old yacht Kurtz had named after his dead wife. Barely visible on the stern were the words: **Sweet Priscilla**. Cait stared at the yacht, trying to reconcile the rotting old derelict in front of her with the sleek ocean-going vessel she had seen in the old photographs.

She got out of the car and walked toward the vessel, which had been drawn up onto land. She could see the sparkle of bay water beyond the marsh that bordered the shore. She walked past another restaurant sign, this one hanging by a single nail, and stopped at the bottom of a wooden ramp leading onto the deck. She tested the ramp with her foot to make sure it wouldn't break under her weight, and walked up it.

Cait stopped in front of a gaping doorway. The doors lay in pieces on the deck. She stuck her head through the portal only to recoil at the over-powering smell of rot and mold. Her eyes could pick out interior details in the light coming through the windows and holes in the walls. She saw some old beer cans and assumed they had been tossed there by fishermen. There were broken tables and chairs, indicating that this once had been a dining room. Birds had built nests in the ceiling beams and decorated the floor with their droppings.

She was overcome by a sense of incredible sadness. Despite the nastiness of her surroundings she found herself being drawn further into the boat.

If only this old wreck could talk, what a story it would tell, she thought.

She walked through the dining room into a space that must have been a lounge.

Light streamed through the windows illuminating the old bar and overturned tables and stools. She tried to picture the bar filled with alcohol-fueled laughter and the clink of glasses, but the task was beyond her imagination. It was clear that this was a fool's errand. The interior of the boat had been gutted of any trace of Kurtz or his treasure.

She turned and walked out of the lounge, engrossed in her thoughts.

As she stepped through the doorway into the dining room, her heart jumped at a glimpse of movement off to her right and the sound of a creaking board. Before she could react, she felt a quick stabbing pain hitting her shoulder.

Her scream caught in her throat as the intense searing pain surged through her body. Her legs turned to rubber, her knees buckled, and the floor came up to meet her. As she lay on the floor with her limbs twitching involuntarily, she had the vague sensation of something hard and cold pressed against her neck, then came a soft puffing sound and a black curtain fell over her eyes.

CHAPTER FIFTY-FOUR

Kurtz was dressed like a gangly version of World War II tank commander General George Tecumseh Patton. Twin pearl-handled revolvers hung from his hips. Three white stars emblazoned his shiny black helmet. The short-waist Eisenhower jacket buttoned tightly across his narrow chest was festooned with a rainbow of military service ribbons. Tan riding pants drooped from his thin legs. The steel-shod heels of his leather knee-high boots clacked as he strode across the wooden floor. He whacked the side of Sutherland's bunk with his riding crop.

"Time to move out, corporal."

He gestured with his crop to Krause, who unlocked the handcuffs from the bunk. He pulled Sutherland to her feet and re-cuffed her hands in front of her, then prodded her toward the door with his rifle. The skin between her shoulder blades was tender from previous jabs and the gun's muzzle hurt. She stopped and turned to Kurtz.

"General, please tell your soldier boy that if he pokes me one more time with his make-believe manhood, I will take his weapon and stick it where the sun don't shine."

Krause blinked at the low, menacing voice coming from the pudgy round face, and then he laughed and turned to Kurtz for reinforcement. The general chuckled and smacked his thigh with the riding crop:

"Do as the prisoner requests or she'll hit you over the head with the Geneva Convention."

Krause used his hand instead of his rifle to push Sutherland through the door and out into the gray darkness. The World War II army Jeep was parked outside the barracks with its motor running. A big Ford 250 pick-up with four militia men was parked behind the Jeep.

The general told Sutherland to get in the back seat. Sergeant Paine sat beside her. Kurtz climbed into the passenger seat and Krause got behind the wheel. Kurtz raised his riding crop in the air and pointed forward.

As they drove past the deserted barracks, Kurtz said airily, "You think I don't know why you came here, corporal? Well I know all about my grandfather and Prester John. You came here to steal our property. Admit it."

Sutherland answered with her name, rank and made up serial number.

"Military rules? I'm okay with that, but you might not be."

Sutherland didn't like his tone, which was smug and threatening, but she kept her mouth shut.

The two-vehicle convey drove past the mansion and through the ghost town. After about a mile the road began to climb through the woods, becoming steeper as it meandered back and forth in a series of ascending switchbacks. The road surface was dirt and gravel and studded with boulders, but the slow-moving vehicles made steady progress. After traveling nearly an hour, they emerged from the woods into an open area at the base of a high ridge.

The general studied a large rectangle of paper for a few minutes and told the driver to keep going another hundred yards.

"This is it," he said. "*Stop.*"

The headlights picked out a crumbling shed and behind it, rails emerging from the side of the hill. The mine entrance itself was almost invisible, a rectangular shadow partially obscured by brush that had grown around the opening. Kurtz got out of the Jeep and walked up to the entrance. He flashed his light on, showing a wall of weathered gray boards, and then ordered his men to give him a hand.

At the general's orders, a couple of his men used crow bars to remove the barrier. The boards easily pried away from the rusty nails holding them in place.

Kurtz consulted the mine diagram again.

"The main shaft goes straight in. There are four tunnels off to the right. We want the third one. Saddle up."

He strode into the mine with Krause, then came Sutherland and Sergeant Paine, followed by the militiamen. The tunnel sloped down at a gradual angle. The blockade had protected the interior of the mine from moisture and destructive forest creatures and the timbers supporting the walls and ceiling were mostly intact.

They trudged in silence between the narrow tracks and encountered the first side tunnel about an eighth of a mile in. They kept moving, passed another opening after a few hundred yards, and after a slightly longer walk came to the third. A few yards beyond the opening, the main shaft ended in a blank wall.

"Something's not right," Kurtz growled.

He studied his diagram, and then wheeled about and with his entourage following, slowly retraced his steps, playing the beam of his flashlight on the walls. He stopped and studied a section of wall that seemed to be slightly indented. He borrowed a crowbar and pried away a slab of rock that was no thicker than a flagstone. Wood could be seen through the hole where the rock had been.

He stepped back and handed the crowbar to a militia man, who pried away more of the flat rocks. Behind the façade was a wooden plank blockade similar to the barrier at the mine entrance.

Kurtz led the way. The tunnel was smaller than the main passage, and went in for a couple of hundred feet before it ended in a wall of steel plates. Painted on the wall in red paint was a primitive drawing of a skull.

"What the hell is that?" Krause said.

"Indian hex sign," Kurtz said. "Figures. They say Grand pop Hiram hired a bunch of Utes to keep an eye on the more valuable mines. They weren't interested in gold or silver and could keep their mouths shut." He stepped back. "That hoodoo won't bite you. Take 'er down."

The men took turns working the crowbars through gaps in the plates. Once one section was pried off, the others came down easily. After about ten minutes a gap around three feet wide, reaching from ceiling to floor, was opened in the barrier.

As soon as the gap was opened Kurtz pushed through. There was silence, then something that sounded like a choking cry.

"You all right, general?" Krause said.

A mad cackle of laughter issued through the opening.

"I'm *more* than all right."

The voice had a ghostly echo, as if it were coming from the inhabitant of a sepulcher. The militia men exchanged puzzled glances and nervously clutched their weapons.

Krause said, "You want us to come in, general?"

Kurtz answered simply. "No. I'm coming out."

He squeezed through the opening, an object wrapped in shreds of cloth clutched close to his chest. He removed the cloth and cradled in his arms was a cross around three feet long that seemed to glow with a green and yellow fire.

The horizontal arms were shorter than the main shaft, and the entire surface was covered with swirling filigrees of gold. The beams from the flashlights reflected off the finely-cut facets of dozens of emeralds inlaid into the gold. At the top of the cross was an emerald as large as an egg.

Kurtz slowly raised the scepter high above his head like a medieval warrior clutching a broadsword. The militiamen stared at the object as if hypnotized by its unearthly glow.

Clearly visible where the arms crossed, inlaid in smaller diamonds, was the letter J.

Sutherland had been brought up in a religious family, but her army experiences had left her cynical and her world had become one of technology rather than superstition. But even she could feel the magical power that radiated from the scepter and seemed to flow down through Kurtz's upraised arms and into his body. The light from the precious stones reflected in the general's eyes, which burned with a supernatural glitter.

The subterranean surroundings with the shadowed walls, the vacant stares of the armed militiamen, and most of all, the cross in the hands of a fanatical madman, all seemed part of an unholy ceremony that mocked good and celebrated evil.

Sutherland's literal mind could not comprehend the totality of what was going on. But she knew from the shivers dancing along her spine that she had every reason to be very afraid.

Hawkins swooped down and emerged below the wooly layer of clouds. He was going too fast so he brought the glider's nose up, precipitating a string of beeps from the variometer warning him of a stall. He pushed the control bar forward and stabilized his flight. He was still having trouble keeping the wing level when Calvin dropped out of the clouds seconds later.

Hawkins pressed the finger switch on his radio. "How do I look?"

"Like a drunken condor. But you're headed in the right direction. Down."

Hawkins glanced at the forest below, then at the GPS screen. "Our LZ is directly ahead. Check out the lights at eleven o'clock."

"I count two vehicles moving up the mountain," Calvin said. "What do you want to do?"

Hawkins had to make a quick choice. They had targeted a clearing near the camp as a landing zone. But if Sutherland were with the vehicles advancing up the side of the mountain, it could take hours to climb to her.

"Scrub the original plan. We'll land on the mountain."

Hawkins scanned the slope for an opening in the trees.

"Off to the left," Calvin said.

Hawkins saw a knob of gray rock that protruded from the forest in the shape of a human shoulder. The promontory was shrouded by misty threads and looked about the size of a dime. Hawkins hoped that it just seemed small from a distance.

"Good for a sparrow perch, maybe, but I'll give it a try."

"Just wheel around in a gradual curve, approach the target, ease out of the hammock, keep it slow, and push your bar up at the last second as you get your feet under you. Pieceofcake."

Hawkins shifted his body weight to put the glider into a turn that pointed the front of the wing directly at the rock. He started moving too fast again, brought the nose up, and then down, making sure the wings were steady. It was a smooth save, and Hawkins began to feel more confident. His cockiness ended as he made the approach and saw the deep fissures in the promontory. Rather than being smooth and flat on top, the rock was lumpy and uneven.

It was too late to veer away.

He had already slipped his legs out of the cocoon, and had them under him, knees bent slightly. A few feet from the ledge he brought the wing up and slowed almost to a stop. His feet hit the hard ground. The shock on his bad leg was greater than he expected, and the impact, and the weight of the gear he was carrying, threw his center of gravity off.

He wobbled dangerously, but by using every ounce of strength in his arms and shoulders, he managed to keep his footing on the uneven surface and immobilize the wing.

He unsnapped the harness and lifted the wing over the side. The glider landed in the trees about a hundred feet below the knob. Then Calvin came in and landed lightly beside him, took a few steps in, and brought the wing down. Hawkins helped him out of the harness and they pushed the wing over the side to join the other hang-glider.

Hawkins and Calvin turned toward the mountain and pushed their way through the brush into the woods. They headed in the direction of the last headlight sighting. After trekking through a murky forest, they stepped out onto a road. Fresh tread marks could be seen in the dirt in the light from the rising sun.

They started hiking up the steep-angled road, but after ten minutes of walking, Hawkins put his hand up to signal a halt. As if on cue, a series of angry shouts shattered the morning stillness.

Then a gunshot echoed throughout the forest.

Hawkins and Calvin began to run.

CHAPTER FIFTY-FIVE

Kurtz had ordered the militia men to tear down the rest of the wall and within minutes the Indian hex sign was a pile of splintered wood. Behind the barrier was a space about five feet deep. Black ebony chests of ancient design, each inlaid with gold swirls, were stacked in rows of four against the wall at the back of the space.

Kurtz went over to a chest that sat on top of the pile. It was longer in shape than the others and the lid was up, revealing faded purple and gold brocade.

"That's where I found her," he said. "Waiting for me."

He moved the container off the pile and ordered Krause to open the next one. Krause undid a simple snap latch and lifted the cover.

"Nothing in here but a couple of old books, general."

He reached in and handed Kurtz a volume bound in dark red leather, around eight by eight inches in size. Kurtz opened the book to the flyleaf. Written in black ink, the letters connecting in an elegant script, were the words:

Magisterus Phillipus.

Kurtz knew the name from his reading. Magister Philip was the physician the Pope sent to find Prester John. He opened the book, eager to examine its contents, but furrowed his brow in disappointment when he saw the tightly written and densely packed Latin script. He put the book back in the chest and lifted out the second volume. It was twice the size of the first, and seemed of more modern production. Kurtz read the gold words embossed on the cover:

The Afghan Expedition

1920-22

By Hiram Kurtz

He flipped the cover back and found a sheet of yellowed paper tucked into the book. Typed on the paper was a simple message:

"To the person who has found this cache. Use it only for good and good will always come your way. Evil begets evil."

It was signed: Hiram Kurtz.

The general held the paper up for his men to see. "This is a note to me from my granddaddy. He owned this mine. As his rightful heir, I claim everything in it. He has given this to me."

Kurtz went over to the stack and with the scepter touched a chest lightly as if he were confirming knighthood.

Two militia men moved forward to carry out his unspoken command. The box was only around sixteen inches long and twelve inches wide and deep, but the militia men grunted with exertion as they lifted it from the stack and set it on the floor.

"Open it!"

A militia man undid the scrolled metal latch and pushed the cover back.

There was a collective intake of breath at the shimmering contents. The chest was filled to the rim with gold coins each the diameter of an old American silver dollar and twice as thick.

Kurtz leaned over, plucked a coin from the chest and held it close to his face to read the inscription **Presbyter Johannes** under the profile of the bearded man. He tossed the coin back into the pile and touched another box with the scepter.

The chest was set on the floor and opened. And once more there was a sharp intake of breath. The chest was full of uncut and cut diamonds. The sight launched Kurtz into a crazed frenzy. He touched box after box, and each was opened to reveal its singular contents.

Rubies. Lapis lazuli. Sapphires. Jade. Opal. Amber. Garnets. Pearls. And Emeralds.

The radiance burst from the opened chests, reflecting off the hard faces of the militia men who stared at the fabulous treasure as if in a trance. Sutherland was equally transfixed, but at the same time, she was wondering if she might be able to steal away while her captors were distracted. That hope was cut short when Kurtz shouted a command.

"This stuff won't do any good lying here," he said. "*Move* it."

The sharp order broke the men out of their trances. They hefted the heavy chests out to the entrance of the side tunnel and placed them in an abandoned ore cart. The contents of an oil can that lay next to the cart were used to lubricate its wheels. With the militia men pushing and pulling, the treasure boxes were moved to the mine's main entrance.

Kurtz came over to Sutherland, who was being watched by Krause.

"Well corporal, it looks like I won't need that money you stole from our bank account. We'll be able to buy all the guns and ammo we want. We can recruit trainers to turn my volunteers into a formidable force. We can buy bombs and explosives. Rockets that'll bring down aircraft. We'll be able to hit the government before they can hit us. We'll have the biggest private army in the U.S. We'll be able to take our country back.

Thanks to you. "

Sutherland blinked away the spittle blasting her face.

"That's nice. If you don't need me, I'd like my motorcycle."

"Not so fast, corporal. You're the one who likes rules and regulations. In my book that means a court martial."

Sutherland had had enough. "You can't court martial me," she shouted. "This is a fake army and you're a fake general."

He seemed to recoil at the comment and a flicker of sanity entered the mad eyes, but it passed quickly. He scowled and with his free hand he patted one of the pearl-handled revolvers. "The bullets in this gun aren't fake, corporal."

He drew the revolver from the holster and fired it into the air.

"Gather around gentlemen, we're going to have us a court martial. Corporal Sutherland here is charged with serious offenses under the uniform code of military justice. We've got, insubordinate conduct, mutiny and sedition, theft, failure to obey, fraudulent enlistment."

Sutherland had had enough. "*You're* the fraud here."

"Whoops, hear that boys? She just added disrespect toward a superior commissioned officer to the list."

Sutherland ignored the laughter coming from the militiamen. Her eyes narrowed behind her glasses.

"You're an idiot as well. Do you think I'm on my own? If you don't let me go my friends will wipe you and your country club off the map."

"No way, corporal. But you just convicted yourself. The added charges are treason and espionage."

Sutherland saw where Kurtz was going. "Under the code, I'm entitled to legal representation."

"No problem." He turned to Krause. "You're appointed to represent the corporal."

The militiaman smiled. "She pleads guilty to all charges."

"In that case, this court martial has no choice. Guilty as charged. Sentence is death by firing squad to be carried out at dawn."

Krause squinted at the rising sun. "Close enough. Let's do it."

Kurtz seemed to snap out of a daze. "Hold on here, Sergeant. We're not killing any of our own soldiers."

"You said it yourself, general. Treason and espionage. Punishable by death under military code."

"Yeah, but I just wanted to scare her."

"She's scared. Now we do our duty."

Krause tugged on the handcuffs around Sutherland's wrists.

The general grabbed his subordinate's shoulder.

"I'm not letting you do this."

"Try and stop me, you crazy old man." Krause turned to the other men. "General Kurtz here seems to have turned yellow. And he wants to keep all these goodies for himself. I say we divvy them up. What do you say we vote me in as four-star general?"

There was a roar of approval.

"You can't—" Kurtz began. He stopped in mid-sentence and clutched at his chest. His face slowly turned blue, then he dropped the scepter and crumpled to the ground. He convulsed once and became still. Krause bent over the general and felt for a pulse in Kurtz's neck. When he stood up again he was holding the scepter and he had a grin on his face.

"Looks like I've just been promoted."

There was another roar of approval. With his free hand, he dragged Sutherland to the mine and slammed her against a slab of boulder next to the opening. The back of her head hit the rock and her knees buckled, but she stubbornly remained on her feet.

She heard Krause yell, "Ready!"

Through blurred eyes she saw the militiamen assemble into a ragged line, facing her.

"Aim!"

She couldn't believe this was happening to her.

"*Fire!*"

As Hawkins loped up the mountain road he cursed the war injury that had shattered his left leg. He and Calvin came to a sharp bend, then ran up another stretch of road to yet another hairpin turn. Which is when they heard the loud crack of several rifles being fired at the same time.

Hawkins felt a nameless dread pulling him back, but he kept on pushing ahead even though he feared it was too late.

An instant before Krause gave the order to fire, Sutherland saw movement out of the corner of her eye.

It was Sergeant Paine. She threw herself in front of Sutherland, her rifle aimed toward the line of militiamen, and yelled, "Stop!"

The firing squad's blood was up, but at the sight of their comrade they raised their rifles into the air and let off a harmless volley.

Krause strode over to Paine. He towered over her, his face contorted in fury.

"What the hell do you think you are doing?"

The sergeant's rifle was still aimed toward the squad.

"You can't do this, sir. It's murder. The general would never approve."

Krause snatched the rifle from her hands and tossed it aside.

"I'm the general now. You have interfered with a court martial sentence against a traitor."

"This isn't a court martial. It's a farce."

"You tell him, girl," Sutherland yelled.

Krause was practically foaming at the mouth. "If you do not remove yourself from the line of fire immediately you will be guilty of aiding and abetting treason and subject to capital punishment."

"I'm not moving until you stop this," Paine said with a stubborn set to her jaw.

Krause stepped behind Paine, brought the scepter under her chin and used it to choke her as he dragged her back to stand next to Sutherland.

As soon as he had her in place, Krause stood back and said, "We will proceed with the execution. Shoot anyone who does not obey my order."

Krause raised his arm with the scepter.

"Ready!" Not pausing, he followed with a quick. "Aim!"

The next command never left his lips. There was a small *thut* sound and a round hole appeared in Krause's forehead below the visor of his cap. His mouth stayed open in an expression of abject surprise, then his legs collapsed and he pitched face forward onto the ground.

Holding his sound-suppressed rifle to his shoulder, Hawkins stepped out of the woods and Calvin emerged from the other side with his CAR-15 at waist level.

Calvin snapped an order. "You know the drill, grunts. Toss your weapons in a pile and get down on your tummies. Hands behind you."

While Calvin corralled the militia men, Hawkins went over to Sutherland. She planted a wet kiss on his cheek.

"I *knew* you'd find me."

"You didn't make it easy for us."

"Sorry, Matt. I got angry because I hadn't heard from you."

"We were out of contact. Didn't get your message until we got back to Kabul. What happened to that man lying on the ground?"

"That's Kurtz. He had a heart attack trying to save me. This is my new friend Sergeant Paine. Sergeant, this is my old friend Matt. The general wasn't all bad. Just a little crazy." She glanced over at Krause. "Can you get the key to the cuffs? It's in the front pocket of the guy you shot."

Hawkins retrieved the key and unlocked the handcuffs. Then he picked up the emerald scepter, his fingers wrapped under the cross-bars.

"So this is what all the fuss is about."

"Careful with that thing. It might get you killed," Sutherland said.

"It wouldn't be hard to find someone who'd kill to get his hands on a treasure like this," Hawkins said.

"You don't know the half of it, Matt."

She led him to the ore carrier and lifted the lid on the box full of diamonds.

He shielded his eyes against the sparkle of sunlight reflecting off the gems. He was even more stunned when he looked into the boxes with the coins and emeralds. He handed Sutherland his rifle and told her to keep an eye on the militiamen. Calvin came over and stared at the treasure and deep laughter roared from his throat.

"Yeah, I know," Hawkins said. "Joke's on us."

Calvin wiped the tears from his eyes. "You've got to admit that it's pretty funny, chasing our asses around Afghan-land while the treasure's sitting here." He pursed his lips. "Now what do we do with it?"

"Not doing any good sitting up here on the mountain. Let's see how strong these cub scouts are."

Hawkins put the scepter back in its chest, retrieved his rifle, and then ordered the militia men onto their feet. He told them to move the boxes from the ore hauler into the back of the truck. When they were done, he and Calvin piled the seized weapons into the truck with the boxes.

"Thanks boys," he said. "One more thing. Take your boots off and throw them in the truck. Socks, too."

"You can't do that," one man protested. "It'll take us days to get down the mountain."

"You'll all have a tenderfoot merit badge waiting for you at the bottom. *Do* it."

The militia men grumbled, but did as they were told. Calvin got behind the wheel of the truck. Hawkins asked Paine to drive the general's Jeep. Sutherland would ride in front. He climbed into the back seat to cover their retreat in case the militiamen decided to be fool-hardy. He'd call the police as soon as they were in the clear and let the authorities sort things out.

During the descent Hawkins called in a report to Abby on his phone. The two-vehicle caravan made it down the mountain side in half the time it had taken to climb up to the mine. As they drove through the camp they passed a number of recruits in training. Some may have wondered who Hawkins was but the general's Jeep was a potent symbol of authority. At Sutherland's direction, Paine drove to the Kurtz mansion. Sutherland got out of the Jeep and said she would be back in a minute. She dashed into the big house and emerged moments later with her computer bag slung over her shoulder.

Hawkins called Abby on the hand radio, gave their position and requested extraction.

Minutes later, they heard a thrumming sound. A shadow passed overhead. Hawkins got out of the Jeep and waved at a helicopter that was circling a couple of hundred feet over the mansion.

The helicopter landed on the weed-choked lawn. The door opened and Abby climbed out into the rotor blast.

"That was fast," Hawkins said in greeting.

"We were waiting in a meadow a couple of miles from the gate." She smiled when she saw Sutherland. "Looks like we're one big happy family again. Who's the lady in the soldier suit?"

"Sergeant Paine. Sutherland's new friend. You've just been discharged from the militia, sergeant."

Paine didn't seem to hear him. She was staring at the helicopter.

"It's black," she said.

"Best we could do on short notice, sergeant."

"Just like the general said would happen. Black helicopters."

He pressed the Jeep's keys into her hand. "That's right. Now go home. Find a boyfriend. Get married and have kids. Shoot squirrels."

Moments later Paine was in the Jeep, glancing in the rear view mirror as she drove toward the gate at full tilt.

"That was a sexist thing to say," Abby chided. "You wouldn't have told a man to get married and have children."

"I told her to shoot squirrels, too."

Abby shook her head. "Ready to fly?"

"After I show you something."

He led her around to the back of the truck and opened the box that held the scepter. She touched the egg-size emerald and the diamond J.

"The scepter of Prester John. It's unbelievably beautiful," she said.

"And slightly lethal," Hawkins said. "There's more to see."

He enjoyed Abby's wide-eyed expression as he opened the chests one after the other.

Calvin backed the truck up to the cargo door and they moved the chests onto the helicopter. When they were done, Hawkins looked around the deserted old buildings. Sutherland had vanished.

Hawkins picked up his CAR-15 and started walking toward the buildings, which is when he heard a staccato blast and turned to see a motorcycle speeding his way.

The Harley skidded to a stop only a few feet from where he was standing. Wearing an ear-to-ear grin, Sutherland got off the motorcycle and pushed it toward the cargo door.

"Hope you've got room for one more item."

They loaded the Harley onto the helicopter and lifted off. Within minutes, they had left Camp Kurtz far behind.

CHAPTER FIFTY-SIX

Cait lay on her back on the old cast-iron bed. Her wrists and ankles were tied to the frame even though she was in a deep drug-induced sleep. There was a faint sheen of sweat on her upper lip. Her breathing was shallow.

Marzak sat in a wooden chair next to the bed studying Cait's finely-sculpted features. At one point, he leaned forward and lifted her head, brought a glass to her mouth and gently poured a trickle of water past her parched lips. His tender gesture had nothing to do with sympathy. It was like watering a plant. The drug in Cait's system could cause dehydration and he didn't want her kidneys to shut down. Cait was no use to him as dead bait.

He had passed what appeared to be an abandoned cottage while he was tailing her. The property was only a few miles from the turn-off leading to the Kurtz yacht, and he had returned there with his prize after knocking her out.

The cottage was indeed abandoned, though some furniture remained, and its remote wooded location was exactly what Marzak wanted. He had lifted Cait's limp form from the trunk of his car and carried her into the bedroom. As she lay on the musty-smelling mattress, Marzak administered an antidote to restore her to consciousness. She gurgled like a baby and her eyes snapped open.

If she had not been on drugs, she would have screamed in terror at the sight of the killer at her bedside. But the drug had a calming, truth serum effect.

Marzak looked familiar, but she couldn't place where she had seen him. He seemed friendly, helping her to sit up and plumping a thin pillow for her neck.

"My shoulder hurts," she said, unaware that Marzak had used a Taser on her.

"The pain will go away soon. You'll feel groggy for a minute, and your tongue will be thick." He handed her a plastic water bottle. "It's important that you drink."

She glugged the water down in almost a single gulp and handed him the empty bottle. "More please."

"After you answer a few questions. Do you remember Hawkins?"

A dreamy smile came to her face. "Oh yes."

"When did you see him last?"

She struggled to recall. "We were flying from Afghanistan with some of his friends. They were very nice." Her voice was slurred.

"Why were you with Hawkins in Afghanistan?"

"Seems so long ago." She furrowed her brow. "I was looking for the Prester John treasure, and so was he. We met by accident at an ancient caravan stop."

"Did you find the treasure?"

"It was gone. Kurtz took it."

"Who is Kurtz?"

"An old explorer. He led an expedition to find the treasure. Moved it out of the cave years ago."

Marzak gave her another bottle of water and while she drank he pondered the answer. Interesting. So Hawkins didn't find the treasure after all.

"Why were you at the boat?"

"It was the Kurtz yacht. I'm writing a book. I wanted to see the vessel that may have carried the treasure back to the United States."

Marzak's pulse quickened. He leaned forward. "The treasure is in the U.S.? Where?"

The abrupt movement and change of voice stirred a faint eddy of fear in Cait's memory. Her instincts told her there was reason to be afraid of this man.

"I don't know," she said, almost in a whisper.

"Where is Hawkins now?"

"In Colorado."

"Is that where the treasure is? I must tell you that I will kill you if you say you don't know again."

She nodded. "He thinks Kurtz took the treasure there and hid it in a mine."

"Have you heard from Hawkins since you parted?"

She shook her head and looked around as if she had lost something. "My phone."

Marzak took a phone from his jacket pocket. "Is this what you're looking for?"

"Yes," she said with relief. "It has Matt's number in it."

"Would you like to call Matt to say hello?"

"Yes," she said eagerly. She took the phone and looked up Hawkins' number in the contact list and pressed the call button. When a voice answered at the other end, she smiled and said, "Matt. It's me, Cait."

Marzak reached forward and pressed the drug injector to her neck. There was a soft puff as the vapor entered her skin at high pressure. She blinked her eyes and frowned, then her head lolled and she slumped back onto the bed. Marzak took the phone from her limp fingers and brought it to his ear.

"Hello, Hawkins," he purred.

The call came when the jet carrying the treasure east from Colorado was about an hour out from Washington.

Abby and Sutherland were stretched out asleep in their own rows near the front of the cabin. Hawkins and Calvin were at the rear of the cabin hashing out a strategy to find Marzak before he could set off the Prophet's Necklace.

He couldn't believe it when he answered the phone. It was Marzak. And he had Cait.

Keeping his voice as neutral as possible, he said, "Hello, Marzak. Thought you were still back in Afghanistan."

"I arrived in the United States not long after you, and immediately arranged a reunion with Dr. Everson."

"I want to talk to her," Hawkins said.

"Not possible. She's under the influence of a potent drug and will be asleep for another few hours."

Calvin was looking at Hawkins with a curious expression on his face. Hawkins put his finger to his lips and pressed the speaker phone button.

"What do you want, Marzak?"

"You're very impatient, Hawkins."

"Why waste time on the small talk? Let's cut to the chase."

"I agree. Dr. Everson told me the treasure wasn't in Afghanistan."

"We struck out, sad to say."

"Don't play games, Hawkins. She told me about Kurtz bringing the treasure back to Colorado. You have it."

"Only part of it," Hawkins said. "The Prester John scepter. I'm looking at it now."

"How do I know you're telling the truth?"

"Hang up and I'll send you proof."

"Make it fast. Dr. Everson's vital organs will shut down if I don't administer an antidote."

Hawkins severed the connection. "You heard him. We'll have to do some fancy footwork if we're going to get Cait out of this alive."

"He'll kill her and try to kill you no matter what we do," Calvin said.

"That's why we need to stall and control the situation as much as possible. He's using Cait to lure me in."

Calvin's lips tightened in a grim smile. "And we were worried we wouldn't be able to find him."

"I never expected Cait to be in the middle, but he's not the only one who knows how to set a hook." He handed his phone to Calvin and opened the box on the seat next to him. He lifted out the scepter and held it up.

"Say cheese," Calvin said. The phone's camera flashed.

Hawkins sent the photo to Cait's phone. Marzak wasted no time calling back.

"Congratulations, Hawkins. You have succeeded where I failed."

"Dumb luck, Marzak. Here's the deal. I give you the scepter. I get Cait. Alive."

"You must think a lot of Dr. Everson to give up something worth millions."

"It's nothing to me. My mission was to find the treasure, not decide what to do with it. I'll need time, though."

"Make it fast. You're not the only one who's impatient."

"True, but we are both realists. I'm in an airplane on my way from Colorado. We're not due to land for another couple of hours. Pick a place for the exchange that's not far from Washington."

"I'll call later with the location."

Hawkins had no intention of improvising his plans last-minute.

"Uh-uh. Now or never."

There was a pause at the other end of the line, then Marzak said, "We will meet in three hours at the old Kurtz yacht. It's on the Eastern Shore of Maryland. Come alone."

He gave Hawkins directions.

"I'll be there with the scepter," Hawkins said.

Cait's phone went dead.

Hawkins had a determined set to his prominent jaw. "You heard him. We've only got a few hours to put this thing together. Marzak will spend that time setting the trap with Cait as the cheese."

"He'll be a lot more careful than the last time we met him," Calvin said.

Hawkins placed the scepter back into its box. "Yes, but this little bauble has a way of clouding a man's mind. We can use Marzak's scepter obsession against him. And he doesn't know about our secret weapon."

"That's good, man." Calvin wrinkled his nose. "Only I didn't know we *had* one."

Hawkins cocked his ear to the soft snores coming from the sleeping women. "Actually, we have *two*."

The old yacht had so many possibilities for an ambush that Marzak had difficulty narrowing them down. As he walked onto the rotting hull he focused on two potentials. The strategic and the poetic.

He scouted the woods around the wreck but it was obvious that anyone trying to come that way would have to cross the marsh and hack his way through heavy undergrowth.

Carrying a leather satchel, he walked out onto a rickety pier. Hawkins and his friend were former navy SEALs and a water approach was not out of the question, but the soft muck of the mud flats bordering the shore cut down possible access. Anyone coming from the bay would have to use the dock.

He retraced his steps and found a loose plank around half way back. He pulled it up, armed a small but powerful mine and slipped it under the board. The weight of a footstep on or even near the board would depress the pressure plate and trigger the explosion.

He went back to the yacht and strolled through the dining room. A few feet from the bar he detected a sponge-softness to the deck. He pried up several planks. A miasma of rotting plants rose through the opening. He explored the bilge with a flashlight, then he removed several supporting boards and replaced the single layer of deck.

In his mind, he created the poetic scene that would greet Hawkins.

Hawkins would drive down the only road, park, and walk into the yacht. He would be armed, of course. Marzak would be surprised if he weren't. Hawkins would approach the bar with scepter in hand and fall through the deck to his armpits. Marzak would pluck the scepter from his hands and proceed to kill him after they had a talk.

Sheer poetry.

CHAPTER FIFTY-SEVEN

Though Hawkins was painfully aware that the gang of misfits at his command was no SEAL Team Six, he could not have been prouder, or more amazed, at the way they had come together in Afghanistan. But for all his brave talk about secret weapons, he knew that the rescue attempt needed the skills of an elite counter-terrorism team versed in the refined elements of assault, like the group that took down Bin laden.

Marzak was a ruthless and experienced opponent and the fact that he had a hostage complicated things exponentially. Cait would be caught between competing forces. Luck simply could not be part of the equation. Nor could blunt force.

Hawkins had designed dozens of SEAL missions. Some had succeeded. Some hadn't. But every one of them was a work of art as well as an exercise in military science. He knew that a successful mission had to be a combination of desperate creativeness and painstaking planning.

"We're going by the book," Hawkins said. "First, Molly," he turned to Sutherland, who was munching on her second blueberry muffin, "you're intel. We'll need an instant summary of everything there is to know about the Kurtz yacht."

"I've already got a folder in my Prester John file."

"Good. Narrow it down to what we need."

Sutherland stuffed her mouth full of muffin and booted up her computer.

"Next, operational strategy. It has to be delicate. I've—"

Abby cut him off. "C'mon, Matt. You're stating the obvious. We're all very aware that we can't bomb the crap out of the target and then send in the marines. The objective is simple. Get in. Neutralize Marzak. Save Cait. Get out."

"That's about right, Abby." Hawkins silently cursed the insanity that had persuaded him to reunite with his ex-wife. "But if you'll let me continue, I've already ruled out dropping in by fast-rope."

"Not fast enough," Calvin said. "Marzak would have too much warning."

Hawkins said, "A land assault would be limited as well. Not enough options. My guess is that, no matter how I come at him, Marzak will use Cait to draw me in where he'll have something nasty planned."

Sutherland had been listening with one ear. Not taking her eyes off the screen, she said, "Here's the CV on the yacht. Steel-hulled, built by Camper and Nicholson boatyard back in 1919. One of their early diesels, switching over from steam engines. It was a hundred-forty-five feet long. Here's a photo."

The computer screen showed a white yacht with a single smokestack, three decks and the almost straight-up-and-down bow typical of ships of its day. There were several photos of the luxurious interior, with its classic salon and spacious stateroom.

"How did the yacht get to Maryland?" he asked.

"After Hiram died his family sold it. It was used as a cruise boat on the Chesapeake, then went to a buyer who gutted the interior and turned the yacht into a waterside restaurant. The owner went bankrupt, the restaurant closed and it went into real estate trust. This picture shows the yacht in 1979."

"Ouch," Calvin said. "The old gal must have had some hard times."

The paint on the vessel had peeled off and huge rusty blotches ravaged the hull like the effects of disease. The tall windows were broken. Sections of deck had been unevenly cut away with torches.

"Got anything on the restaurant interior?" Hawkins asked.

Sutherland clicked the computer cursor. "These photos are from a newspaper article."

The grainy black-and-white pictures showed the dining room and the bar. Hawkins paid particular attention to a diagram of the restaurant's lay-out.

"What's your assessment, Cal?"

"Lots of places to set up an ambush. But there are a dozen ways to sneak on board, too."

"You're going to have to be the 'sneakee.' Marzak is expecting me, and he's got Cait."

"I'm going to like being back in my natural habitat. H. 2. O." Calvin tightened his lips and turned to Sutherland. "You got an overview showing where the boat is in relation to its surroundings?"

A satellite photo of the Maryland shore appeared on the screen. Sutherland zoomed in until the outline of a peninsula appeared.

"Kinda looks like a lollipop," she said.

The narrow section of the peninsula was a causeway leading to the widening, roughly circular tip of land. It was surrounded by shallows between the upland and the darker open water. The elongated lines of the yacht became visible. "Newspaper story says a hurricane pushed the yacht onto land and washed in silt that made it impossible for boats to come in and tie up." Sutherland enlarged the image up, showing a long dock sticking out into a marsh.

Calvin said, "You come in by land, I make it by water. Classic pincers maneuver. You distract him here." He pointed to the dining room. "I come up through the marsh, sneak aboard the boat here and come in the kitchen. Might even stop at the bar to order a rum coke."

"You really think it will be that easy?" Hawkins said.

"Naw. I was kidding about the rum coke." Calvin asked Sutherland for a geological survey chart of the Eastern Shore. The water showed only a foot or two of average depth close to shore.

"There's almost no water close to the upland," Hawkins said.

"If this wetland is anything like a Louisiana bayou, it'll be mostly mud. No way to walk across it. And no telling what shape that dock is in, but it's sending off real bad vibes."

"Marzak vibes?'

"He likes to play with explosives and he'd expect us to try something funny. If I were him, I'd figure you to come in across the causeway. But he knows you've got back up with me, so he'd booby trap the only other access."

"Makes sense. What about placing explosives in the swamp?"

"Be tough to lay down charges in the water. Big area to cover and he'd figure it's too shallow for a boat and too muddy for walking."

Hawkins pictured the scene in his mind. Driving across the causeway. Climbing onto the yacht. Looking for Marzak, who'd lay down a trail for him to follow to a trap.

"Let's use Marzak's MO against him."

He outlined his thoughts.

"Might work," Calvin said. "It would depend on precision timing, no margin for error and luck, but it would make a hell of a distraction. What if the dock isn't booby-trapped?"

"Then you'll have to come up with your *own* distraction."

Abby had been listening to the back and forth.

"Is this as close to surgical precision as you can get?"

" 'Fraid so, Abby. A lot can go wrong. But we'll look at all the eventualities and build layers of backup. That's all we can do."

She nodded, but the expression on her face showed she was still worried.

"Matt, there's something I have to say to you."

"Uh-oh," Calvin said. "I feel another one of those tender moments coming on. Hey Sutherland. Let's get us a couple of muffins."

Sutherland grinned, the computer cover snapped shut, then she and Calvin headed for the galley.

"I'm waiting," Hawkins said when they were gone.

"Matt, I've really grown to like Cait and I'd hate to see anything happen to her."

"Same here, Abby. That's why we're going to make this work."

"I know you will, but I've got to ask you something that sounds really stupid. You'd be willing to give up the scepter for her. Would you do the same for me?"

"No," Hawkins replied, his mouth widening into a grin at her crestfallen expression. "I'd exchange the whole Prester John treasure for you."

Abby smiled. "Damn you, Hawkins!"

He threw his palms wide. "What?"

She leaned over, kissed his lips and headed for the front of the cabin. Then, abruptly, she turned and said, "Excuse me. I've got to make some phone calls."

Hawkins watched with a puzzled expression in his eyes as Abby settled into a seat with a phone against her ear. Then he punched out a number on his own phone and when a voice answered, he said, "You were right about the snake pit, Commander Kelly."

"Hawkins! Damn. Hope you had plenty of snake repellent."

"We used so much that we ran out."

"That bad?"

"Worse, commander."

"Sorry, Matt. What can I do to help?"

Hawkins told him what he wanted and when he was arriving in Washington.

"I'll have it waiting at the airport," Kelly said. "Anything else?"

"I'll let you know."

"Good luck, whatever you're into."

"Thanks," Hawkins said, "I'm going to need it."

CHAPTER FIFTY-EIGHT

The Eastern Shore, Maryland

Calvin backed a pick-up truck up to an abandoned boat ramp, and Abby and Sutherland unloaded a five-foot-long black rubber raft from the bed and carried it to the water's edge. Calvin tied a nylon tow line running from the prow of the raft to his air tank. He stripped down to a body-fitting Speedo bathing suit and got into his custom-fitted black neoprene wetsuit.

He waded into the water and tested his closed-circuit re-breathing SEAL rig which was designed not to emit bubbles like conventional SCUBA gear. Then he and his helpers loaded a waterproof zipper bag onto the raft. He gave them each a quick peck on the cheek, and donned his mask, hood and flippers.

Abby watched him breast-stroke ahead of the raft, pulling it from shore, and as soon as he submerged, she called Hawkins to let him know that Calvin was on his way.

Hawkins acknowledged the message with a thank you, clicked the phone off and waited.

He was sitting in a car parked a quarter of a mile from the turn onto to the yacht driveway. A chart of the local waters was spread out in front of him. He tried to picture where Calvin would be, but he knew he could only guess at his friend's progress. He broke into a broad smile of relief at the chirp of his hand radio.

A slow drawl came over the phone.

"Fish ain't bitin' on the crab meat I'm usin' for bait. Anybody got any suggestions?"

Calvin was telling him that he had arrived at the boat dock.

"Try hangin' a night crawler on your hook," Hawkins said in lazy tone that had more Maine than Maryland in it.

"Thanks, Cap. Let you know how it goes."

The cornball code may have been overcautious, but with Cait's life at stake, Hawkins didn't want the faintest possibility of a screw-up.

Now it was his turn.

He started the car engine and drove to the restaurant driveway, turned in at the No Trespassing sign and bumped along the cratered road to the weed-grown restaurant parking lot. The old yacht that loomed in the headlight wash was in even worse shape than the boat in the photo Sutherland had dug up.

He snapped the lights off, re-checked the load in his Heckler and Koch P-9 and slid the pistol back into the carbon fiber hip holster that was concealed by the hem of his long-sleeve black T-shirt. He slipped the strap holding a thermal imaging monocular around his neck and pulled on a navy baseball cap.

He got out of the car and reached into the back seat to open the ebony case. He removed the scepter, tied a nylon rope around the nexus of the relic's arms, and slung the loop over his right shoulder. The scepter hung at his left side like a sword.

Hawkins took his time examining the yacht from stem to stern through the monocular, letting his gaze linger at each of the vacant windows. All was quiet except for the *ka-chunk* of a bullfrog's bass against the soprano insect chorus. Hawkins started walking slowly toward the boat only to halt after a few steps. The phone in his pocket was vibrating.

"Right on time, Hawkins," said the voice at the other end of the line.

"Hello, Marzak." He squinted through the monocular. "This place suits you."

"It appealed to my sense of the poetic. Dark and mysterious, like the human soul."

"Actually, I was thinking about how it smells rotten." Hawkins slid the scepter from his shoulder and held the jewel-encrusted relic above his head. "Let's do the deal, Marzak."

"Yes, let's. Walk toward the boat and climb onto the deck at the midships gangway."

Hawkins lowered the scepter and slung it over his shoulder again. His hand dropped to his pistol holster and unsnapped the flap as he approached the base of the wooden gangway. He tested it with his foot to see if it would support his weight. The planks sagged and groaned, but didn't break, so he continued onto the deck and stood in front of the doorway leading to the dining room.

The stench that issued from the dark portal was a combination of mold, rotted wood and bird and animal droppings.

This must be what the doorway to hell looks like, he thought.

Calvin was less worried about Marzak than the mud.

After he had surfaced and called Hawkins, he had slipped off his re-breather and put it and the Pegasus in the raft. Calvin hauled on the tow rope and pulled the raft with him through the saw grass until the water was less than half a foot deep.

It was no use, though. The muck was like quicksand. He pulled back until the water deepened and heaved himself onto the raft which sank almost to the bottom with only a few inches to spare.

He paddled through the grass until the front of the raft bumped into something hard. He reached out and found the edge of the floating platform that had been connected to the permanent dock. It rested on the mud with no room underneath for booby traps. The plastic foam pontoons sank even deeper into the mud when he rolled from the raft onto the platform. He placed the Pegasus unit and SCUBA gear on the platform.

He examined the old pier the platform had been secured to. The dock had once been level, elevated around four feet between twin lines of pilings, but now broken sections of planking sagged all along its length. He leaned over and looked at the underside of the stationary pier.

A red dot glowed beneath the dock. He rolled off the platform into the mud and slithered closer until he was under a small black box attached to a cigarette-sized packet of plastic explosives.

His eyes followed a wire that disappeared through the boards. Probably attached to a pressure plate device.

He checked for other booby traps and found none, and then he pushed himself back through the mud and climbed onto the platform. Calvin heaved the waterproof bag from the raft onto the floating dock and unzipped it, revealing what looked like a miniature tank.

The PackBot had been waiting at the airport as Kelly had promised.

The machine was a mobile robot that had been developed by a company called IRobot and its first operational job was to probe the wreckage of the World Trade Center. Later, it was given to soldiers in Iraq and Afghanistan. Calvin and Hawkins had been introduced to it as a way to see into enemy caves without getting their heads blown off. But its most popular use was by soldiers who employed the tough little robots to clear away Improvised Explosive Devices, or IEDs as they were called.

The forty-two pound robot was about the size of a lawnmower without the handle, and it moved on polymer tracks that were designed to flip up and down, allowing the machine to climb stairs or rocks and even go underwater. Calvin unpacked the joystick controller and switched on the PakBot's batteries.

With the gear removed, the raft might be buoyant enough now to skim over the shallow water to the shore. He radioed Hawkins with an update and then turned his attention back to the robot.

No SEAL operation Hawkins had ever been involved in had gone off without a glitch. Including this one. He thought he had prepared for every eventuality only to discover that he was wrong.

As Hawkins stood on the deck in front of the door to the yacht's interior, Marzak called again.

"Welcome aboard, Hawkins. Come in. Don't be shy."

"Let's deal out here in the open, Marzak. I want you where I can see you."

"You're being disingenuous, Hawkins. You've been using a night vision device. You're also armed, no doubt. So what are you worrying about?"

"I jump at shadows. Sometimes I shoot at them."

Marzak chuckled. "I'll light the way for you. Keep your phone on."

A moment later there was a soft flickering glow in the windows.

Marzak's order to keep the phone on hadn't been in the plans. Hawkins' intention was to keep in touch with Calvin on their radios until the last second when he could signal that the time was right.

He had to alert Calvin that the plan had changed. He switched on the radio so Calvin could hear his every word and said, "I'm coming in, Marzak."

Then he stepped through the doorway.

He saw the source of the light. A dozen votive candles were arranged in two clusters on the bar. One group of candles was burning at Cait's head and the other at her feet. She was covered with a sheet.

Marzak had turned the bar into an altar. He stood behind Cait like the high priest at a pagan sacrificial ritual. He wore a sweatshirt with the hood over his head, intensifying the image. The candlelight reflected off the shiny blades of a long, two-edged knife he held raised in his hand.

"Where should I start carving? Would you like a wing or a leg, Hawkins?"

Hawkins kept his eye on the knife. Marzak could lop off Cait's head in the time it would take to draw his pistol. He forced a laugh.

"Very theatrical. What are you supposed to be, some sort of satanic demi-god?"

Marzak pushed the hood back. Grotesque shadows danced on his face.

"Is this devilish enough for you?"

"Now you look like a creep out of a Grade B horror movie."

Marzak's smile suggested that he was more amused than insulted by the comment.

"I'm not the only one with a flair for theatrics. I recall the elaborate helmet you wore when you almost shot me down in Afghanistan. That was quite the close call. You nearly killed me."

"That was my intention."

Marzak chuckled and said, "Let bygones be bygones. Please step forward and hand me the scepter. Then I'll back away. The woman will be yours."

Hawkins clutched the scepter closer to his chest. "Not yet. I want to make sure she's alive."

"See for yourself." Marzak moved back from the bar, putting himself at the edge of the halo of light.

Hawkins took another step toward the altar. He tried not to stare at Cait's face. He had to be alert to his surroundings. The sacrificial offering, the candles, the sly tone of Marzak's voice, all screamed the word *trap* at him. He had to stall until he figured it out.

"We've got more to talk about first, Marzak. The professor told me about the Prophet's Necklace."

"I'm not surprised. The professor seemed a man of divided loyalties. What did he tell you?"

"That the necklace is a string of sarin-laden explosives you placed near crowded population centers. And that you are the only one that can set them off. He called it connecting the strands and that it could be done with a phone call."

"You're correct about my role in placing the sarin, and the phone call, but I'm not the one who controls the clasp."

"The Shadows?"

"I don't work for the Shadows, even though they think I do."

"Who *do* you work for?"

"Anyone who pays me."

"In that case, I can make you rich beyond your dreams. The scepter is only part of what I found. I'll trade the scepter for Cait. And I'll give you the rest of the treasure if you identify who's giving you orders."

Marzak glanced down at Cait's supine form and a thoughtful look came to his face.

"Tell me about it," he said.

Calvin was tying a flashlight to the top of the robot when the voices started coming over the radio. Something had gone wrong.

As he listened, he activated the robot's forward control. It moved forward slowly, navigating the undulating boardwalk, and stopped around a foot from where he had seen the booby trap. He climbed back into the raft and pushed away from the platform until he was a safe distance off shore.

Hawkins slid the scepter off his shoulder.

"This bauble is only part of it," he said. "There are twenty chests of treasure. Each one is filled with a different type of gem. Diamonds, rubies, emeralds, lapis lazuli. You name it. You could retire in splendor to your own island."

"Tempting, Hawkins. How do I know you're telling the truth about the treasure?"

"Easy. I can lead you to it."

"Agreed. The scepter for now, please. Then we'll talk about the rest of it."

He's agreeing much too fast, Hawkins thought.

"OK. Your call. Just hope this thing doesn't blow up in your face."

"What are you talking about, Hawkins?"

He held the scepter up. "I'm talking about the explosive nature of this thing."

"You're talking like a crazy man."

"Maybe, but this thing has already caused a lot of fireworks."

Calvin finally realized what Hawkins was trying to tell him.

Duh. He pushed the forward button. The robot's treads hit the pressure plate.

Kaboom!

The middle of the dock disappeared in a blinding ball of fire. Flaming splinters of wood fell from the sky like rain.

Calvin was already on the move.

Cait moaned at the noise of the explosion and tried to lift her head.

Marzak cocked his ear as the echoes faded. "I forgot to tell you. I set up a surprise for anyone attempting to come ashore at the old dock."

"You killed Calvin, you sonofabitch! The deal is off."

Hawkins backed up. He wanted to draw Marzak away from Cait.

Marzak came around the side of the bar, holding the dagger forward like a fencer, and advanced slowly. Hawkins raised the scepter and swung it like it was a Louisville Slugger. Marzak jumped back out of the way.

Cait was up on one elbow, taking in the confrontation with bleary eyes. She pushed herself off the bar, stood on shaky legs and tried to walk. She was only vaguely aware of knocking something over with her knee as she made her way unsteadily around the bar.

Marzak thrust the knifepoint at Hawkins, who sucked his gut in and took another swing with the scepter. Marzak circled, trying to drive Hawkins toward the weakened floor in front of the altar. He dodged another swing, and got in a quick swipe of his knife that caught Hawkins in the ribs.

Marzak saw Hawkins wince with pain and lower the scepter. The next cut of the blade would catch Hawkins below the Adams apple.

Cait was still unsteady on her feet, but she made it around to the front of the bar. Her groping hand accidentally pushed a candle over the edge. There was a *plouff* sound as the gasoline she'd knocked over a moment earlier ignited.

Flames roared up, enveloping the back of the bar and the rotten deck.

Hawkins jumped back to avoid another knife thrust. He felt a warm wetness in his chest where he'd been cut. He instinctively moved to protect Cait only to feel his feet break through the rotten planks. He crashed through the deck up to his armpits and struggled to keep from falling in any further. His pistol holster was inaccessible.

Marzak sheathed his dagger and extended a hand.

"Give me the scepter, Hawkins. I'll pull you out."

Hawkins lifted the relic, but when Marzak moved closer, Hawkins swung it at his ankle. The cross arm connected with skin and bone. Marzak yelled in pain and backed off. His hand went to his belt holster and he drew his pistol and pointed the muzzle at Hawkins' face.

Speaking quietly, he said, "Fine, I'll just go ahead and kill you now, Hawkins. Matter of family honor for killing my brother. Too bad. We're arrows from the same quiver, you know."

"What are you talking about?"

Marzak smiled, but instead of firing the gun, he shuddered, as if he'd been hit by a blast of wind, and his mouth dropped open in a look of shock. His free hand groped at his shirt where two holes had appeared as if by magic. He squinted through the flames roaring around the bar, fired his gun at something unseen then turned and ran into the dining room and out onto the deck.

Flames were rapidly spreading through the lounge and the air was thick with smoke. Cait rushed forward to give Hawkins a hand, but then a familiar voice was yelling at her to stand aside.

Calvin stepped past her and reached for the scepter, wrapped his hands around it and pulled Hawkins out like a cork from an old bottle of wine.

With Calvin in the lead, they ran through the dining room, weaving their way through the swirling pockets of flame dancing around like fiery wraiths. Tongues of yellow fire licked at their heels, but then they were out the door and down the gang plank.

The massive bonfire consumed the boat from stem to stern and blistered the air with its heat.

As they hastily made their way to the truck in the undulating light from the blaze, Hawkins scanned the old parking lot and the surrounding woods

Marzak was nowhere to be seen.

CHAPTER FIFTY-NINE

Northern Virginia, Twenty-Four Hours Later

The conference room in the office labyrinth of Global Logistics Technologies was unremarkable, but the same could not be said about its four occupants.

Hawkins stood in front of a blank presentation screen holding a laser pointer. He had bagged his quasi-military outfit in favor of Woods Hole casual: jeans, chambray work shirt and work boots. Hawkins' big-boned physique and craggy features would have been an imposing presence anywhere, but the Afghan sun and wind had brought out the reddish skin tint he'd inherited from his Micmac ancestors and the rigors of the Afghan mission had hardened his features, especially around the dark eyes.

Seated at a table directly in front of Hawkins was Calvin, who looked like an entertainment lawyer in his thousand dollar Armani suit. Next to him was Abby, smartly dressed in a beige pants-suit and lavender blouse. They both wore a watchful wariness that wasn't there at the start of the operation.

The only one not to have changed was Sutherland who sat at a table with her battered laptop open in front of her. She wore her standard outfit of jeans and sweatshirt. With the slight smile under her pudgy cheeks and innocent eyes blinking behind her glasses, she could have been a bank teller about to cash a check at the drive-up window.

"Cait is still recovering from her drug hangover," Hawkins announced. "She'll be okay in another day or so. Unfortunately, Marzak is still on the loose and he's got the capability to detonate the sarin bombs at any time."

"Should we let the authorities know what's going on?" Calvin asked.

"Since we don't know the target cities, there's not much the authorities could do short of evacuating whole cities. People could be killed in the panic. I think the key here is still the treasure. Abby?"

"I had the scepter and other chests crated and stored in a temperature controlled vault on the floor below. I've authorized vault access for everyone in this room."

"Thanks, Abby. With the treasure removed from circulation, we've torpedoed the Shadows' plans for now. But if we believe what Marzak told me, he's not working for the Shadows and the decision to tie the clasp on the Prophet's necklace isn't his. He's working for someone else."

Abby nodded. "Makes sense, Matt. He could have set the plot in motion the second he was clear of the boat, but he didn't, and he hasn't since, which means that he's either biding his time or telling the truth about the sarin attack being out of his hands."

Hawkins nodded. "Marzak is only one piece of a jigsaw puzzle that looks like a Pollock painting. That's why I've asked Molly to work on a forensic search to help us assemble the pieces as fast as we can."

On cue, Sutherland clicked the computer mouse, and dozens of facial images filled the screen. At the center of the photo-montage was the image of the emerald scepter.

"These are the faces of every individual, including us, who has a connection to the Prester John mission," Hawkins said. He pointed the laser dot at a square that had a close-up picture of a rat. "What's this?"

"That's Rashid," Sutherland explained. "I didn't have a photo of him."

"That rat's a lot better looking than ol' Rash," Calvin said. "Good picture of me, though. Handsome and mean at the same time."

"That other one looks like Omar Sharif, the actor," Abby said.

"It *is*. That's supposed to be Amir," Sutherland said.

"Not bad," Abby said. "But how is this going to help us find Marzak?"

"I'll explain. When I first started digging into the lives of people who interested me, I'd go through search engines like Google. What I got was collard greens, turnips and beans."

"Pardon me?" Abby said.

Sutherland blushed. "Sorry. That's my West Virginia talking. You throw all those things in a frying pan back home and you get a dish called a *mess*. There's no way to separate one thing from the other. Same thing online, too, only it's a mess of *data*. Lot of it is useless. That's when I came up with Snoopster."

Abby glanced at Hawkins with an expression of distress on her face. He responded with a shrug.

"My guess is that Snoopster is a computer program," he said.

"That's right. I named it after Snoop Doggy Dog. They use a data miner like this in some human resource departments to figure out someone's character. It uses a huge list of key words to help sift the weevils out of the flour. In my program the key word at one extreme is **Bad-ass**. At the other end, it's **Saintly**. I came up with a big list of things to measure a person by, and gave each one a point score. I tweak it with stuff that isn't on the record, but that I know."

"That seems pretty subjective," Abby said.

"I know it's not rocket science, but sometimes what I *feel* about someone is more accurate than what I know."

Hawkins said, "It's called instinct, Molly, and it's kept me out of a lot of trouble."

Sutherland smiled at the praise. "Depending on the point score, the person is dumped into files labeled **Good Guy**, **Bad Guy** and **Maybe**. Then I smooth out the rough files and come up with an estimate of what a person is."

Suddenly intrigued, Abby leaned forward. "Could you give us an example, Molly?"

"Sure. I'll use me. I got math awards in high school, and good marks for my army service. They gave me an honorable discharge, so that makes me a **Good Guy**. You take Rashid up there on the screen. Lies, steals, tries to kill and hurt people, and he's an easy **Bad Guy**."

"What about a **Maybe**?" Hawkins asked.

Sutherland smirked. "That would be you, Matt. You did *good* in the navy, but got screw-up points when you went before a board of inquiry that had you cashiered for being crazy."

"That would make me a **Bad Guy**, wouldn't it?"

She shook her head. "You went on to be an engineer who made some contributions to science. The fact that you were evaluated by a Bad Guy like Trask gave you goodie points too, but not enough to move you out of the Maybe category. That's where I come in. I add in feelings, which could push you to the Good Guy category."

Hawkins had to admit that Sutherland's simple explanation made perfect sense. "Thanks, Molly. Can this program help us locate Marzak?"

"Not exactly, but it can give us an idea who he hangs out with. Like my mama used to say, 'Tell me your friends and I'll tell you who you are.'"

"Hey, sounds like what my mama used to tell me when I got in with the bad crowd," Calvin said. "Birds of a feather flock together."

"Too bad you didn't listen to your mama, or you wouldn't be hanging around me," Hawkins said. "Go on, Molly."

"Sure. It's all about connections. Watch." She clicked the computer and the montage of faces was covered with a web of black lines. "It's the Kevin Bacon thing. Everybody's connected to everybody else. But *how* you're connected makes a big difference. Amir is a drug guy, and has bad connections, but he's also connected to you and he helped find the treasure and fight the bad guys."

The lines disappeared and the photos were grouped on two sides of the scepter in clusters that were labeled Good Guys and Bad Guys.

"No more maybes?"

"Not when you factor in the details. The program connects the dots and arranges the photos depending on the strength of the link."

Hawkins was disheartened that the bad guys greatly outnumbered the good, but he scanned the faces, moving from one side of the screen to the other. Most were pretty obvious, like Rashid and Murphy, who were paired side by side with the baddies, and Cait and Abby on the other side. Then there was him and Calvin.

But his wandering gaze rested on one photo in particular. He placed the laser dot on the photo.

"Are you sure this is accurate?" he said.

"As much as it can be," Sutherland replied. "You take what you know and apply it to what you don't know. The computer connects the dots."

Hawkins couldn't believe what he was seeing. The man in the photo had the same necktie he had seen when he met with the Newport Group. Then there was the cottony hair, the goatee and the lips pursed in perpetual disapproval.

And next to the man's photo was an all-too familiar face.

Marzak.

A thought occurred to Hawkins. "Molly, could you Google the word Arrowsmith?'

"The rock band?"

"No. Arrow as in Arrowhead corporation."

The first listing that came up was for the Sinclair Lewis novel by that name. He asked Sutherland to click on the next listing, a Wikipedia link.

Arrowsmith may refer to: A person who makes arrows (see fletching)

Why hadn't he seen it before?

Fletching is the art of putting feathers on arrows.

And the person who attaches the feathers is a *fletcher*.

CHAPTER SIXTY

Newport, Rhode Island, Three Hours Later

The sprawling mansion built on a promontory that jutted defiantly into the dark waters of Narragansett Bay could have been the setting for a Gothic novel. With its octagonal turrets and soaring chimney stalks, the massive pile of granite looked as foreboding as a Norman keep. Surf whipped up by an offshore storm smashed the rocky bulkhead and spray pelted the mansion's lower level windows, but all was serene in a second floor room that resembled the dark-paneled study of a London gentlemen's club.

Five people sat in plush dark leather chairs gathered around a massive fireplace framed in mahogany taken from the gun deck of an 18th century British man-o'-war. Brown-black shellac covered the once blood-soaked timbers that had been carved with scenes romanticizing the ship's victories at sea.

Charles Fletcher sat at the center of the half-circle, allotting his time precisely to those on his left and his right. Like the others, he swirled a snifter of Louis Royer brandy and smoked a His Majesty's Reserve cigar infused with Louise XIII cognac and worth about the same as the median weekly wage of the U.S. worker.

His audience of middle-aged men all wore tuxedoes, a dress code Fletcher required of his male dinner guests. Their facial features differed, but they glowed with the powerful good health of the wealthy, and their eyes shared the same avaricious hardness.

Fletcher had been continuing his dinner discussion of naval power and the Big Game, as Kipling called the competition among the Great Powers in the days of tsars and kings.

"The world outside of Europe and American was nothing more than a big garden full of ripe fruit and vegetables. The Great Powers were the gardeners who carved whole countries out of virgin land. Occasionally, they got into border spats, went at each other with pitchforks, and after a sufficient period watering the plants with blood, they joined together to battle the poachers."

"You have a gift for metaphor," one of the men said. "I would have loved to have gotten my hand on a pitchfork back in those days."

"My point is, things really haven't changed that much," Fletcher said. "The main difference is the lightning speed at which events move now. We're in one of those accelerated time warps." He paused to let his audience chew on his words. "Now, if you gentlemen will all follow me into the media room we will talk about the important matter you came here to discuss." Ever the thoughtful host, he said, "I've sent my cooking staff home. You'll have to bring your own brandy."

They entered a small auditorium and took their seats in the banked armchairs that faced a stage. Fletcher sat in the first row and tapped a control console in the arm of his chair. The lights dimmed and the curtains behind the stage parted to reveal a large wall screen that displayed a satellite picture of the earth. At a touch of a button, the image zoomed in on Asia, showing territorial borders in white.

"Here we are above Afghanistan, courtesy of Google earth," Fletcher said. "This ancient and fabled land is often called the Graveyard of Empires for reasons our own military has discovered. Afghanistan is many things to many people, but I will wager that this is how the people in this room see it."

Superimposed over the map was the familiar little man with the sly smile and white handle-bar mustache who symbolized the capitalist in the game of Monopoly. He was leaning on a dollar sign almost as tall as he was. The image triggered laughter that ended abruptly when the picture changed. The capitalist was frowning and he was leaning on a red rectangle with five gold stars. The flag of China.

The image brought forth a round of hoarse boos.

Fletcher smiled. "I can see there is unanimity of opinion in this room."

"Is it *that* bad, Charles?" said Frank Sturmer, president of a vast minerals cartel and spokesman for the group.

"As I tell my navy students, without understanding the past we can't change the future. Let's go back a few years." The red flag became a hammer and sickle. "The Soviet Union invades Afghanistan. With the help of the CIA and U.S.-supplied Stinger missiles, the *Mujahideen* send the Russians packing. The military invasion was a failure, but the Soviets left their mark in other ways."

"What ways?" Sturmer asked.

"I'm going to let an expert tell you," Fletcher said. "Do you hear me, Dr. Davis?"

"Loud and clear," a voice said over the speakers.

A man's face appeared on the screen. He had thinning hair and a beard of matching gray. His crevassed features had the deep tan of someone who spent a great deal of time in the sun.

"Would you please introduce yourself to my friends?"

"No problem. My name is Lee Davis. I'm a geologist and I've been working for a number of years with the Pentagon."

"Thank you, Dr. Davis. Can you please pick up where I left off?"

"Sure. As mentioned, Russian troops left Afghanistan in 1989. They had teams of specialists, including mining experts, scattered throughout the country, and many of these teams had to evacuate before they could collect all of their data. Inevitably, much of the mining data was lost, but some of it ended up with the Afghan geological survey library."

"And what happened to it from there?"

"Three years after our guys drove the Taliban out of Kabul, a group from the U.S. Geological Survey went to Afghanistan to help with reconstruction. In the Afghan survey offices they stumbled on old survey charts and mining data. Stuff that looked important. So in 2006, they outfitted a navy Orion P-3 plane with advanced gravity and magnetic measuring gear and flew over around seventy percent of the country."

"Did they find anything promising?"

"Enough to bring them back the next year for a deeper look using equipment that produced 3-D pictures of mineral deposits under the surface. They turned the data over to a small group of geologists."

"And what was the reaction?"

"We were astonished."

"*We?*"

"I was part of the group."

"Go on."

"The government sat on its hands for two years. No one looked at the findings. The Pentagon had a task force to create business opportunities, but they were focused on Iraq. With things winding down there, they transferred the task force to Afghanistan. They looked at the surveys and measured the potential economic value of the deposits. The Pentagon guys couldn't believe their eyes, so they brought in American mining experts to take a look on the ground. Next they briefed the Secretary of Defense and the president of Afghanistan."

"It must have been a pretty big deal," Fletcher said.

"A *very* big deal," Davis said with a grin on his face. "They figured the potential value of the mineral deposits they had found was nearly a *trillion* dollars."

"That's a lot of money," Fletcher said.

"Hell yes. The country is bursting at the seams with all sorts of goodies. The iron and copper alone could make the country a major world producer. There are big deposits of niobium for use in making superconductor steel, rare earths, and huge gold reserves. Under the dry salt lakes in some areas of the country, there could be as much lithium as in Bolivia, which has the biggest deposits now."

"Could you put the extent of the lithium deposits in perspective?" Fletcher said.

"Someone at the Pentagon said Afghanistan could one day become the Saudi Arabia of lithium! The Pentagon is helping the Afghans develop a system to put mineral rights out to bid. Unfortunately, not much has happened in that regard yet, especially in the south and east with all the fighting."

"Suppose we had a magic wand that could end the fighting," Fletcher said. "Based on your findings, what is the likely scenario for minerals development?"

"The development money would come pouring in. It would dwarf the opium trade. Minerals would become the backbone of their economy. Afghanistan could become a powerhouse."

"And who might these investors be?"

"U.S. mining companies. Multi-nationals. But mostly developing countries that need important minerals to sustain their growth."

"What about China?"

"Already a player. They bribed the Afghan minister of mines to let them place the winning bid on a copper operation. He got fired, but the Chinese are in charge of the Aynak copper mine in Logar province. They're hungry for more and will probably come in using proxies."

"Very interesting and insightful. Thank you for your time, Dr. Davis."

"My pleasure."

The screen went blank. Fletcher turned to Sturmer.

"I think Mr. Davis just answered your question about how bad it is with his comment about the Chinese copper mine. This goes beyond economic interests. Control of minerals is of strategic value. China has used its control of rare earths to push Japan around. The U.S. is heavily dependent on Chinese minerals, which means we could be next in line for blackmail."

"But our army is in charge of the country now," Sturmer said. "The only way the Chinese can come in is if they choose to go up against our guys in combat."

"The Chinese know that and are working with elements of the Pakistani intelligence service to broaden their influence in Afghanistan. This has been made easier by the fact that some Pakistani intel people see China as a counterweight to their arch enemy India. The Chinese are aware of this and are using the Pakistanis to cultivate links with insurgent groups as a strategic hedge so they'll have influence in Afghanistan once the U.S. leaves Kabul."

"Looks like the Chinese are making an end run," Sturmer said.

The satellite picture of Afghanistan reappeared and the camera zoomed in on a body of water shaped like a long figure eight.

"Exactly. They hope to score a goal. *Here.* The salt flats around this lake cover some of the biggest lithium deposits in the country. This province is a lynchpin. If the Chinese-Pakistani cartel takes control of it, it will become increasingly difficult to stop them from doing the same in other parts of the country where they can negotiate with the locals or corrupt central government officials. Companies like yours and the others here in this room would be nudged out."

"By God! We've shed blood to hold onto this piece of real estate," Sturmer said. "The men in this room represent some of the biggest minerals extraction companies in the world. We deserve exclusive rights."

Fletcher raised an eyebrow. He was aware that the only blood Sturmer and his colleagues had ever shed came while they were shaving and that they regarded the U.S. armed forces as an appendage in the service of their corporate interests.

"Calm down, Kurt," he said. "No one is going to walk into that province with a handful of *Renminbi*. It's controlled by a drug warlord named Amir Kahn."

"Can't our guys take him out?'

"That would be unwise. He's connected by family ties to the ruling government and the *Haqqani* network that has been supporting the insurgents. Elements of the Pakistani intelligence services recently tried to remove Amir. Our intention was to let them do the dirty work for us, then move in. Unfortunately Amir survived the assault."

"That *is* unfortunate," said a guest. "How do we pry this guy out?"

"Simple. With a carpet-bombing campaign and permanent occupation of the border regions that puts up a big No Trespassing sign telling the poachers they will be shot on sight."

Sturmer laughed. "I like it, Charles. There's only one problem, the

U.S. government wants to get out of Afghanistan and the voters are tired of the whole war. We're going broke. Bridges, roads and schools have become a priority. People in Afghanistan want us out. *Our* metaphorical gardener is tired from tending the cabbage patch."

"What if we made him *un*tired?" Fletcher said. "What if something happened that would marshal public opinion to put aside its misgivings, reorder those priorities and get behind the massive effort I'm talking about?

"Last time that happened was after 9/11."

"What if something happened that was even more horrendous than 9/11?"

"Is that a possibility?"

"As an intelligence officer, I would say that it is very much a possibility. And we had better be prepared."

Sturmer made his voice heard above the murmurings.

"What do you need from us?" he asked.

"Your discretion, to begin with. Then the usual things. Money. Influence on Capitol Hill, so that when the time is ripe, you can move in with your heavy equipment at an instant's notice."

"I think I can speak for the others when I say that we have implicit trust in you, Charles."

He went around one-by-one to the others in the room and got their agreement.

"Thank, you gentlemen," Fletcher said. "I will keep you informed through my old friend Kurt. I've arranged for a car to take you back to the airport."

Fletcher saw his guests to the front door, and watched the stretch limo until its taillights vanished down the long driveway which was still wet from the rain. He went back to his study, poured a couple of fingers of cognac into a snifter and sat in a leather chair in front of the windows.

The rain scratched against the glass and the rumble of thunder had grown louder. The storm was moving fast. His favorite weather. He took a sip of brandy and glanced toward the fireplace at the far end of the study where he saw a purple plume of cigar smoke rising above the back of the chair he'd been sitting in earlier. He realized that he was not alone.

CHAPTER SIXTY-ONE

Fletcher put the snifter down on his desk, quietly opened a drawer and filled his hand with a compact SIG Sauer P228 semi-automatic pistol. He eased the safety off and pointed the muzzle at the back of the chair.

"Turn around so I can see you," he said in a calm voice. "I have a gun."

Slowly, the chair swiveled around. There was a red glow as the silhouetted intruder exhaled a cloud of smoke.

"Who are you?" Fletcher said. "Be quick with your answer!"

"Don't tell me you've forgotten my face so soon."

Fletcher lowered the pistol.

"Damnit, you could get yourself shot, Hawkins." He turned a desk lamp on.

Hawkins got up and came over to settle into a chair facing the desk. Moisture matted his thick hair and beaded his black windbreaker. He swirled the liquid in the snifter and took a sip.

"Damned fine brandy. Good smoke, too. Helped myself. Hope you don't mind."

"Glad you appreciate my hospitality," Fletcher said. "What are you doing here?"

"I came for my discharge papers according to our agreement."

Fletcher opened the drawer that had held the gun. He pulled out a thick brown envelope and placed it on the desk blotter. "You are now officially sane as far as the navy is concerned. How did you get in?" he said.

"Standard SEAL insertion. Fast-roped in by helicopter."

"I never heard—"

"Just joking, Dr. Fletcher. I climbed the *porte-cochere* to a second-floor window."

"It would have been far easier if you rang the doorbell."

"I didn't want to interrupt your fireside chat and movie show."

Fletcher's eyes narrowed. "How much did you hear, Hawkins?"

"Enough so that I know what it was all about. Professor Saleem said there was a bigger prize here than the Prester John treasure. I'd say a trillion dollars in minerals qualifies for that designation."

"That's not *all* it was about, Hawkins. This was about national security."

Hawkins' cutting laugh brought a frown to Fletcher's jowly face.

"So those tuxedoed fat cats are just patriots taking up arms to defend their bank accounts?" Hawkins said.

"They are wealthy mining officials, but in their own way they are foot-soldiers in a worldwide struggle in which our country is engaged."

"Do tell."

"I understand your skepticism. What do you think would happen if the Chinese gained monopolistic control of the rare minerals like lithium? We and China both devour natural resources to fuel our economies, which support our military. Being denied access to those resources would fatally weaken us as an economic and military power."

"So by plundering Afghanistan, you and your rich pals defend the U.S."

"You seem troubled because someone will make money off this arrangement."

"From the look of this mansion and the quality of your liquor cabinet, you, apparently, are not troubled in the least."

"People have always gained wealth by conflict or the threat of conflict. We need symbiotic relationships with those who provide us with the means to be secure."

"Relationships like you have with Arrowhead?'

"Quite correct." He eyed Hawkins like a poker player. "How did you know?"

"You left latent fingerprints all over the place. It was only a question of lifting the partials and assembling them into a full set. Real CSI stuff."

"Impressive. What else do you know?"

"Bits and pieces. Maybe you'd like to fill me in on the whole story."

"You've played cozy with me, lieutenant. Why should I tell you anything?'

Hawkins shrugged. "It's the only way you'll learn how a psychotic ex-SEAL has been able to give you nightmares."

The two men locked stares. Hawkins was not surprised that Fletcher was the first to back off. The man was consumed by his self-importance and would want to tell Hawkins how smart he was.

"We had three main goals. Eliminate the Shadows as a threat. Torpedo Pakistan's effort to ease Chinese exploitation of the lithium fields and beyond. Gain control of the mineral wealth for the U.S. We would accomplish the first goal by luring the Doctor, the Shadows' head, and his friends out into the open. The treasure was a bonus because the Shadows would eliminate Amir, clearing the way for us to move into the vacuum thus created."

"What was Arrowhead's role in all this?"

"You have to go back to 9/11 to understand the whole picture. The nation was frightened and confused. No one knew if another attack was coming. The CIA was empowered to use unusual methods to find and interrogate suspects."

"Torture."

Fletcher dismissed the comment with a wave of his hand. "They couldn't let their methods be known, so they hired contractors who were willing to dirty their hands."

"The Arrowhead corporation provided those contractors."

Fletcher nodded. "I had been an intel consultant for Arrowhead. I set up an enhanced interrogation team."

"Archer?"

"Archer. When news of the CIA interrogation methods went public, we were officially disbanded, although in reality our talents were used in Afghanistan in the intimidation program against the Taliban."

"Intimidation? Another euphemism."

"Assassination and torture, if you will. We were trying to persuade the Taliban to come to the bargaining table." Even Fletcher had to smile at the irony of his statement.

"Tell me about Trask and McCormick."

"Trask was head of our psychological unit. He oversaw how far a suspect could be pushed before breaking or dying. McCormick was in charge of delivering counter-punches."

"What about Murphy?"

"He was a strong-arm man. An enforcer, if you will. He relayed your message about a trade for Trask and McCormick, by the way. Murphy is prone to error and loose talk, which is why he is no longer with us."

"Dead?"

"I prefer to say he is longer in our employ. He told you the truth about

Honest Abe. He warned the warlord that you were coming. The ambush was entirely out of our control."

"But the cover-up and the slime job against me were not."

"Your investigation could have led to our unit. Trask suggested the psychiatric discharge. People had already started asking questions as a result of your probe, so we left Afghanistan. We came back together when rumors of a very nasty group, the Shadows, surfaced, but we were revamped a bit."

"Murphy called it a think tank with muscle."

"That's right. We had almost carte blanche at a high level of authority. The government was making progress against *Al Queda*, but was worried about unaffiliated splinter groups less easily identified. The Shadows were particularly dangerous. Their fanaticism went beyond the whole caliphate nonsense. They had lost family in drone attacks and wanted pure revenge against the U.S. They were run by a leader who had ties to the Pakistani intelligence service. We wanted to wipe out the Shadows leadership. The challenge demanded new strategy. You know how difficult it was to hunt down and kill *Bin Laden*, but he was an outlaw. The people we wanted were part of the fabric of society.

"We had to draw the Doctor and his friends out. Our only leads were the contacts they had made trying to radicalize U.S. citizens. They had grown tired of seeing the FBI roll up amateur young radicals over stupid mistakes, so we decided to give them people who had military skills to organize attacks in the U.S."

"That's where the Marzak twins came in," Hawkins said.

"That's right. The Marzaks had been on the fringes of Arrowhead, taking jobs no one else had the stomach for. They made it known to the Shadows that their skills were for hire. The Shadows wanted proof, so the twins performed an assassination on one of their enemies as a demonstration."

"A marketing demo?"

"A good description. It worked, and the Shadows formed a connection with the Marzaks as we planned. But they were skittish. We were going round and round. The Marzaks attempted to lure them with a ruse called the Prophet's Necklace, but they were still suspicious. It seemed the whole thing would fall apart. We needed to think outside the box."

"Dr. Everson provided you with a path when her research uncovered the location of the Prester John treasure."

"Correct. We knew they would be intrigued by the symbolic value of the treasure and the emerald scepter in particular."

"Where did Saleem figure in this?"

"A useful fool. The ISI had sent him to the U.S. as a spy. Professor Saleem related the odd little story he had heard from his colleague to his cousin at ISI, who in turn told his contacts in the Shadows. The emerald scepter was like a piece of the True Cross, something mystical and powerful they could use to recruit new followers. The treasure would buy weapons and foot-soldiers."

"But Dr. Everson messed up their plans when she told the State Department as well."

"State was aware of the significance of the treasure's location near a huge lithium deposit originally surveyed by the Soviets. The State Department passed the treasure information to the CIA. Eventually it made its way to Archer."

"Saleem said he regretted telling his cousin about the treasure."

"He became irrelevant after that point. The Shadows told the Marzaks to kidnap Dr. Everson so she could help find the treasure and then kill her to prevent her from talking to others. That was fine by us. We had visions of using her to lure their leaders someplace to view the treasure, and—"

He snapped his fingers.

"Sounds like a police sting. The cops tell the fugitive to come collect his lottery prize."

"Not far off the mark. They wanted the treasure in the worst way. When Dr. Everson disappeared, they hired the Marzaks to put together the mercenary expedition to wipe out Amir and dive on the treasure."

Hawkins leaned back in his chair and laced his fingers behind his head.

"You're making me feel like a real Mickey the Dunce. I risked my ass on your crazy treasure hunt for nothing."

"Don't run yourself down, Hawkins. Your mission served a purpose. Word that a U.S. expedition was going in to find the treasure was a charade that would persuade the Shadows to send in their own people."

"How did you pick me?"

"From our acquaintance with your previous Afghan service."

"A certifiably insane guy with a messed up record?"

"You fit the job description. And you were expendable. Nothing personal about it."

"It became personal when the Marzaks tried to kill me. Your call, too?"

"Regretfully. We assumed that your mission would fail, and were prepared to give you back up that would make sure that was the case. But you immediately took control of the operation, forming your own team and looked prepared to succeed. We forgot that even a crippled hawk has a sharp beak, so we had to clip your wings."

"When that didn't work you brought in Murphy who happened to bump into me at the airport and gave us Rashid."

"Murphy was just a hastily devised back up plan."

"Was Marzak's ambush in Maryland part of that back up?"

"I don't know what you're talking about."

"Didn't Marzak tell you? He kidnapped Dr. Everson and held her hostage. We were able to free her."

"I had nothing to do with that. It would have been a distraction. It troubles me that he went off the reservation."

"Here's something else to trouble you. We found the emerald scepter and the Prester John treasure in a Colorado mine."

"Well, congratulations, but it means nothing to me compared to the country's mineral wealth. If the Chinese gained control of Sheik Amir's holdings, more takeovers would follow."

"A new domino theory."

"Correct. But revelation of the treasure's existence would be an undesirable loose end that must be tied up. You see where I'm going?"

"You want me to tell you where to find it. But there's another loose end that needs tying. The Prophet's Necklace." He turned in his chair and spoke into the shadows. "Isn't that right, Marzak?"

A figure holding a gun stepped into the light. Hawkins stood and held his arms in the air while Marzak frisked him, then sat down again.

"You evidently have eyes in the back of your head, Hawkins."

"The ones in the front work quite well. I saw Fletcher glance over my shoulder the same time he dropped his arm down to the alarm button on his desk. Welcome back from the dead," Hawkins said.

"Death was not in the cards. I was well protected with my Kevlar vest. How did your friend set off the booby trap without getting killed?"

"Not very difficult. He sent in a robot that triggered the bomb."

"Ingenious. Your friend ruined a good shirt, however."

Hawkins touched his ribs where Marzak's dagger had taken a slice out of his flesh. "That makes us even." He turned back to Fletcher. "At what point did the Prophet's necklace go from being a ruse to the real thing?"

"What makes you think that's the case?"

"You confirmed it when you bragged to your friends that something was in the works that would surpass 9/11. Marzak told me he set it up, but he wasn't the trigger man."

Fletcher snarled. "You talk too damned much, Marzak."

"He never identified you. He said he and I were arrows in the same quiver. In other words, we were both fashioned by the same arrowsmith. From what I know, the necklace also qualifies for that dubious honor. How many victims will you kill in the sarin attack?"

"Enough to provoke the anger and the determination to mount a major strike."

"Pakistan might object to a carpet bombing campaign and occupation of its borders, and they have nukes," Hawkins said.

"They will be told that their nuclear storehouses have been targeted and will be destroyed if they try to stop us."

"So we're in the region forever?"

"If need be. Decades are nothing in the history of occupations."

"I was in Iraq," Hawkins said. "We learned that occupations are a lot harder to maintain than they used to be."

"We also learned a lesson from Iraq when we had to compete for the oil after sacrificing so much blood and money. This time we will secure the lithium fields first and use this as a bargaining chip to control the rest of the mineral riches for the U.S."

"The American public isn't going to like more fighting."

"That will work in our favor. Instead of regular troops we will fill the ranks with contractors sent by Arrowhead and other security companies. This will give us even tighter control."

"People are going to die, no matter who is involved," Hawkins said.

"What of it? We're talking about an international chess game in which pieces are often sacrificed for the greater good."

"You're insane, Fletcher. Those are your countrymen you're sacrificing so you can control mineral wealth that doesn't belong to you."

"Then why don't you ask your countrymen what they'll think when China controls the lithium that goes into the batteries that will power their smart phones and electric cars. Ask people what they think of an economic catastrophe that will reduce our country to a third-world beggar state."

"Too bad for you the Prophet's Necklace is not going to happen."

"Really?" Fletcher's eyes narrowed to slits. He picked up his phone and quickly punched out a number. "It *has* happened." Hawkins tweaked up the right side of his mouth in a lop-sided grin and reached for the envelope containing his discharge. He plucked a pen from a holder, wrote down a series of numbers, and pushed the envelope across the desk to Fletcher.

Fletcher's jowls quivered as he read off the numbers. "How did you know?"

"I had Marzak's phone number from our chat at the boat. He used his own phone to talk to me."

"That's right, Hawkins," Marzak said. "I thought you might try to ping my location if I used Dr. Eversons' phone."

"Too bad. A friend who is very good at this kind of thing used it to track the slave numbers that would activate the explosives. The phone network has been neutralized, the FBI alerted and the bomb sites are being cleared."

Fletcher turned his fury on Marzak. "You fool! Your carelessness has ruined months of planning."

Marzak tucked his gun into his belt and started toward the study's exit.

"I will take that as a dismissal. Congratulations, Hawkins. Till we meet again."

"Hawkins killed your brother," Fletcher said. "Don't you want revenge?"

"That was your responsibility as much as Hawkins', so you might want to temper your call for vengeance. I'm off to buy an island. You and Hawkins work it out. My contract is terminated."

Fletcher aimed his pistol at Marzak's back and in a quiet voice said, "So are *you*."

Marzak spun around gun in hand, but Fletcher's first shot caught him in the side when he was halfway into the pivot. The second bullet crashed into his rib cage and penetrated his heart. He crumpled to the floor.

Hawkins let out the breath he'd been holding. "Nice shooting for a history professor, Doc."

Fletcher glanced at the body and back at Hawkins.

"You set this up," he said, his voice quivering with rage.

"It's getting so that you can't trust anyone these days," Hawkins said. He rose from his chair. "Thanks for the brandy and the smoke. I'll be going along now."

Fletcher brandished the gun. "I'm afraid this isn't over."

"It is for you." Hawkins pulled out the microphone from inside his shirt. "My partner has monitored our entire conversation."

Fletcher replied with a feral smile. "Recordings can be doctored. You think anyone will believe your crazy ramblings?"

"Maybe not. Which is why my partner is calling 911 to say there's been a shooting at the Fletcher mansion. Dead man. Your gun. Your fingers on the gun. Even if you stay out of jail, your days as a wheeler-dealer are done."

He picked up the envelope with his discharge and started for the door.

"Come back, Hawkins. Let's talk. We can work this out."

Fletcher's shouts became fainter, drowned out by thunder as Hawkins descended the wide stairs to the first floor. He stepped out under the *porte-cochere*. Headlights were approaching through the slanting rain. Calvin was coming to pick him up.

As the storm raged around him, he realized something was missing.

For the past five years, even on bone dry days, he had lived with a gnawing sensation in his bum leg, and with this much moisture in the air the old wound should have been cranking out knife-edged spasms. But as the car stopped in front of him and he opened the passenger side door, his lips spread in a gargoyle grin and he let out a cry of joy.

"Hoo-ha!"

The pain that had plagued him for five years had vanished.

CHAPTER SIXTY-TWO

Georgetown University, Two Days Later

The antique Cadillac touring car arrived at the warlord's house in the gray light of the pre-dawn. Amir had assigned two of his most trusted men to escort me to the ruins. Their names were Ghatool and Baht. Both men were armed with automatic rifles, and from their belts hung pistols and knives. Although the air was cool, we drove out of the village with the convertible top down and traveled for about an hour through the rugged countryside until we came to the remnants of an ancient paved road that led to the front gate of the abandoned *caravanserai*. As I gazed with wonder and excitement at the centuries-old caravan stop, I had no idea of the mystery, and the danger, waiting beyond the silent walls.

Cait leaned back in her in her chair and stared at the words she had typed into her computer. Her mind was thousands of miles and hundreds of years away from her Georgetown University office. She only half-heard the soft knock at the door and assumed it was the graduate student helping with her research.

Without taking her eyes from the screen, she said, "Come in and put the files on my desk if you can find room."

The door opened and clicked shut. Someone approached and a deep voice said, "Sorry to interrupt. I happened to be in the neighborhood and hoped you could sign this."

She looked up over the neatly-stacked piles of paper, books and folders that rose above the desktop like castle ramparts. Hawkins stood there holding her Silk Roads book. He had a wide grin on his wind-burned face. Her heart skipped a couple of beats. She smiled with pleasure, told Hawkins to have a seat and took the book from his hand.

Turning to the title page, she said, "Anything in particular you'd like me to say?"

He nodded. "Please dedicate it to your biggest fan."

Her smile grew impossibly wider. She wrote in the book and passed it back to Hawkins, who read her words aloud:

"To Matt, my biggest fan, from *his* biggest fan."

"Perfect," he said, a gleam of amusement in his dark eyes. He thanked her and tucked the book into a canvas rucksack he had slung over his left shoulder. He surveyed the stacks covering her desk. "You didn't waste much time getting back to work."

"Research material." Pointing at the computer screen, she said, "I'm sketching out a first draft of my book on the Prester John treasure."

Hawkins shifted his tall body in his chair, glanced out the window, and brought his attention back to Cait.

"About that treasure," he said.

"Is there something wrong?"

"I met with the rest of the team before I came over here."

"And—?"

"Before I tell you what we talked about, maybe you could answer the question we asked ourselves. What do you think would happen if news of the treasure's discovery went public?"

"It would be the biggest archaeological event since King Tut's tomb was found. It would be all over the news. Every major museum in the world would compete to put the treasure on display. There would be television specials galore. It would change our view of history." She tapped the computer screen. "And there would be dozens of books written."

"That was pretty much our assessment," Hawkins said. "Have you given any thought to who owns the treasure and the income it might produce?"

"I'm not a lawyer, but I can follow the historical trail of ownership. Prester John intended the treasure as a gift to the Pope, so the Vatican might put in a claim. Hiram Kurtz found the treasure; it's possible his descendants would say it belongs to them. The families of the archaeologists on his expedition might want a piece. The government of Afghanistan could say it is rightfully theirs. It was found on Amir's property and he might say he owns it."

"Which means that given the treasure's murky history, the litigation would involve dozens of lawyers worldwide."

"It would take years and the ownership issues might never be resolved," Cait agreed, but she wasn't going to give up without a fight. "Even so, there is no reason the treasure couldn't be displayed and its earnings put in trust until the ownership is cleared up."

Hawkins was well acquainted with Cait's persistence, and was prepared to deal with it.

"That might work." He pointed to the computer screen. "But the treasure didn't materialize out of nowhere. How did you plan to describe its discovery without mentioning me or the rest of my team?"

Her stubborn smile vanished. "That would be extremely difficult."

"To say the least. Especially if you factor in the fact that our mission was top secret."

"In that case it would be virtually impossible to tell the complete story," she admitted. "But—"

"One more question. What would be the political reaction to the scepter?"

"That's even more complicated than the ownership issue. The scepter symbolizes the ancient divide between the Christian and Islam worlds."

"And that symbolism is why the Shadows wanted the scepter, hoping to stir up long-held animosities," Hawkins said.

"It's hard to say what would happen, with all the changes in the works stemming from the Arab spring. Everyone hopes that despotic regimes will be replaced with democratic rather than extremist governments."

"This doesn't seem to be a good time to turn up the heat," Hawkins said.

She sighed. "I see where you're going, but I can't say I like it."

"Sorry Cait, but it was the team's unanimous decision that the scepter and the rest of the treasure remain secret. Abby will keep it stored in her vault. Only five of us will have access."

Cait blinked. "Five?"

"We'd like to include you."

"I appreciate your trust," Cait said. She stared bleakly at the screen. "Damn. I would have loved to have wiped the smug smiles off the faces of my colleagues who scoffed at my claim that Prester John was real."

"Maybe you still can. There is more than one kind of treasure. "

He reached into his canvas bag and pulled out a rectangular package wrapped in transparent plastic. He handed the packet to Cait who read the title on the leather bound volume.

"This is the journal of Master Philip!"

"We also voted that you should have access to this. Using the journal, you can backtrack to Prester John and his kingdom. Hell, maybe you can find Prester John's tomb. You won't have to mention the mission."

"Where would I say I found the journal?"

"If anyone asks, say it was given to you by an Afghan warlord who found it in a cave."

"That might work," she said. "I could tell the story up to the time the treasure disappears. The revelations would rock the foundation of the historical establishment."

"That should be very satisfying after all the doubt your research has met with."

"Of course. But more satisfying would be setting the historical record straight and giving the participants their due."

Cait's eyes took on a dreamy look. She had left the present and her thoughts were being drawn to the past like metal filings to a magnet.

"About that dinner I promised you," Matt said.

She snapped out of her daze. "Oh, Matt. I'm so sorry. I've got to get the journal translated immediately."

"Is that a no?"

"I'm sorry, Matt. You know how hard this is to say after all we've been through together. It's not forever?"

Hawkins smiled and said, "You're not off the hook. I want a signed copy of your next book."

He rose to say good-bye. Cait sprang from her chair, came around the desk, wrapped her arms around him and planted a kiss on his lips that curled his toes.

Abby was waiting for him outside.

"How did it go?" she asked.

"Okay. A little difficult."

"Difficult? Then why do you look like the cat that swallowed the canary?"

He put his arm around her shoulders. "I was thinking about an idea I wanted to discuss with you."

When he explained what he had in mind it was Abby's turn to smile.

"It's about damned time, Hawkins."

Camden, Maine, Six Hours Later

The sleek red-hulled lobster boat glided out of the picturesque harbor, passing some of the windjammers that carried passengers to give them a taste of what it was like in the days of sail.

Hawkins was at the wheel and Abby stood on the deck taking photos of the tall-masted boats. Not a wisp of a cloud marred the luminous blue sky. The air was heavy with the salty scent of the sea. Squadrons of sharp-eyed gulls wheeled over the fishing boats searching for scraps of food. The breeze ramped up several knots as the boat entered the open waters of Penobscot Bay, but the bow cut through low mounding waves like scissors through blue silk.

Hawkins' father had the wooden-hulled boat custom built for his lobster business. When he retired from fishing and became a shore-bound lobster distributor, he converted the forty-two-foot-long workboat into a comfortable pleasure craft that was ideal for island-hopping along the Maine coast. When Hawkins had called and asked to borrow the boat, he had felt like a teenager asking Pop for the keys to the family car, but his father had happily obliged, especially when he learned Abby was coming with him.

After the meeting with Cait, Hawkins and Abby had dashed home to pack their overnight bags and rendezvoused at the airport. Abby had arranged for a small jet that flew them to Portland, Maine where they picked up a rental car. Two hours later, they pulled up to the low-slung Hawkins family home on a rocky point. His father came out to wrap Abby in a bear hug and his mother beamed with delight. She still considered Abby as a daughter. Hawkins stayed long enough to be polite, eat some homemade apple pie and catch up on local gossip before saying that he wanted to get moving so he could make landfall before dark.

His father said the boat was fueled up, well-stocked with food and booze and ready to go. Within minutes of boarding, Hawkins and Abby set a course to Vinal Haven, southwest of Camden, and when they arrived they found an anchorage in a quiet cove. While Hawkins grilled a couple of rib eye steaks and sweet potatoes, Abby made a salad and opened a bottle of 2007 Bordeaux.

Abby had suggested that they dress for dinner. She had exchanged her shorts and polo-shirt for a diaphanous strapless cocktail dress of lavender. Hawkins changed from his cargo shorts and T-shirt into an olive cotton blazer, fresh jeans and a dark green shirt. They sat at a table on the wide deck, enjoying their food and wine by candlelight, watching the sun dip behind the island, and chatting about Calvin and Sutherland.

After their meeting in Washington, Hawkins had asked Calvin and Sutherland what they planned to do. Calvin had grinned like a mischievous kid.

"I've been talking to Abby about transporting Amir's bomber if I can persuade the old bandit to part with it."

Sutherland simply said, "I'll let you know," before she got on her

Harley and rode off like the Lone Ranger.

"Do you think we'll ever hear from Molly again?" Abby said.

"When she's ready. In the meantime she'll be watching every move we make." Hawkins took a sip of wine and stared up at the star-spattered sky. "We're damned lucky the gods look out for fools." He realized his *faux pas* and said, "No offense, Abby."

Abby laughed softly. "None taken. I'm glad you asked me to go on the mission."

"We couldn't have done it without you, Abby."

"I'll have to admit I had my doubts."

"Can't imagine why. Having Crazy Matt arrive on your doorstep asking you to go on a dangerous treasure hunt seems like a perfectly normal request."

"I think Crazy Matt is no more," she said.

"And I think that we're out of wine."

Hawkins opened another bottle and filled their glasses. They sipped their wine in silence for a few minutes, enjoying the rhythmical tap of waves against the hull and the piney scent of the warm Maine night. Abby broke the silence.

"We know what Calvin and Molly's plans are. Where do we go from here?" Abby said.

"I'll head back to Woods Hole and play with my robotic toys. I assume you'll go back to running your company."

"I didn't mean professionally. I was talking about *us*. About *our* future."

"*Ah*," Hawkins said. "Excuse me for being brain dead. It's a male thing. What's your take on the situation?"

She put her glass down on the table and got up. She walked to the stern, staring out at the land lights sparkling against the blue darkness, then turned and said, "There may be a chance for us. There may not be. We're both different than we were. It's as if we've got to get to know each other all over again."

Hawkins got up and went over to Abby. The soft breeze was blowing the tender folds of her dress against the curves of her body. He put his arms around her and kissed her neck, her ear, her cheek and finally her lips. He ran his hands down from her shoulder blades to the small of her back, exploring the valley of her vertebrae, the firm roundness of her buttocks, the curve of her thighs. She shivered at his touch although the night was warm as his searching fingers brought back tactile recollections of times past.

"No time like the present to get to know each other again," he said.

They climbed down into the cabin, leaving a trail of clothes behind them, slipped beneath the sheets of the V-shaped berth in the bow of the boat, made love with a frantic urgency, fell asleep, awoke and made love again, slower and more deliberately, and slept until they were awakened in each other's arms by the squalling of gulls and sunlight through the portholes.

After they got dressed, Abby took the wheel and they headed south to Matinicus Island where they anchored again and Hawkins whipped up a masterful omelet. They rowed ashore, spent the day exploring the rocky island and later that evening explored each others' bodies again.

The next morning, they set a direct course back to Camden. Hawkins called ahead to his folks and said that he and Abby would love to visit, but they had to get back for an appointment. After returning the boat, they drove to Portland. Abby summoned her jet and Hawkins caught a commercial flight to Boston. Before taking off, they exchanged the lighthearted kiss and hug of old friends and vowed to keep in touch.

The pain of parting stayed with Hawkins during his flight. When his plane landed in Boston, he caught a bus back to Woods Hole. He had called ahead and Snowy was waiting at the bus stop to give him a ride home in the red pick-up. They made small talk on the ten-minute ride. The afterglow of Hawkins' cruise with Abby was wearing off, sadly. He realized that their romantic interlude had been only that, with no resolution to what he called their *situation.* He was still thinking about Abby when they pulled up in front of his house. He glanced at the second floor. The bullet-shattered picture window had been replaced.

"Forgot to mention that there's a surprise waiting for you," Snowy said.

As Hawkins got out of the truck, Quisset emerged from around a corner of the house and limped over. One of her back legs wasn't working quite right, and she wore a collar to prevent her from getting at the bandage on her head, but there was nothing wrong with her wagging tail and she did her best to knock Hawkins over with her usual thigh slam.

Hawkins knelt and gave Quisset a big hug that set off a squirming fit.

It was good to be home.

POSTSCRIPT

Mohamed sat in the passenger seat of the unmarked ISI vehicle parked on the side of a hillside road, watching the walled-off villa through the lenses of his night-vision binoculars.

Four cars had disappeared through the wall gate, which was guarded by two men armed with automatic weapons. He couldn't see what was going on in the villa hidden behind the walls, but he could picture the scene from past experience attending meetings of the Shadow leadership.

The Doctor and his lieutenants would be sitting cross-legged on the bare floor, their backs to the walls of the room. The Doctor would be haranguing them, lacing his tirade with frequent religious references. In this case, the Doctor would be discussing the failure of the Prophet's Necklace and the disappearance of the man who was going to carry out the plot.

Mohamed knew this because his commander was the one who had told the Shadows that the ISI could no longer provide cover for them. The treasure mission had failed. The Chinese deal had fallen through. Amir was still alive and in control of the lithium fields. The old warlord was looking for the highest bidder, but the U.S. was sweetening its offer by bringing in troops to protect Amir's village.

Mohamed had heard from a CIA contact that Marzak and not Hawkins had killed his cousin. He had been fond of Saleem, and felt a load of guilt about bringing the professor into the dirty business of intelligence. His contact had said Marzak was dead, but Saleem knew there were others who were complicit in his cousin's murder. When the commander told him to tie up loose ends, he had no hesitation carrying out the orders.

Mohamed knew that the Doctor was ultra-cautious. He would arrive in one car and leave in another, one of four that would speed off in different directions. Any attacker would have to go after all four cars if he didn't know the right one.

What the Doctor didn't know was that one of the men at the gate was in the employ of the ISI. When the gate opened after a few minutes, Mohamed kept his eye on the guard, who dropped his hand and tapped the rear fender of the third vehicle as if sending it on its way.

Mohamed smiled and punched out a number on his cell phone.

"Black Mercedes. Heading east," he said.

The call was patched through to a dimly-lit windowless room in Tampa, Florida. The pilot in charge of the Predator that had been circling high above the villa worked the joystick and sent the drone winging after its prey. Within minutes the drone's nose camera picked up the smudge moving in an easterly direction. The operator's supervisor gave the command to fire, and seconds later two Hellfire missiles streaked out from below the wings of the drone and transformed the Mercedes into a ball of white fire.

The explosion that destroyed the Doctor and his car was soundless in the operations room, but thousands of miles away Mohamed heard the thud and saw the flare in the distance.

He instructed his driver to get moving and said in a low voice, "A torch to light your way to paradise, dear cousin."

THE END

Made in the USA
Lexington, KY
27 November 2013